IN THE REALM OF GODS AND KINGS

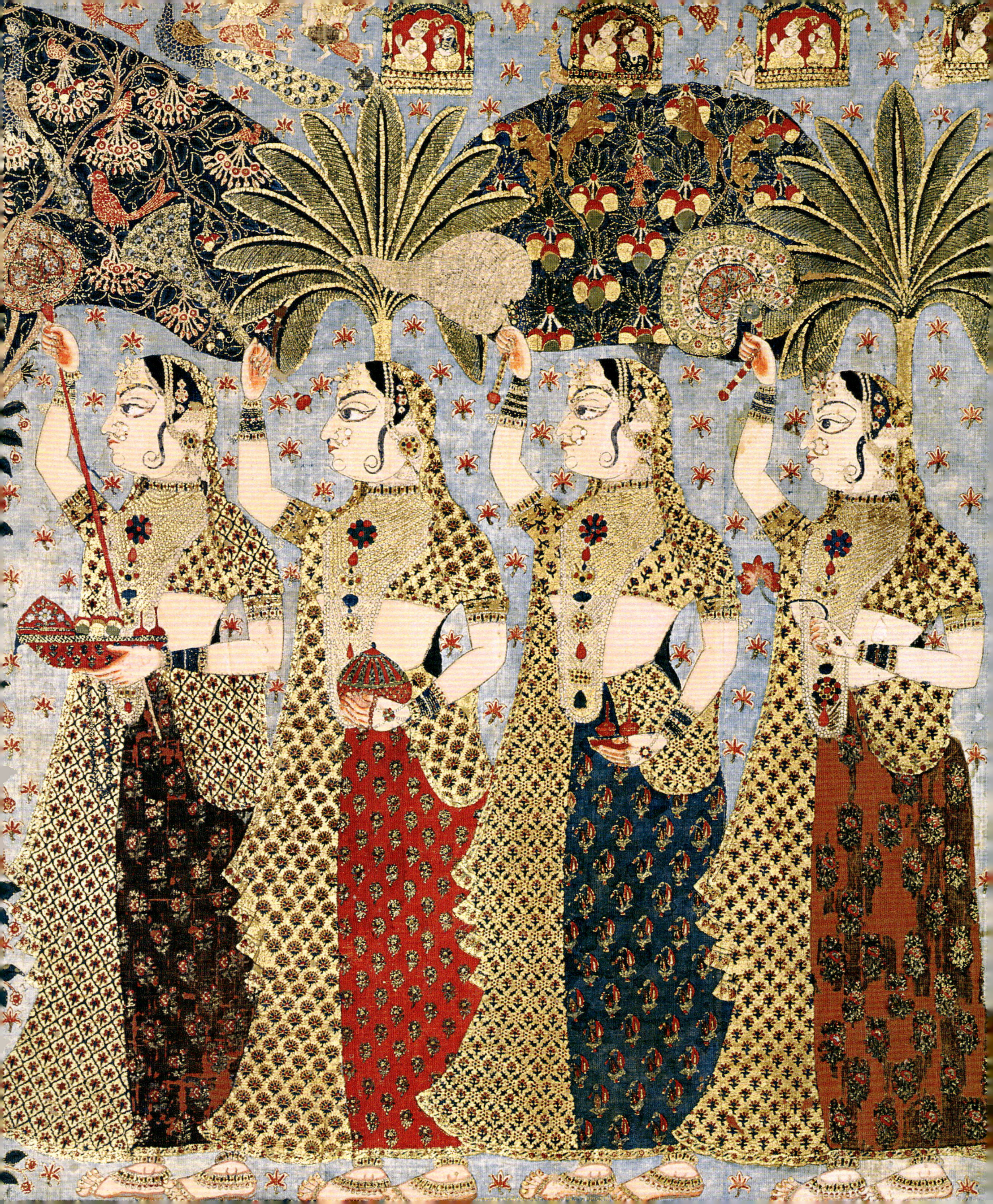

IN THE REALM OF GODS AND KINGS

Arts of India

EDITED BY ANDREW TOPSFIELD

PHILIP WILSON PUBLISHERS

New revised paperback edition published in 2013 by
Philip Wilson Publishers
an imprint of I.B.Tauris & Co Ltd
6 Salem Road
London W2 4BU
www.philip-wilson.co.uk

Distributed in the United States and Canada
exclusively by Palgrave Macmillan
175 Fifth Avenue, New York NY 10010

First published in 2004 by Philip Wilson Publishers

Designed by Peter Ling
Printed in China

ISBN 978-1-78130-014-5

A copy of the CIP data is available from the British Library upon request
A full CIP record is available from the Library of Congress

Library of Congress Catalog Card Number: available

CONTENTS

ACKNOWLEDGEMENTS

I would like to express my gratitude to those at The Metropolitan Museum of Art and at the Asia Society Museum who assisted with the preparation of this book and the related exhibition at the Asia Society Museum, September 13, 2004 – January 2, 2005.

To Philippe de Montebello, Director of The Metropolitan Museum of Art, for his encouragement and assistance and to the following individuals at The Metropolitan Museum of Art for their cooperation and assistance:

Doralynn Pines of the Office of the Director, Sharon Cott of the Office of the Vice President, Secretary and General Counsel, Deanna Cross of the Photograph and Slide Library, Annick Des Roches of the Department of Islamic Art, Hwai-ling Yeh-Lewis and Michael Rendina of the Department of Asian Art, Frederick Sager of the Department of Objects Conservation, John O'Neill of the Editorial Department, as well as the staff of the Department of Photographs

To: Dr. Vishakha Desai, President, the Asia Society, for her contribution to this book and to Mirza Burgos, Helen Abbott, and the staff of the Asia Society for their assistance.

I am grateful to Andrew Topsfield for his essays and contributions to this book and to the contributing authors John Falconer, Dr. Navina Haidar, Jeremiah Losty, and Michael Spink. I wish to thank, as well, John Eskenazi, Martin Lerner, and Terence McInerney for their participation.

To: Philip Wilson of Philip Wilson Publishers, Cangy Venables, Managing Editor, Norman Turpin, Production Manager, and Peter Ling for the editing, design and production of this book and for their enthusiasm for the project.

To: my assistant, Karen Maguire, for her devoted attention to all the detail in the preparation of the manuscript.

To: Sheldan Collins for his thoughtful and excellent photographic work and to his assistant, Eva Haggdahl.

To my son, Nicholas Polsky and to John Eskenazi and Jill Spalding for their helpful advice.

In addition, I am grateful to know and to have known fine scholars, curators, collectors, and art dealers who have been generous in sharing their knowledge and expertise with me. These have included: Dr. Pramod Chandra, Dr. Vidyia Dehejia, Dr. Joseph Dye, Dr. Daniel Enbohm, Dr. Eberhard Fisher, Anthony Gardiner, Dr. B. N. Goswamy, Pulpul Jayakar, Dr. Karl Kandalawala, Subash Kapoor, Steven Kossak, Dr. Stella Kramrisch, Peter Marks, Dr. Barbara Stoler Miller, Dr. Pratapaditya Pal, Amy Poster, Dr. Marhrukh Tarapor, Daniel Walker, Paul Walter, Stuart Cary Welch, Doris Wiener, Nancy Wiener, and William Wolff.

CYNTHIA HAZEN POLSKY
New York City

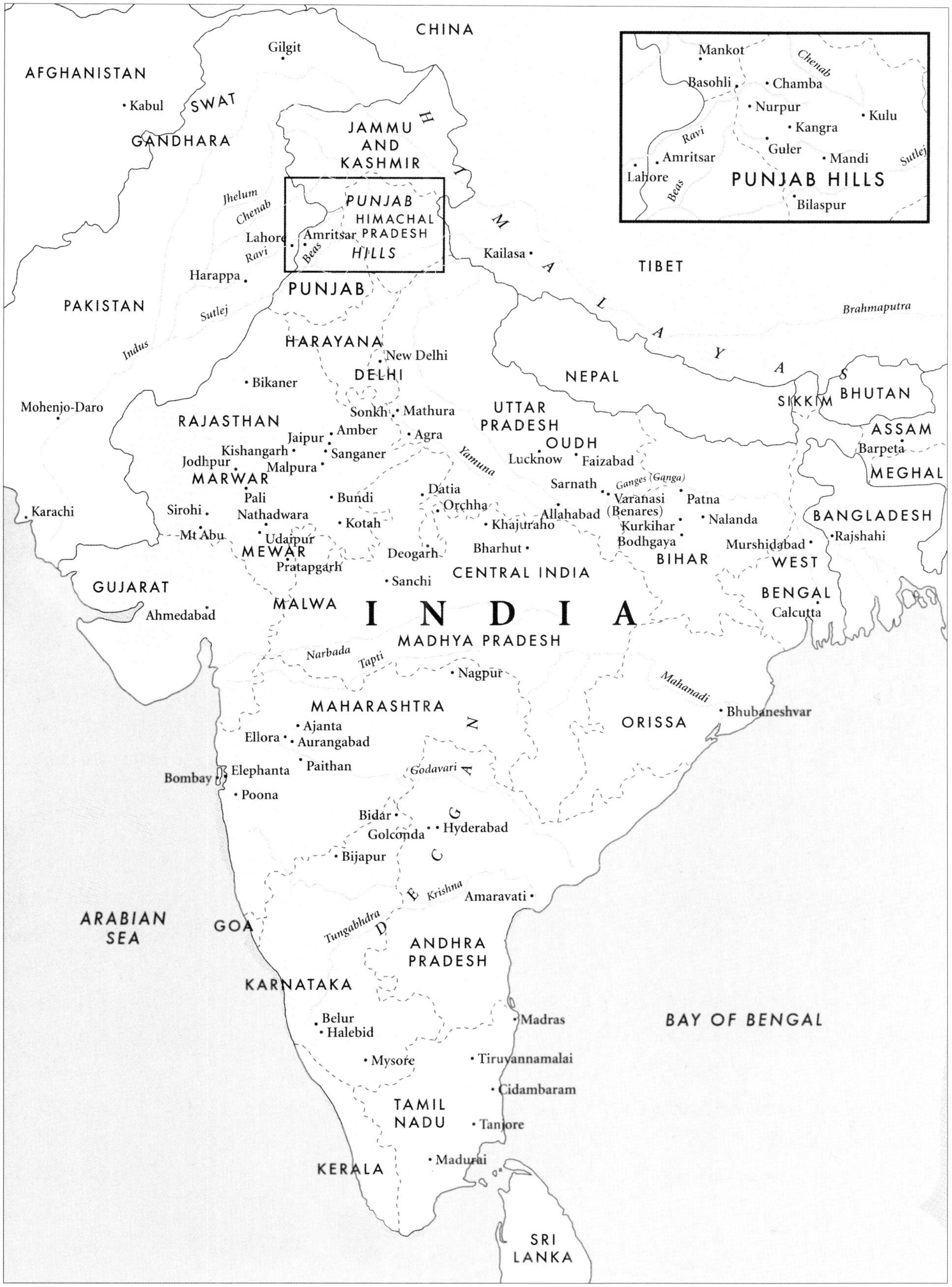
CHINA
AFGHANISTAN
Gilgit
Kabul
SWAT
GANDHARA
JAMMU AND KASHMIR
HIMALAYAS
Jhelum
Chenab
PUNJAB
HIMACHAL PRADESH
HILLS
Lahore
Amritsar
Ravi
Beas
Kailasa
TIBET
Harappa
PUNJAB
PAKISTAN
Sutlej
Brahmaputra
Indus
HARAYANA
New Delhi
DELHI
NEPAL
Bikaner
BHUTAN
SIKKIM
Mohenjo-Daro
RAJASTHAN
Sonkh
Mathura
UTTAR PRADESH
ASSAM
Amber
Agra
Barpeta
Jaipur
OUDH
Kishangarh
Sanganer
Lucknow
Faizabad
Jodhpur
Malpura
Yamuna
MEGHAL
MARWAR
Sarnath
Ganges (Ganga)
Pali
Bundi
Datia
Varanasi (Benares)
Patna
Karachi
Sirohi
Orchha
Allahabad
BANGLADESH
Nathadwara
Kotah
Khajuraho
Kurkihar
Nalanda
Mt Abu
Udaipur
Bodhgaya
Rajshahi
MEWAR
Deogarh
Bharhut
Murshidabad
Pratapgarh
BIHAR
WEST
GUJARAT
Sanchi
CENTRAL INDIA
BENGAL
MALWA
Calcutta
Ahmedabad
INDIA
MADHYA PRADESH
Narbada
Tapti
Nagpur
Mahanadi
MAHARASHTRA
Bhubaneshvar
Ajanta
ORISSA
Ellora
Aurangabad
Paithan
Bombay
Elephanta
Godavari
Poona
DECCAN
Bidar
Golconda
Hyderabad
Bijapur
Krishna
Amaravati
ARABIAN SEA
GOA
Tungabhadra
ANDHRA PRADESH
KARNATAKA
Madras
BAY OF BENGAL
Belur
Halebid
Mysore
Tiruvannamalai
Cidambaram
TAMIL NADU
Tanjore
Madurai
KERALA
SRI LANKA
Mankot
Chenab
Basohli
Chamba
Nurpur
Kulu
Kangra
Ravi
Guler
Amritsar
Mandi
Sutlej
Lahore
Beas
PUNJAB HILLS
Bilaspur

FOREWORD

Most collectors of Indian art tend to specialize in one particular medium, either sculpture or painting, or perhaps the decorative arts. Few have created so richly comprehensive a collection as that of Cynthia Hazen Polsky. The distinguished works published in this book, drawn from the Polsky collection and augmented by loans from The Metropolitan Museum of Art with Polsky connections, cover an exceptionally wide range of collecting interests.

The book embraces fine early Indian terracotta sculptures, as well as later works in stone; superb ivory carvings from South India, Orissa, and Sri Lanka, and examples of the Mughal decorative arts; a strong selection of paintings representing many of the major schools of the Mughal period; and, not least, a revealing group of contemporary photographs of Indian subjects, including several by the late Raghubir Singh. The generous-spirited inclusiveness of these collections has much to do with Cynthia and Leon Polsky's keenly felt engagement with India and its culture ever since their first visit in 1960. Their various Indian encounters over the years have also been enriched by a fruitful association with scholars and curators of Indian art and their active support of art institutions with Indian collections. This book and the accompanying exhibition are therefore a testimony to Cynthia Hazen Polsky as a collector, supporter, and student of Indian art.

When Cynthia Hazen Polsky first discussed with me the idea of creating a book centered around her collection, both we and Steven Kossak of The Metropolitan Museum of Art were soon agreed that it should be structured in such a way as to suggest unusual and stimulating connections between disparate works, not unlike the sometimes incongruent realities of India itself. As the Polsky collection, augmented by loans from The Metropolitan Museum, was broad in historical scope, but with a strong focus on paintings, it seemed most instructive to organize the book along thematic rather than chronological lines.

The two principal strains of Indian art—works dealing with religious themes and those dealing with courtly subjects—would best serve as the primary thematic divisions. But how to recognize the fact that in India, a king could imagine himself as a devotee in the heavenly abode of gods, and gods can take the guise of courtly lovers? And what about literary romances, illustrated for rulers and courtiers, but dealing with the god of love, Krishna? We soon realized that in any such exercise there must be an element of arbitrariness. Thus some of the paintings relating to Krishna appear here in the section dealing with the god in his own right, while others come in the section dealing with courtly manuscripts. We felt, however, that such inconsistencies or unexpected juxtapositions could in fact prove interesting and thought provoking. Ultimately, our goal has been to suggest such unusual associations, and to open up a more creative engagement between the viewer and the works.

It is natural that this book and exhibition should include many works loaned from The Metropolitan Museum of Art: not only the objects given by Mr and Mrs Polsky, but also those bought by the

Museum's curators with funds provided by the Polsky family. As a trustee of the Museum since 1984, Mrs Polsky has been closely involved with the Departments of Islamic and Indian Art as well as of Photography, and has supported the acquisition program of all three departments.

It is fitting, too, that this project should have a special connection with the Asia Society Museum. Cynthia Hazen Polsky has been a long-term supporter of the institution, as a trustee, honorary life trustee, and active member of the Museum's Advisory Committee. The support from the Polskys was instrumental in the development of a series of lectures and related publications by leading scholars of Indian art at the Society in the 1980s. For me personally, it is also heartening to be able to celebrate a relationship that has grown over more than two decades from professional acquaintance to close friendship.

A project of this scope involves a close partnership among many different people. Cynthia Polsky has acknowledged many of them, but I want to add my personal thanks to Philip Wilson and Cangy Venables for their commitment to create this beautiful book, and to Andrew Topsfield for acting as its general editor.

We are most grateful to The Metropolitan Museum of Art, especially Philippe de Montebello, the Director, and the curatorial staff of the Islamic and Indian Art sections for facilitating the loans from the Museum.

At the Asia Society, the staff of the museum and cultural programs has worked hard to create a beautiful installation and to organize related public programs. Special thanks go to Helen Abbott, Mirza Burgos, Amy McEwen, Deanna Lee, and Joshua Harris of the Museum staff, and Rachel Cooper and Linden Chubin of public programs and performances. We are also grateful to Merrill Lynch for their support of India-related programs at the Asia Society in the fall of 2004.

From its inception, the Asia Society has made a commitment to present the best of Asian art in ways that can open up broader vistas of Asian cultures. The exhibition *In the Realm of Gods and Kings* continues and strengthens our efforts to create innovative approaches to appreciating Asian cultures through artistic traditions.

Vishakha N. Desai
PRESIDENT
Asia Society

TO BECKON THE MODERN EYE

Who can say why it is that the arts of a distant place and a culture removed from our own can communicate to us deeply? My first glimpse of India was in the pages of a small book about Indian arts and crafts given to me by a family friend when I was eight or so years old. I remember a grainy black and white photograph of a sari-clad woman walking with elegance across a bare field holding a *lota* on top of her head with one hand. Decades later I thought I saw her again as I watched groups of people walking in the fields near Sanchi in the late afternoon—"the hour of cow dust," as it was named in the *Bhagavata Purana*. Carved into the walls of temples, she is at the heart of the sense of the mythic that pervades the life and arts of traditional India.

Buddhist, Hindu, Muslim, and Jain visual cultures have harmonized in the extraordinary outpouring of architecture, sculpture, painting, and decorative and folk arts that are India's rich heritage. My husband, Lee, and I have been fortunate to spend time in India traveling with family and friends who share our fascination with the region and its extraordinary culture. The presence of Indian art in our home has been our way of maintaining a continuity with the ways of thought and visions of the world that are unique to India. For my sons and now for my grandchildren the delight of Indian art has been part of our family life.

My experience as a Trustee of The Metropolitan Museum of Art and participation in the development of the Museum's collections of Indian art with curators Martin Lerner and Steven Kossak of the Department of South and South East Asian Art, as well as with Daniel Walker and Navina Haidar of the Department of Islamic Art, has immeasurably enhanced my knowledge, as has my friendship and dialogue with other scholars, experts, and collectors in the Indian field.

My trusteeship since 1984 at the Asia Society has made possible the close friendship that I am fortunate to share with Dr. Vishakha Desai, President of the Asia Society. It has been a particular pleasure for me to work in collaboration with her on planning this book and the related exhibition at the Asia Society, September 13, 2004–January 2, 2005.

My interest in the art of India covers a wide range of periods, media, and styles ranging from the lively ivory plaque of the second century BC depicting a procession of musicians, dancers, and elephants (cat. no. 106), to the great gilt copper sculpture of Nagaraja of the fifteenth century (cat. no. 26) and the enchanting picchavai of the eighteenth century (cat. no. 70), as well as the Raghubir Singh photograph of 1989 showing Sadhus returning from bathing at the Kumbh Mela (cat. no. 87); however, the heart of my collection is painting.

It is considered that certain traditions of Indian manuscript and folio painting of the sixteenth through nineteenth century are part of traditions distantly related to fifth- through ninth-century Hindu and Buddhist wall painting as seen in the Ellora and Ajanta caves. Two styles developed from this common source: a naturalistic Buddhist painting style, found in ninth- to twelfth-century manuscripts from Bihar and Bengal, and a distinctive abstract, schematic style seen in eleventh- to fifteenth-century manuscripts of southern Rajasthan and Gujarat. Common motifs, symbols, and aesthetic conventions relate the more naturalistic style to foreign-influenced Sultanate and Mughal school paintings of the fourteenth through nineteenth century, to nineteenth century paintings of the Punjab Hills, and to Company school paintings of the late nineteenth and early twentieth century. The paintings in this volume, collected over a thirty-year period, reflect a sampling of the splendid variety of Mughal and Rajput painting.

The world of Indian painting, fresh, intimate, and emotive, presents us with royal portraits and depictions of celebration, war, devotion, asceticism, eroticism, and romance. These subjects, which are similar to many in Western medieval and post-medieval manuscript illustrations and works on paper, describe histories and epics such as the *Akbarnama*, the *Ramayana*, India's great epic, and the *Bhagavata Purana*, a key religious text. They are classic to the Indian world but relatively unknown in the West.

In the cosmopolitan Mughal courts, Persian paintings and Chinese blue-and-white porcelain were known, as were Western European prints and drawings. Elements from these sources appear in the paintings produced in their ateliers, giving familiar aspects to the unfamiliar world shown. Vibrant in color, small in scale, and once the possessions of emperors and nobles, courtiers and merchants, there is much in these paintings that unexpectedly draws the modern eye.

The abstract, schematic styles of southern Rajput painting, which are distinctive for their emotive rather than descriptive use of color, and for a concentration on abstract, symbolic forms, have a particular appeal to modern tastes because abstraction and iconic imagery are important aspects of twentieth-century painting traditions. These were aspects of Indian painting of particular interest to me in the 1960s and 1970s, when I was active as an artist. There are some remarkable similarities between certain Rajput styles and aspects of the Fauve, Symbolist, and Expressionist styles of nineteenth- and twentieth-century European painting. Works by European artists such as Gauguin, Nolde, and Matisse portray inner realities through the use of simplified forms and expressive color in a manner that seems to echo paintings of the Malwa and Mewar schools. Gauguin's statement of purpose, "instead of working with the eye, we search in the mysterious center of thought," could also apply to the Rajput artist, who sought to convey thought and feeling through the use of a formalized vocabulary of imagery and color references. Paintings from Kotah are distinctive for their depiction of luxuriant foliage, dense gardens, and jungles without horizon that enclose their inhabitants. Particularly coincident with these is a work such as *The Hunt* (cat. no. 118), which curiously anticipates Henri Rousseau's painting *The Dream* (1910).

Some collectors of contemporary art and certain contemporary artists have found Indian paintings sympathetic to their interests. In particular, Howard Hodgkin and Francesco Clemente have integrated aspects of Indian painting traditions into their own works. Hodgkin, long a collector of Indian painting

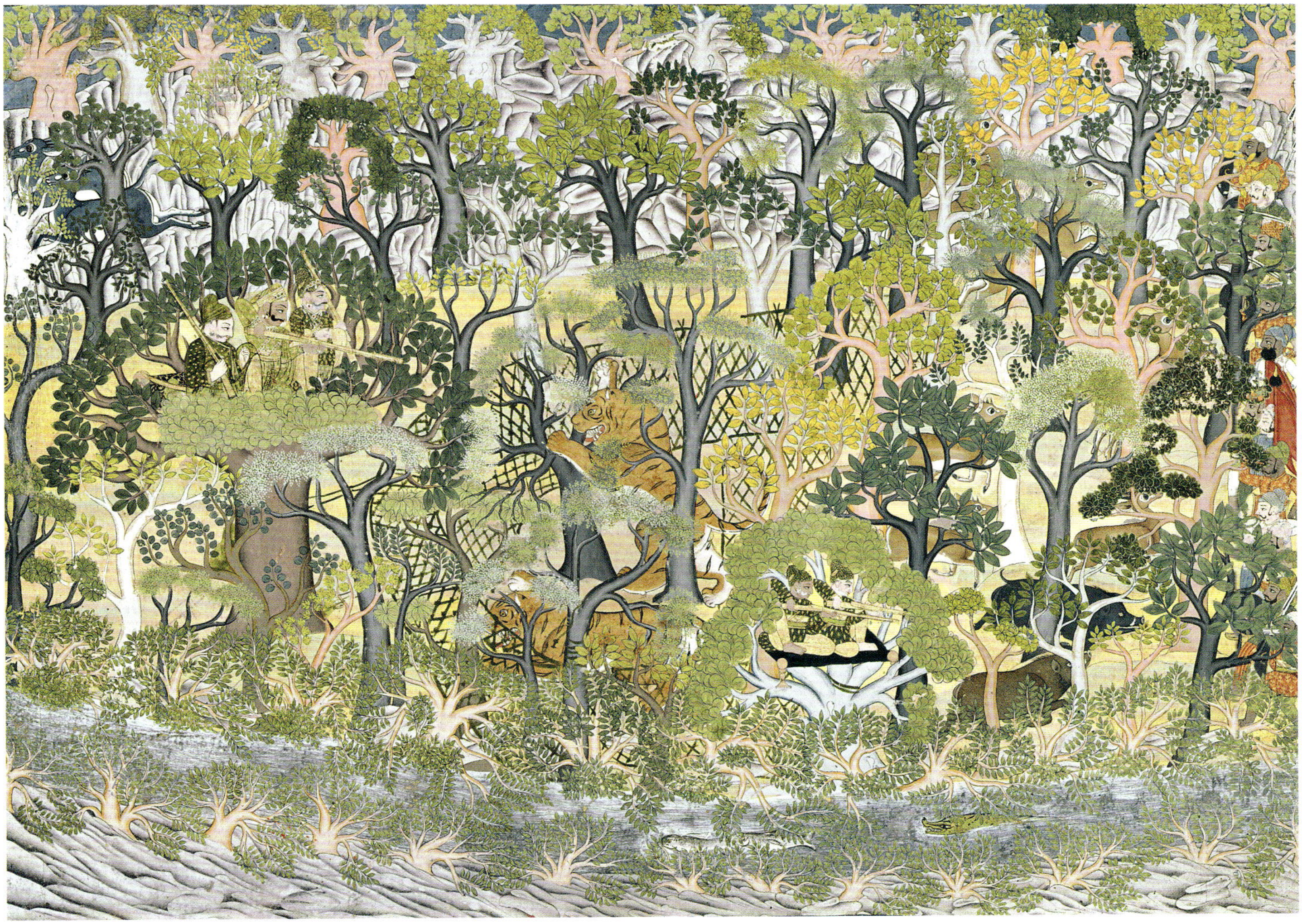

A tiger hunt, Kotah, Rajasthan, dated 1773, by Hansraj Joshi (cat. no. 118)

and a frequent visitor to India, is thought to reflect aspects of Indian painting in many of his works. Michael Taylor, curator of the 2001 exhibition "Philadelphia Collects Hodgkin," noted:

> Hodgkin's preference for rich, saturated color, his pictorial language of eloquent compression, and ambiguity of surface and depth, can be linked to his fascination with Indian painting. In speaking of Indian painting, Hodgkin has praised its ease in depicting a "whole world in a way which is completely convincing but totally separate, a world in which everything is precise and visible and yet somewhere else.

The Italian artist Francesco Clemente began in 1973 to spend part of each year living and painting in India. He has collaborated with Indian artisans and used Indian materials for some of his works. He frequently chooses Hindu and Buddhist themes as subject matter and includes references to both traditional and contemporary Indian art. In an interview with Michael Aupling, he commented:

> What we are talking about is the relation between what is in movement and what is static. My main affinity with India and the Eastern traditions is my sympathy for the contradictions that exist between these poles. The tenet in the East that I totally accept is that everything is real and everything is changing.

Clemente's interest is part of a modern tradition that began in the nineteenth century, when works such as Sir James Frazer's *The Golden Bough* stimulated the interest of artists and intellectuals in the mythologies and religions of the non-Western world. Despite this receptivity, an appreciation and understanding of Hindu temple sculpture was slow to grow among Western travelers and art historians. Some early travelers to India commented that images of multi-limbed deities were "monstrous." Now, however, as many aspects of Indian culture from yoga to cuisine have become part of Western life, certain Hindu images, too, have become familiar and almost iconic for us.

Shiva represents multiple forms of divine power; when shown in his manifestation as Lord of the Dance, he is associated with both creative and destructive forces. While he dances, he is said to hold the world in equilibrium (cat. no. 39). The renowned late scholar Dr. Stella Kramrisch wrote:

> He dances in the evening twilight to the music of the Gods...this elation has all the rhythms of the cosmos. He dances the cosmos into and out of existence.

In search of a reference to convey the magnitude of the moment, Robert Oppenheimer said when viewing the first nuclear explosion:

> Now we have become Shiva, breaker of worlds.

As is the case with Shiva, representations of the Goddess in paintings may have resonance for the present moment. Derived from fertility figures and early rites, the worship of the Great Goddess was established by texts of the sixth, tenth, and eleventh centuries AD. In India as well as parts of South Asia, the Goddess became and remains a central focus of worship, not only for Hindus but for Jains and Buddhists as well. She can be envisaged not only as primordial mother but also as warrior and destroyer. A seventeenth-century Basoli manuscript page (cat. no. 72) depicts her as Devi seated radiant and benign upon her lotus; in an eighteenth-century Guler drawing she is shown as Kali (cat. no. 74), the ferocious, avenging deity; and in a nineteenth-century Pahari painting she appears as Parvati, the beautiful bride of Shiva. She inhabits myriad identities that a modern heroine might envy.

Gods, kings, and princes, goddesses and royal women have many continuities of aspect and attributes, as the realms of the sacred and secular are deeply intertwined. Gods appear among mortals and mortals can be shown as godlike. In a Bikaner painting of the seventeenth century, Krishna enters the lives of a group of cowherds, and in a romantic seventeenth-century South Indian ivory sculpture, a couple is shown in postures suggesting Shiva and Parvati. Continuities with traditional painting exist in color-drenched images of the contemporary photographer, Raghubir Singh, who framed fragments of these enduring themes, which are alive today. The arts of India are given grandeur by the portrayal of these and other complex deities embedded in epic, mythic, and religious themes. They invite and reward contemplation.

CYNTHIA HAZEN POLSKY
New York City

SEEING THE EYES OF THE GOD
THE EXPERIENCE OF CREATIVITY IN INDIAN ART

VISHAKHA N. DESAI

The vision and capacity to find new uses or create new forms out of old materials is one of the prevailing characteristics of traditional Indian culture. Even the first-time visitor to India will be struck by the roadside displays of small toys and bicycles made out of old metal wires, or forty-year-old cars painted new. Similarly, neon-lit shrines in the midst of high-rise cities and ancient rituals as integral parts of high-tech factory inaugurations, are fundamental aspects of contemporary Indian life.

One might argue that this phenomenon is prevalent in most developing societies where the throwaway mentality and the cult of the new have not yet taken hold, and that in time it too will be swept away by the passion for novelty. Even so, a persistent emphasis on incremental change, and the simultaneous presence of multiple pasts, remains more intense and prevalent in India than in most other societies at the beginning of the twenty-first century. The dynamic adherence to traditions and a search for the "new" in the "known" in India is based on elaborately articulated and millennia-old concepts of time, individuality, and creativity. An understanding of these concepts is crucial to our appreciation of Indian art and culture.

Throughout the history of pre-modern Indian art, one can find corollaries to those recycled roadside toys and high-tech shrines. A temple sculptor or a court painter would continue to create a previously known form, but with a fresh insight. This can be seen in relation to the works in the Polsky collection, such as the various illustrations to the *Ramayana*, both from the Mughal court (cat. nos. 158–64) and one of the small Hindu courts in the Punjab Hills (cat. nos. 48–49). The story of the epic is, of course, well known; what we appreciate is the way the scenes are enacted on paper. We look for the special ways in which the army of monkeys is treated, or the unique qualities imparted to depictions of the hero Rama. This is not just about new formal qualities, but about the ways we can go deeper into the story itself. It is also less about the individuality of the artist and his personal interpretation of the story and more about whether he manages to open the eyes and minds of the viewer to those aspects of the narrative that can provide special insight into the human condition.

Even today, one is very aware of this cultural preference in India for defining aesthetic quality or creative excellence through "insight" rather than "innovation", especially in relation to practices with pre-modern and pre-colonial origins. This was brought home to me very vividly about two decades ago. An impressive-looking Jain temple was being built near our family home in Ahmedabad. The patrons of the temple were very proud to have brought the most renowned sculptors from Rajasthan to create the architectural details and carve the sculptures for the main niches of the temple.

With a friend, I decided to document the building process and talk to the artists about their definition of excellence and creativity. Without exception, they talked about the ability of the artist to bring forth the special "power" of the deity or the image in a physical form. For human forms, they focused on the elegance of the proportions and the quality of the facial expression, especially the carving of the eyes. Similarly, after the completion of the temple, as the devotees started coming in, the older temple-goers often talked about what they particularly treasured in the temple. While they appreciated the fact that it had a large *mandapa* (outer hall), it was once again the expression on the faces of the main images of the three Jinas, and the "inner spirit" as expressed in the eyes of the sculptures, which allowed them to declare that these particular images were superior to others.

DEFINITIONS OF CREATIVITY

A number of scholars have pointed out that such values lie at the heart of the definition of creativity in Indian culture.[1] In India as well as in the West, the creative act is defined as a formation of a distinctive unit out of a fusion of disparate elements. Both Western and Indian definitions of creativity share the notion that to create is to bring into being something unique that would not have evolved naturally or have been made by ordinary processes.[2] However, they disagree profoundly about the dynamics of the process and about the ultimate goal of the creative act.

In the West, there is a strong emphasis on the value of novelty and uniqueness in the creative process. While no one actually creates something out of nothing or without some reference to what has come before, the final result must be transformational, not merely a rearrangement of what was already known. The scientific and mathematical models in the West focus on problem solving, which can stand for inventiveness. Beginning with the Renaissance and through the discourse of the Enlightenment in the eighteenth century, Western ideas of creativity became firmly associated with individuality and ultimately separated from spiritual concerns. The rise of the romantic tradition in the nineteenth century, particularly in music and literature, further emphasized personal expression over collective symbols. In the visual arts, this privileged position of uniqueness became particularly strong in the late nineteenth century, when the idea of the avant-garde artist took hold. As the modernist ideology began to permeate artistic productions all over the world, the idea of a creative individual as an independent thinker, non-conforming in outlook and willing to go against the grain of society to pursue new ideas and new forms, has become a universal norm.

By contrast, the idea of newness, fundamental to the Western notion of creativity, is accorded a low priority in Indian ideas of creative activity. For most of Indian history until the advent of colonial rule and the subsequent modernist practices, the artistic creative act was generally associated with spiritual self-realization and insight rather than invention. Since the discussion of creativity and artistic endeavor in India is mainly tied to spiritual and philosophical theories, one has to look to texts of this kind for a better understanding of cultural notions of creativity. The lowly status of novelty can be related to Indian concepts of time and space. The formulations of Indian cosmology do not allow for an understanding of the universe as generating novelty as it moves through time and history.[3] Time is seen as being cyclical, a continuum in which history repeats itself, thus allowing for no original quality. The quest then is to find the non-changing elements in life and to discard those that are impermanent. This also means that for an individual, the goal is not to strive for unique achievement that sets him or her apart, but rather to find the ultimate Self, which goes beyond the individualistic ego and connects to all humanity.

This idea is abundantly evident in early texts, especially the Upanishads, which form the backbone of Indian thought. In the *Isha Upanishad*, an emphasis on change and novelty for its own sake is seen as almost antithetical to true creativity. The world of differences existing separately from ourselves, one of the central tenets of individual creativity in the West, is understood to be a low level or "normal" state of awareness in the Upanishads, and is associated with "ignorance."[4] Creativity is connected with the experience of an Enlightened Self that can see the "unity-in-difference" and appreciate that "each transitory experience is a celebration of eternity." The *Mundaka Upanishad* further elaborates on the idea of lower self as ego and the quest for a True Self:

Like two golden birds perched on the selfsame tree,
Intimate friends, the ego and the Self
Dwell in the same body.
The former eats the sweet and sour fruits of the tree of life
While the latter looks on in detachment.
As long as we think we are the ego,
We feel attached and fall into sorrow.
But realize that you are the Self, the Lord of life,
And you will be freed from sorrow.
When you realize that you are the Self,
Supreme source of light, supreme source of love,
You transcend the duality of life
And enter into the unitive state.[5]

The assumption is that novelty or originality, as understood in the West, is associated with the transitory satisfaction related to the ego. The true quest has to be to find the non-changing, archetypal Self, beyond individualistic manifestations. In this sense, the ultimate act of creation involves energizing known forms, to intuit the inner essence of the thing depicted, rather than to suggest a new reality. This "aha" or intuitive moment, resembling the Satori in the Zen tradition, is also comparable to the "inspiration" stage in the Western theory of creativity.[6] As philosophers such as Nietzsche have pointed out, inspiration is the most dramatic stage in the creative process, appearing as a revelation, or otherworldly.[7]

In India too, there is a comparable awareness of this transformative moment in the creative process; but there, significantly, the idea of inspiration is connected to deep intuition and not to inventive creation; the artist's goal therefore is not so much to create a form that is unique and separate from all precursors. As pointed out by Stella Kramrisch:

> The Indian artist…did not think of wanting to be known as different from others—as unique; on the contrary, he wanted to be known as conveying surpassingly well what other artists then and in the future would endeavor to convey. His singularity does not stress or seek otherness, but strives for intensity of realization and for power in giving form to content experienced and approached by all those for whom he works.[8]

THE EXPERIENCE OF CREATIVITY

Since art is communicative, all creative acts have to be depicted in some outward form. Forms have to be tested, arranged, and rearranged, until they adequately convey the creative insight. Consequently, the process of translating intuitive knowledge or awareness into a meaningful form requires a total mastery of the craft, or art-making technique. All texts on Indian arts, from the *Bharata Natyashastra* and *Abhinaya Darpana* to the *Vishnudharmottara Purana*, are clear about the relationship between mastery of technique and true insight. One of the principal verses of the *Abhinaya Darpana* vividly describes this relationship:

> *Wherever the hands go, follow the eyes, where the eyes go, follows the mind,*
> *With the mind goes the inner expression, and with that emerges the true rasa.*[9]

Intended as a guideline for dancers, the verse connects the physical technique with the expression of a creative aesthetic experience. It is understood that superior technique is necessary, but not synonymous with the intuitive knowledge. Since the goal is to fuse the known archetypes with fresh vitality, it is important for the artist to learn the archetypes well to imbue them with fresh insights. The value lies in how well the performer or the artist is able to find that inner quality and communicate it with those who partake of the art as performers or as viewers.

The responsibility for making manifest that which is not ordinarily known or visible lies not only with the artist but also with the viewer. In other words, creativity, as understood in the pre-modern Indian context, is associated not only with the artist but also with the audience. The *rasa* theory, as described in ancient texts and analyzed by scholars of Indian art, makes this clear.[10] Aesthetic delight, the experience of creative beauty, is an interactive process that involves not only the insight of the artist made evident in a form, but also the ability of a viewer to perceive the inner truth, the artistic intuition. Although some early theoreticians maintained that this capacity to feel the true *rasa* of a work is not acquired by study, but is gained from the virtues of a past life,[11] other references to art-making practices, as well as to the idea of a *rasika* or connoisseur, suggest that sustained experience of works of art can in fact yield a greater capacity for appreciation.

Such discussions of creativity and the experience of art might seem too essentialist or to imply that for most of two millennia or more, art making in India remained unchanged. Similarly, it could be observed that a lack of emphasis on individual creativity was part of many other cultures, including the medieval world of Europe and the societies of the Islamic world.[12] Both observations have merit, but it is equally true that there is a persistence of older forms and a corresponding lack of emphasis on radical innovation in Indian art and theory throughout its pre-modern history.

Even in the contemporary art world, there have been artists and writers who have questioned the singular status awarded to the value of originality. One of the foremost contemporary Indian painters, K. G. Subramanyan, has written eloquently about the problematic of seeking novelty above all other elements in his book *Creative Circuit.* He acknowledges that it is hard for individual artists in the current situation to lay aside "the mantle of idiosyncrasy and innovation," given the fact that one is always placed as an "individual among individuals and pushed into competition with the rest."[13] But he places much higher value in finding one's place between the ability to create and to respond to one's own cultural context:

> That an artist is not burdened today with predispositions coming from society or prevalent cultural forms may be true, but he is not functioning in a vacuum either. When he uses this freedom to find his personal moorings and work-circuit, he is coming into certain relationships with whatever is around; some that he shares with other artists of his time, some cultural, some personal and individual. It falls to a responsive observer, critic or connoisseur to be aware of this. So to find real access to a work or to get something out of it, he will have to go to the *norms* behind the *forms.*[14]

What is striking about Subramanyan's comments is that while acknowledging the modern condition of an artist in India as being fundamentally different from that of the pre-modern artist, he still places much less value on creativity as a thing separate from culture and looks to find a space between the two tendencies: an individual choice of what one wants to do, and making sense of it in the context of the world one finds oneself in. For him, "the most rewarding and hopeful thing in the modern art world is the eventful courtship, even quarrel, of these two tendencies and the opening of exciting horizons in-between."[15] In other words, even in the contemporary Indian art world there is a strong sense of skepticism about pursuing the latest fashion or putting too much weight on distinctive newness as a value in itself.

THE EXPERIENCE OF THE POLSKY COLLECTION

These observations are, again, relevant to our appreciation of the Polsky collection. A large majority of these works of art date from the later historical periods, when the subcontinent had thoroughly integrated Islam into its cultural fabric. Under the influence of rulers such as the Mughals, art-making practices of non-Indian Islamic origin had been assimilated. Even so, such elements did not radically change the basic notions of art making, nor did they really alter the role of artists and their relationship to their patrons.[16]

We may find, in contrast to earlier periods, a greater emphasis on individual artists at the Mughal court, and visible elements of Safavid court painting in the early Akbari period style. Yet, by and large, the effect is that of an incremental change, and of innovation through assimilation, rather than of total transformation. The ancient stories such as the *Ramayana* persist, but are given fresh interpretations, by adding Persianate mountains to a landscape or by imparting a greater degree of naturalism to the main iconic characters. New ideas about portraiture flourish at the Mughal and Rajput courts, but soon after the Westernized notions of naturalism are introduced, the portraits once again revert to being iconic, symbolizing larger meanings. Even the idea of visual specificity or "observed reality" can take on an iconographic meaning. Thus, the blindness of the ruler Sital Dev of Mankot, along with his known devotional spirit, is treated more as an exaggerated visual element than an observable or contextual reality (cat. no. 137). While his face may have the kind of sensitive naturalism that we find in the more humanized paintings of the Mughal court, it is placed against the bright, two-dimensional patterns of turmeric gold, vermilion orange, and an unlikely pinkish mauve. It is this capacity to absorb the new and make it into an archetype, and the ability to live with the incongruent juxtapositions of the foreign and the indigenous, that leads people to remark that Indians live in many centuries at once, or that the past is ever present in India.

The works of art in the Polsky collection reflect this essential reality of India in many ways. Even some of the most modern works, the contemporary photographs of Raghubir Singh, take on an iconic air when seen beside the paintings and decorative arts of earlier eras. Rather than being representations of a fleeting moment, they create an atmosphere where time stops, almost becoming archetypes of India where the past and present come together and develop a fluid relationship to one another. As I have suggested in my foreword, the thematic organization of the Polsky collection in this book and exhibition is intended to suggest just such recurrent archetypes and past-present connections. It is hoped that our readers and viewers will experience these works in a similar vein.

1 Several major scholars of Indian art have written about the role of art, artists, and creative powers in Indian culture; much of what is written has been colored by the writings of Ananda Coomaraswamy and Stella Kramrisch in particular; e.g. see A. K. Coomaraswamy, *The transformation of nature into art*, Cambridge, Mass., 1934; and *The dance of Shiva*, New York, 1924; and Barbara Stoler Miller ed., *Exploring India's sacred art: Selected writings of Stella Kramrisch*, Philadelphia, 1983.

2 Some of the observations made here are based on the writings of Ralph J. Hallman, particularly: "The necessary and sufficient conditions of creativity," *Journal of Humanistic Psychology*, Spring 1963, pp. 17–19; "Toward a Hindu theory of creativity," *Educational Theory*, n.d., pp. 368–76.

3 Hallman, "Towards a Hindu theory of creativity," p. 369.

4 See A. Shearer and P. Russell tr., *The Upanishads*, New York, 2003, pp. 51–59.

5 *Mundaka Upanishad*, III, 1–3: E. Easwaran tr., *The Upanishads*, Berkeley, 1987, p. 115.

6 In the West, the creative process is seen as a series of four chronological stages, each one making a special contribution to the overall process. Hallman describes them as follows: 1) preparation: the accumulation of data, meanings, and imagery; 2) incubation: commingling and fusing of these data in unconscious levels of the mind; 3) inspiration: the sudden insight into new connections among the data; and 4) verification: the use of craftsmanship or cultural tools which can externalize these insights: Hallman, "The necessary and sufficient conditions of creativity." He points out that Indian traditional literature also refers to comparable stages, but places no particular emphasis on their causal or chronological connection, and sees the entire process primarily in spiritual terms.

7 Hallman, "Towards a Hindu theory of creativity," p. 372.

8 S. Kramrisch, "Artist, patron and public in India," in Miller ed., *Exploring India's Sacred Art*, p. 55.

9 See Manubhai Bhatt, *Abhinaya Darpana of Nandikeshvar*, Ahmedabad, 1965 (in Gujarati); and A. K. Coomaraswamy, *Mirror of Gesture*, 1935.

10 One of the clearest descriptions of *rasa* theory is given by B. N. Goswamy in the exhibition catalogue *Essence of Indian art*, San Francisco, 1986.

11 A. K. Coomaraswamy, "That beauty is a state," in *The Dance of Shiva*, Bombay, 1956 (third ed.), p. 68.

12 Coomaraswamy has written eloquently on the subject in *The Christian and Oriental or true philosophy of art*, London, 1943.

13 K. G. Subramanyan, *The Creative Circuit*, Calcutta, 1992, pp. 76–79.

14 *Ibid.*, pp. 67–68.

15 *Ibid.*, p. 67.

16 Partha Mitter argues that the status of the artist and his relationship to his patron did not really change until the mid-nineteenth century, under the influence of the British colonial education system, when the older systems of patronage broke down and a new educated middle class of artists in the Western sense emerged: P. Mitter, *Art and nationalism in colonial India 1850-1922*, Cambridge, 1994.

In the Realm of Gods

Executed in a wide range of media and styles, the works of art in the Polsky collections also represent many different periods of Indian history, from Kushan times or earlier (ca. 100 BC–AD 300) to the present day, as well as greatly differing cultural milieux: mainly Hindu, Buddhist or Jain, but also Islamic and European. Yet despite their diversity, these works constantly touch on or illumine certain recurrent, unifying strands of Indian life and experience, so creating a rich, kaleidoscopic pattern from apparently disparate elements. These fundamental themes are set out in the various section headings of this book, from Nature to Courtly Manuscripts. These sections are also grouped in two divisions, which mainly represent religious works of art and those relating to courtly life: it should, however, be noted at once that distinctions between the sacred and the secular are generally less clear in India—and often far more permeable—than would be the case in a European context.

Throughout the Indian subcontinent, a sense of the numinous remains more universal and more inclusive than in the post-medieval West. The towering, complex edifice of Hindu belief, myth, and practice has evolved gradually over five millennia, yet it also remains timeless. Despite constant metamorphosis, nothing essential has been lost in the process; all of its constituent stages of development remain in some sense valid and related. Thus the divine may be found and venerated in a simple country or wayside shrine, perhaps originally founded on a distinctively shaped rock or an ancient tree, as much as in the huge temple complexes that have developed over the last two thousand years, with their wealth of sculptural representations of the gods, created in response to the major theistic cults that grew from the Kushan period, continuing to expand in response to *pervasive currents of* bhakti *devotionalism. A resurgence of Vishnu* bhakti *centered on the avatars Krishna and Rama, which continues to flourish, similarly gave rise to a vigorous later flowering of the Hindu manuscript painting tradition, from around 1500 until the early nineteenth century. Many examples of such paintings are found in the Polsky collections, along with similar works which celebrate the longer established cults of Shiva, Vishnu, and the Goddess, whether in painting or earlier stone and bronze sculpture and refined decorative objects in ivory and other materials.*

Finally, and felicitously, these varied works of art reflecting the main strands of Indian religious culture are augmented here by landscape, architectural, and other subjects carefully documented in nineteenth-century British photographs, and—more expressively still—by the contemporary photographs of Raghubir Singh. In his life's work he brought an acute, Cartier-Bressonian eye to capturing revelatory instants from the overwhelming transient spectacle of Indian life: moments of time which are often also informed by his intuitive perception of the seemingly incongruous or paradoxical cohabitation between India's timeless aspect and the strident manifestations of modernity.

AT

NATURE

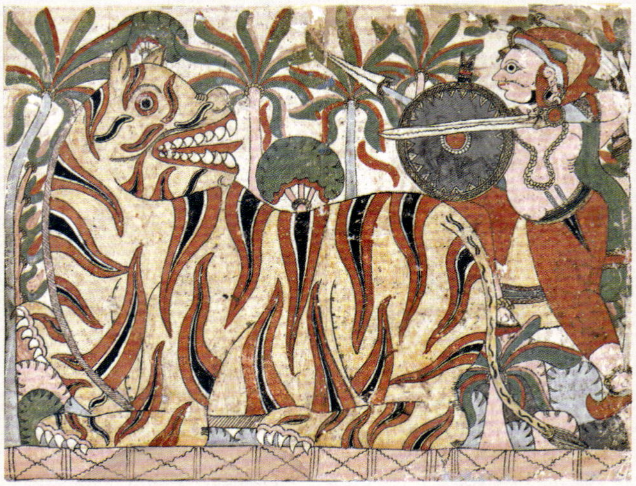

More than all the themes of this book, that of nature permeates not only this section but most others also. With its awesome manifold energies, both benign and destructive, nature has always played an elemental role in Indian life and art. Its seasonal power is manifested most dramatically in the monsoon rains, which inundate and regenerate the earth after the searing summer heat. This life-giving transformation of the landscape has been celebrated in most ages by poets in classical languages such as Sanskrit, as well as in the later vernaculars:

> *The fire has left the mountain range*
> *and the blackened woods grow back;*
> *the horizon now is serrate with fresh clouds*
> *and the sky is clear of dust;*
> *what's more, the beautiful* kadamba
> *is thickly covered with its waves of buds,*
> *and peacocks at long last have broken*
> *their vow of silence.*

BHAVABHUTI, CA. AD 725[1]

In Indian sculpture and painting, the bountiful abundance and sheer life force of nature are universally celebrated in traditional decorative imagery of birds, animals, plants, and trees, or in continuous panels of sinuous flowering plant stems and scrolls, especially the undulating stalk of the lotus flower, a symbol of purity and enlightenment. Trees and shrubs too—remnants of the primordial forests which once covered the land—were venerated for their fruits, shade, and medicinal or auspicious properties, and were represented in art as the teeming abode of snakes, birds, and animals such as monkeys. Birds, animals, and even serpents were loved or respected in their own right, even when (like deer) they were also hunted and eaten. The horse especially was esteemed by the nobility, who relied on it as their mount in battle, and likewise the elephant. In general, man was traditionally seen as being close to the animal and natural worlds, as also to the supernal worlds of the gods (*devas*) and demons (*asuras*): all these various realms formed a hierarchical continuum of being and reincarnation, according to one's individual karma.

As well as being carved, modeled, and painted with great sympathy and insight by artists, animals and birds played a major role in myths, stories, and fables. The *Jataka* tales of the supposed earlier lives of the Buddha center on his incarnations in animal or bird form, and in the *Ramayana* epic, Rama's allies in his quest to find Sita and defeat the demon Ravana included the eagle Jatayu, Hanuman the monkey-god, and whole armies of monkeys and bears. Each of the major gods had his vehicle (*vahana*) or cult animal: Shiva, the bull; Vishnu, the man-bird Garuda; Brahma, the goose (*hamsa)*; Devi, the lion. As a plentiful provider, the cow attained a huge cultural significance (and inviolability), and later became associated particularly with the cult of Krishna. Some birds and animals also grew in the human mind to assume a powerful symbolic importance, such as the auspicious hamsa or sacred goose, or the water-dwelling, crocodile-like monster of the deep (*makara*). Sometimes birds, animals, and plant forms would become amalgamated and transformed into fantastic composite creatures such as the leogryph (*vyala*), symbolizing the awesome fecundity and potential ferocity both of the outer, natural world and of the inner world of the human psyche. Through such potent images man and nature are seen as one and inseparable.

During the period of Islamic rule in Northern India, the Mughal Emperors Babur (1526–30) and Jahangir (1605–27) wrote vivid memoirs which record with keen observation the diversity and splendor of India's flora and fauna. Mughal artists, who had learned their skills from Iranian and European as well as Indian models, excelled at representing birds, beasts, and flowers in manuscript illustrations or album paintings. Flower imagery, moreover, became the central motif of Mughal decoration. Arrays of poppies and other blooms are found almost everywhere, in architectural decoration, the borders of paintings, the embellishment of woodwork and ivory, carpets and textiles, metalwork and glass. Later Hindu painters, as a rule, aspired less to close observation than to sympathetic imagination in their treatment of the plant and animal worlds, as is seen in the expressively ferocious tigers lurking in vibrant jungles of a Maharashtran folk artist (cat. no. 16) or the court artists of Kotah in Rajasthan (cat. nos. 118–19).

AT

1 Ingalls, D. H. H. tr., Sanskrit poetry from Vidyakara's "Treasury," Cambridge, Mass, 1972, no. 225.

1

Virabadra Drug

LINNEAUS TRIPE (1822–1902)

Virabhadradurgam, Tamil Nadu, 1857–58
Albumen silver print from a waxed calotype negative
27.7 × 38.2 cm (10 7/8 × 15 1/16 in.)
Published: Linneaus Tripe, *Photographic views of Ryakotta and other places in the Salem District*, Madras, 1858, pl. 7
Metropolitan Museum of Art, New York, Purchase, Cynthia Hazen Polsky and Lila Acheson Wallace Gifts (1997.382.60)

TRIPE'S PHOTOGRAPHIC FAME as one of the great calotype photographers of the nineteenth century rests largely on the series of slim folio volumes of South Indian architectural studies published in 1858, containing the results of his work as Government Photographer in the Madras Presidency from 1856 to 1859. The creation of such a post, short-lived as it proved to be, was the result of the growing scholarly interest in the antiquities and archaeological heritage of the subcontinent, which in 1854 had led the East India Company to issue a minute offering official encouragement of the "useful art"of photography in the documentation of Indian architecture.[1] Tripe, an officer in the Madras Army, was the natural candidate for any such post in the Madras Presidency, having just produced a remarkable and well-received series of views while acting as official photographer to a diplomatic mission sent by the Indian Government to the Burmese court at Ava in 1855.

This view of the "drug" or hill fort at Virabadra is one of ten prints pasted into his *Photographic views of Ryakotta*, issued by the Madras Government in 1858. In contrast to the Daniells's sharply delineated aquatint of the same fort made half a century before, Tripe sets his more distant view in a hazy landscape emphasizing the surround-ing vistas of sharply rising wooded hills. The grainy texture of the paper negative and the rich purplish toning of the image, together with the light cloud effects painted directly onto the negative, are all characteristic of Tripe's work. The prints in the Ryakotta volume are distinctive in locating his subjects more fully within the context of their distinctive rugged environment, in contrast to his more usual closer concentration on the architectural structure itself. For J. A. C. Boswell, author of the descriptive notes that accompanied the photographs, such views could also be pressed into service to point out a moral lesson, over and above their pictorial value. For Boswell, writing in the shadow of the recent Mutiny, such images served as visual evidence both of a barbarous past "now crumbling in the dust," and of the promise of "Christian European Civilization," in which "everything speaks in language that cannot be mistaken that a brighter day has already dawned in India."

JF

1 Bombay public despatches, 26 December 1854.

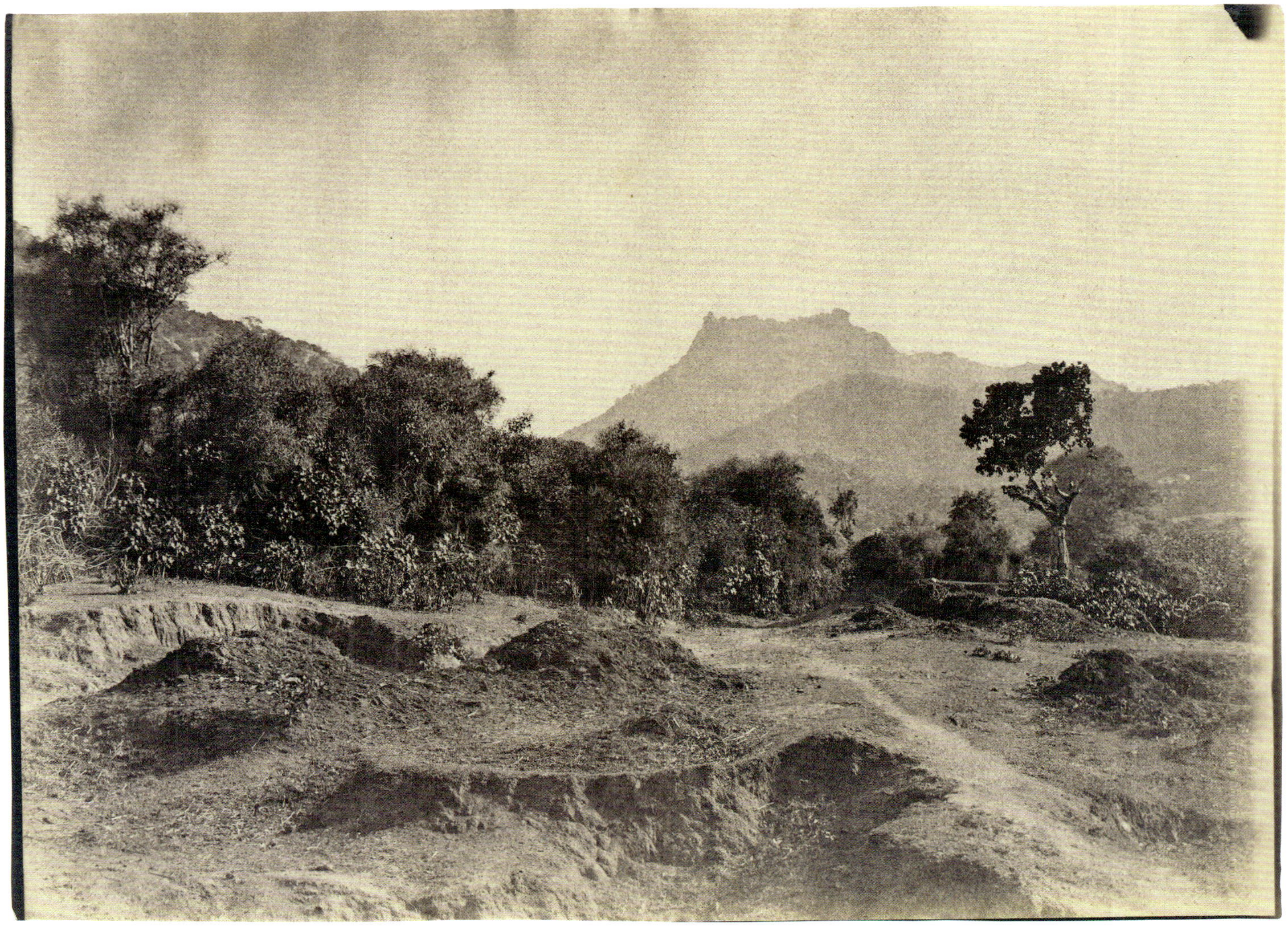

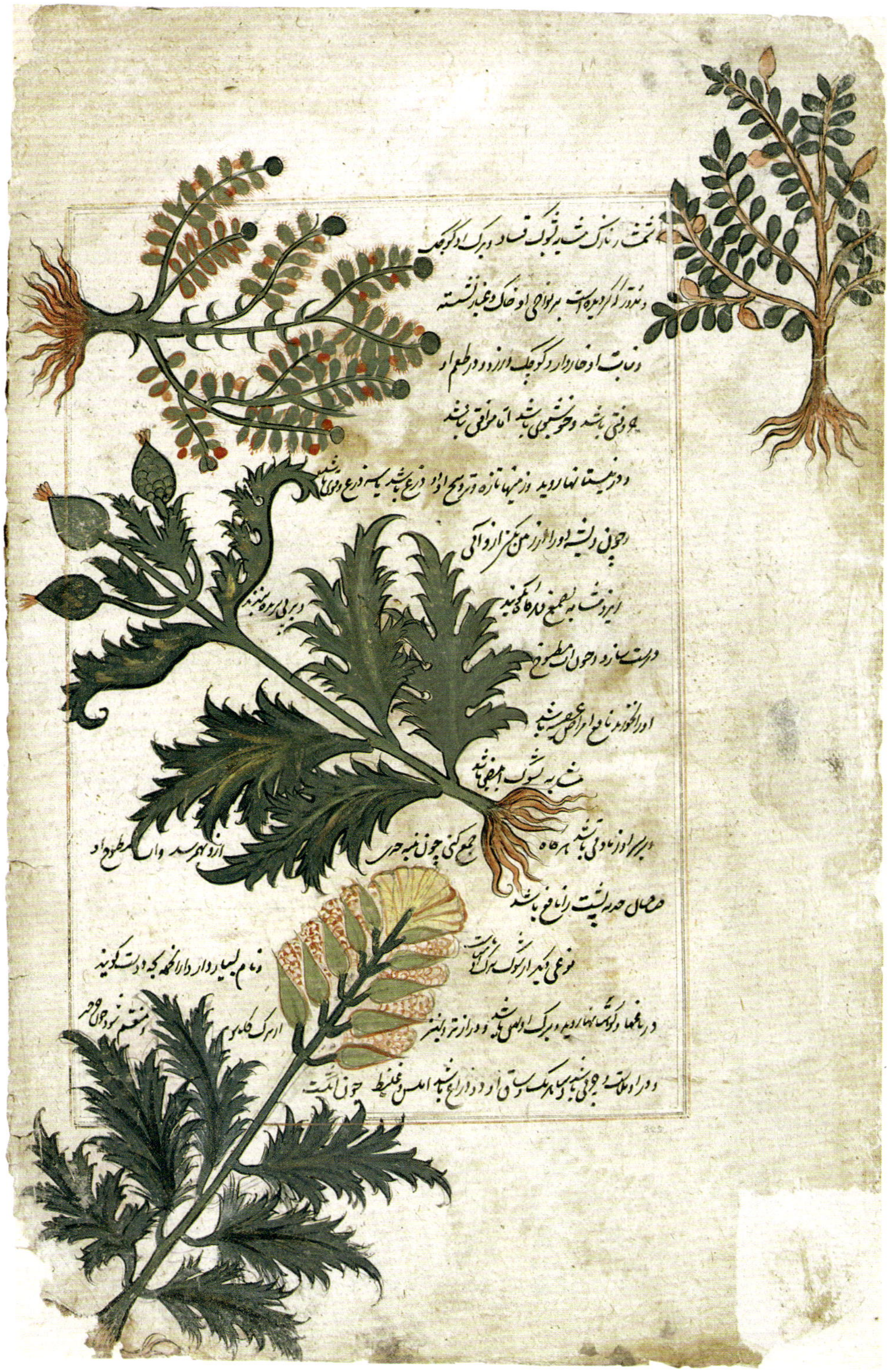

2

Thistles and other medicinal plants

FOLIO FROM A MANUSCRIPT OF KITAB-I HASHA'ISH (DE MATERIA MEDICA OF DIOSCORIDES), TRANSLATED FROM THE ARABIC INTO PERSIAN BY GHIYAS AL-DIN MUHAMMAD RIZAVI

Probably from the Deccan, 1645
Ink and watercolor on paper
Image 40 × 24.5 cm (15 ½ × 9 ¾ in.);
page 40 × 25.5 cm (15 ½ × 10 in.)
Private collection

THIS DISPERSED MANUSCRIPT IS REMARKABLE for the arrangement of the plants on the page, which crowd in among the fifteen lines of the Persian text in *nasta'liq* script in a free and almost unprecedented manner, in contrast to the more formal arrangement of drawing and text in earlier manuscripts. It is possible that the plants, which here include two specimens of thistle, were drawn first and the text then fitted in around them. A page in the Hodgkin Collection has simply three clumps of bamboo on the page, without any text.[1] Roots, stems, leaves, and flowers are all shown in the drawings.

Dioscorides's work on medicinal plants was one of the most important legacies of the classical age to the Middle Ages, and survived in Greek in the famous manuscript of Juliana Anicia of 512 now in Vienna. A Syriac version was used as the basis of the Arabic translation by Mihran ibn Mansur, done in what is now south-eastern Turkey for the Artuqid Prince Najm al-Din Alpi (1152–76). This is one of the most famous of the illustrated manuscripts of Dioscorides, and was deposited in the Shrine Library at Mashhad in north-east Iran by Shah 'Abbas I (1588–1629), who before doing so ordered Ghiyas al-Muhammad Rizavi to make a Persian translation. The original of this translated version is now lost, but the text survives in other copies.

Two copies of it were prepared in 1645, one now in Dublin, and the second the dispersed copy from which this folio comes.[2] Barbara Schmitz writes that these copies resemble in layout the Mashhad manuscript, but in fact in this folio this is not the case; it has four illustrations rather than the two which are on the related Mashhad page.[3] Text and illustrations are interwoven with a great freedom in this manuscript, more so than in the somewhat stilted layout of the Dublin manuscript in the only so-far published page.[4] The way in which the space has been utilized to give primacy to the illustrations is very Indian, and has led various authorities to attribute this version specifically to Bijapur. There was extensive Iranian influence on the Deccani kingdoms in the sixteenth and seventeenth centuries.

JPL

1 Topsfield and Beach, 1991, no. 7; further pages from this manuscript are published in McInerney, 1982, no. 17, and Lawton and Lentz, 1998, pp. 184–85.

2 The date has also been read as 1004/1595 (McInerney, *loc. cit.*) rather than the more likely 1054/1645, but the colophon page is unpublished. Massumeh Farhad suggests that this is in fact a different Persian translation (Lawton and Lentz, p. 184), and this point awaits clarification.

3 Schmitz, 1992, p. 14.

4 S. Carboni, "The Arabic manuscripts," in *Pages of perfection: Islamic paintings and calligraphy from the Russian Academy of Sciences, St Petersburg*, Lugano, 1995, p. 90.

3

A wandering ascetic and a fox seek the fruit of a tree

FROM THE FIRST IMPERIAL COPY OF THE BABURNAMA, CUT FROM ITS TEXT AND MOUNTED AS AN ALBUM PAGE WITHIN A BORDER

Mughal, ca. 1590
Opaque watercolor on paper.
Image 8.6 × 12.4 cm (3 ⅜ × 4 ⅞ in.)
page 10.8 × 14.6 cm (4 ¼ × 5 ¾ in.)

THE BABURNAMA, OR MEMOIRS OF THE MUGHAL EMPEROR BABUR (r. 1526–30), is one of the greatest and most interesting of pre-modern autobiographical books.[1] He records in detail not only the events of his own tumultuous life, but also his reactions to India on first coming into that fabled land in 1526, and to its people, its flora, and its fauna. It was written in Turki, the ancestral language of the Mughals, and his grandson Akbar ordered it to be translated into Persian for the better comprehension of his court. This work was entrusted to Akbar's friend Mirza 'Abd al-Rahim Khan-i Khanan, who presented the finished translation to Akbar in November 1589. Court artists immediately set about producing an illustrated version. Most of this text is now dispersed, but twenty folios are in the Victoria and Albert Museum, London.[2] At least three more illustrated manuscripts based on this first version were produced within the next ten years, which are now in the British Library; divided between the Moscow State Museum of Eastern Cultures and the Walters Art Gallery, Baltimore; and in the National Museum, New Delhi.

Babur in his memoirs describes those fauna and flora of India that differ from Central Asia just after relating how his forces defeated those of the Sultan of Delhi, Ibrahim Lodi, at the Battle of Panipat in 1526. In the dispersed manuscript, this section occupies thirty folios: whole folios measure 26 × 15.3 cm most with paintings on both sides, some of them arranged two to the page in horizontal format, as would have been the case here. Miskin, Kanha, and Tulsi the Younger are the artists who are known to have worked on this section.[3] The tree seems to be the lote-fruit or *ber* tree (*Zizyphus jujuba*), which produces lots of plum-like fruits during the winter months, but which were not much to Babur's liking. Our illustration shows the tree in fruit, with an ascetic, his worldly possessions wrapped up in a cloth hung over his shoulder, and a fox staring expectantly at it. The unknown artist has treated this subject with the fresh and spontaneous brushwork common to many artists of this manuscript, suggestive of the great haste with which much of it was illustrated.[4] It is still a far more elaborate painting than the same subject in the British Library manuscript, in which the artist Mani shows just the tree in a rocky landscape.[5]

JPL

1 Tr. A. S. Beveridge, *The Babur-nama in English*, London, 1912–22.

2 Stronge, 2002, pp. 86–91; E. Smart, "Six folios from a dispersed manuscript of the *Babur-Nama*," in *Indian painting*, London: Colnaghi & Co, 1978, pp. 109–32.

3 *Ibid.*, p. 113.

4 A full-page miniature for this manuscript still took one artist fifty days (*ibid.*, p. 113).

5 BL Or. 3714, f. 399v, reproduced H.Suleiman, *Miniatures of the Babur-Nama*, Tashkent, 1970, p. 78.

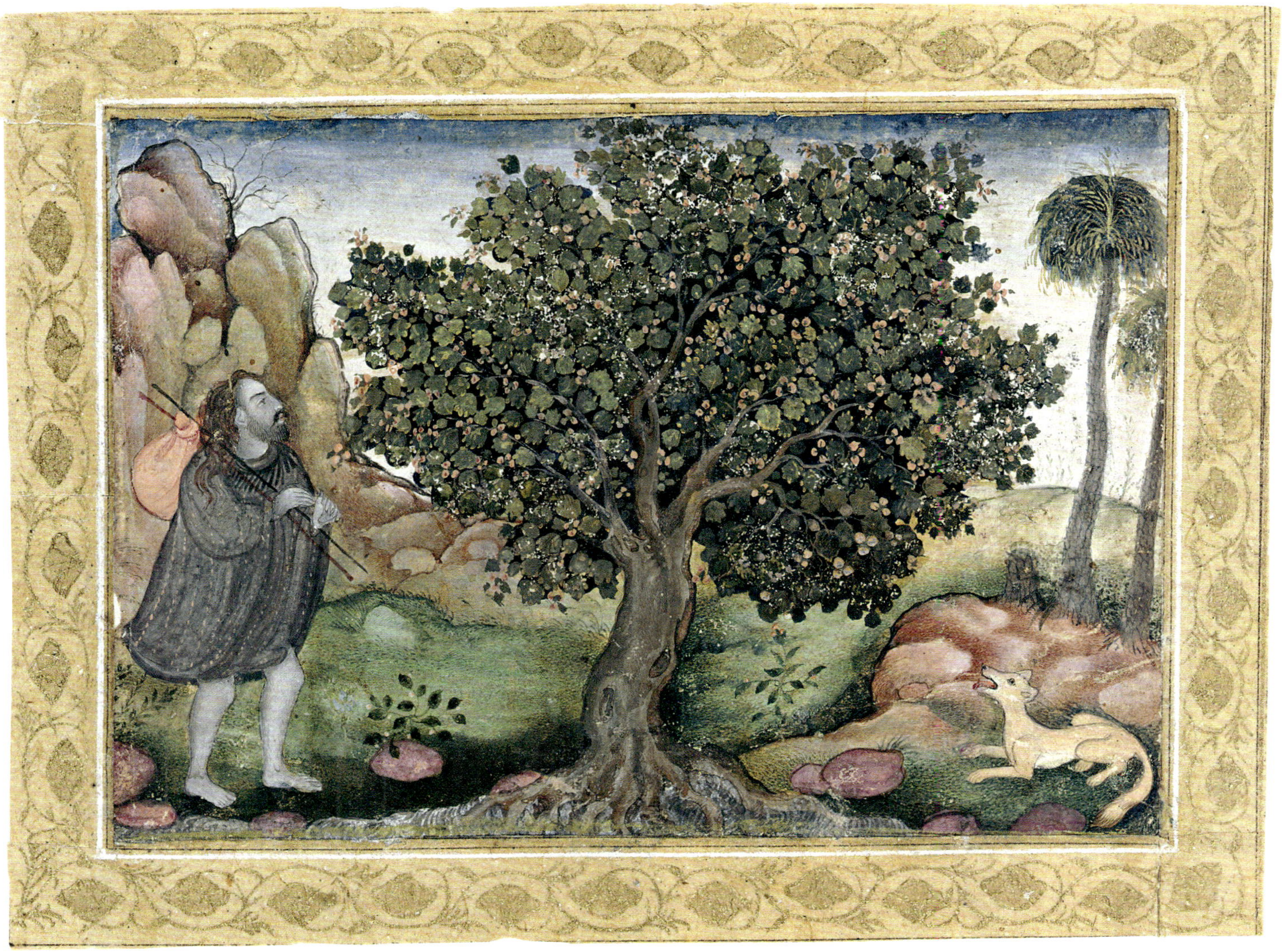

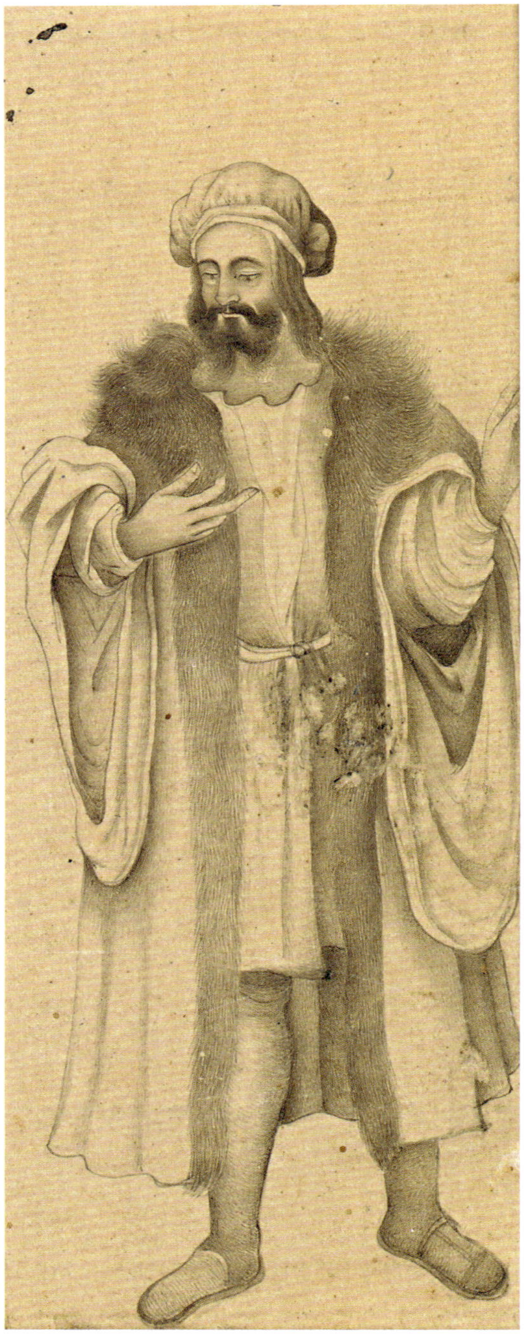

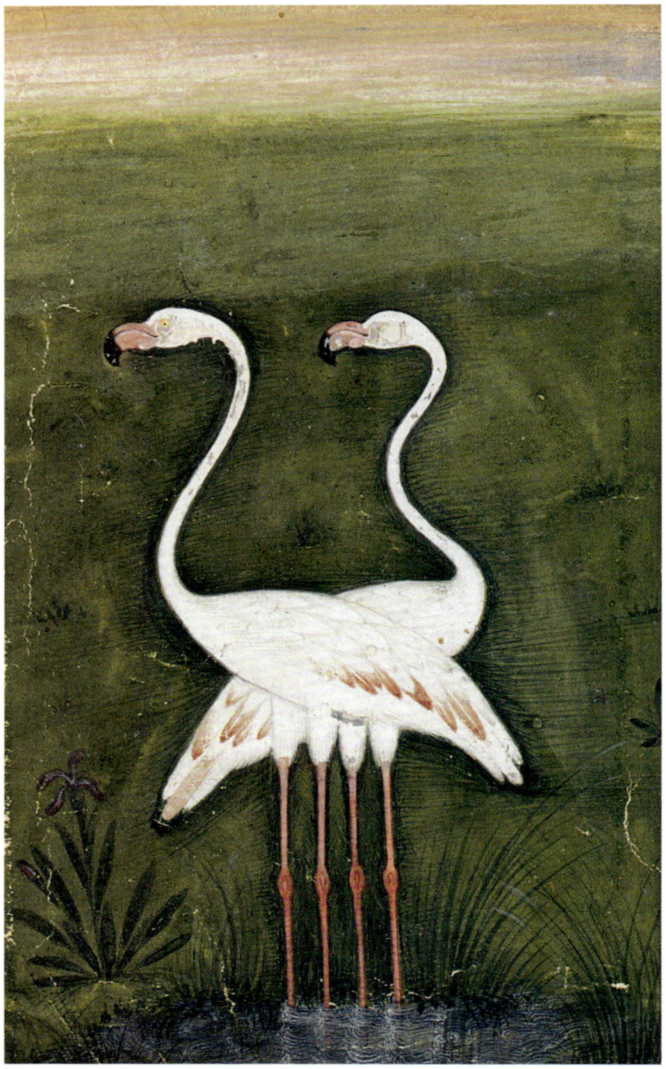

4

Two-sided image:

Two flamingos standing in a pool

MUGHAL, 1630–40

Opaque watercolor on paper
8.3 × 6 cm (3 ¼ × 2 ⅜ in.)
Published: T. McInerney, *Indian paintings from the Polsky Collections*, Princeton, 1982, no. 4

A European in fifteenth-century costume

MUGHAL, CA. 1650

Brush drawing in ink on paper
17.1 × 6.4 cm (6 ¾ × 2 ½ in.)

TWO FLAMINGOS STAND WITH THEIR FEET IN A POOL, their legs parallel, their bodies facing opposite ways, but one twists its neck around to form a serpentine line parallel to its friend's neck. The pool is beautifully handled, with some rushes and an iris on its bank, but the landscape is treated more broadly as it retreats to a streakily colored sky at the top of the page.

The Mughal Emperor Jahangir (1605–27) was particularly fond of telling his artists to draw natural history subjects, and had his chief specialist in this field, the artist Mansur, draw many now-famous images, especially of such exotic imports as a zebra and a turkey-cock. These subjects were extensively copied for inclusion in later Mughal albums, right up until the nineteenth century. In this instance, our pair of flamingos seems based on a similar study of two flamingos in a more extensive landscape, datable to about 1620, now in the Cowasji Jehangir Collection in Bombay.[1] A mallard in the same collection[2] gives a clue as to the purpose of such a copy, since this subject reappears in the album in the British Library compiled by Prince Dara Shikoh for his wife Nadira Banu Begum between 1633 and 1642.[3] Although in the particular case of the mallard the extensive landscape has also been copied, many of the subjects in Dara Shikoh's album have been given backgrounds very similar to that of our flamingos. The painting must once have graced an album of the reign of Shah Jahan (1628–58). At some later stage, it was extracted and placed in an album back to back with a mid-seventeenth-century Mughal brush drawing of a European in fifteenth-century costume. This is a fine and sensitive copy, noteworthy for the rendering of the texture of the fur.

JPL

1 Khandalavala and Chandra, 1965, no. 20.

2 *Ibid.*, no. 21.

3 Falk and Archer, 1981, pp. 72–81, reproduced pp. 379–400. The mallard is f. 10, while backgrounds similar to our flamingos are seen particularly on ff. 6 and 16. See also Pal, 1993, no. 82, for a mid-Aurangzeb period portrait with this type of landscape.

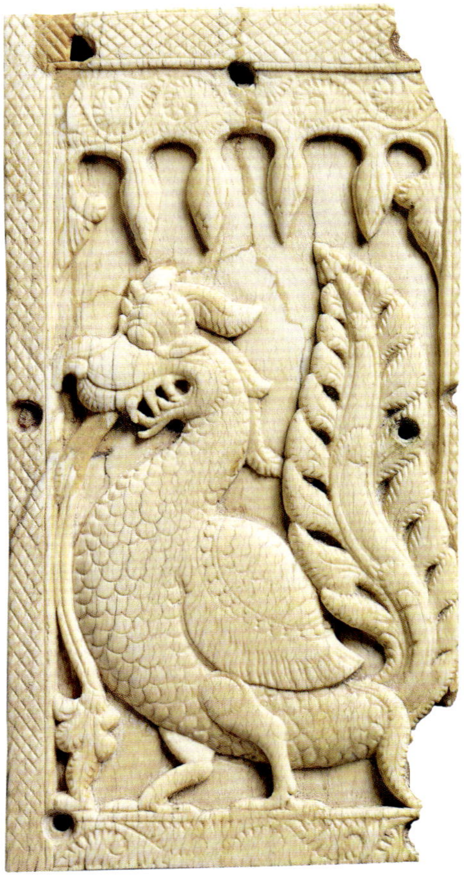

5

Ivory panel depicting a fantastic bird

EASTERN INDIA, ORISSA,
SEVENTEENTH CENTURY

H. 14.9 cm (5 ⅞ in.)

THIS IVORY PANEL DEPICTS a fantastic bird with the head of a lion, a feathered body, and the long tail of a peacock; a long palm frond issues from its mouth. Four buds and two half-opened leaves hang from a scrolling row of palmettes, which are also found on the lower border, with a hatched outer border to the left and top. The panel was probably originally attached to a box or a piece of furniture. Another furniture panel with a rearing lion, also with a palm frond issuing from the mouth, is in the Los Angeles County Museum.[1] The lion is a symbol of royal power and majesty, and the image reinforces the authority of the owner of the object.

Fantastic animals form a rich part of the Indian decorative vocabulary. Animals formed from elements of various creatures are found in both sculpture and paintings. Composite animals which combine humans and creatures in contorted attitudes to form another animal such as an elephant, camel, or horse occur in Mughal, Rajput, and South Indian painting.[2] Interpretations of these figures vary, and range from the literal representation of female acrobats to mythological depictions.[3] Tavernier describes a group of nine acrobats who represented themselves as an elephant at Masulipatam.[4] Other fantastic animals include the leogryph (*vyala* in Sanskrit), a rampant lion with horns and foliate tail which decorated Western and Central Indian temples between the seventh and tenth centuries,[5] and the *gajasimha*, a lion with an elephant's head.[6]

MCS

1 Pal, 1981, fig. 77.

2 Okada, 1986, nos. 132–33, 135.

3 For discussion, see R. del Bontà, "Indian composite paintings: A playful art," *Orientations*, January 1996, pp. 31–38; for a drawing of acrobats, see Welch, 1976, no. 48.

4 *Ibid.*

5 Pal, 1997, nos. 346–47.

6 The Freer Gallery ivory throne leg is a *gajasimha*: A. Lippe, 1970, pp. 41–46.

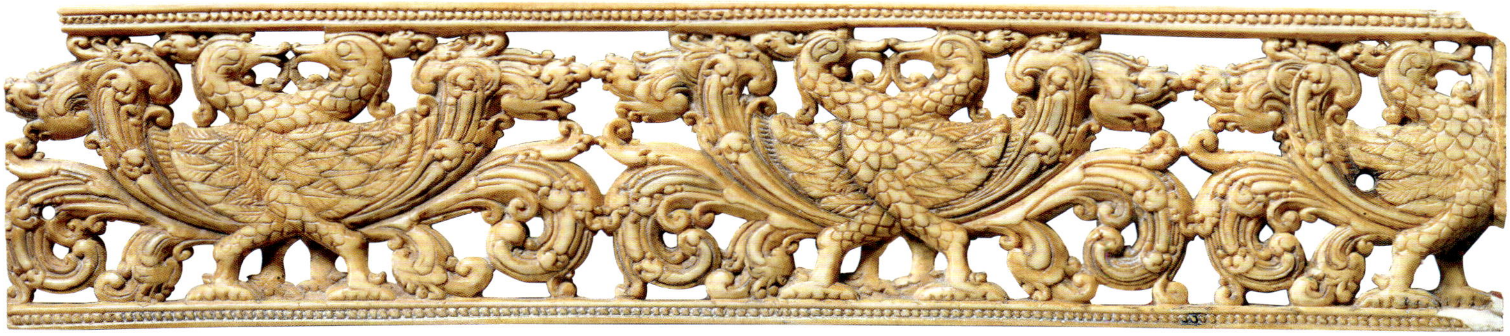

6

Ivory panel with geese

SRI LANKA (CEYLON),
SEVENTEENTH CENTURY

5.1 × 25.4 cm (2 × 10 in.)

THIS IVORY OPENWORK PANEL SECTION depicts two pairs of geese amid scrolling foliage, with a further single goose at the right-hand end. The birds are depicted with their necks entwined and facing each other, the single bird facing right, with further decoration of a line of beaded decoration along the top and bottom edges. This panel was originally part of a longer section, and was probably attached to a piece of furniture. A seventeenth-century box with a panel of birds is in the British Museum,[1] while a very similar design of two birds with necks entwined is found on a later comb, also in the British Museum.[2] The scrolls are characteristic of those found in South India and Sri Lanka. The range of decorative devices employed by the ivory carvers was wide, and included birds, lions, and floral motifs. Narrow panels such as this would be assembled over the wooden core of the box, together with the larger principal decorative panels. The panels could be openwork as here, or solid ivory with floral scrolls and figures.[3]

These boxes were probably destined for export to Europe, to the Portuguese or Dutch markets. The eagerness of Europeans to acquire ivory boxes was evident as soon as the Portuguese reached Sri Lanka. Dom João de Castro (governor of Portuguese India, 1545–48) received chests from the King of Kotte and other rulers, and he gave chests to Queen Catherine, wife of Dom João III of Portugal (r. 1521–57). The 1550–52 inventory of her possessions includes "an ivory casket in the shape of a small box, all worked with imagery and foliage with lock and key made of gold . . . sent from India to the Queen by Dom João de Castro."[4]

MCS

1 Acc. no. OA 1892.2–16.25: M. Willis, "Early Indian ivory," *Arts of Asia*, 28, no. 2, March–April 1998, fig. 126.

2 Acc. no. OA 1919.11–4.54: *Ibid*, fig. 124, attributed to Sri Lanka, nineteenth century.

3 Tchakaloff et al., 1998, nos. 26, 52.

4 A. Jaffer and M. A. Schwabe, "A group of sixteenth-century ivory caskets from Ceylon," *Apollo*, CXLIX, March 1999, no. 445, p. 8.

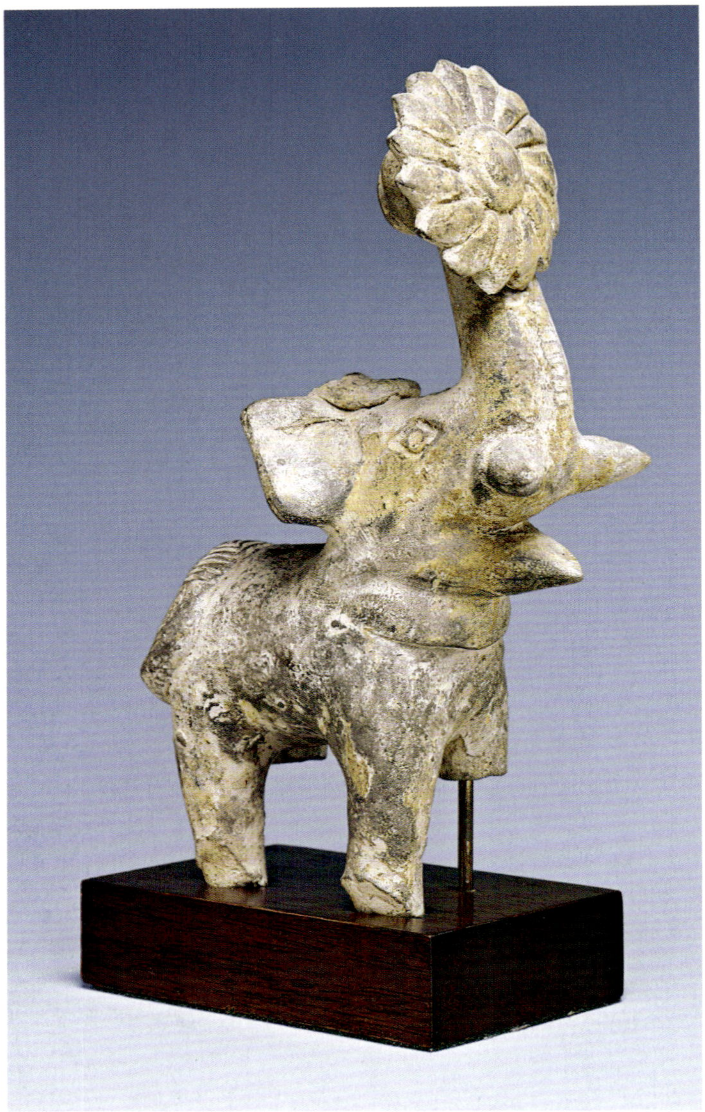

7

Elephant with a raised trunk

MATHURA AREA, UTTAR PRADESH, SECOND CENTURY BC

Terracotta
H. 17.8 cm (7 in.)

IN THIS BLACK CLAY TERRACOTTA FIGURE of an elephant, his trunk is raised high and holds a large rosette. His legs are strongly defined, his ears are held forward, his tail curls over his back, his mouth is open and his tusks project forward. The sculpture displays the great energy and strength of the elephant, although it is not realistically modeled. It is an example of the three-dimensional figures of elephants dating from the Mauryan period and after, a number of which were excavated at Taxila.[1] Other examples include an elephant without riders in the Paul Walter Collection,[2] while a figure of an elephant with two riders is in the Kanoria collection[3] and another, also with riders, is in the Los Angeles County Museum.[4] The function of these images is not clear. Pal has suggested that they may have been used for household decoration[5] or as votive sculptures. Others, with a curved base and a lug for fitting a wheel or rocker, were clearly intended for use as toys.[6]

Sculptures of various single free-standing animals have also been found in other excavations of Mauryan and post-Mauryan period sites, such as Chandraketugarh in Bengal. The subject matter includes horses, rams, bulls, and dogs.[7] The decoration on these figures includes applied rosettes or other vegetation, and punched and incised motifs. Terracottas found in the Mathura area are generally of a dark grey color, while those found in the Chandraketugarh area are made from a yellowish or orange material.[8]

MCS

1 Marshall, 1951, vol. 3, pl. 134, nos. 72, 75, 78.
2 Pal, 1981, no. 29.
3 Bautze, 1995, pl. XXXVIb, pp. 23, 37.
4 Pal, 1986, no. S13, p. 135.
5 *Ibid.*
6 *Ibid.*, no. S18, p. 139.
7 Bautze, *op. cit.*, pl. XXXVIa, c; also Poster, 1986, no. 21.
8 Bautze, *op. cit.*, pp. 1–2.

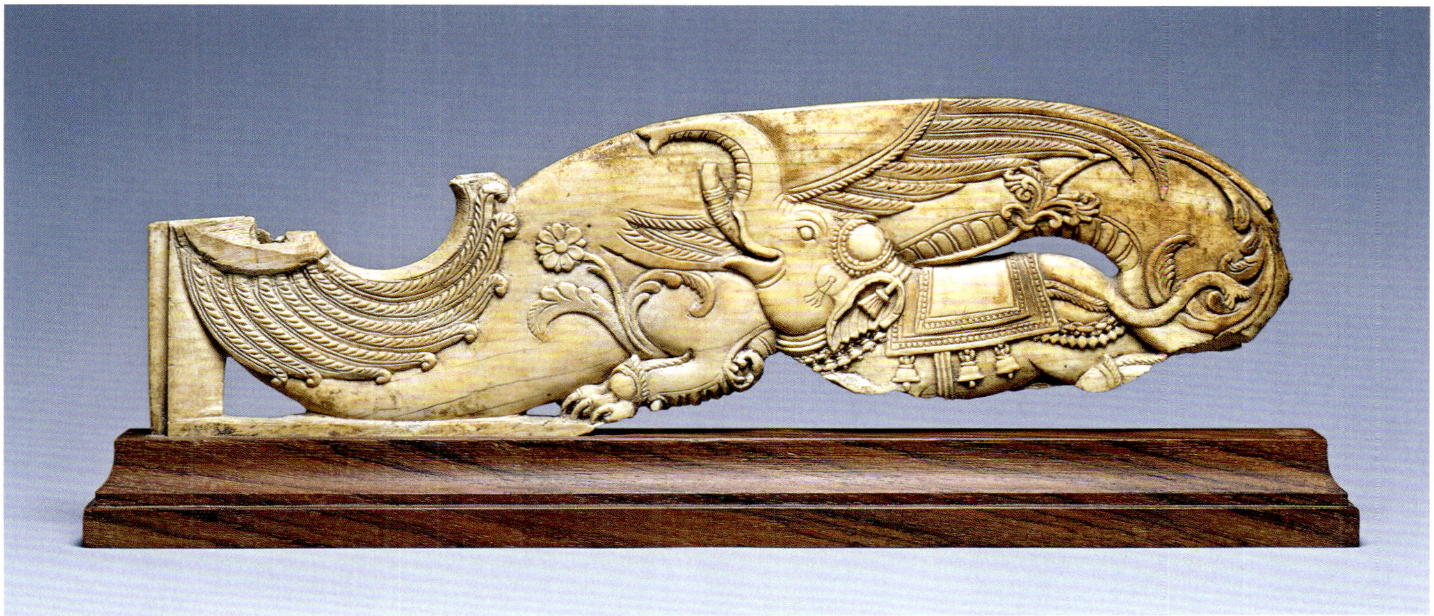

8

Ivory panel depicting an elephant and a fantastic creature

ORISSA, SIXTEENTH OR SEVENTEENTH CENTURY

8.9 × 31.1 cm (3 ½ × 12 ¼ in.)

THIS FRAGMENTARY IVORY PANEL depicts an elephant and, alongside it, a fantastic creature with long tail feathers and an extended scaly tail, a clawed foot (under which is a flowering plant), and long feathers at the neck. The elephant moves alongside the tail, with a saddle-cloth decorated with bells, and a further string of bells around its neck. The panel was originally part of a piece of furniture, possibly a chair. The subject matter is obscure, as is the identity of the fantastic animal. While the design may be simply decorative, it could also be a representation of the *Gajendramoksha* story (the Deliverance of Gajendra) from the *Bhagavata Purana*. In this tale, the king of the elephants is ensnared by an aquatic monster while bathing in the Ganges. Despite his struggles Gajendra remains trapped for a thousand years, until eventually he invokes Vishnu and is saved through the intervention of the god (cat. no. 43).

Orissa was well known for fine-quality ivory carving. A fifteenth-century inscription on the Jagannatha temple at Puri records a gift of eight ivory thrones, confirming the existence of this important regional school of ivory carving.[1] This is borne out by a series of magnificent ivory throne legs depicting rearing lions, the earliest of which is attributable to the thirteenth century and is now in the Freer Gallery of Art, Washington, D.C.[2] Depictions of such ivory throne legs are found in stone sculpture at Konarak.[3] The development of the Orissan style of ivory carving can be followed through further examples of throne legs, including one in the Norton Simon Museum, Pasadena,[4] and another formerly in the Alsdorf Collection.[5] The robustness of the earlier pieces becomes more stylized over the passage of time, with greater emphasis on surface decoration. A powerful Orissan ivory figure of Ganesha, attributable to the fourteenth to fifteenth century, is in The Metropolitan Museum of Art, New York.[6]

MCS

1 Lippe, 1970, p. 45.
2 *Ibid.*, pp. 41–46, pls. 41–55; another leg from the same throne is in the Philadelphia Museum (*ibid.*).
3 Donaldson, 1987, vol. 3, pl. 1412.
4 P. Pal, 2003, no. 163.
5 P. Pal, *1997*, pp. 236, 239.
6 Acc. no. 64.102: Lippe, *op. cit.*, figs. 53–55.

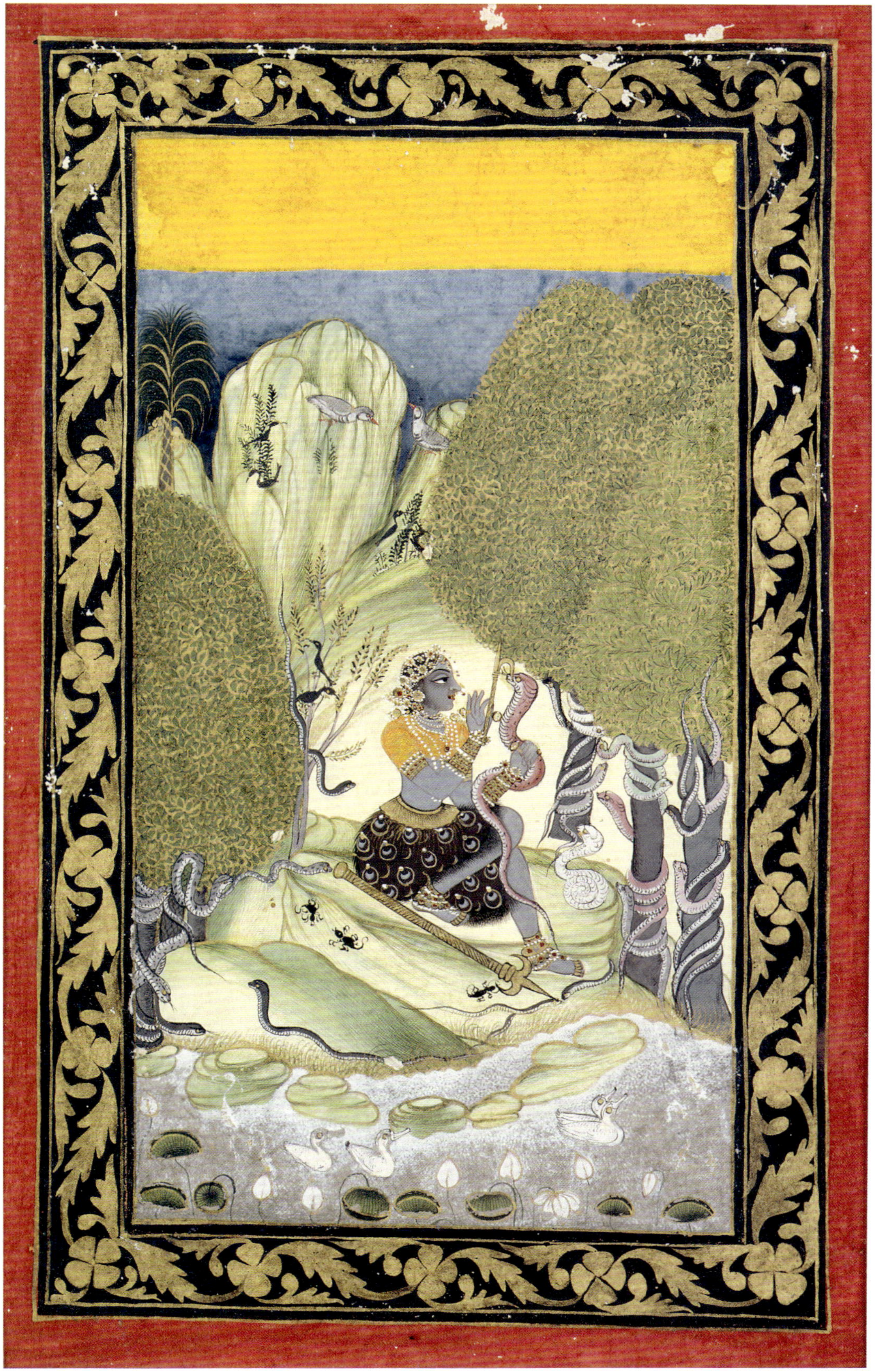

9

A tribal lady charms the forest snakes

ILLUSTRATION TO THE MUSICAL MODE ASAVARI RAGINI

Kotah, Rajasthan, ca. 1760
Opaque watercolor with gold on paper
20.3 × 11.4 cm (8 × 4 ½ in.)

IN THIS PAGE FROM A *RAGAMALA* (The Garland of The Ragas) series, the female raga (*ragini*) Asavari is depicted as a tribal lady, wearing a peacock feather skirt, seated on a rock by a forest pool. Her charms are such that the very snakes come down from the trees to pay court to her. Asavari is a plaintive musical mode of Hindustani music, played in the early morning hours. It is said to originate in a snake-charmer's melody, hence perhaps the iconography of a lady charming snakes. At the same time, she is wearing the jewelry and accoutrements of a court lady, and as such she also represents the solitary idealized poetic heroine (*nayika*), whose lover has not come to their tryst in the forest. In his absence, she holds a spellbound snake in her hand, as well as a small elephant goad (*ankus*) which further emphasizes her mastery over it. Another longer goad or staff lies beside her. Her solitude is contrasted with the burgeoning natural setting, with its happy pairs of ducks, quail, and other birds, and even of scorpions.

The painting shows a considerable degree of finish, with much gold outlining of the trees and landscape. The subject would have been a very familiar one to the artist, as ragamala was one of the most popular painting themes at the Hara Rajput courts of the Bundi-Kotah region of south-eastern Rajasthan in the seventeenth and eighteenth centuries. *Ragamala* series comprising the basic thirty-six subjects, or occasionally many more, were executed both as works on paper[1] and as wall-paintings.[2] In most cases their iconographies follow a prototype *ragamala* illustrated by Mughal-trained artists in 1591 at Chunar, near Varanasi, under Bundi royal patronage.[3] The Chunar version of Asavari already shows most of the compositional details seen here.[4]

AT

1 E.g. Archer, 1959, fig. 10; Waldschmidt, 1975, fig. 110, pp. 323–24.

2 E.g. Bautze, 1987, p. 177, col. pl. VII: a mural painting of Asavari at Indargarh.

3 Ebeling, 1973, p. 155; Beach, 1974, pp. 6–10; Bautze, *op. cit.*, pp. 58–61.

4 Christie's, London, 22–23 November 1984, lot 182.

10

Ivory bracket with a monkey, parrots and scrolling leaves (two views)

SOUTH INDIA, NAYAK PERIOD, FIRST HALF OF SEVENTEENTH CENTURY

8.9 × 5.1 cm (3 ½ × 2 in.)

THIS IVORY BRACKET IS CARVED WITH A CORBEL with a pendant lotus and on either side the figure of a monkey, which crouches under the top of the bracket among leaves, holding up its hand, while its tail snakes across the architectural decoration. This carving was once part of a larger piece of furniture or another construction that was carved from solid ivory, to be assembled using fine dovetail joints. Surviving solid ivory furniture, as opposed to ivory veneer, is relatively scarce. Examples include the throne legs from Orissa made from single pieces of ivory, dating from the fourteenth to fifteenth centuries and later,[1] an ivory settee-back from Mysore,[2] and chairs and other furniture in solid ivory that were made in Murshidabad in the eighteenth century, including a set presented to Warren Hastings by Mani Begum and brought to England in 1784.[3]

The bracket is a miniature version of those found surmounting columns in buildings built under Nayak patronage in the seventeenth century, such as the Kudal Alagar Perumal temple[4] or the secular Pudu Mandapa (literally, New Hall) or choultry of Tirumala Nayak (r. 1623–59),[5] which has corbels with pendant lotus flowers, and a crouching lion in place of the monkey.[6] In addition to those carved in stone, similar brackets are also found on the great wooden sacred chariots (*rathas*) used in processions during religious festivals.[7] Medieval Indian building manuals link the architecture and iconography of the temple and the chariots, indicating that the chariot was considered to be a mobile temple.[8] The bracket may have formed part either of a miniature shrine, or a luxurious chariot that was mounted in ivory.

MCS

1 See cat. no. 8 for discussion.

2 Watt, 1903, pl. 78.

3 Jaffer, London, 2001, p. 238.

4 Michell, 1995, p. 105, and fig. 68, p. 106.

5 *Ibid.*, p. 104; J. Guy, "Tirumala Nayak's Choultry and an eighteenth century model," in C. Bautze-Picron ed., *Makaranda: Essays in honour of Dr James C. Harle*, Delhi, 1990, pp. 207–13.

6 Guy, *op. cit.*, fig. 14. A similar ivory capital with a makara instead of the monkey is to be found in a group of ivories presently in the Madurai Museum.

7 G. Michell, "Chariot panels from Tamil Nadu," in G. Michell ed., *Living Wood: Sculptural traditions of Southern India*, Bombay: Marg, 1992, fig. 9, p. 38; fig. 11, p. 41.

8 *Ibid.*, p. 36.

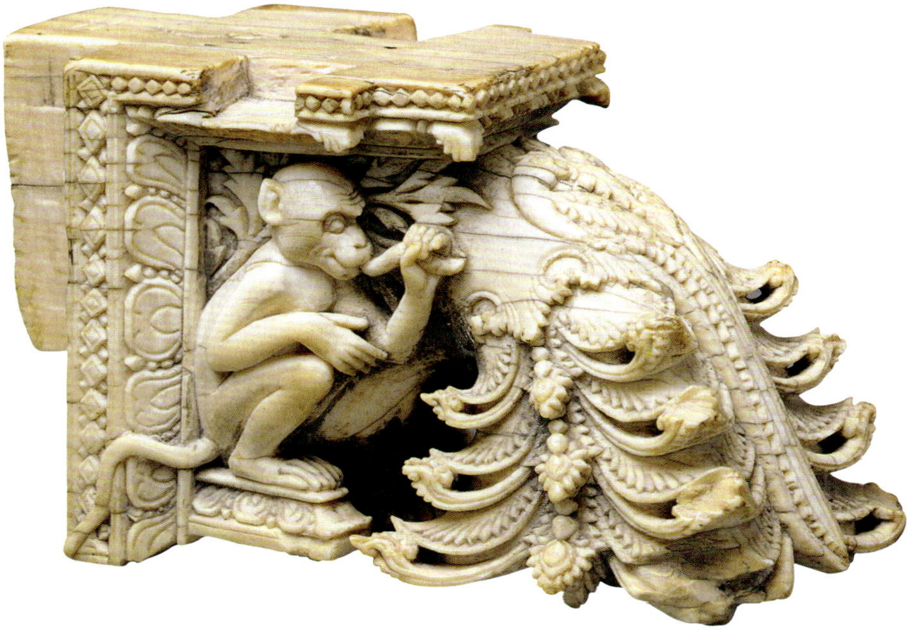

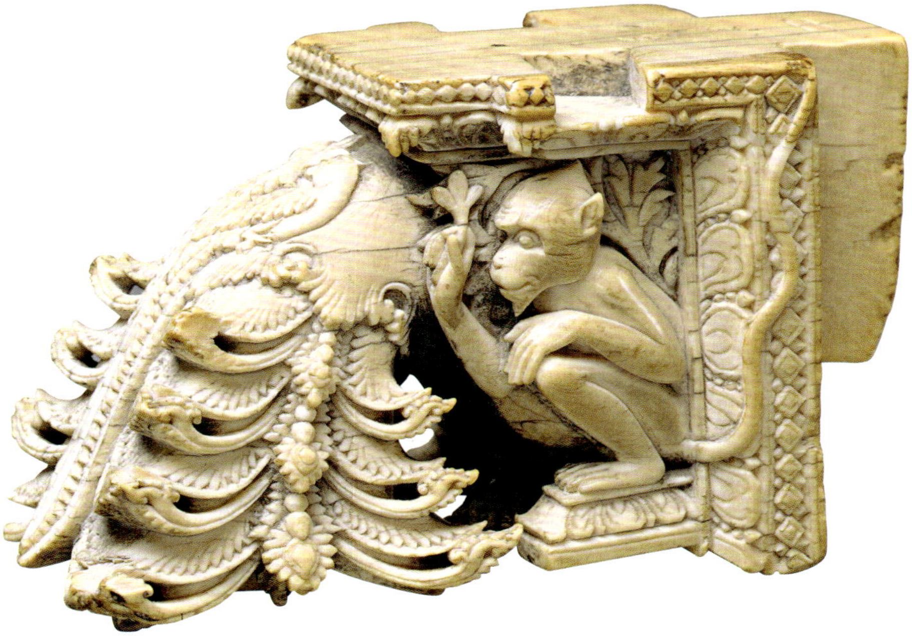

11

A blackbuck

MUGHAL, CA. 1650, WITH LATER OVERPAINTING

Opaque watercolor with gold on paper
20.3 × 14.9 cm (8 × 5 ⅞ in.)
Published: P. Pal et al., *Romance of the Taj Mahal*, Los Angeles, 1989, fig. 104

A BLACKBUCK STANDS ON A DARK GREEN SWARD, boldly silhouetted against a golden sky. A tame animal, it carries the usual halter on its head, but is furthermore obviously a favorite pet, with its necklaces of pearls and shells and its tassels. Blackbuck were used in Mughal India to draw carts, especially those used to carry cheetahs off to the hunt,[1] while there are some well-known early seventeenth-century studies of blackbuck with their keepers.[2]

While portraits of animals of the Jahangir period normally have minimal backgrounds, and are in essence scientific studies driven by Jahangir's curiosity to record the natural world around him, by the period of Shah Jahan (1628–58) decorative qualities in such studies had become more important, while more attention was paid to line and to the setting. Their backgrounds had become more naturalistic, a green ground perhaps stretching up to near the top of the page, with minimal treatment of the sky.[3] Here our buck stands instead on a sharply defined piece of green grass beside water, of a type found more often in later eighteenth-century painting from Lucknow. This impression that the background has been repainted is confirmed by the treatment of the sky, which is found in paintings from Delhi and Lucknow in the second half of the eighteenth century.[4] Many earlier portrait studies had their plain backgrounds repainted in Lucknow around 1770–90, or else were copied in this newer style. Another version of this painting with the same landscape and sky, perhaps done entirely in Lucknow, is in the Bodleian Library, Oxford.[5]

JPL

1 Falk and Archer, 1981, figs. 30, 63.

2 *Ibid.*, fig. 31; Leach, 1995, p. 464; and Stronge, 2002, pl. 102.

3 As in cat. no. 4 above, or a study of a nilgai published in Pal et al., *op. cit.*, fig. 102.

4 E.g. a portrait of Mirza Shah Rukh painted by Miskin Muhammad in Lucknow, 1775–80 (Falk and Archer, *op. cit.*, fig. 276).

5 Stchoukine, 1929, pl. LXXXXVIb.

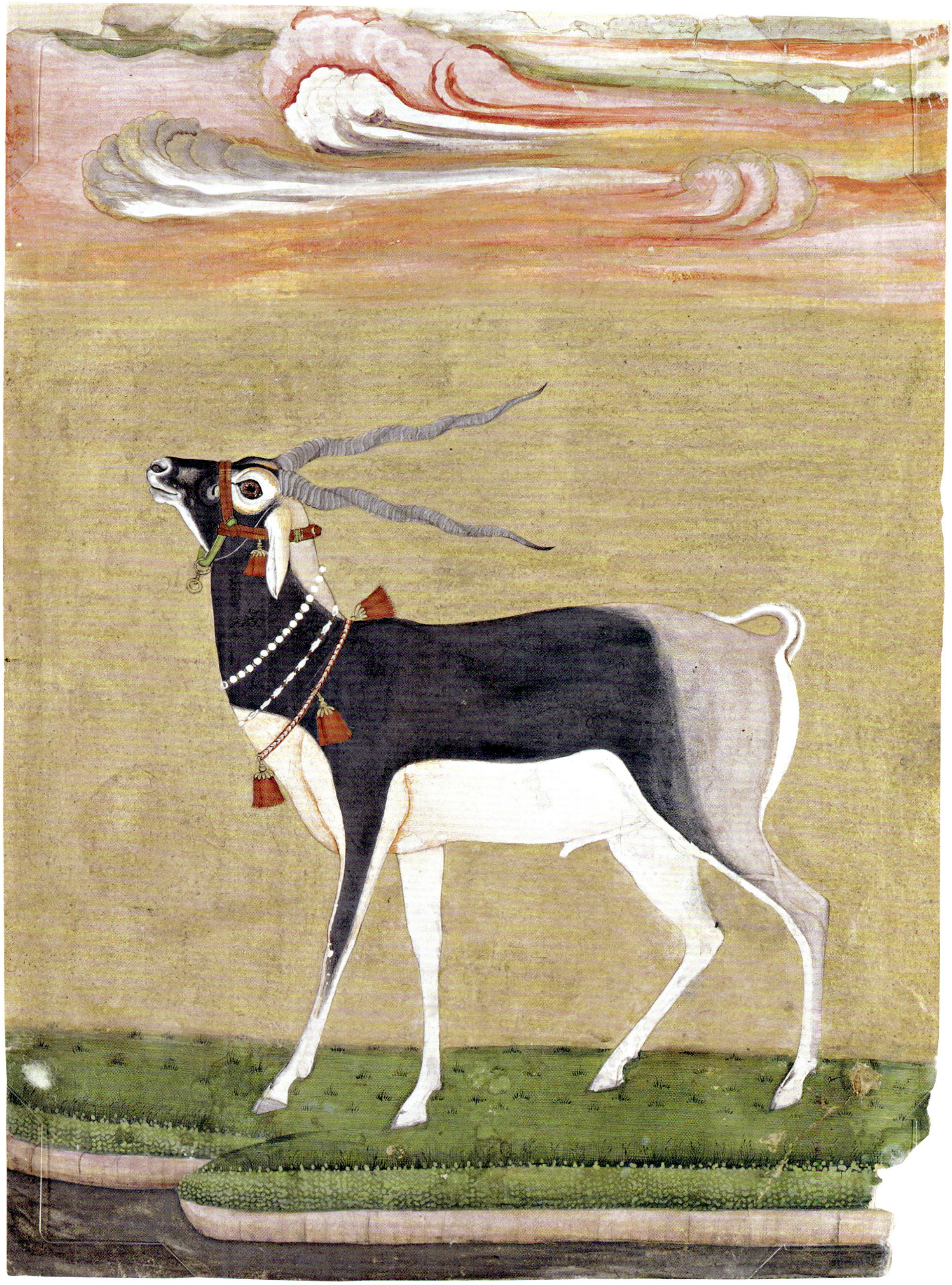

12

Album page with cut-paper decoration

MUGHAL, CA. 1625–50

Cut paper on paper, watercolor and gold
26 × 18.1 cm (10 ¼ × 7 ⅛ in.)
Metropolitan Museum of Art, New York, Purchase, Cynthia Hazen Polsky and Leon B. Polsky Fund (2002.222)

THE LIGHT, SILHOUETTED FORMS OF PLANTS, delicate birds, animals, and ornamental calligraphy on this album page are not painted or stenciled; they are instead cut and pasted onto the dark blue ground from paper so fine that the seam can barely be discerned by eye or touch. While a cut paper technique was well known in Ottoman tradition, particularly in "decoupage calligraphy," in Mughal albums such cut-paper works are much more rare, this being one of only two similar known examples.[1] The fully flourishing profile of the plant forms suggest a date for this page in the reign of Shah Jahah (1628–57), when the decorative borders of picture albums made for the Emperor often contained comparable painted flower shapes, frequently executed in gold against a blue background.[2] The calligraphy on the lower part of the page is vertically arranged along the stem of a plant in a mirror arrangement that gives the impression of foliage and which reads: *'amal-i baz (?) khan* ("work of Baz? Khan"). On the upper part of the page an Arabic phrase, also vertically placed and sinuously curving, may be read as: *inna illa 'ali kull* ("that except … 'Ali… every.."?). Later Hyderabad traditions showed a renewed interest in this cut-paper technique, which, notwithstanding, remained a rare accomplishment in Indian art.[3]

NHH

1 A late sixteenth-century Mughal cut-paper work is reported in a London private collection.

2 Welch et al., 1987, p. 118, no. 20.

3 A cut-paper composition with trees from Kishangarh is in the Jagdish and Kamla Mittal Museum, Hyderabad. The Gol Gumbaz Museum in Bijapur contains two unusual decoupage pages where the folio "negatives," or the page from which the calligraphy has been very precisely cut out, are mounted on a burnished page which can be seen through the shapes of the letters, thus giving a two-dimensional effect (no. 123 B 68: Surat al-Fatiha as described above, and inscribed: *al 'abd al muznib haji beg sipahi*; and no. 65 B 10, inscribed: *sayyid 'ali bukhari ghafarallah*).

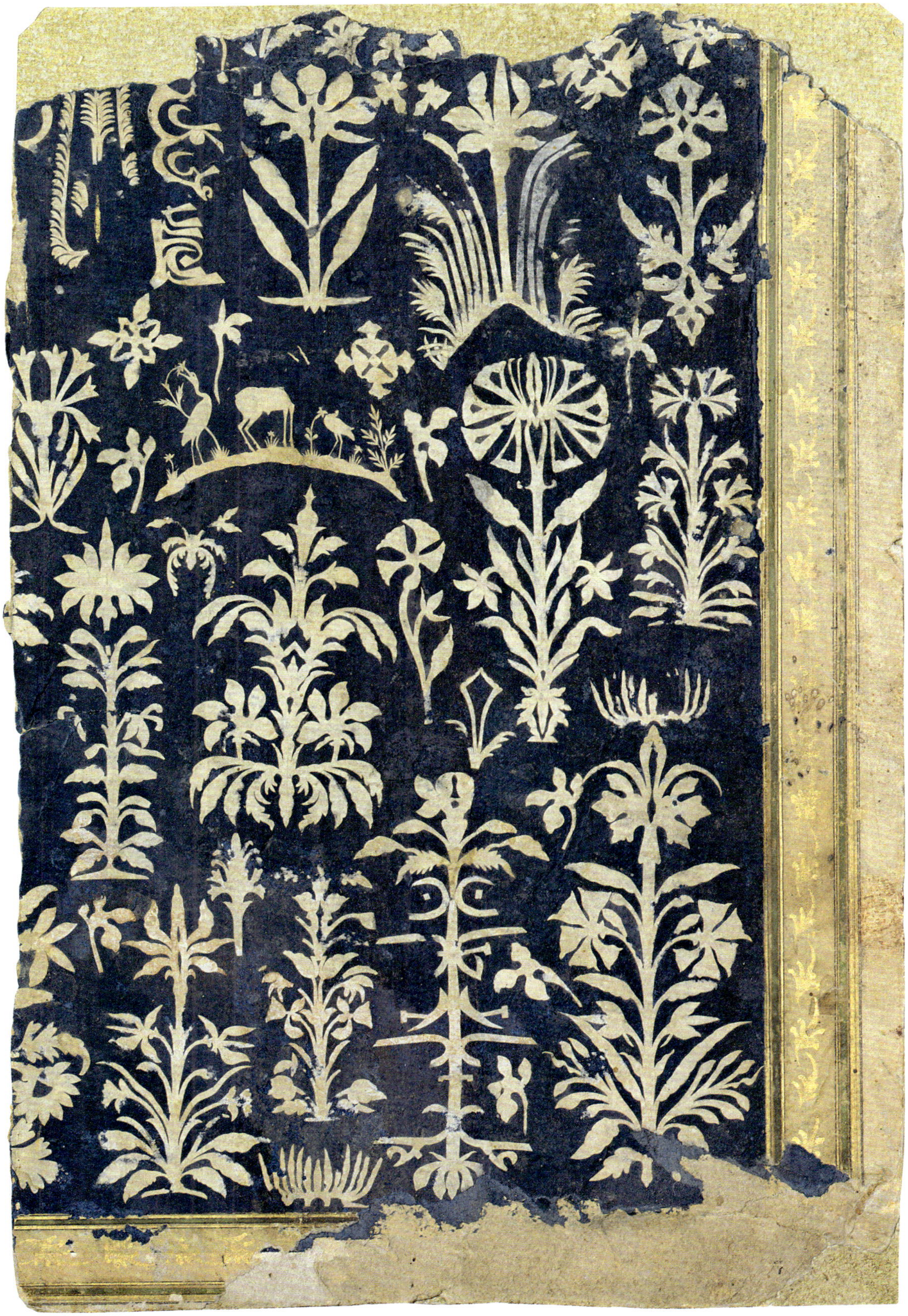

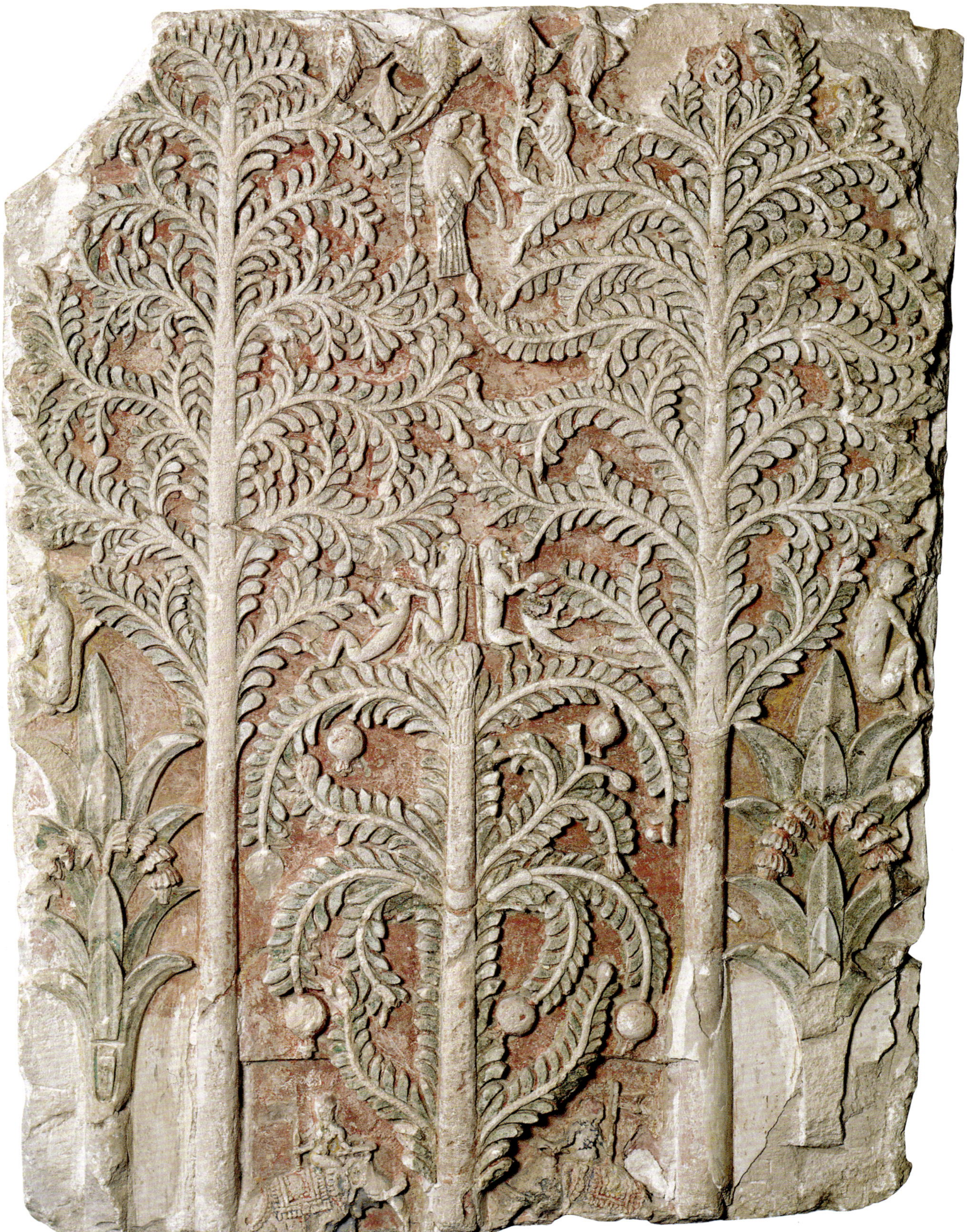

13

Stone panel with trees in relief

GUJARAT OR RAJASTHAN, EARLY EIGHTEENTH CENTURY

109.2 × 73.7 cm (43 × 29 in.) (including base)
Metropolitan Museum of Art, New York,
Gift of Cynthia Hazen Polsky (2005.373)

THIS STONE PANEL IS CARVED IN RELIEF with a close-packed series of trees, including pomegranate and plantain. The branches teem with monkeys and birds eating fruit, and elephants and riders appear below. The panel is painted in green on the trees against a red background, with yellow and blue on the elephants and riders. This lush jungle scene captures the busy Indian landscape, with noisy birds in the trees helping themselves to fruit; birds such as parakeets are a common feature of the Indian countryside, seen wherever they can find food. The greed of the monkeys is almost palpable, as they stuff fruit into their mouths. The relative scale of the trees, the animals, and the tiny figures of the elephants and their riders below emphasizes the luxuriance of the forest and reduces the importance of man in the natural landscape.

This panel may have formed part of a wall frieze within a palace, where the rooms would combine the use of painted murals, carved architectural elements, and surface decoration perhaps enhanced with the use of inlaid mirrored glass and stucco. The combination of relief carving and pigmentation make the panel virtually a three-dimensional painting rather than a sculpture. Although carved in stone, the detail and treatment of the surface gives the impression of stucco work.

The origin of this panel is uncertain, though a resemblance has been observed with wooden carvings on domestic *haveli* architecture in Gujarat, where the panel might have come from a series decorating a courtyard, with an overhanging roof structure to protect them. However, the long thin trees and the profusion of animals are also motifs found in Deccani paintings of the late seventeenth century,[1] as is the eccentric spatial perspective of the landscape. It also has echoes in Bikaner paintings. There were strong links between the Deccan and Bikaner in the late seventeenth century, when Maharaja Anup Singh (r. 1674–98) spent his entire reign in the Deccan in service to the Mughal emperor, some of it as governor of Adoni (1689–98). A number of Deccani paintings were formerly in the Bikaner Royal Collection, in particular paintings from Golconda.[2] This panel could therefore perhaps have been designed by a Deccani artist working in Rajasthan, or by a local Rajasthani artist working within a Deccani fashion.

MCS

1 Zebrowski, 1983, fig. 188, illustrates a page from a manuscript dated 1698 by a Deccani artist who may have worked for Maharaja Anup Singh of Bikaner.

2 *Ibid.*, p. 207.

14

Sculptural fragment depicting two hamsas

RAJASTHAN, EIGHTEENTH CENTURY

Sandstone
21.6 × 30.5 cm (8 ½ × 12 in.)

THIS SMALL STONE FRIEZE DEPICTS TWO GEESE (*HAMSAS*), with polychrome decoration in blue and yellow against a red background. The two birds carry flower stems in their beaks.

The hamsa occupies a special place in Indian decoration and religious iconography. It is the vehicle (*vahana*) of Brahma and is seen as such in Hindu temples throughout India. Geese are believed to be able to extract the milk from a mixture of milk and water,[1] and to be able to travel between earth and heaven, thus linking the celestial and earthly worlds. The hamsa also is significant in Buddhist iconography: the *Hamsa Jataka* recounts the birth of the Buddha and his chief minister in a previous life as the king and chief minister of a herd of golden geese, who were able to explain to Brahmadatta, King of Varanasi, the virtues of ruling righteously.[2]

The hamsa also occurs frequently as a decorative motif. The present frieze originally belonged to a longer section of decoration, probably forming part of a molding in a temple. The use of bright color to enhance architectural detail is a common feature of Indian temples. Another frieze with geese, formerly part of a domed ceiling, is in the Art Institute of Chicago,[3] and geese are seen on many of the terracotta tiles from Harwan (cat. no. 78), where they may represent the freedom of the ascetic to wander.

MCS

1 Pal, 1997, p. 249.

2 Pal, 1988, no. 80. Another panel from the same monument, depicting the Peacock Jataka (*Mayura Jataka*), is in the Norton Simon Museum: Pal, 2003, no. 136.

3 Desai and Mason eds., 1993, no. 39; also illustrated in Pal, *Collecting Odyssey*, no. 360, pp. 264, 352.

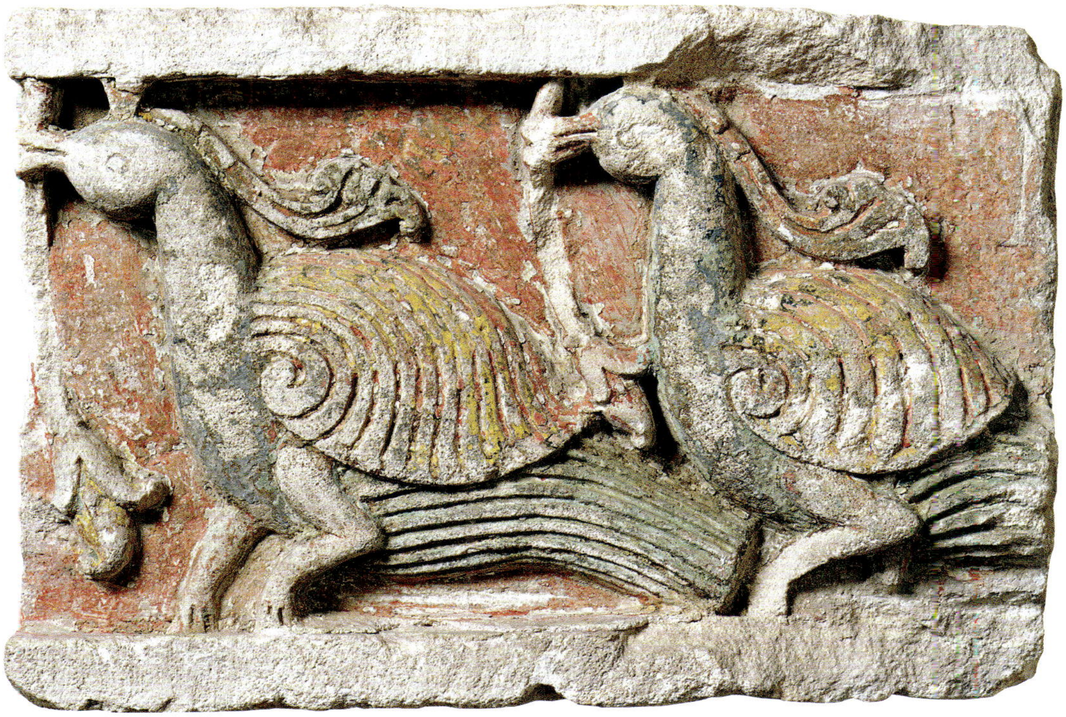

15

Radha goes to meet Krishna in the grove

KOTAH, RAJASTHAN, CA. 1760

Opaque watercolor and gold on paper, with some later restoration
Image 25.1 x 15.6 cm (9 7/8 x 6 1/8 in.); page 27.9 x 19.1 cm (11 x 7 1/2 in.)
Published: P. Pal et al., *Pleasure gardens of the mind: Indian paintings from the Jane Greenough Green collection*, Los Angeles, 1993, no. 9

IN THE LUSH, BIRD-THRONGED FOREST with a river in spate, Radha is seen twice as she goes to Krishna. Watched by her fellow cow-maidens (*gopis*) through the trees, she first demurely approaches her divine lover, half-hiding her face and gazing down like a new bride. The warm colors of her clothing contrast with the jungle verdure and suggest the mood of passion. The lovers sit together on a raised platform, resembling those used by the Rajput nobility for hunting and shooting game. Krishna, with a nimbus and in princely dress, holds a cowherd's crook in one hand.

This page is without text and comes from an unidentified series.[1] Its subjects show a general similarity to episodes in the *Gita Govinda*, in which the Sanskrit poet Jayadeva hymns the love between Krishna and Radha in vernal forest settings (cat. no. 64).[2]

AT

1 Sotheby's, New York, 15 December 1978, lots 141–46; compare also Welch, 1973, no. 19; Colnaghi & Co, 1978, no. 67; Isacco and Dallapiccola, 1982, pl. 4; .Kramrisch, 1986, no. 54.

2 Miller tr., 1977.

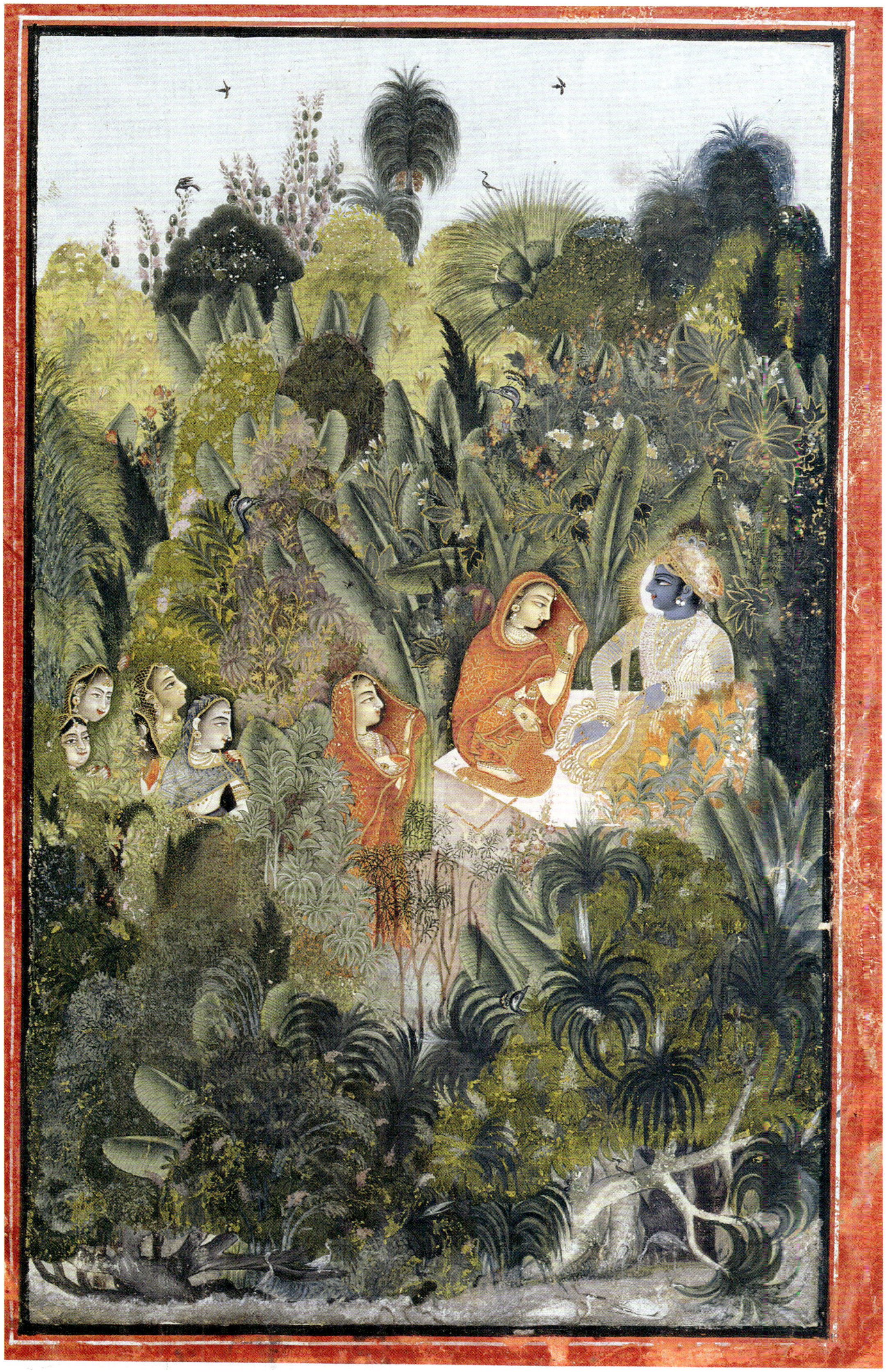

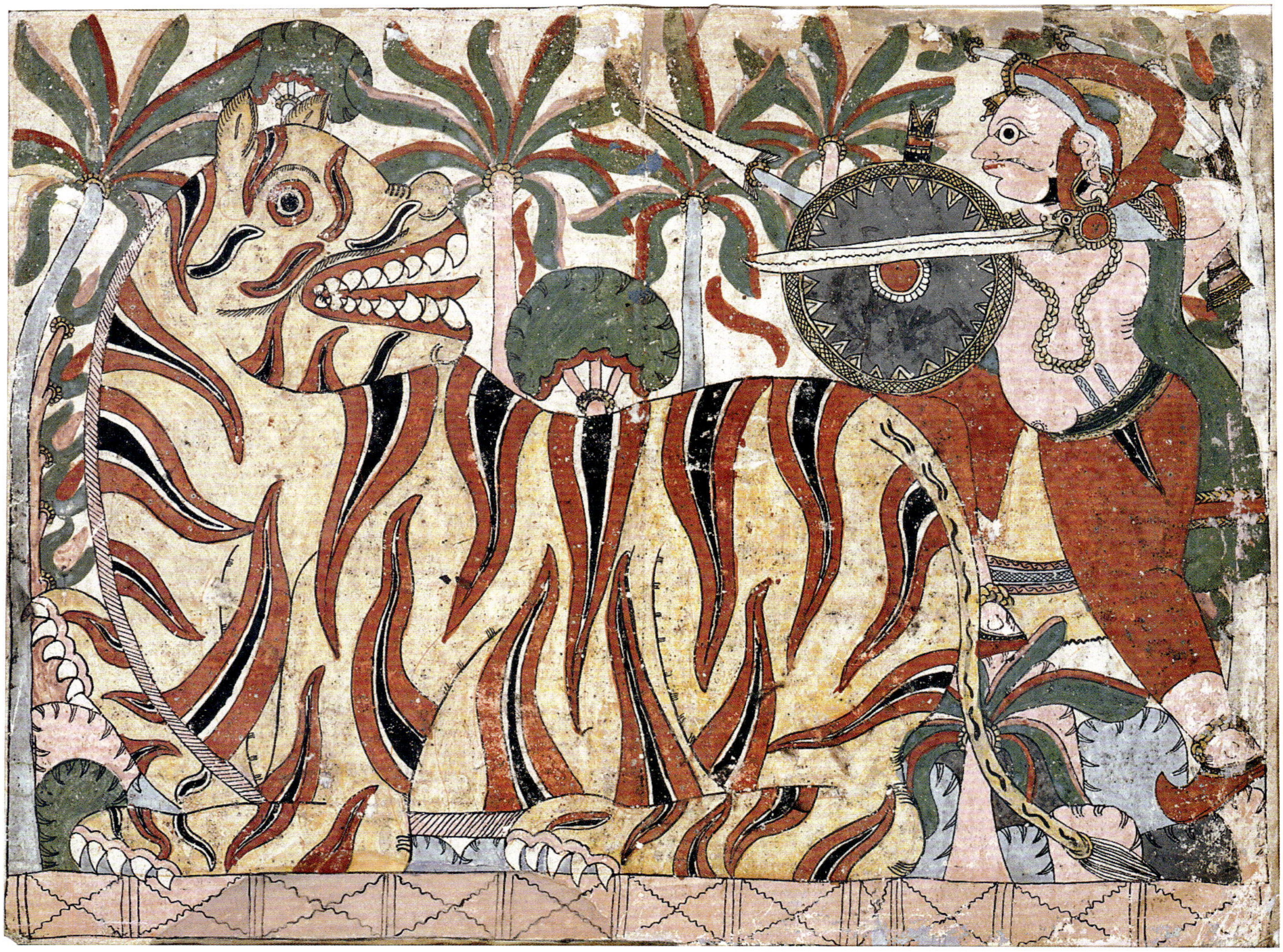

16

A tiger pursued by a warrior

PAGE FROM A STORY-TELLER'S SERIES OF *MAHABHARATA* EPISODES

Western Deccan (Maharashtra or northern Karnataka), ca. 1840–50
Opaque watercolor on paper
30.5 × 41 cm (12 × 16 in.)
Published: T. McInerney, *Indian paintings from the Polsky collections*, Princeton, 1982, no. 27; B. Rossi, *From the ocean of painting: India's popular paintings 1589 to the present*, New York, 1998, no. 54
Joseph Polsky Collection

THIS DYNAMIC FOLK PAINTING belonged to a narrative series used by a traditional itinerant storyteller (*chitrakathi*) in Maharashtra or northern Karnataka. A warrior brandishing his sword, spear, and shield mounts a low rocky promontory as he stalks an immense tiger. The fearsome beast turns to face him with bared fangs and lolling tongue. The mounting drama is heightened by the jagged rhythms of the tiger's massive, flame-like stripes, complemented by the tremulous patterns of the palm-tree fronds behind. It has been suggested that this scene may belong to the horse sacrifice (*Ashvamedha*) episode in a Marathi version of the *Mahabharata* epic: when a tiger tries to attack the black horse Shyamakarna which is under Arjuna's protection, his warriors pursue and kill it.[1] A closely related painting, probably from the same series and showing a similar giant tiger killing a boar, is in the Jagdish and Kamla Mittal Museum, Hyderabad.[2]

AT

1 J. Jain-Neubauer, "Citrakathi paintings of Maharashtra," in J. Jain and J. Jain-Neubauer, *Treasures of everyday art: Raja Dinkar Kelkar Museum*, Bombay, 1978, p. 115; see also A. L. Dallapiccola, "'Paithan paintings': The epic world of the Chitrakathis," in J. Jain ed., *Picture showmen*, Bombay: Marg, 1998, pp. 66–73, and for a more extensive study of this type of painting: *Dallapiccola, Die "Paithan"-Malerei: Studie zu ihrer stilistischen Entwicklung und Ikonographie*, Wiesbaden, 1980.

2 Acc. no. 76.483: Mittal, 1990, no. 46, illus. p. 13; also nos. 40–45, for six more paintings from this series.

THE TEMPLE

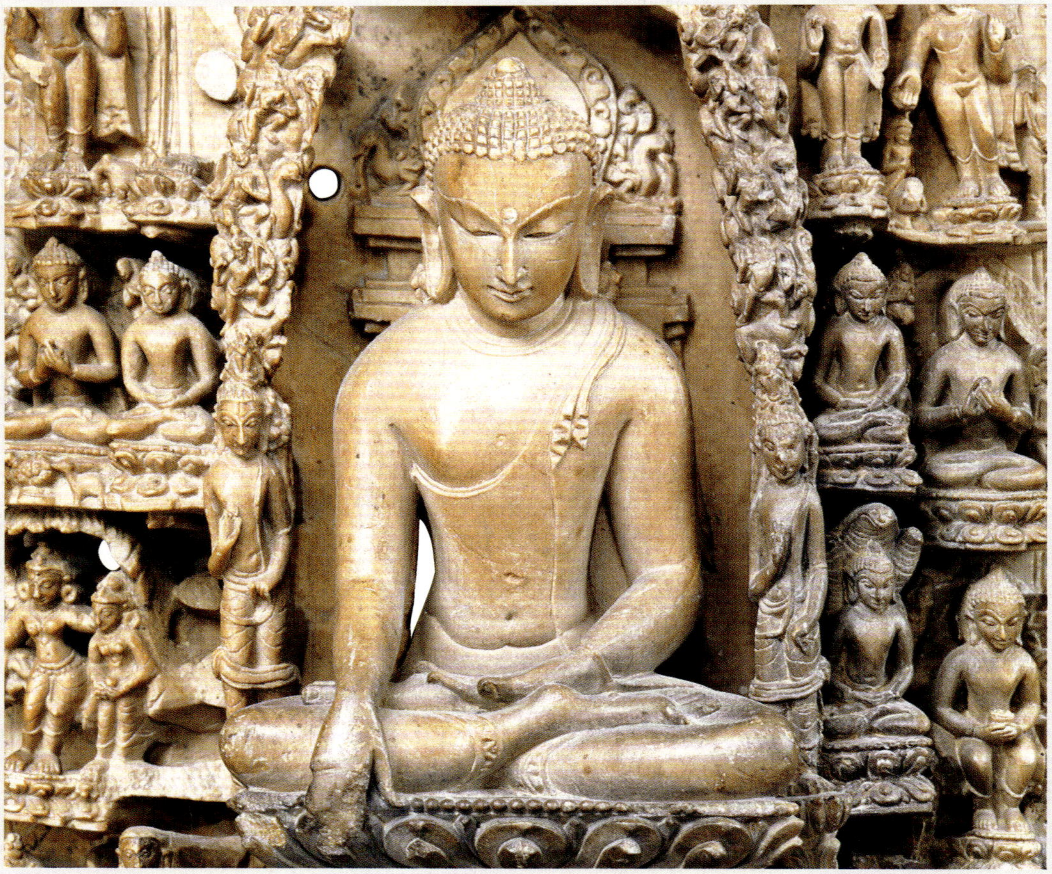

Varying from wayside shrines to huge building complexes covered with sculptures and enclosed by walled courtyards and imposing gateways, the Hindu temple is the abode of a deity, the meeting-place between the worlds of man and the gods, and, in its more developed forms, a symbolic representation of the universe in a three-dimensional mystical palace (*mandala*). The image of the presiding deity is installed in a small, plain sanctuary or "womb chamber" (*garbhagriha*), above which rises the temple's *shikhara*, a tapering tower superstructure which symbolizes the sacred mountain Meru.

Adjoining the sanctuary there will be at least one pillared hall (*mandapa*), and possibly an ambulatory to allow devotees to circumambulate the shrine in the auspicious clockwise direction (*pradakshina*). The sculptural decoration around the sanctuary and other doorways may include protective images of door-guardians (*dvarapala*) and deities such as the goddess Lakshmi, the river goddesses Ganga and Yamuna, and Ganesha, the god of beginnings and remover of obstacles. Elsewhere, on pillars, ceilings, door surrounds, and outer walls, a whole heavenly host may be depicted, including gods, celestial beings, warriors and musicians, amorous couples, human donor figures, mythical beasts, and endless luxuriant bands of foliage.

Devotees visit the temple above all for vision (*darshan*) of the deity, manifested especially through beholding the eyes of the divine image. Their offerings such as fruit, flowers, or incense are received by the officiating priests, who will later return blessed offerings (*prasada*) to them as they leave. The Brahmin priesthood alone can officiate in invoking the deity through chant and use of the *arati* lamp, censer, and other ritual instruments, and in attending the image and dressing it in fine clothing and jewelry, according to the occasion. Many larger temples, particularly in the south, also maintain a richly carved wooden chariot (*ratha*), a virtual temple on wheels, in which the image of the deity is taken out in procession on annual festival days. The immense ratha of Jagannath, a form of Krishna, at Puri in Orissa, which is pulled in proces-sion by a vast number of devotees, has passed into English in the word "juggernaut."

Buddhism hardly survived in its Indian homeland following the destruction of the monasteries by Muslim invaders around 1200, though its traditions were preserved and developed in Sri Lanka (Ceylon) and the Himalayan regions of Nepal and Tibet, as well as throughout South-east Asia and the Far East. However, the Jain religion, founded by the Buddha's near-contemporary Mahavira in the sixth century BC, has maintained itself successfully to the present day, particularly in parts of Western India. Jain temples have much in common with their Hindu counterparts and include some of the most intricately carved interiors in India, notably those of the Dilwara temples at Mount Abu in southern Rajasthan, built entirely in marble from the eleventh century onward. Tending strongly to asceticism in its doctrine, Jainism has always been supported by a prosperous merchant class. Jain laymen have traditionally sought to gain spiritual merit and offset their adverse karma through donations, and often they would present to the temple libraries (*bhandar*) opulently illustrated and embellished copies of the Jain scriptures such as the *Kalpasutra*. Numerous examples of these manuscripts have been preserved into modern times in the bhandars of Gujarat and Rajasthan.

AT

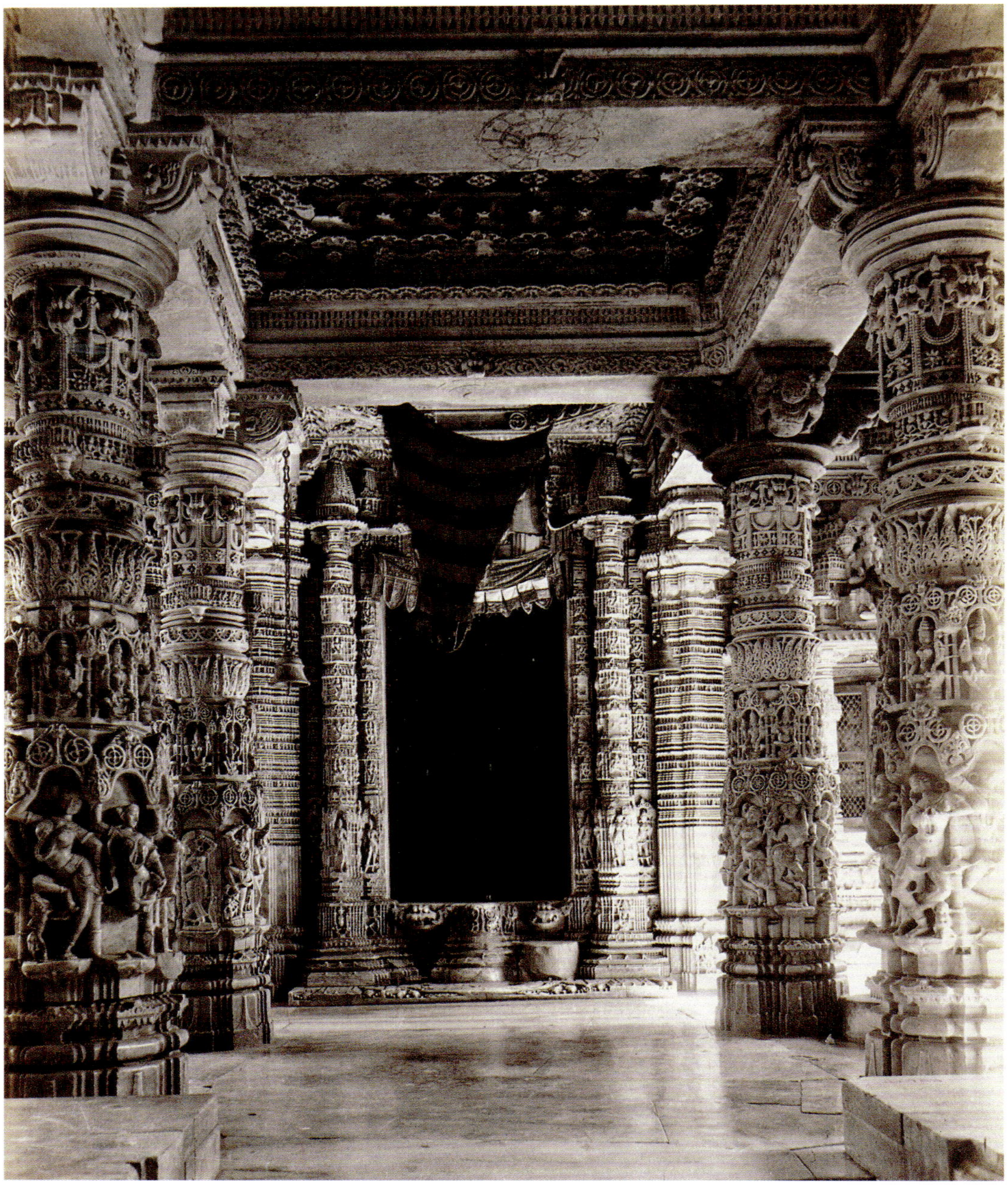

17

Dilwara Temple, Mount Abu

UNKNOWN PHOTOGRAPHER

Mount Abu, Rajasthan, ca. 1870s
Albumen silver print
28.1 × 23.9 cm (11 1/16 × 9 7/15 in.)
Metropolitan Museum of Art, New York, Gift of Cynthia Hazen Polsky, 2000 (2001.624.3)

THE ORNATELY CARVED INTERIORS of the Jain temples on Mount Abu in Rajasthan were a popular subject for many commercial photographers in the last quarter of the nineteenth century. This view, the work of an unknown photographer, looks from the mandapa toward the sanctuary door of the Luna Vasahi Temple, one of the group of four large temples at Dilwara, just to the north-east of the town of Abu. The mountain was a holy place to both Shaivites and Jains from an early period, but is especially sacred as a place of pilgrimage to the latter, since Mahavira, the "Great Hero" and twenty-fourth Tirthankara of Jainism, is supposed to have visited the site. Dedicated to Neminatha, the twenty-second of the twenty-four Tirthanakaras (teachers or saviours) whose worship lies at the core of the Jain religion, the Luna Vasahi temple was erected by two wealthy merchants named Vastupala and Tejapala and was built and added to from 1230 onward.

Based on the premise of the sacredness of all life, the Jain religion enjoins its followers to live by peaceable occupations such as trading and banking, rather than from the spoils of war, and extensive trading links with the Arab and European worlds made this part of Western India the wealthiest region in the subcontinent during the Solanki period, between the tenth and thirteenth centuries. Much accumulated wealth was therefore available to be lavished by Jain patrons on some of the most elaborately decorated temples in India. All the temples at Dilwara present characteristically plain and unembellished exteriors, but these give way to lavishly intricate sculptural decoration inside the shrines, with almost every surface covered in sharply detailed carving representing dancers, musicians, soldiers, horses, and elephants, as well as geometric designs, all executed in glowing white marble. While architecturally similar to the older Adinatha temple in the same group, the Luna Vasahi temple is distinguished by the extraordinary richness of its sculptural decoration.

JF

18

Statuary from the Central Museum, Madras

LINNEAUS TRIPE (1822–1902)

Madras, Tamil Nadu, May–June 1858
Albumen silver print from a dry collodion glass negative
23.3 × 29.9 cm (9 3/16 × 11 3/4 in.)
Published: Linnaeus Tripe, *Photographs of the Elliot Marbles; and other subjects; in the Central Museum Madras*, Madras, 1859, pl. 46
Metropolitan Museum of Art, New York, Purchase, Cynthia Hazen Polsky and Horace W. Goldsmith Foundation Gifts (1991.1152)

THIS STUDY OF SCULPTURES FROM THE MADRAS MUSEUM is one of seventy-five photographs taken by Tripe in May and June 1858. Completed during a break in his eight-month photographic tour of Southern Indian architectural sites, the collection constitutes the earliest surviving photographs of these important pieces.[1] Tripe's work, as seen in this print, included other work from the museum's collections as well as the sculptural fragments from the Buddhist stupa at Amaravati, popularly known as the "Elliot Marbles" (after Sir Walter Elliot, the civil servant largely responsible for their recovery).[2] The series was published the following year in an edition of seventy copies, with a title page, brief introduction, and list of plates. This is clearly an early print, since examined copies of the issued work show that the negative was broken at some stage during production and prints show clear evidence of several cracks. The print was made before the negative suffered this damage. The practicalities of the project forced a technical departure from Tripe's usual method of working with large paper negatives. As an apologetic introductory note explains, "Many of the subjects being heavy masses, and therefore not to be easily transported into the open air, were taken as they were lying, in the rooms of the Museum. In order to attend them at all, he was obliged to use a dry collodion process with which he had only recently made acquaintance.[3] He would point to both these circumstances to account for the unsatisfactory pictures he has made of some of these sculptures." This, the note continues, "also increased the liability to yellowness in the [high]lights, so much complained of in toning a print on albumenised paper with gold." Despite this disclaimer, many of these studies form arresting compositions, with the form of the sculptures dramatically set off against the painted-out backgrounds.

JF

1 The survival or present whereabouts of an earlier set of photographs of some of the sculptures, taken in 1855 by Dr, A. J. Scott while the pieces lay in the open in front of the museum, are unknown.
2 Many of the Amaravati sculptures were later transferred to England and now form part of the British Museum collections. For a full history, see Knox, 1992.
3 The development of a successful "dry" collodion process, by which a prepared glass negative would remain sensitive for several months, rather than having to be prepared, exposed, and developed on the spot, was the subject of much research throughout the 1850s: the first reasonably successful dry plates had only become commercially available a year or so before Tripe's work with them in Madras. Although much slower than wet collodion plates, they allowed considerably shorter exposures than Tripe's customary calotype (paper) negatives.

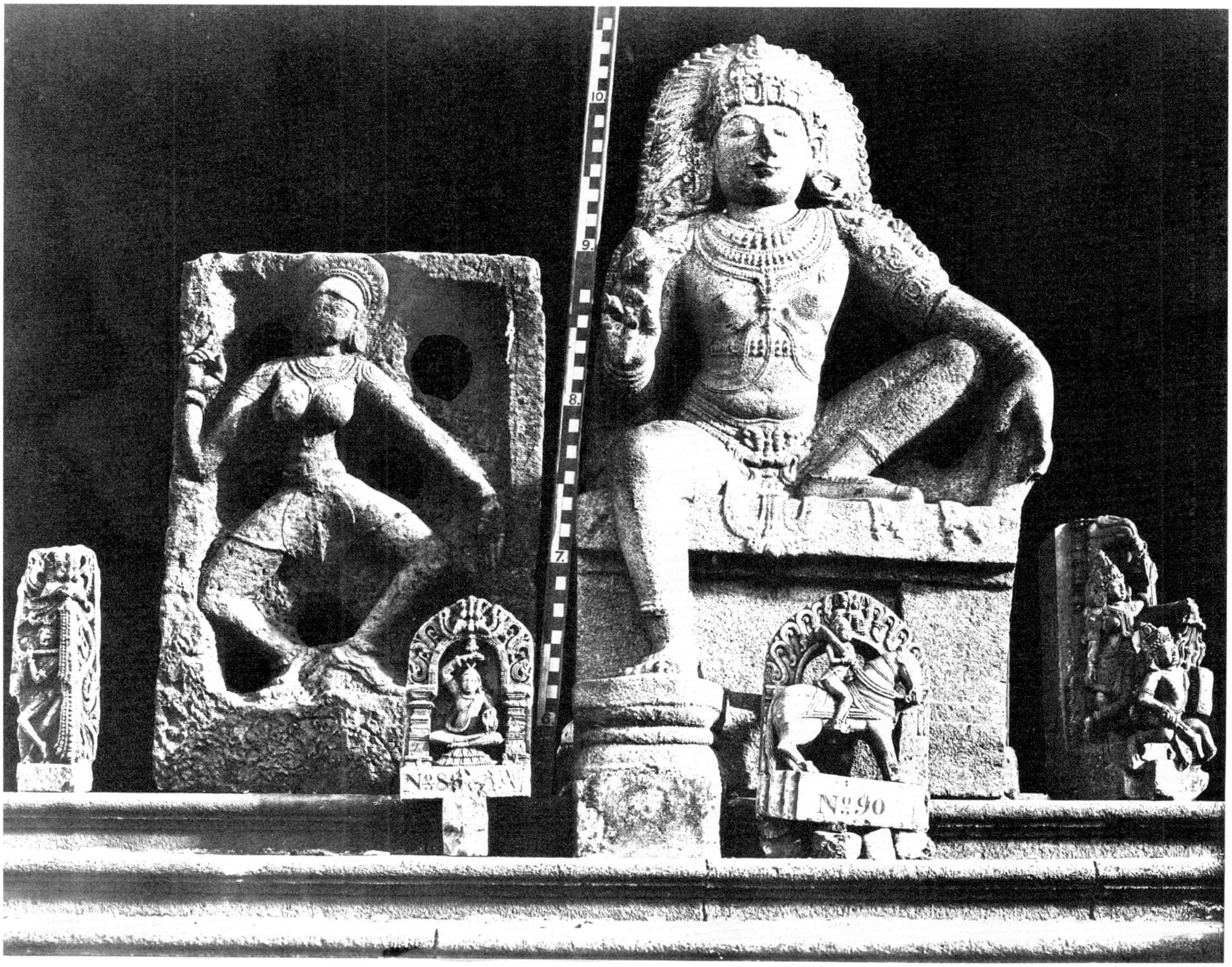
Nº 90

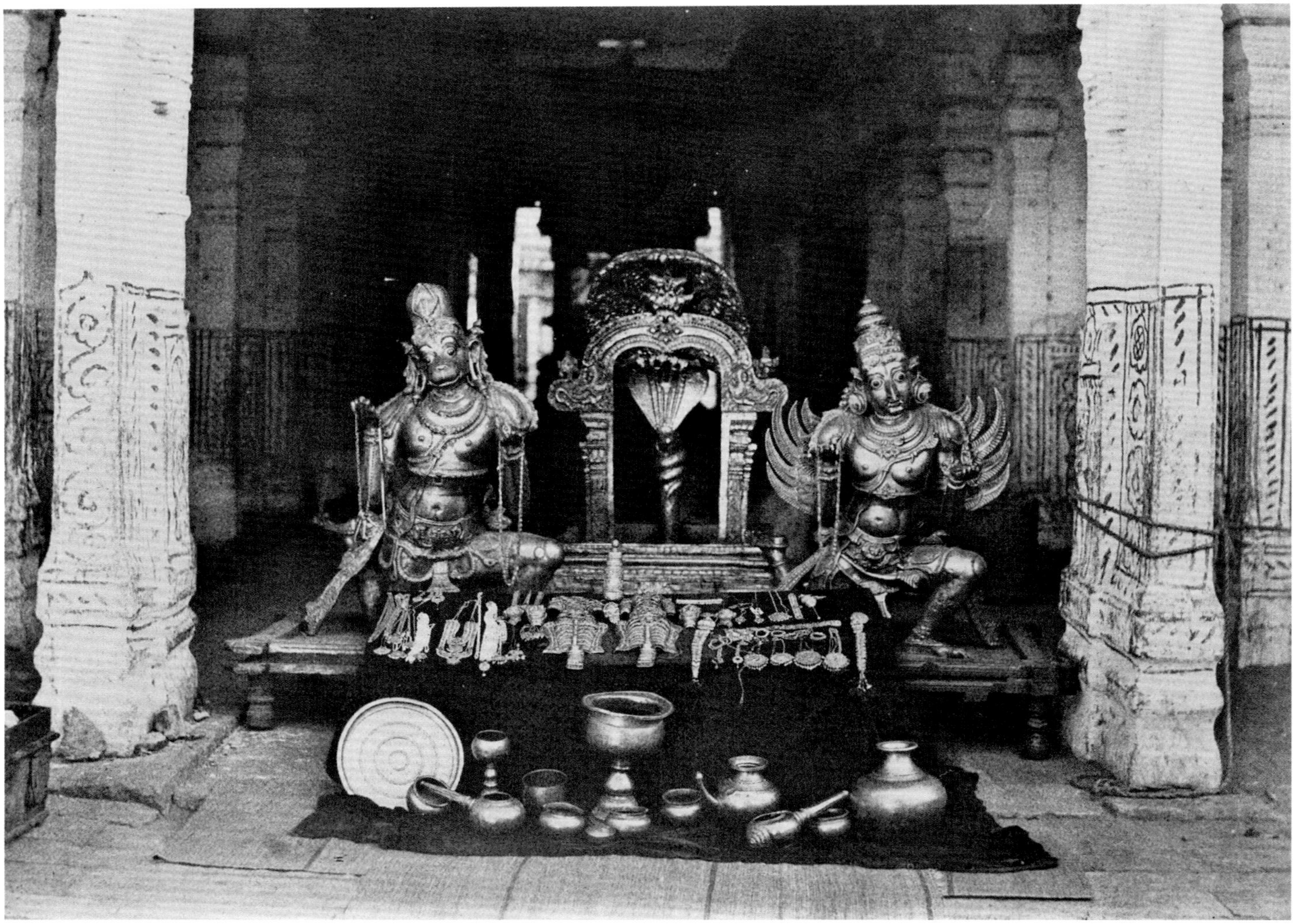

19

The Great Pagoda at Seringham: Jewels of the Pagoda

LINNAEUS TRIPE (1822–1902)

Srirangam, Tamil Nadu, 1858
Albumen silver print from a waxed paper negative
26.4 × 36.9 cm (10 ⅜ × 14 ½ in.)
Published: Linnaeus Tripe, *Photographic views of Seringham*, Madras, 1858, pl. 6
Metropolitan Museum of Art, New York, Gift of Cynthia Hazen Polsky (1988.1048)

THIS IMAGE OF THE TEMPLE JEWELS of the great Ranganatha Temple at Seringham is an unusual close-up study. All of the remaining eight views of the Rangunatha and Jambukeshvara temples at Seringham published in the *Photographic views of Seringham* consist of general architectural studies and, with the exception of his Elliot Marbles series (cat. no. 18), Tripe seems rarely to have been attracted to the close view in his work.

Tripe's reputation as one of the finest practitioners of calotype photography in the mid-nineteenth century rests almost entirely on two bodies of work, the portfolio of 120 views of Burma taken during the diplomatic mission of 1855 and some 100 large architectural studies taken as Government Photographer during the first half of 1858. It is tempting to speculate how much more he might have achieved had his post become established. Tripe himself certainly lobbied hard for permanent status as Government Photographer and nursed ambitions to create over time a comprehensive photographic record that would encompass the architecture, topography, and natural and commercial products of the country, as well as "illustrations of the races under this government, of their customs, dress, occupations."[1] But such hopes were dashed in early 1859. On seeing the accounts of Tripe's expenses, which included premises and staff in Bangalore for producing prints in bulk, the Governor of Madras Charles Trevelyan ruled that such projects, in the financial austerity of the post-Mutiny period, were "an article of high luxury which is unsuited to the present state of our finances."[2] An order was shortly issued abolishing his photographic establishment, despite Tripe's passionate defense of his work and its value (including a probably unrealistic attempt to argue that it could be made self-financing). Henceforward, the authorities ordered, the documentation of Indian architecture should more properly be undertaken by amateur initiatives, rather than falling on the shoulders of government.[3]

JF

1 Tripe to the Secretary to the Governor of Madras, 22 July 1856, East India Company Board's Collections, in British Library IOR/F/4/2725.

2 Madras public proceedings, 19 April 1859.

3 Madras public proceedings, 18–24 June 1859.

20

Two ivory dvarapala plaques

KARNATAKA (MYSORE) OR TAMIL NADU, LATE EIGHTEENTH CENTURY

8.3 × 3.8 cm (3 ½ × 1 ½ in.)
Metropolitan Museum of Art, New York, Gift of Cynthia Hazen Polsky
(2011.576.1; 2011.576.2)

THESE PLAQUES DEPICT FIERCE DOOR-GUARDIAN FIGURES (*DVARAPALAS*). The right-hand plaque shows a four-armed standing figure with the left leg raised, wearing elaborate jewelry and a tall headdress. Flanked by architectural elements of pilasters and capitals, he stands on a plinth with lotus leaves. The second panel is similarly decorated, with the design reversed. These ivory pieces can be compared to wood carvings from Southern India. Dvarapala guardian figures such as these commonly adorn temple architecture and are found on the huge wooden temple chariots used in ceremonies. They are also placed on the door lintels of houses: one example, with central figures of the gods including Lakshmi flanked by dvarapalas trampling on lions, is from a mansion in the Chettinad district of Tamil Nadu.[1] The dvarapalas on this panel are very similar to our ivories.

Mysore and Travancore were major centers of ivory carving in Karnataka, an area that fell within the former Madras Presidency.[2] Large and lively openwork ivory panels decorated with fantastic creatures were carved at Mysore, including a magnificent settee or throne back,[3] and it is possible that the panels came from these workshops.

Ivory carvings with architectural settings may also have been used in miniature domestic shrines,[4] and a number are known, such as an ivory sculpture with a recumbent Vishnu in the Asian Art Museum, San Francisco.[5] On this carving, the central divinity is flanked by dvarapala figures in similar postures to our examples, while the architecture represents the temple doorway at Srirangam, a temple near to Madurai in Tamil Nadu.

MCS

1 D. Thiagarajan, "Doors and woodcrafts of Chettinad," in G. Michell ed., *Living wood: Sculptural traditions of Southern India*, Bombay: Marg, 1992, fig. 11, p. 66; *ibid.*, p. 156 (cat. no. 48).

2 Watt, 1903, p. 189.

3 *Ibid.*, pl. 78.

4 Michell, 1995, p. 209.

5 *The Asian Art Museum of San Francisco: Selected works*, San Francisco, 1994, p. 39; acc. no. B82 M4.

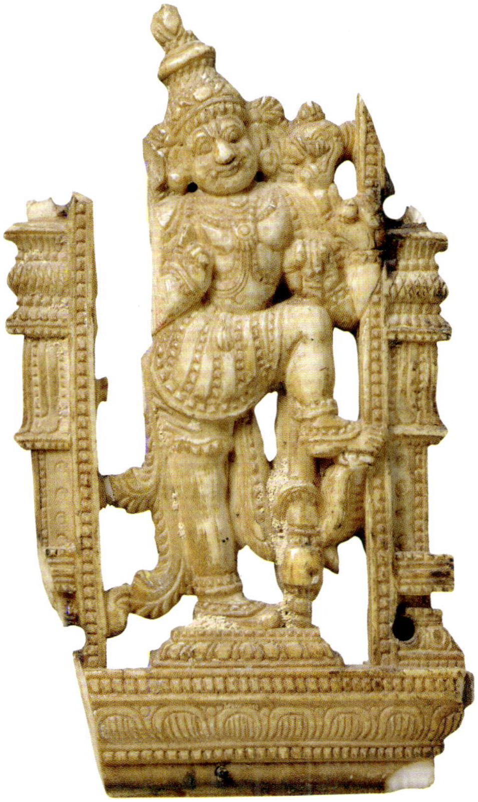

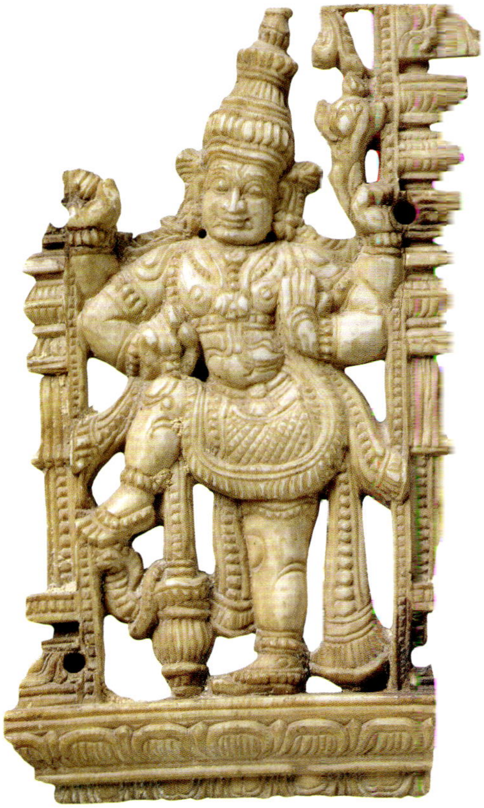

21

Gold necklace

KERALA, LATE NINETEENTH CENTURY

H. (each element): 9.5 cm (3 ¾ in.)
Metropolitan Museum of Art, New York, Gift of Cynthia Hazen Polsky (1991.32.2)

THIS GOLD NECKLACE consists of a series of forty-one elements strung on a black thread, each element in the form of a long tapering bud with concave faces issuing from a faceted pod, and each set with a ruby. The buds could represent either jasmine (*Jasminium sambac*) or *champa* flower (*Michelia champaca*). Other examples of a jasmine bud necklace, with slightly different finials, are in the Freer Gallery of Art, Washington D.C.,[1] and the Barbier-Mueller Museum, Geneva.[2] A similar necklace is seen, worn by a Bengali lady, in a painting of 1787 by Francesco Renaldi (1755–ca. 1799).[3] Necklaces of this type were made in silver and brass as well as gold.[4]

The bud and garland motif echoes the use of garlands in Indian ritual. *Champa* bud necklaces were given as offerings to Shiva and other deities,[5] and the flowers are commonly used in shrines and temples. Flowers are considered to be pure, and therefore suitable for use in the temple and for adorning images. They are also used in marriage ceremonies and were considered a means by which a wife might keep her husband's attention.[6]

The necklace would have formed part of a bride's dowry. Jewelry given at the time of marriage was her share of the family property, and an investment. It could be passed from mother to daughter. Even though constructed from sheet, the amount of gold contained in such jewelry is often substantial. Necklaces made of coins (*kasumala*) are a visible and easily convertible form of wedding dowry, and may be up to a meter long.[7]

MCS

1 C. R. Bolon and A. Vohra Sarin, "Metaphors in gold: The jewelry of India," *Asian Art*, VI, 4, Fall 1993, fig. 5, p. 22; acc. no. 1990.4.

2 Untracht, 1997, fig. 37, p. 35.

3 *Ibid.*, fig. 41, p. 37.

4 *Ibid.*, fig. 43.

5 *Ibid.*, fig. 35, p. 34.

6 *Ibid.*, p. 33.

7 Bolon and Sarin, *op. cit.*, p. 22.

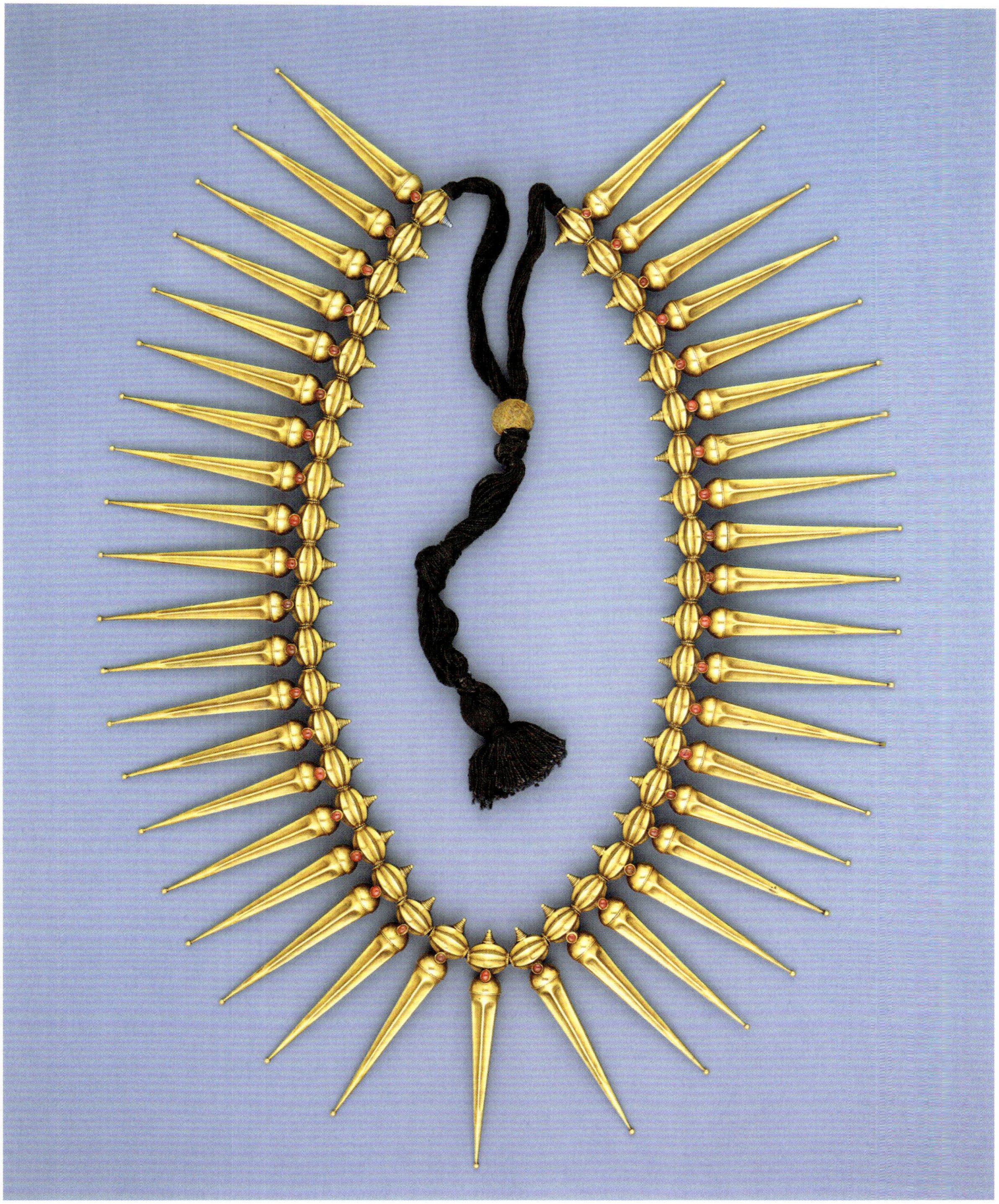

22

Gold marriage necklace

TAMI NADU, LATE NINETEENTH CENTURY

L. 48.5 cm; (33 ¼ in.)
Metropolitan Museum of Art, New York,
Gift of Cynthia Hazen Polsky (1991.32.3)

THIS GOLD MARRIAGE NECKLACE, known as a *kalata uru* (*kala* means neck and *uru* means bead)[1] is of a type worn by Nattukottai Chettiar women in Tamil Nadu. It comprises a series of twenty-one elements strung on black thread. The central pendant (*thali*) depicts Shiva with Parvati riding on the bull Nandi, flanked by dancing figures. Around this is a series of paired cylindrical beads with crosshatched surfaces, four elements each with four fingers, a pair of square section beads, and two beads to tie off the thread.

The Chettiars are a Shaivite merchant sect who are often wealthy bankers. The necklace would have been part of a bride's dowry, and would be tied around her neck by her new husband. Subsequently her jewelry would all be taken to her husband's home, where it would be examined and valued by her female in-laws. The necklace was also worn at a ceremony held when a Chettiar man attained the age of sixty, at which his wife once again wore her bridal jewelry, possibly including a second necklace commissioned for the occasion.[2] Similar necklaces are in the Freer Gallery of Art, Washington, D.C.,[3] the Ivory Collection[4] and the Victoria and Albert Museum, London.[5]

The Sanskrit word *thali* is derived from the local name for the palmyra palm (*thala*), as it was traditional to tie fronds from the palm around the neck of a bride, and the term was transferred to the gold element.[6] Thalis can be made in a wide variety of shapes and sizes. They can be phallic symbols in Tamil Nadu, and some have images of Lakshmi[7] or Shiva and Parvati, as here.[8] The four hand-shaped elements, known as *athanams* in Tamil,[9] are said to represent the hands of the bride and groom, while the four fingers represent the four Vedas.[10]

MCS

1 C. R. Bolon and A. Vohra Sarin, "Metaphors in gold: The jewelry of India," *Asian Art*, VI, 4, Fall 1993, p. 19.

2 Untracht, 1997, p. 158, fig. 282.

3 Acc. no. 1991.4; Bolon and Sarin, *op. cit.*, fig. 4.

4 Untracht, *op. cit.*, fig. 284.

5 Stronge, Smith and Harle, 1988, no. 69, pp. 76–77.

6 Untracht, *op. cit.*, p. 168.

7 Ibid., fig. 306; Bolon and Sarin, *op. cit.*, fig. 4.

8 Also Stronge et al., *loc. cit.*

9 Bolon and Sarin, *op. cit.*, p. 19.

10 Untracht, *op. cit.*, p. 158.

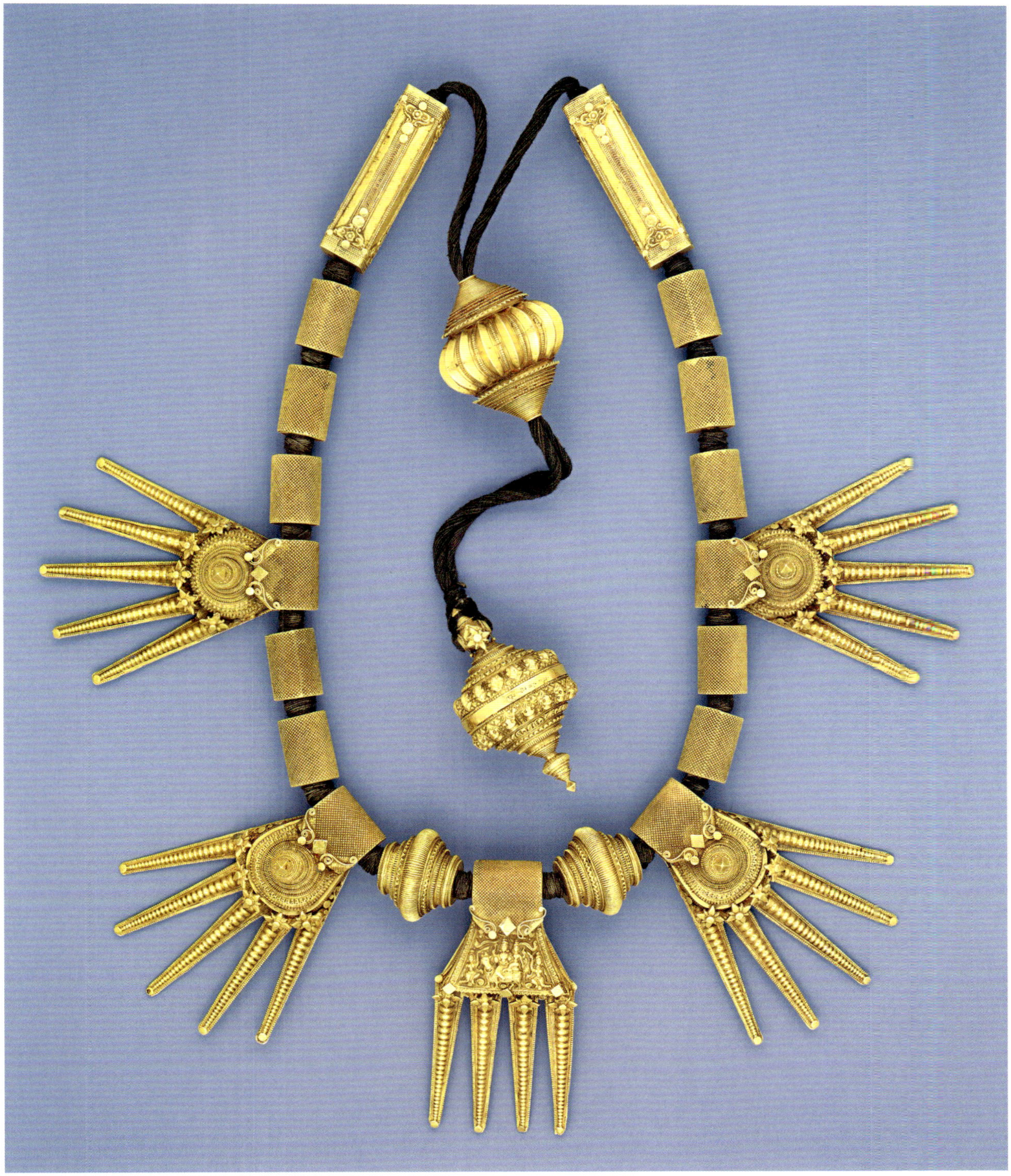

23

Gold earring

KERALA, LATE NINETEENTH CENTURY

H. 10.2 × W. 6.4 cm (4 × 2 ½ in.)

ONE OF A PAIR, this gold earring (called in Tamil *andi bhaden kathija*) is designed to hang from the lobe of the ear, and is constructed from gold sheet soldered onto a core, embellished with applied gold wire, granulation, and small, diamond-shaped pieces of sheet which are soldered to the main body. Earrings such as this were worn in distended earlobes, often with a cluster of other earrings. This particular example is of a type worn by Muslim Malayalam women in Cochin Division (Kerala).[1] Although appearing massive, they are quite light in weight. The earlobes of young girls were pierced shortly after birth and then stretched, using cloth followed by lead weights, so that by the time of marriage the ritual earrings could be attached.[2] The custom and style is not restricted to Muslims, and Hindu women in Tamil Nadu wear earrings of geometric and cubic forms, often with multiple piercing of the ear.[3] The custom is ancient and found throughout India, being seen in sculpture from Kushan times, but it is now dying out as a result of Western influence.[4]

The other earring from this pair is in The Metropolitan Museum, New York, and similar examples are in the Freer Gallery of Art, Washington, D.C.[5] The range of jewelry in Southern India is as diverse as it is in the rest of India, and is quite distinct from Mughal jewelry traditions.[6] The gold used is generally 22 carat. The use of enamel (*minakari*) is not usually found, with a preference instead for decorated gold sheet and inlaid precious stones. Marriage jewelry formed the dowry of the bride, while temple jewelry was attached to the image of the deity during festivals and processions.[7]

MCS

1 Untracht, 1997, p. 225, fig. 460, for similar earrings.

2 *Ibid.*, p. 220.

3 *Ibid.*, p. 218.

4 C. R. Bolon and A. Vohra Sarin, "Metaphors in gold: The jewelry of India," *Asian Art*, VI, 4, Fall 1993, pp. 28–29; fig. 13, p. 30.

5 Metropolitan Museum acc. no. 1990.100; a closely similar pair of earrings is in the Freer Gallery: 1990, 3a, b.

6 Stronge, Smith and Harle, 1988, pp. 38–43, discusses Southern Indian jewelry.

7 Filliozat and Pattabiramin, 1966, illustrates a wide range of Southern Indian temple jewelry.

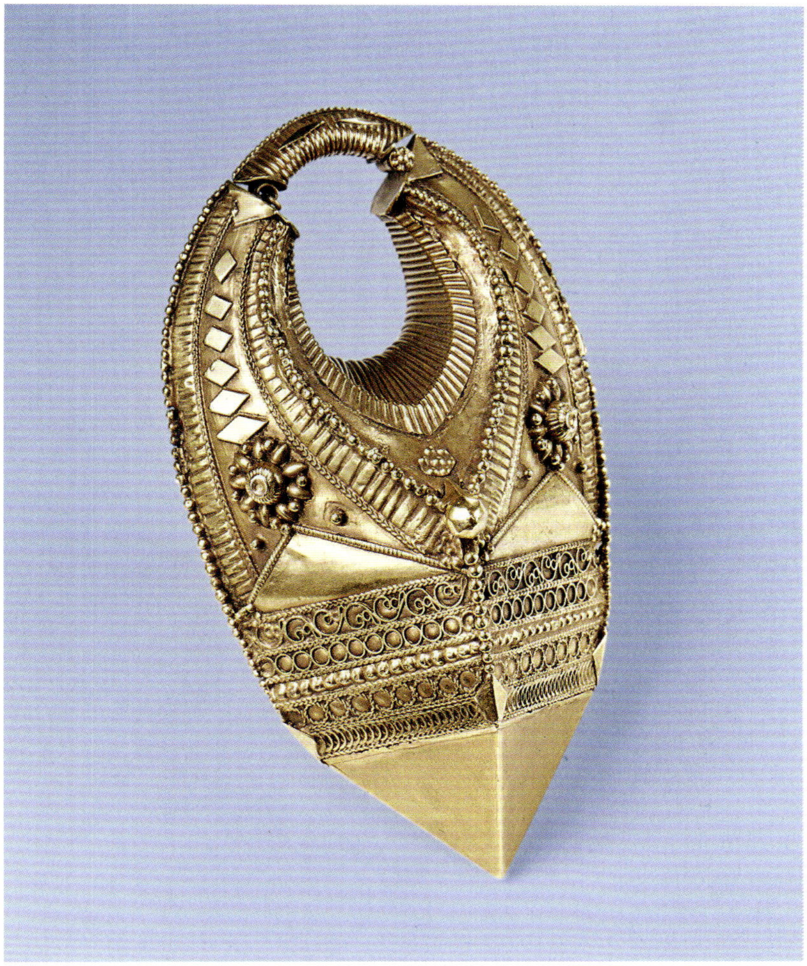

24

Juggernaut car (temple chariot), Madras

FREDERICK FIEBIG (FL. 1840S–50S)

Madras, Tamil Nadu, 1852
Salted paper print from a paper negative
23.9 × 18.3 cm (9 7/16 × 7 3/16 in.)
Metropolitan Museum of Art, New York, Purchase, Cynthia Hazen Polsky and Horace W. Goldsmith Foundation Gifts (1989.1033)

THIS IS ONE OF THE SEVERAL VIEWS of elaborately carved temple cars (*ratha*) photographed by Frederick Fiebig during his visit to Madras in 1852. This example is additionally adorned with flags and other decorations, in preparation for processing the image of the god through the streets. Although elaborate temple vehicles are widely seen throughout India, the massive chariot used to convey the image of Jagannatha through the street of Puri in Orissa during the famous annual festival led to the epithet Juggernaut being applied by Europeans during the nineteenth century to temple cars in general.

A large collection of some 600 hand-colored prints by Fiebig, including a colored version of this image, survives in the British Library. Uncolored examples of his work, however, which are generally much more richly printed and toned, are extremely rare. The British Library collection of Fiebig's prints was originally purchased from the photographer in 1856 by the East India Company, but the somewhat mystifying absence of any other significant quantity of his work is mirrored in the tantalizingly little that is known about the man himself. Fiebig's work appeared at around the time that photography was starting to challenge other media as the prime means of visual documentation and Fiebig himself is an example of this trend. In the 1840s he was working as a topographical artist and lithographer in Calcutta, and in later correspondence with the East India Company he states that he took up photography in the late 1840s as an amateur pastime during his travels in the subcontinent.[1] It seems likely, however, that the commercial potential of the medium had played some part in the creation of such a large portfolio. In 1852 Fiebig visited Madras, where he showed a large portfolio of views as well as giving some tuition in the calotype process, and a short article that appeared in a local journal praised the work of this "expert German professor of the art."[2] His correspondence with the East India Company negotiating the sale of his photographs indicates that he spent at least some time in England, but from that point this important early photographer disappears into a complete and intriguing obscurity.

JF

1 East India Company, miscellaneous letters received, vol. 193, 1856.

2 *Illustrated Indian Journal of Art*, Madras, 1852, p. 32. This article also states that Fiebig had traveled and photographed extensively in China and Burma, but no evidence of this work appears to have survived.

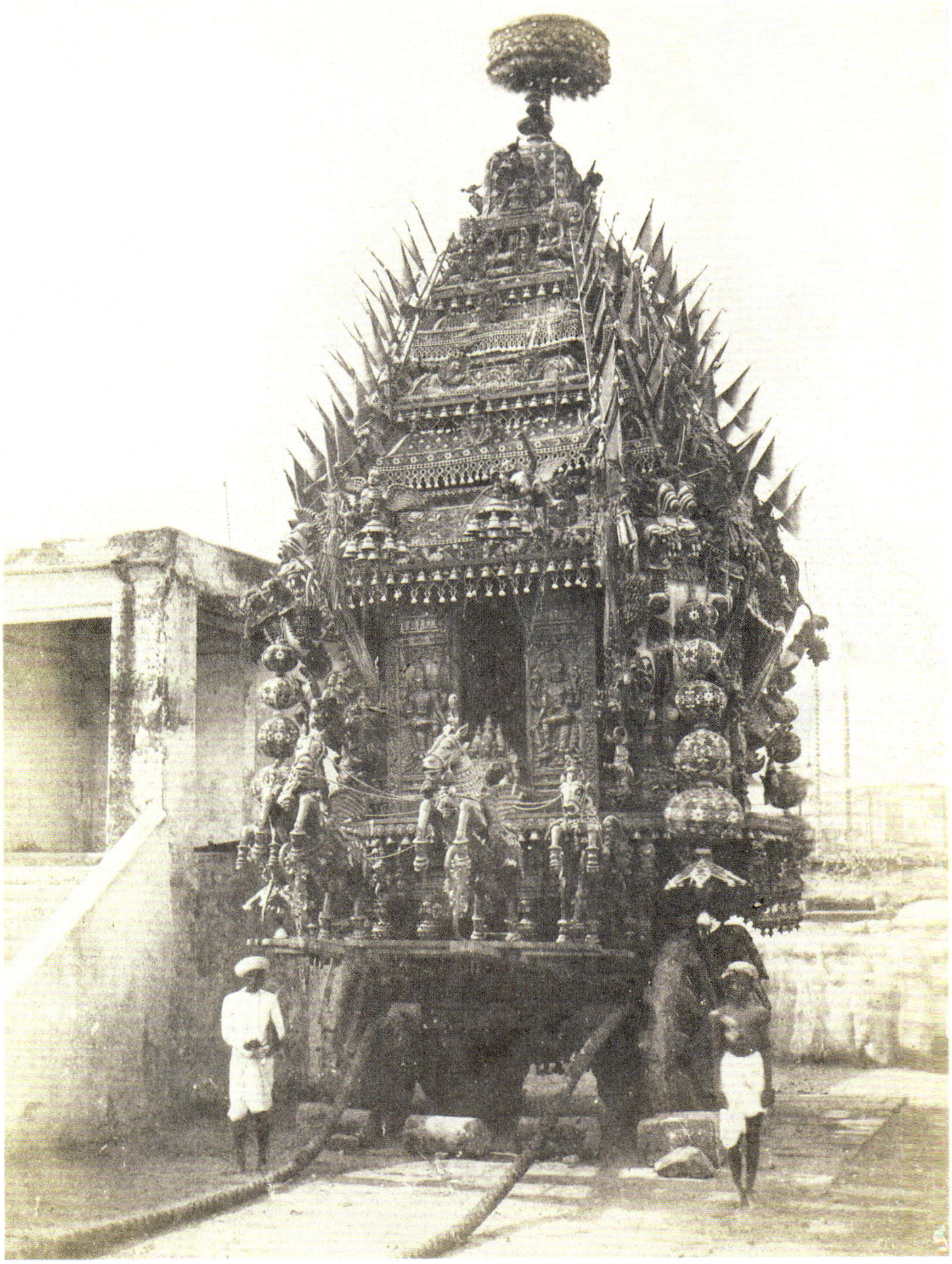

25

Two donor figures

GANDHARA, PROBABLY HADDA AREA
AFGHANISTAN, THIRD TO FOURTH
CENTURY AD

Stucco with remains of pigment
30.5 x 15.2 cm (12 x 6 in.)

THIS STUCCO SCULPTURE IN RELIEF depicts a standing couple, probably donor figures, with the female standing to the fore. She has a high hair arrangement held in place with a plain band, large earrings and a torque or necklace around her neck. She wears a shorter tunic over a long garment; the male figure also wears a tunic and holds an offering in his hands. Their costume is a form of nomad dress.[1] Their identification as straightforward donor figures is more probable than that they depict the auspicious deities Panchika and Hariti, although the latter have a diverse iconography.[2]

Visible remains of pigment indicate that the sculpture was once brightly painted. It probably comes from the region near Hadda, now in the Jalalabad district of Afghanistan, a site well known for its stucco sculptures. The site was famous in antiquity, being described by Chinese pilgrims including Faxian around AD 400. Stucco, introduced from Alexandria, became the main material used for sculpture at Hadda by the fourth century. It has a coarse core of lime plaster and small stones, covered with finer stucco and finally coated in a layer of gypsum plaster which was often painted.[3] Molds were sometimes used. Much of the known material consists only of heads, possibly due to the fragility of stucco, and this pair of figures is a relatively unusual survival.[4]

The site of Hadda was extensively excavated by the French between 1923 and 1928, particularly the monastery of Tapa-Kalan, and much of the material is now in the Musée Guimet, Paris.[5] The Kabul Museum, Afghanistan, received many objects from the excavations, which are now presumed destroyed. Stucco sculpture was also found at other sites, including the monasteries of Jaulian and Mora-Moradu at Taxila.[6]

MCS

1 Zwalf, 1996, vol. 1, p. 56.

2 Zwalf, *op. cit.*, vol. 1, p. 44; also Allchin et al., 1992, nos. 136, 144.

3 Rowland, 1966, p. 73.

4 Zwalf, *op. cit.*, vol. 2, figs. 545–635.

5 Béguin, 1992, p. 104; Kurita, 1990, vol. 2, pp. 138–44, illustrates some of the Guimet material, including a pair of monks (fig. 396, p. 139).

6 Marshall, 1951.

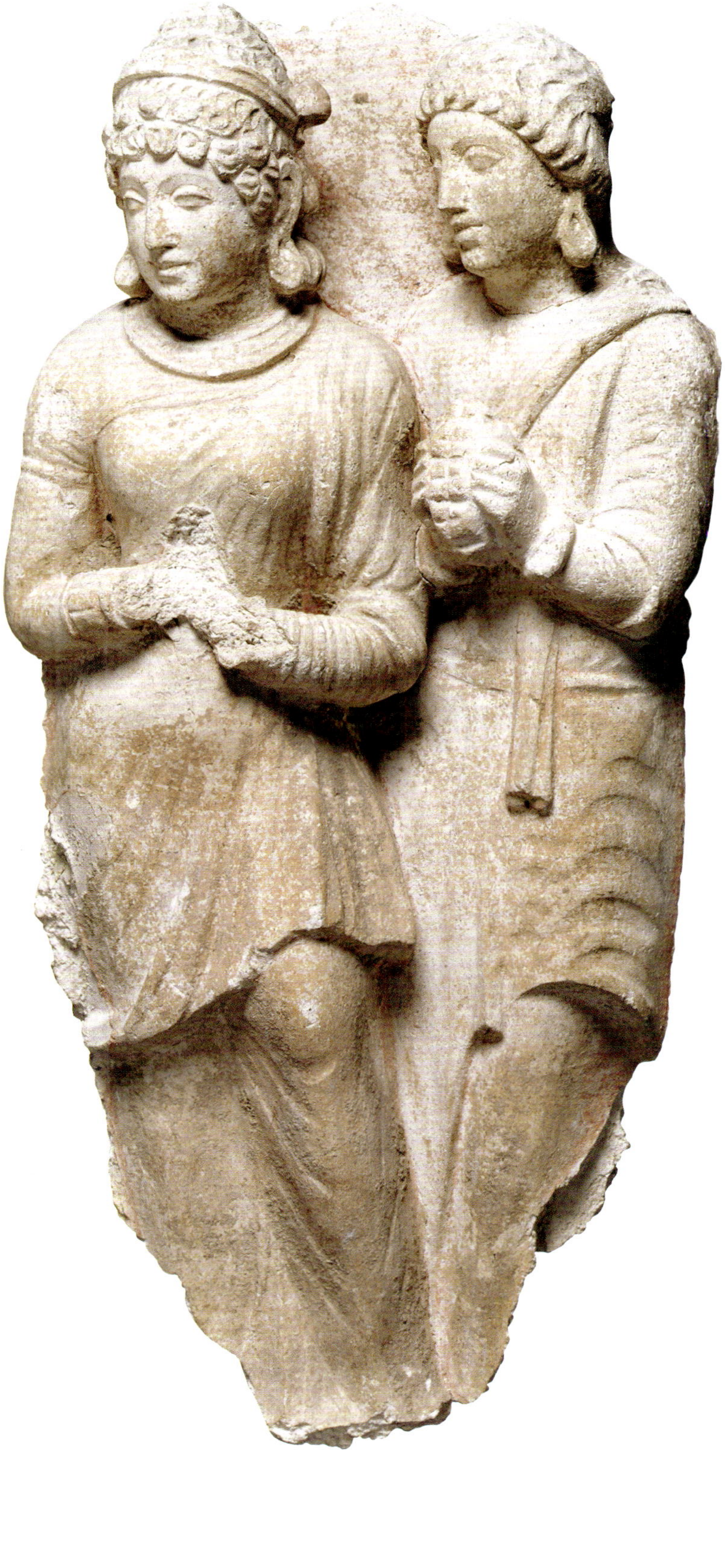

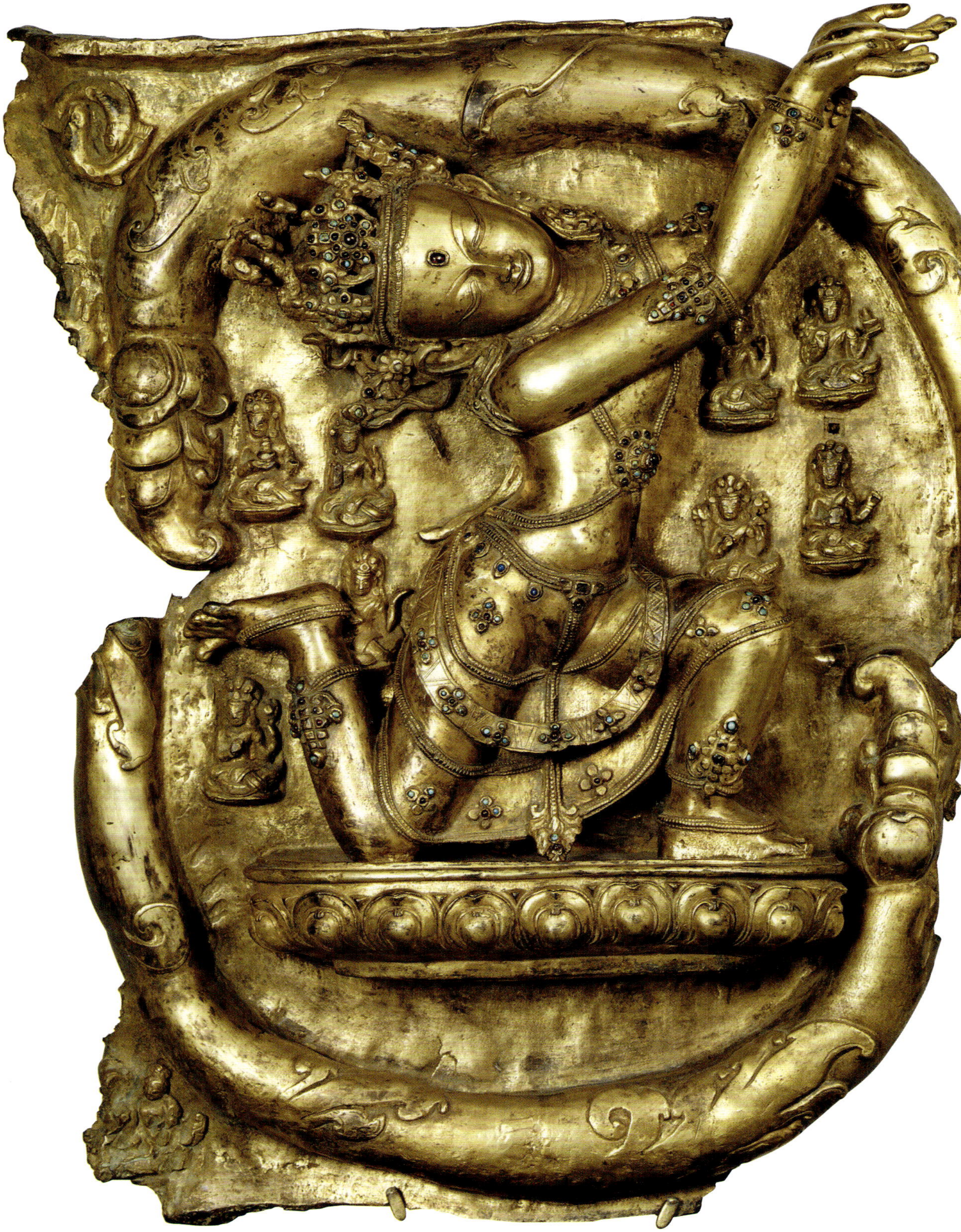

26

Nagaraja

TIBET, DENSATIL, EARLY FIFTEENTH CENTURY

Gilt bronze inlaid with semi-precious stones
58.4 × 45.7 cm (23 × 18 in.)

THE SERPENTS (*NAGAS*) ARE BENEVOLENT GENII, friendly to humans, providing protection against lightning and controlling rainstorms. They also protect the Buddha's Law. The supreme Nagaraja (King of the Nagas) is the Lokapala Virupaksha. Another of their kings is Nanda, sometimes depicted as half man and half serpent, and yet another, Muchalinda, protected the meditating Buddha during a storm. This gilt bronze and inlaid plaque depicts a Nagaraja kneeling on a lotus, with both arms raised to offer gifts to the Buddha. He is crowned and wears elaborate jewelry. Eight miniature figures are seated on lotuses in the background. Around the figure of the Nagaraja are the thick, sinuous bodies of two crocodile-like aquatic beasts with long snouts (*makaras*), which were originally part of a tendril that united the long frieze to which this piece belonged.

It is a fragment from one of the great reliquaries from the monastery of Densatil, a site to the south-east of Lhasa. There were originally eighteen stupas, the first being founded in 1198. The abbots were from the powerful Lang (*glangs*) family, and under their patronage stupas were erected by each abbot to honor his predecessor. The use of gilded bronze indicates that the craftsmen who made the frieze were Nepalese working for their Tibetan patrons. A stupa for the first abbot was built in 1255. Four stupas were built between 1370 and 1400, another in 1431, a silver stupa in 1434, and three more between 1440 and 1450, one in 1489, and five between 1564 and the early seventeenth century.[1]

The monastery was one of many sites destroyed by the Chinese during the Cultural Revolution. However, it had been visited by the 1948 Tucci expedition, and photographs were taken by the Italian photographer Pietro Mele,[2] giving us an insight into the splendor that has been lost. Fragments of the friezes are now in public and private collections, including other Nagaraja panels, and panels showing musicians and dancing goddesses.[3] These panels have inlay, as in this example, of turquoise, garnets and other semi-precious stones.

MCS

1 Eskenazi, 1995, pp. 36–37.

2 Mele, 1975.

3 von Schroeder, 1981, pp. 430–31, no. 113G (musicians); Eskenazi, *op. cit.*, nos. 25–26.

27

Seated Buddha, with scenes from his life

BENGAL OR BURMA, ELEVENTH TO TWELFTH CENTURY AD

Mudstone
22.5 × 12.7 cm (9 × 5 in.)
Published: S. Kossak, "A group of miniature Pala stele from Bengal," *Orientations*, vol. 29, no. 7, July–August 1998, pp. 19–27, fig. 7; C. Bautze-Picron, "Between India and Burma: The 'Andagu' style," in *The art of Burma: New studies*, *Marg*, vol. 50, no. 4, June 1999, fig. 10, p. 44

THIS BEIGE MUDSTONE SCULPTURE depicts the Buddha seated in earth-touching gesture (*bhumisparshamudra*) on a double lotus throne, with a Bodhisattva to either side, and the host of Mara arched above him in the Bodhi tree. He is flanked by a double column of figures in three tiers. The outer column and the main and topmost figures represent the Eight Great Events from his life; the inner figures and again the main figure represent the Buddha's actions at Bodhgaya at the Seven Stations in the seven weeks after the Enlightenment. The scenes, depicted clockwise from the Buddha's knee on the left, are the birth of the Buddha, the First Sermon, and the Buddha taming the elephant Nalagiri; at the top is the Death of the Buddha (*Parinirvana*), above which would have been a stupa (now missing), the descent from the Tavatimsa heaven, with Brahma and Indra shown beside him, the scene of the Twin Miracles, with the Buddha seated in teaching gesture (*dharmacakramudra*), and the Buddha being offered a bowl of honey by the monkey. The inner figures (also clockwise, with two figures missing) show the Buddha meditating, and being protected by the Muchalinda Naga. The lotus throne is supported by two Naga kings, and further supported by lions and crouching Gods (*devas*) below, while the foot of the base has miniature figures possibly representing the Seven Jewels.

This finely carved and minutely detailed sculpture is one of a group of carvings depicting the life of the Buddha, known as *andagu* stelae, the Burmese name for the very fine-grained yellow-beige stone, known as mudstone, which includes the form known as pyrophyllite.[1] Examples have been found in Burma, India, Thailand, and Sri Lanka (Ceylon).[2] Another example close to this piece is in the collection of the Asia Society, New York.[3] They fall into three groups, with a developing iconographic complexity,[4] this example being in the third and most complex group. The whole series has been generally assigned to Burma, but recent scholarship has questioned this, placing some or all of the objects within an Indian context.[5]

MCS

1 S. Kossak, "A group of miniature Pala stele from Bengal," pp. 19–27.

2 Luce, 1969–70, vol. 3, pls. 400–04; C. Bautze-Picron, "Between India and Burma: The 'Andagu' style," pp. 37–52; includes a list of forty-seven examples with references (this example is no. 36). A further nine examples are identified in Schroeder, 2001, pp. 400–05, pls. 129–31.

3 Acc. no. 1979.90.

4 Bautze-Picron, *op. cit.*, pp. 40ff.

5 *Ibid.*, arguing for an Indian provenance for some of the known sculptures, with the later examples being made in Burma; H. Woodward, "The Indian roots of the 'Burmese' Life of the Buddha plaques," in *Silk Road Art and Archaeology* 5 (1997/98), argues that the sculptures could originate from the Bodh Gaya region. Huntington, 1990, no. 61, pp. 217–20, discusses the Asia Society example and argues for a Burmese provenance; whereas Kossak prefers a Bangladesh or West Bengal provenance.

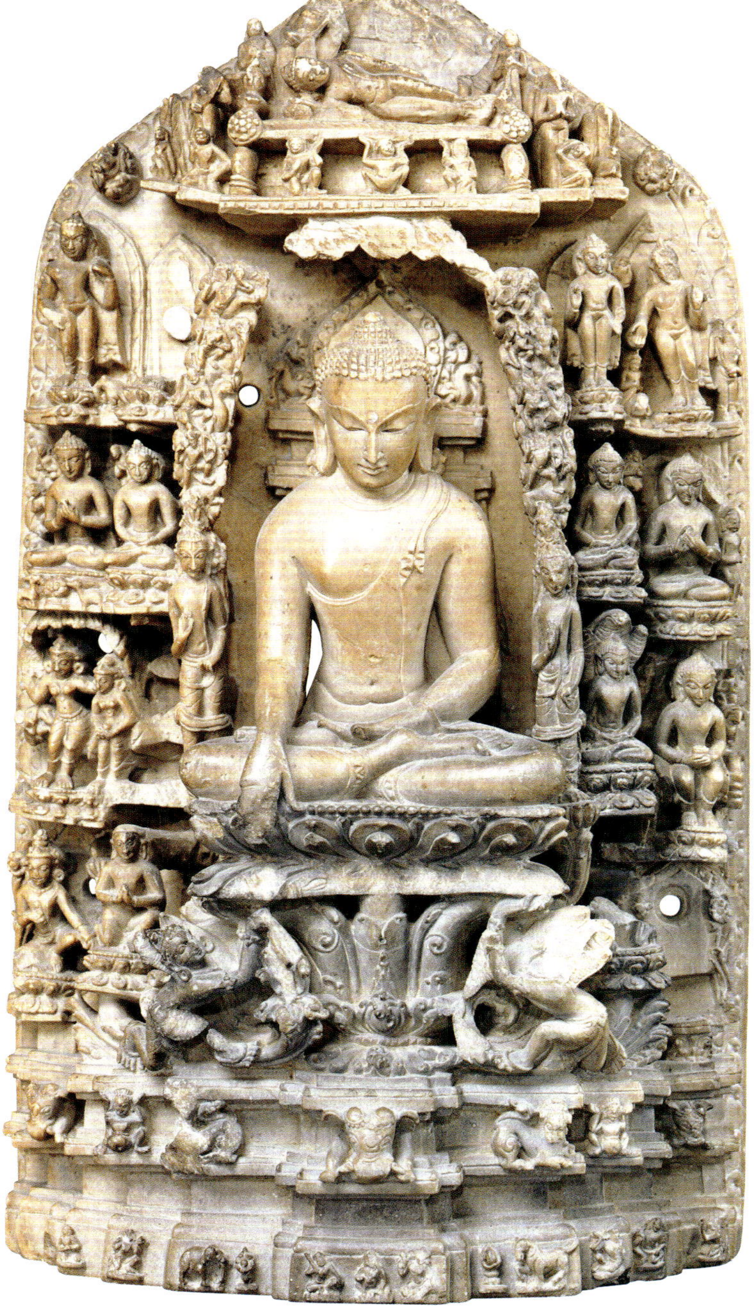

28

Standing Tirthankara in a Jain shrine at Gwalior

UNKNOWN PHOTOGRAPHER

Gwalior, Madhya Pradesh, 1860s
Albumen silver print from a glass negative
27.3 × 22.6 cm (10 ¾ × 8 ⅞ in.)
Metropolitan Museum of Art, New York, Purchase, Cynthia Hazen Polsky Gift (1993.126)

THE CLIFF FACE OF GWALIOR FORT is dotted with numerous Jain shrines, cave temples, and images. The most extensive series of sculptures is situated in the Urvahi valley—commonly known as "Happy Valley" by Europeans in the nineteenth century—a steep-sided gorge on the sheer western face of the hill. Here, between the seventh and fifteenth centuries, Jain devotees carved from the rock face a large group of devotional images unique in India for both their number and size. The most dramatic of these sculptures is the group of twenty-two colossal standing Tirthankaras, carved during the first half of the fifteenth century. This image, the largest of the group and sixty-two feet high, exhibits the stylized, rounded modeling characteristic of the group as a whole. Many of the images were severely damaged on the orders of the Emperor Babur, after his visit to Gwalior in 1528. Although impressed by the size of the sculptures, his religious sensibilities were outraged by their representation of the human form and by their nakedness, and he swiftly ordered their destruction. In most cases, however, the images were merely mutilated and were later restored in stucco by Jain devotees. The dramatic location of Gwalior's palaces and temples, perched on a long, steep-sided plateau overlooking the town, received extensive photographic coverage in the nineteenth century. These Jain images, however, situated in the narrow gorge running between the cliff face and the roadway, represented something of a technical challenge for the photographer, and were consequently photographed less frequently.

JF

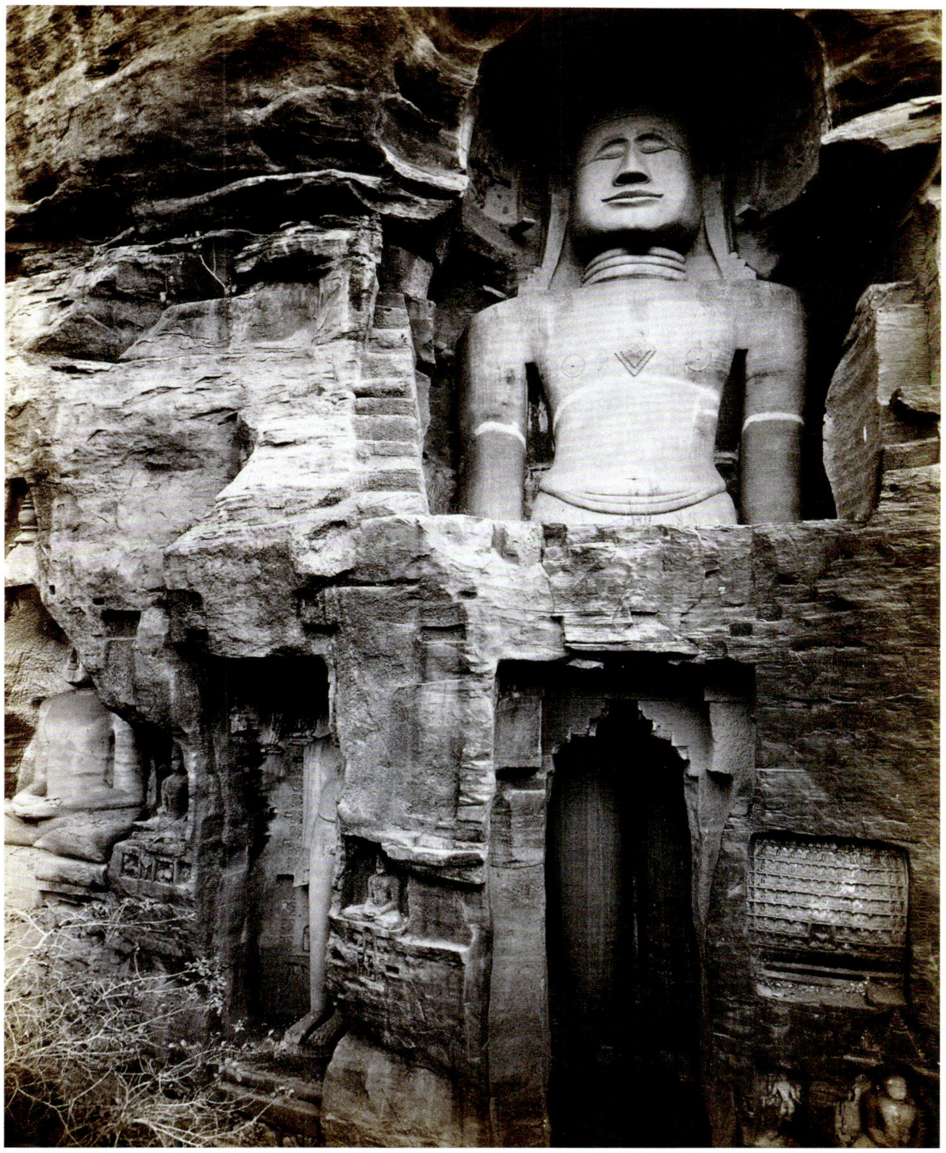

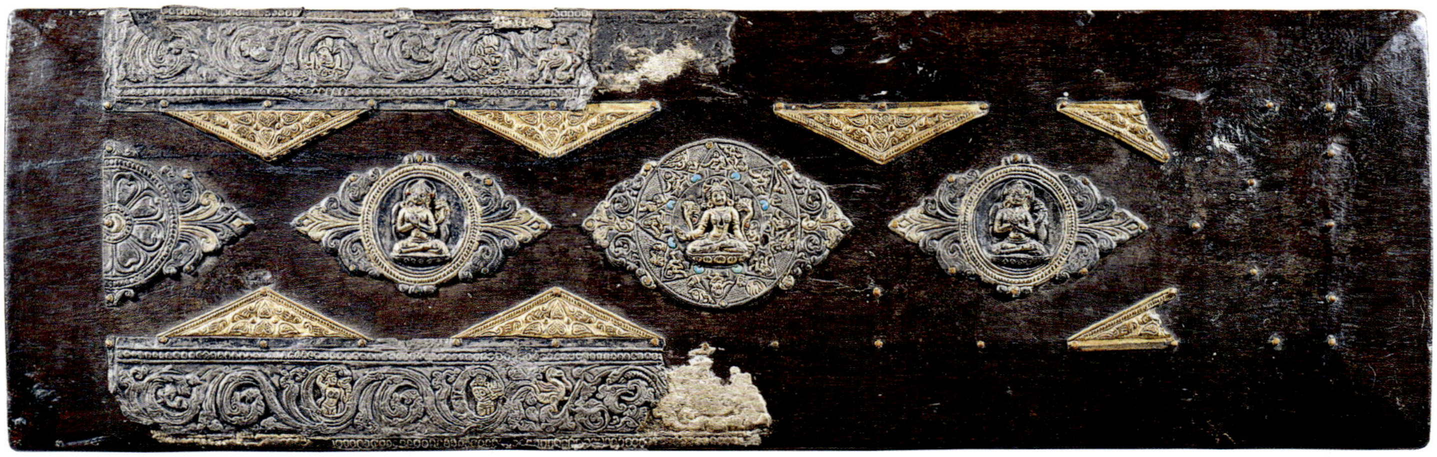

29

Pair of bookcovers for a Buddhist text

EASTERN INDIA, PALA STYLE
(COMMISSIONED FOR TIBET),
ELEVENTH TO TWELFTH CENTURY

Silver and gilt copper alloy with traces of pigment and semi-precious stones on wood
Each cover 70.5 × 22.5 cm (7 ¾ × 8 ⅞ in.)
Metropolitan Museum of Art, New York,
Gift of Cynthia Hazen Polsky (2005.436.1a, b)

THIS UNIQUE AND MAGNIFICENT PAIR OF BOOKCOVERS was probably made by Eastern Indian artists for a Tibetan patron. While the style and craftsmanship of the repoussé work is unquestionably Pala, the size of the covers is typical of Tibetan translations of Sanskrit Buddhist texts. (Indian manuscripts were traditionally written on palm leaf, usually not higher than six centimetres, and not on paper like Tibetan examples.) In the eleventh and twelfth centuries Tibetan Buddhists sought to deepen their understanding of Buddhism and to "purify" their practice by apprenticing themselves to the great masters and monastic universities of India, and it is likely that a Tibetan merchant-pilgrim or monk-translator of that period[1] commissioned these book covers from Indian artists. Both covers are adorned with repoussé metalwork attached to the wood by copper-alloy nails. The decoration features large medallions depicting deities, placed at regular intervals along the central axis of the inner rectangle. Gilt copper-decorated triangles are arranged along the intersection between the inner rectangle and the sloping border.

At the centre of cover A is the Buddhist goddess Tara in her form as Ashtamahabhaya ("She who protects from the Eight Great Perils"). Surrounding her in an eight-pointed star are eight Taras, each protecting a devotee from one of the Eight Perils: floods (depicted as a body of water marked by conch shells and a fish); false imprisonment in foreign territories (represented as an official holding a baton); and attack by wild elephants, lions, forest fires, bandits (here a figure with a knife), poisonous snakes, and demons who cause diseases. Both flanking medallions show another form of Tara, in teaching gesture (*dharmachakramudra*). Along the sloping wooden border,

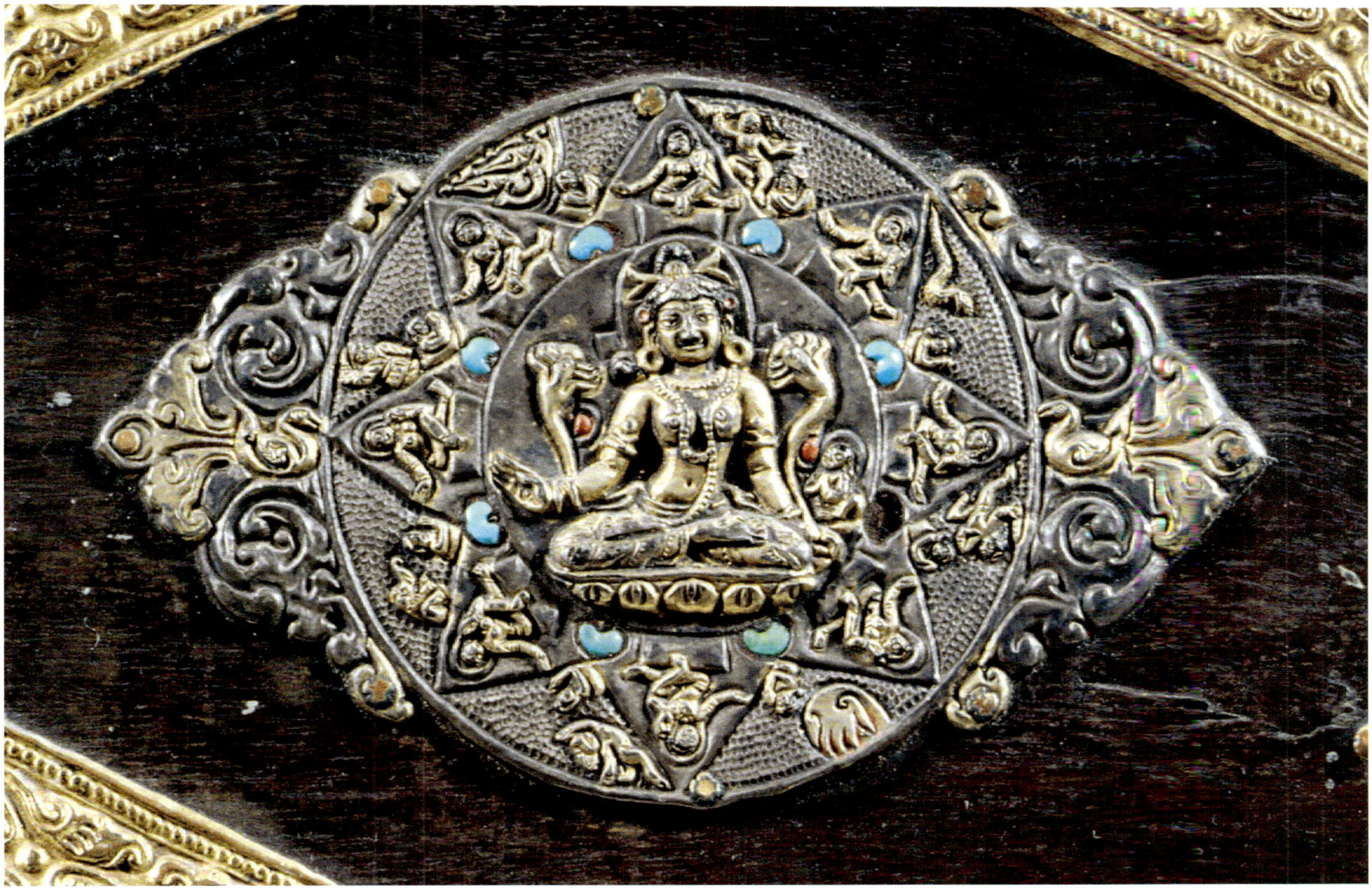

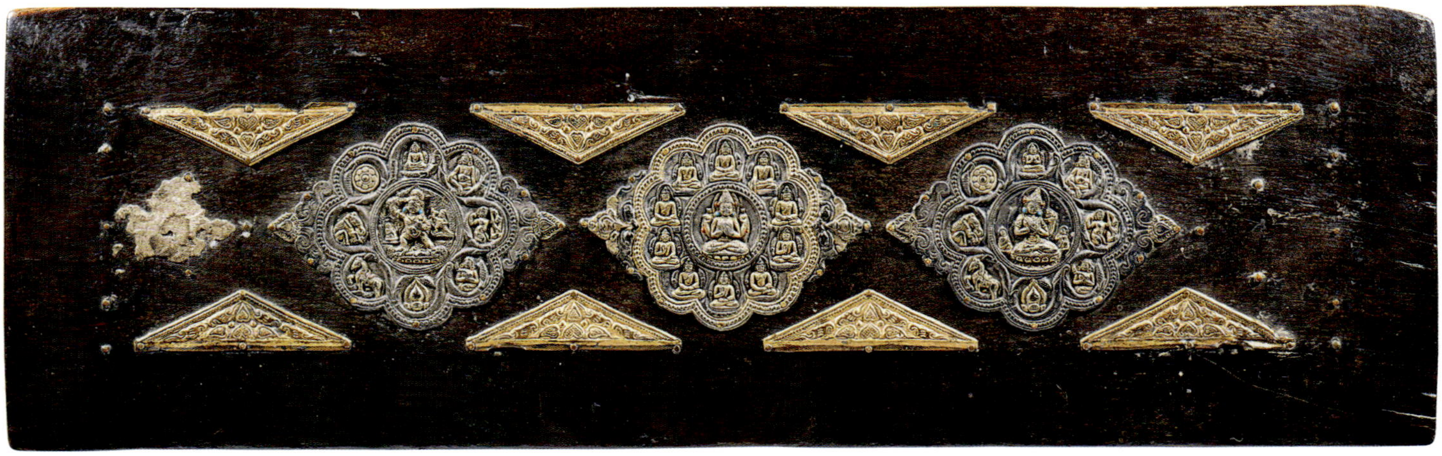

fragments of a repoussé frame feature foliate scrolls which emerge from the tails of geese and support bare-breasted offering goddesses.

At the centre of cover B is the goddess Prajnaparamita ("Perfection of Wisdom") in teaching gesture and surrounded by ten Buddhas. In the medallion on the left is Achala holding a sword surrounded by an image of the Buddha and seven auspicious symbols associated with the enlightened World Ruler: minister, general, queen, gem, horse, elephant, and wheel. In the medallion on the right is Shri Potalake Lokanatha, a form of the Bodhisattva Avalokiteshvara, surrounded by eight symbols identical to those described.

The style of the images is typically Eastern Indian, as are the beaded medallions and the foliate scrollwork in the border. Faces have large, heavily hooded eyes with deeply incised pupils, full lips and puffy cheeks; bodies are fleshy and rounded. Eastern Indian works such as this not only inspired the style, composition, and motifs used in Tibetan painted and carved wooden covers, but the repoussé technique also was simulated by Tibetan artists.

JE/JC

1 The dating given here is supported by a radiocarbon-14 test performed by the Institute of Particle Physics in Zürich.

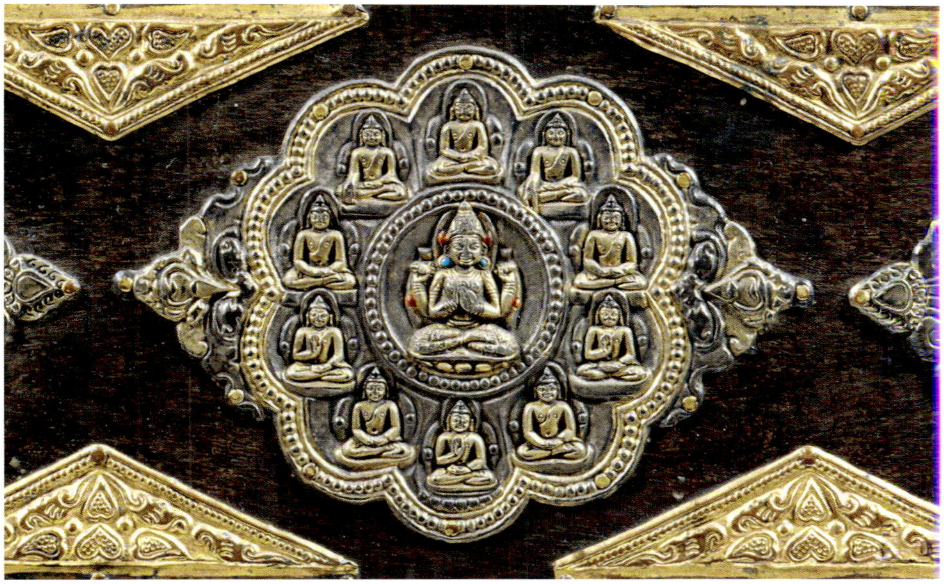

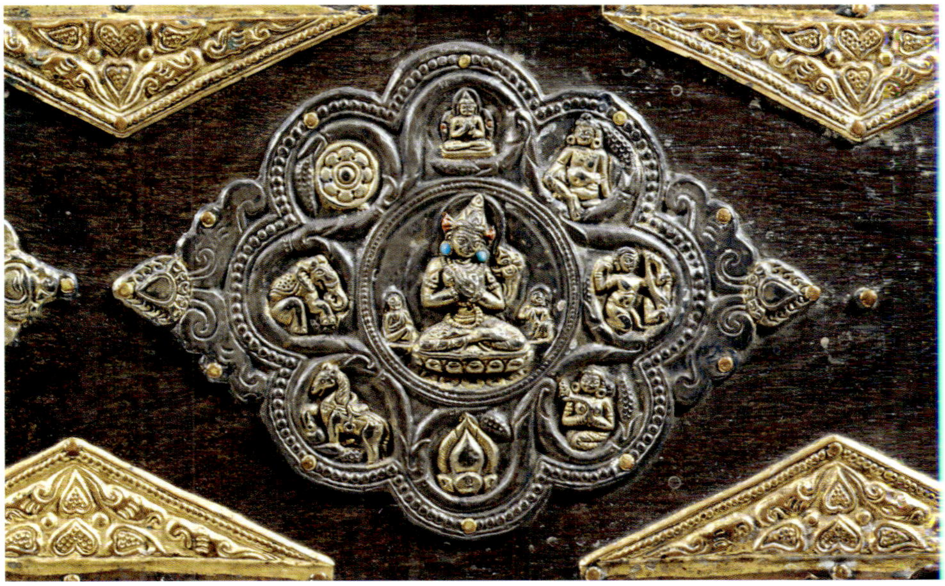

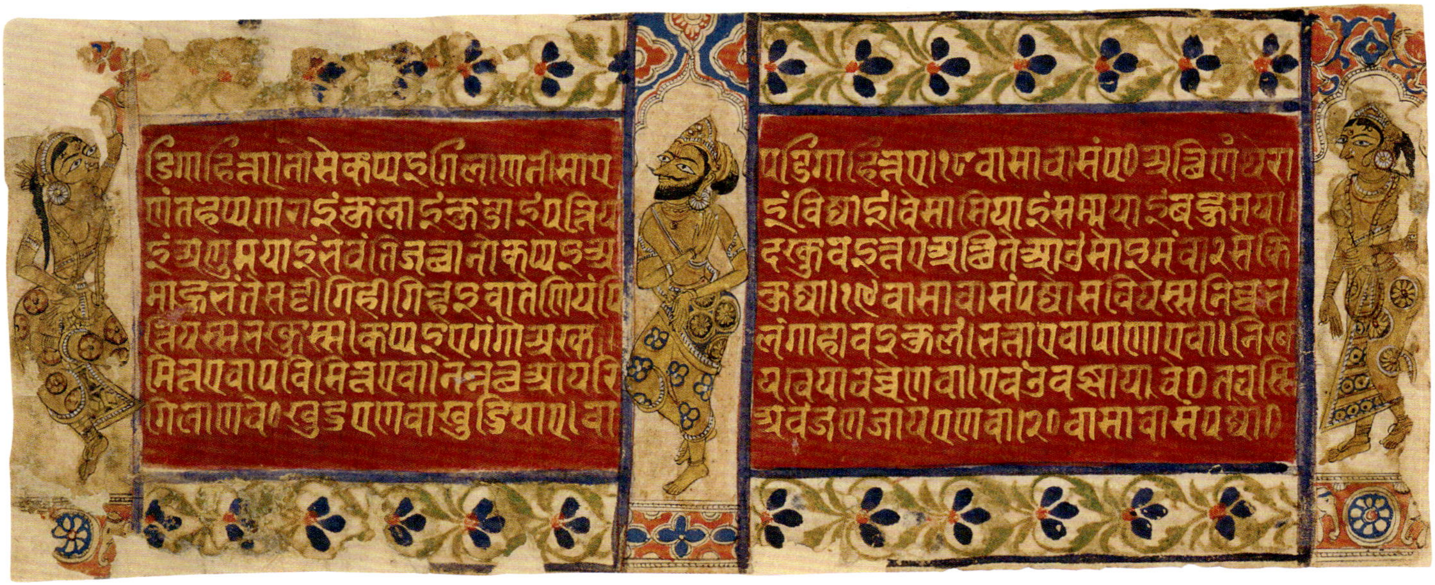

30

Decorated page from a Jain manuscript

FOLIO 85 FROM A MANUSCRIPT OF THE KALPASUTRA

Gujarat, ca. 1500
Opaque watercolor with gold on paper
11.4 × 29.2 cm (4 ½ × 11 ½ in.)
Metropolitan Museum of Art, New York, Gift of Cynthia Hazen Polsky (1985.398.9)

THIS PAGE BELONGED TO A MANUSCRIPT OF THE *KALPASUTRA*,[1] the Jain canonical text in Prakrit, from the Sthaviravali section on the succession lists of the Jain pontiffs. Although somewhat damaged and unfinished, it is distinguished by its lively decorations. Floral meanders at the top and bottom of the page are intersected by vertical margins containing dancing figures in architectural niches. All three are drawn with great liveliness and delicacy, and the artist, while aware of the iconographic need of the projecting farther eye, nonetheless anchors it securely into the facial structure instead of letting it hang out completely as in cat. no. 32. The verso decoration of this page consists of floral meanders in all the margins.

The most famous Jain manuscript with dancing figures in the margin is that from the Gujarati city of Broach of about 1500, originally from the Devaseno Pado Bhandar (temple library) in Ahmedabad but from which various folios are now dispersed. In this the female dancers bear inscriptions naming the particular dancing pose.[2]

JPL

1 Other pages from this manuscript are published in Leach, 1986, no. 5; and Pal, 1993, no. 30.

2 Khandalavala and Chandra, 1969, pp. 29–43; Losty, 1982, pp. 61–62; Goswamy, 1999, pp. 12–13.

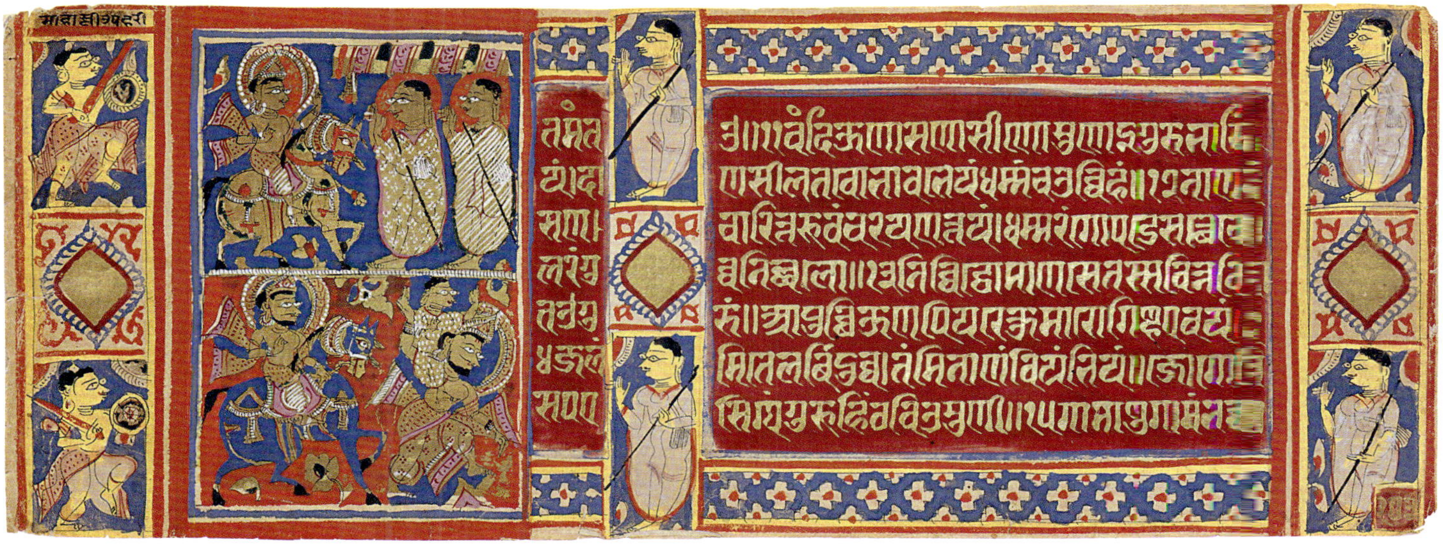

31

The abduction of Kalaka's sister by the King of Ujjain

VERSO FOLIO (NUMBERED 103) FROM A MANUSCRIPT OF THE KALAKACHARYAKATHA, THE STORY OF KALAKA, A JAIN PRAKRIT TEXT

Gujarat, 1475–1500
Opaque watercolor with gold on paper
Page 11.4 × 30.2 cm (4 ½ × 11 ⅞ in.)
Inscribed: *maha stri apahari* ("abduction of the nun") on top-left corner, indicating the subject

THE MINIATURE IS IN TWO REGISTERS. In the upper register, King Gardhabhilla of Ujjain comes upon two Jain nuns, and in the lower, he orders an attendant to carry off one of the nuns, who turns out to be Sarasvati, the sister of the monk Kalaka. The story of Kalaka is a popular one among Jains, and exists in several different medieval Prakrit and Sanskrit versions.[1] In order to rescue his sister, Kalaka persuaded the Sahi, or Saka, king to invest the city of Ujjain, a story that links up with the presence of a kingdom of the Sakas (Scythians, who came to India from Seistan in Iran) based on Ujjain in Malwa in the first century BC. The story is sometimes appended, as here, to manuscripts of the *Kalpasutra* (see cat. no. 32), since it was the monk Kalaka (although actually a different person of the same name from the one in the story) who changed the date of the Paryushana or rainy season festival, the rules for which form the last part, *Samachari*, of the *Kalpasutra* text.

This manuscript, like cat. no. 32, is decorated lavishly, with the text in gold ink on a crimson ground, and geometrical decorations in the top and bottom margins. In the vertical margins are two Sahi warriors on the left, and opposing them in the central and right margins, four Jain monks. The city of Pattan in Gujarat was famous for the production of manuscripts fully illuminated in such a way.[2]

JPL

1 For other illustrated manuscripts of this text, see Brown, 1933.

2 One such dated 1428 is in the British Library, IO San 3177 (Losty, 1982, p. 59).

32

The Fourteen Dreams of Queen Trishala

FOLIO 16 FROM A MANUSCRIPT OF THE KALPASUTRA PROBABLY FROM JAUNPUR, EASTERN UTTAR PRADESH, MID-FIFTEENTH CENTURY

Opaque watercolor with gold on paper
Page 11.7 × 29.2 cm (4 5⁄8 × 11 1⁄2 in.)

MAHAVIRA, THE LAST OF THE TWENTY-FOUR JINAS OR TIRTHANKARAS, was born to Queen Trishala. On the night of his conception, she dreamed the fourteen auspicious dreams which foretell the birth of a Universal Emperor or else of a Buddha or Jina. These are: 1) an elephant, 2) a bull, 3) a lion, 4) the goddess Shri, 5) a pair of garlands, 6) the moon, 7) the sun, 8) a banner, 9) a full pot, 10) a lotus lake, 11) the ocean of milk, 12) a celestial palace, 13) a heap of jewels, and 14) a brilliant smokeless fire.

The miniatures in manuscripts of the *Kalpasutra*, the Jain canonical text in Prakrit on the lives of the twenty-four founders of Jainism, conform generally to a rigid iconography, especially in Gujarat and Rajasthan, whence most of the fourteenth to sixteenth century examples come, and are stylistically standardized. Such manuscripts were normally deposited in Jain temple libraries (*bhandars*) as votive offerings. The more costly examples use gold ink for the writing of the text against grounds made from expensive pigments such as crimson and ultramarine, and are decorated in the margins with geometric or floral designs. A small number of more individual manuscripts of this text is known, sometimes from outside Western India, e.g. from Mandu in Central India and from Jaunpur in Eastern India, both capitals of Muslim Sultanates exposed to the manuscript illustrations of Iran. Such Jain manuscripts are both more refined and more progressive in casting off the rigidities of the traditional iconography and of figural style.[1]

This page comes from a now dispersed manuscript[2] which is stylistically very close to a famous manuscript written and illuminated at Jaunpur in 1465.[3] Although the iconography is traditional, the artist's line is more refined than usual, and he has pushed Trishala's projecting farther eye so far out that it is ready for the next stage, of being dropped off, thereby producing by the end of the century the characteristic early Rajput face in full profile. The strange feature of the projecting eye seems originally to have been caused by artistic reluctance to let so important a feature as the farther eye disappear, during the slow migration of the head in medieval painting from three-quarter to full profile. The recto here has static floral motifs in the margins, while the verso has floral meanders in the top and bottom margins, but sprays of tulips in the outer margins. This must be one of the earliest occurrences of this flower in Indian art.

JPL

1 See Losty, 1982, pp. 43–46, for a discussion of the format and styles of Jain manuscripts.

2 Other pages from this manuscript are published in Chandra and Ehnbom, 1976, nos. 9–10; and Poster et al., 1994, no. 15.

3 K. Khandalavala and M. Chandra, "An illustrated Kalpasutra painted at Jaunpur in AD 1465," Lalit Kala, 12, 1962, pp. 9–15.

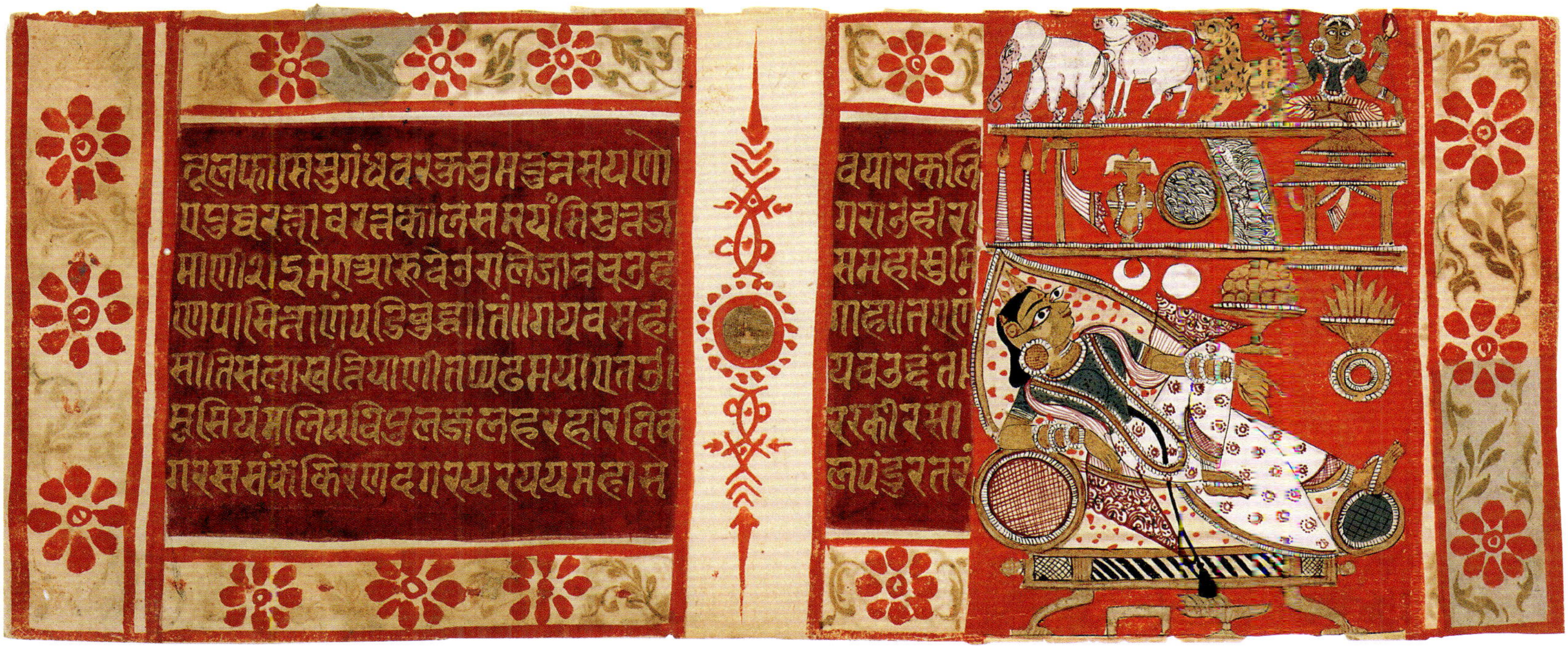

SHIVA

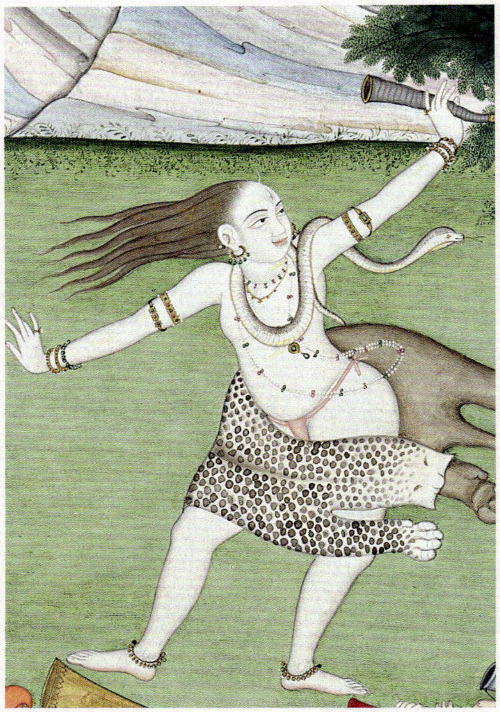

The three principal Hindu deities, whose cults have become the most ramified and widespread in India over the last two millennia, are Shiva, Vishnu, and Devi (the Goddess). Of the three, Shiva ("the Auspicious"), also known as Mahadeva ("the Great God"), is in many ways the most complex and ambivalent figure. He is at the same time the divine yogi, skilled in meditation and austerities, and the lover of his spouse or *shakti*, who embodies the cosmic energy which sustains the world. Shiva thus unites within himself the polar opposites of male and female, asceticism and eroticism, creation and destruction. His origins in the Vedic period (ca. 1500–1000 BC) or perhaps earlier remain obscure, but his early cult absorbed elements of those of the Vedic storm-god Rudra ("the Howler"), as well as of Agni and Indra. Shiva is commonly worshipped in the form of the phallus *(linga)*, a symbol of cosmic energy and generative power which can be traced as early as the Indus Valley civilization (ca. 2500–1700 BC); often, in later times, the linga image was set in a base or pedestal symbolizing the *yoni* (female organ). Shiva's cult animal or divine "vehicle" (*vahana*) is the bull, also an ancient symbol of fertility. Images of the couchant bull Nandi are usually placed in Shiva temples to face the shrine sanctuary with its linga icon.

In his human form, Shiva is generally represented as the Great Yogi, a mountain-dwelling ascetic with ash-smeared body and long matted locks from which the river Ganges at its source cascades to the earth. Shiva has the third eye of yogic insight, bears a crescent moon at his brow, wears animal skins and garlands of snakes, and is sometimes armed with a trident. He has numerous other names and iconic forms, benign or terrible, many of which are represented in sculpture and painting. One of the more famous is that of Nataraja, the Lord of the Dance, the form in which Shiva dances out the periodic destruction of the universe at the end of each cycle of time. The sculptures and paintings shown here mainly reflect Shiva's less awesome aspects, for example as a family man. In the superb Chola bronze group from The Metropolitan Museum (cat. no. 32), he appears with his consort Uma (or Parvati) and their son Skanda (or Karttikeya), and in the stone fragment from Kashmir (cat. no. 33), their other son Ganesha also appears.

The elephant-headed Ganesha in particular remains one of the most universally popular of India's deities, as a god of wisdom and as the remover of obstacles who is invoked by Hindus at the beginning of any enter-prise. The home life of this unconventional holy family is charmingly shown in the painting of Shiva dancing wildly in his mountain abode, to a musical accompaniment provided by his family members and other attendant figures (cat. no. 39). Shiva himself, however, is never a truly domesticated figure, always remaining the wild archetypal outsider. In another of his multiple forms, he is the naked wandering mendicant and lord of the dead, who roams the earth with a skull for his begging-bowl. At the best of times his nature remains volatile, and he is given to fiery discharges of energy which incinerate those who incite his wrath, such as the seductive love-god Kama. Shiva is always in the end the supreme Destroyer, with fire as his weapon.

AT

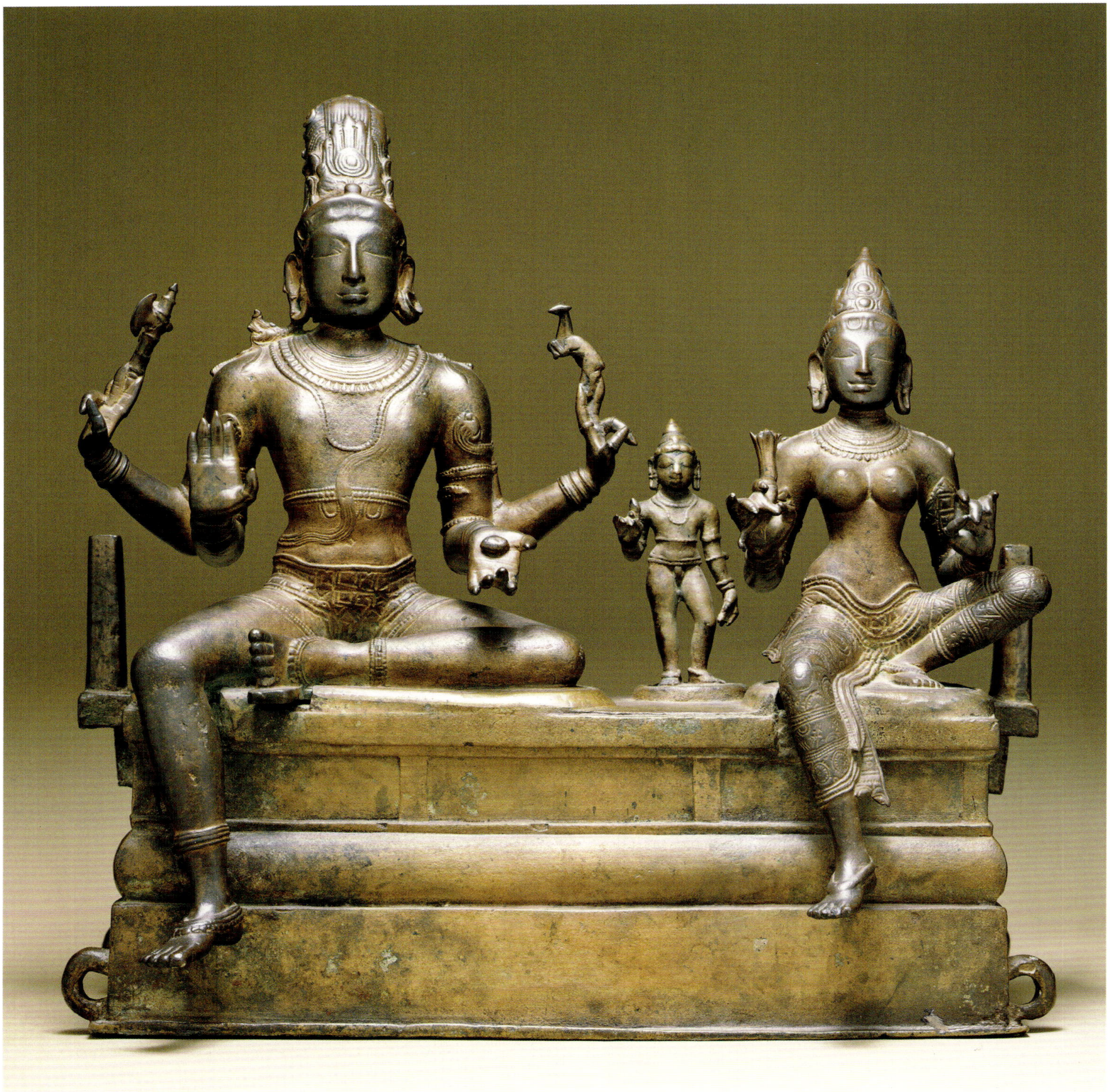

33

Shiva, Uma, and their son Skanda (Somaskandamurti)

TAMIL NADU, CHOLA PERIOD, EARLY ELEVENTH CENTURY

Copper
H. 54.6 cm (21 ½ in.)
Metropolitan Museum of Art, New York, Purchase, Lita Annenberg Hazen Charitable Trust Gift, in honor of Cynthia Hazen and Leon Bernard Polsky (1982.220.10)

SOUTHERN INDIAN SOMASKANDA GROUPS, while having a common iconography, vary considerably in detail. Some of these variations are a function of date, such as costume and jewelry, others represent the sculptor's artistic skill and sophistication. Subtle shifts of Shiva's and Uma's body, variations of expression, and minor compositional adjustments change both the visual appearance of the sculpture and the psychological tension between Shiva and Uma.

The demands made by this iconic type have here been very admirably met. There is no direct interaction among the figures, but they are clearly a family unit, each seemingly aware of the others' proximity. They are beautiful images by themselves, but it is clear that the presence of one reinforces the impact of the others, both compositionally and psychologically. The Somaskandamurti iconography was very popular in Southern India, and quite a few Chola bronze representations have survived. Within that group, this sculpture is a most distinguished example: sensitive, sensual, significant in size, and outstanding in quality.

Seated on an oblong, tiered pedestal, the four-armed Shiva has one leg pendant; the other rests on the top of the pedestal. His consort Uma (Parvati) sits gracefully with her raised leg bent, the foot set on top of the pedestal; her right leg, paralleling Shiva's, is suspended. Between them stands their nude son Skanda, bejeweled and holding a lotus bud in his raised right hand. Shiva and Uma are adorned with the usual jewelries of the period and, in orthodox fashion, Shiva holds the battle-axe and blackbuck in his upper hands and a citron in his lower-left hand; with his raised lower-right hand he makes the fear-allaying gesture. Uma holds a water lily in her right hand. The fingers of her left hand are arranged in exactly the same manner as those of her right hand, but the hand is vertical. Four rings at the lower corners of the pedestal would have allowed the sculpture to be secured in a temple and provided for the insertion of poles for carrying the icon in procession. As is usual, the figures are cast separately and then secured to the pedestal.

ML

34

The holy family of Shiva

NORTH-WEST INDIA, KASHMIR, NINTH CENTURY

Stone
H. 15.9 cm (6 ¼ in.)

IN THIS GREY-GREEN STONE IMAGE OF THE HOLY FAMILY, Shiva and Parvati stand side by side in a graceful triple-flexed posture (*tribhanga*). They appear here almost on equal terms (she is nearly as large as he is). Shiva's bull Nandi and his son Ganesha appear to the left, his other son Karttikeya (Skanda) in the center, and a *gana* attendant to the right. The four-armed figure of Shiva holds a trident (*trishula*) in his upper-right hand, his lower-right hand is raised in a fear-dispelling gesture (*abhayamudra*), and his upper-left arm rests on Parvati's shoulder. He wears jewels and a crown with an aureole behind his head, and a thin garment from which projects his erect phallus. Parvati, shown with two arms, wears large earrings, a thin garment, garlands, and a crown with a crescent moon. Her right hand is also raised in abhayamudra, and her left hand holds a garland.

This sculpture is a later and more hieratic version of a portable shrine in the Metropolitan Museum, New York, showing Shiva and Parvati in a relaxed posture.[1] It can be compared with a Brahmanical Triad in the Metropolitan datable to the eighth–ninth century[2] and a sculpture of Shiva and Parvati attributable to the eleventh century, formerly in the Pan-Asian Collection.[3] The modeling and posture of the figure of Shiva can be also be compared to the standing brass Vishnu in the Los Angeles Museum, datable to ca. AD 850, and a standing stone Vishnu also in the same museum.[4] Our sculpture can be placed into the second half of the ninth century, when the Karkota dynasty's rule was replaced by the Utpala dynasty under Avantivarman (r. 855–83).[5]

MCS

1 Lerner and Kossak, 1991, p. 112, no. 81.

2 *A decade of collecting 1984-1993: Friends of Asian Art Gifts*, Metropolitan Museum, 1993, p. 49.

3 Pal, 1977, no. 28, pp. 54–55; Kramrisch, 1981, no. 47, p. 56.

4 Pal, 1988, pp. 70–72, no. 14a–b.

5 R. E. Fisher, "Later stone sculpture (ninth-twelfth centuries)," in P. Pal ed., *Art and architecture of ancient Kashmir*, Bombay: *Marg*, 1989.

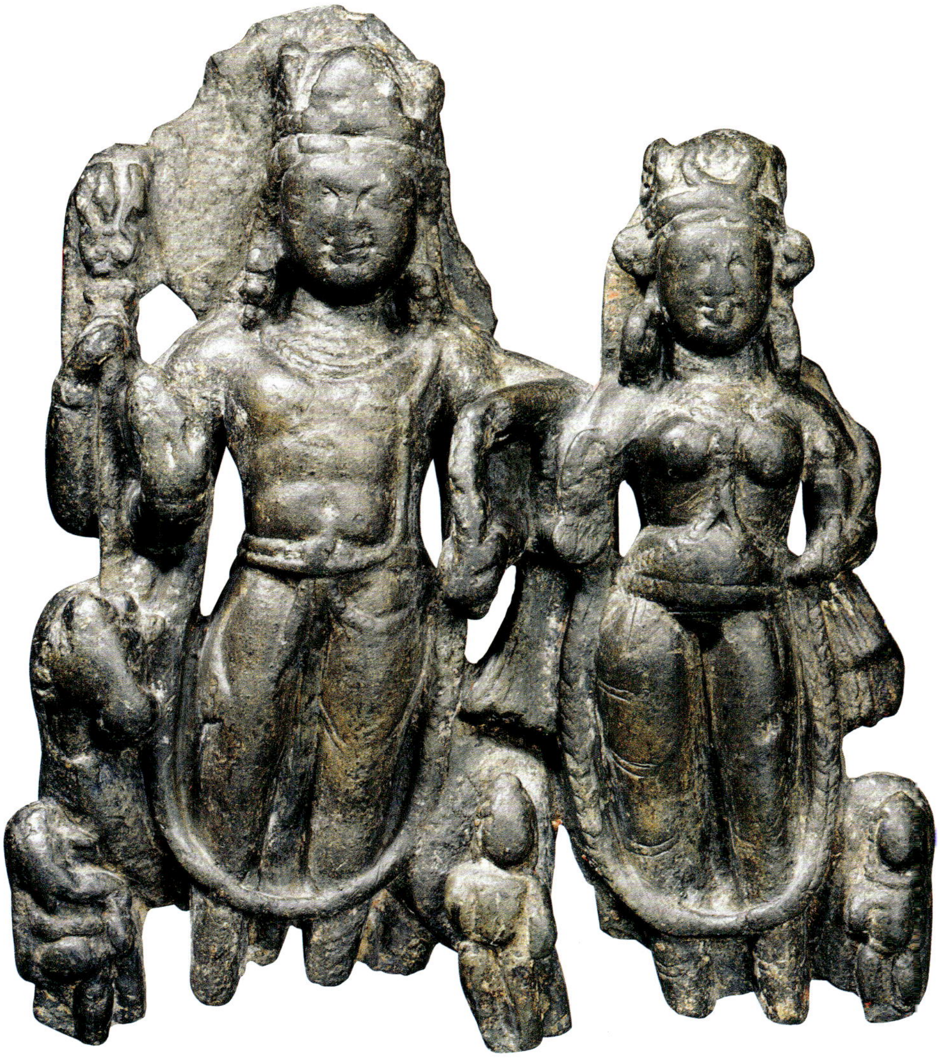

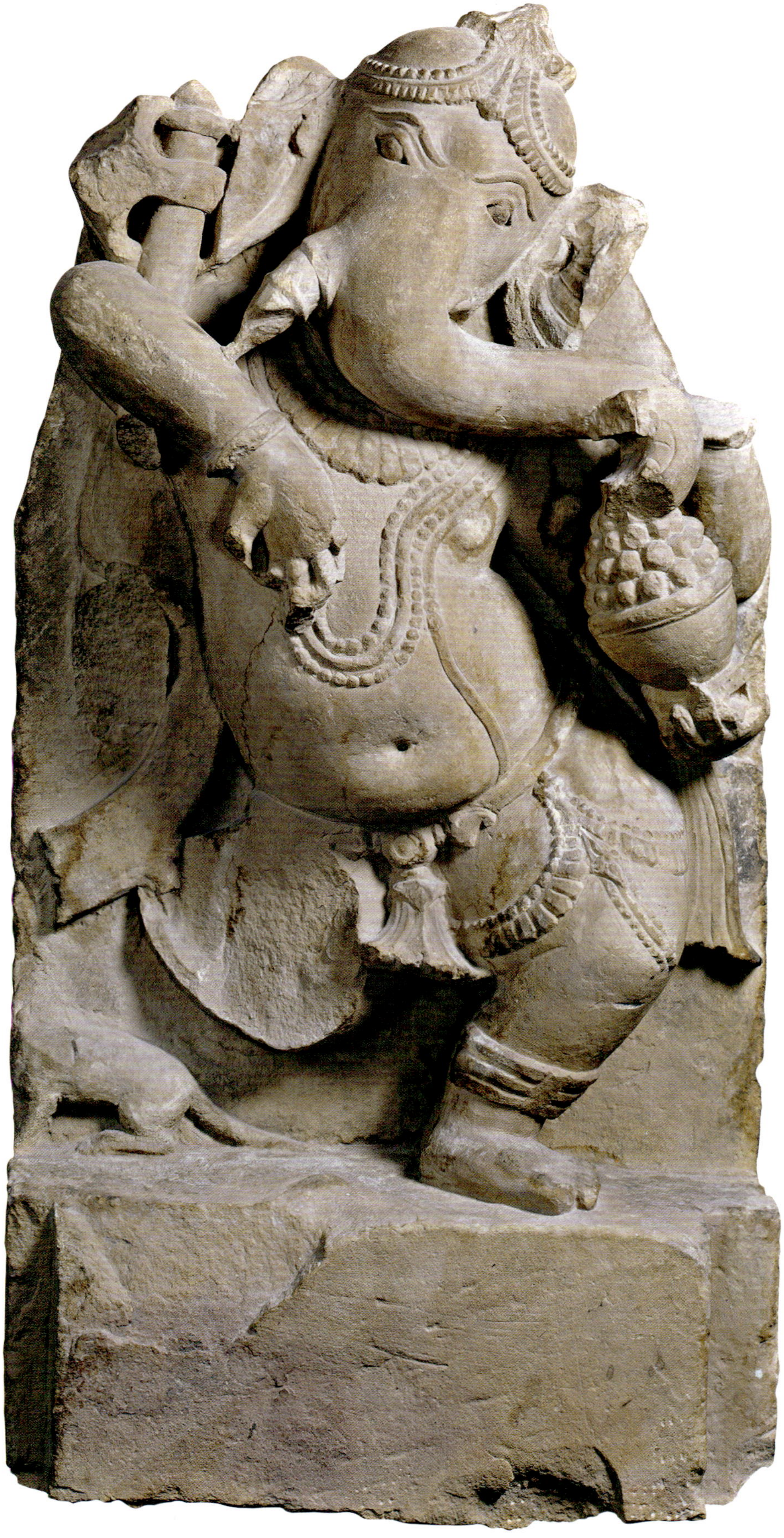

35

Dancing Ganesha

MADHYA PRADESH, CA. AD 1000

Buff-colored sandstone
H. 86.8 cm (30 ¼ in.)

CARVED IN HIGH RELIEF IN A BUFF SANDSTONE, Ganesha, the elephant-headed son of Shiva, is shown in dancing pose. Wearing jewelry and a short garment, he holds a bowl of sweetmeats in his lower-left hand to which he is helping himself with his trunk, and his axe under his upper-right arm, which is turned in toward the body with the hand pointing downward in gesture of knowledge (*chinmudra*). His vehicle (*vahana*), the rat, appears on the left of the stele. Originally sculpted with four arms (two are now missing), he also usually holds a broken tusk or radish in one of his right hands, while his upper-left hand would have held a book, conch, or lotus bud. He has a fat belly and short fat legs.

Ganesha is one of the most popular of the Hindu deities. He is one of the sons of Shiva (the other being Karttikeya, known also as Skanda or Kumara), though accounts vary as to his exact parentage and the source of his elephant head.[1] He is the god of auspicious beginnings, and his axe—sometimes shown as an ankus or elephant goad—is used to remove obstacles, for he is invoked at the beginning of every undertaking to remove any difficulties.

Ganesh is depicted in sculpture in a number of poses: seated, dancing, and standing. By the eighth century the dancing posture (*nritya-ganapati*) could be found in temples in north-central India, Uttar Pradesh, and Madhya Pradesh.[2] This sculpture is almost certainly from a Shaivite temple and would have been placed in a niche on the southern wall.[3] Examples of Ganesha sculptures are in many museums and private collections, including the Norton Simon Museum, Pasadena,[4] and the Alsdorf Collection.[5] Here Ganesha is shown dancing alone, while on other examples he may be shown with attendants or musicians.

MCS

1 Kramrisch, 1981, p. 74.

2 Pal, 2003, no. 81, pp. 122–23.

3 Desai and Mason eds., 1993, p. 129, and no. 16, p. 166 (Asia Society no. 1979.13).

4 Pal, *loc. cit.*

5 Pal, 1997, nos. 70–72, pp. 60–62, 287–88.

36

Head of Shiva

RAJASTHAN, ELEVENTH CENTURY

Sandstone
H. 18 cm (7 in.)

CARVED IN A PINKISH BUFF-COLORED SANDSTONE, this head of Shiva (or a Shaivite guardian figure) would once have adorned a temple. His bearded face has the third eye of divine insight carved just below the hairline. His yogi's matted hair (*jatamukuta*) is shown in tight coils, rising from the swept-back hair on his forehead, which is held by a plain band running across the head. The expression is peaceful, and this head may have belonged to an Uma-Maheshvara group, in which Shiva embraces his wife Parvati. It could also have been from a single figure of Shiva, perhaps on an overdoor panel,[1] or from a guardian figure which would have stood at the door of the temple.[2] A head with similarly swept-back and tightly coiled hair, but depicting Shiva as the ferocious Bhairava, is in the Ford Collection.[3]

First known in early Vedic myth as Rudra, the "Wild God," Shiva has many manifestations, as creator, protector, and above all destroyer. He is the Lord of the Cosmos, Destroyer of Demons, and Lord of the Dance. Much of his power derives from his mastery of austerities, and he is often depicted as an ascetic with matted hair.[4] His third eye, which appeared when Parvati playfully covered his eyes and plunged the world into darkness, can be used to destroy his enemies.

MCS

1 Desai and Mason eds., New York, 1993, no. 58, p. 236.

2 Pal, 1988, no. 45a–b, pp. 116–18.

3 Kramrisch, 1981, no. 27, p. 31.

4 *Ibid.*, pp. xiv–xxiv.

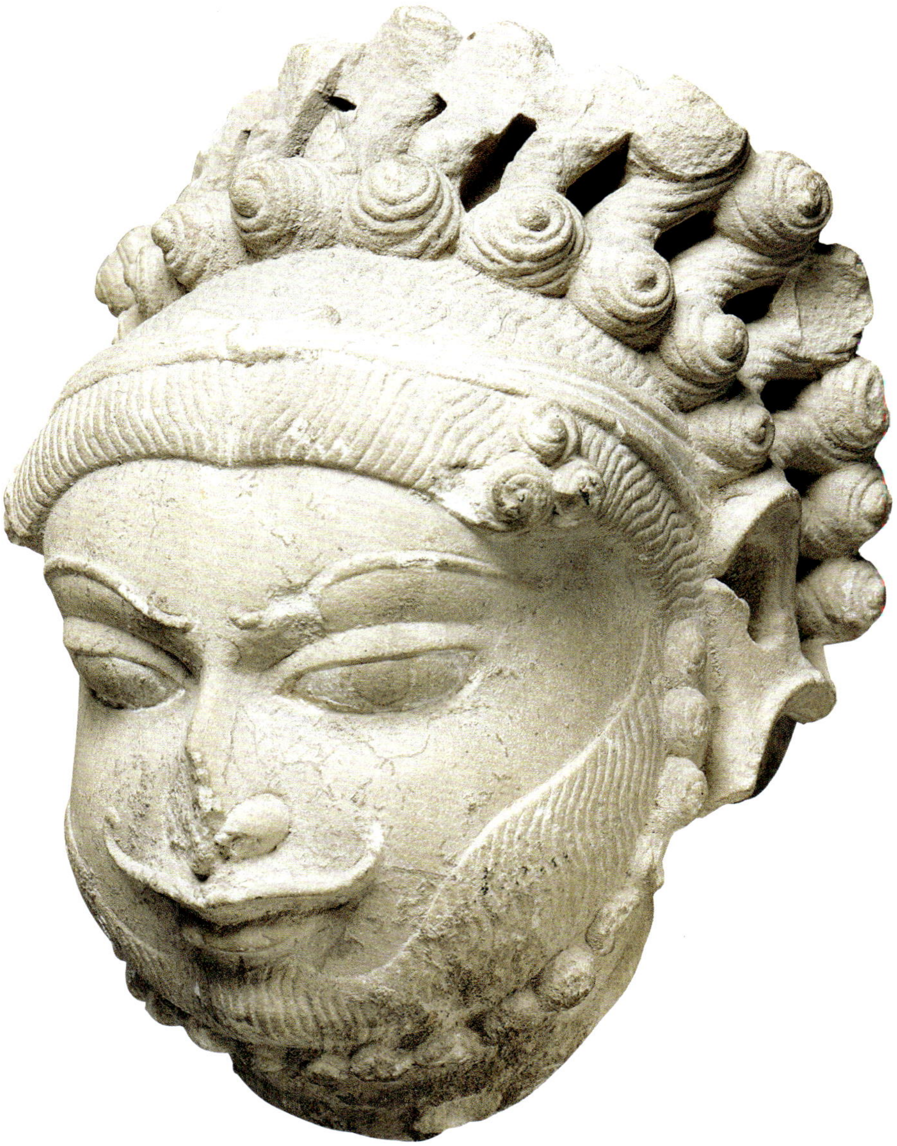

37

Devotees worshipping Agni

SOUTH-EASTERN RAJASTHAN (AT RAGHUGARH?), CA. 1780

Opaque watercolor with gold on paper
39.4 × 20.3 cm (5 ½ × 8 in.)

AGNI OR FIRE (THE WORD IS RELATED TO LATIN *IGNIS*) is one of the most ancient Indian deities, celebrated in the hymns of the *Rig Veda*, the earliest and most revered of the four Vedas (ca. 1500–1200 BC). As deity of the sacrificial fire, Agni plays the role of mediator between the worlds of men and gods. As the natural element of fire itself, Agni embodies the vital spark of life in men, beasts, fish, plants, and trees. He is still invoked today by Hindus whenever a sacred flame is lit. He is also one of the protector deities of the eight directions, being guardian of the south-east. In Vedic times, his more aggressive counterpart was Rudra, a forerunner of Shiva, but elements of both deities were to contribute to the later, dominant cult of Shiva.

While Agni appears, in anthropomorphic form, in later Indian sculpture, he is less often seen in painting. In this late eighteenth-century Rajasthani picture, he appears as the sacred flame itself. His shrine is set symbolically in a lake with lotuses, reflecting an ancient polarity between the elements of fire and water in Hindu mythology. While priests or devotees venerate the flame, auspicious white blossoms shower down on it, as offering and blessing, from the flowering creepers which entwine the row of trees above.

AT

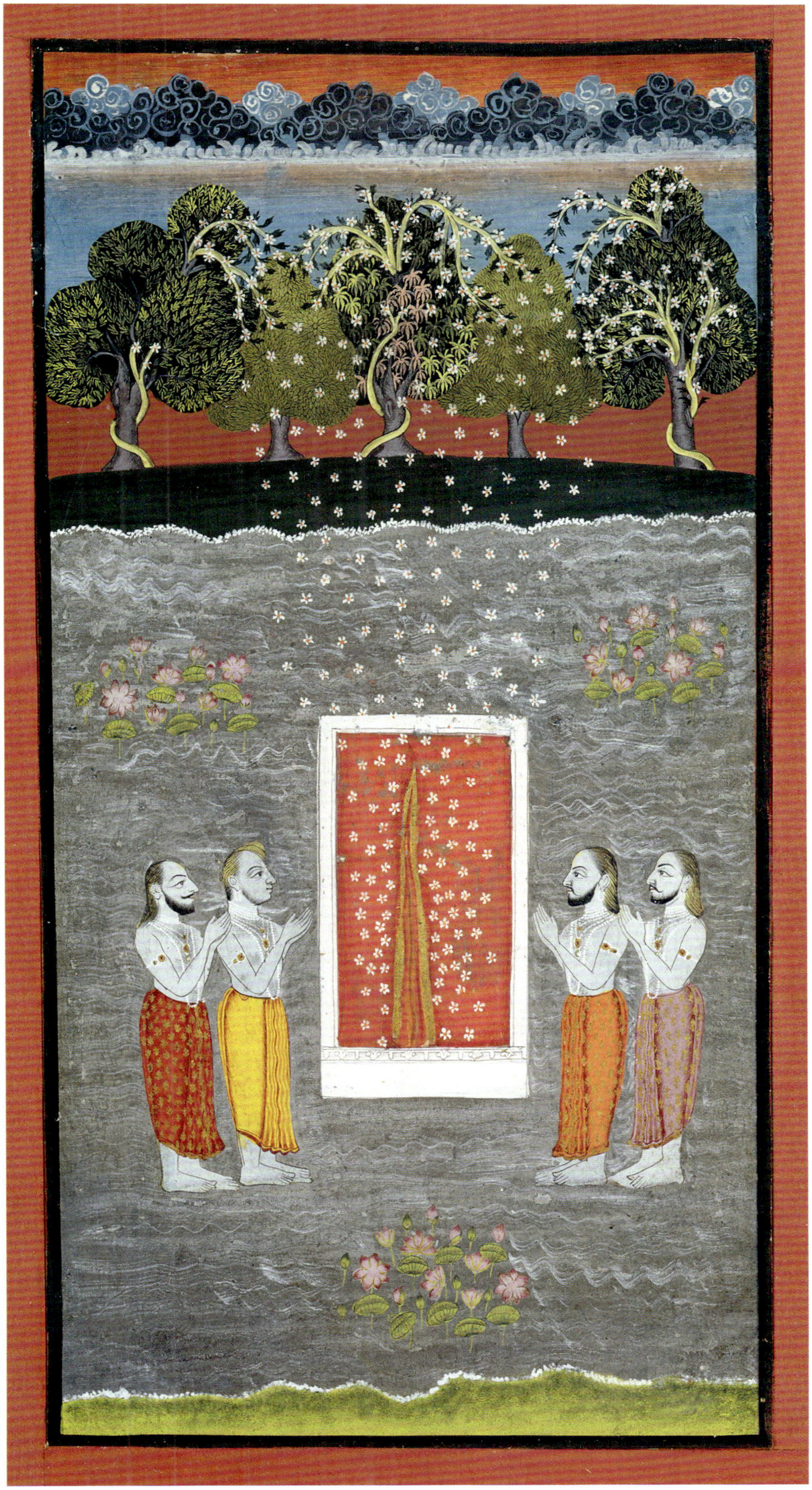

38

The heavenly durbar of Shiva

MANDI, PUNJAB HILLS, CA. 1810;
STYLE OF SAJNU

Opaque watercolor on paper
23.5 x 26.7 cm (9 ¼ x 10 ½ in.)
Published: T. McInerney, *Indian paintings from the Polsky Collections*, Princeton, 1982, no. 24

SHIVA PRESIDES OVER A HEAVENLY DURBAR OR AUDIENCE, at which his fellow-gods and holy sages (*rishis*) pay homage to him. Standing on a lotus throne in the central pavilion, Shiva holds a bow and arrow and Parvati holds a flower, while chowry (fan)-bearers and maids stand behind. Vishnu, holding a conch, and the four-headed Brahma lead the ranks of deities and rishis who stand respectfully in attendance. Rishis and women bow or prostrate themselves, while a troupe of animal or bird-headed celestial musicians provides a resounding accompaniment, with the long cylindrical drum (*pakhavaj*) and kettle-drums (*naqqara*) to the fore.

As a mountain-dwelling ascetic, Shiva usually appears far removed from worldly or courtly life in paintings. But here, in a regal guise and dwelling in an opulent celestial palace deriving from earlier Mughal pictorial models, the god appears in a form with which the Pahari royal patron could identify. The painting is in the style of Sajnu, an influential Hill artist, active ca. 1790–1830, who practiced his own angular and elaborately detailed version of the late eighteenth-century Guler-Kangra tradition.

A closely related painting in his style, showing a similar celestial durbar of Vishnu's avatar Parasurama, is in the Ackland Art Museum, Chapel Hill.[1]

AT

1 Acc. no. 82.5.2: *Ackland Art Museum, Intimate views: Indian miniature paintings from the 16th to the 19th century*, Chapel Hill, 1995, fig. 4.

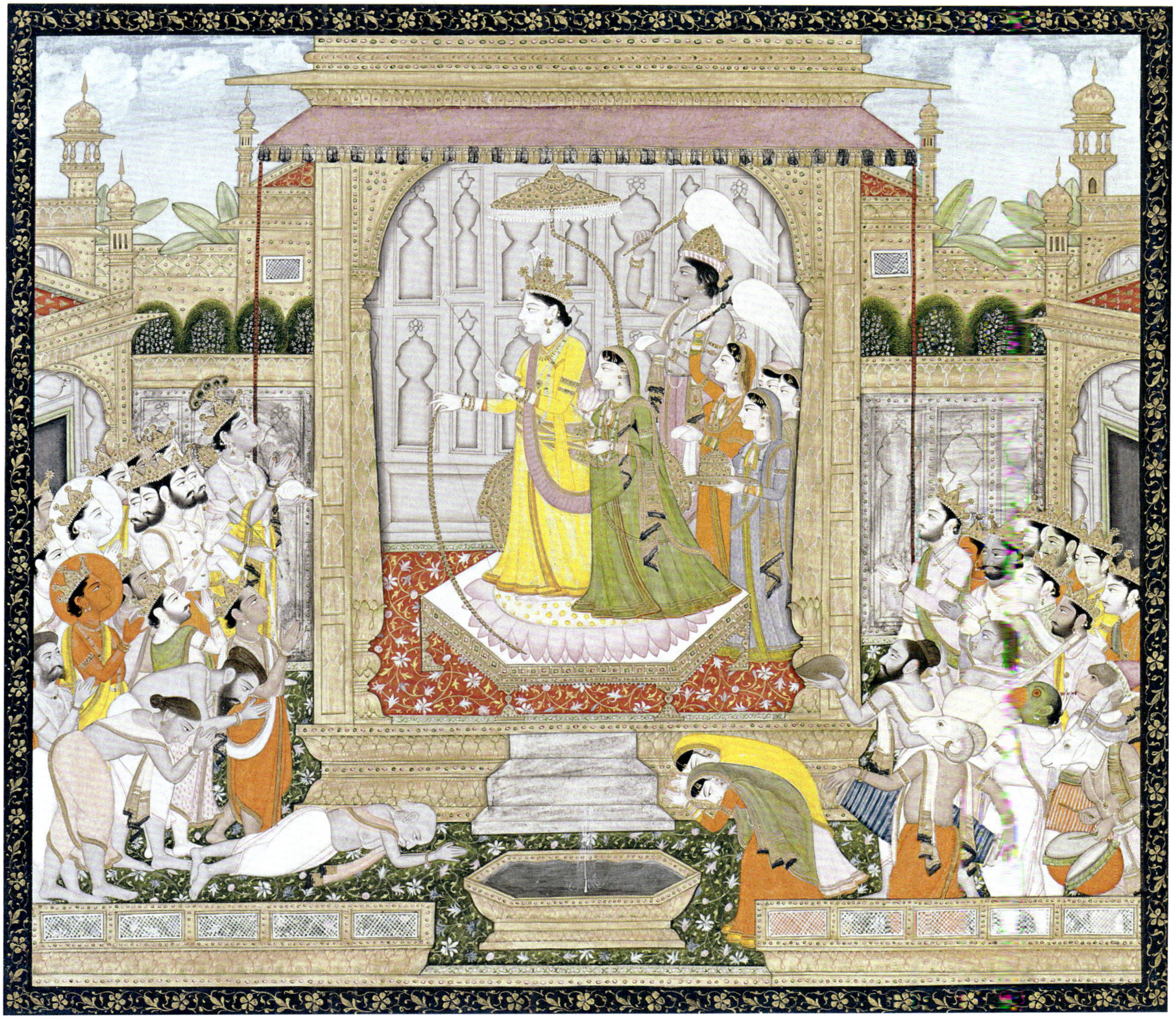

39

Shiva dancing in the mountains

KANGRA, PUNJAB HILLS, CA. 1790–1800

Opaque watercolor on paper
20.3 x 26.7 cm (8 x 10 ½ in.)
Published: S. Kramrisch, *Manifestations of Shiva*, Philadelphia, 1981, no. P-24, p. 186

THE DANCE OF SHIVA PLAYS A MAJOR PART IN HIS MYTHOLOGY. In its most fearsome form, perfected above all in South Indian bronze sculpture, Shiva appears as the awesome Nataraja (Lord of the Dance), symbolically dancing out the destruction of the Universe at the end of each cycle of four world ages (*yuga*). Here, more intimately observed with his family and close attendants in a pleasant Himalayan valley, Shiva dances his ecstatic dance with arms flung wide, one hand holding a horn. He wears a cobra around his neck and leopard and elephant skins, which whirl around him. To the left, Parvati demurely plucks an Indian stringed instrument (*vina*), while their sons Karttikeya and Ganesha dextrously play a variety of instruments with their multiple arms. Animal-headed *gana* attendants of Shiva play horns and percussion, and his thousand-armed devotee Banasura artfully thumps a whole battery of *pakhavaj* drums. The stirring sound of this divine ensemble can only be conjectured.

This charmingly observed composition of Shiva's family accompanying his dance is known in other versions in the National Museum, New Delhi, and the Allahabad Museum;[1] related drawings are in the Bharat Kala Bhavan, Varanasi,[2] and the Paul Walter Collection.[3]

AT

1 Sivaramamurti, 1974, repr. 1994, figs. 238–39.

2 *Ibid.* (1994 ed.), p. 147, fig. 4; Krishna ed., 1971, fig. 480.

3 Pal and Glynn, 1976, no. 54.

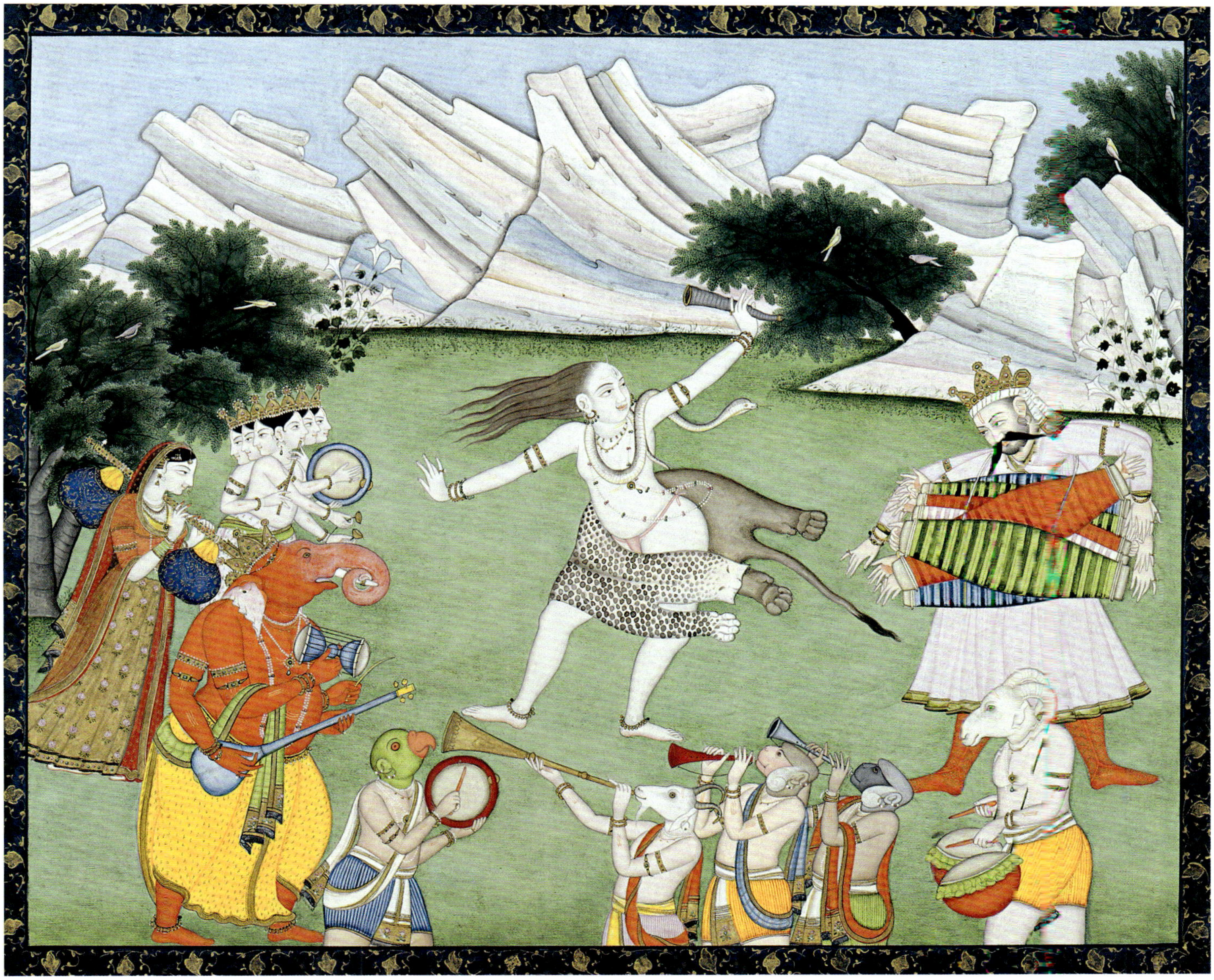

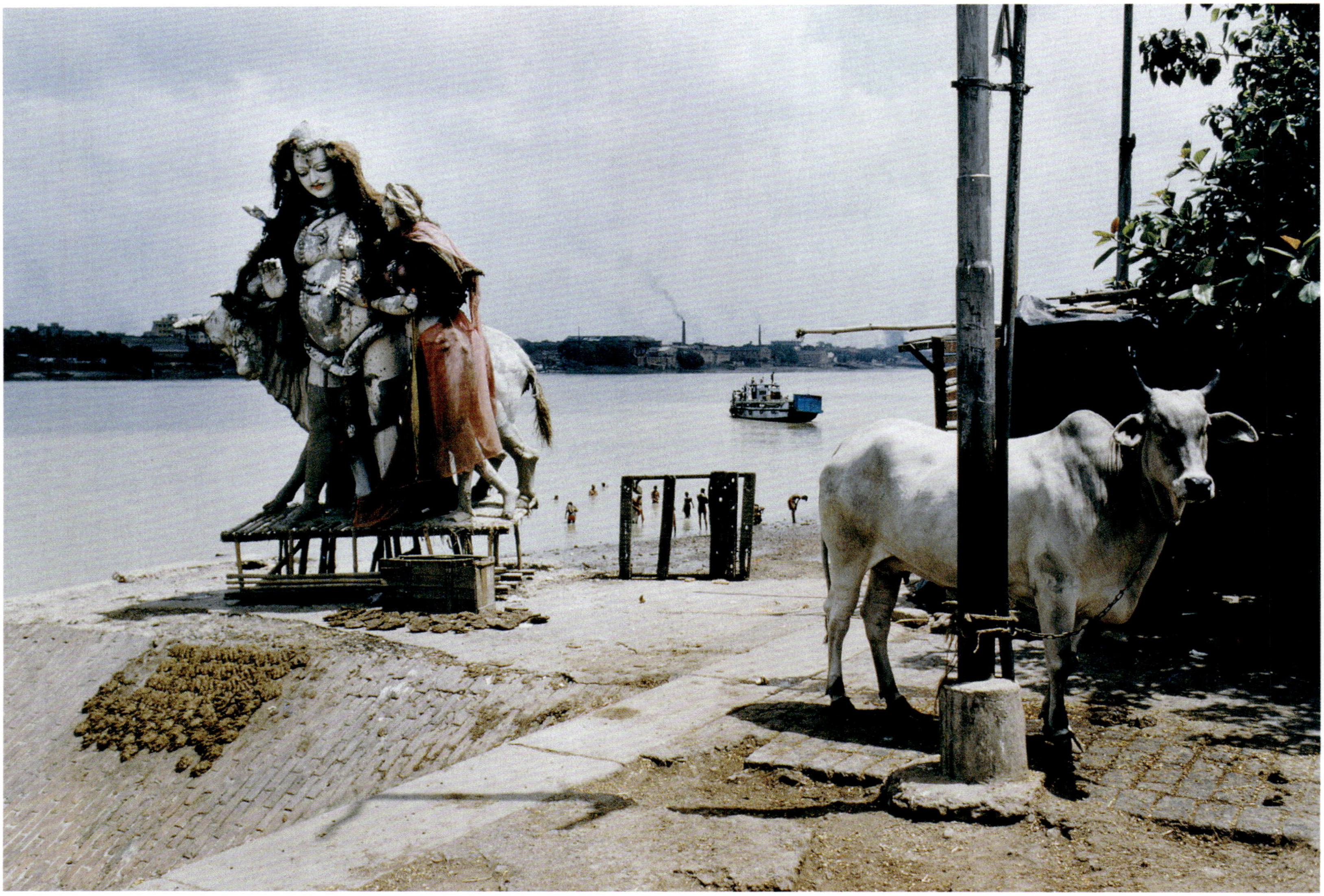

40

Shiva image and cow beside the Ganges at Calcutta

RAGHUBIR SINGH (1942–99)

Calcutta, West Bengal, 1988
Chromogenic color print
25.4 × 37.4 cm (10 × 14 ¾ in.)
Published: Raghubir Singh, *River of colour: The India of Raghubir Singh*, London, 1998, p. 92
Metropolitan Museum of Art, New York, Purchase, Cynthia Hazen Polsky Gift (1991.1284)

MANY OF RAGHUBIR SINGH'S IMAGES illustrate the pervasive presence of religious life as it intersects with the mundane. Here, an elaborate representation of Shiva leaning against his garlanded bull Nandi stands on the bank of the Hugli (an arm of the Ganges) at Calcutta, while cow-dung cakes dry in the foreground and bathers wade into the river beyond. Mirrored in the other half of the frame, the live counterpart to Shiva's companion stands tethered to a post. The naturalness of such a scene is fully in keeping with Singh's vision of an India in which the whole chain of creation—both human and non-human—is absorbed into daily life. Such photographs form an integral part of Singh's dedication to recording and allying himself with the inclusive spirituality of India, rather than with a Western world-view that considers the human world to stand outside and above the rest of nature.

JF

VISHNU

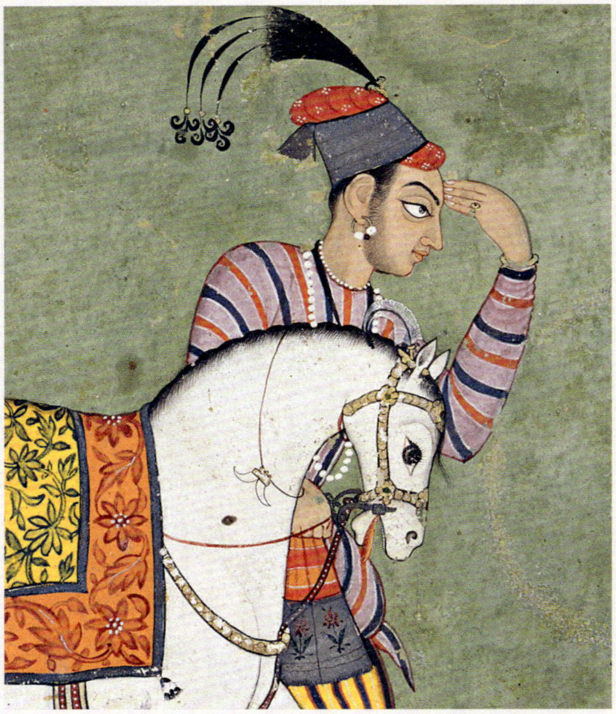

Although the conventional triad of principal Hindu deities is conceived as Brahma the Creator, Vishnu the Preserver, and Shiva the Destroyer, the worship of Brahma has never become widespread in India. Of the two other major gods, the cult of Vishnu ("the Pervader") in his various forms and incarnations has probably enjoyed the greater popularity in recent centuries. In contrast to the wild, solitary, ascetic, and unpredictable nature of Shiva, Vishnu stands for the more solid, reassuring. and communal virtues of maintaining the cosmic order and saving the world from evil. In iconography, Vishnu is represented as a youthful, four-armed, kingly figure, wearing a tall crown and holding in his hands the attributes of a conch shell, lotus, discus, and club. His mount (*vahana*) is the bird or man-bird Garuda ("Devourer"), on whom he rides into battle. Vishnu's consort is Lakshmi, the beneficent goddess of wealth and prosperity, who is also commonly invoked and worshipped in India in her own right.

As a Preserver and Saviour figure, Vishnu returns to the earth periodically in a succession of incarnations or avatars, to vanquish disruptive evil forces, save his devotees from peril, and restore universal order. Vishnu's avatars probably incorporate some of the regional deities or hero-gods whose cults had become assimilated into his cult over the ages (including even the Buddha, not a god but a historic religious teacher who lived around 500 BC). According to one widely accepted system, Vishnu's ten avatars (*dashavatara*) are: 1) Matsya the fish;

2) Kurma the tortoise; 3) Varaha the boar; 4) Narasimha the man-lion; 5) Vamana the dwarf; 6) Parashurama ("Rama with the battle-axe"); 7) Rama (hero of the *Ramayana* epic); 8) Krishna; 9) Buddha; and 10) Kalki, the white horse or horseman who will come to destroy the Universe at the end of time. Among these avatars, the cults of Rama and above all Krishna, fuelled by the powerful *bhakti* devotional movement, have attained an immense popularity during the last millennium. Their respective myths and deeds have been celebrated constantly in literature and in works of art, as will be seen in the two following sections of this book.

For many Krishna *bhaktas*, Krishna himself has indeed come to be regarded as the supreme deity. But it is as Vishnu incarnate that Krishna declares his nature and mission to Arjuna on the battlefield, in the *Bhagavad Gita* (IV.5–8):[1]

Many a birth have I passed through, and many a birth have you: I know them all but you do not.

Unborn am I, changeless is my Self, of all contingent beings I am the Lord! Yet by my creative energy I consort with Nature—which is mine—and come to be in time.

For whenever the law of righteousness withers away and lawlessness arises, then do I generate Myself on earth.

For the protection of the good, for the destruction of evil-doers, for the setting up of the law of righteousness I come into being age after age.

AT

1 Zaehner tr., 1969, pp. 182–84.

41

Narasimha kills Hiranyakashipu

VIJAYANAGARA, SIXTEENTH TO SEVENTEENTH CENTURY

Ivory
H. 16.8 cm (6 ⅝ in.)

NARASIMHA (THE MAN-LION) was the fourth incarnation of Vishnu. To defeat the demon King Hiranyakashipu, Vishnu assumed the form of the lion-headed Narasimha, because Hiranyakashipu could not be killed by either man or animal, inside or outside a house, by night or day, on earth or in water, or by any weapon. Narasimha (neither man nor beast) killed him on a verandah (neither inside nor outside) at twilight (neither day nor night), by holding him on his knees (neither land nor water) and disemboweling him with his claws.

This ivory panel is carved in relief with a four-tiered temple and three images of Narasimha killing Hiranyakashipu down the left side, increasing in size from the lowest to the highest image. The details of the temple are intricately carved, with a cusped arch rising to the second level and small figures riding birds around the edge. At the top of the arch is a standing figure (probably Vishnu) in a niche, above this a further figure in a niche, and at the top a central lion mask, flanked by two further masks to the left representing other corners of the temple. Further niches appear on each of the temple tiers. The architecture can be compared to buildings at Vijayanagara of the sixteenth and seventeenth centuries. The cusped arch owes its origin to Deccani architecture and was unknown in Southern India before the Vijayanagara period,[1] while the curved roof relates to the architectural developments of the early sixteenth century such as the mandapa extension at the Virupaksha Temple, Hampi, carried out under Krishnaraya (r. 1510–29) in 1510.[2] It is interesting to note that his two predecessors as emperor (*raya*) were named Narasimha. The panel may have been attached to a box with corresponding sections for the rest of the architecture, for use in a temple or at worship, or it could have formed part of a door lintel.[3]

MCS

1 Michell, 1995, fig. 88, p. 131.

2 *Ibid.*, fig. 14, p. 41.

3 D. Thiagarajan, "Doors and woodcrafts of Chettinad," in G. Michell ed., *Living wood: Sculptural traditions of Southern India*, Bombay: *Marg*, 1992, fig. 12, p. 68.

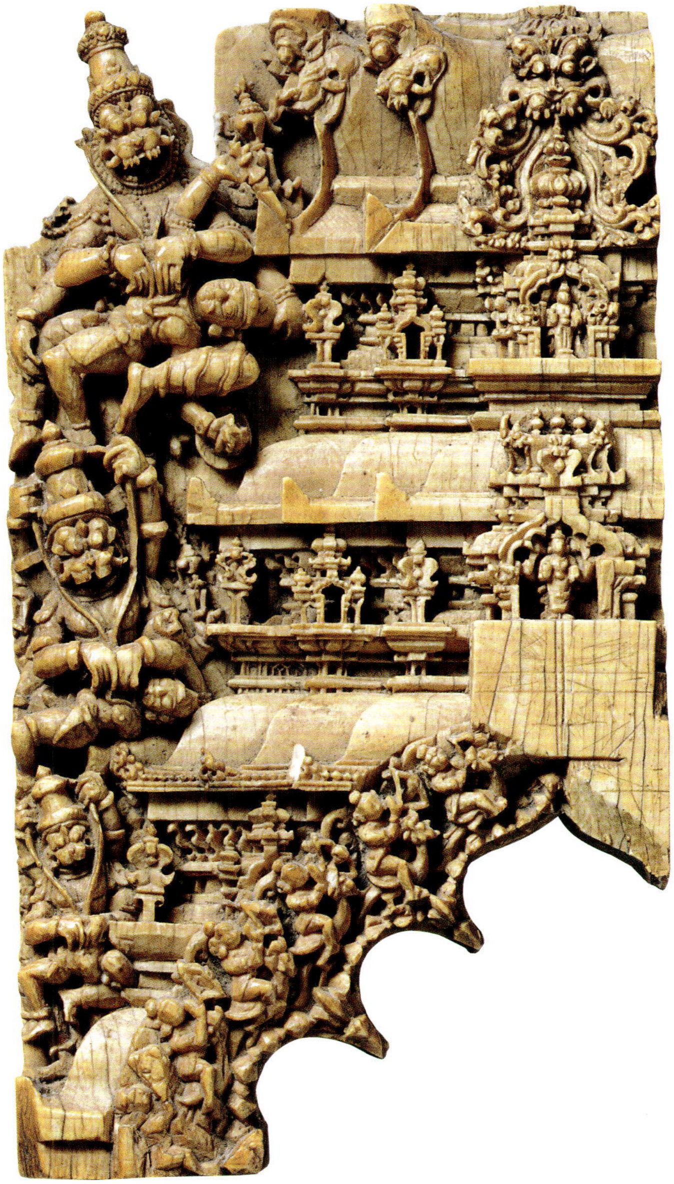

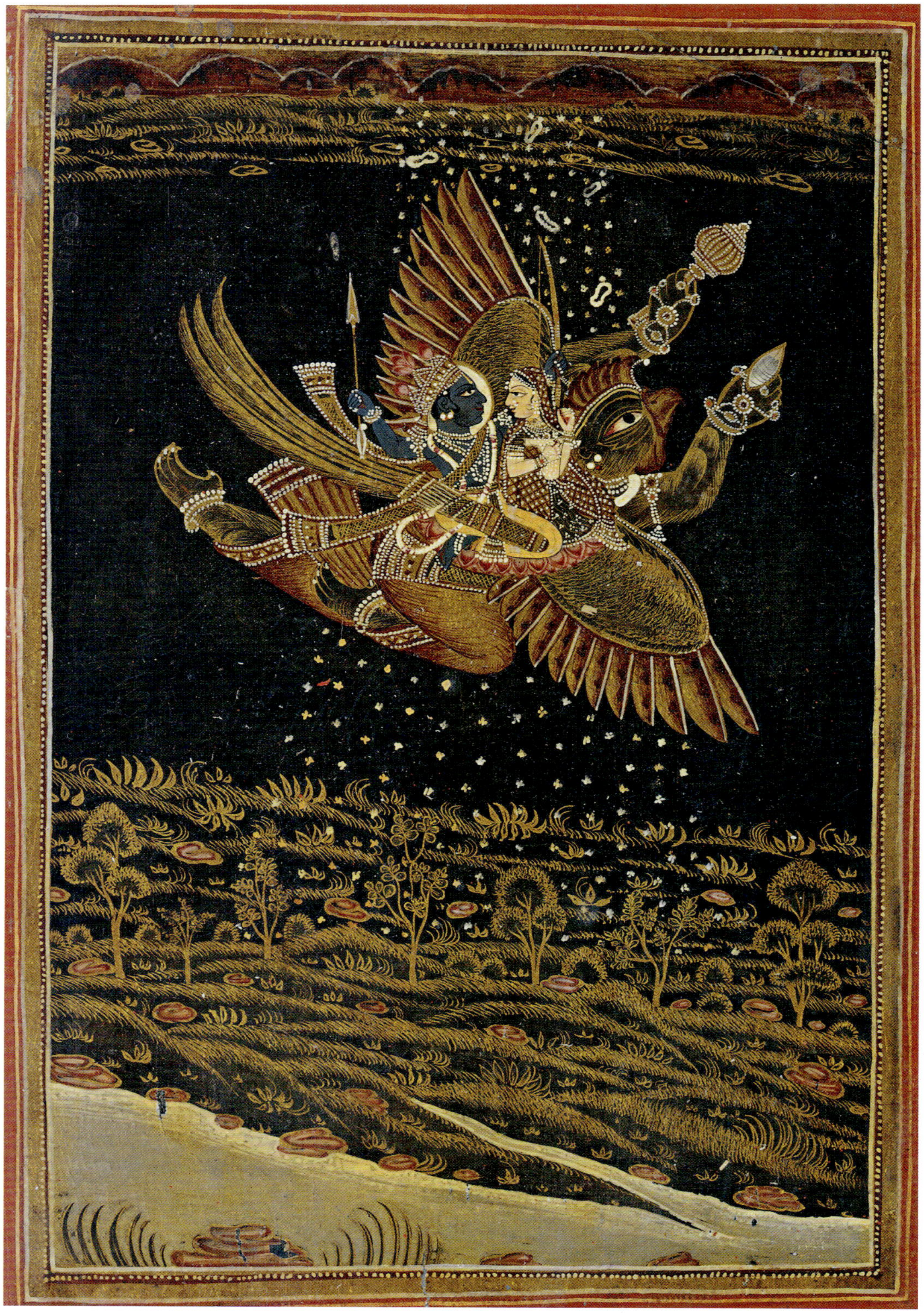

42

Vishnu and Lakshmi flying on Garuda

BUNDI-KOTAH REGION, RAJASTHAN, LATE EIGHTEENTH CENTURY

Opaque watercolor with gold on paper
22.9 x 15.6.cm (9 x 6 ⅛ in.)

GARUDA, KING OF BIRDS, DESTROYER OF SERPENTS and remover of obstacles, is the vahana associated with Vishnu. Half-bird and half-man, he carries the god into battle or wherever wrongs are to be righted, as when Vishnu liberates the elephant King Gajendra from a crocodile's grasp (cat. no. 43). Here he bears Vishnu, with his consort Lakshmi, in stately flight. Garuda carries Vishnu's mace and conch-shell, while the god (who here has two arms, not four) holds a bow and arrow.[1] The divine couple gaze at one another with serene devotion. As blossoms and garlands shower from the sky, they fly over a landscape which has been very heavily embellished with gold.

The subject of Garuda bearing Vishnu and Lakshmi became a popular one in Rajput painting from at least the sixteenth century, particularly at the courts of the Bundi-Kotah region in south-east Rajasthan, where it is found in palace wall-paintings of the seventeenth century[2] and later, as well as in works on paper.[3] From the eighteenth century Garuda (on his own) became the state emblem of the Kotah rulers and thus appeared on their royal standards.[4]

AT

1 The arrow has a pointed not sickle-shaped tip, as in most examples of the subject, e.g. Sotheby's, *Fine oriental miniatures* sale cat., 10 October 1977, lot 60.

2 E.g. J. Bautze, "Eine Garudastandarte aus Kota im Linden-Museum," *Tribus*, no. 35, Stuttgart, 1986, figs. 3–4.

3 E.g. Archer, 1958, fig. 21; Archer and Binney, 1968, no. 15; also, Welch et al., 1997, no. 42.

4 Bautze, *op. cit.*, figs. 1, 7–8; Brijraj Singh, 1985, p. 14, fig. 23; Pal and Glynn, 1976, no. 21.

43

The Liberation of Gajendra

BIKANER, RAJASTHAN, CA. 1630–40

Opaque watercolor with gold and silver on paper
Image 23.5 × 18.7 cm (9 ¼ × 7 ⅛ in.); page 32.7 × 25.4 cm (12 ⅞ × 10 in.)
Inscribed with a Sanskrit verse above; on the reverse: four lines of Hindi verse; also crudely inscribed: *3 / narayin* [Narayan?] */gajagraha...*
Published: P. Pal et al., *Pleasure gardens of the mind: Indian paintings from the Jane Greenough Green Collection*, Los Angeles, 1993, no. 2

WHILE BATHING WITH HIS HERD in a pleasant lotus lake, Gajendra, lord of the elephants, was suddenly seized by the leg by a lurking *makara*, a crocodile-like aquatic beast. Despite his struggles he could not free himself and stood trapped in its grip for a thousand years. But when finally he prayed to Vishnu, the god swiftly appeared on his vahana, the man-bird Garuda and, in his *karivarada* form ("bestowing a grace on the elephant"), slew the water-monster with his *chakra* (wheel or discus). The Liberation of Gajendra (*Gajendramoksha*) became a popular theme of Vaishnava devotional literature, the elephant's plight symbolizing the inexorable entrapment of the human soul by worldly illusion, from which the invocation of Vishnu brings release.

The artist has interpreted this edifying story in a lively composition, to some extent based on earlier Mughal studies of wild elephants bathing. Surrounded by his family or herd members who wade in the lake, Gajendra looks up joyfully at Vishnu and offers him lotus flowers with his trunk. Vishnu, here shown with two arms, is poised to throw his chakra, while Garuda flies alongside in an attitude of respect. This page seems to have belonged to a series of illustrations of the exploits and avatars (incarnations) of Vishnu,[1] illustrated for a Maharaja of Bikaner, a kingdom in the deserts of north-west Rajasthan where strong Mughal and Deccani pictorial influences prevailed in the seventeenth century.

AT

1 Pal, *Pleasure gardens, loc. cit.;* also T. McInerney, 1982, nos. 21–22.

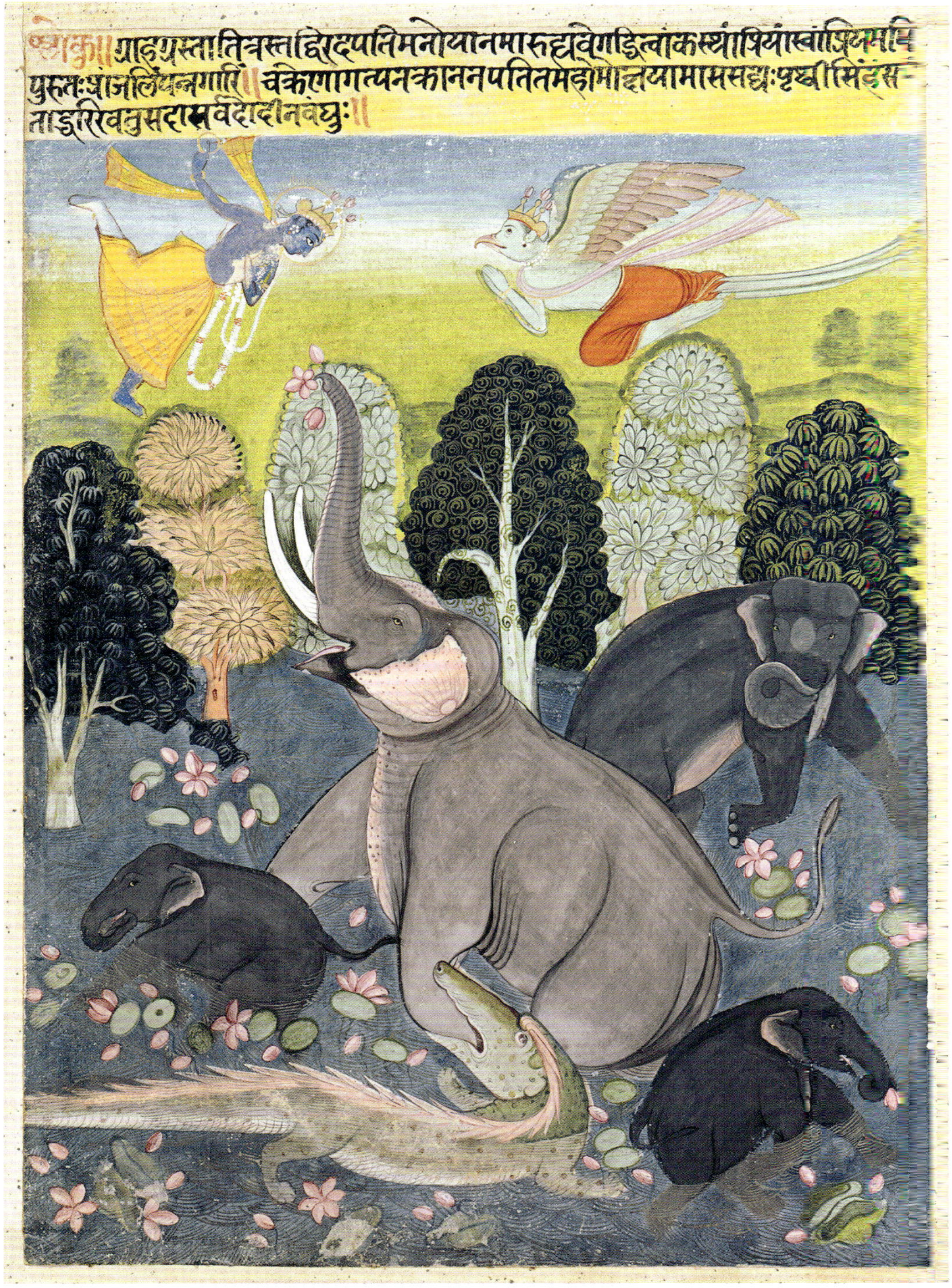

44

The demon Hiranyaksha departs

ILLUSTRATION TO A SERIES OF THE BHAGAVATA PURANA (BOOK 3)

Guler, Punjab Hills, ca. 1735–40
Attributed to Manaku
Opaque watercolor and gold on paper
Image 18.1 × 28.9 cm, (7 1/8 × 11 3/8 in.); page 21.9 × 32.7 cm (8 5/8 × 12 7/8 in.)
Inscribed on the reverse with Sanskrit text and Mandi State stamp and inventory number
Metropolitan Museum of Art, New York, Cynthia Hazen Polsky and Leon B. Polsky Fund (2002.179)

IN VISHNU'S THIRD INCARNATION AS VARAHA, the boar, he rescues the world when it is seized by the demon Hiranyaksha ("Golden-eyed") and dragged down to his abode below the waters. Hiranyaksha has been granted the boon of invulnerability to every creature except (though an oversight) the boar. In this form, therefore, Vishnu descends into the depths, slays the demon, and saves the earth. Here, Hiranyaksha, green-skinned and holding a mace, departs from the palace, presumably to confront Varaha, after taking leave from his elder brother the demon-king Hiranyakashipu ("Golden-robed"). The latter, pink-skinned and seated on his royal throne, would himself later be slain by Vishnu's fourth avatar Narasimha (cat. no. 41). When the balance of the cosmos is periodically disturbed by evil influences and destructive energies, the forces of good will eventually prevail and restore order: thus all such arrogant demons (symbolizing spiritual ignorance) will ultimately be overcome by almighty Vishnu. Despite their horns, fangs, tails, clawed feet, and staring eyes, these demon brothers in their neat drawers have a certain humanity as well as a comic grotesqueness and even pathos. Similar demonic types are found elsewhere in the family workshop production of Manaku of Guler (ca. 1700–60),[1] to whom the extensive dispersed *Bhagavata Purana* series to which this page belongs can largely be attributed.[2]

AT

1 For a recent study of Manaku, see Goswamy and Fischer, 1992, pp. 239–65.

2 For a preceding page in the narrative sequence, see Sotheby's New York cats., 25 March 1987, lot 182; 3 March 2002, lot 41. For scenes of the subsequent battle leading to the death of Hiranyaksha, see Archer, 1973, s.v. Basohli, no. 23 (i); Aijazuddin, 1977; s.v. Basohli, nos. 7 (iv–ix); Goswamy, 1986, no. 112; Goswamy and Fischer, *op. cit.* no. 106.

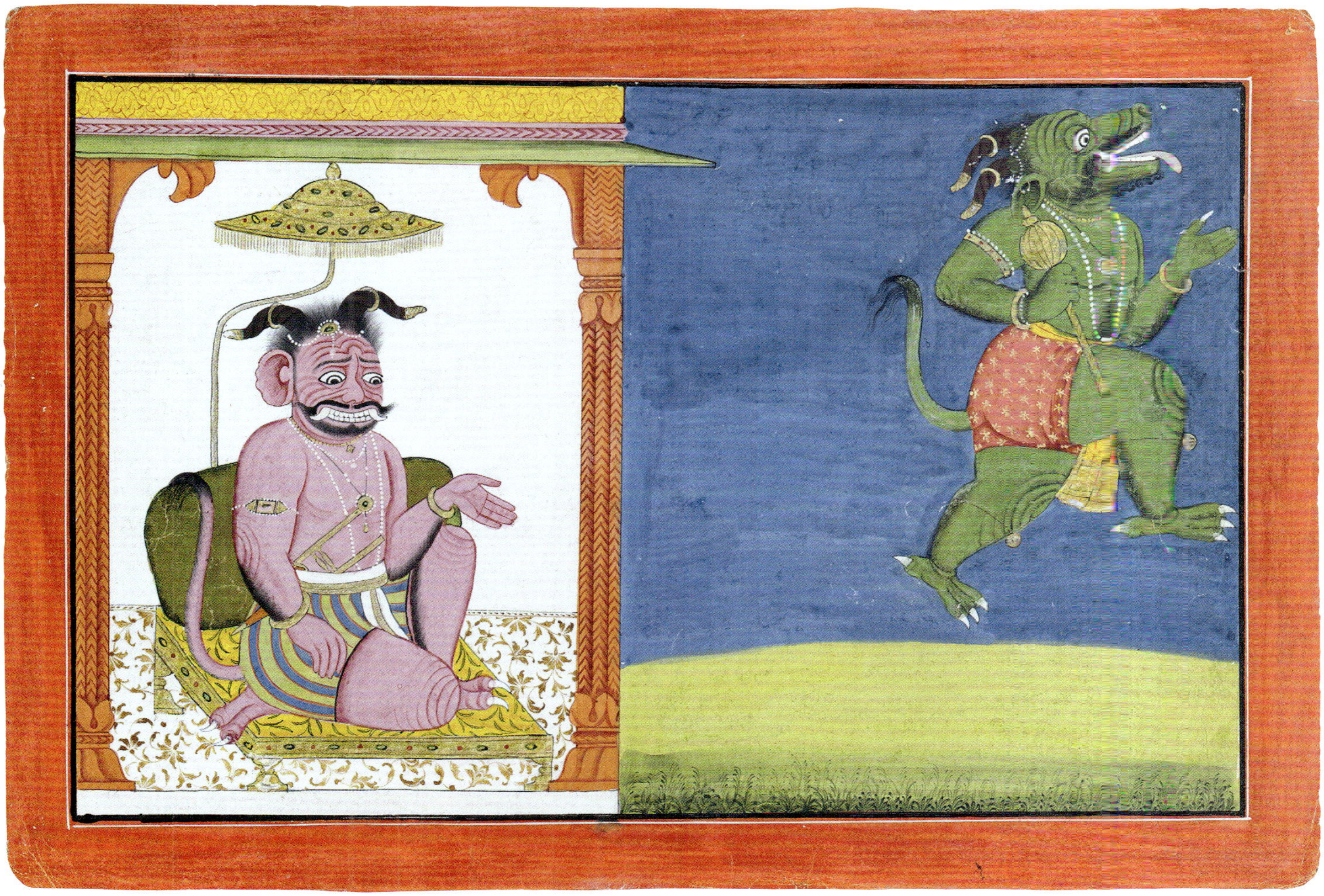

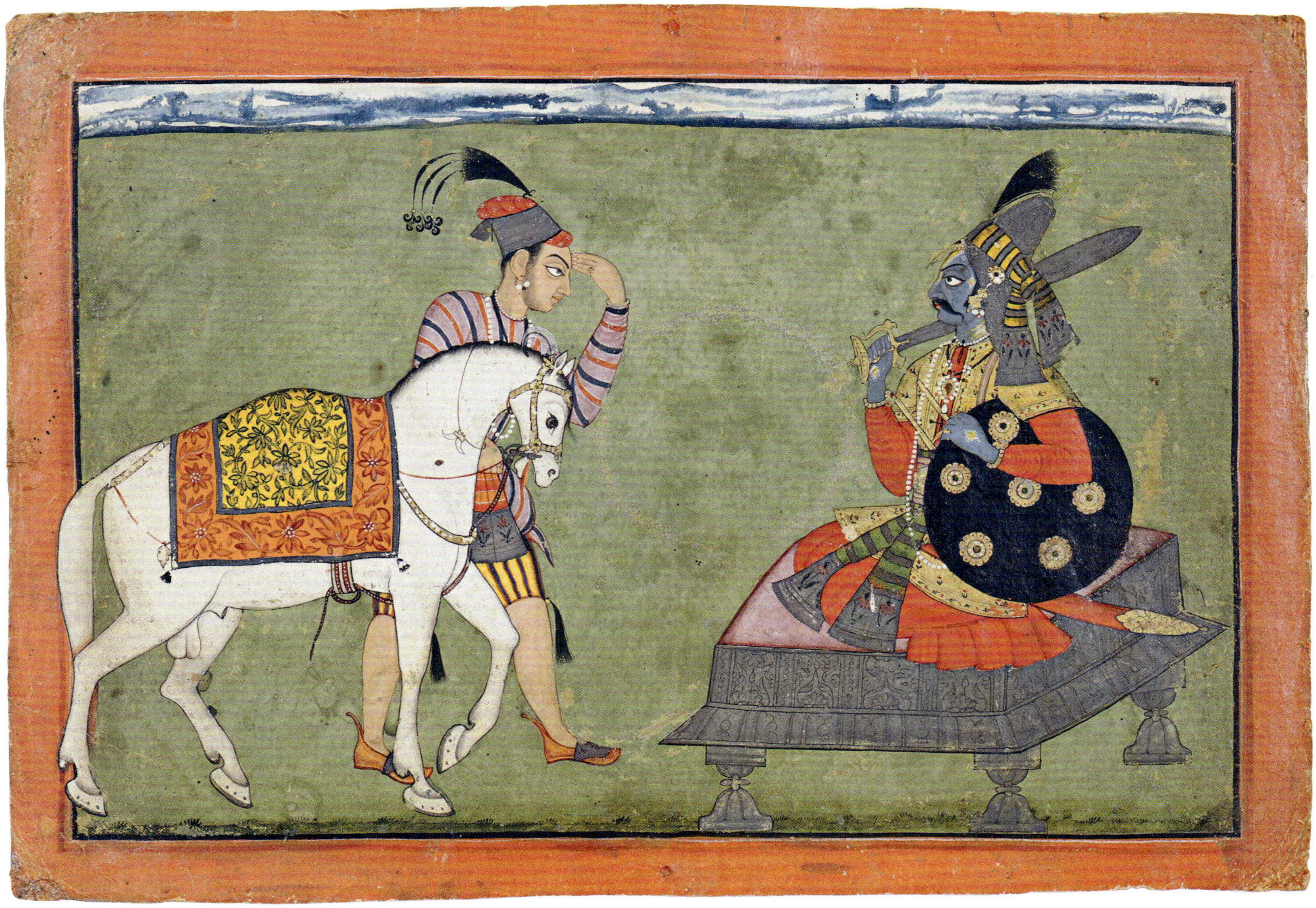

45

Kalki Avatar, the future incarnation of Vishnu

BASOHLI, PUNJAB HILLS, CA. 1700

From a *dasavatara* series of illustrations of the ten incarnations of Vishnu
Opaque watercolor with silver, gold, and beetle-wing cases on paper
Image 17.2 × 26.7 cm (6 ¾ × 10 ½ in.); page 20.1 × 30 cm (8 1⁄16 × 11 15⁄16 in.)
Published: P. Pal, *The classical tradition in Rajput panting from the Paul F. Walter Collection*, New York, 1978, no. 54
Metropolitan Museum of Art, New York, Gift of Cynthia Hazen Polsky (1991.32.1)

KALKI, THE TENTH AND FINAL INCARNATION OF VISHNU, will appear at the end of time, in the form of a fearsome rider on an apocalyptic white horse. His coming will bring to an end the Kali Yuga, the present degenerate and final world age (said to date from the death of Krishna), in which the moral and spiritual values and quality of existence established in the three earlier world ages have been in constant decline. Wielding a blazing sword, Kalki will come to punish the wicked, comfort the virtuous, and restore the rule of Dharma (law), before he finally destroys the Universe. Then, after a period of rest, yet another long cycle (*mahayuga*) of the four world ages will begin again.

Kalki is shown by the artist as a keen-eyed, mustachioed Rajput lord, seated on a low throne. Blue-skinned as befits an avatar of Vishnu, he is armed for battle. He wears a rich gold tunic over a bright red coat (*jama*) and holds his sword and shield at the ready. In a scene reminiscent of the daily life of a Rajput court, his groom (syce) bows and makes a gesture of respect to his royal master as he leads the white stallion of the apocalypse forward for inspection, in its harness and floral saddle-cloth. The horse, with a curious hump, is accorded a relatively modest size within the grouping; in later Pahari versions of the subject it would become steadily more imposing.[1]

AT

1 E.g. Skelton, 1961, no. 49; Archer, 1973, s.v. Bilaspur, nos. 25, 37; Topsfield, 1986, no. 26.

R A M A

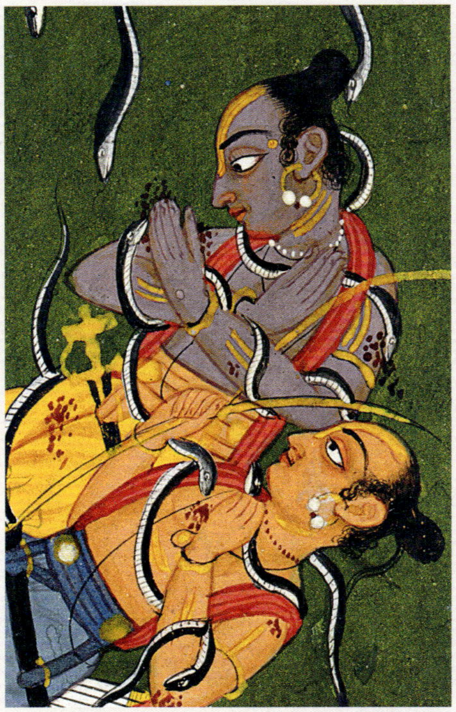

The god-king Rama ("Pleasing") is the seventh avatar of Vishnu and the hero of the *Ramayana* epic; he is also known as Ramachandra ("Rama the moon"), a reference to his moon-like beauty. Probably in origin a historic chieftain of the Ganges valley, Rama became incorporated as an avatar of Vishnu, developing into the divine personification of the ideal, righteous ruler and the vanquisher of evil, personified by the demon-king Ravana. Rama's wife Sita, whom Ravana had abducted and imprisoned, herself later became a major Indian cultural archetype of steadfast wifely virtue.

The Sanskrit *Ramayana* verse epic attributed to the sage Valmiki is a lengthy composition in seven books, which reached its present form some time during the period ca. 500 BC – AD 200. Its second to sixth books represent the earlier epic core, Rama's divine nature being emphasized more in the additional first and seventh books. Other, later versions in various regional languages also became popular, including those of the Tamil poet Kamban in the tenth century and the Hindi poet Tulsi Das in the sixteenth century. The essential story of the epic may be briefly summarized. Born the eldest son of Dasharatha, king of Ayodhya, Prince Rama is unjustly banished from the court, through the intrigues of his stepmother Kaikeyi who wishes her own son to be heir to the throne. Following, as ever, the path of duty and obedience, Rama goes into exile in the forest, accompanied by his devoted wife Sita and loyal brother Lakshmana. One day, Sita is abducted by the wicked Ravana, demon king of

Lanka, and Rama's long struggle to regain her then begins. Rama and Lakshmana are aided in their search for Sita and in their culminating campaign against Lanka by the monkey army and other helpers, including above all the resourceful monkey-god Hanuman. After long battles and the defeat of the demon champions such as the giant Kumbhakarna, King Ravana is finally overcome and killed. The liberated Sita then successfully undergoes a fire ordeal to prove her chastity while in captivity. At last, they return in triumph to Ayodhya, where Rama is installed as king.

Attaining universal popularity throughout the subcontinent, as well as in South-east Asia, the Rama story has become an enduring, integral element of Indian culture and the visual and dramatic arts. *Ramayana* episodes are frequently found in temple relief sculptures, and later provided some of the most frequently depicted themes in court and folk painting, though never quite rivalling Krishna subjects in this respect. Besides the eighteenth-century examples of *Ramayana* illustrations in the Pahari (Punjab Hill) styles included here (cat. nos. 47–50), earlier Mughal examples appear elsewhere in this book (cat. nos. 157–64). Devotion to Rama remains extremely strong in modern times. Invoking his name in a mantra (as Ram) is considered equivalent to invoking God, and such an invocation was the assassinated Mahatma Gandhi's last utterance. In recent years, a television dramatization of the *Ramayana* brought the country almost to a standstill at the transmission times of its sixty or more episodes.

AT

46

Rama's victory over Kumbhakarna

SOUTH INDIA, SEVENTEENTH CENTURY

Ivory
H. 7.6 x W. 6 cm (3 x 2 ½ in.)

THIS IVORY PANEL depicts an episode from "The Book of Battle," the sixth book of the *Ramayana*, in which Rama and the monkey army led by Sugriva engage with the demon army of Ravana, king of Lanka, who has kidnapped Sita. Ravana employs every weapon at his command in vain: Rama shoots all of them down with his arrows. At one stage of the battle, Ravana succeeds in waking his brother, the formidable giant Kumbhakarna, from his perpetual slumber. Kumbhakarna lumbers forth to do battle with Rama, but he is eventually decapitated by Rama's arrow. Ultimately, Rama unleashes his final weapon, only to be used when all other means have failed, and Ravana too is killed.

Rama is shown seated on the body of the defeated Kumbhakarna, his right knee raised as he holds up his bow in his left hand. His brother Lakshmana stands beside him, Garuda holds his left arm, and Hanuman stands in front of him. Monkeys and other figures gather round, while above to the left a monkey flies in a mountainous landscape, and to the right the ten-headed and twenty-armed Ravana flies in his airborne chariot. The whole group is supported on a base with engraved florets.

This type of composition, with crowded and piled up figures arranged in distinct blocks of action, is found in Southern Indian paintings of the seventeenth and eighteenth centuries,[1] and it is to this period that the ivory can be attributed. The tiered headdresses of Rama and Lakshmana are seen on seventeenth-century ceiling paintings and in a *Ramayana* manuscript from Mysore dated 1670.[2] The *Ramayana* theme holds a significant place in surviving ceiling paintings and the relatively few known manuscripts from Southern India,[3] particularly as many events in the epic are associated with the city of Vijayanagara.[4]

MCS

1 Mittal, 1969; e.g. fig. 27, depicting Rama in a very similar pose.

2 Ehnbom, 1985, no. 43, p. 100; Michell, 1995, figs. 169, 177.

3 *Ibid.*, pp. 234, 241.

4 A. Dallapiccola,"'The city of Vijayanagara: Kishkindha, the Monkey Kingdom," in V. Dehejia ed., *The legend of Rama*, Bombay: Marg, 1994, pp. 61–72.

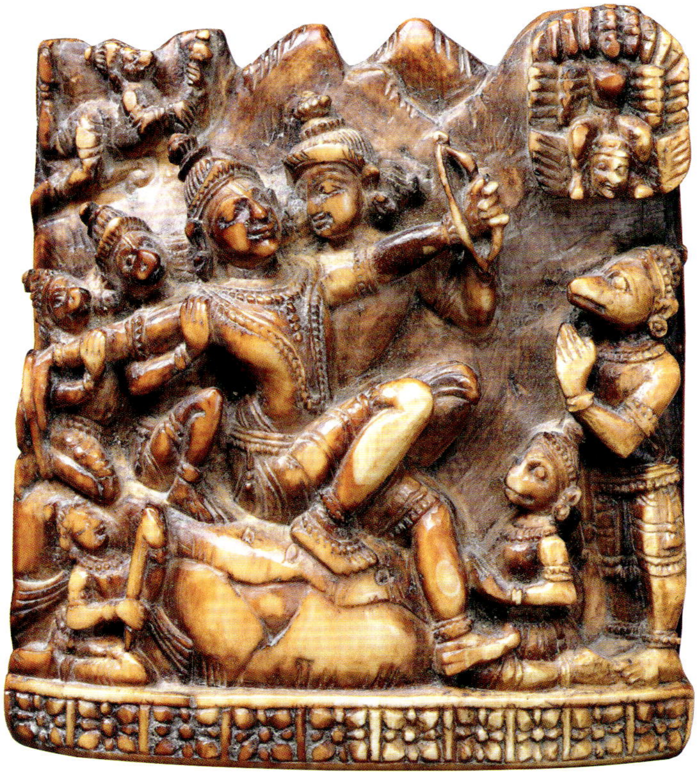

47

Rama and Lakshmana on Mount Prasravana

FOLIO FROM THE DISPERSED SHANGRI RAMAYANA SERIES, BOOK IV (KISHKINDHAKANDA)

Possibly Nurpur or Bahu, Punjab Hills, early eighteenth century
Opaque watercolor with silver on paper
24.4 × 34.6 cm (9 5/8 × 13 5/8 in.)
Inscribed in devanagari on verso: *118 kiskindha* (numerals also in takri)
Metropolitan Museum of Art, New York, Purchase, Cynthia Hazen Polsky Gift (1999.400)

IN THE FOURTH BOOK OF THE *RAMAYANA*, the "Book of Kishkindha," Rama and Lakshmana continue to search for the abducted Sita, aided by the monkey-king Sugriva who becomes their ally. At one point they take up their abode in a cave on Mount Prasravana, whose natural beauties delight Rama. Valmiki's text extols the mountain's innumerable trees and flowering creepers and its abundance of bird and animal life.[1] Here it is shown by the artist in a characteristically conceptual manner, as a simplified rocky outcrop with a single protruding tree standing for the verdant forest. This device emphasizes not the distracting beauties of nature, in which Rama may find passing solace, but instead the underlying mood of desolation following his loss of Sita. On this wavy, pink rock, Rama and Lakshmana sit in conversation under a full moon and stars.

The lengthy and unfinished Shangri *Ramayana* series (see also cat. nos. 48–49) is so called from its place of discovery in the 1950s, at a minor court in the Kulu Valley region of the Punjab Hills.[2] One of the most ambitious and important documents of early Pahari painting, it is now dispersed in many collections, notably that of the National Museum, New Delhi. This page is by an artist working in a relatively naive and simplified manner (classified by Archer as Style III).[3]

AT

1 Shastri tr., 1952, II, pp. 234ff.

2 See e.g. W. G. Archer, 1973, s.v. Kulu, no. 1; Goswamy and Fischer, 1992, pp. 75ff.

3 E.g. compare Mason et al., 2001, no. 29 (with a Mandi attribution).

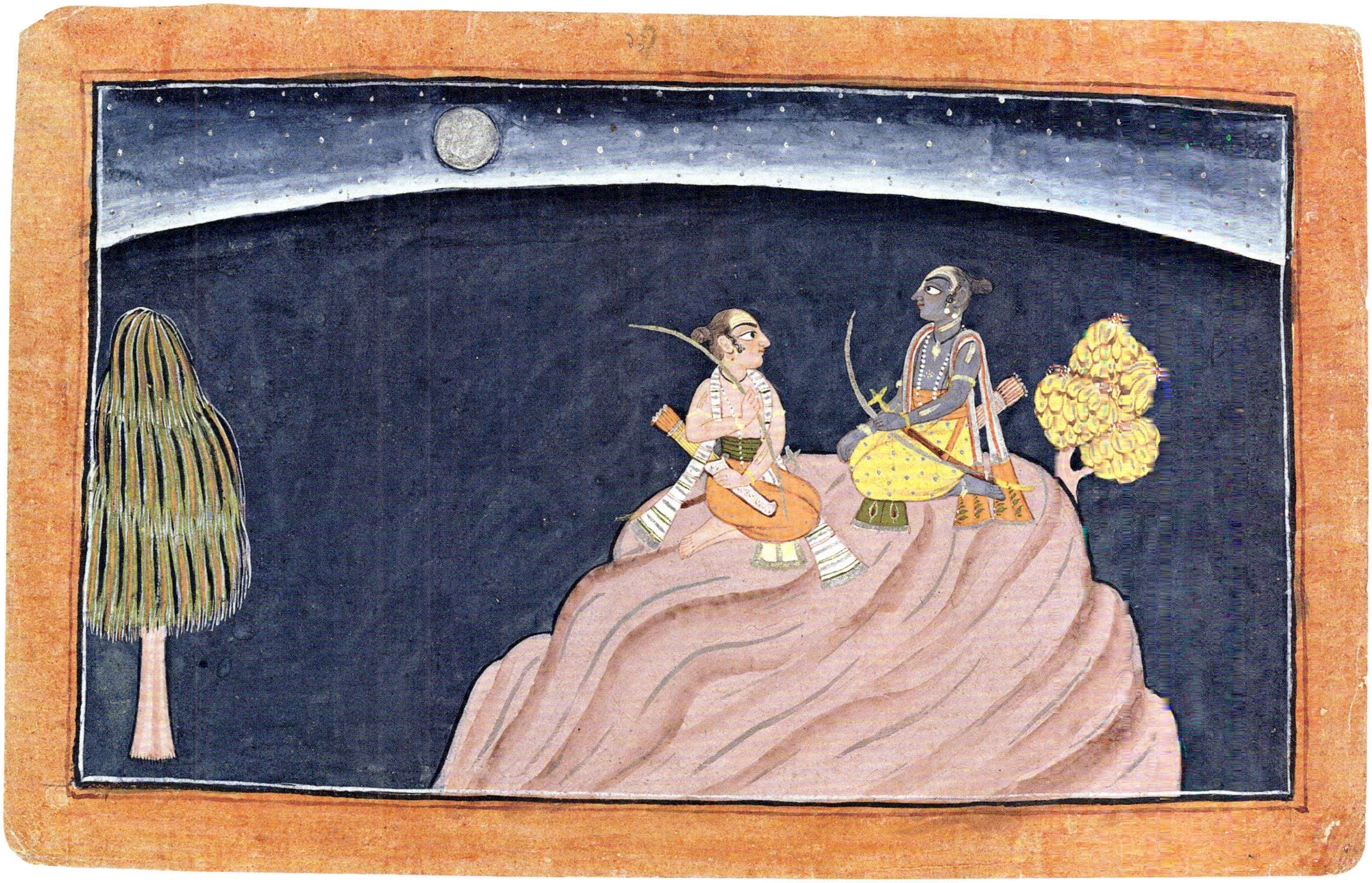

48

Bharata and Shatrughna take leave of King Dasharatha

FROM THE SHANGRI RAMAYANA SERIES, BOOK II (AYODHYAKANDA), 1, VV.3–4

Possibly Nurpur or Bahu, Punjab Hills, ca. 1700
Opaque watecolor with silver and gold on paper
Inscribed on upper border in takri with number (2) and names of the figures; on verso, in devanagari: *2 ayodhya*
21.6 × 33 cm (8 ½ × 13 in.)

AGAINST A GLOWING YELLOW GROUND, as often found in the Shangri *Ramayana* series (cat. nos. 47, 49), King Dasharatha, in an orange jama, presides over a small gathering of princes and courtiers. Standing before him, armed with bows, his sons Bharata and Shatrughna take their leave of him. They are departing to escort to his home their maternal uncle Yudhajit who has been visiting the court; he stands behind them, in a white jama. Dasharatha waves his hand in courteous approval of their leave-taking. His other sons Rama and Lakshmana, also with bows, sit in attendance beside him. Syces hold the horses ready, and two royal attendants to the left hold a chowry (fly-whisk) and a ceremonial canopy, and a cloth-wrapped sword and a ewer or hookah. The simplified palace in the background terminates in two domed turrets, one of brick and the other with spiral stripes.

This untroubled scene of court life, displaying the typical formal etiquette of the Rajput nobility, comes at the very beginning of Book 2, the "Book of Ayodhya." Soon after this, through the intrigues of Dasharatha's youngest queen Kaikeyi, who wished to see her own son Bharata installed as heir to the throne, Rama would be sent into his unjust exile from Dasharatha's court.

AT

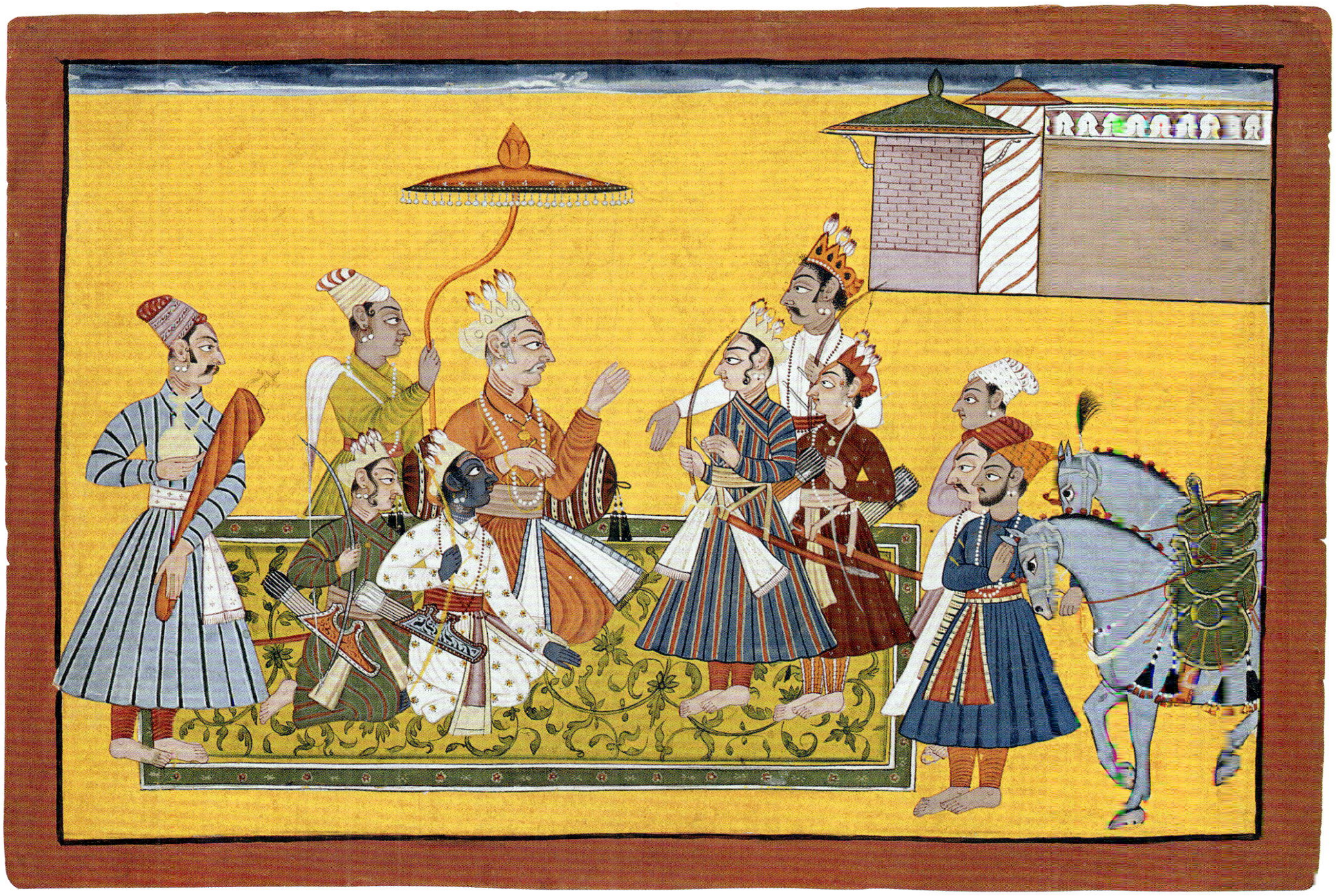

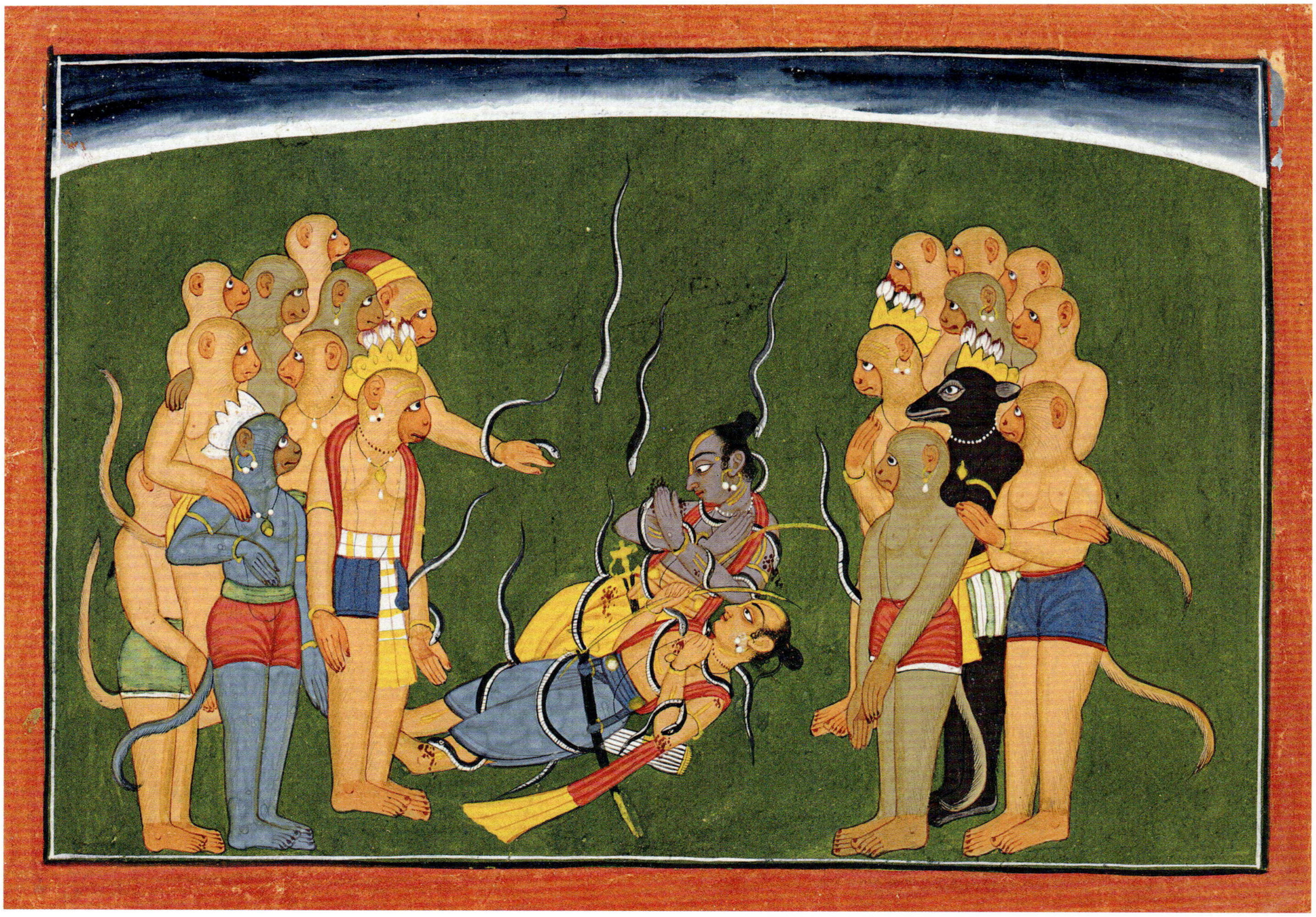

49

Rama and Lakshmana bound by serpent arrows

FROM THE SHANGRI RAMAYANA SERIES, BOOK VI (LANKAKANDA OR YUDDHAKANDA)

Possibly Nurpur or Bahu, Punjab Hills, early eighteenth century
Opaque watercolor on paper
Inscribed on verso in devanagari: *61 lanka* (numerals also in takri); numbered 3 on border
21.3 × 30.5 cm (8 ½ × 13 in.)

DURING THE LONG BATTLE BETWEEN RAMA and his allies and the armies of Ravana, demon king of Lanka, the latter's son Indrajit plays a cunning trick firing powerful magic arrows at Rama and Lakshmana which turn into snakes. Indrajit who has the gift of invisibility, thus succeeds in bringing down the two brothers in a tight mesh of serpents (*nagapasha*). Here, against a plain dark green ground, the pair lie wrapped in snakes and apparently dead on the battlefield. Their friends, the monkey-king Sugriva, Hanuman, and other monkey and bear warriors, gather in two clusters around them, making sorrowful gestures. Rama, however, has just regained consciousness and will himself lament the apparent death of Lakshmana, still prostrate beside him. But Lakshmana too revives, and the brothers then fight on to ultimate victory.

Several related pages from this dispersed manuscript (see cat. nos. 47–48) show different stages of the nagapasha episode: for example, in the Los Angeles County Museum; Bharat Kala Bhavan, Varanasi;[1] Museum Rietberg, Zurich;[2] and the National Museum, New Delhi.[3]

AT

1 Krishna ed., 1981, fig. 543.

2 Boner, Fischer and Goswamy, 1994, no. 303.

3 Acc. no. 62.118; also Sotheby's New York, 6 October 1990, lot 115, numbered 60 in devanagari on the reverse, which may precede the present painting.

I am grateful to Alka Bagri for these and other references.

50

Ravana converses with a demon by the sea

ILLUSTRATION TO A DISPERSED RAMAYANA SERIES

Kangra, Punjab Hills, ca. 1780
Opaque watercolor on paper
24.8 x 35.6 cm (9 ¾ x 14 in.)
Published: T. McInerney, *Indian paintings from the Polsky Collections,* Princeton, 1982, no. 21
Metropolitan Museum of Art, New York, Gift of Cynthia Hazen Polsky (1985.398.14)

THE TEN-HEADED AND TWENTY-ARMED DEMON-KING RAVANA, clutching a multitude of weapons in his hands, converses with a demon, whom he is probably instructing to go forth and do battle with Rama, in the course of the sixth book ("Yuddhakanda") of the *Ramayana.* The yellow-faced and orange-bodied demon gesticulates with hands raised, while leering horribly. In the background, Ravana and the demon move off in the royal chariot. Ravana's golden palace at Lanka appears in the distance, and the sea swirling in the foreground teems with the heads and tails of fantastic fish and water-beasts.

The relative smallness of the figures in relation to the sensitively rendered landscape is typical of this finely painted *Ramayana* series, which may have been commissioned soon after his accession by the noted connoisseur Maharaja Sansar Chand of Kangra (r. 1775–1823). More than a hundred pages survive from this series and are now widely dispersed;[1] a number of pages with gold-decorated, dark blue inner margins, not the plain black band seen here, appear to be from a closely related, near-contemporary series.

AT

1 E.g. Archer, 1976, nos. 40–42; Pal, 1976, no. 6; Pal, 1978, nos. 67–68; Ehnbom, 1985, nos. 116–18; Kramrisch, 1986, no. 120; Goswamy, 1986, no. 122; Goswamy and Fischer, 1992, nos. 143–45; Poster, 1994, nos. 215–16; Kossak, 1997, no. 62*; Indian paintings and manuscripts*, London: Sam Fogg, nos. 73 (i–ii); Goswamy, 1999, nos. 189–90; Mason et al., 2001, no. 81; Hurel and Okada, 2002, no. 46.

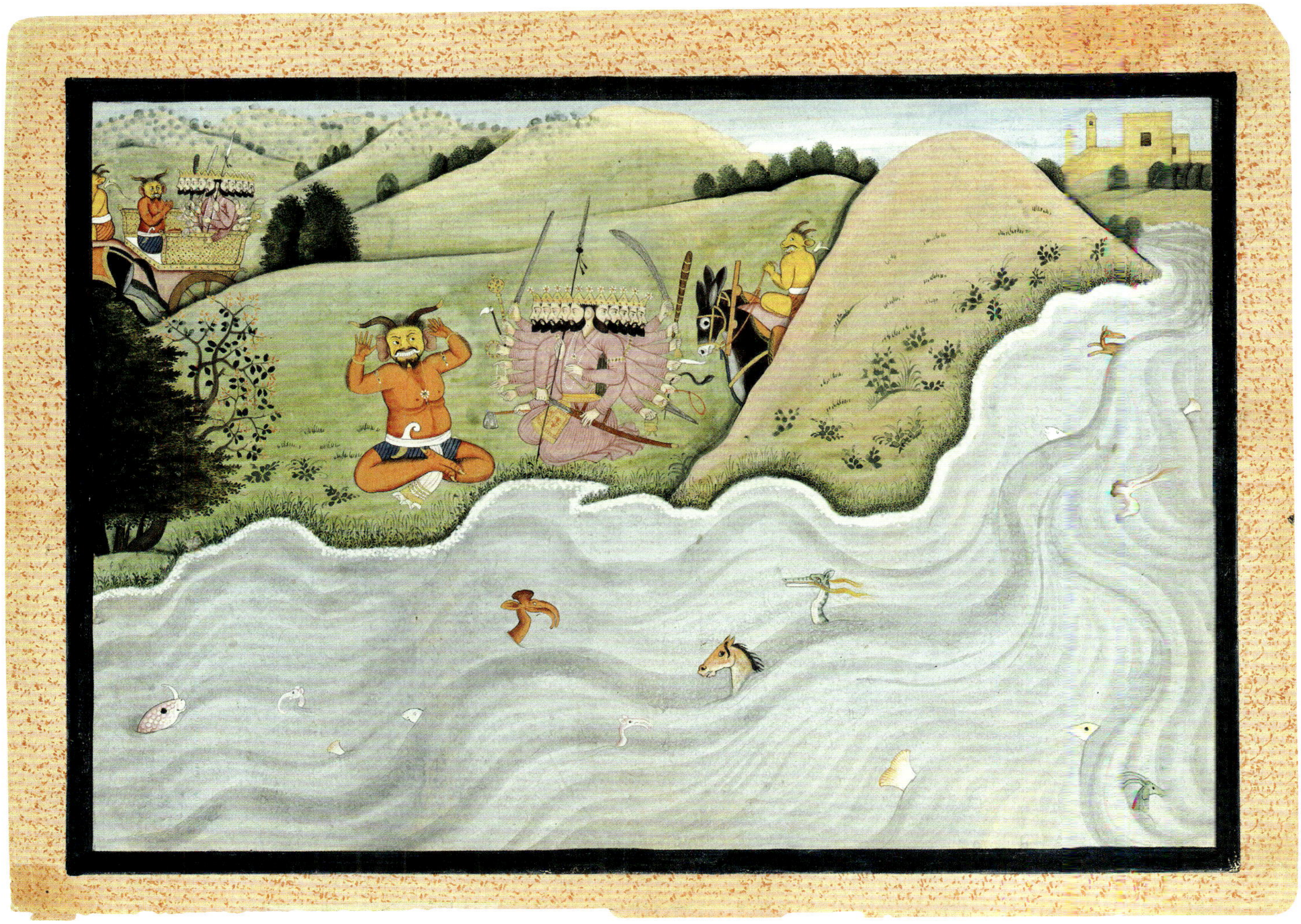

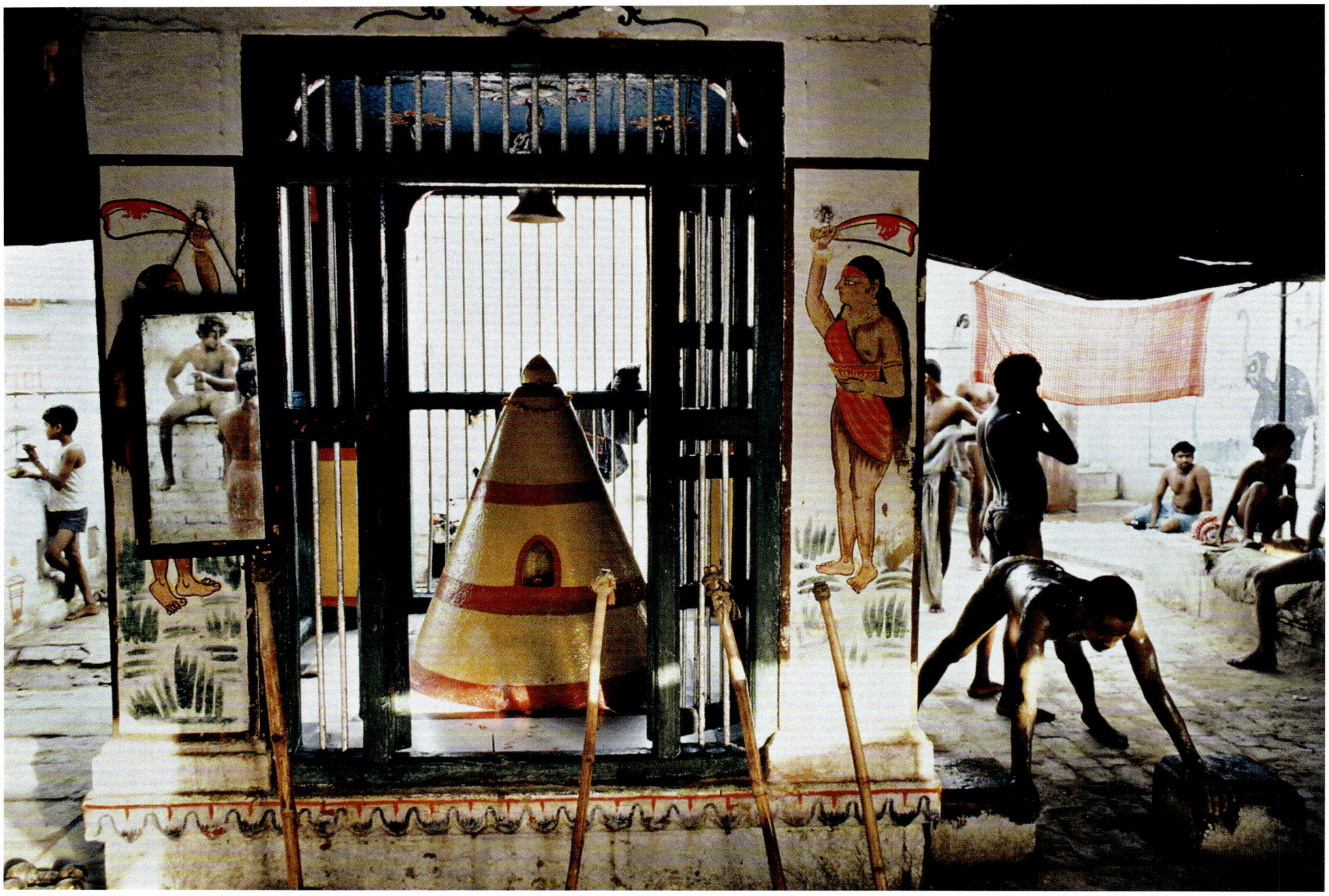

51

Wrestlers exercising at the Hanuman Shrine, Benares

RAGHUBIR SINGH (1942–99)

Varanasi (Benares, or Banaras),
Uttar Pradesh, 1983
Chromogenic color print
25.4 × 37.7 cm (10 × 14 13⁄16 in.)
Published: Raghubir Singh, *Banaras: Sacred city of India*, London, 1987, pl. 40
Metropolitan Museum of Art, New York, Purchase, Cynthia Hazen Polsky Gift (1991.1286)

THIS IS ONE OF A NUMBER of Raghubir Singh's Benares photographs to feature wrestlers, and the compositional potential of these glistening bodies was clearly attractive to the photographer—they appear at temple shrines, elegantly and somewhat surreally counterpoised on a riverbank, or practicing in a sand pit. Here, the athletes exercise at the shrine to the monkey god Hanuman, one of the most popular Indian deities and the protector of wrestlers and acrobats. While almost all of Singh's published work was a geographically arranged examination of Indian life, his Benares book, composed from photographs taken over a number of years, is a particularly intense and successful compilation, evoking the religious intensity, human variety, and the often anarchic vitality of one of the oldest cities in the world. As a portrait of India's holiest city, the book is inevitably much concerned with the mingling of everyday life and religious observance on the ghats and temples along the Ganges, but the work as a whole is equally successful in presenting the whole spectrum of city life, in a series of acutely observed images whose spontaneity is coupled with Singh's instinctive eye for composition. While "bewitched by the myth and mystery of Banaras,"[1] Singh's work was never sentimental. Indeed, in his preface to the book he discusses frankly his love-hate relationship with a city that alternates between aggression and gentleness. But it is these tensions and contradictions that ultimately supply the cumulative force in his photographic exploration of the City of Light.

JF

1 Raghubir Singh, *Banaras: Sacred city of India*, introduction, p. 7.

KRISHNA

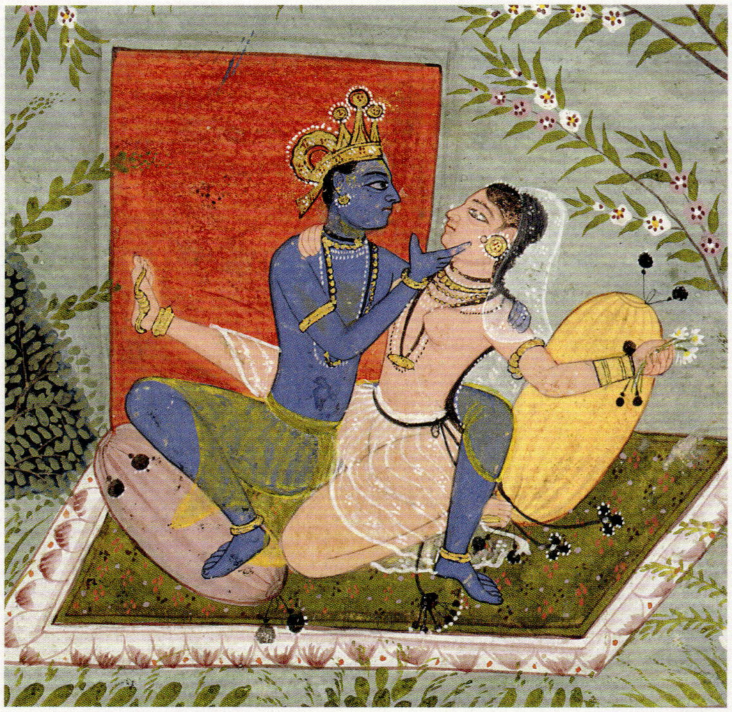

Krishna ("black" or "dark blue") is the eighth and most widely venerated of all the avatars of Vishnu. His mythology reveals several distinct strands, reflecting the early assimilation of different regional deities to his cult, and a progressive development of his character from his appearance in the *Mahabharata* epic (ca. 200 BC – AD 200) to the fuller narratives of his life in the *Harivamsha* (ca. AD 400) and, above all, the tenth book of the *Bhagavata Purana* (ca. AD 900), after he had become a main focus of the widespread *bhakti* devotional movement.

As an avatar, Krishna's central mission was to destroy the evil tyrant King Kansa of Mathura. Kansa had been forewarned that a child of his cousin Devaki would grow up to kill him, so he imprisoned her and Vasudeva, her husband. But despite his merciless slaying of Devaki's children, the infant Krishna was miraculously saved and carried to Vrindaban, where he grew up in a cowherding village in the home of Nanda and his wife Yashoda. As a child who was at the same time divine, Krishna perpetrated many mischievous pranks such as stealing his mother's butter, when he was not slaying the demons sent by Kansa to destroy him, or outwitting the occasional ploys of the displaced rival god Indra. As Krishna grew to manhood, all the *gopis* (cow-maidens) were captivated by him and spellbound by the music of his flute. Still mischievous, he teased them by stealing their clothes one day while they bathed in the river. But eventually he rewarded their devotion by performing a miraculous round dance, in which each of them danced with him as their own partner at the same time. Krishna eventually left behind the pastoral life of Vrindaban and the distraught gopis, when the time came for him to fulfil his destiny by slaying Kansa at Mathura. After that climactic deed, he established himself as a prince at Dwarka on the west coast of India, where he undertook further heroic exploits, while also settling down with his wives, who numbered 16,108 in all.

Later devotional literature dwells mainly on the events of Krishna's childhood and his dalliance with the gopis. By the time of the poet Jayadeva in the eleventh century, Radha had been identified as Krishna's favorite gopi, and his great poem, the *Gita Govinda*, describes their love and its consummation in a forest setting in richly wrought imagery. Later still, the love between Krishna and Radha became a standard theme of Hindi devotional poetry and rhetorical treatises such as the late sixteenth-century *Rasikapriya* of Keshav Das. Drawing on earlier literary tradition, Keshav examines the nuances of emotion and behavior experienced by idealized lovers (*nayakas* and *nayikas*) who are personified as Krishna and Radha. The simple pastoral idylls of Braj were thus transposed to the urbane, cultured milieu of the Rajput courts, in which any real association between the sexes was prevented or circumscribed by the prescriptions of purdah. Hence, in part, the great popularity with the princes and their ladies of the court artists' versions of these more romantic than devotional themes.

AT

52

Yashoda and Krishna

KARNATAKA (?), VIJAYANAGAR PERIOD, CA. FOURTEENTH CENTURY

Copper
H. 43.1 cm (17 in.)
Metropolitan Museum of Art, New York, Purchase, Lita Annenberg Hazen Charitable Trust Gift, in honor of Cynthia Hazen and Leon B. Polsky (1982.220.8)

IN ANY SURVEY OF GREAT REPRESENTATIONS of mothers and children in world art, this extraordinary and moving image of Yashoda nursing Krishna must be assigned a high ranking. Among the various art traditions of all of Asia, it is without peer. Representations of the theme of the baby Krishna in the arms of his foster-mother are in fact rare, particularly in sculpture. Here Yashoda, seated with her left leg resting on a flat oblong base and her right leg pendant, is shown nursing the infant god. With her left hand she cradles Krishna's head, and with her right she encircles the baby below his waist. She is dressed in a long skirt and simple jewelry and wears her hair in a chignon. A nose ring was once attached to her left nostril. Krishna is seated on her left leg, touching the nipple of Yashoda's right breast with his left hand. His right arm is placed around her. This depiction is surely one of the most intimate and tender portrayals in all Indian art. Transcending the secularity of this ancient theme, the gentle, compassionate expression Yashoda presents to the viewer suggests a paradigm for universal maternal love and sublime grace.

Occasionally a unique work of art appears, to challenge the standard scholarly paraphernalia of stylistic yardsticks. Such an object gathers around itself a network of conflicting scholarly opinion so diverse that the only subject of unanimous opinion is the object's uniqueness. Such is the case with the present sculpture. The identification of the subject is clear, as is the fact that the sculpture originated in Southern India, but precisely where has been a matter of some speculation. The state of Tamil Nadu has been suggested but it is more likely the product of a workshop in Karnataka. The dating of this great sculpture has also been decidedly problematic. It has been dated as early as the eleventh to twelfth century and as late as the sixteenth century or later still. We believe that a rewarding source for stylistic comparisons are early Vijayanagar wall paintings, and instead of being a product of the Chola dynasty, this sculpture was probably not created earlier than the fourteenth century—during the earliest phase of sculptural activity of the Vijayanagar dynasty. It is additionally conceivable that it could be as late as the fifteenth century.

ML

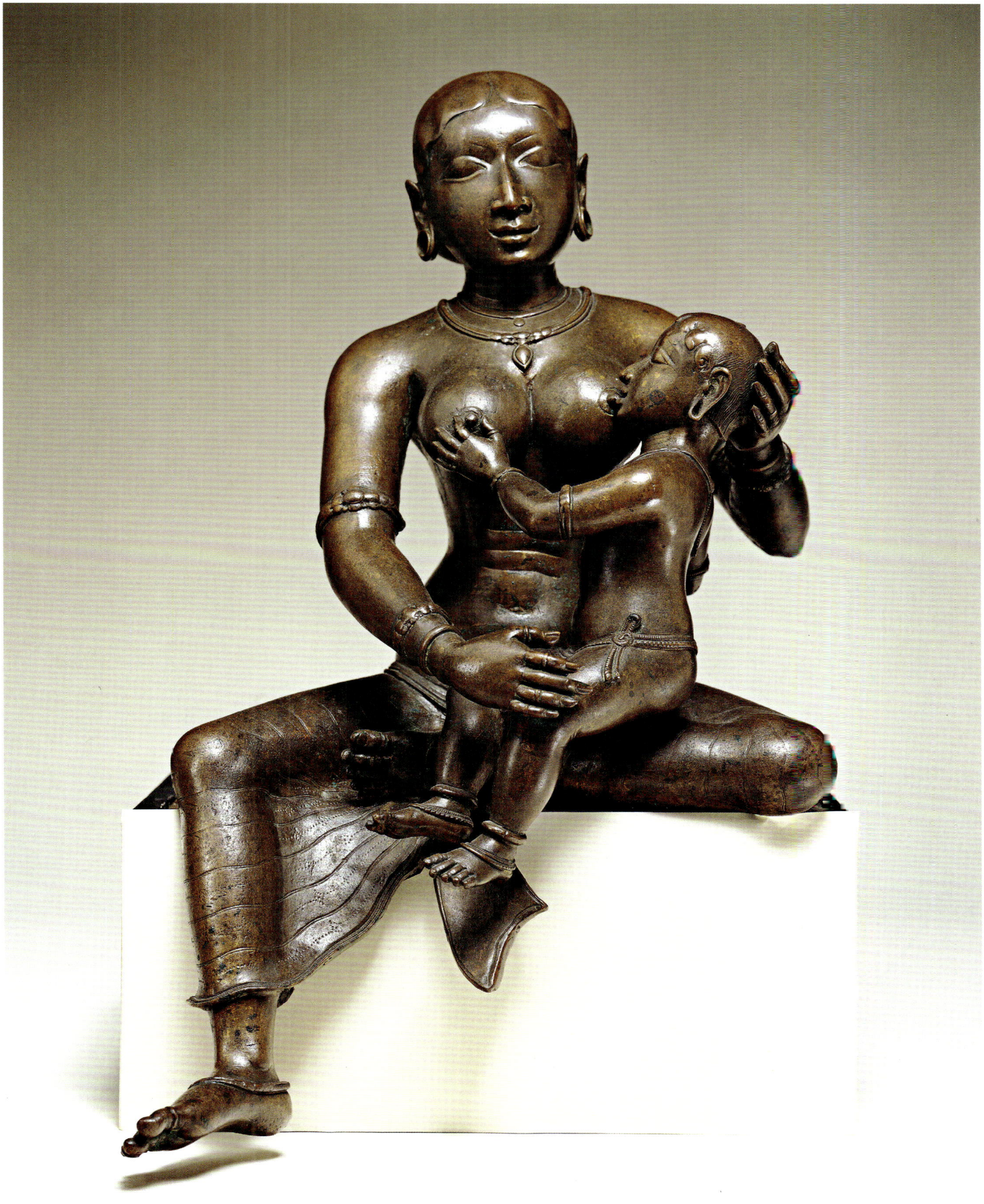

53

Ivory comb depicting Yashoda and Krishna

SRI LANKA (CEYLON), EIGHTEENTH CENTURY

H. 11.4 cm (4 ½ in.)

THE IVORY COMB (*PANAVA*) HAS A CENTRAL PANEL on both sides with similar scenes of a baby suckling at each of his mother's breasts. These figures probably represent the infant Krishna with his foster-mother Yashoda, though no specific incident in the early life of the child-god is alluded to. Krishna is naked, and his mother, seated on a low double-lotus throne, wears elaborate jewelry, large earrings, a necklace, and armbands. Her hair is gathered in a knot behind her head, and she wears a long flowing skirt, with floral scrolls to either side of her. At each side of the central panel is a section with four florets and, above and below, a panel with a diamond-patterned design (*kundi rakkan*), with a further band of beading around the whole, from which the teeth of the comb are then cut at both ends. The scene is reversed from the front to the back to allow the same sections of ivory to be identically carved, and there are remains of blue and red pigments showing that the comb was once brightly colored.

Krishna themes were popular on combs, and particular episodes from his life that are represented include his theft of the butter as a child, and (in his early manhood) the playful theft of the gopis clothes.[1] Other popular auspicious motifs represented on combs include Lakshmi, the goddess of wealth and fertility,[2] and dancing women.[3]

MCS

1 Welch, 1985, no. 11.

2 Archer et al., 1987, nos. 122–23.

3 Pal, 1981, no. 63; *The Asian Art Museum of San Francisco: Selected works*, San Francisco, 1994, p. 40 (acc. no. B60 M345).

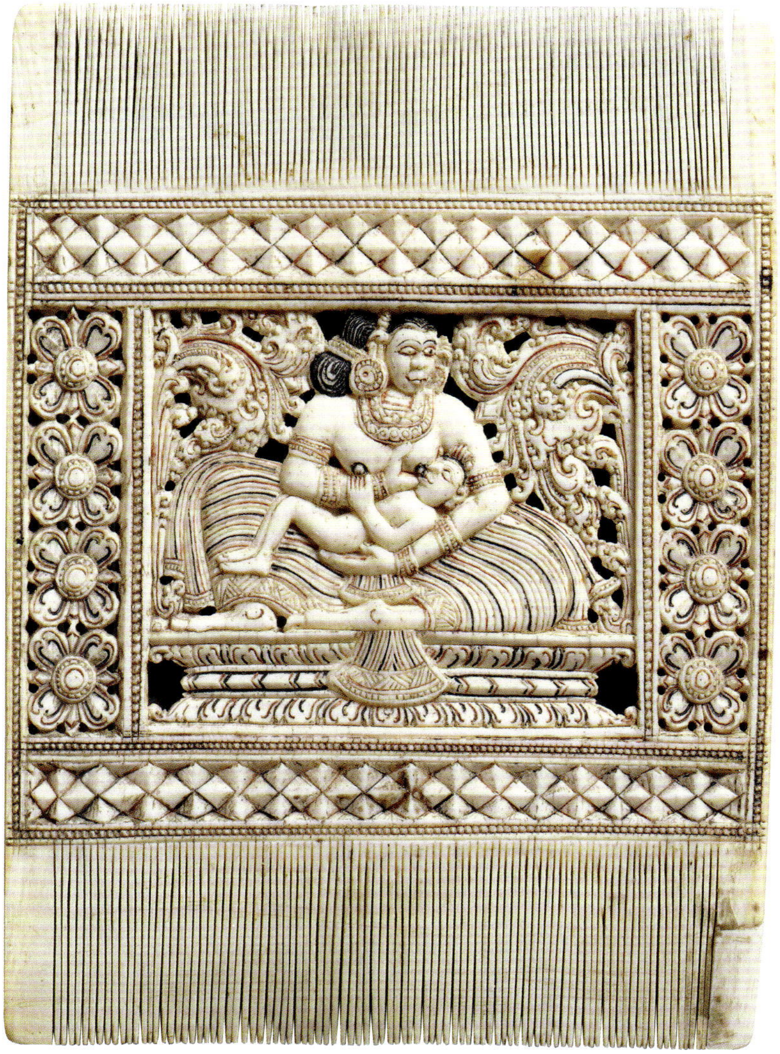

54

Krishna departs for Mathura

FOLIO FROM A DISPERSED BHAGAVATAPURANA, BOOK X, CH. 39, VV. 32FF.

Early Rajput style, possibly in Mewar, ca. 1520–25
Opaque watercolor on paper
17.1 x 22.2 cm (6 ¾ x 8 ¾ in.)
Inscribed on verso with Sanskrit text; and in devanagari above with names of some figures shown, also the names *sa nana* and *hirabai*[1]
Published: T. McInerney, *Indian paintings from the Polsky Collections,* Princeton, 1982, no. 1

IN THE COURSE OF KRISHNA'S EARLY LIFE, spent among the cowherds of the Braj country, he grew from a playful infant with miraculous powers to the youthful slayer of demons and the lover of the gopis. Eventually the time came for him to leave for Mathura and fulfil his destiny by slaying the evil King Kansa, who lay in wait for him there. Firm in this purpose, Krishna rides forth with his brother Balarama in an ornate chariot with an aquatic-beast (*makara*) head finial holding a three-pointed flag. In front sit Akrura, who is conducting Krishna to Kansa's court, and a diminutive charioteer. Krishna's foster-father, the cowherd Nanda, follows behind in a cart laden with jars of milk products. To the left, two rows of gopis sit poignantly lamenting the departure of their divine lover. Above, a messenger sent by Krishna offers the women a consoling promise of his return; but in reality, Krishna would not come there again. As he departed, "the gopis, like painted figures, followed him in their minds for as long as the banner and the dust of the chariot could be seen."[2]

This page is from a famous illustrated series, now widely dispersed, of the tenth book of the *Bhagavata Purana.*[3] It is painted by a number of different hands belonging to a single atelier, in a vigorous form of the sixteenth- century Early Rajput style, with its bold, rhythmical drawing, simplified coloring, and division of the picture space into flat planes and layered registers. Opinions have long differed as to the principal centers of the style, but in the case of this manuscript, Chitor, the fortress capital of the Maharanas of Mewar up to 1568, is a possible candidate.[4]

AT

1 These names, recurrent in the series, may be those of former owners of the manuscript.

2 Bryant tr., 2003, p. 164.

3 The doctoral thesis by D. J. Ehnbom, *An analysis and reconstruction of the dispersed Bhagavata Purana from the Caurapancasika Group*, University of Chicago, 1984, provides a full study; see also e.g. Beach, 1981, pp. 46–55; Mason et al., 2001, nos. 7–9.

4 As suggested in Topsfield, 2002, Ch. 2.

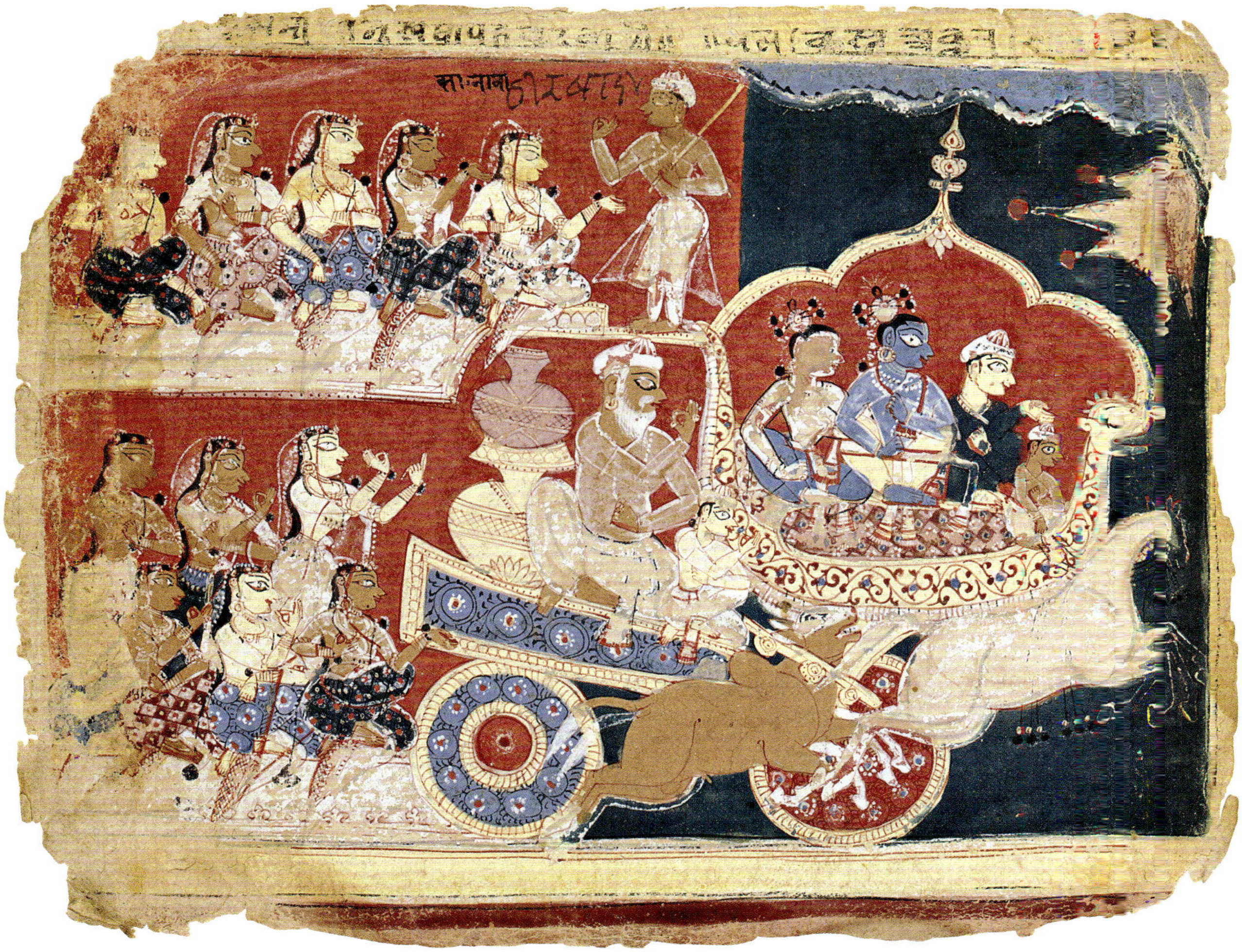

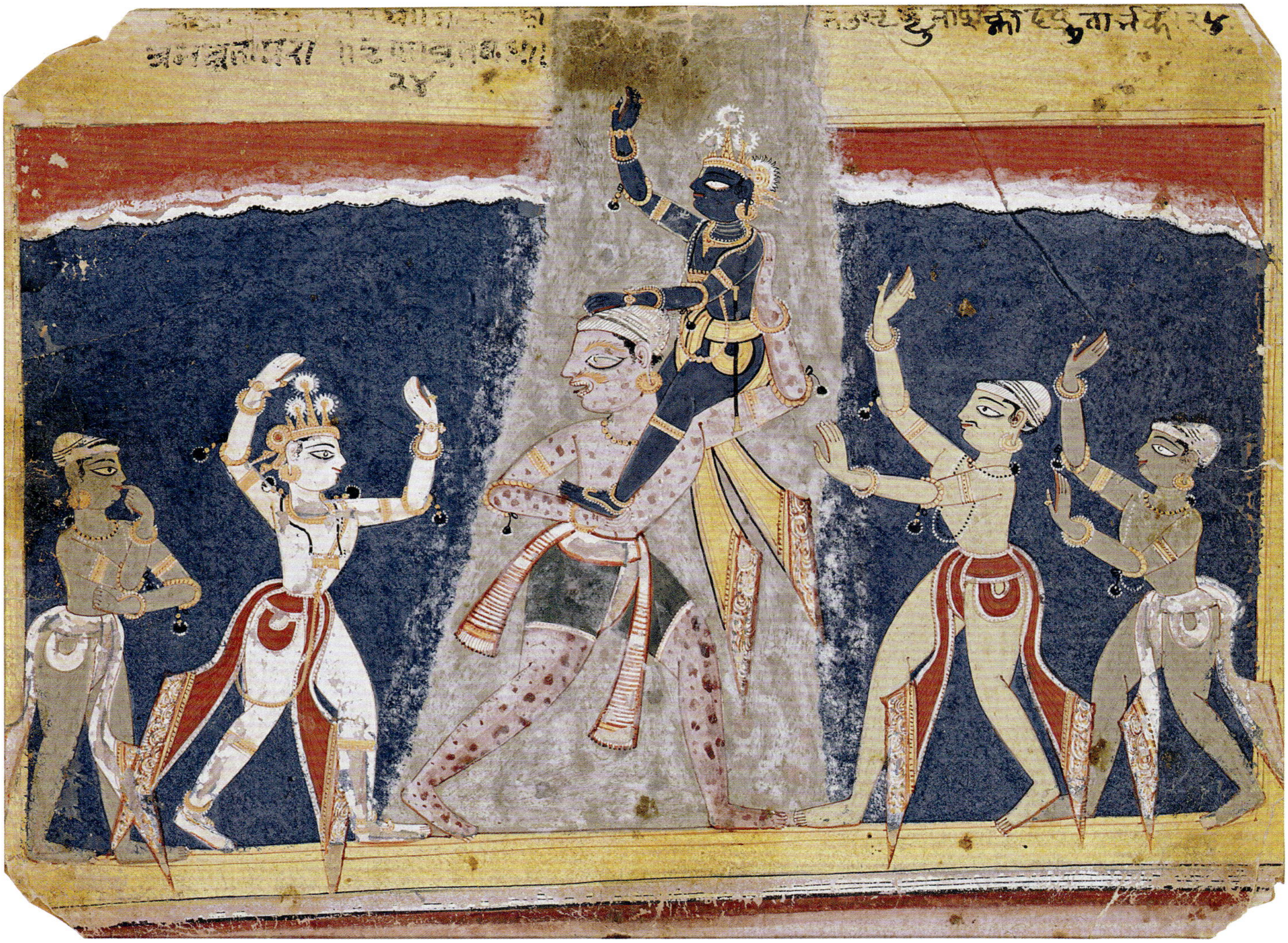

55

Krishna overcomes the whirlwind-demon Trinavarta

FOLIO FROM A DISPERSED BHAGAVATA PURANA SERIES, BOOK X, CH. 7

Early Rajput style, probably in Rajasthan, ca. 1565–70
Opaque watercolor on paper
Abraded Hindi text above describing the scene, numbered 24; inscribed in devanagari on verso: *trinavarta* 16, also a partly obscured Rajasthani Hindi inscription
19.4 × 26.4 cm (7 ⅝ × 10 ⅜ in.)

SURVIVING KING KANSA'S MASSACRE OF THE INNOCENTS, the infant Krishna found refuge as foster-son of the cowherd Nanda and his wife Yashoda. But even in their quiet village he was soon attacked by a series of demons sent by Kansa to destroy him. He vanquished them with miraculous ease, beginning with the ogress Putana (cat. no. 57). His third attacker was Trinavarta, the whirlwind-demon. Arriving in a storm of dust, Trinavarta snatched Krishna from Yashoda's side and carried him high into the sky. But overwhelmed by the colossal weight of the child-god, he fell to his death on a rock with Krishna still hanging safely on to his neck.

Here the doomed demon, with mottled pink skin, hoists Krishna on his shoulder, while Balarama and three gopis show their astonishment by raising their hands: one "bites the finger of surprise," in the manner of Persian or Mughal painting. Trinavarta's whirlwind surges dramatically out of the picture space and into the text panel above; similar irruptions into the picture borders, by the Jumna river, are found elsewhere in this series. With its simplified composition, confident but stiff figure drawing, flat color areas, and mannerisms such as the prominent trailing sash ends, this is a typical page of the Isarda *Bhagavata Purana*, so called after its modern place of discovery in the Ajmer region of Rajasthan. Half a century later in date and less exuberantly inventive than the earlier dispersed *Bhagavata* series (cat. no. 54), it reveals the beginnings of Akbar period Mughal influence on the Early Rajput style.[1]

AT

1 The series has been often published: e.g. K. Khandalavala and J. Mittal, "The *Bhagavata* MSS from Palam and Isarda, a consideration in style," *Lalit Kala*, 16, 1974, figs. 1–4; P. Chandra, *The Tutinama manuscript of the Cleveland Museum of Art and the origins of Mughal painting*, Graz, 1976, pls. 85–86; Leach, 1986, no. 9; and, among more recent publications, Kossak, 1997, nos. 5–6; Goswamy, 1999, nos. 19–21; Mason et al., 2001, nos. 11–12.

56

Krishna and Radha in a grove

ILLUSTRATION TO A DISPERSED SERIES OF THE BHAGAVATA PURANA

Bikaner, Rajasthan, ca. 1600–1610
Opaque watercolor with gold on paper
Short devanagari inscription on verso (obscured)
16.5 x 24.1 cm (6 ½ x 9 ½ in.)

IN A GROVE BY THE JUMNA RIVER, Krishna embraces a favoured gopi with whom he makes love in the forest at night, while the other gopis wander in search of him.[1] This gopi is identified by later tradition as Radha. Sitting astride Krishna's thigh, she raises one leg in an abandoned posture. Her companion nearby keeps watch, or is perhaps another gopi searching for Krishna herself. Both subject and setting are typical of illustrations to the *Gita Govinda* of Jayadeva, celebrating the joyful union of Krishna and Radha, which became a popular subject in the sixteenth-century Early Rajput school and in many later styles of Indian painting. However, this page belongs to a more wide-ranging *Krishnalila* series, generally identified as a *Bhagavata Purana*, although it apparently bears no Sanskrit texts.[2] In this *Purana* (ca. AD 900 or earlier) Radha is not yet named as Krishna's special consort, but by Jayadeva's time (ca. 1100) she had become the pre-eminent gopi.

The red rectangular backdrop highlighting the figure of Krishna is a common convention in Early Rajput painting, as well as in some later series, such as this one, in a more Mughal-influenced idiom. Features of the hybrid sub-imperial (or Popular) Mughal style had spread from Delhi and Agra to the Rajasthani courts by the end of the sixteenth century. Formerly in the royal collection at Bikaner in north-west Rajasthan, this series may well have been painted there also.

AT

1 Cf. Bryant tr., 2003, p. 133.

2 E.g. Goetz, 1950, fig. 91, p. 100; Pal, 1978, nos. 4a–b; Ehnbom, 1985, nos. 17–18; Goswamy and Bhatia, 1999, no. 84; *Indian Paintings and Manuscripts*, London: Sam Fogg, 1999, nos. 23 (i–ii); Mason et al., 2001, no. 18.

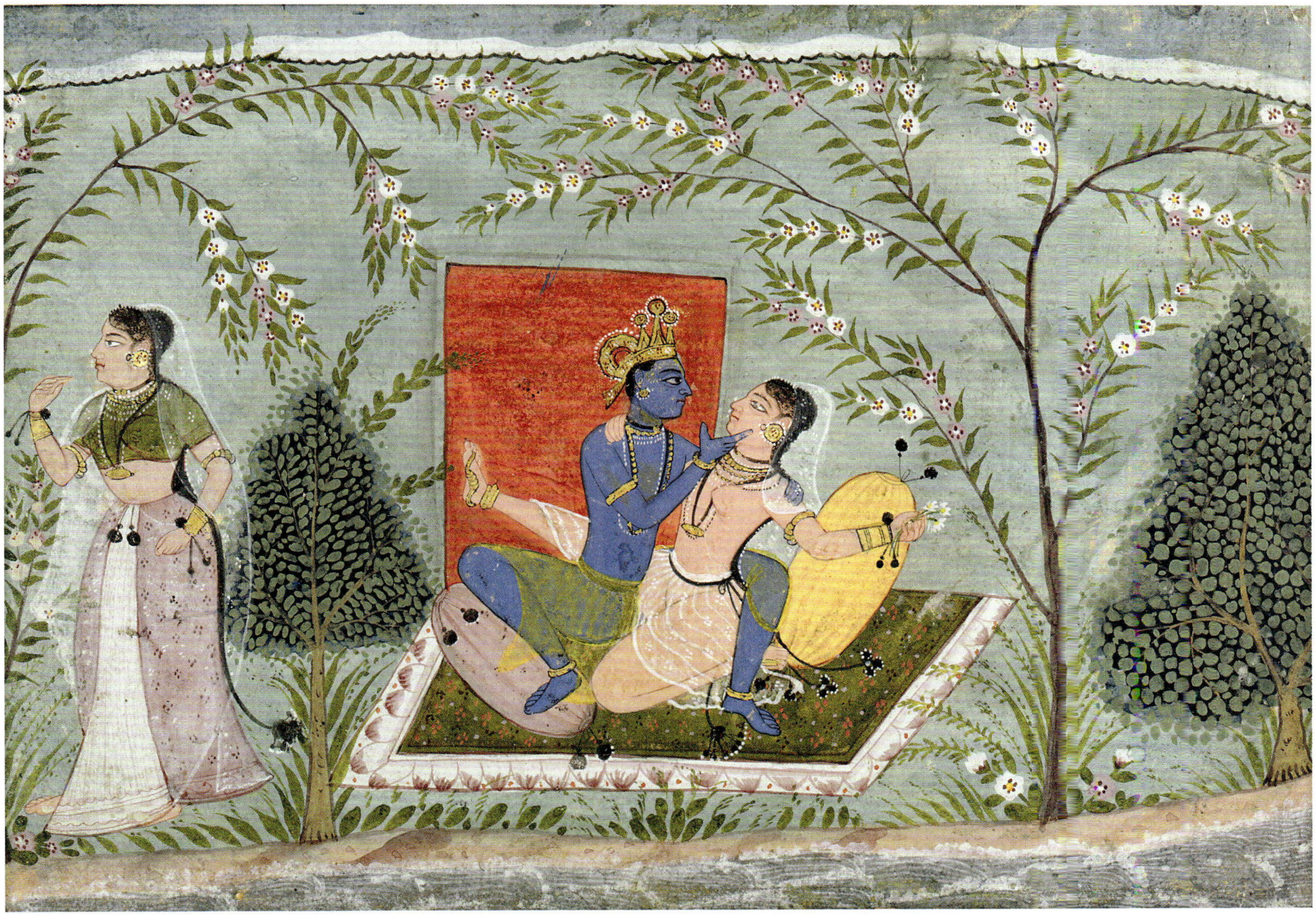

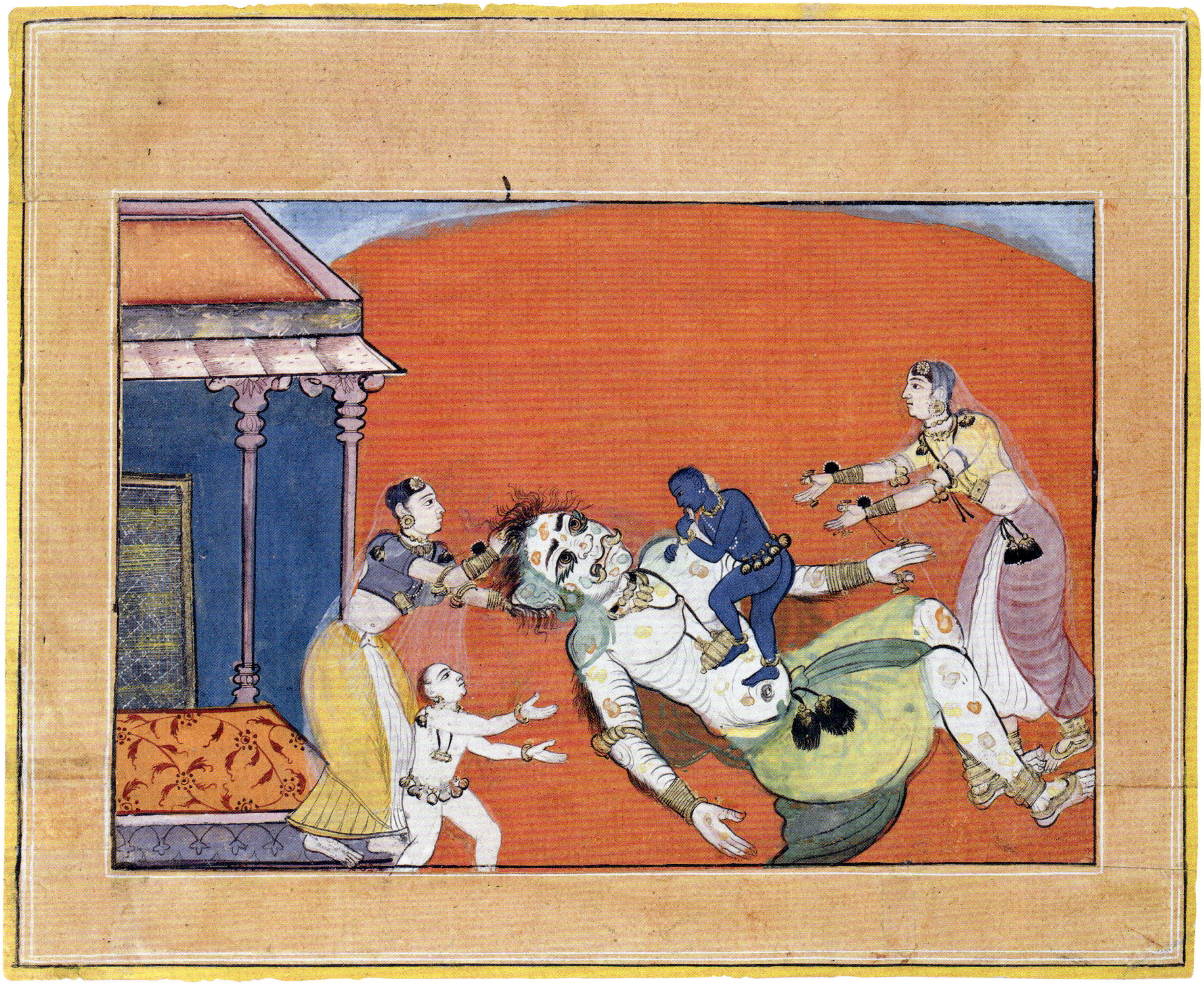

57

The infant Krishna slays the demoness Putana

ILLUSTRATION TO A DISPERSED BHAGAVATA PURANA SERIES, BOOK X, CH. 6

Bikaner, Rajasthan, ca. 1600–10
Opaque watercolor on paper
Image 17.1 × 24.8 cm (6 ¾ × 9 ¾ in.);
page 20.2 × 28.1 cm (7 15⁄16 × 11 1⁄16 in.)
Inscribed in devanagari on verso:
putanabadha 22; also another similar inscription, a number (18), and deleted stamp (of Bikaner State)
Metropolitan Museum of Art, New York, Cynthia Hazen Polsky and Leon B. Polsky Fund (2002.176)

THE DEMONESS PUTANA, DEVOURER OF CHILDREN, was sent by King Kansa to roam the country in the form of a beguilingly beautiful woman. Passing by Nanda's house and seeing the infant Krishna, she picked him up and gave him her breast, imbued with deadly poison. But with his divine insight he knew her evil intent "Squeezing [her breast] tightly with both hands, the furious Lord sucked it, along with her life breath."[1] Drained of life by the suckling child-god, the expiring ogress reverted to her true hideous form.

In this page from a *Bhagavata Purana* series, probably painted at Bikaner under sub-imperial Mughal influence (see cat. no. 56), the scene is set with simple economy against an intense red ground. As Putana falls to the ground, Krishna's foster-mother Yashoda reaches out for him. But the mighty child sucks on remorselessly. On the left, Rohini and her son Balarama also hasten to help. Nanda's house nearby resembles a stylized palace pavilion with its columns and projecting eaves. This version of the subject is expressive in its Mughal-influenced way, but lacks the concentrated drama of the earlier treatments in the *Bhagavata Purana* of ca. 1520–25 and the Isarda series of ca. 1570[2] (cat. nos. 54–55).

AT

1 Bryant tr., 2003, p. 33.

2 Both are in the Goenka Collection, Bombay: Goswamy and Bhatia, 1999, nos. 13, 19.

58

Krishna steals the gopis' clothes

ILLUSTRATION TO A DISPERSED BHAGAVATA PURANA, BOOK X, CH. 22

Bikaner, Rajasthan, ca. 1600–10
Opaque watercolor with gold on paper
Inscribed in devanagari on verso: *vastraharan* ("stealing of clothes"); numbered: *an* 56, with another number (43) and deleted Bikaner State stamp
Image 17.1 x 24.8 cm (6 ¾ x 9 ¾ in.); page 20.2 x 28.1cm (7 15/16 x 11 1/16 in.)
Metropolitan Museum of Art, New York, Cynthia Hazen Polsky and Leon B. Polsky Fund, 2000 (2001.437)

AS KRISHNA GREW TO RESPLENDENT MANHOOD, the young gopi maidens all fell in love with him. On their way to bathe in the river each morning they would sing of him. One day as they bathed, Krishna playfully gathered their clothes from the riverbank and climbed a tree. Before he would return their garments, he compelled the bashful girls, who were shivering in the water, to come before him one by one in their nakedness, and with hands held high in obeisance to him. Despite being thus robbed of their modesty, the gopis "were not really upset with Krishna. They were delighted to be in the company of their darling."[1] Later in the year, Krishna would fulfil their prayers and they would all enjoy union with him in their great Round Dance.

Against a pale yellow landscape with leafy clumps, Krishna is highlighted by a red background panel, as found elsewhere in this and comparable series (cat. no. 56). As he addresses the gopis from his tree perch, they stand in the river imploring him for mercy. The water is covered with semi-naturalistic billows of a kind first found in early Akbar period Mughal painting.

AT

1 E. F. Bryant tr., *Krishna: The beautiful legend of God*, London, 2003, p. 105.

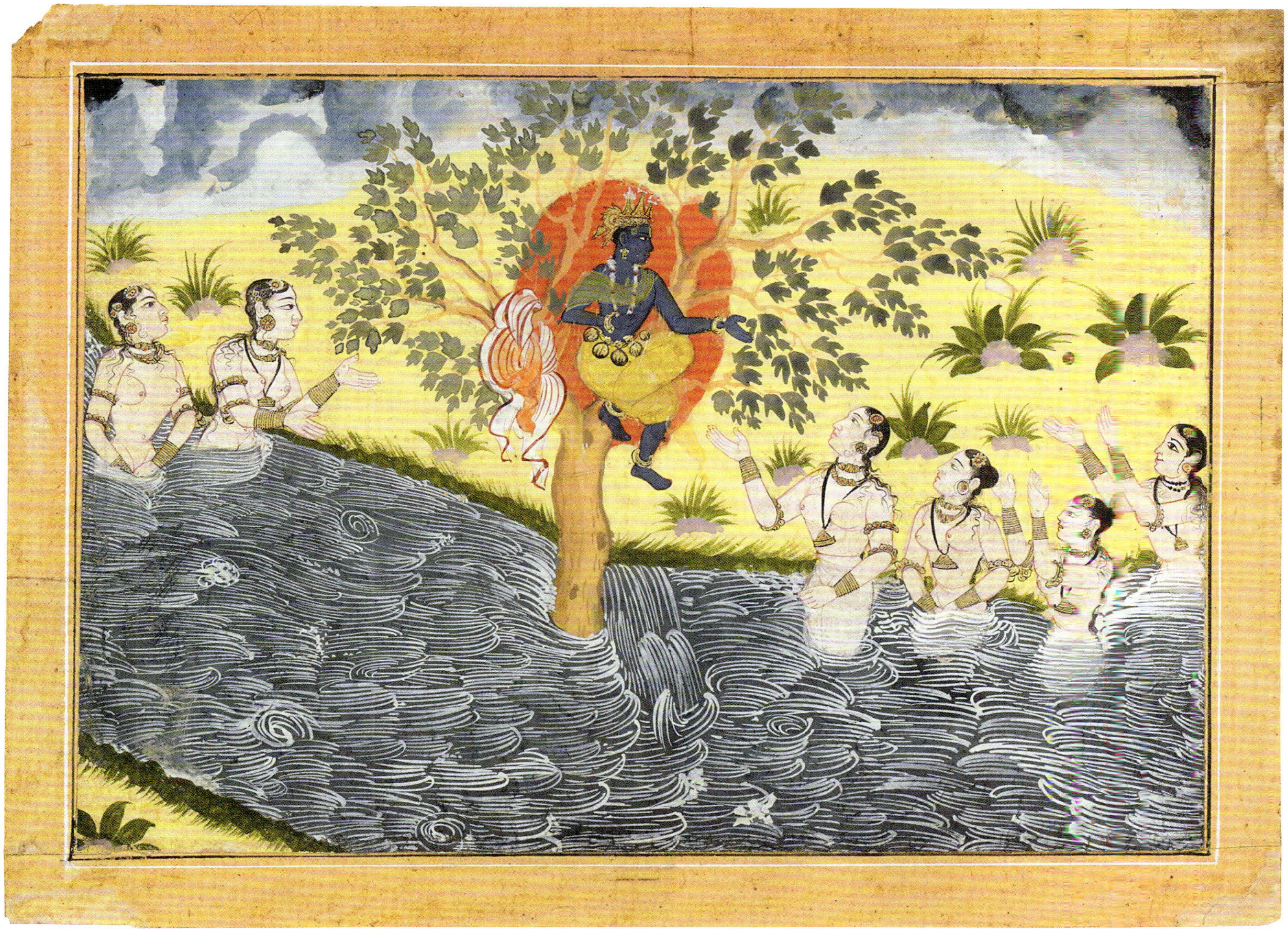

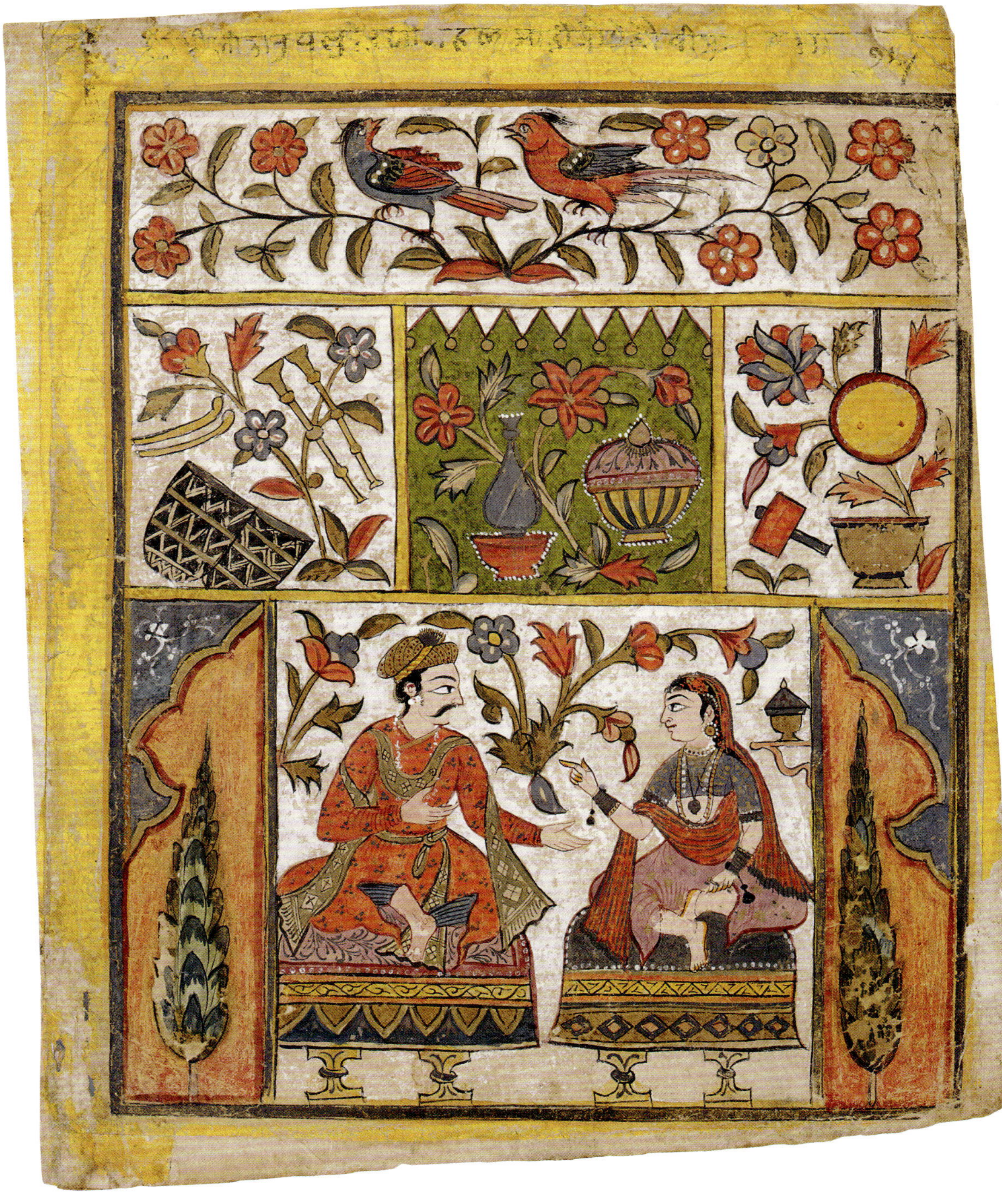

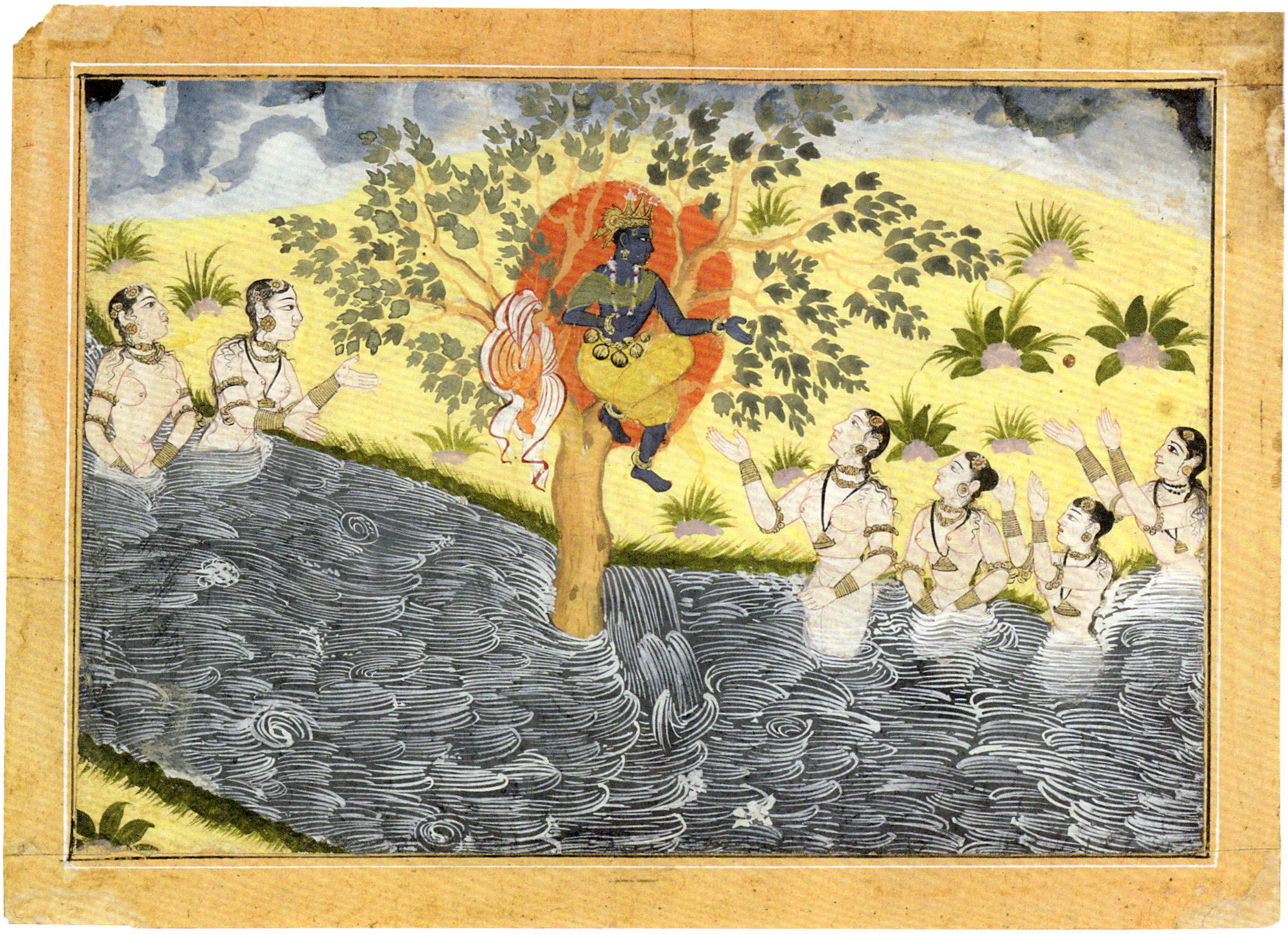

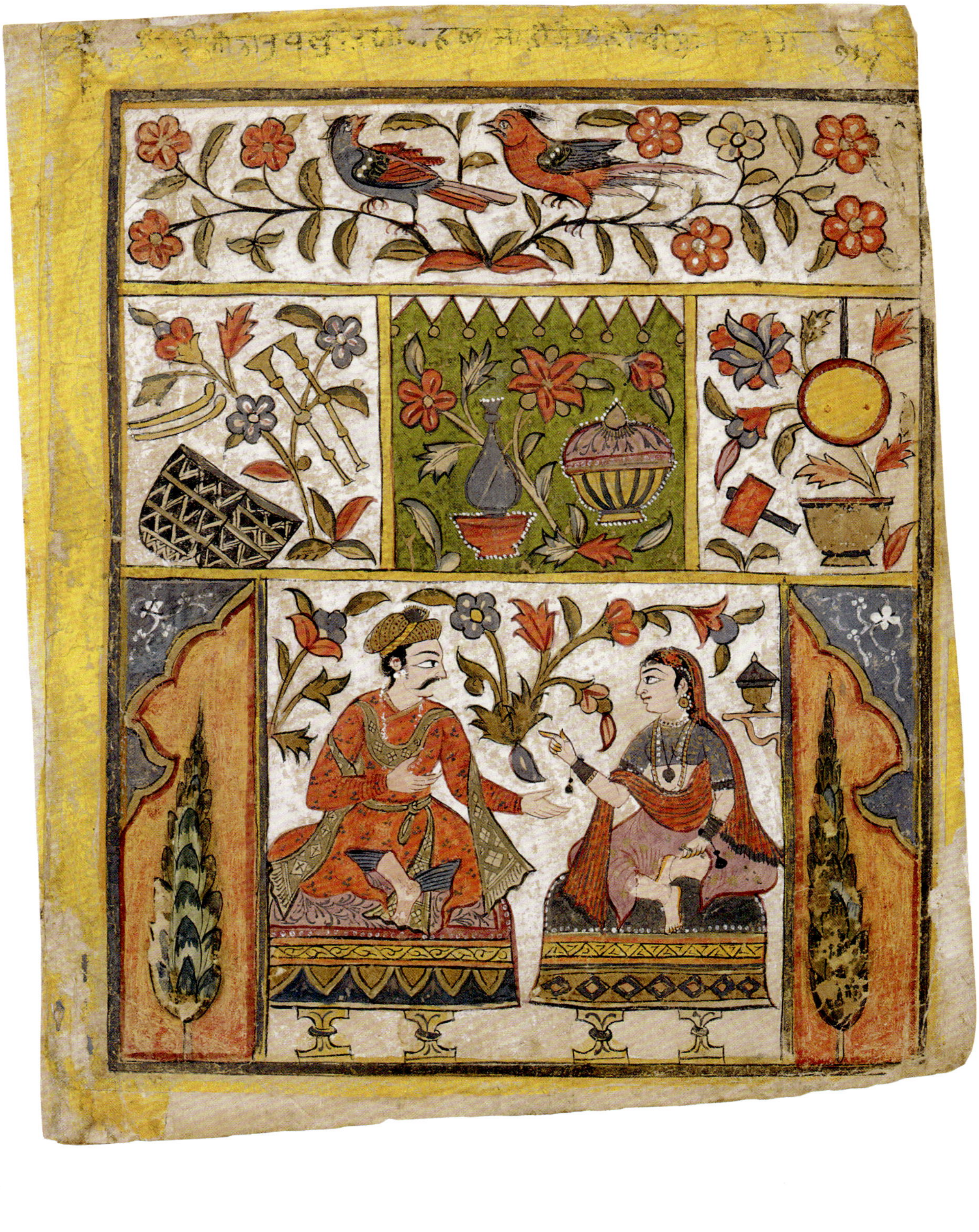

59

A couple in conversation

ILLUSTRATION TO A DISPERSED SERIES OF THE BHAGAVATA PURANA, BOOK X

Gujarat, probably at Surat, early eighteenth century
Opaque watercolor on paper
Indistinct, abraded devanagari inscription above, numbered 7..?
26.7 × 21.6 cm (10 ½ × 8 ½ in.)

SEATED ON ADJACENT THRONES IN A CHAMBER, a couple in courtly dress converse, with appropriate hand gestures. They may perhaps be the parents of Krishna: Vasudeva, minister of King Kansa, and his wife Devaki. Huge flowering tendrils fill the white space around them, and a lidded vessel stands on a wall-bracket. The scene is framed by a broken arch, with flanking cypress trees. In three rectangular panels above, more flowering plants appear, interspersed with auspicious vessels in the center, and *naqqara* kettledrums, horns, and other instruments to the sides. In the upper panel, two birds perch on a flowering shrub.

This page belongs to a *Bhagavata Purana* series from Gujarat in Western India. Said to have comprised seventy pages before its dispersal around 1950 by a Delhi dealer, it is sometimes called the Tula Ram series after him.[1] Vigorously painted, if somewhat rustic in style, this compartmented assemblage of semi-decorative vignettes bears out Kramrisch's observation that "spontaneity and archaism commingle" in the execution of this manuscript.[2] Its floral, vegetal, and figural elements, unusually set against pallid whitish or yellow grounds, suggest a close aesthetic relationship with the decorative repertoire of contemporary Gujarati printed and embroidered textiles.[3]

AT

1 H. Goetz, "A new key to early Rajput and Indo-Muslim painting: A unique Bhagavata Purana (Dasama Skandha) album from south western Marwar," *Roopa-Lekha*, XXIII, 1–2, 1952, p.2; also e.g. Welch and Beach, 1965, no. 15; Spink, 1971, figs. 25, 51; Welch, 1973, no. 15; Pal, 1978, no. 9; Isacco and Dallapiccola, 1982, fig. 40; Tandan, 1982, fig. 14; Kramrisch, 1986, nos. 39–42; Beach, 1992, fig. 162; Poster, 1994, no. 182; Dye, 2001, no. 126.

2 Kramrisch, *op. cit.*, p. 165.

3 As noted by Beach, *op. cit.*, p. 206, who first attributed the set to Surat, by comparison with a *Devi Mahatmya* series of 1719 (*ibid.*, fig. 163).

60

Krishna manifests himself as the cowherd boys and calves

ILLUSTRATION TO THE BHAGAVATA PURANA, BOOK X, CH. 13

Bikaner, Rajasthan, ca. 1690
Opaque watercolor on paper
24.8 x 33.7 cm (9 ¾ x 13 ¼ in.)
Hindi inscription on verso describing the subject (beginning: *dasama rai adhyay 13 panau 51*; "tenth book, chapter 13, page 51")
Published: T. McInerney, *Indian paintings from the Polsky Collections*, Princeton, 1982, no. 9

ONE DAY, WHEN KRISHNA'S PLAYMATES, the young cowherd boys (*gopas*), took their calves out to pasture, the powerful god Brahma stole them away and hid them, as a challenge to the child-god. Realizing the nature of this trick, Krishna miraculously transformed his own self into the living forms of the missing boys and calves, through his divine power of illusion (*maya*).[1] He then led them all home to Vrindaban, where the new-made boys and calves were received as their own by their mothers, and thus life carried on as usual. When Brahma returned, after an instant of his time (which is a year in human time), he was amazed at this divine impersonation. Restoring the original captives to their homes, he paid homage to Krishna.

In this page from a dispersed *Bhagavata Purana*, Krishna leads home the gopas and herd that he has just created. In the distance, the four-headed Brahma sits imperturbably enthroned, while the real gopas and calves slumber before him. This refined and elegant series was produced over a long period at the court of Bikaner, where strong Mughal and Deccani pictorial influences prevailed in the latter half of the seventeenth century.[2] Bikaner itself is surrounded by desert, and the distant, semi-barren country and luminous sky here evoke the local light and landscape.

AT

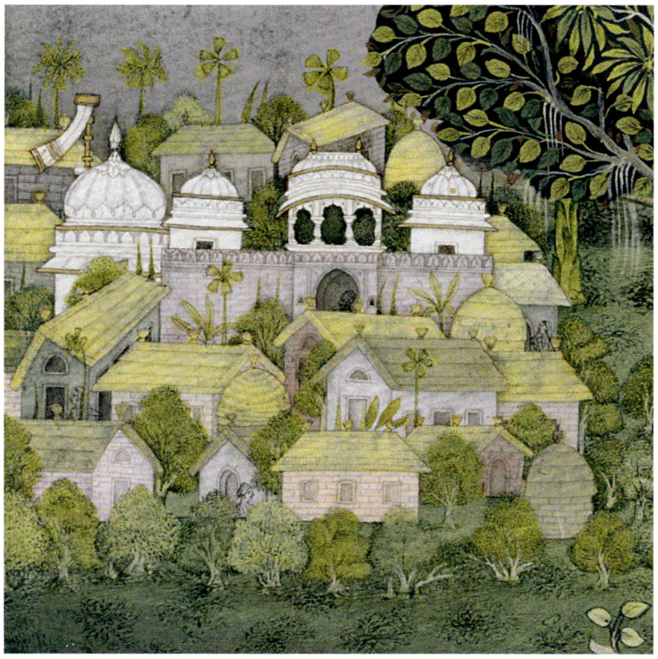

1 Bryant tr., 2003, p. 64.

2 For further Bikaner *Bhagavata Purana* pages, see e.g.: Barrett and Gray, 1963, illus. p. 156; Welch and Beach, 1965, no. 29; Pal, 1978, no. 25; 1978, no. 61; Binney, 1979, no. 24; Ehnbom, 1985, no. 68; Goswamy and Bhatia, 1999, nos. 120–23.

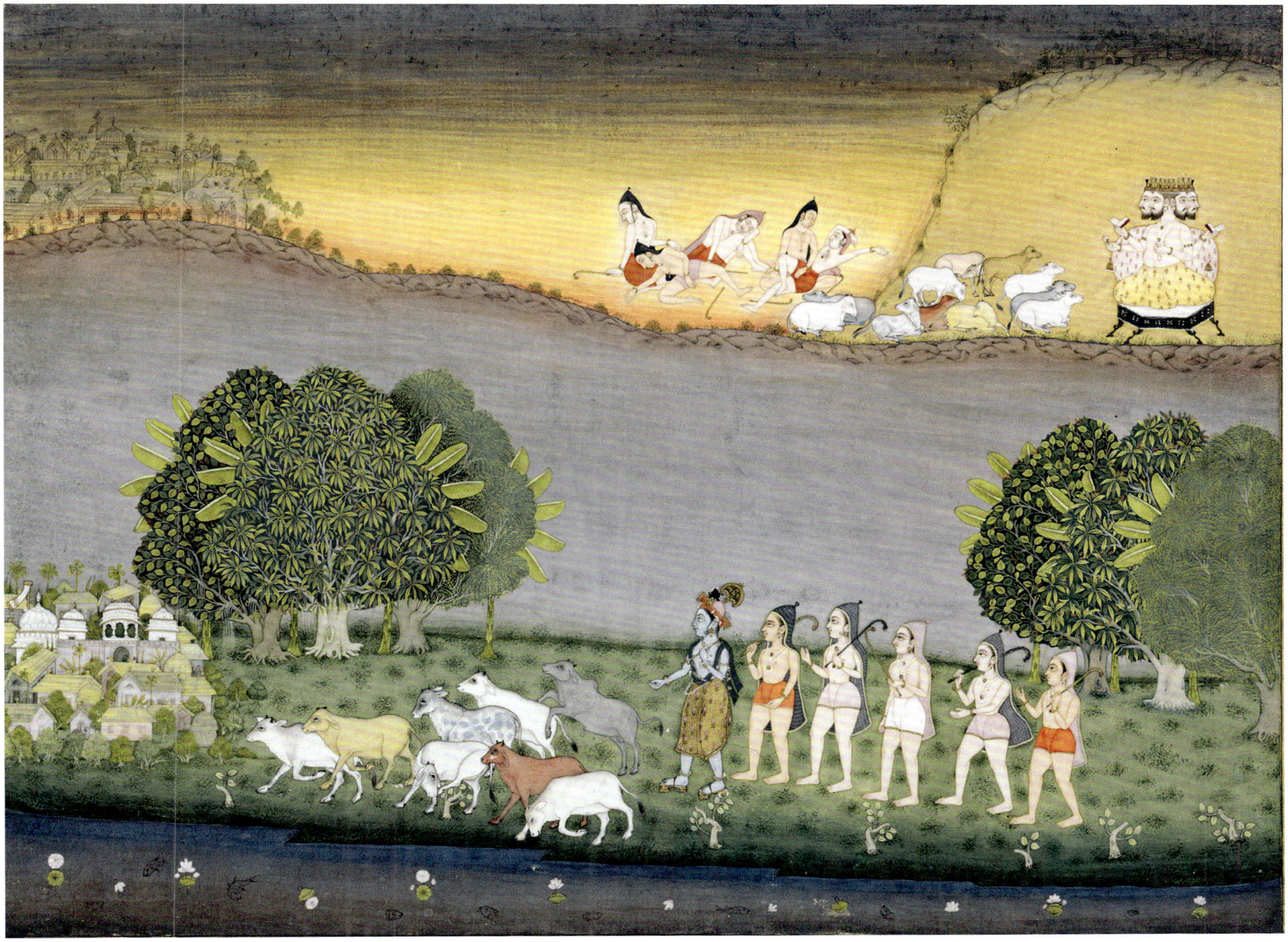

61

Krishna as nayaka is addressed by the sakhi

ILLUSTRATION TO A SERIES OF THE RASIKAPRIYA OF KESHAV DAS

Malwa, Central India, ca. 1640
Opaque watercolor on paper
21 x 17.8 cm (8 ¼ x 7 in.)
Page numbered 255 above; 7 lines of Hindi text on verso (*RP*, ch. 13, vv.1-2)
Published: T. McInerney, *Indian paintings from the Polsky Collections*, Princeton, 1982, no. 5

THE *RASIKAPRIYA* OF KESHAV DAS IS A TREATISE classifying idealized types of lovers (*nayakas* and *nayikas*) and their emotions and behavior, according to traditional poetic theory. Here the nayaka, personified as the archetypal lover Krishna and dressed as a prince, sits holding a betel (*pan*) and a lotus stem within a forest grove. In the absence of his lover, the heroine (*nayika*)—who is similarly personified as Radha), he is here addressed by her companion (*sakhi*). She has the important role of mediator between the lovers. This illustration comes at the beginning of the thirteenth chapter, which deals specifically with the role of the sakhi: "To instruct, entreat, unite, adorn; to stoop, and chide—these are the acts which bosom friends for lovers perform".[1] In the extract, the sakhi then goes on to encourage the nayika in her love, but this is not illustrated here. Instead the nayaka appears, and the sakhi likewise exhorts him to go to his lover and help to adorn and beautify her.[2]

This page is from a lengthy, dispersed series,[3] painted in the robustly expressive style of seventeenth-century Malwa and Bundelkhand, where Mughal pictorial influence was slighter than in nearby Rajasthan. Local artists continued to work in a simplified version of the Early Rajput style of the previous century, employing schematic palace and landscape compositions characterized by strong color combinations. In the pages of the series, yellow backgrounds alternate throughout with dark blue. In this simple but effective composition, there is a charming contrast between the serious demeanor of the human figures, preoccupied with the eternal complexities of human relations, and the spontaneity of the frisky deer and monkeys leaping between the symmetrical flowering trees.

AT

1 Bahadur tr., 1972, p. 208.

2 *Ibid.*, pp. 208–9.

3 For other pages, see Isacco and Dallapiccola, 1982, pl. 161; Bautze, 1991, nos. 56–58 (with references); Mason et al., 2001, no. 21 (also Kramrisch, 1986, no. 90).

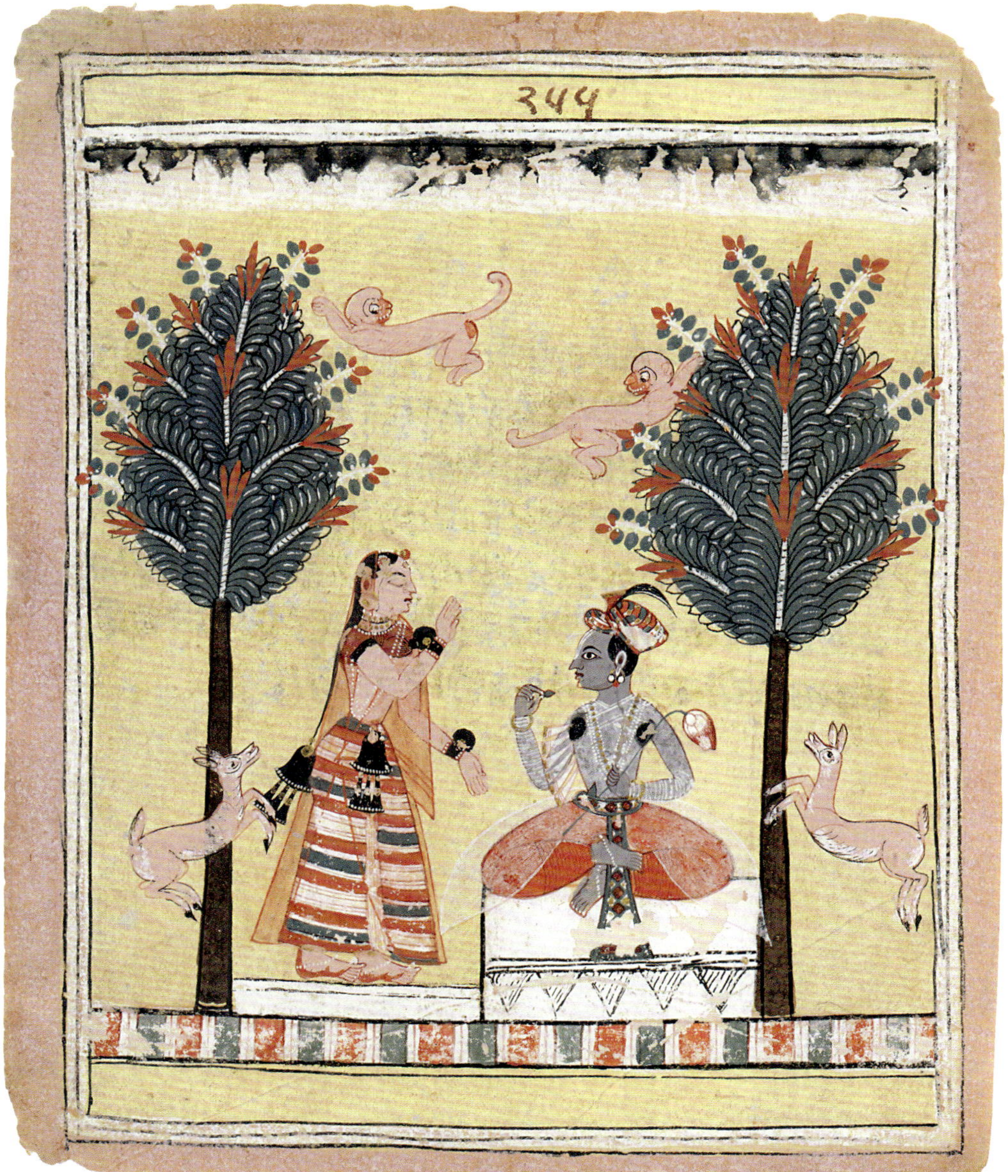

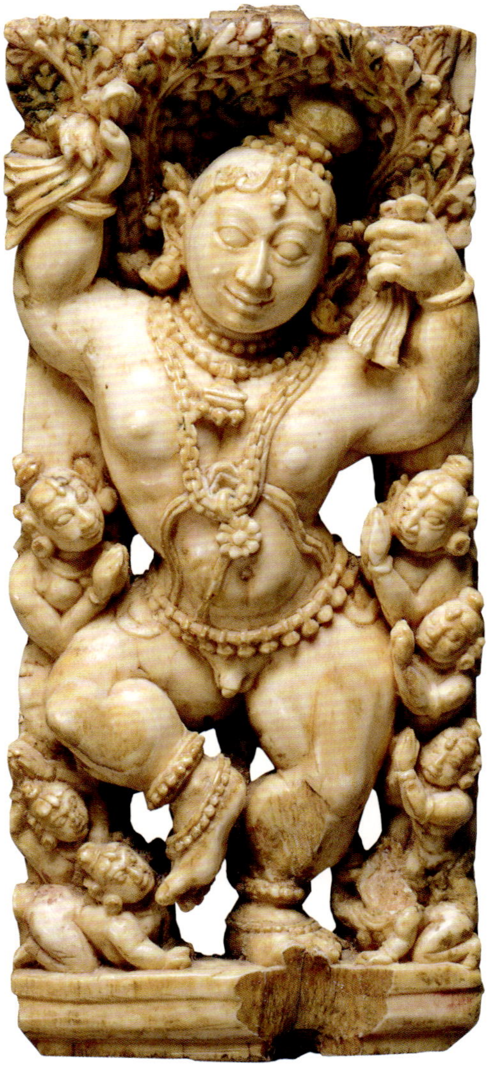

62

Krishna with the gopis' clothes

KARNATAKA, MYSORE, SEVENTEENTH TO EIGHTEENTH CENTURY

Ivory with traces of color
12.1 × 7 cm (4 ¾ × 2 ¾ in.)

THIS FINE IVORY PANEL DEPICTS KRISHNA, in the form of Balakrishna ("child Krishna"), dancing, with right leg raised. He is naked apart from his elaborate jewelry, consisting of earrings, an array of necklaces (one with an amulet), a jeweled belt, ankle bands and wristbands. The child-god's dance sometimes refers to his victory over the serpent-demon Kaliya, on whose head he danced in triumph. But here, with arms raised, he holds garments in his hands. Beside him are seven smaller figures representing the gopi girls, whose clothes he stole as a young man while they bathed in the river, so compelling them to reveal their nakedness to him (cat. no. 58). Their hands are clasped together in modest entreaty. An arch of thick foliage appears overhead.

This sculpture would originally have been placed in a small shrine, dedicated to Krishna or to Vishnu, of whom he is an incarnation. Its quality is outstanding, with sensitive modeling of the body and crisp definition of the jewelry of Krishna. The carving is almost three-dimensional, with the plaque cut through around the dancing god. The jewelry is an accurate representation of known examples: for instance, the amulet case.[1] An ivory panel with the same subject matter is in the British Museum.[2] A sixteenth-century ivory figure of Balakrishna holding two butter balls, also carved in Karnataka, is in the Los Angeles County Museum;[3] it shows Krishna facing forward toward the viewer, without the movement of this example.

MCS

1 Untracht, 1997, pp. 126–35.

2 M. Willis, "Early Indian ivory," *Arts of Asia*, 28, no. 2, March–April 1998, no. 136, p. 116.

3 Pal, 1988, no. 133, p. 255.

63

Ivory comb depicting Krishna as butter thief

ORISSA, SIXTEENTH CENTURY

8.9 × 7.6 cm (3 ½ × 3 in.)

THIS IVORY COMB (*PANAVA*) HAS A SINGLE ROW of teeth and a prominent decorative panel. The central dancing figure of a plump child represents the young Krishna (Balakrishna), holding the balls of butter which he has stolen from his foster-mother Yashoda's larder. Flanked by two dancing female musicians playing a drum and castanets or cymbals, Krishna wears jewelry and a tiered headdress and holds a butterball in each hand. A framing arch appears above, with two hanging swags or tassels. The remains of a red pigment indicate that the comb was originally polychromed.

An Orissan bronze figure of a dancing Krishna with a similar headdress is in the Los Angeles County Museum,[1] and an Orissan ivory sculpture in the round of Krishna fluting is in the National Museum, New Delhi.[2] Attributed to the seventeenth century, the Delhi figure has more elaborate and detailed jewelry than is shown on this comb and was probably made later. Another comb from Orissa with one row of teeth and depicting an episode from the life of Krishna is in the National Museum, New Delhi.[3] Orissan ivory carving was featured in the nineteenth century exhibitions of Indian art and manufactures, along with ivory carving from other centers. Among these, Murshidabad and Travancore were considered the main centers of ivory carving by the late nineteenth century.[4]

MCS

1 Pal, 1988, no. 116.

2 Dwivedi, 1976, fig. 101.

3 Welch, 1985, no. 11, depicting Krishna stealing the gopis' clothes.

4 Mukharji, 1888, repr. Delhi, 1974, p. 275; Watt, 1903, p. 189.

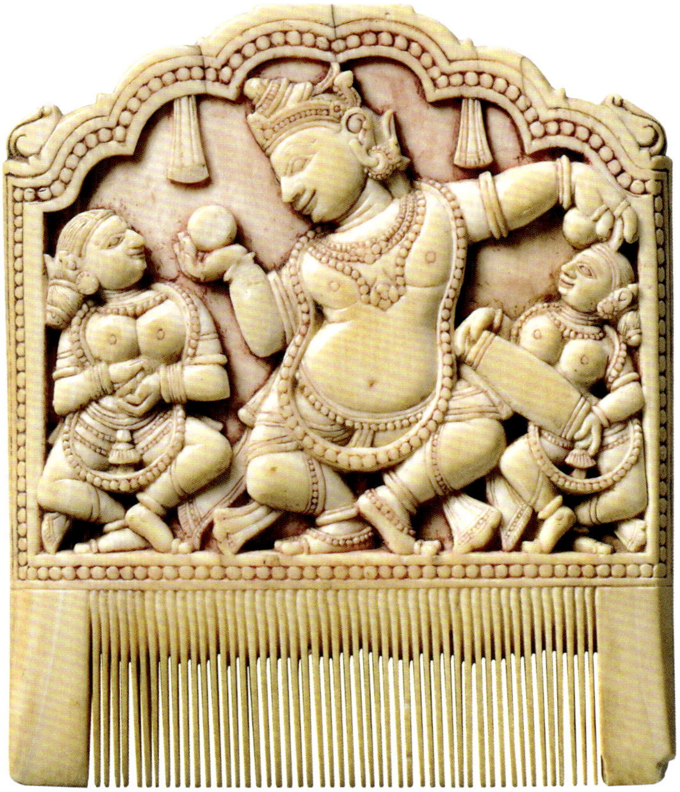

64

Radha makes love to Krishna in the grove

ILLUSTRATION TO THE GITA GOVINDA OF JAYADEVA

Kangra, Punjab Hills, late eighteenth century
Opaque watercolor on paper
(Page trimmed to) 15.4 × 14 cm (6 × 5 ½ in.)
Fragmentary Sanskrit verses on verso

IN THE TWELFTH AND FINAL CANTO of Jayadeva's great lyric poem, Radha goes to her tryst with Krishna in a forest grove at night. To culminate their love-making, she mounts Krishna and takes the active role, until exhaustion finally overcomes her:

Displaying her passion
In loveplay as the battle began,
She launched a bold offensive
Above him
And triumphed over her lover.
Her hips were still,
Her vine-like arm was slack,
Her chest was heaving,
Her eyes were closed...[1]

This inversion by Radha and Krishna of male and female sexual roles became a popular theme in later devotional literature and exegesis.

The painting has been severely trimmed from a horizontal to a square format and rebordered in red, to isolate the amorous scene from its wider landscape setting. In this, it can be related to several other square-cropped (and differently rebordered) scenes of Krishna and Radha's love-making, which were at some time cut down from pages of the Kangra *Gita Govinda* of ca. 1775–80 (cat. nos. 69, 176).[2] The present subject relates quite closely to one such composition in the Museum Rietberg, Zurich,[3] and could perhaps be a later and somewhat less sensitive reworking of it. Krishna here unusually wears a yellow turban not a crown, and the figures of the embracing couple have been inverted. The arbor around them is also simplified, so that the encircling trees no longer provide the lovers with an artful degree of semi-concealment, but act merely as a framing device.

AT

1 Miller tr., 1977, p. 123.

2 E.g. Mason et al., 2002, no. 83; for the Kangra series, see Randhawa, 1963.

3 Goswamy and Fischer, 1992, no. 137; cf. also Archer, 1973, s.v. Kangra, no. 33 (vi).

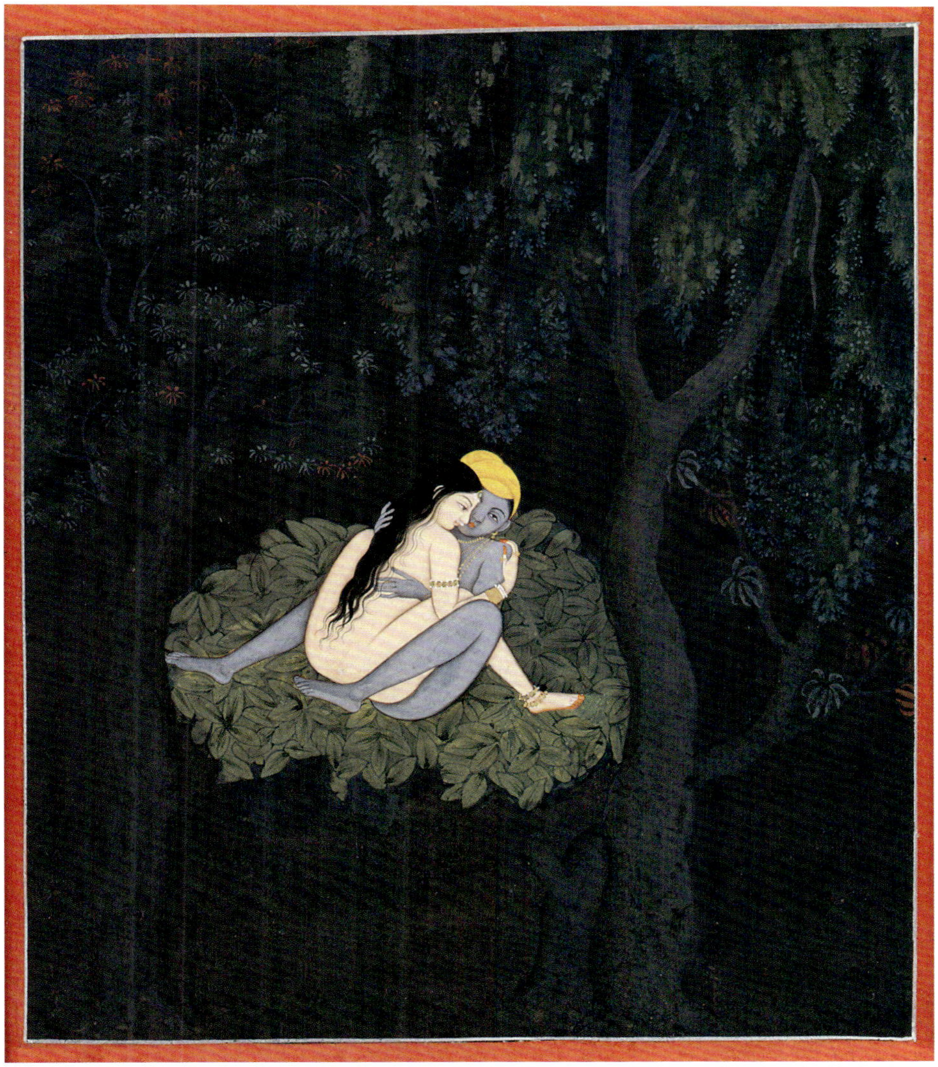

65

Krishna as a prince approaching the village girls

KISHANGARH, RAJASTHAN, CA. 1735–40

Opaque watercolor on paper
28.6 × 43.2 cm (11 ¼ × 17 in.)
Published: T. McInerney, *Indian paintings from the Polsky Collections*, Princeton, 1982, no. 12

AT THE EIGHTEENTH-CENTURY COURT OF KISHANGARH in central Rajasthan, a remarkable stylistic development resulted from a marriage of imperial Mughal painting technique with the emotional intensity of the cult of Krishna and Radha, as exemplified by the devotional poetry of Nagari Das, the pen-name of Prince Savant Singh of Kishnagarh, who succeeded his father Maharaja Raj Singh in 1748. The naturalism of the received Mughal tradition was transformed by a growing stylization of the human figure, with elegantly exaggerated forms, such as the elongated human eye. Horses too were reinterpreted (not least by the leading artist Bhavani Das) with rhythmical curves and exquisitely pretty heads. The results were often aesthetically sublime, but later became perilously sweet and finally overblown.

In this painting, a conventional subject of the later Mughal school—the encounter, with romantic undertones, between a prince on horseback and village beauties at a well[1] —is imaginatively reinterpreted in a classic Kishangarh idiom. Krishna, in princely dress and with royal nimbus, rides a magnificent stallion with henna-stained lower quarters, attended by a retinue of parasol and *morchal* (peacock-feather fan)-bearers. The gopis, who have come to draw water from a river, gaze wonderingly at him. One of them, presumably intended for Radha, half-swoons on seeing him. Beyond, a great plain stretches away in the manner of contemporary Mughal painting of the Muhammad Shah period, with an elaborate walled reservoir, distant villages and hills, royal elephants at play, and army encampments on the horizon. Krishna here is not only the devotional hero but a majestic monarch, commander of all he surveys.

AT

1 E.g. Falk et al., 1979, no. 26; for an orthodox Kishangarh version of the same subject, Welch and Beach, 1965, no. 33 (col. pl.).

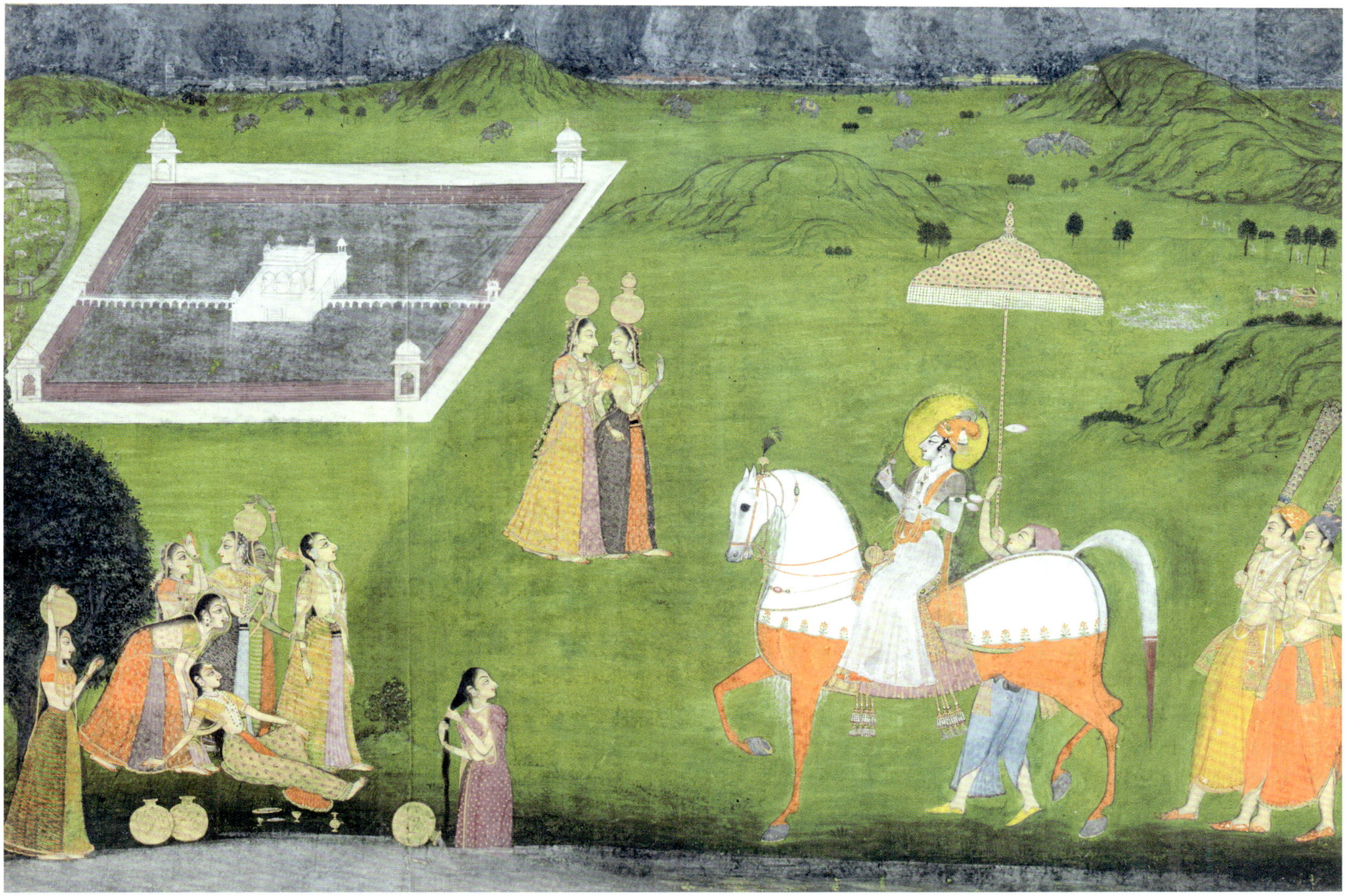

66

Krishna requests the Syamantaka jewel from Satrajit

ILLUSTRATION TO THE BHAGAVATA PURANA, BOOK X, CH. 56

Guler-Basohli style, Punjab Hills, ca. 1760–65
Opaque watercolor on paper
28.6 × 39.4 cm (11 ¼ × 15 ½ in.)
Two lines of Sanskrit text on the verso, with further devanagari and gurmukhi inscriptions
Published: T. McInerney, *Indian paintings from the Polsky Collections*, Princeton, 1982, no. 20

WHEN KRISHNA, IN LATER LIFE, ruled by the sea at Dvaraka, a prince of the Yadava clan named Satrajit was granted the Syamantaka jewel by the Sun-god. This magic gem brought wealth and protection to the virtuous but misfortune to the wicked. One day Krishna requested the jewel from Satrajit, to present it to the king of Mathura. "But, addicted to his wealth, Satrajit did not give it. Nor did he reflect upon what his refusal might mean."[1] Subsequently, the jewel was lost by his brother, killed by a lion. Krishna, wrongly implicated in this death, then recovered the jewel from the bear Jambavan.[2] He returned it to Satrajit,[3] who in shame offered it back to Krishna, together with his daughter Satyabhama. Krishna accepted the latter and she became one of his eight principal wives.

The fateful moment which initiated this chain of events is shown with dramatic simplicity. In a stately pavilion (recalling the palace architecture of Mughal Delhi) set in isolation among woods, Krishna has asked for the gem but Satyabhama crosses his wrists, implying his refusal. This page is from the "large" *Bhagavata Purana* in Guler-Basohli style,[4] painted a generation later than the ca. 1740 series by Manaku of Guler, and attributable in part to his son Fattu.

AT

1 Bryant tr., 2003, p. 241, v.12.

2 Welch and Beach, 1965, no. 54, for this scene, from the same series.

3 Archer, 1973, s.v. Basohli, no. 22 (XII).

4 E.g. Archer, *loc. cit.*, nos. 22 (i–xiv); Archer, 1976, nos. 8–10; Ehnbom, 1985, no. 112; Kramrisch, 1986, nos. 102–4; Mason et al., 2001, no. 80.

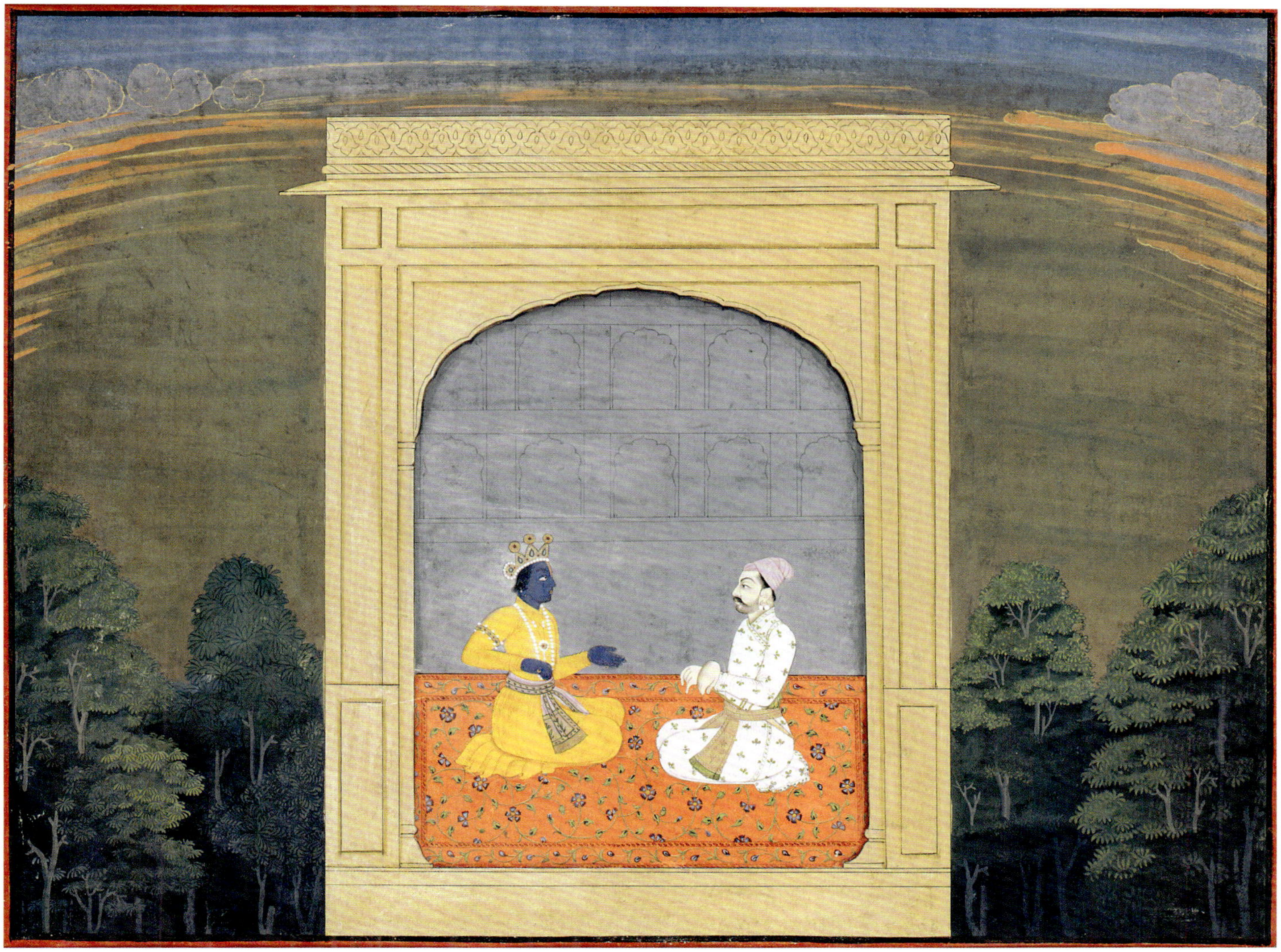

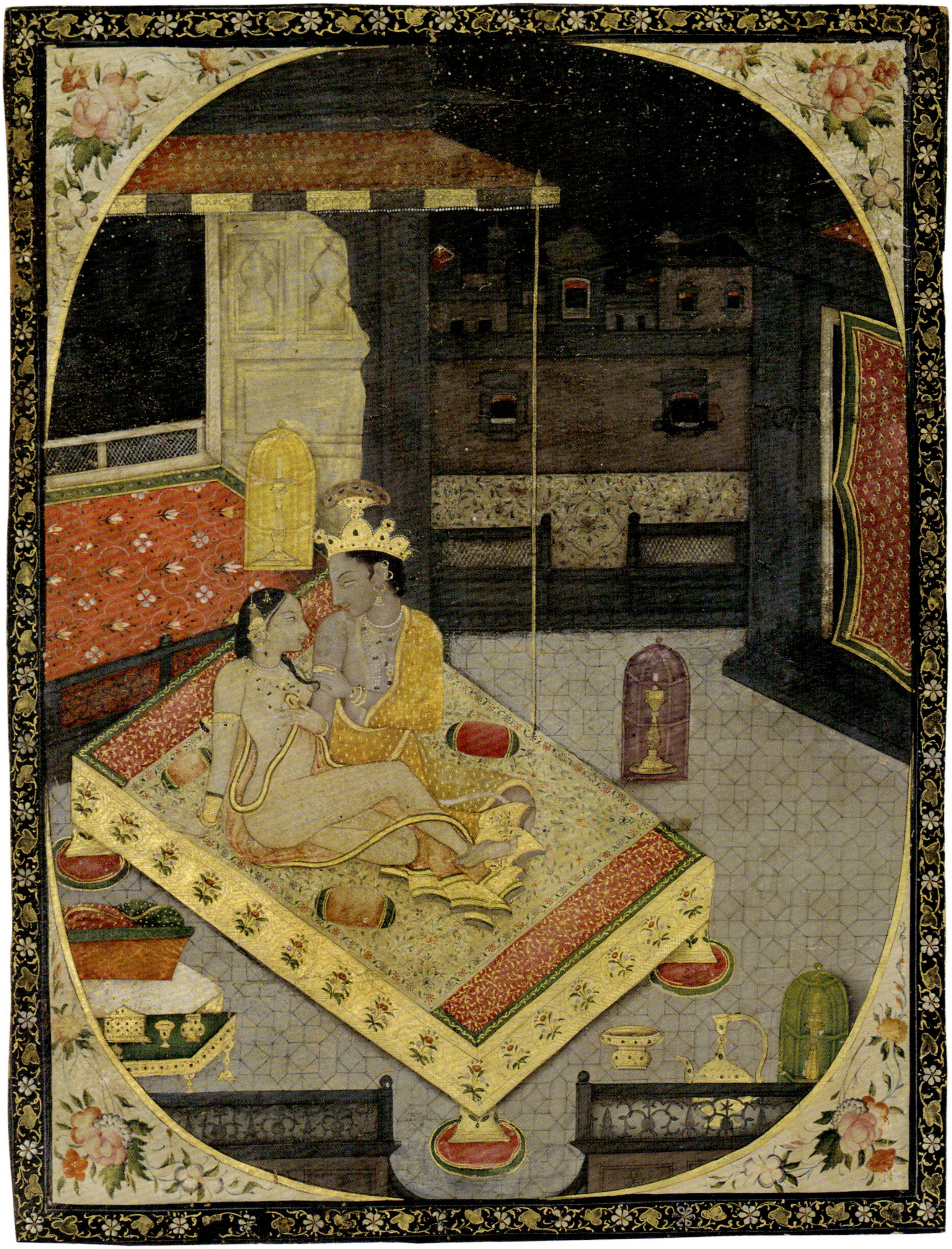

67

Krishna and Radha on a bed at night

SIRMUR (NAHAN), PUNJAB HILLS, CA. 1830

Opaque watercolor with gold on paper
24.8 × 18.7 cm (9 ¾ × 7 ⅜ in.)
Published: W. G. Archer, *Visions of courtly India*, Washington, D.C., 1976, no. 80;[1]
T. McInerney, *Indian paintings from the Polsky collections*, Princeton, 1982, no. 25
Metropolitan Museum of Art, New York, Gift of Cynthia Hazen Polsky (1985.398.13)

IN A COURTLY SETTING FAR REMOVED from the bucolic forests of Vrindaban, Krishna and Radha exchange a tender glance after making love on a palace terrace at night. As Radha gathers her flimsy garment to her breast, Krishna fondles a strand of her hair. Around their gilded and painted bed stand oil-lamps in shades, a ewer and basin, a pan-box, and other vessels. With its sensitive drawing and muted, nocturnal tones, the painting powerfully evokes the rapt atmosphere of the still watches of the night. The composition is framed within an oval cartouche, with European-influenced floral decoration in the spandrels. This very refined example of later Pahari painting has been attributed by W. G. Archer, the eminent authority who once owned it, to the kingdom of Sirmur, with its capital at Nahan.

AT

1 Also: Archer, 1967, no. 43; Archer, 1975, pl. 40.

68

Krishna swallows the forest fire

KANGRA, PUNJAB HILLS, CA. 1790

Illustration to the *Bhagavata Purana*, Book X, Ch. 19
Brush drawing with preliminary coloring on paper
26.6 x 23.5 cm (11 ¼ x 9 ¼ in.)
Picture surface inscribed in devanagari with abbreviated color notations

ONE DAY WHEN KRISHNA, BALARAMA, and the young gopas were playing, their cows strayed and became lost. After a long search, the gopas discovered them in the forest. But then a great forest fire, fanned by the wind, threaten to encircle them. The frightened cowherds turned to Krishna, who calmly told them to close their eyes and not to fear. "When they had closed their eyes, Bhagavan, the supreme Lord of *yoga*, consumed the terrible fire with his mouth, and freed them from danger."[1] In this fluently executed preparatory drawing, with some preliminary coloring in white and red, the gopas huddle trustingly around Krishna and the cows gaze up at him devotedly, in contrast to the terrified birds and beasts of the forest. The great conflagration, which unusually emanates here from the mouth of a flying demon,[2] is calmly scooped into his own mouth by Krishna.

AT

1 Bryant tr., 2003, p. 95, v.12.

2 For earlier, more conventional versions of the subject, see e.g. Archer, 1973, s.v. Basohli, no. 22 (iv); Chamba, no. 29.

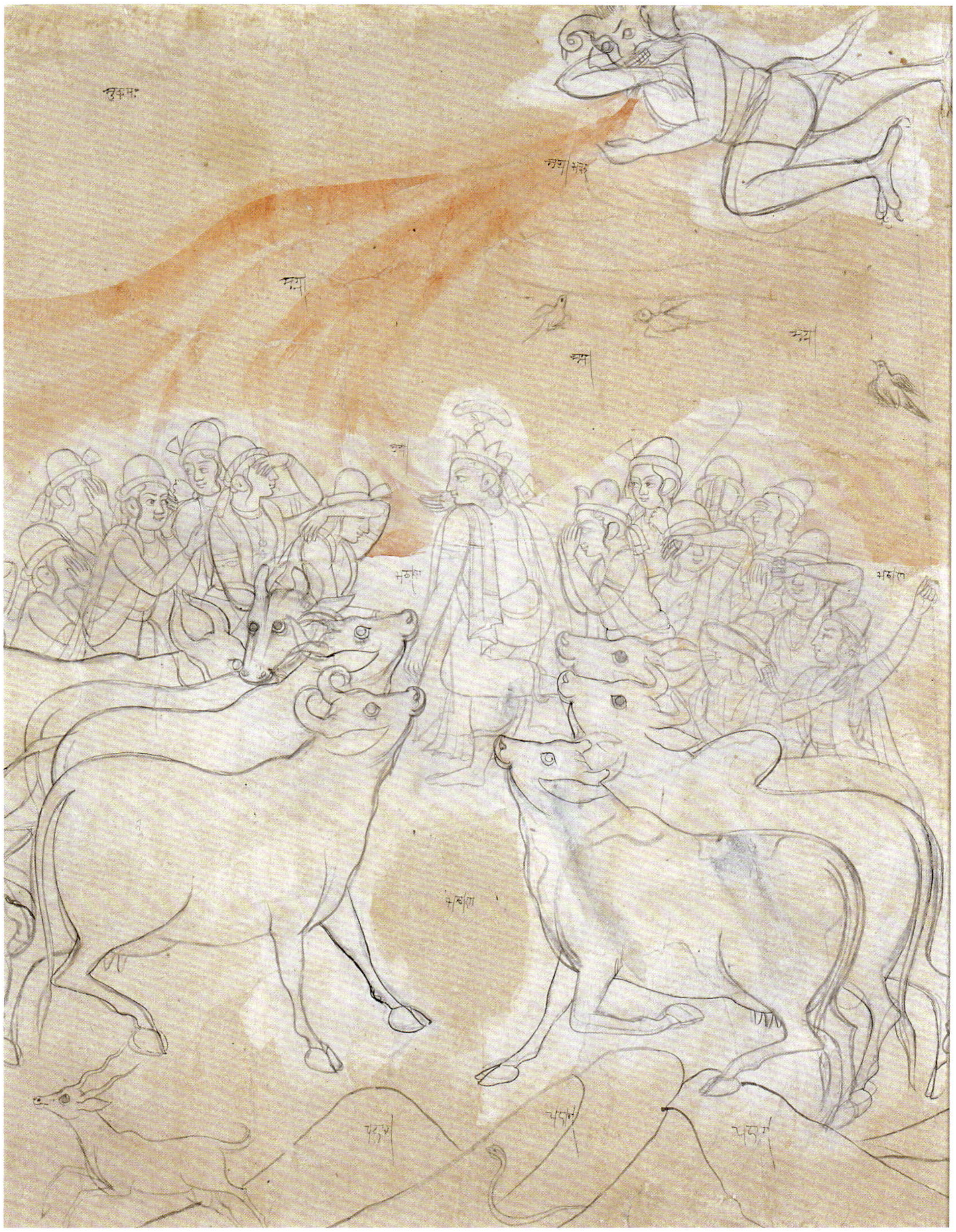

69

Krishna adorns Radha after their love-making

ILLUSTRATION TO THE GITA GOVINDA, BOOK XII

Kangra, Punjab Hills, ca. 1775–80
Opaque watercolor with gold on paper
15.9 x 25.4 cm; (6 ¼ x 10 in.)
Inscribed on verso with fragmentary Sanskrit text (*GG* XII, v.14)
Published: M. S. Randhawa, *Kangra paintings of the Gita Govinda*, New Delhi, 1963, pl. 17

IN THE FINAL CANTO OF JAYADEVA'S *GITA GOVINDA*, Krishna and Radha have passed their climactic night of love in the forest (cat. no. 14). In this final song, Radha, "secure in her power over him," tells the languid Krishna to dress her and adorn her body for her in various ways.[1] In the verse illustrated here, she tells him:

My ears reflect the restless gleam of doe eyes, graceful Lord.
Hang earrings on their magic circles to form snares for love.
She told the joyful Yadu hero, playing to delight her heart.[2]

Radha turns her head aside as Krishna obediently arranges her earrings. They sit close together by the swirling river issuing from rounded, wooded hills. The flowering tree and slender, sinuous willow, which almost touch above them, mirror the serene rapport between the lovers. This famous series, with its tender evocations of love in idyllic landscape settings, was formerly in the Tehri-Garhwal Royal Collection, and may have been among a distinguished group of manuscript series painted for Maharaja Sansar Chand of Kangra soon after his accession in 1775.[3] Opinions have differed as to the hands mainly responsible for it, the most recent suggestion being that it was mainly designed by the great Pahari master Nainsukh.[4]

AT

1 See e.g. Goswamy and Fischer, 1992, no. 134, in which Krishna paints her breast; and Archer, 1973, s.v. Kangra, no. 33 (vi), where he places her anklets on her feet.

2 Miller tr., 1977, p. 124.

3 Randhawa, *Kangra paintings of the Gita Govinda*; Archer, *op. cit.*, Kangra no. 33 (i–vii); see also e.g. Ehnbom, 1985, no. 119; Mason et al., 2001, no. 82.

4 Goswamy, 1997, p. 244.

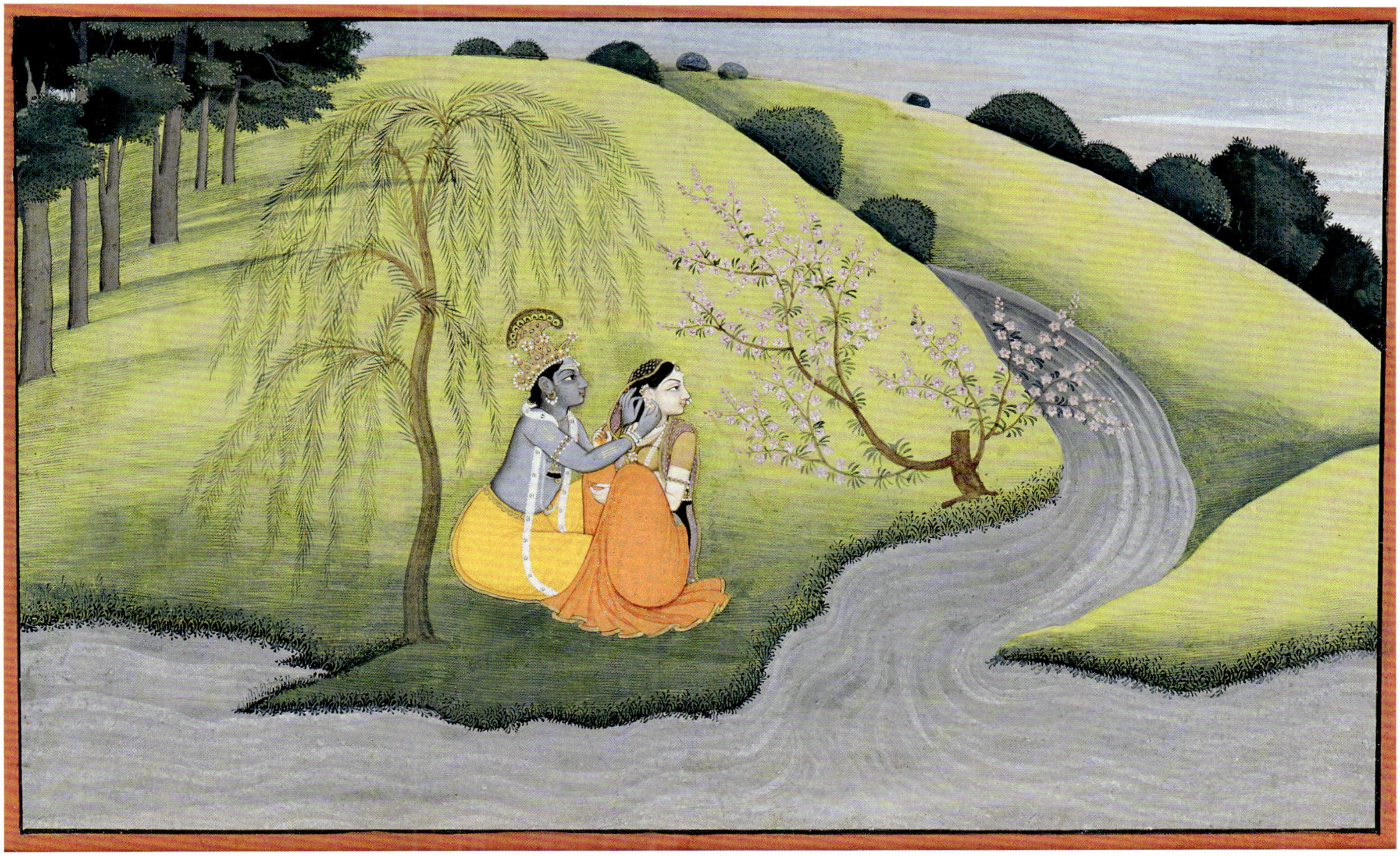

70

The gopi handmaidens of Krishna

PICCHAVAI (PAINTED TEMPLE HANGING)

Deccan, probably Masulipatam, late eighteenth century
White cotton, hand-painted and block-printed
Two devanagari inscriptions in the lower field

DOMINATING THE CENTRAL FIELD, the gopis—more princesses than village milkmaids—present offerings to Krishna. They stand beneath fruit-laden trees, populated by sporting monkeys and birds. The sky is filled with winged angels and celestial chariots transporting gods and goddesses. To the left in the lower field, Krishna is teasing a gopi for her jug of milk; while to the right of the gopis, gopas, and cows stand in attendance at two shrines, one consecrated to Krishna, the other to his brother Balarama.

This remarkable painted cotton is the right section of an imposing temple hanging. The present location of its left section, published in 1976, is unknown. The two sections would have flanked an empty or undecorated central panel of cloth. A sculpted image of the fluting Krishna would have been placed in front of this central void, as a focus for the inner temple sanctum, with the painted gopis as a backdrop, visible to either side.

Hangings of this type are connected with the Vallabhacharya sect of Krishna devotees. Although adherents of the Vallabha sect are found mostly in Northern India, they are also found in small enclaves in the Deccan, established by wealthy trading communities from Gujarat and Rajasthan. This painted hanging must have been made for an important temple or palatial chapel, as it stands apart from the mass of Krishna cult picchavais in richness of materials and pictorial finesse. In terms of style it is virtually unique, apart from a slightly later, iconographically related example with separate added borders, in the Tapi Collection, Bombay.[2]

TM

1 Neven, 1976, pp. 58, 112, no. 154.

2 Barnes et al., 2002, no. 81, pp. 202–3; two later, nineteenth-century pichhavais in the same general style are in the Prince of Wales Museum, Bombay, and the Jagdish and Kamla Mittal Museum, Hyderabad: S. Andhare, "Notes on some recent acquisitions," *Bulletin of the Prince of Wales Museum*, 11, 1971, pp. 66–68, figs. 65–67; Gittinger, 1982, p. 78, no. 69.

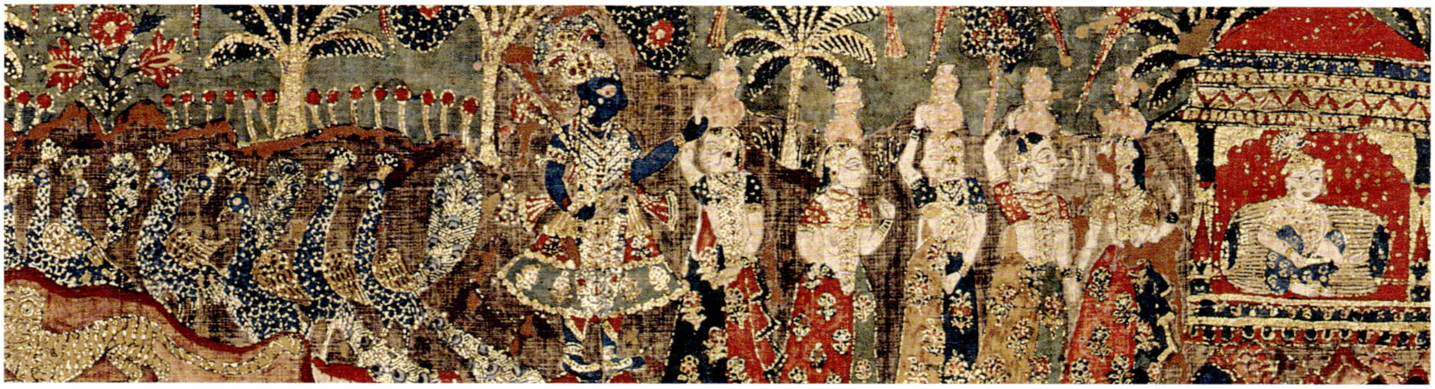

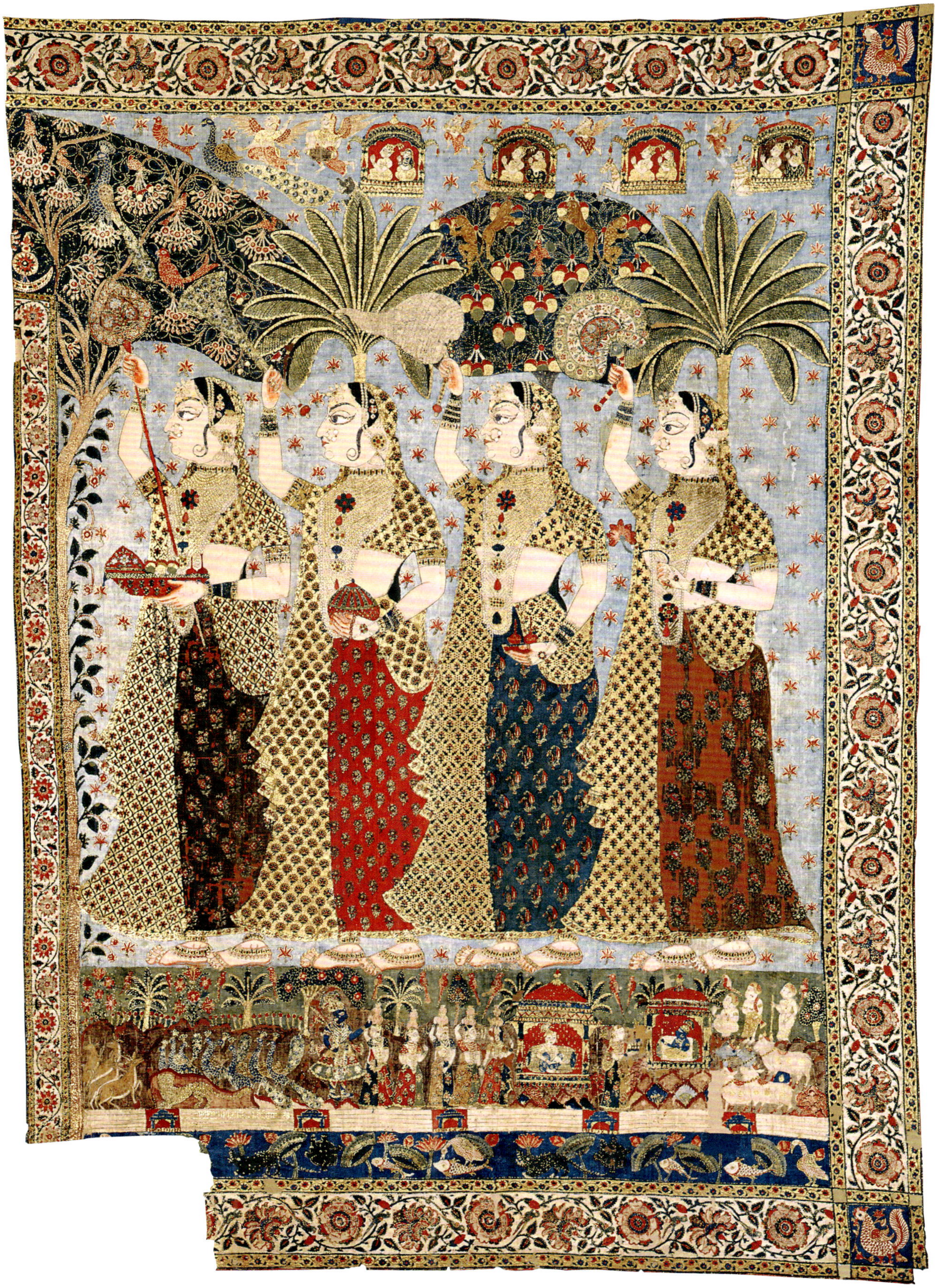

71

Krishna and Radha in a grove

KOTAH, RAJASTHAN, CA. 1720

Opaque watercolor on paper
19.1 × 11.1 cm; (7 ½ × 4 ⅜ in.)
Metropolitan Museum of Art, New York, Cynthia Hazen Polsky and Leon B. Polsky Fund (2003.178a, b)

NOBLE LOVERS, OFTEN PERSONIFIED AS KRISHNA AND RADHA, standing in close embrace in a flowering grove or hastening to a woodland tryst, were a popular pictorial theme in the Bundi-Kotah region of Rajasthan. Carrying floral garlands, Krishna and Radha gaze into each other's eyes as they promenade in a grove under a vivid sky. The forest setting is a masterpiece of luxuriance, with its deep verdure textured with stippled shading, its explosive palm trees, bursting blossoms, and flowering sprays, its perching birds and peacocks and clustered pairs of ducks and waterfowl in the foreground lotus pool. This bravura treatment of a familiar theme, as well as the facial types and other elements, suggest the style of the early eighteenth-century painter called by Welch the Kotah Master,[1] or else a close follower. Although there is no indication that the picture illustrated a manuscript series, its subject is a classically literary one, in a poetic tradition going back several hundred years to the time of Jayadeva.

On the reverse of this painting, a later eighteenth-century Jaipur painter has added another, very different image of Krishna. Here he is shown with nimbus and in full face, more like an icon to be worshipped, as he plays the flute whose music seduced the gopis.[2]

AT

1 S. C. Welch, "Kotah's lively patrons and artists," in Welch et al., *Gods, kings and tigers: The art of Kotah*, Munich, 1997, pp. 17–30.

2 At the Jaipur court of this time the devotional cult of Krishna was expressed particularly in the form of *Raslila* dance dramas, in which female or boy dancers enacted the divine plays (*lilas*) of Krishna with the gopis for the Maharaja. Similar figures were also depicted in large and boldly delineated cartoons for wall-paintings. With his statuesque dancer's pose, balancing easily on one foot, his trailing side-locks and widely flaring jama skirt, this Krishna has the air of a contemporary *Raslila* player who assumes the cowherd god's iconic pose in a palace setting.

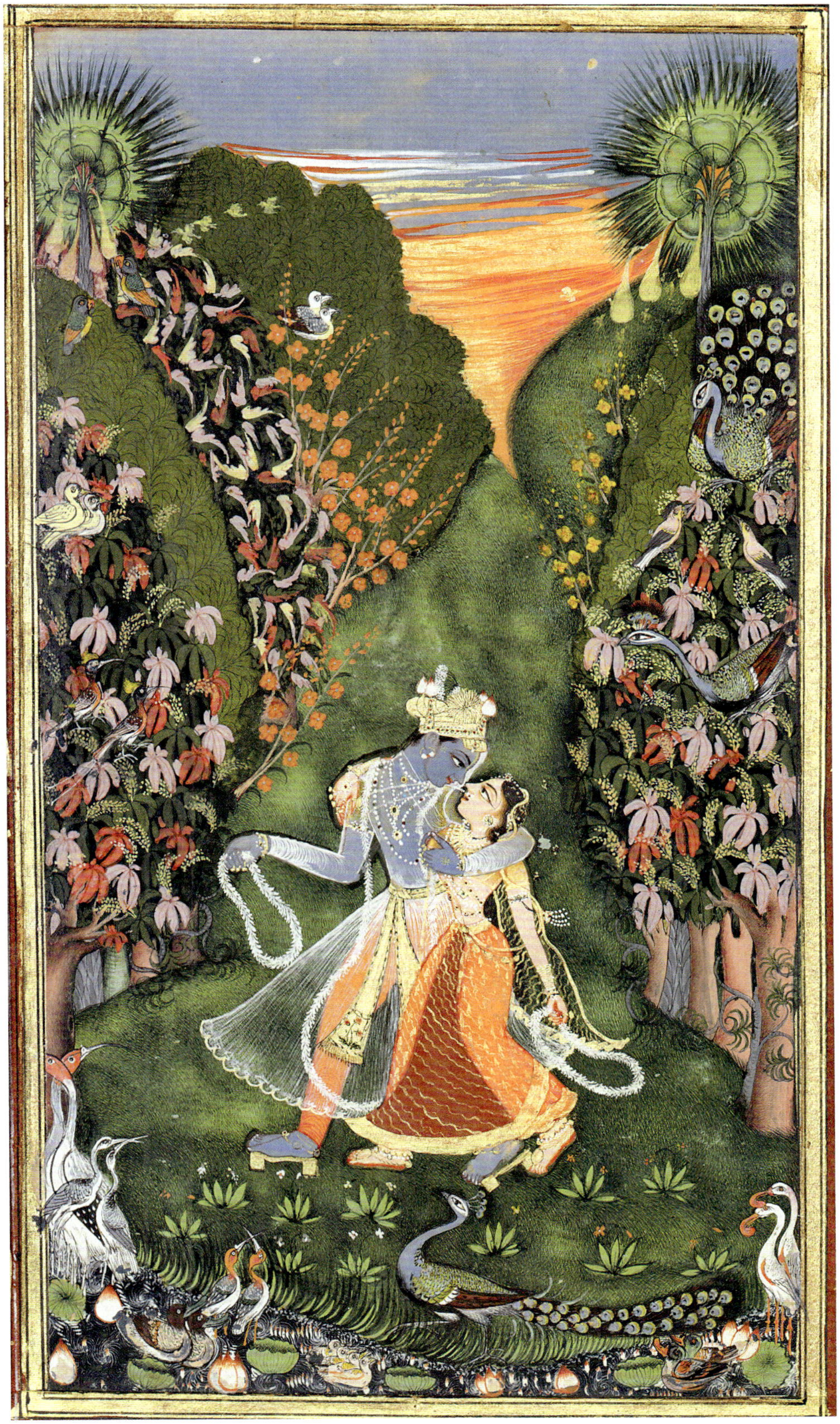

GODDESSES

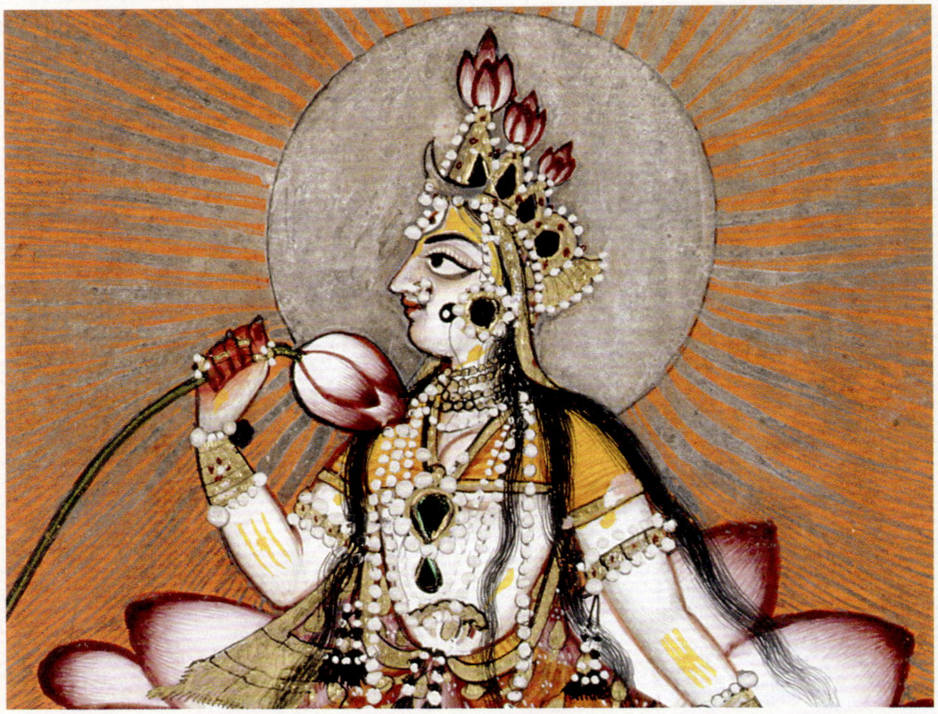

Worship of the Mother Goddess is very ancient in India. It is attested by the many surviving terracotta female figurines or carved ring-stones, presumably representing nature or fertility goddesses, which date in some cases from the Indus Valley civilization (ca. 2000 BC) and, in greater numbers, from the period ca. 200 BC – AD 200. But in the absence of any docu-mentation, little is known about their cults. The later generic Sanskrit word for a goddess is *devi*. This may refer to a primitive local nature deity, or to such a deity who has been promoted to wife of one of the principal gods, or else to those goddesses who, for example, personify the earth (Bhu), the dawn (Ushas) and night (Ratri), or the sacred rivers (Ganga, Yamuna, and others). During the early centuries AD, various goddess figures, benign or destructive, were absorbed into the mythology of the Great Goddess (Mahadevi), who represents the *shakti* or cosmic energy of Shiva. This syncretism partly accounts for the strongly contrasting characteristics of the Devi's divine nature: she is at once the alluring maiden and the fierce hag; the loving mother and the bringer of disease and death. She is the mild consort Parvati, the warrior Durga, the horrific destructress Kali, the smallpox goddess Shitala, and she has many other forms besides.

The systematic elaboration of the active female divine principle is first expressed in a text of the fifth to sixth century, the *Devi Mahatmya*. A central episode is the story of the Goddess's incarnation as Durga, in order to destroy the giant buffalo-demon Mahisha, who through the practice of austerities had gained sufficient power to drive the gods out of their heaven. Durga, the fierce martial form of the Goddess, is a beautiful, yellow-skinned woman who rides a lion (or tiger). Her ten arms hold the various weapons entrusted to her by the gods, who created her and invested her with their joint powers so that she could challenge Mahisha and other arrogant demons: thus she wields Vishnu's discus, Shiva's trident, Agni's flaming dart, and so on. Despite his protean power of changing his form at will, the mighty Mahisha is outmatched and slain by the invincible Goddess. She also wages successful campaigns against another usurping demon called Durga (from whom she derives her own name), and finally the demon brothers Shumbha and Nishumbha. Against them, Durga leads a massed army of *shakti* goddesses into battle, before she finally slays the two brothers in single combat. When all is over, the assembled gods unite in a hymn of praise:

O Goddess, who takes away the sufferings of those who take refuge in you, be gracious:
be gracious, O Mother of the entire world.

Be gracious, O queen of all, protect all; you are the queen, O Goddess, of all that does and does not move.

You have become the sole support of the world, for you abide in the form of earth.
By you who exist in the form of water, all this universe is filled up, O one of inviolable valor...

All the various kinds of knowledge, O Goddess, are portions of you, as is each
and every woman in the various worlds... [1]

AT

1 Tr. T. B. Coburn, in V. Dehejia ed., *Devi: The Great Goddess*, Washington, D. C., 1999, p. 52.

72

Devi on the lotus

ILLUSTRATION FROM THE TANTRIC DEVI SERIES

Basohli or Nurpur, Punjab Hills, ca. 1660–70
Opaque watercolor, gold, silver and beetle-wing cases on paper
20.3 x 20.6 cm (8 x 8 ⅛ in.)
On verso, a Sanskrit verse in praise of the Devi; on the borders a number (38) and identifying inscription in takri script
Published: T. McInerney, *Indian paintings from the Polsky Collections*, Princeton, 1982, no. 18; T. McInerney, "Mysterious origins: The *Tantric Devi* series from Basohli," in V. Dehejia ed., *Devi: The Great Goddess*, Washington, D. C., 1999, fig. 1, p. 125

DEVI, THE GREAT GODDESS, who embodies the cosmic energy (*shakti*) of Shiva, sits resplendent, enthroned on an open lotus rising from the waters. She is crowned, bejeweled and adorned as a princess; small cut fragments of iridescent beetle-wing cases simulate her emeralds. In her hennaed right hand she holds a lotus flower, the attribute of the bountiful goddess Lakshmi. Her nimbus radiates in glory over the hot orange background, with a narrow band of sky above. The Sanskrit shloka on the reverse invokes her thus:[1]

Mother of the three worlds
radiant as a crore of suns
adorned with variegated ornaments.
In my heart I meditate on that goddess
that Absolute One

Devi, whose cult was strong in the Punjab Hill region, has many forms and faces, benign and terrifying. This page belongs to one of the earliest and most powerfully expressive of all Pahari manuscripts, known as the Tantric Devi series.[2] Originally comprising around seventy pages, of which less than half are known to survive, it is a unique iconic sequence of illustrations to short Sanskrit verses invoking the many and diverse esoteric forms of the Goddess. In each page the Devi presides in a different form, either on her own (as here) or with attendant figures. The series may once have served as a book of *darshan* ("seeing," or contemplation of a deity) for a princely devotee, created with true visionary intensity by an exceptionally gifted court painter. With its arresting subjects, vigorous line and vibrant color harmonies, his style has been described by Archer as one of "barbaric magnificence and wild sophisticated luxury."[3]

AT

1 Tr. V. Dehejia, in Dehejia ed., *Devi: The Great Goddess*, p. 391.

2 For a study of this series, see McInerney, "Mysterious origins," in Dehejia, *op. cit.* (and cat. nos. 27–42; pp. 390–91); see also e.g. Archer, 1973, s.v. Basohli, nos. 1 (i–iii); Aijazuddin, 1977, s.v. Basohli, nos. 1 (i–iv); Ehnbom, 1985, no. 87; Goswamy and Fischer, 1992, nos. 7–12; Kossak, 1997, no. 38; Mason et al., 2001, nos. 23–24.

3 Archer, *op. cit.*, I, p. 34.

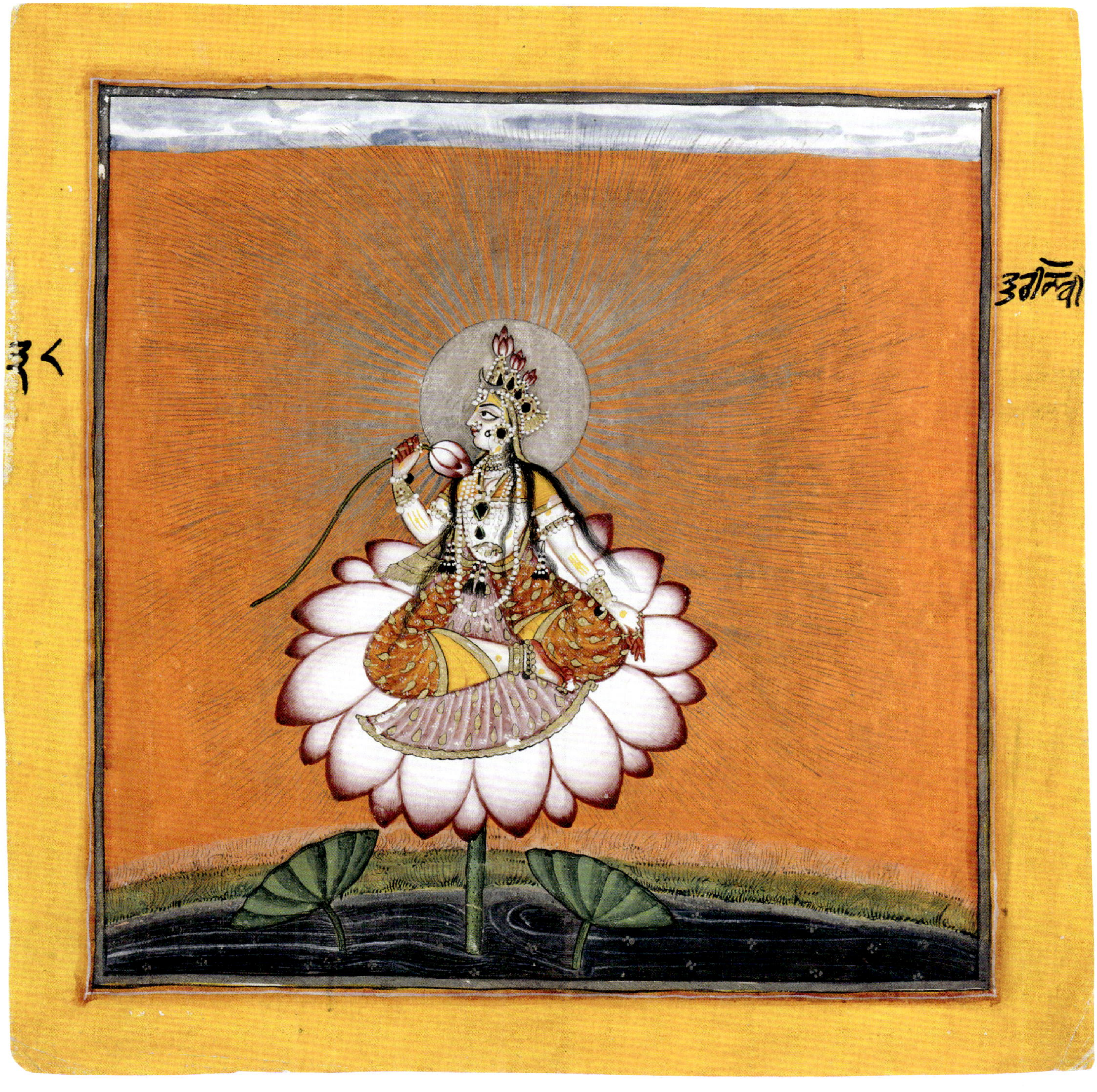

73

Chandika confronts Mahisha the Buffalo-demon

ILLUSTRATION TO THE DEVI MAHATMYA, BOOK 3

Guler, Punjab Hills, ca. 1770
Brush drawing with preliminary color on paper
Abraded devanagari inscriptions on picture surface, numbering above obscured
19.3 x 29.3 cm (7 13/16 x 11 3/4 in.)
Metropolitan Museum of Art, New York, Gift of Cynthia Hazen Polsky (2005.436.2)

THE MAHADEVI OR GREAT GODDESS was created by the gods, in the form of Durga, and invested with their joint powers in order to slay the Buffalo-demon Mahisha who was usurping their celestial kingdom. This was was to be her most famous exploit.[1] In this unfinished drawing,[2] the warrior Goddess, who became known henceforth in this context as Chandika ("the Wrathful"), rides her lion onto the battlefield and challenges Mahisha to single combat. In her many hands she bears the weapons and attributes of Vishnu and other deities, as well as a cup and vessel of strong liquor. Mahisha, who was able to change his form at will, appears as a gigantic buffalo, tearing up mountains with his horns and trampling warriors underfoot, while dark clouds swirl ominously behind him. Soon Durga in her righteous wrath will take a draught of liquor and leap on Mahisha's back. Then, as he changes into his human demonic form, she will decapitate him, to the applause of the assembled gods.[3]

This subject in sculpture and painting has been venerated in India for at least two millennia, as a major religious symbol of the triumph of good over evil. It would also have been of particular inspiration to the martial Rajput nobility, who prized victory in battle as one of the main goals of life.

AT

1 For this narrative, see T. B. Coburn, "The threefold vision of the Devi Mahatmya," in V. Dehejia ed., *Devi: The Great Goddess*, Washington, D. C., 1999, pp. 43–47.

2 For a related drawing from the same series, see Pal, 1978, no. 71; also *ibid.*, no. 62, for a probably later painted version of the present subject, and Aijazuddin, 1977, s.v. Guler, no. 41 (vi).

3 Pal, *op. cit.*, no. 69, for a Guler drawing of this subject.

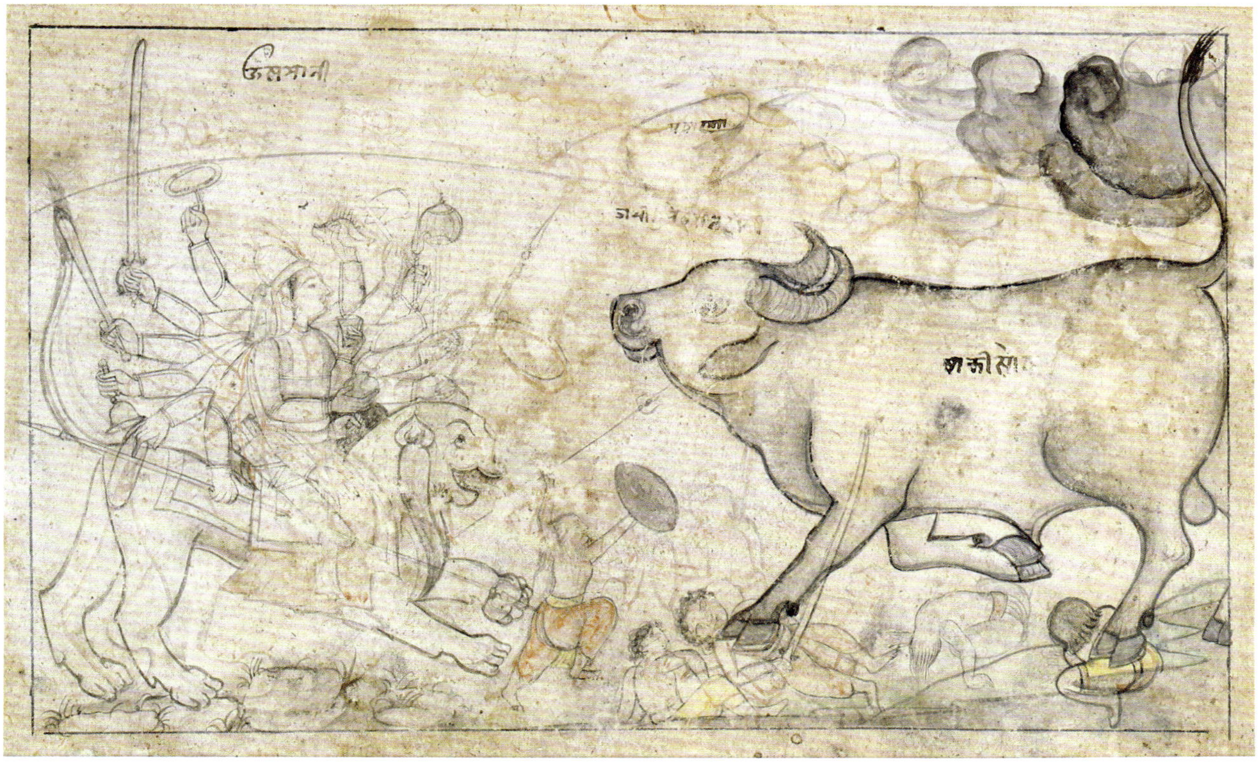

74

Kali advances on Shumbha's army

ILLUSTRATION TO THE DEVI MAHATMYA, BOOK VIII

Guler, Punjab Hills, ca. 1780
Brush drawing with some color on paper
Numbered 33 above; abraded and obscured devanagari inscriptions on upper picture surface
19.8 x 29.8 cm (7 13/16 x 11 3/4 in.)
Metropolitan Museum of Art, New York, Gift of Cynthia Hazen Polsky (1997.390)

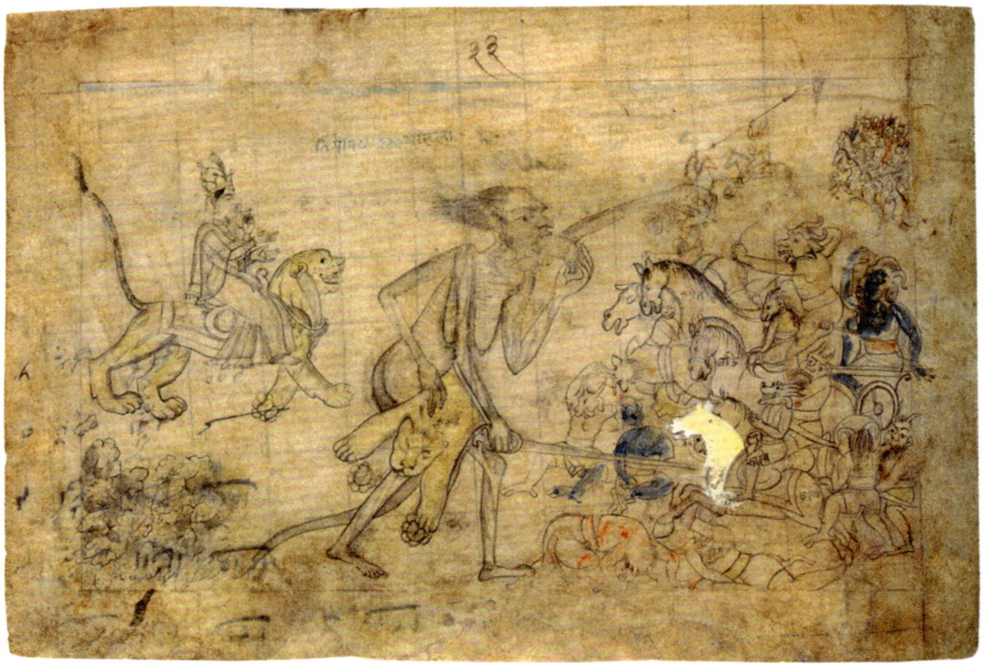

IN THIS DRAWING DEVI, the Great Goddess in the form of Ambika, sits astride her tiger drinking a cup of strong liquor, as she watches the fearsome goddess Kali advance on the armies of the demon Shumbha. Kali has just sprung forth from Ambika's wrathful brow: "with her dreadful face, carrying sword and noose . . . she was shrouded in a tiger skin and looked utterly gruesome with her emaciated skin."[1] Wild-haired, bony, and with sagging breasts, Kali advances remorselessly with sword in hand into the enemy ranks; with another hand she devours an elephant, and with a third she reaches out to seize a pair of chariot-horses. The composition resembles in much of its detail a painted version in the Lahore *Devi Mahatmya* series of 1782,[2] and it may have served as a preparatory drawing for that or a similar series.[3]

AT

1 Tr. T. B. Coburn, in V. Dehejia ed., *Devi: The Great Goddess*, Washington, D. C., 1999, p. 49.

2 *Ibid.*, fig. 6, p. 49; Aijazuddin, 1977, s.v. Guler, no. 41 (xvi).

3 For a later version, see Zimmer, repr. 1963, fig. 57; another, variant composition is in the Victoria and Albert Museum: Dehejia ed., *Devi*, no. 15; Archer, 1973, s.v. Guler, no. 61 (ii).

75

Ivory foot-scraper with Durga and lion

BENGAL, NINETEENTH CENTURY

11.4 × 5.7 cm (4 ½ × 2 ¼ in.)

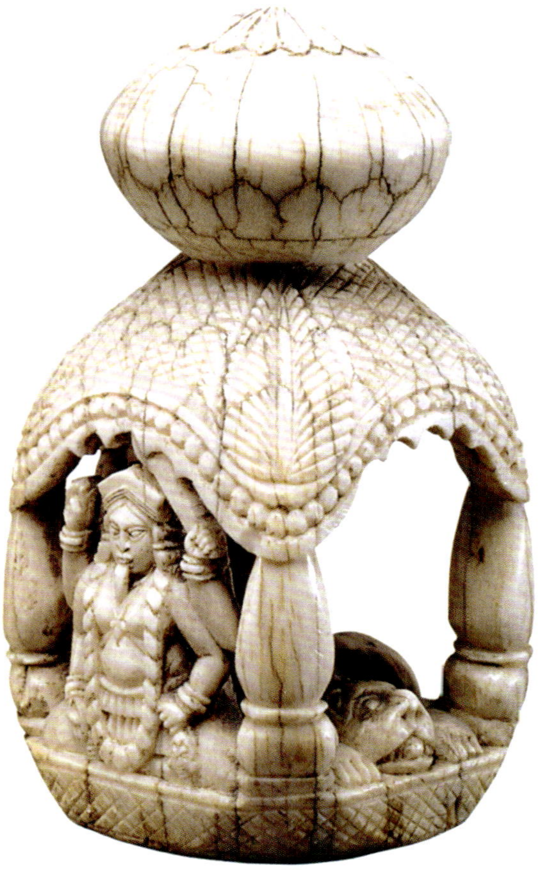

THIS IVORY FOOT-SCRAPER is of architectural form, with four columns at the corners, rising to a sloping curved top with palm fronds and a hatched design across the surface and with a large bulbous finial. At one of the openings is a seated, four-armed goddess holding attributes including a sword, and with a garland of skulls around her neck. At another opening a seated musician plays a stringed instrument, while inside lies a recumbent lion. The presence of the lion and the attributes held by the goddess identify her as Devi in the form of Durga, with her vahana the lion.[1]

The foot-scraper could have had a secular function, as it was not unusual to decorate objects in daily use, such as combs, with religious subjects.[2] It could also have been made for use in the temple, at a ritual cleaning ceremony. An implement in such an expensive material must have been owned either by a senior priest or a Maharaja. Ritual objects of various kinds play an important role in Hindu worship.

The architectural form of the foot-scraper is itself almost temple-like, but also recalls the Mughal imperial marble throne (*jharoka*), with baluster columns and curved (*bangla*) roof, at which the emperor would present himself to his nobles.[3] The iconography of the throne was intended to portray the emperor as semi-divine, and this powerful imagery has been transferred to a Hindu context, in which it is appropriate for the Devi to reside in such a structure.

MCS

1 T. B. Coburn, "The threefold vision of the *Devi Mahatmya*," in V. Dehejia ed., *Devi: The Great Goddess*, Washington, D. C., 1999, pp. 37–58.

2 Pal, 1981, no. 65, p. 76, for a comb with an image of Vishnu.

3 Asher, 1992, pp. 194–95, pl. 119.

76

The smallpox goddess Sitala being worshipped, Calcutta

RAGHUBIR SINGH (1942–99)

Calcutta, West Bengal, 1988
Chromogenic color print
25.3 × 37.5 cm (9 15/16 × 14 7/8 in.)
Published: Raghubir Singh, *The Ganges*, London, 1992, pl. 100
Metropolitan Museum of Art, New York, Purchase, Cynthia Hazen Polsky Gift (1991.1283)

THE HAND OF AN UNSEEN WORSHIPPER scatters an offering to the goddess Sitala at a riverside shrine on the banks of the Hugli at Calcutta. The image of the goddess herself is probably the only partially seen mounted figure in the background, since Sitala was commonly represented as seated on horseback. Smallpox is identified with this goddess across much of Northern India, where she is known as Sitala ("the cool one," possibly in euphemistic avoidance of reference to the intense fever characteristic of the disease) and often simply as Mata ("Mother"). The goddess is equally widely revered in Southern India, where she is worshipped as Mariamman. Although not a part of the original Hindu pantheon, the prevalence of the disease has led to the acceptance of this folk deity in Brahmanical Hinduism and she is considered pre-eminent among the seven disease goddesses. Sitala was seen both as the source of the disease and, by correct religious practice, the means of gaining protection from it, or at least experiencing it in a "benevolent" form, since the smallpox sufferer was also commonly believed to be possessed by the goddess. While there are few temples specifically dedicated to Sitala in Bengal, shrines to the goddess are widespread, ranging from a symbolic pot or decorated stone, to this more elaborate representation.

JF

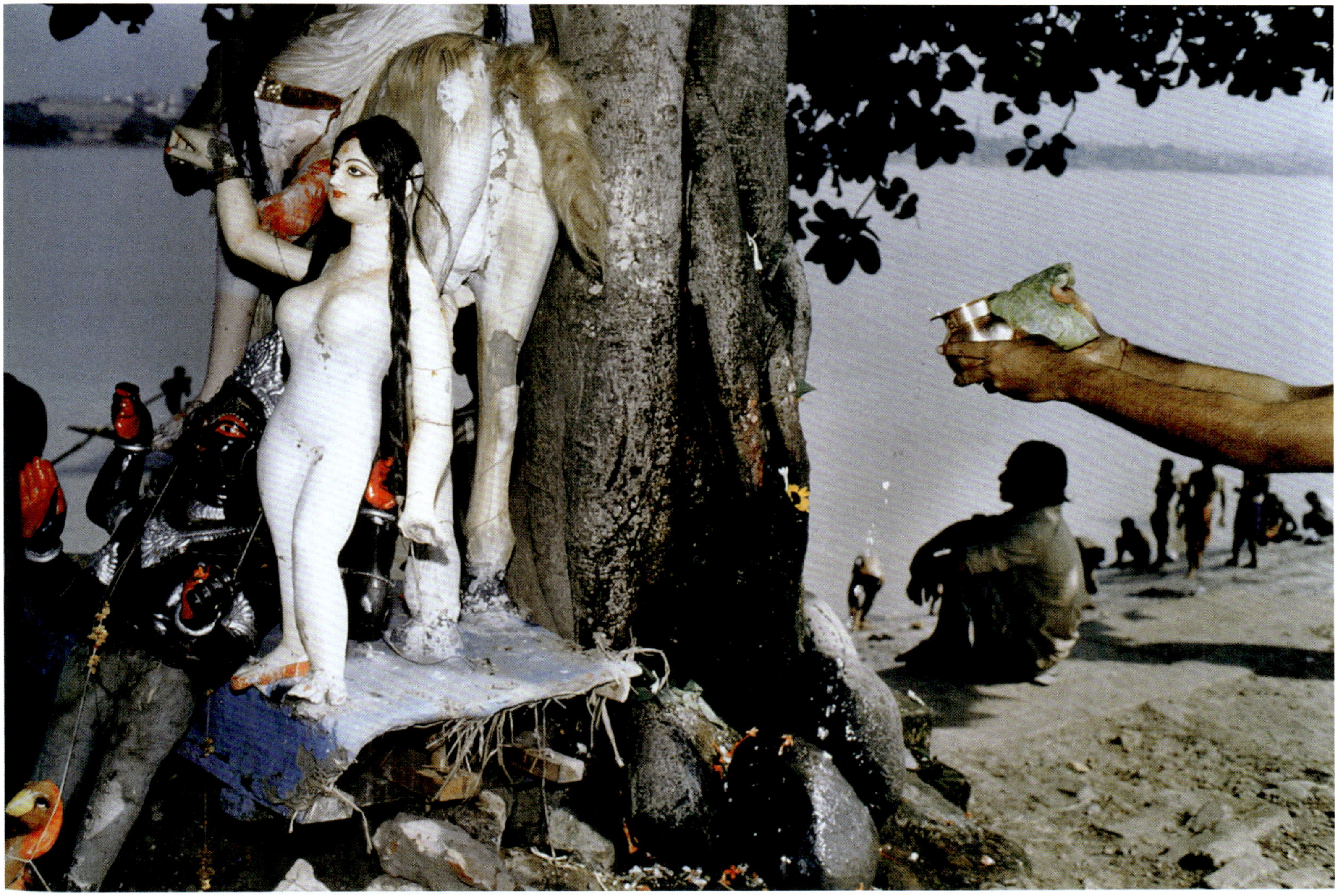

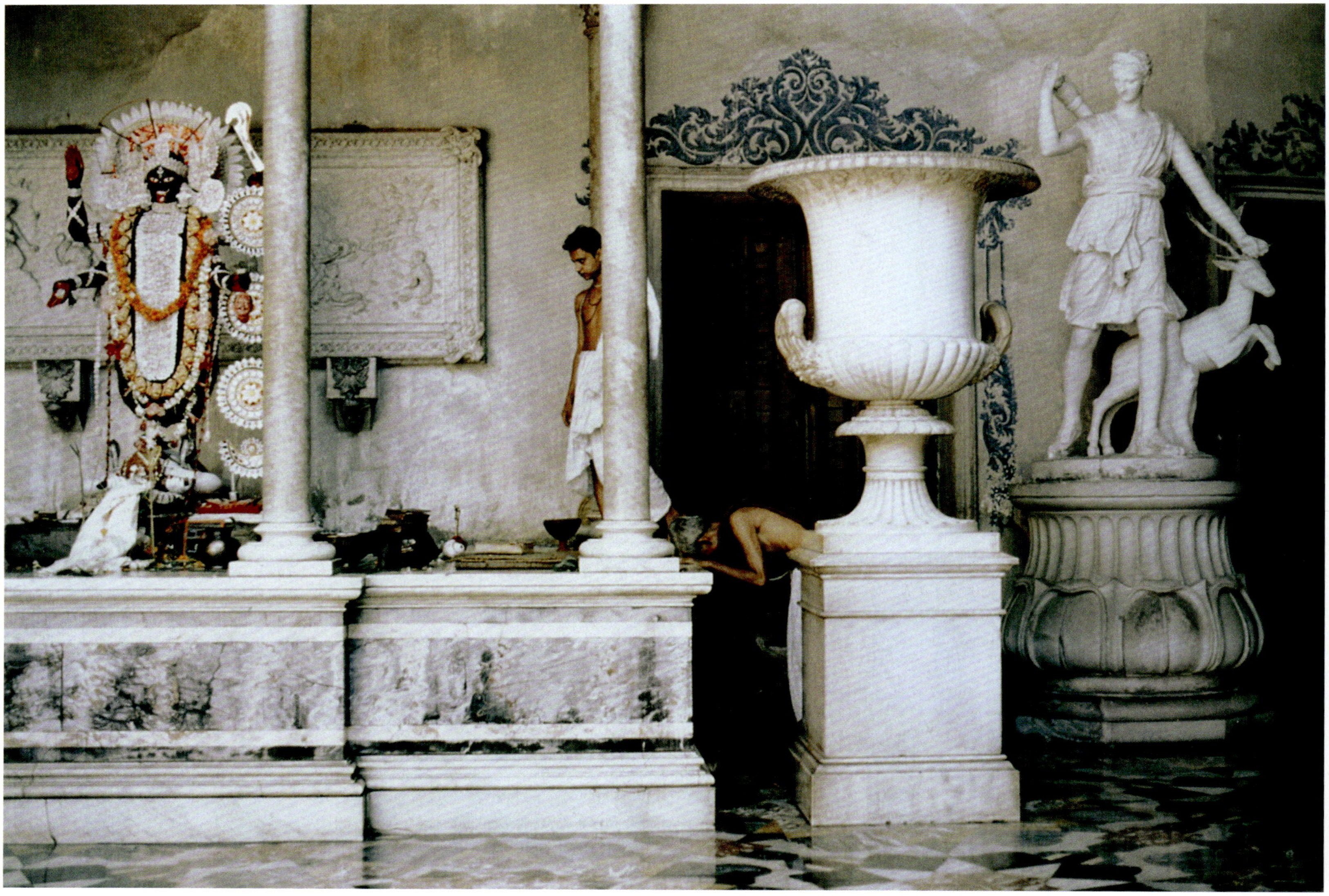

77

Kali Puja in the Marble Palace, Calcutta

RAGHUBIR SINGH (1942–99)

Calcutta, West Bengal, ca. 1975
Chromogenic color print
30.5 × 41.9 cm (12 × 16 ½ in.)
Published: Raghubir Singh, *Calcutta: The home and the street*, London, 1988, pl. 20

THE JUXTAPOSITION OF AN IMAGE of the goddess Kali with a high Victorian statue of the huntress Diana wittily exemplifies perhaps the most intriguing architectural legacy of the European presence in Calcutta. Built by wealthy babu families of nineteenth-century Calcutta—those enterprising Bengali dynasties who had allied themselves to the British and often built up substantial fortunes in the process—a number of vast classical mansions survive in Calcutta. Most have seen better days, their stucco peeling beneath the onslaught of heat and rain, crumbling into a picturesque decay and often now little more than slum dwellings, their interiors divided up and rented out in sections. A few remain in the ownership of the builders' families, their interior furnishings of "chipped marble busts, dusty chandeliers, creaking columns"[1] evoking the eclectic assimilation of a once-fashionable foreign style adapted to Indian tastes. Raghubir Singh, whose writings were much concerned with the artistic and cultural cross-fertilization between East and West,[2] was clearly fascinated by these hybrids and his work includes a number of studies of the interiors of these survivors. For the outsider, the Marble Palace is perhaps the only easily accessible example of these eccentric islands of Victorian taste in the bustle and noise of modern Calcutta. Now an established point on the Calcutta tourist circuit, the palace built by Raja Rajendra Mullick between 1835 and 1840 preserves, in penumbral and dusty aspic (frozen in time by the stipulations of a family trust), an astonishing collection of porcelain, statuary, paintings, and bricabrac, including a massive statue of the Queen Empress herself.

JF

1 R. S. Gupta, introduction to Raghubir Singh's *Calcutta: The home and the street*, p. 19.

2 Most notably in the introductory essay to his *River of colour: The India of Raghubir Singh*, London, 1998.

SAINTS & SADHUS

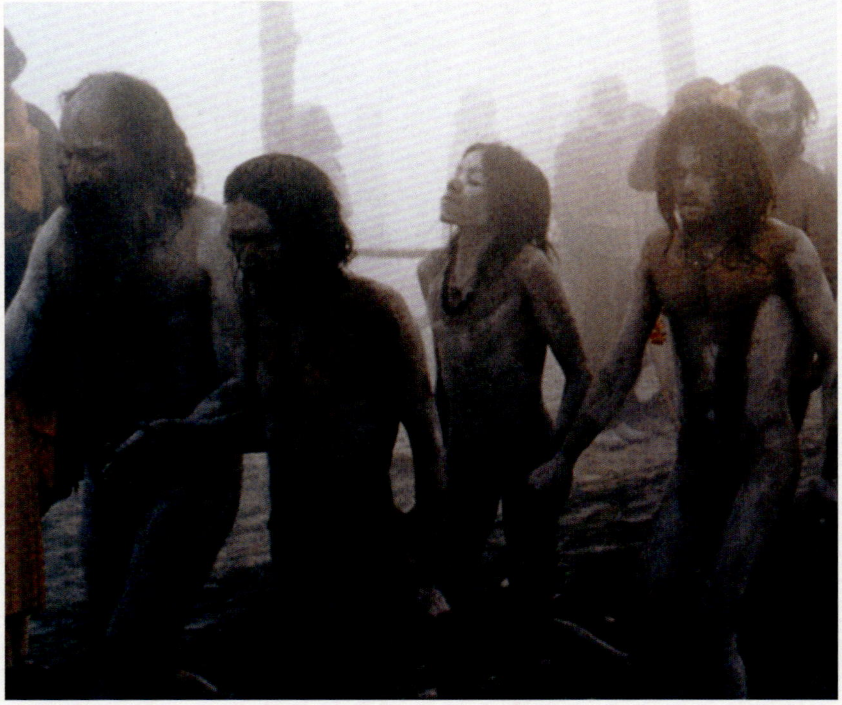

While much of Indian art is devoted to celebrating nature and its energies and to the more joyous sides of human life, the corresponding ascetic impulse, toward the renunciation of the world and its seductive illusions, also forms a main strand of Indian life and culture. To the religious ascetic, the world is indeed a dangerous and unwholesome place, an idea well evoked in the Jain parable of a man who, fleeing a mad elephant, finds himself trapped in the shaft of a well, hanging precariously to a few reeds growing from its side. With the elephant trying to kill him up above and deadly snakes awaiting him below, he can only watch as two mice (representing time) nibble through the reeds to which he clings (representing his life-span). His doom is inevitable and imminent. Bees, whose overhanging nest has been dislodged, then begin to sting him mercilessly. Yet when a stray drop of their honey falls by chance on his lips, he licks it greedily and hopes for more.

For Jains and Buddhists, the escape route from this world of Samsara, or the bondage of karma and rebirth, impermanence, and suffering, was the preserve of specialist monks practicing meditation and other disciplines in monastic communities supported by the laity, who could thereby gain merit for themselves. For Hindus, in theory, liberation (*moksha*) is the ultimate of the four goals of human life, the three which precede it being: righteousness (*dharma*), gaining wealth (*artha*), and sensual enjoyment (*kama*). According to another fourfold theory, the ideal life of the male Brahmin proceeds through the stages of the celibate student or disciple (*brah-machari*), the mature householder (*grihastha*), the forest-dwelling recluse (*vanaprashtha*), and finally the homeless mendicant who renounces worldly life and all its ties (*sannyasi*). However, those who do not wish to wait so long can take vows of renunciation at an early age and be initiated by a guru into one of India's hundreds of (predominantly Shaivite) sects of yogis or sadhus. The initiate will take a new name and adopt the customs of his sect. In appearance, he may be shaven-headed or grow thick, matted locks and a beard. He may go naked except for a covering of ash, or be half-clothed, or wear a robe dyed an auspicious saffron color. His few possessions may include a staff, rosary, begging-bowl, water-pot, and an arm-rest for meditation. He may live in a settled community, as a solitary recluse in the wilderness, or wander the country begging and giving instruction.

In Mughal India, as in earlier ages, charismatic holy men—Muslim Sufi teachers, Hindu yogis, or Jain acharyas—were generally venerated by the emperors, sultans and maharajas, who in many cases would go to visit them to seek their advice or blessing. The Mughal ruling family had important relationships with the saints of the Chishti, Qadiri, and other Sufi orders, and the more free-thinking among them, notably Akbar and later the ill-fated Prince Dara Shikuh, were also unusually receptive to the wisdom of Hindu sages. In modern India, a number of well-known gurus have attracted a world-wide public following, and at a more commonplace level the wandering sadhu remains a familiar figure. The great periodic religious festivals such as the Kumbh Mela at Allahabad bring together, along with millions of pilgrims, huge numbers of sadhus, who wade into the river en masse at the auspicious time, in one of the most remarkable of human spectacles.

AT

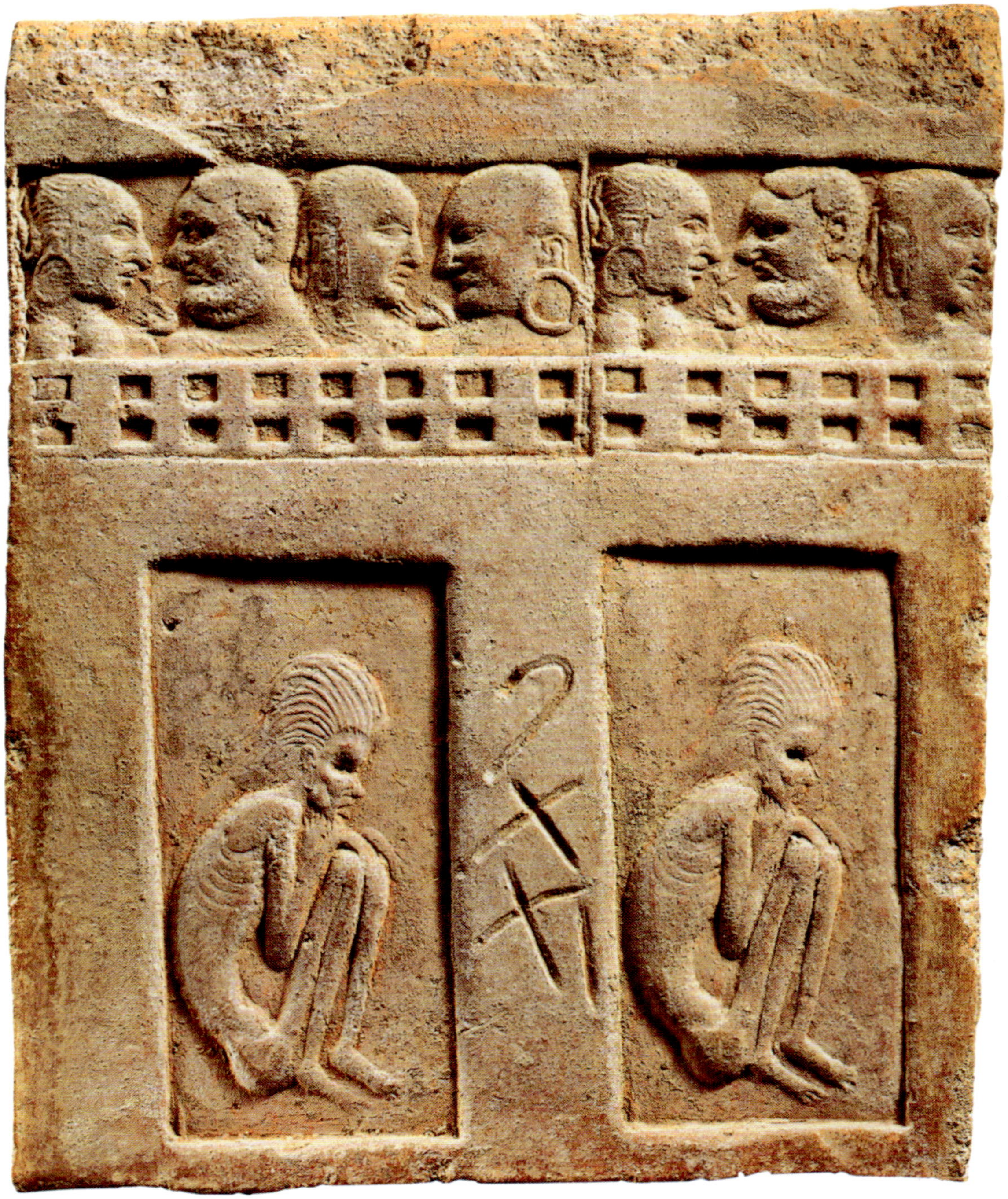

78

Terracotta tile with ascetics

HARWAN, KASHMIR, THIRD TO FOURTH CENTURY AD

40.3 × 33.6 cm (15 ⅞ × 13 ¼ in.)
Published: A. Poster, *From Indian earth: 4,000 Years of terracotta art*, New York, 1986, no. 63
Metropolitan Museum of Art, New York, Gift of Cynthia Hazen Polsky (1987.424.26)

THIS STAMPED TERRACOTTA TILE is one of a large series that comes from Harwan, a site in Kashmir with Buddhist remains. It is decorated in two bands, the lower depicting two crouching bearded ascetics, the upper with a frieze of paired heads looking over a parapet. The tile is numbered in Kharoshthi script between the figures.[1] The iconography of such tiles is unusual in a Buddhist monument, and it has been suggested that the Harwan site was occupied prior to the Buddhist phase by the Ajivika sect, who went naked and practiced severe austerities. The ascetics on the wall tiles have been linked to the yogic practices of the Ajivikas, who were known to adopt a squatting posture, often inside large clay pots.[2] The paired heads, which have Central Asian features, are also found on Kushan sculpture.[3]

Terracotta tiles were found on the upper terrace of the site, both on the floor and around the edge of a courtyard as risers to a low wall or bench seat.[4] Motifs found on the floor tiles include male and female figures, animals such as horses, stags, elephants, and birds, and flowers and abstract designs.[5] Tiles such as this one are all from the wall. Other similar tiles, also with pairs of crouching ascetics and a row of paired heads, are in various museum and private collections. In addition, many examples also have a register of geese (*hamsa*) below the crouching figures,[6] which may represent the freely wandering ascetic. The tiles were numbered in Kharoshthi script, which had fallen into disuse before the end of the fifth century,[7] presumably to allow them to be assembled in the correct order.

MCS

1 The Kharoshthi numerals are 10, 4, 4, and 1, to be read together as 19; see Kak, 1933.

2 R. E. Fisher, "The enigma of Harwan," in P. Pal ed., *Art and architecture of ancient Kashmir*, Bombay: Marg, 1989, pp. 1–17.

3 Pal, 1986, no. S55, p. 178.

4 Béguin, 1992, p. 109, illustrates one of the photos taken at the excavation in the 1920s, after Kak, *op. cit.*

5 Fisher, *op. cit.*, pp. 5–7.

6 Examples are in the Los Angeles County Museum (Pal, *op. cit.*, no. S98, pp. 223–24); Ashmolean Museum, Oxford (Harle, 1974, pl. 144, p. 57); Victoria and Albert Museum, London (Poster, *From Indian earth*, p. 130); Musée Guimet, Paris (Béguin, *op. cit.*, p. 109), which also does not have the lower band of geese.

7 A dating prior to the end of the fifth century is bracketed by thermoluminescence tests on one of the tiles, giving a date of between the second and sixth centuries (Fisher, *op. cit.*, p. 16, n. 5).

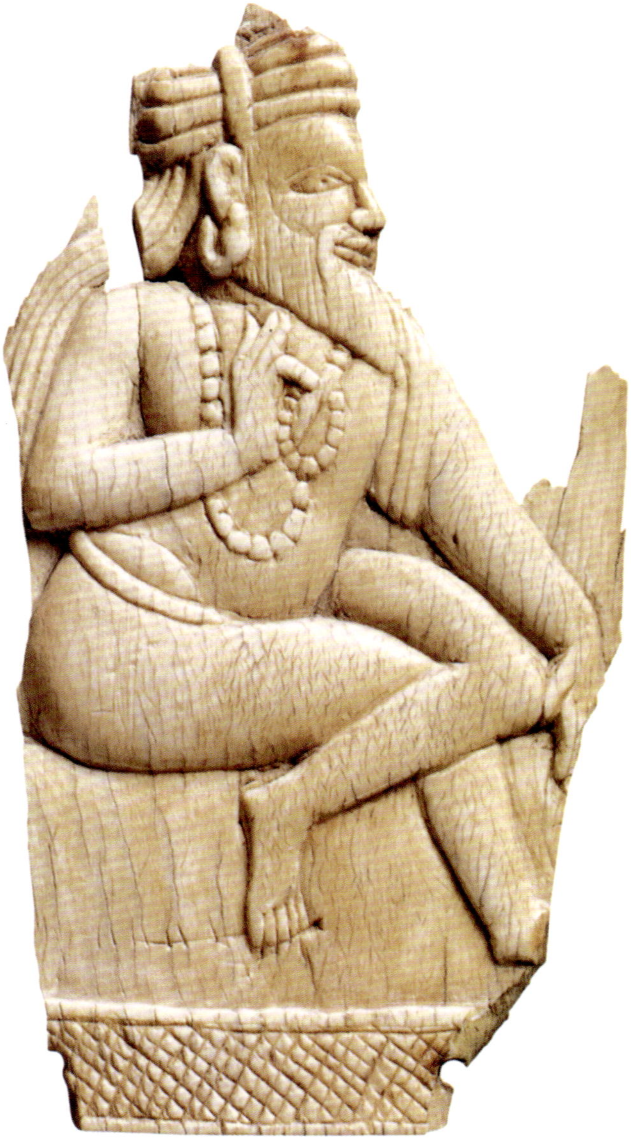

79

Ivory panel with a seated sadhu

ORISSA, SEVENTEENTH OR EIGHTEENTH CENTURY

12.7 × 6.4 cm (5 × 2 ½ in.)
Metropolitan Museum of Art, New York, Gift of Cynthia Hazen Polsky (2011.576.3)

THE SUBJECT OF THIS IVORY PANEL carved in relief is a sadhu or holy man. Middle-aged, bearded, and slightly plump, he sits cross-legged, holding a rosary (*mala*) in his right hand. He is naked apart from a narrow belt, his necklace, and his turban, which has two long tassels over the shoulders. A very similar figure, wearing a comparable turban with long sashes to either side, appears on an ivory plaque, also with a cross-hatched border, in the Los Angeles County Museum.[1]

Offering an implicit contrast between the rich material of the ivory and the asceticism of its subject, this panel may perhaps have decorated a piece of furniture to remind its owner of his duty toward the yogi. Ascetics and sadhus, representing many varied religious groups, hold an honored place with all levels of Indian society. Both Hindu and Muslim rulers would often seek the advice of holy men and offer them patronage, and such meetings were sometimes recorded in Mughal and Rajput painting. The Mewar Maharanas, for example, supported the Kanphata and other orders of yogis, and a large mid-eighteenth-century painting depicts an audience between a group of yogis and Maharana Jagat Singh.[2]

MCS

1 Pal, 1981, fig. 73, p. 81.

2 A. Topsfield, "Udaipur paintings of the eighteenth and nineteenth centuries," in *Indian miniature painting*, London: Spink and Son, 1987, no. 42; Mason et al., 2001, no. 61.

80

Sultan Ibrahim ibn Adham of Balkh visited by angels

ATTRIBUTED TO THE LUCKNOW/FAIZABAD ARTIST HUNHAR, 1760–70

Opaque watercolor with gold on paper
21 × 20.5 cm (8 ¼ × 8 ⅛ in.)
Inscribed on verso in devanagari: *kalam honhar ki 200* ("Hunhar's brush; 200 [rupees]")

SULTAN IBRAHIM IBN ADHAM (d. 776–77) gave up the kingdom of Balkh in order to become a dervish. According to the legend related by Farid al-Din 'Attar, he was visited by angels who brought him ten dishes of food, arousing the envy of the poor dervish depicted here in the lower corner, who was only granted one dish. The subject is a well-known one in eighteenth-century Mughal painting,[1] and the various versions are linked by their being dependent on European imagery for the figures of Sultan Ibrahim and the angels, going back to a now lost seventeenth-century version. Gauvin Bailey writes that the figure of Ibrahim is derived from that of Christ in "The demon tempts Christ in the wilderness" and that the angels are derived from "Angels minister to Christ," from the "Poor Man's Bible" of 1593, a book which arrived in the Mughal court in 1595.[2]

The figures of the two dervishes in our version are painted with considerable sensitivity to their seventeenth-century origins, while the costumes of the angels have been subtly Mughalized (front-opening coats and sashes, rather than the European tunics of the St. Petersburg version for instance). But the landscape here is quite remarkable. This is a naturalistic wood with hillocks and folds in which one could get lost. A painting signed by Puran Nath, an alias often used by Hunhar, of about the same date in the Binney Collection, shows a similar naturalistic interest in trees.[3] An interest in more naturalistic landscape is common to the styles of both Murshidabad and Lucknow at this time, derived often from European eighteenth-century engravings.[4]

JPL

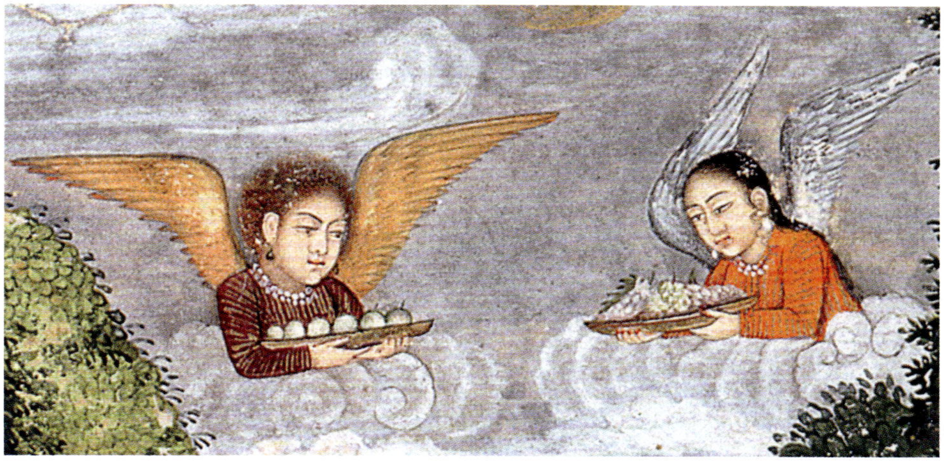

1 As in *The St. Petersburg Muraqqa'*, Milan, 1996, pl. 90, and in Falk and Archer, 1981. nos. 325 (from Lucknow) and 367 (from Murshidabad).
2 Engraved illustrations by Adrien Collaert, pls. 12 and 14 from Jerome Nadal's *Evangelicae Historiae Imagines*, Antwerp, 1593: see Gauvin Bailey's catalogue description in *The St. Petersburg Muraqqa'*, p. 81.
3 Binney, 1973, no. 97. For portraits by Hunhar II known as Puran Nath, see Falk and Archer, *op. cit.*, nos. 269–74, which are in a rather different style.
4 See J. P. Losty, "Towards a new naturalism: Portraiture in Murshidabad and Avadh 1750–80," in B. Schmitz ed., *After the Great Mughals*, Bombay: Marg, 2002, pp. 34–55.

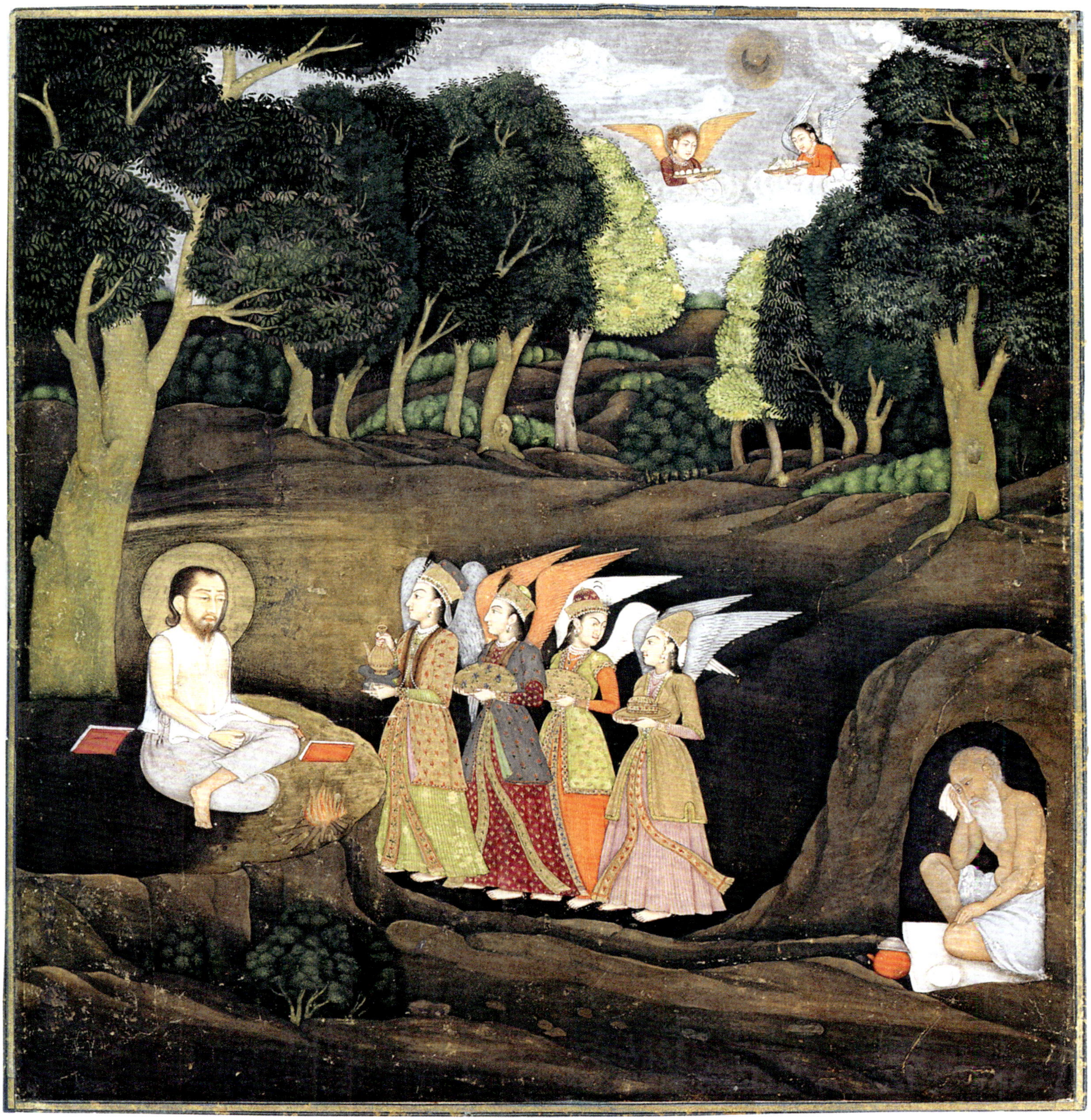

81

A gathering of ascetics preparing bhang

MUGHAL, 1600–10, WITH LATER ADDITIONS

Brushed drawing in ink and watercolor on paper
19.5 x 11.8 cm (7 ¾ x 4 ¾ in.)

GATHERINGS OF ASCETICS, NORMALLY HINDU ONES of the Kanphat or Split-eared variety of yogis, were among the most popular subjects for Indian artists to draw in the seventeenth century. The connection lies perhaps in the opportunity it gave artists to practice their drawing of a near-naked body, and to assemble those bodies into meaningful groups without color to help with the perspective. This group of Hindu ascetics is observed with that sharpness of vision, and indeed wit, with which Indian artists normally depicted their holy men, whether Hindu or Muslim.[1] They are here entirely devoted not to spiritual activities but to the preparation of *bhang*, a drink made from Indian hemp, i.e. marijuana. Below, we see the bringing in of the raw materials and the pounding of the leaves, which are then boiled and strained to produce the liquid narcotic. This is then presented in a cup to the leader of the group, who with the other elders sits beneath the tree around the traditional ascetics' fire. Several miniatures are devoted entirely to the effects on the ascetics of the consumption of bhang.[2]

The drawing where original is very fine (all those figures down the left-hand side of the composition, in particular the cross-legged ascetic with the dog), but it has been compromised by a later hand apparently trying to strengthen the line.

JPL

1 A tradition begun in a drawing by Basawan in the 1580s; see Losty, 1986, no. 23.

2 See Khandalavala and Chandra, 1965, pl. G, and Leach, 1995, p. 513, for examples.

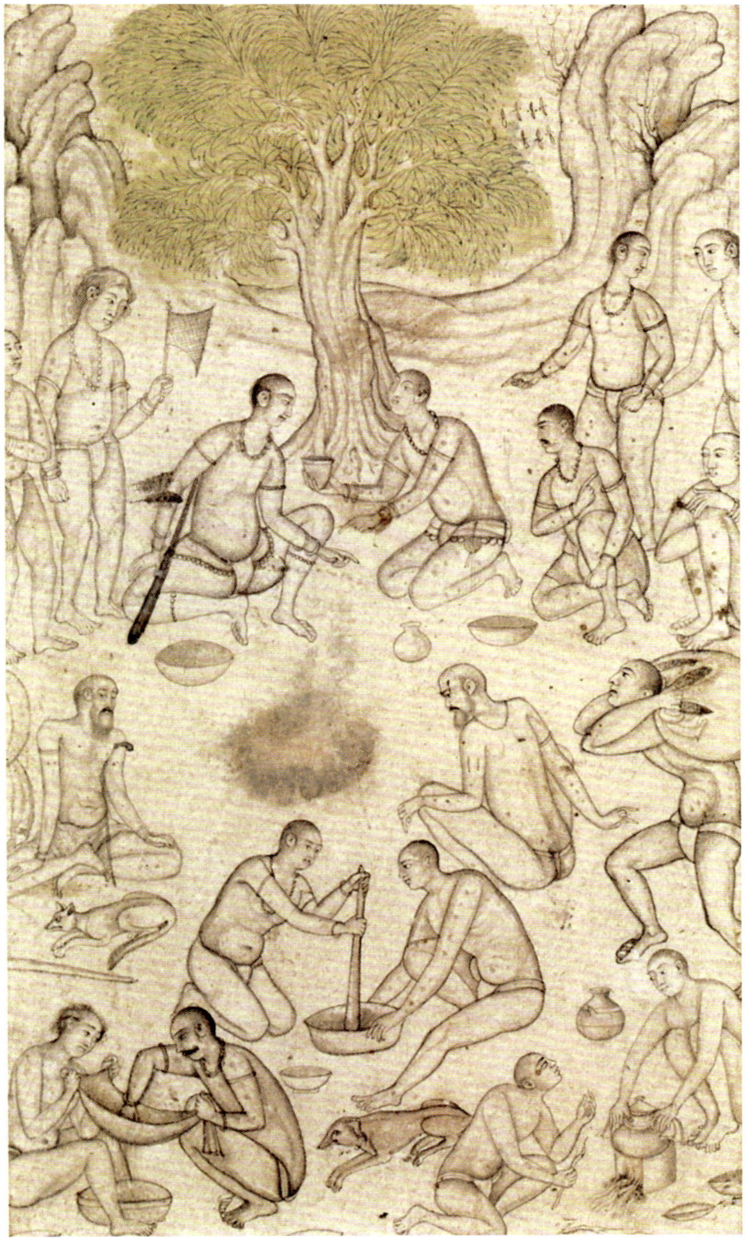

82

The acolyte and the jujube tree

GULER, PUNJAB HILLS, CA. 1760,
ATTRIBUTED TO NAINSUKH

Opaque watercolor on paper
17.8 x 26.7 cm (7 x 10 ½ in.)
Published: B. N. Goswamy, *Nainsukh of Guler*, Zurich, 1997, no. 86

TO THE LEFT, A YOUNG *BRAHMACHARI* (an acolyte who has made a vow of abstinence) is first seen near a water tank, where he may have just bathed. A barber is intently giving his head a shave, leaving only his ritual topknot. Wearing a loincloth, *mala* beads, and Vaishnavite sectarian marks, and carrying his drinking-vessel, the acolyte then passes a jujube tree (*ber*) and gazes longingly at the ripening fruit above him. The plum-like fruit of the jujube seem to have perennially attracted ascetics, as a comparable scene occurs in a Mughal *Baburnama* illustration (cat. no. 3). Up in the branches of the tree, another brahmachari is already reaching down the fruit with the help of an *ankus* (elephant-goad). Although our man appears to resist such temptation, he does not pass unscathed. On the right, he looks back finally with a pained expression as he hastens to avoid bombardment by tumbling jujubes.

Now somewhat damaged, this witty and original painting may illustrate a popular proverb[1] or some anecdote satirizing priestly greed.[2] The figures' postures are acutely observed and the continuous narrative sequence is elegantly conceived. The execution shows an assured fluency, particularly in the freely brushed tree with its laden branches. Evidently in the style of the great Pahari painter Nainsukh, this picture has been attributed by Goswamy to the master himself.

AT

1 E.g. some variant of "Hailstones falling as soon as the head is shaved;" as suggested by Goswamy, *Nainsukh of Guler, loc. cit.*

2 For other Pahari satires on greedy Brahmins, see e.g. Goswamy, 1986, no. 78; Topsfield and Beach, 1991, no. 33.

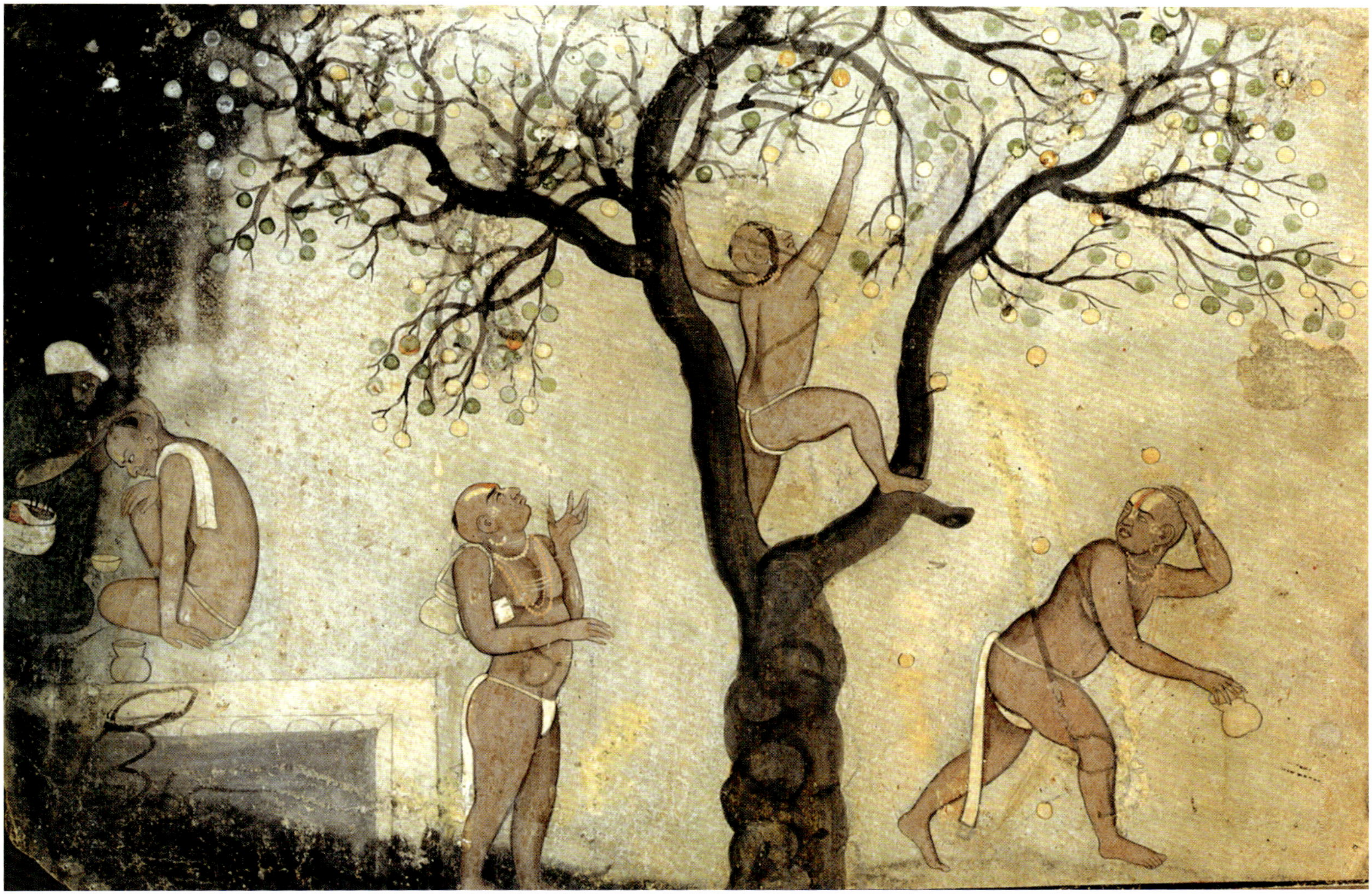

83

Himalayan pilgrimage of the five siddhas

FROM A SERIES OF THE KEDARA KALPA

Guler, Punjab Hills, early nineteenth century
Opaque watercolor on paper
Inscribed with folio number 6 on upper border
29.8 x 42.5 cm (11 ¾ x 16 ¾ in.)
Published: D. J. Ehnbom, *Indian miniatures: The Ehrenfeld Collection*, New York, 1985, no. 127

AMONG THE ROCKY RANGES OF THE HIMALAYAS, five Shaivite *siddhas* (ascetics or sages) are seen four times, in the course of their pilgrims' progress. In the foreground, four of them bathe in a holy river, while one has his head shaved by a barber. Then, clad in dhotis and animal-skin shawls, they worship at the Shiva temple nearby, bowing before the lingam in the inner shrine. The tree with perching birds nearby stands in pleasant contrast to the otherwise chill and jaggedly barren landscape, unpopulated except for a herdsman fluting to his goats and a traveling Hill couple, who carry their baby and belongings in baskets on their backs. To the left, the five siddhas bathe a second time in another river, then set out again on their long upward journey.

This complex and rewardingly detailed composition belongs to a well-known series, recently identified by Goswamy as illustrating the *Kedara Kalpa*, a Shaivite text expounding the merits of pilgrimage to the Kedara-Kailasha region, the legendary abode of Shiva.[1] In one of its stories, as told by Shiva to Parvati and their son Karttikeya, five sages perform a Himalayan pilgrimage and encounter great hardships but also wondrous sights, including golden cities where celestial maidens sing. Numbered 6, this page illustrates an early stage of the journey, with the sages still ascending from the Himalayan foothills; in the next page, they will emerge among boulder-strewn, icy heights.[2] Although the topography of their pilgrimage is to a large degree fantastic, it has been suggested that the holy rivers depicted here might be the Ganges and Jumna near their sources. The shrine also could plausibly be the Shiva temple at Gangotri, an important traditional pilgrimage site.[3]

AT

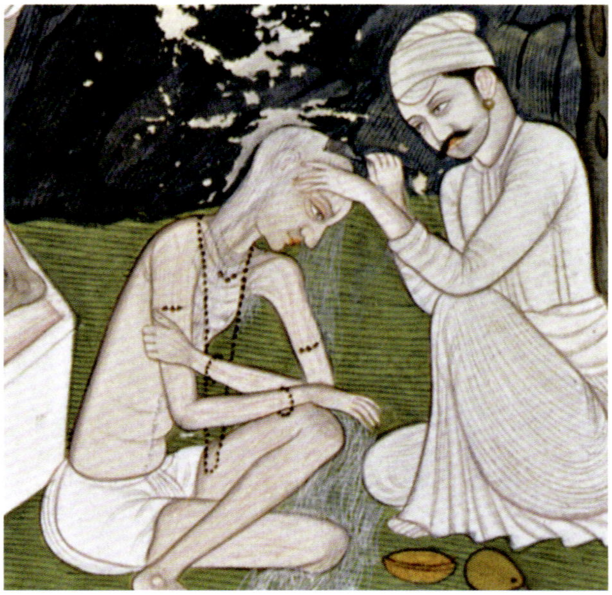

1 Goswamy and Bhatia, 1999, no. 216; for other published pages, see Pal, 1978, nos. 72a–b; Kramrisch, 1981, nos. P-52 (a–c); *Indian Paintings and Manuscripts*, London: Sam Fogg, 1999, no. 68; Pal, 2001, no. 50; Mason et al., 2001, no. 86; Dye, 2001, no. 149. A related, slightly later series is in the National Museum, New Delhi: Archer, 1973, s.v. Hindur, no. 5; Dye, *loc. cit.*, figs. 87–89.

2 Dye, *loc. cit.*

3 Sotheby's, New York, 6 October 1990, lot 57, with reference to the contemporary aquatint view of Gangotri by James Baillie Fraser (in 1815): Archer and Falk, 1989, pl. 27. Compare also the similar view photographed by Raghubir Singh, *The Ganges*, London, 1992, pl. 11.

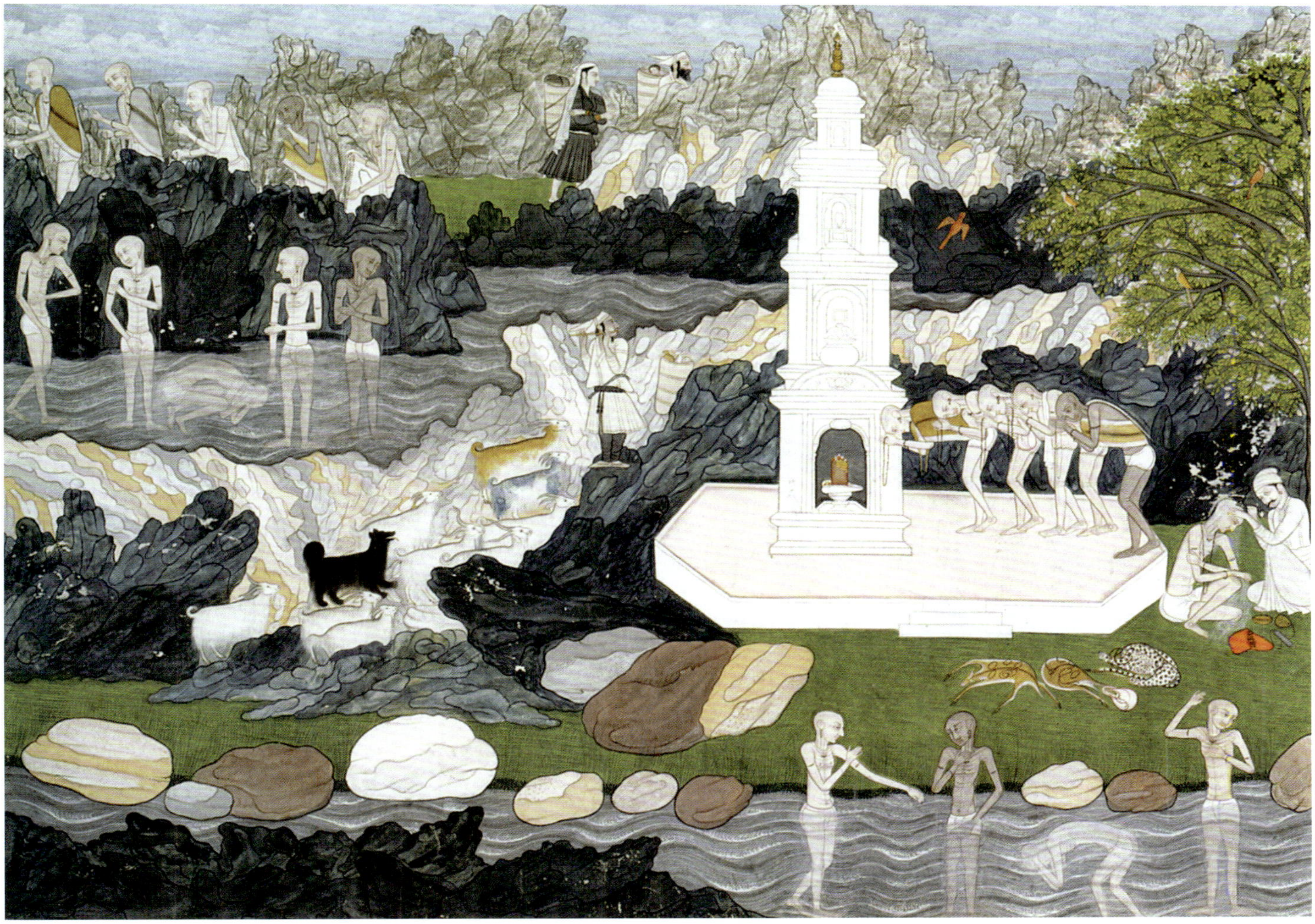

84

Portrait of a sadhu

KEVIN BUBRISKI (B. 1954)

India, 1985–89, printed 1996
Platinum palladium print
25.4 × 20.3 cm (10 × 8 in.)
Metropolitan Museum of Art, New York,
Purchase, Cynthia Hazen Polsky Gift
(1996.120.2)

KEVIN BUBRISKI'S RICHLY TONED and contemplative portrait of a Hindu sadhu or ascetic looks back to an earlier tradition of photographic practice and print-making. Favoring the use of larger format cameras which by their technical nature impose slower and more considered working methods, the choice of the platinum palladium process for print-making similarly reflects a concern to expand the aesthetic breadth of the photographic print in the face of a continually diminishing range of commercially available materials. The last two decades have witnessed a resurgence of interest, particularly in the United States, in the expressive possibilities of a number of photographic printing processes widely used in the late nineteenth and early twentieth centuries, but considered obsolete in the following half-century. The platinum processes, in particular, have become the preferred medium for a number of photographers and craft printers. Using light-sensitive salts of platinum rather than silver, the platinum print was extensively used from the 1870s until World War One, when escalating prices made the metal prohibitively expensive. The process was never revived as a commercially available option, but the very delicate and subtle gradations of tone that the process allows in comparison to the silver-based print has made it increasingly attractive to fine-art photographers. The addition of palladium to the print chemistry further deepens the tonal range of the material and this, together with a range of chemical controls not available with commercially produced papers, has led to its use among a growing number of photographers.

JF

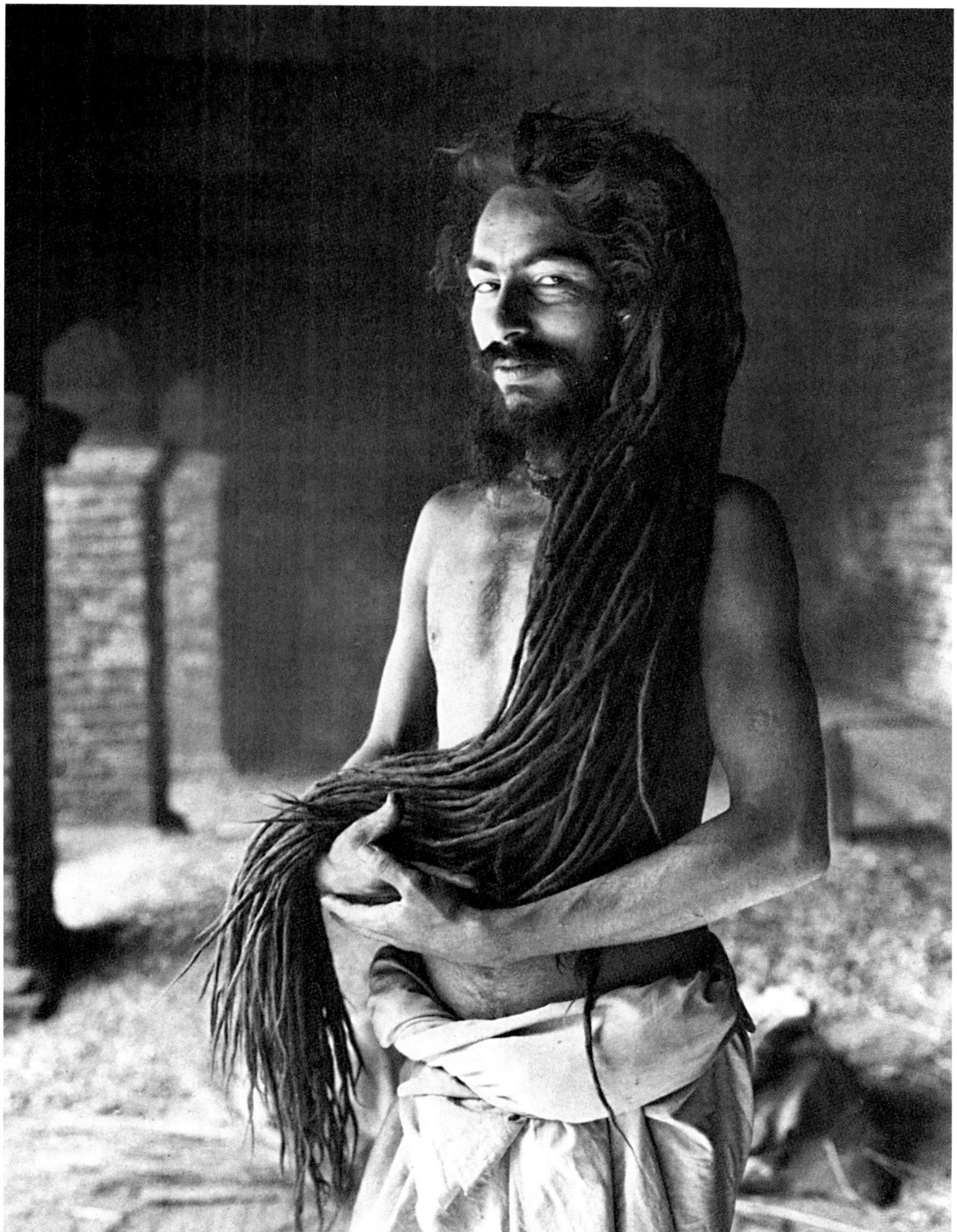

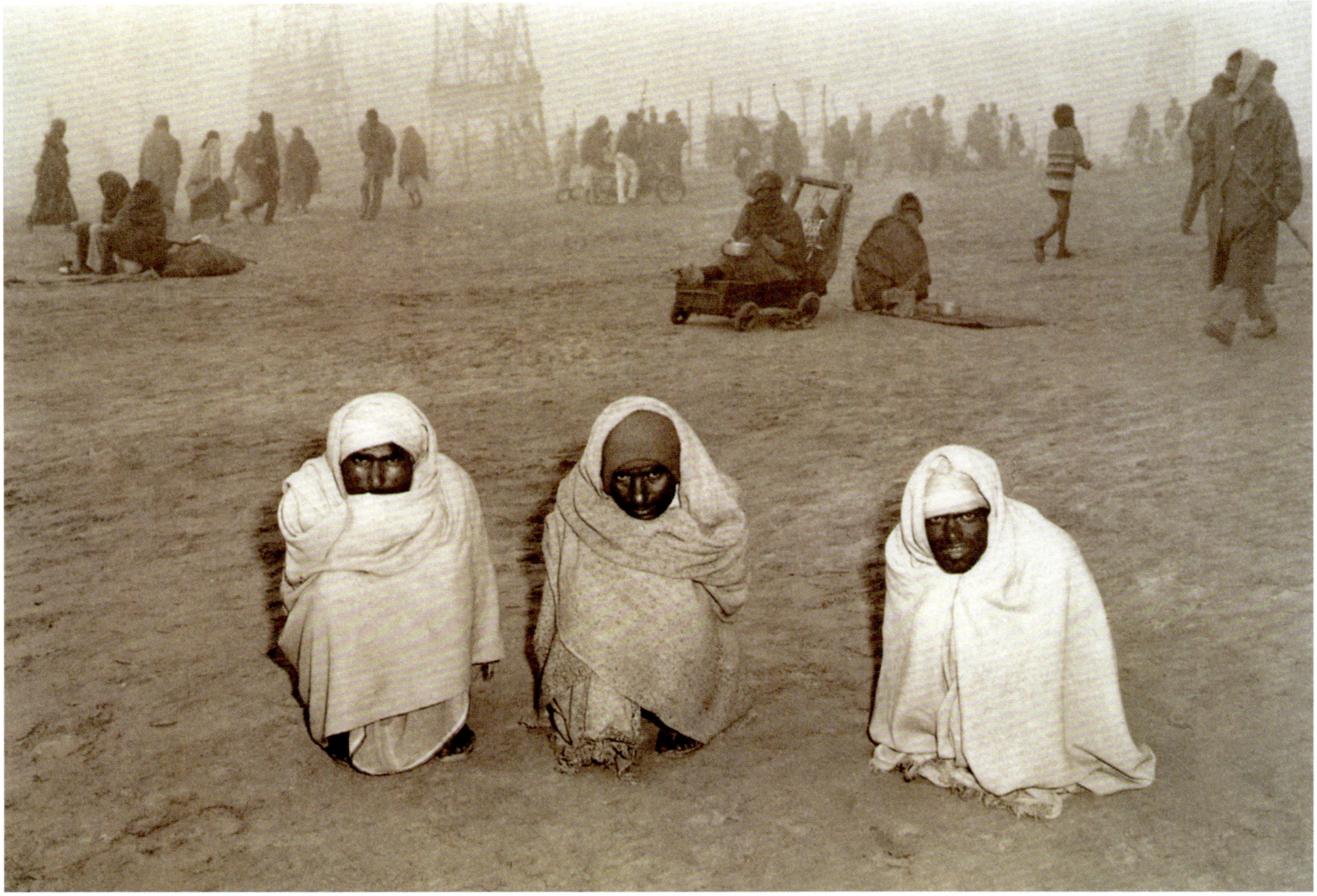

85

Three pilgrims at the Sangam, Kumbh Mela, Allahabad

KEVIN BUBRISKI (B. 1954)

Allahabad, Uttar Pradesh, 1985–89, printed 1996
Platinum palladium print
15.2 × 22.9 cm (6 ⅛ × 9 in.)
Metropolitan Museum of Art, New York, Purchase, Cynthia Hazen Polsky Gift (1996.120.14)

IN CONTRAST TO MOST PHOTOGRAPHIC COVERAGE of the Kumbh Mela gatherings, which concentrate on the vast numbers of pilgrims who converge at the festivals, Bubriski's study, characteristic of his meditative photographic approach, focuses on an isolated group of three pilgrims at the *Sangam*, the holy spot most propitious for bathing. The Kumbh Mela, which can roughly be translated as "pot festival," has it origins in antiquity, and the name refers to drops from the pot holding the nectar of immortality spilled by the warring gods. These fell to earth at four sites—Prayag (Allahabad), Haridwar, Ujjain, and Nasik—and every three years over a twelve-year cycle a Kumbh Mela is held at one of these places, each a huge religious festival that attracts millions of worshippers (and, nowadays, tourists). Of the four Mela locations, that held at Prayag is the most important, since the festival is located at the confluence of holy rivers, the Ganges, the Jumna and, according to Hindu belief, a third, the mythical Saraswati. Even in the late nineteenth century, over a million people attended the Prayag Kumbh Mela. On the latest occasion it was held, in 2001, it is estimated that seventy million people were present over the course of the festival, the largest single gathering in world history, and that in one day alone, fifteen million people bathed at this holy and auspicious spot.

JF

86

Wrestlers exercising at Rama Ghat, Benares

RAGHUBIR SINGH (1942–99)

Varanasi (Benares), Uttar Pradesh, 1983
Chromogenic color print
24.8 × 37.5 cm (9 ¾ × 14 ¾ in.)
Published: Raghubir Singh, *Banaras: Sacred city of India*, London, 1987, pl. 35

ALTHOUGH APPARENTLY UNPOSED, this beautifully composed study shows Raghubir Singh's remarkable ability as a photographer to create an elegantly balanced image without sacrificing a sense of the spontaneity of people going about their daily lives. Exercising at a riverside ghat above an image of Bhima,[1] the graceful figures of these wrestlers are caught in a series of fluid movements that capture a sense both of pictorial and human unity. The tension of this frozen moment recalls the work of Singh's early hero Henri Cartier-Bresson who, despite his contempt for color photography,[2] was revered by Singh throughout his career, both for the humanistic sympathy of his vision and for his ability to seize the significant moment in the flux of events. Indeed, in the essay accompanying his last book, Singh deliberately echoes Cartier-Bresson in his description of "the Zen of sight and sense, the archer's oneness with the subject,"[3] which ultimately lies at the heart of true photographic expression. In his most eloquent images, Singh's appropriation of the words of the French photographer appear not arrogant but rather those of a worthy follower in a great photographic tradition.

JF

1 Son of the Wind God Vayu, the coarse and violent Bhima plays a conspicuous role in the *Mahabharata*.

2 Singh recalls visiting Cartier-Bresson early in his career and showing him his work, only for the master to put the books aside after looking at only a few images. "I knew he had no love for colour photography. But this attitude, and my own fear of failure, made me redo the two works." Singh, 1998, introduction, p. 14.

3 *Ibid.*, p. 17.

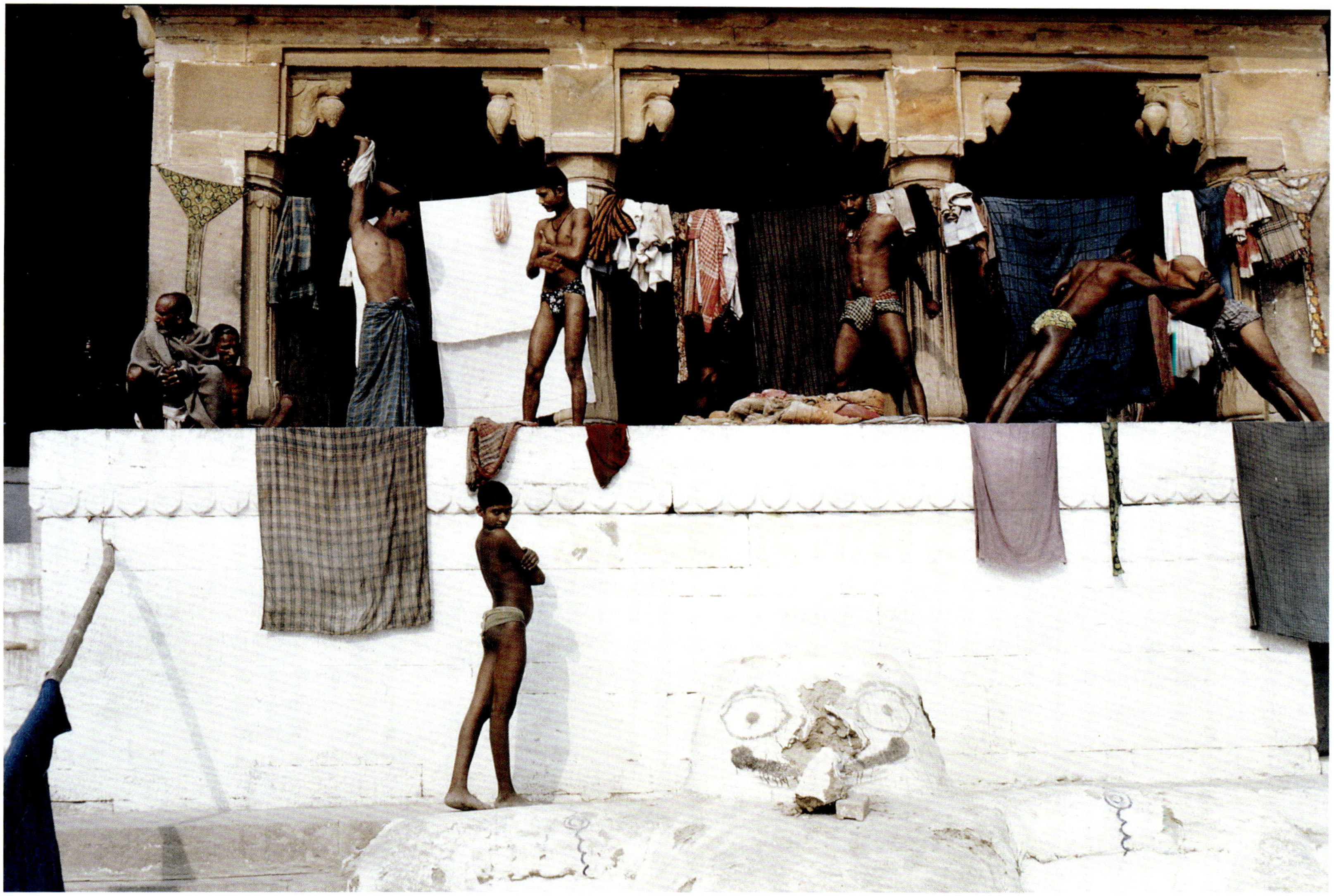

87

Sadhus returning from bathing at the Kumbh Mela, Prayag

RAGHUBIR SINGH (1942–99)

Prayag (Allahabad), Uttar Pradesh, 1989
Chromogenic color print
25.1 × 35.6 cm (9 ⅞ × 14 in.)
Published: Raghubir Singh, *River of colour: The India of Raghubir Singh*, London, 1998, p. 35; Raghubir Singh, *The Ganges*, London, 1992, pl. 44

RAGHUBIR SINGH VISITED THE GREAT KUMBH MELA FAIRS many times over a number of years, capturing the excitement, spiritual exhilaration and the sheer scale of these religious gatherings. This photograph is unusual in his work in the uncharacteristically muted colors of the image. Clearly the reasons are partly technical: the scene is lit only by a weak early morning sun, and in the grainy under-exposure of the scene the figures in the background merge into ghostly undifferentiated shapes. But this, if anything, only increases the sense of spiritual mystery and exoticism of this view, in which a group of *nagas* (naked ascetics), their hair matted and bodies smeared with ash, are seen returning from bathing in the cold and hazy January dawn. The Kumbh Mela festivals are the occasion when potential nagas are initiated into the sect, after having lived nine years as one who has renounced earthly pleasure (*brahmachari*).

This photograph was taken at the same Kumbh Mela as Kevin Bubriski's image of pilgrims at the Sangam, and the two images make an intriguing contrast between the photographic styles of these two contemporary photographers.

JF

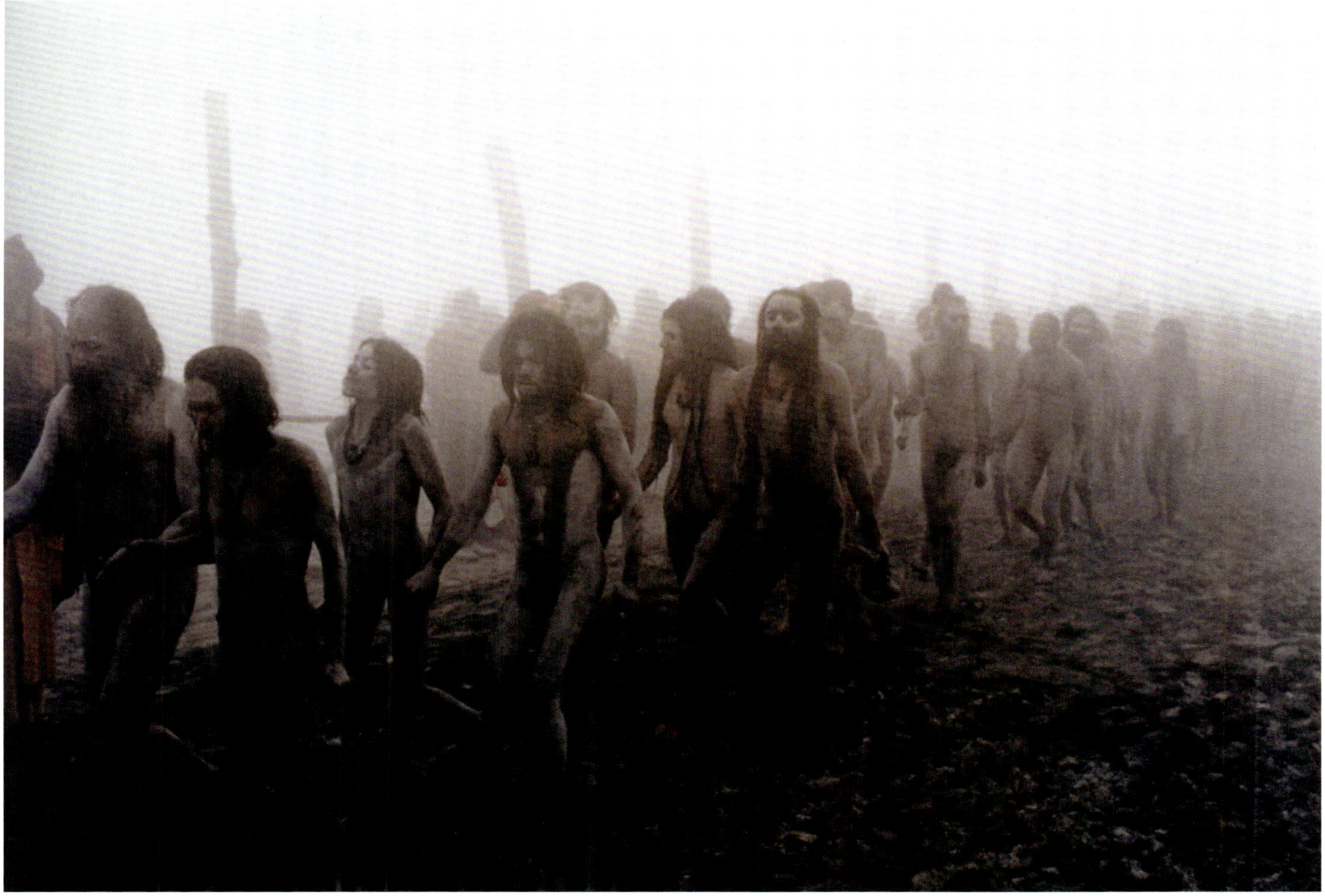

In the Realm of Kings

If most surviving early Indian art is primarily religious in inspiration, much of it was also commissioned by kings. In most ages the Maharajas (Great Kings), who belonged to the Kshatriya (warrior) class, represented the principal source of high artistic patronage, while the wealthy merchant classes also commissioned work at a less exalted level. Such royal ascendancy was only natural. From early times, kings were considered to be divinely appointed. The god Indra, riding his elephant Airavata, was a prototypical ruler of heaven and leader of the gods in battle, and later came to embody the power of the Kshatriya class. In ancient times, a royal consecration involved many religious sacrifices investing the ruler with the magical power of kingship. This power could be further renewed by undertaking the major ritual of the horse sacrifice, in which, before being sacrificed, a sacred horse was freed to wander for a year at will, followed by warriors who laid claim to all the lands it entered. In later ages, the Rajput rulers of western India claimed explicit descent from the Sun and Moon gods, or from the heroic god-king Rama, in the genealogies composed by their bards.

Many royal commissions—most obviously, of temple shrines or illustrated religious manuscripts—were inspired by the rulers' devotion to particular deities. But even seemingly profane commissions could be viewed in a similar light. For example, when a series of the Rasamanjari of Bhanudatta (a Sanskrit treatise on the classification of ideal lovers, and thus a precursor to Keshav Das's Hindi Rasikapriya), was illustrated in 1695 at Basohli in the Punjab Hills, its colophon inscription stated: "In order to see the creation of God and to realize the hollowness of this world, this illustrated Rasamanjari, containing many pictures, [which are] the wealth of the mind, was caused to be prepared by Raja Kirpal

Pal…" Irrespective of the worldliness of the Rasamanjari *text, the opening words here suggest that the enlightened enjoyment of fine art and poetry is itself conducive to a foretaste of moksha , the liberation from earthly attachment which is the ultimate goal of human life.*

Piety also gave rise to many of the commissions of the Muslim Mughal emperors, most clearly in the construction of mosques and the tombs of saints or the nobility (of which the Taj Mahal is the most famous example), although increasingly, in the time of Jahangir and Shah Jahan, the elaborate symbology devised by their artists came to be centered as much on their own imperial mystique. The greatest Mughal contribution to later Indian painting, however, was the careful and sensitive observation of human, animal, and plant life that the Mughals encouraged in their artists. This revolutionary pursuit of naturalism rather than idealization in the art of portraiture and court reportage was imitated and modified at most other Indian courts, so providing the rich surviving record of Indian royal life in all its guises from the seventeenth until the late nineteenth century, when Western pictorial influences and the novel art of photography finally prevailed.

AT

COURTLY LIFE

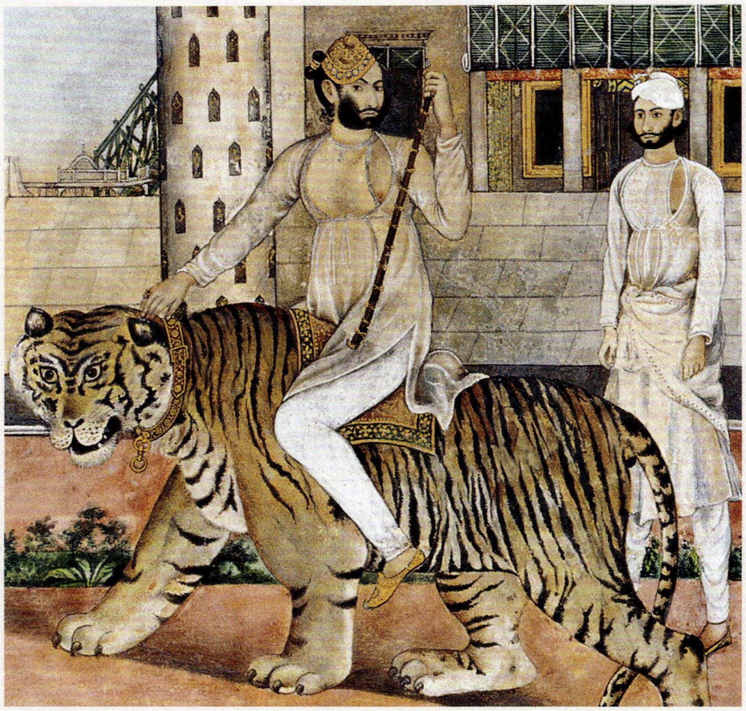

Scenes of court life—royal processions and assemblies or more intimate domestic groups—appear quite early in Indian art, surviving mainly in the form of stone relief sculptures, as well as in wall-paintings at the Ajanta caves. Though often highly evocative, they tend to be as idealized and conventional in treatment as the contemporary literary descriptions of such scenes in Sanskrit and other sources. The detailed, first-hand reportage of events at a specific, historical court was one of the naturalistic innovations of Mughal painting in the late sixteenth century. The Emperor Akbar's studio became a dynamic forcing-house, in which the most gifted painters learned their art from newly available European models as well as from more traditional sources. Among their main commissions were illustrated historical manuscripts of the lives of Akbar and his grandfather Babur, in which the painters' observations of the court milieu around them were judiciously modified by the need to tell a story and by the propagandist requirement to aggrandize the personality of the ruler, who is usually shown engaged in battle, hunting, or presiding at durbars and other public occasions. This tendency continued in Jahangir's commissions of finely executed illustrations to his own memoirs and in the *Padhshahnama*, recording the events of the reign of Shah Jahan in a magnificent if highly formalized manner. Even in smaller and more intimate group portraits, which are often more psychologically revealing than these great set-pieces, the Mughals tend almost always to stand on their imperial dignity.

In the outlying kingdoms of the Deccani Sultans in the sixteenth to seventeenth centuries, and of the Rajput Maharajas from the late seventeenth century onward, a more rounded and often more relaxed picture of life at court is presented in painting. In Rajasthan, patrons such as Maharana Amar Singh II and his successors at Udaipur encouraged their artists to show their daily lives—sometimes also including their more private moments in the company of their ladies—in unprecedented, almost documentary detail. A still more candid and revealing record of an individual nobleman of the Punjab Hill kingdoms, Raja Balwant Singh, was created by the outstanding Pahari artist Nainsukh.

Such paintings could embrace most of the typical phases of the daily routine of a Raja. It is likely that he would rise early, bathe, and perform his religious devotions (*puja*). Then, after some refreshment, he might undertake state business, receiving his ministers, nobles, or other visitors in private audience. On more public occasions, a full assembly of nobles, ministers, and courtiers would be held in the palace durbar hall. A communal meal with his nobles might follow. Recreation often took the form of the all-important pursuit of hunting, as will be seen in the following section. For other entertainment, the ruler might watch staged fights between his elephants or his professional court wrestlers. He might promenade in the royal gardens with his ladies, or bathe in a pleasant pool during the hot weather. On religious festival days (which were frequent throughout the year) he might ride forth on his elephant or in cavalcade to visit the appropriate temple for the day, and later he might watch animal fights or picnic in a garden. In the evening, he would perhaps smoke a hookah and drink liquor, while watching his nautch girls dance or listening to his musicians play classical ragas. Finally he would retire to keep company with his numerous queens and concubines in the closely guarded seclusion of the *zenana* (female quarters) wing of the palace. All the while, drummers and shehnai-players blowing their reedy horns above the palace gateway would mark the passing hours of the day, or the Raja's exits and entrances, with their resonant, plaintive airs.

AT

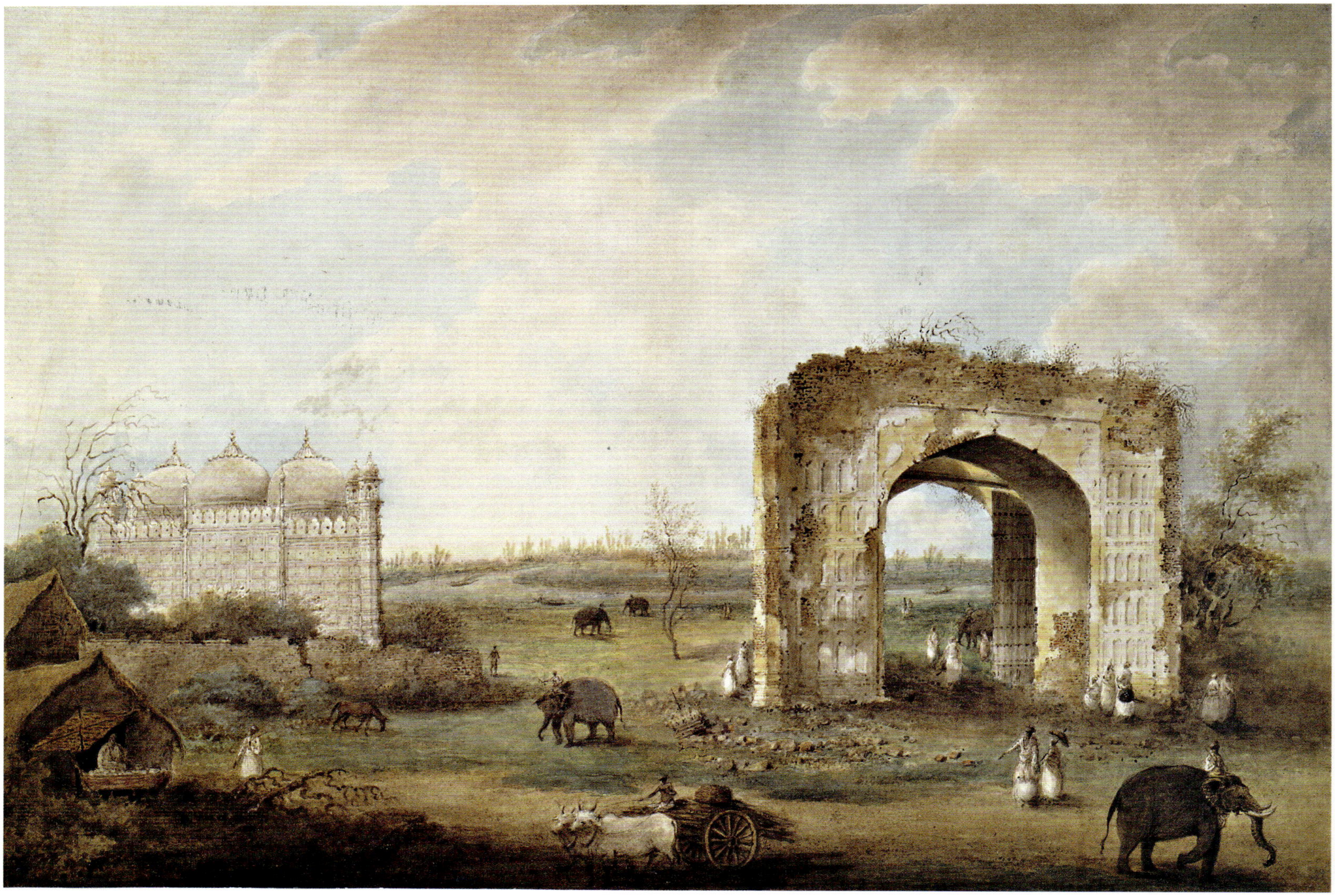

88

View of a mosque and gateway in Upper Bengal

BENGAL, CA. 1820–21
ATTRIBUTED TO SITA RAM

Watercolor on paper
33 × 48.8 cm (13 × 19 ¼ in.)
Published: J. Bautze, *Interaction of cultures: Indian and Western Painting* 1780–1910, Alexandria, Va., 1998, no. 82
Metropolitan Museum of Art, New York, Cynthia Hazen Polsky and Leon B. Polsky Fund (2002.461)

THIS VIEW OF A MOSQUE AND GATEWAY in upper Bengal is attributed to the Bengali artist Sita Ram (fl. 1810–22) and is in all likelihood part of a series from two important, partially dispersed albums consisting of views of the Ganges in Bengal and of monuments in Agra.[1] A further eight albums comprising 184 large watercolors by Sita Ram are housed in the British Library. Together these record a series of journeys made by Francis Rawdon (1754–1826), second Earl of Moira, later first Marquess of Hastings, when Governor-General in Bengal from 1814–21; this picture was most likely painted during Hastings' tour of upper Bengal in 1820–21.[2] Sita Ram accompanied Lord and Lady Hastings in the capacity of a draughtsman appointed to record the memorable and impressive events and sights of the trips, including animal and bird life, architectural studies, and views of nature.

Sita Ram was trained in the Murshidabad school of Company painting, where he mastered techniques of watercolor and the Europeanizing treatment of subject matter. It has been suggested that he might have had direct contact with distinguished European artists such as George Chinnery and Charles D'Oyly.[3] This work reflects his ability as a landscape painter, seen in the subtle rendering of the meandering river in the background and the great sky above. Tiny figures, some possibly English ladies from the traveling party, may be seen below the arched gateway, providing a sense of its scale and proportions. The placement of elephants at intervals in the middle ground gives a further sense of recession and depth to the composition. While Sita Ram's grasp of European technique is plainly evident, his Indian roots can also be discerned, perhaps not so much in this work, but in others where he uses elements such as multiple perspectives and rich color, in response to an influence from Indian painting.

NHH

1 J. P. Losty, "The Governor-General's draughtsman: Sita Ram and the Marquess of Hastings' Album," *Marg*, vol. 47, 2, Bombay, 1995, pp. 80–84.

2 J. Bautze, *Interaction of cultures*, no. 82 and front cover.

3 *Ibid.*, p. 309.

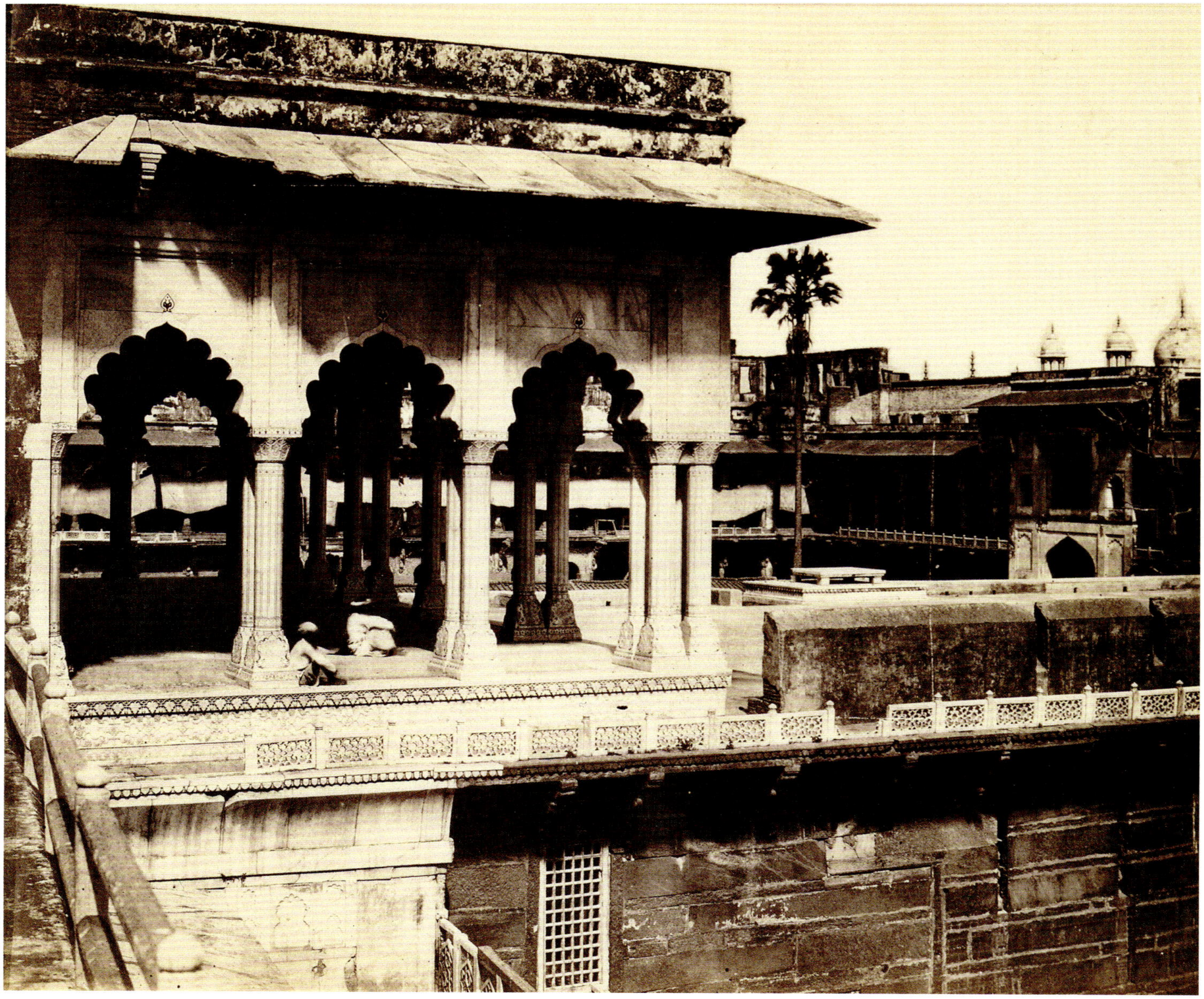

89

The Diwan-i Khas from the Mussaman Burj, Agra Palace

JOHN MURRAY (1809–98)

Agra, Uttar Pradesh, ca. 1862–64
Albumen print from a waxed paper negative (no. CL2)
40.6 × 44.3 cm (16 × 17 7/16 in.)
Metropolitan Museum of Art, New York, Purchase, Cynthia Hazen Polsky Gift (1988.1134.2)

TAKEN FROM THE TERRACE OF THE MUSSAMAN BURJ (octagonal tower) in the palace at Agra, this photograph looks north-west along the northern façade of the Diwan-i Khas, the Hall of Private Audience, completed in 1637 and used for the reception of nobles and high officers of state. On the terrace beyond can be seen the white marble slab, assigned for the use of ministers of state, with the courtyard and range of buildings known as the Macchi Bhawan in the background. An officer of the Bengal Medical Service, Murray devoted himself to photography in the leisure moments of a busy career and in the course of the 1850s established a reputation in India as one of the most distinguished photographers using the paper negative process. His photographic status was considerably enhanced by the exhibition and publication of two collections of views by the London photographic publisher and printseller J. Hogarth.[1] Shown in London at the time of the Mutiny, his work attracted considerable attention, both for its subject matter and technical assurance.

Deliberately narrow in his chosen range of subject matter, Murray's output was largely concentrated on the Mughal architecture of Agra, Fatehpur Sikri, Delhi, and a few other sites in Northern India. The present view strikingly illustrates his almost obsessive practice of re-photographing the same scenes over a period of years, often with only minute compositional variations. A casual comparison suggests that it is almost indistinguishable from a number of views of the Diwan-i Khas taken around the mid-1850s, one of which appears in Murray's second published collection.[2] Both the photographer's vantage point and the placing of figures in the central arch of the audience hall are almost identical. However, the presence here of a low brick wall (erected during or shortly after the Mutiny) on the terrace fronting the river Jumna indicates that this view must have been taken some years later, in the early 1860s.[3]

JF

1 The first, *Photographic views of Agra and its vicinity*, London, 1858, is in the form of a portfolio of thirty loose prints on card mounts, with an accompanying descriptive pamphlet; its sequel, *Picturesque views in the North-Western Provinces of India: Photographed by John Murray …with descriptive letter-press by Major-General J. T. Boileau*, London, 1859, was published as a printed book in folio format, with twenty-four original prints pasted down on pages following Boileau's descriptive text.

2 *Picturesque views*, pl. 7.

3 A further variant in negative form, evidently taken on the same occasion and from an identical viewpoint as this image, but with only one figure placed in the central arch, survives in the British Library (Oriental and India Office Collections, Photo 35, O.N. 43).

90

The Diwan-i Khas from the Mussaman Burj, Agra Palace

JOHN MURRAY (1809–98)

Agra, Uttar Pradesh, ca. 1862–64
Waxed calotype negative
37.1 × 46.4 cm (14 5/8 × 18 1/4 in.)
Metropolitan Museum of Art, New York, Purchase, Cynthia Hazen Polsky Gift (1988.1134.1)

THIS WAXED PAPER NEGATIVE, the original from which the preceding print was made (cat. no. 89), supplies valuable information on Murray's working practice. The enlarging of negatives for printing did not become a practical or common procedure until the end of the nineteenth century, and the production of the large prints favored by Murray required working with negatives of the desired final size. Printing by contact rather than enlargement allowed the photographer only limited control in altering the density of local areas of the image during printing, and such work was therefore most conveniently carried out beforehand on the negative itself. In common with the general practice of Murray and many other photographers, the sky has been completely blocked out with black ink in order to avoid an unattractive and grainily overexposed texture printing through.[1] At the other extreme of the tonal scale, Murray has used gamboge, the yellow resin obtained from the gamboge tree, to hold back the darker areas and retain shadow detail in the interior of the hall and beneath the overhanging dripstones (*chajjas*). The negative itself has also been treated with heated wax, ironed into the negative after processing in order to increase the paper's translucency in printing.

Although he made some experiments with photography on glass, Murray remained faithful to the calotype paper negative process throughout a photographic career in India lasting from 1849 to 1865. By the time he abandoned photography, both technique and taste had moved on and the great creative phase of paper negative photography was drawing to a close. By the early 1860s, the soft-toned, grainy expressiveness of the calotype negative had been largely superseded by the sharp detail and rich contrast of the wet collodion glass negative and the albumen print. Murray's last photographs to be exhibited before the Bengal Photographic Society were shown in 1862, and while the judges praised them as superior examples of calotype photography, they also dismissively remarked that "the process itself cannot compete with the results of more recent discoveries in clearness, sharpness, and artistic effect."[2]

JF

1 Murray does not appear to have followed the common procedure of many photographers (among them Linneaus Tripe) of either painting cloud effects directly onto the negative or of printing-in clouds from a separate negative.

2 *Journal of the Bengal Photographic Society*, September 1862, p. 40. Murray was not the only victim of changing taste: his contemporary Linneaus Tripe, the other great master of paper negative photography in India, was similarly criticized for exhibiting views that, while "as calotypes they were excellent," were "inferior to what might have been expected if collodion had been used." (*ibid.*, p. 6).

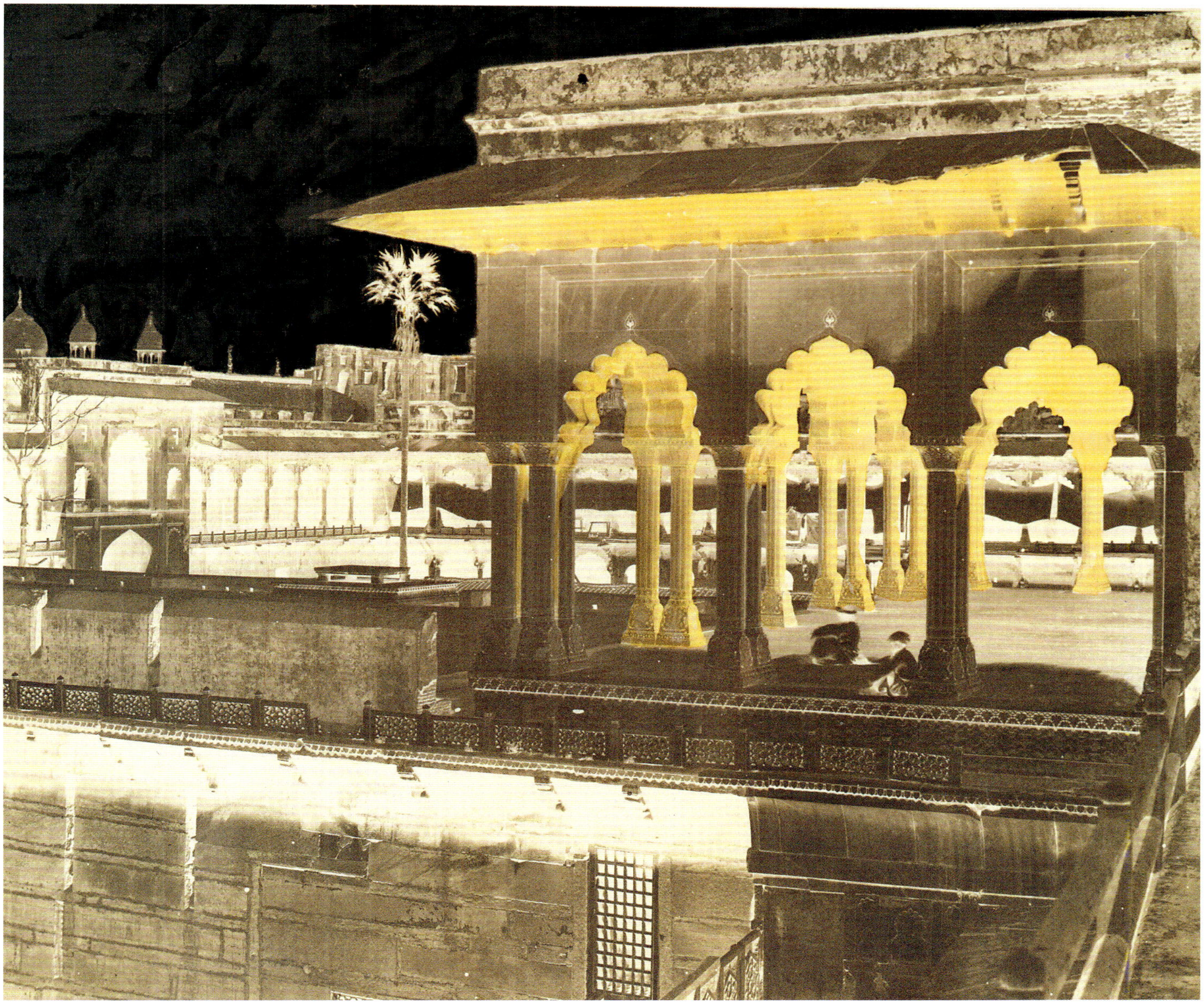

91

The Taj Mahal, Agra

JOHN MURRAY (1809–98)

Agra, Uttar Pradesh, 1864
Waxed calotype negative
38.5 × 47.2 cm (15 3/16 × 18 9/16 in.)
Metropolitan Museum of Art, New York, Rubel Collection, Purchase, anonymous gift and Cynthia Hazen Polsky Gift (1997.382.57)

THIS VIEW, TAKEN FROM THE TOP OF THE ENTRANCE GATEWAY of the Taj, looks northward across the garden toward the tomb itself. Murray was first stationed in Agra as civil surgeon in 1848 (the year before he took up photography) and was based there for the remainder of his career. It is unsurprising, therefore, that the most celebrated monument in India should have become a central theme of his work. Throughout nearly two decades of photographic activity, he repeatedly returned to the Taj as a subject, photographing the complex from every angle and in different lights. While studies of the Taj were becoming a stock item in the catalogues of almost every commercial photographer by the 1860s, no other artist in nineteenth-century India produced such a detailed visual record. This body of work, however, was clearly not intended as an exhaustive documentary inventory: Murray had little interest in photographing close views of decorative detail or architectural elements, his work being almost entirely concerned with capturing the gleaming mass of the building against the dark expanses of vegetation which at this period filled the garden, an approach particularly suited to the broad tonal sweep of the large-format paper negative process.[1] Indeed, from around 1860, he appears to have felt that even his standard print format was insufficient for the grandeur of his subject and in his last years of photographic activity, he turned increasingly to the creation of panoramic views composed of two or three linked prints. The Taj, with its flanking subsidiary buildings to the east and west, lent itself to these triptych-like compositions, and this photograph is almost certainly the central element of such a three-part panorama, one of several almost identical compositions taken in the early months of 1864.[2]

Increased professional commitments following his appointment as Director-General of Hospitals for the North-Western Provinces in 1865 may account for his apparent abandonment of photography at this time, his last known images being a series of views of Simla taken in that year. The lack of appreciation for paper negative photography, by now considered outmoded in its effects, may also have played its part. In any event, his photographic achievement was largely forgotten by his contemporaries, and while he merited an obituary in *The Times* that paid tribute to a distinguished medical career, no mention was made of his photographic achievement.[3]

JF

1 Although from around 1860 and possibly earlier, Murray produced many small-format prints in the form of stereographic halves, the compositional similarities of these to his larger prints, and their often apparently casual technical finish, suggest that their function was primarily that of preliminary studies.

2 A number of these variant images, as well as other panoramic views of the Taj from around this period, are illustrated in the catalogue accompanying the sale of the Murray archive: *Early photographs of India: The archive of Dr John Murray*, Sotheby's sale L09311, London, 18 June 1999.

3 *The Times*, London, 4 August 1898, p. 6.

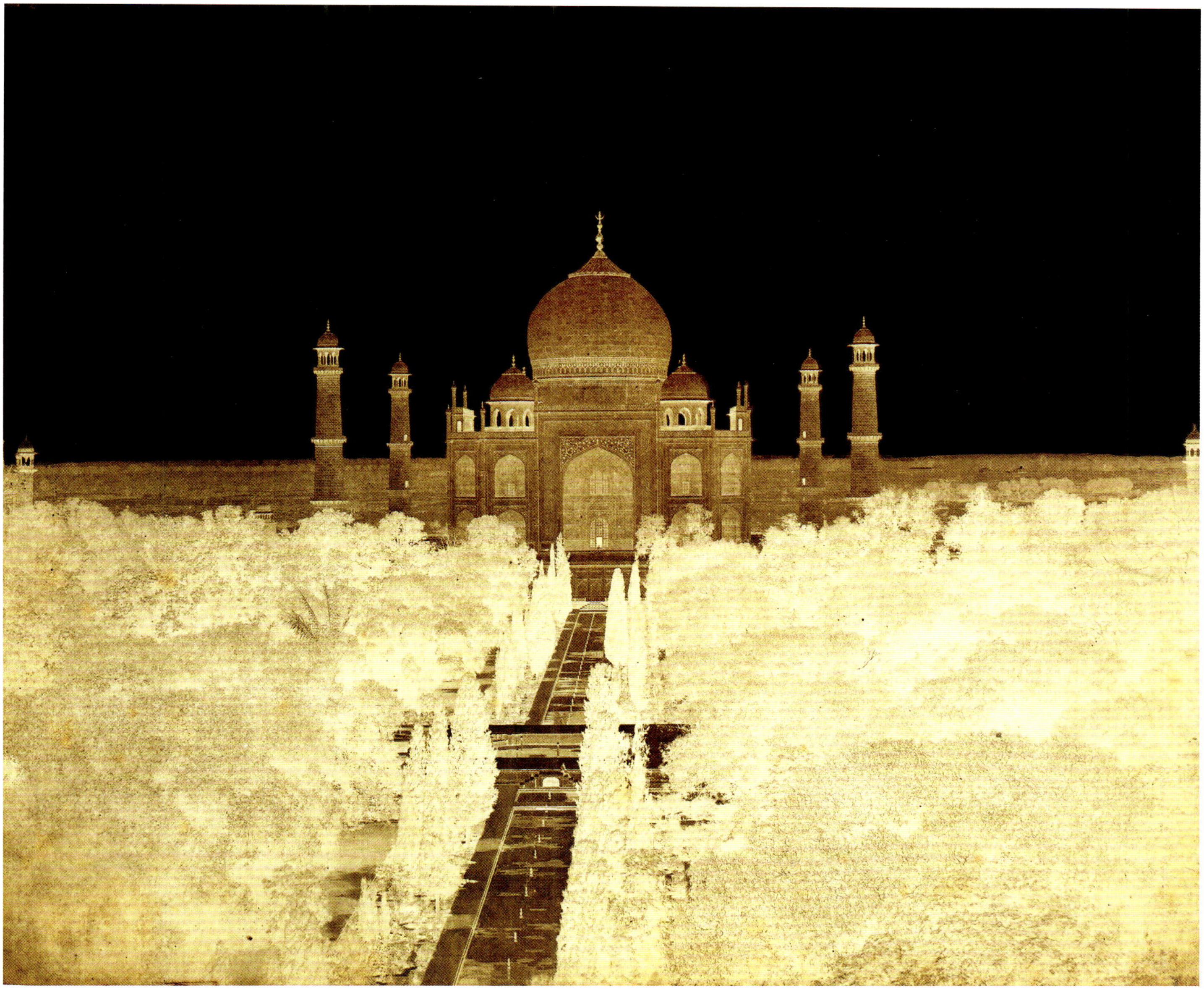

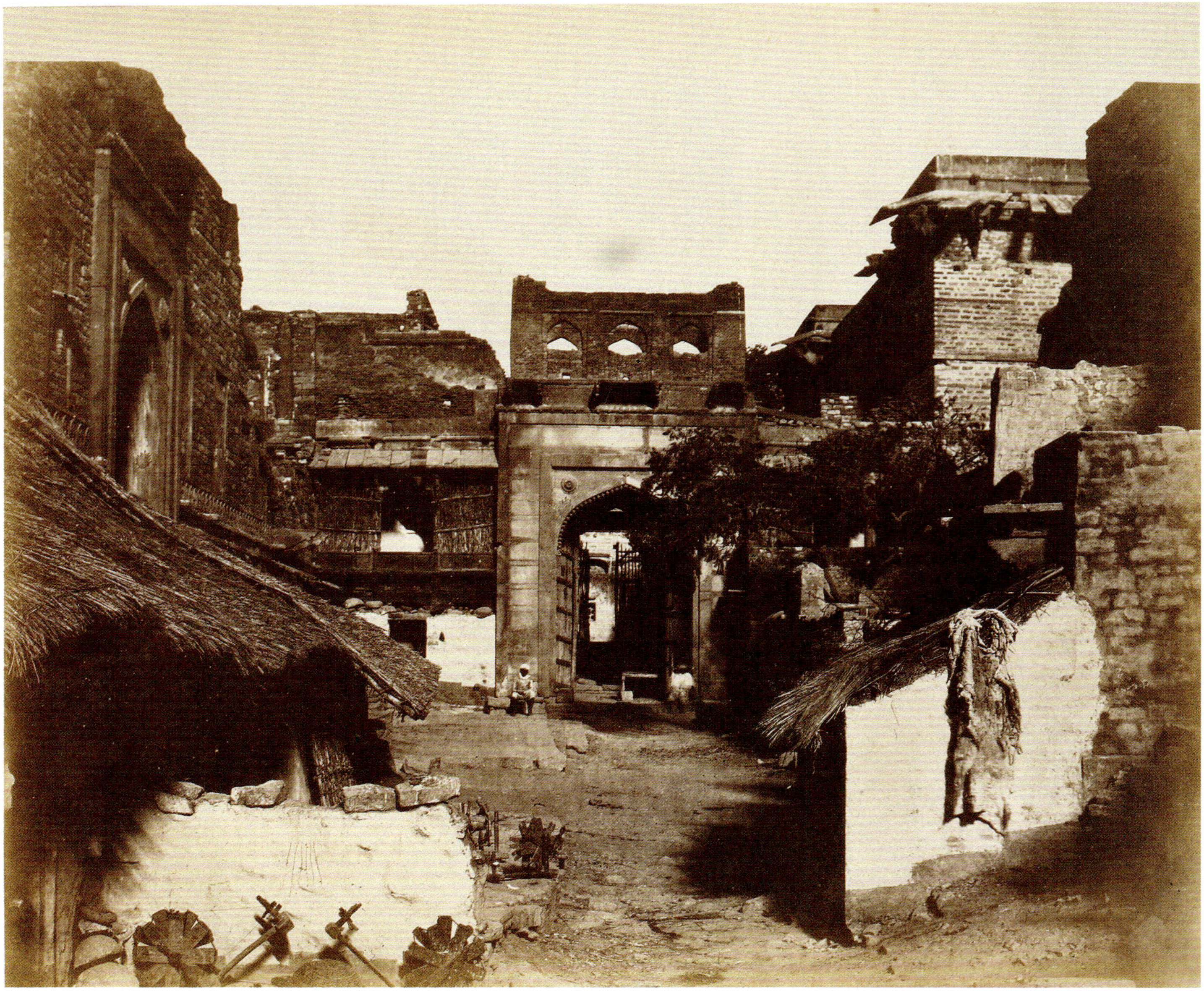

92

Street scene in Fatehpur Sikri

JOHN MURRAY (1809–98)

Fatehpur Sikri, Uttar Pradesh
Albumen silver print from a waxed paper negative
36.8 × 45 cm (14 ½ × 17 ¾ in.)
Metropolitan Museum of Art, New York, Purchase, Horace W. Goldsmith Foundation and Cynthia Hazen Polsky Gifts (1990.1106)

MOST NINETEENTH-CENTURY PHOTOGRAPHERS contented themselves with recording the historical remnants of the city that was briefly the capital of the Mughal Emperor Akbar. When, after only fifteen years' occupation, the Emperor transferred his capital to Lahore in 1584, the city was soon deserted and fell into ruin. From the records of most photographers of Murray's period and later, one would conclude that it was no more than an abandoned archaeological site, but if the city's former glory had long departed, it never wholly ceased to be inhabited. While in common with his contemporaries Murray made an extensive record of all the major monuments of the city, he is rarer in also taking a number of studies of less celebrated parts of the surviving town. The precise location of this view has not been established (it is possible that it looks along a street toward the Shahi Chowk gateway), but despite the empty air, the spinning wheels, and abandoned coat in the foreground testify to continued occupation.

JF

93

Railing with jali pattern of vases and flowers

MUGHAL, AGRA REGION,
MID-SEVENTEENTH CENTURY

Sandstone
44 × 103 cm (17 ¾ × 41 ⅛ in.)

THIS RECTANGULAR OPENWORK SANDSTONE PANEL (*JALI*) has a principal design of three baluster-shaped vases, separated by scrolling leafy tendrils which issue from opening flower buds; the border is carved with a rounded molding. The panel was originally a section from a railing along the edge of a terrace or parapet, with small pillars placed between each section. The red sandstone was mined at a number of quarries from Dholpur to Karauli in Rajasthan, and was the principal building material used by the Mughals from the reign of Akbar onward. The floral scrolls can be compared to an openwork marble screen, resembling those at the Taj Mahal, which has a similar use of opposing scrolls joined with a single bud or bloom at the point of contact, though it shows even more exuberance than the present example.[1] Such a lively floral jali design, incorporating a sense of three-dimensionality, represented a considerable advance in design from the more severe geometric motifs found on slightly earlier monuments, such as the tomb of Jahangir at Lahore (1628–38), and 'Itimad ud-Daula's tomb (1626–28), the latter commissioned by Nur Jahan, the favorite wife of Jahangir.

The vase motif occurs in Mughal art from the early seventeenth century onwards and is found in several media, including textiles, stone, and paintings. It is found for instance at the tomb of 'Itimad ud-Daula both as an inlaid decorative device and as a painted motif [2] while vases with flowers are also carved in relief around the walls of the main mausoleum of the Taj Mahal (1632–43).[3] A variation on the design is also found on the seventeenth-century monuments at the shrine of Nizam ud-Din in Delhi.[4]

MCS

1 Lerner, 1984, no. 60.

2 Okada, 2003, *passim*.

3 Okada and Joshi, 1993, pp. 76–79.

4 Jacob, 1890, part VI (Balustrades), pls. 18, 21.

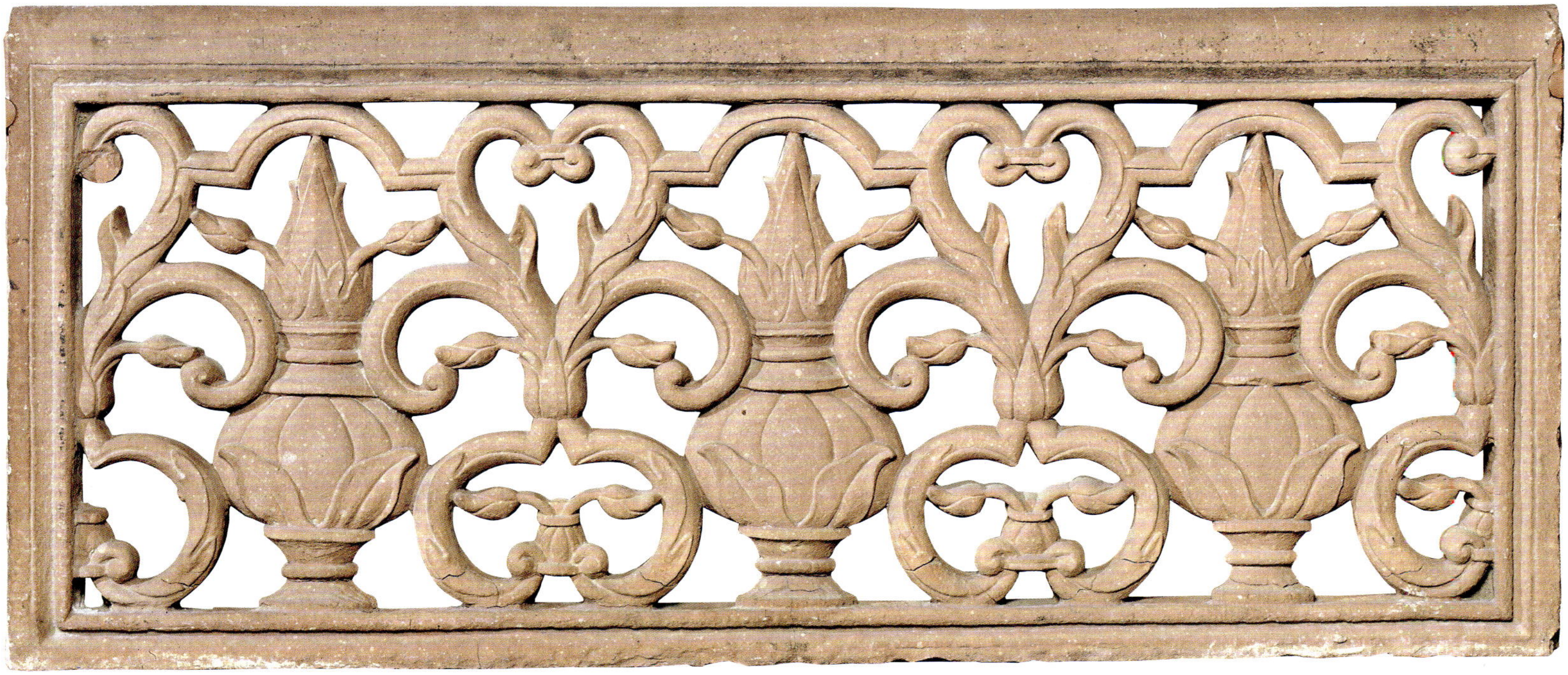

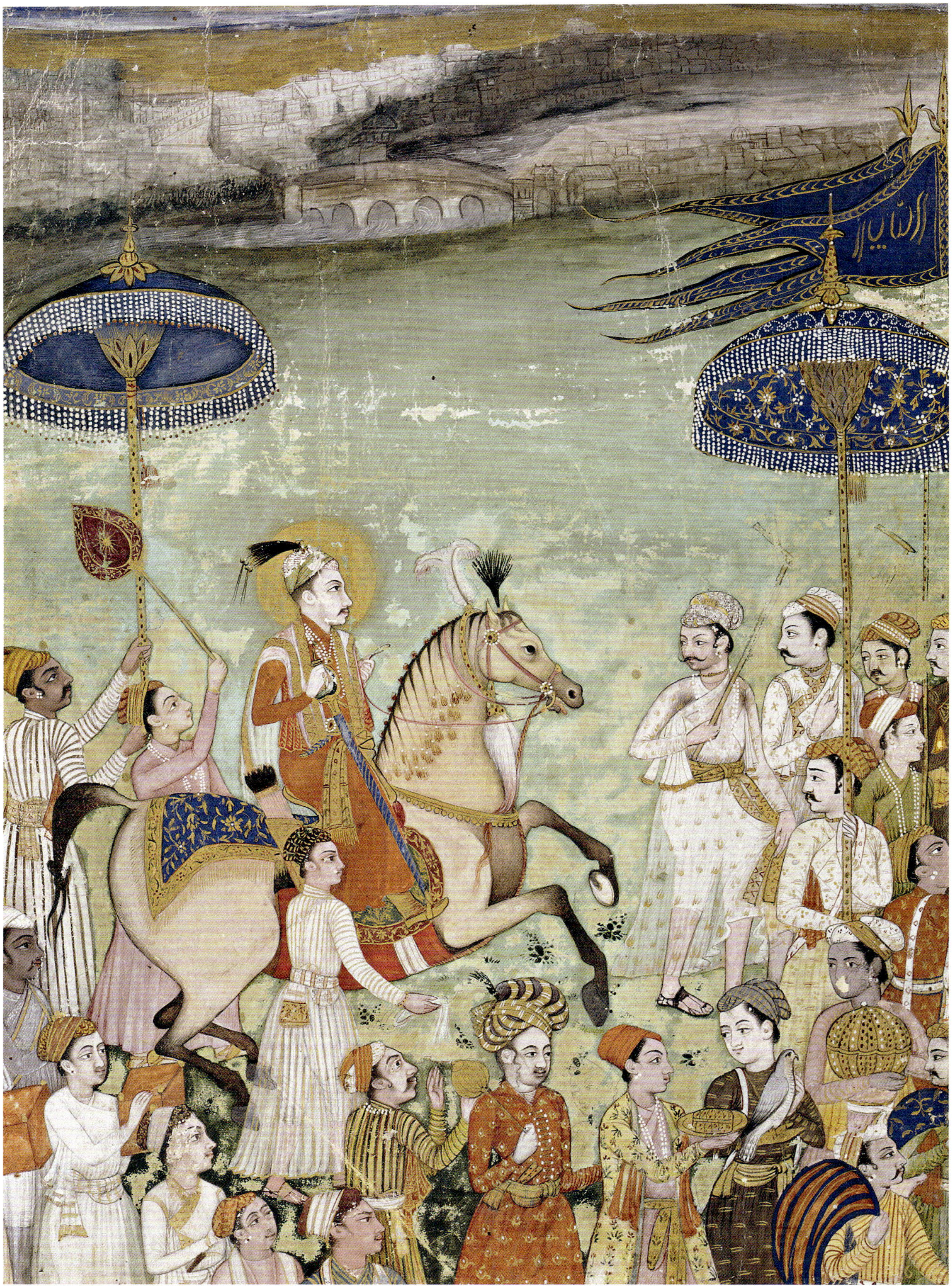

94

Sultan ʻAbdallah Qutb Shah in procession

GOLCONDA, DECCAN, 1635–40

Opaque watercolor and gold on paper
35.3 × 27.7 cm (14 × 10 3/8 in.)
Dutch and French inscriptions on reverse (the French one stating that the painting was brought to Europe in 1665, captain Hugo Hollandais[1])
Published: S. Safrani, "Deccani drawings: Reflections on life," *Marg*, XLIV, 1, September 1992, p. 60, fig. 3

SULTAN ABDALLAH QUTB SHAH (r. 1626–72) came to the throne of Golconda at the age of twelve. His age in this processional scene suggests that the original was done about 1635, as was another standing portrait of him in the Chester Beatty Library, Dublin.[2] Other portraits of him are in the Ashmolean Museum, Oxford, as a mature young man in about 1640,in the Victoria and Albert Museum, London, and in the Ehrenfeld Collection, of about ten years later.[3] The present painting and that in Dublin show him with the long straight Deccani sword and the shawl draped gracefully over his shoulders as seen in portraits of his father Muhammad Qutb Shah (r. 1612–26) and grandfather Muhammad Quli Qutb Shah (r. 1580–1612).[4] In 1635, however, the Mughal emperor Shah Jahan intervened decisively in Deccani affairs, and forced Sultan ʻAbdallah to submit to incorporation into the Mughal empire; his later portraits show him wearing the curved Mughal sword and the shawl wrapped around his upper body instead of draped. The ubiquitous draped shawls seen in the royal portraits of Golconda were apparently the gifts of the Hindu inhabitants,[5] which were, and indeed are, given as marks of respect to individuals, but are also used to drape images of the gods. Hence no doubt the change of sartorial fashion enforced by the sumptuary police of the orthodox Shah Jahan.

The scene is set beside the river Musi, with the new city of Hyderabad founded by the Sultan's grandfather at the top of the painting. The attendants carry spectacular, pearl-fringed, royal umbrellas and standards, while a group to the front, one of whom is dressed in Iranian costume, bears such royal necessities as incense burners, pan-boxes, hawks, and the like. The whole layout of this scene would have been impossible before serious northern artistic influence began to make itself felt in the Deccan in the mid-1630s, when not only Mughal artists but also Rajput ones seem to have been traveling with the Mughal generals of Shah Jahan's armies. Indeed, some of the figures in this processional scene are couched in a Rajput idiom. While such considerations might normally suggest that this is a painting from late in the reign, based on an earlier Golconda painting, there would seem little reason to copy such a work and alter the appearance of the attendants, but keep the royal portrait in exactly the style of 1635.

JPL

1 The proceedings of the first voyages of the French East India Company in 1664–66 make all this impossible (see Weber, 1904, pp. 133–87, for details of ships, their voyages and their captains). No doubt this is a later, somewhat garbled family tradition.

2 Leach, 1995, pp. 938–42.

3 All three illustrated in Zebrowski, 1983, figs. 149–51.

4 *Ibid.*, figs. 142–43, and 145 (the latter published wrongly as ʻAbdallah, whom it does not resemble: it is a youthful portrait of his grandfather).

5 As suggested in Safrani, *op. cit.*

95

Steel dagger hilt in the form of a parrot head

MUGHAL, SECOND HALF OF SEVENTEENTH CENTURY

L. 16.5 cm (6 ½ in.)

THIS DAGGER (*KHANJAR*) HILT is made from finely forged steel with cut and chiseled designs, and with scrolling quillons with recesses for inlaid gems and openwork palmettes. The handle narrows toward the top and curves into a terminal head of a parrot, with a recess for the eye (probably also originally inset with a precious gem) and a strongly curved beak. The use of plain steel for this hilt combines the practical necessity for a strong material with an austere elegance and a pronounced use of linear design instead of the elaborate surface decoration often found on a more extravagant material such as jade. Daggers with angular geometric hilts and a plain form were favored during the reigns of Akbar and Jahangir, and are found in plain steel as well as jeweled gold.[1] The use of zoomorphic motifs on dagger hilts occurs by the 1630s, with horses, camels, lions, rams, and nilgai particularly found on carved jade hilts.[2] Such motifs are less usual on steel hilts.[3] Hilts of this type may be seen in paintings from the *Padshahnama*, the court history of Shah Jahan, worn by Dara Shikoh and Shah Shuja,[4] and were clearly reserved for royal princes or senior nobility, as the vast majority of nobles wear the *katar* (twin-handled, thrusting) dagger in these paintings. A steel sword hilt with a lion head is in the Khalili collection,[5] and sword hilts with tiger heads were among the items from Tippoo Sultan's armory.[6] From the late seventeenth century onward, use of animal heads on weapons became widespread throughout Mughal India and Rajasthan, with a gradual decline in the naturalistic quality of their representation.

MCS

1 Welch, 1985, nos. 98 and 127 for jeweled daggers of this period; and H. Ricketts and P. Missillier, *Splendeur des armes orientales*, Paris, 1988, no. 145, p.90 for the same form in plain steel.

2 Welch, *op. cit.*, no. 168 for a jade nilgai dagger; Ricketts and Missillier, *op. cit.*, has examples of zoomorphic dagger hilts, especially pp. 87–101.

3 Okada, 2000, has a plain steel *khanjar* with a "pistol" hilt, pp. 48–49.

4 Beach and Koch, 1997, fol. 72b (horse head) and fol. 115b (nilgai).

5 Alexander, 1992: for examples of plain steel hilts see nos. 120–22; lion hilt, no. 82.

6 Ricketts and Missillier, *op. cit.*, no. 211, p. 122.

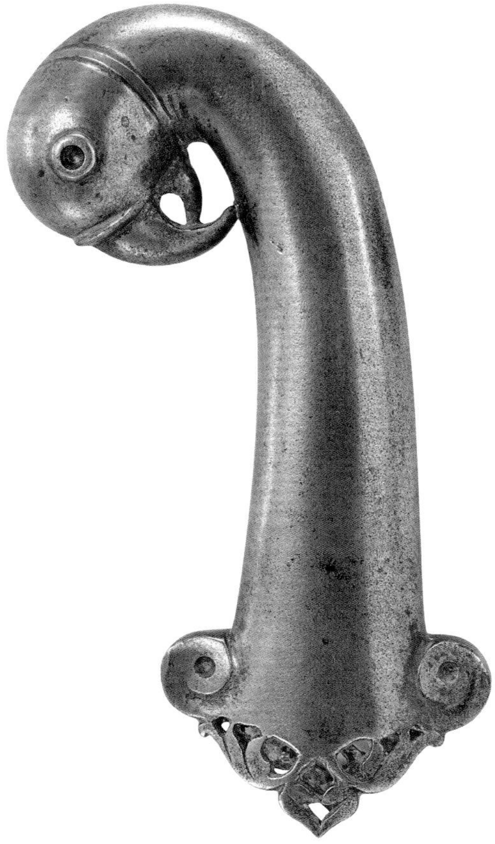

96

Penbox

DECCAN OR KASHMIR, LATE SEVENTEENTH OR EARLY EIGHTEENTH CENTURY, BY MANOHAR

Painted and lacquered papier-mâché with gold
23.2 × 3.8 × 2.9 cm (9 ⅛ × 1 ½ × 13⁄16 in.)
Inscribed in Persian: *kamtarin manohar* ("by the humble Manohar")
Published: N. Haidar Haykel, "A lacquer pen-box by Manohar," in R. Crill et al. eds., *Arts of Mughal India: Studies in honour of Robert Skelton*, London, 2004[1]
Metropolitan Museum of Art, New York, Cynthia Hazen Polsky and Leon B. Polsky Fund (2002.416 a-b)

THIS LACQUER PENBOX IS A FINE EXAMPLE of a combination of Indian, Persian and European elements, first seen in late Safavid painting in Iran, which influenced developments in India. The box is signed by a previously unknown Indian artist, Manohar, and relates closely to a well-known laquered jewel case in the Victoria and Albert Museum, London, by Rahim Deccani.[2] Together these works contribute to growing evidence of a following of this distinct Safavid offshoot in Indian painting of the late seventeenth century. The central motif depicts a young woman with long tendrils of hair, wearing Persian dress and holding a branch above her head in a fertility pose that is familiar from ancient Indian art. Similar compositions are known in the works of the Persian artists Shaikh 'Abbasi and Bahram Sofrakesh and their followers.[3] Above, an amorous couple are in Indian dress, the prince seated on a high-scalloped back chair; again images of lovers similarly dressed and arranged are be found in several late seventeenth-century Persian compositions. Below, a European gallant is seated on rocks and plays his flute to deer grazing nearby. Among the many pastoral scenes on the sides of the box, which include groups of travelers, hunters, lovers, and views of distant architecture, is an allegorical motif of two men carrying an oversized bunch of grapes, based on a work by the French artist Nicolas Poussin.

Two centers in India have emerged as possible areas where Persian and Indian artists, including Manohar and Rahim, may have been practicing this distinctive hybrid style: Golconda in the Deccan and Kashmir in the far north. Several important Persian artists are thought to have spent time at both these centers in the late seventeenth century, giving rise to local painting idioms that followed their influential style. Contact between the Persian and Indian painting traditions was also sustained through the circulation and copying of works, demonstrating a mutual awareness of styles.[4]

NHH

1 Also N. Haidar, in *Recent acquisitions, a selection: 2002–2003*, *Metropolitan Museum of Art Bulletin*, Fall 2003, p. 10.

2 Zebrowski, 1983, pp. 202–203, figs. 169-74.

3 For comparative material see Soudavar, 1992, p. 347, no. 146; Adamova, 1996, p. 242, no. 33.

4 See N. Haidar Haykel, "A lacquer pen-box by Manohar," for further discussion in the context of other Persian and Indian works.

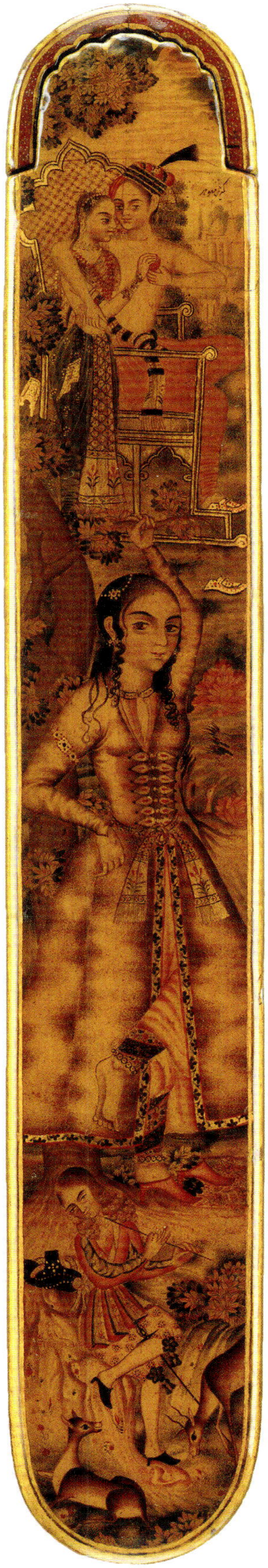

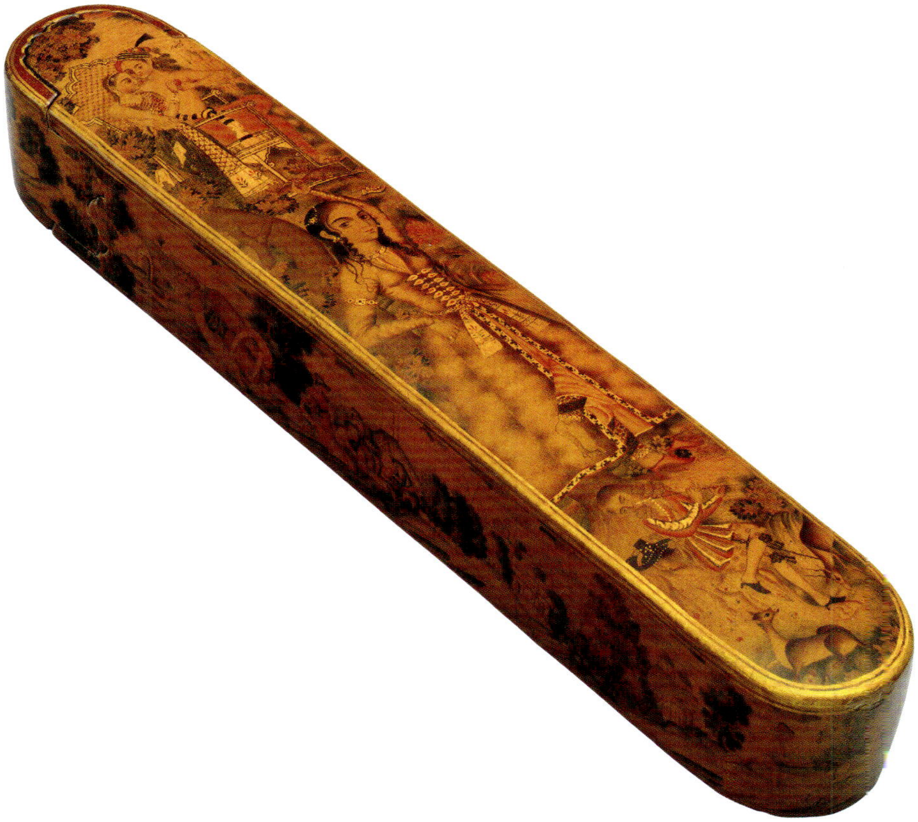

97

Glass bowl and dish

MUGHAL, NORTH INDIA, FIRST HALF OF THE EIGHTEENTH CENTURY

Glass; blown, painted with silver and gold leaf, and fired; tooled on the pontil
H. 12.1, W. 20.3, D. 25.4 cm (4 ¾ × 8 × 10 in.)
Metropolitan Museum of Art, New York, Cynthia Hazen Polsky and Leon B. Polsky Fund and The Annenberg Foundation Gift (2000.490 a-b)

OF ALL THE DIFFERENT CATEGORIES OF MUGHAL GLASS, the milky-white color of this bowl and dish ensemble constitutes the rarest type.[1] The opaque surfaces of the bowl and its matching tray are decorated with identical flowering shrubs enclosed within oval compartments, painted in two shades of gold and silver, now tarnished into a dark metallic gray. Although the cinched waist profile of the bowl is unusual, at least one metalwork example is known, including others depicted in contemporary paintings.[2] The round, flat tray with everted rim, however, follows a classic Indian thali form, recalling earlier examples of bidri ware both in shape and decoration, especially in the radiating arrangement of flowering shrubs in compartments.[3]

While little evidence of glass production from early India survives, the Mughal period saw a flourishing of this industry, in several cases stimulated by European, and in particular British, contact.[4] Glass was fashioned into a number of types of objects including globular and bell-shaped hookah bases (cat. no. 100), square "gin" bottles, and assorted vessels, some of which were imported, and then painted and gilded to luminous effect. Glass workshops were located in Gujarat, Lucknow, Rajasthan, and Sind, where the technique of free blown and mold-blown glass was best known but also was accompanied by a revival in wheel-cut and more rarely twice-fired applied glass.[5] The decoration of Mughal glass followed trends seen in the broader world of decorative arts and painting of the period including, as in this example, the classic combination of floral forms, in profile or silhouette against a plain ground, often incorporated within cartouches of varying shapes. This hallmark Mughal style first developed in floral painting studies of the Jahangir period (1605–27) and was adapted to the decorative arts in general under his successor Shah Jahan (1628–57) by about 1640.

NHH

1 Dikshit, 1969, pls. XVII, XXIV, illustrating two other examples and with an overview of the development of Indian glass.

2 Zebrowski, 1983, fig. 53; also, there is a similarly shaped vessel in the Los Angeles County Museum, in silver and attributed to the eighteenth century (acc. no. AC1994.174.1, illustrated on the LACMA website under "Decorative arts, South and Southeast Asia."

3 Zebrowski, 1997, fig. 433.

4 S. Digby, "A corpus of 'Mughal' glass," *Bulletin of the School of Oriental and African Studies*, London, XXXVI, 1, 1973, pp. 80–96.

5 Carboni, 2001, pp. 381–96; Carboni, 2002, for an overview of Islamic glass.

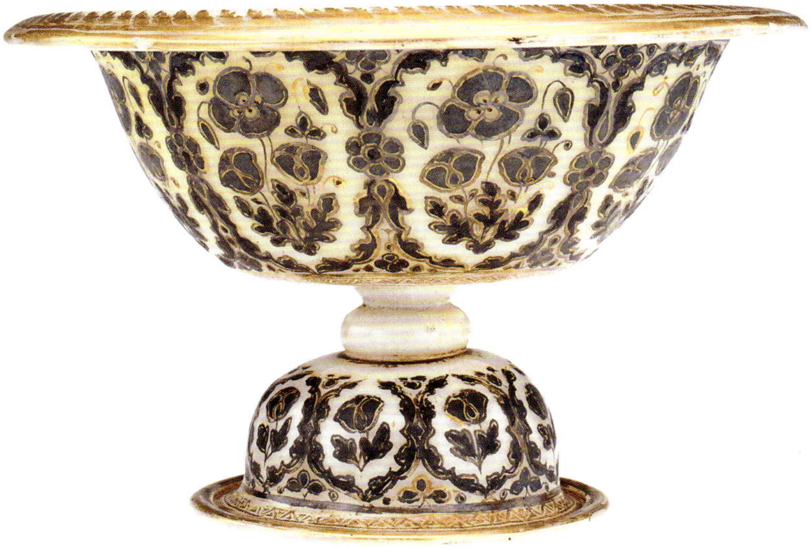

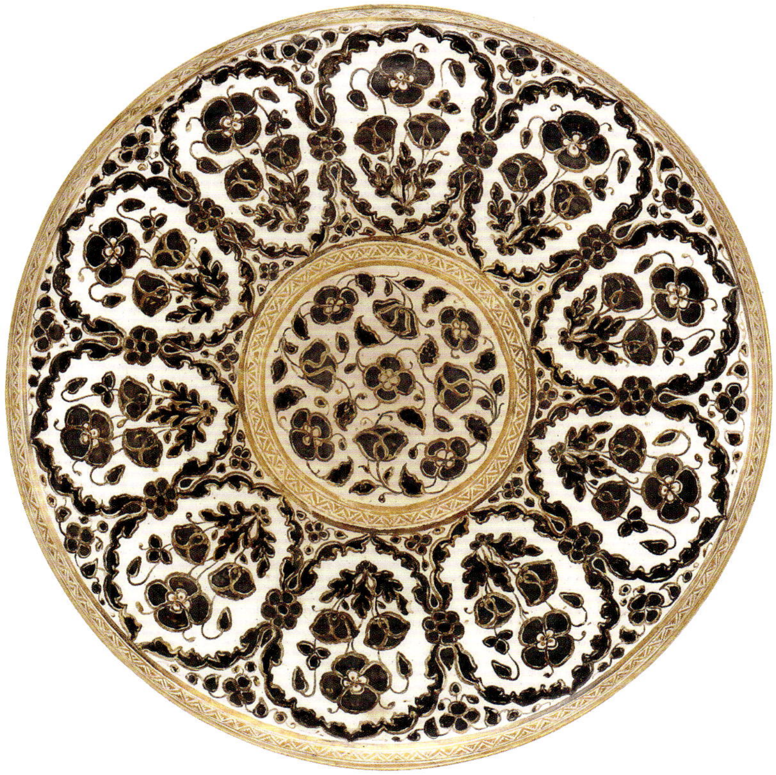

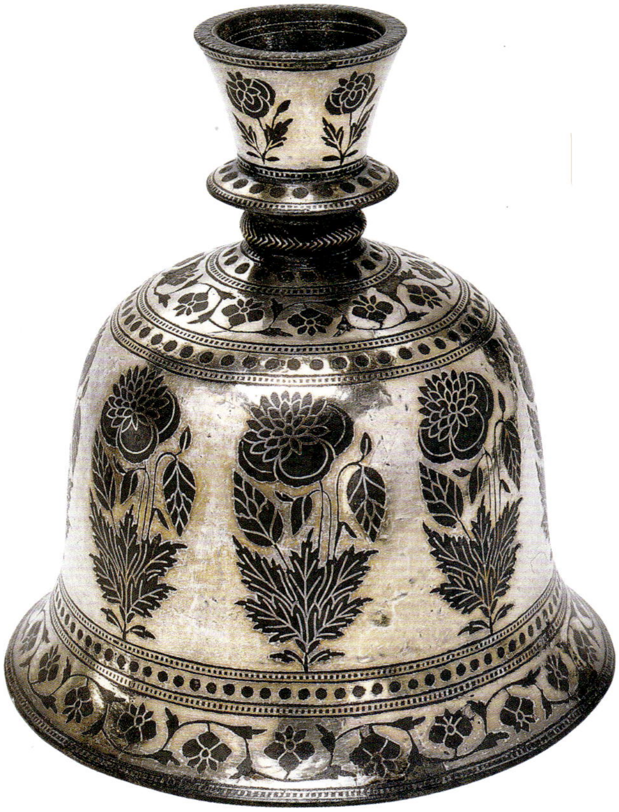

98

Bidri hookah base

BIDAR, DECCAN, SECOND HALF OF THE EIGHTEENTH CENTURY

Bidri ware: base metal alloy with silver
H. 17.1 cm (6 ⅛ in.)

THIS BELL-SHAPED BIDRI HOOKAH BASE is decorated with silver,[1] with eight flowering plants around the body, above and below which are bands of a dot motif and bands of arabesque. The neck has a ridge and a further band of flowering plants, also reserved against the silver ground. The material known as bidri was manufactured in the Deccan, principally at the town of Bidar from which its name derives. The metal consists of an alloy with high zinc content which is cast. The surface is then engraved with the design and the recessed area inlaid in silver or brass, or rarely in gold (*zarboland* technique). Alternatively the design is cut from silver sheet and silhouetted against the dark ground (*aftabi* technique), as in this example.[2] Finally the surface is darkened with a chemical paste and burnished with oil.

A number of surviving objects in bidri can be dated stylistically to the seventeenth century, and are also seen in seventeenth-century paintings, though the earliest literary reference dates from 1759. The illustrated atlas prepared at Faizabad in 1770 for Col. Jean-Baptiste Gentil, military advisor to the Nawab of Oudh, shows bidri manufacture on the map of the district of Bidar, with a variety of items made in the technique illustrated in the margins.[3] Other later centers of bidri production, established by the eighteenth or nineteenth centuries, were Purnea in Bihar, Murshidabad in Bengal, and Lucknow. In miniature paintings from the mid-seventeenth century onward, bidri hookah bases are shown initially with spherical bases, supported on a ring, the later bell-shaped bases appearing by the 1740s. The two forms co-existed for a short period, before the bell-shape gained general popularity, due no doubt to the increased stability it provided.[4]

MCS

1 Stronge, 1985, p. 94.

2 Zebrowski. 1997, pl. 398, for a similar hookah base to this example.

3 Gole, 1988, illustrating the map plates from Col. Gentil's atlas, now in the British Library (Or. 4039).

4 Zebrowski, *op. cit.*, figs. 361–66, 402–5, and ch. 16, pp. 225–45, for a discussion of the evolution of the hookah.

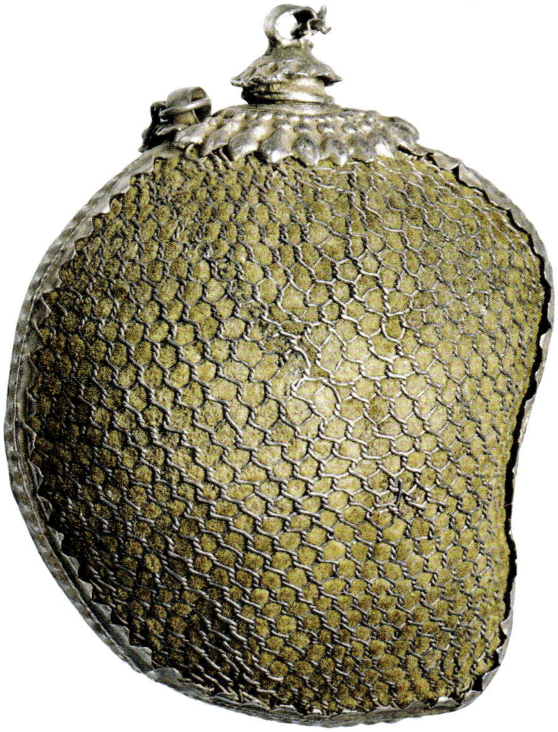

99

A vessel in the form of a mango

NORTH INDIA, EIGHTEENTH CENTURY

Silver and fabric
H. 6 × W. 4.1 cm (2 ⅜ × ⅝ in.)
Metropolitan Museum of Art, New York,
Gift of Cynthia Hazen Polsky (2011.576.6)

THIS SMALL VESSEL IN THE FORM OF A MANGO may have been a container for lime paste (*chunam*), one of the ingredients of pan, and may have been worn on the belt, assuming both a practical and ornamental function.[1] The body of the vessel is covered in green fabric and a fine mesh of silver wire, with silver mounts and a silver stopper, which screws into the top of the vessel, secured by a chain. The mango form was much favored by Indian craftsmen when making small containers and flasks, and is found in various media throughout the Mughal period. Examples include a series of small rock crystal mango flasks and mango-shaped brass and bidri hookah bases.[2] Other vegetable forms used included a jade hookah base carved as a melon, and a jade bowl carved as a half gourd.[3]

A similar use of silver wire forming a mesh around an object is seen on a *pandan* (box for pan) datable to the early eighteenth century.[4] The technique, possibly of Chinese origin, is otherwise very rare. Silver wire is also used in filigree, worked in the eighteenth century at Karimnagar in the Deccan, and datable through a silver filigree dressing table set listed in an inventory of Robert Clive's possessions in 1774.[5] Relatively little silver survives from India from before the nineteenth century. A silver gilt rosewater sprinkler, datable by an engraved coat of arms, establishes the use of silver in the seventeenth century,[6] and silver trays, sword fittings, and boxes survive from the eighteenth century.

MCS

1 It has also been suggested that it could have contained a condiment used in cooking: McInerney, 1982, p. 38.

2 Welch, 1963, no. 54, for a rock crystal mango flask formerly in the Heeramaneck Collection; Zebrowski, 1997, pp. 240–41, for three mango-shaped containers. T. H. Hendley, *Indian jewellery: Journal of Indian Art and Industry*, vol. XII, London 1906–09, pl. 93, no. 629, shows a silver mango-shaped perfume flask from Trichinopoly.

3 Welch, 1985, no. 123, p. 195, for the jade melon hookah base; Victoria and Albert Museum; 1982, no. 355a, p. 119, for the gourd bowl (British Museum 1945.10–17–259).

4 Zebrowski, *op. cit.*, p. 44, nos 19 (a–b), for the silver mesh *pandan*.

5 Archer et al., 1987, and Zebrowski, *op. cit.*, fig. 20.

6 *Ibid.*, p. 41, pl. 12.

100

Glass hookah base

NORTH INDIA, EARLY NINETEENTH CENTURY

Glass, wheel-cut and gilt
H. 17.8 cm (7 in.)

THIS BELL-SHAPED, GREEN GLASS HOOKAH base has wheel-cut and gilt designs of stems and flowers around the body, further bands of wheel-cut and gilt decoration around the base of the body and the neck, and a band of small flowers around the upper neck. Two comparable hookah bases[1] show similar techniques of decoration, though these have a row of single vertical blooms around the body instead of the design of trailing plant stems seen here.

The form and decoration of glass hookah bases are largely derived from metal bidri models (cat. no. 98), but the glass bases have a less clearly established chronology. Some useful dating evidence comes from a mid-seventeenth-century Mandi painting depicting a glass shop in a bazaar.[2] At some point in the eighteenth century, the spherical form gave way to the bell shape, as in the case of bidri ware, though again the two shapes seem to have co-existed for some time.[3]

The history of glass manufacture in India is also complicated by the substantantial imports from Europe in the Mughal period. There was already a well-established Indian production: Abu'l Fazl in the *'Ain-i Akbari* (written 1596–97) mentions glass made in Bihar and at Alwar near Agra,[4] and glassworks were established in Gujarat at Kapadwanj and in the Kathiawar peninsula, and at Ahmedabad, Surat, Bhuj, perhaps Hyderabad in Sind, and at Lucknow in the eighteenth century.[5] However, substantial amounts of glass were also imported from Europe in the sixteenth century and later, with material coming from England, Italy, Bohemia and Holland. *Rhead's Weekly Journal* of September 17, 1737 notes that "6,306 pieces of [English] glass" were exported to India.[6] Such imports included both finished vessels and blocks of glass for finishing in India.[7] The body of our glass hookah could either be of English origin or have been made in India,[8] although the numerous bubbles perhaps indicate an Indian origin.

MCS

1 A colorless bell-shaped base is in the David Collection, Copenhagen: K. von Folsach, *Art from the world of Islam in the David Collection*, Copenhagen, 2001, no. 354 (acc. no. 30/1979), and another in the al-Sabah Collection: Carboni, 2001, no. 104e; see also Dikshit, 1969, pl. XVIA, for an example with the floral decoration running round the body.

2 Topsfield and Beach, 1991, no. 15; S. Digby, "A corpus of Mughal glass," *Bulletin of the School of Oriental and African Studies*, XXXVI, 1, 1973, pp. 80–96, pl. III; S. Markel, "Western imports and the nature of later Indian glassware," *Asian Art*, VI, 4, Fall 1993, fig. 2, p. 37.

3 Carboni, *op. cit.*, p. 381.

4 S. Markel, "Indian and 'Indianate' glass vessels in the Los Angeles County Museum of Art," *Journal of Glass Studies*, vol. 33, 1991, p. 83.

5 *Ibid.*; also Digby, *op. cit.*

6 Markel, *loc. cit.*; Markel, "Western imports," pp. 35–59.

7 Markel, "Indian and 'Indianate' glass vessels," p. 83.

8 Carboni, *op. cit.*, p. 385.

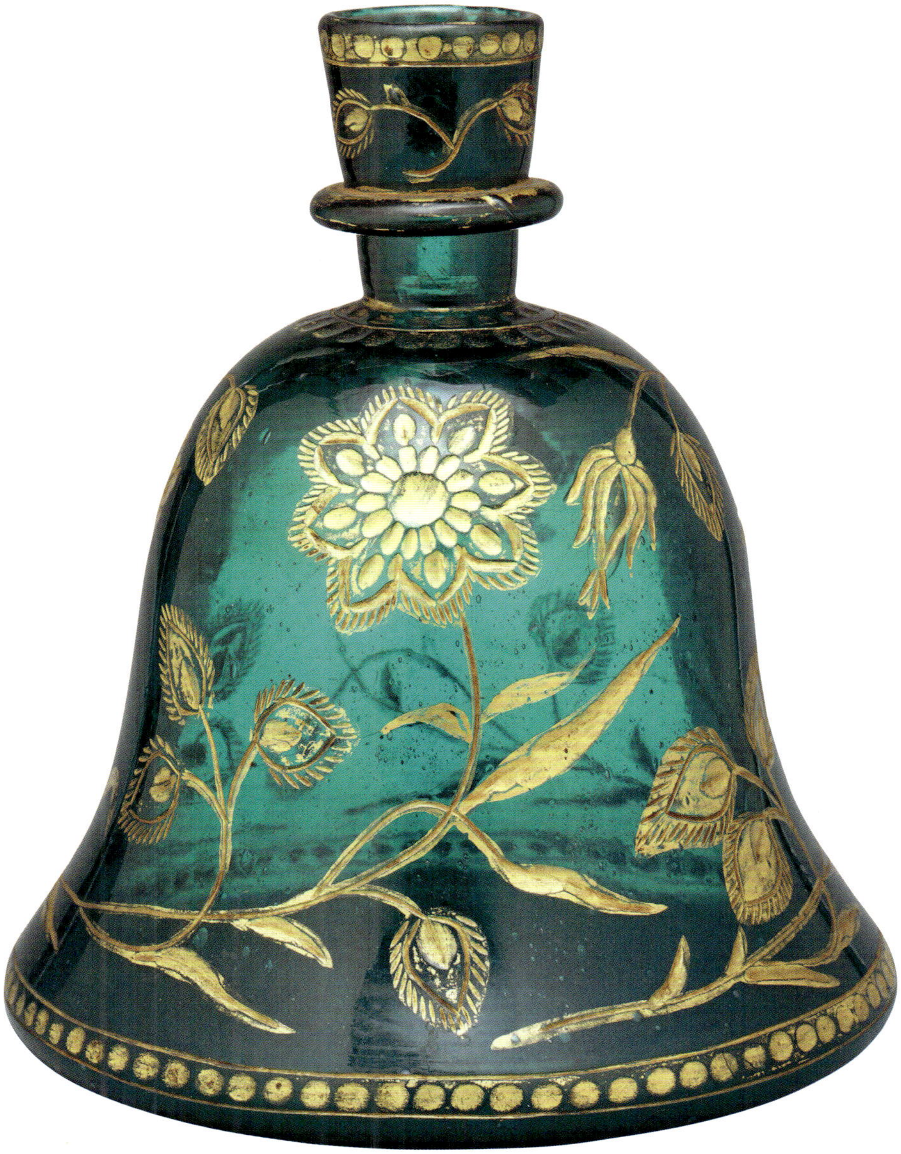

101

A courtesan and some rowdy officers

KISHANGARH, RAJASTHAN,
CA. 1745

Brush drawing on paper
20.3 x 27.9 cm (8 x 11 in.)

THIS ENIGMATIC SCENE THROWS A DROLL LIGHT on the seamy underside of life at court or in camp. An evidently popular prostitute sits as though enthroned on a high seat, smoking a hookah. Before her a table is covered with hookahs standing ready for her visitors. One client, a bearded officer with sword and shield, squats before her, smoking. Two more officers stand in line behind him, one holding a bird.[1] In the foreground, a lively altercation takes place, as two pairs of warriors bicker or incompetently threaten each other (their swords are broken), while their companions look on in puzzlement or exasperation.

Also known in earlier versions,[2] this curious vignette may illustrate an unidentified anecdote or is perhaps a general satire on a drunken and licentious soldiery. Along with the refined romantic paintings of Krishna and Radha in court settings (cat. no. 65), the eighteenth-century Kishangarh school is notable for an earthy and sometimes biting genre of satirical scenes taken from everyday street life (cat. no. 105) or private sexual mores.[3] The gifted master Bhavanidas may well have played a major role in its formation. Evidently one or more of the royal patrons at Kishangarh—Prince Savant Singh, also known as the devotional poet Nagaridas, may well have been the initiator[4]—was as conscious of the ridiculous in human life as of the sublime.

AT

1 Faint outlines of a third man appear on the left, and of another female at far right.

2 E.g. S. C. Welch, "A matter of empathy: Comical Indian pictures," *Asian Art and Culture*, 3, Fall 1994, fig. 12; also Welch, 1997, illus. p. 35.

3 N. Haidar, "Satire and humour in Kishangarh painting," in A. Topsfield ed., *Court painting in Rajasthan*, Bombay, 2000, pp. 78–91; Welch, "A matter of empathy," pp. 92–102.

4 Haidar *op. cit.*, pp. 89–90.

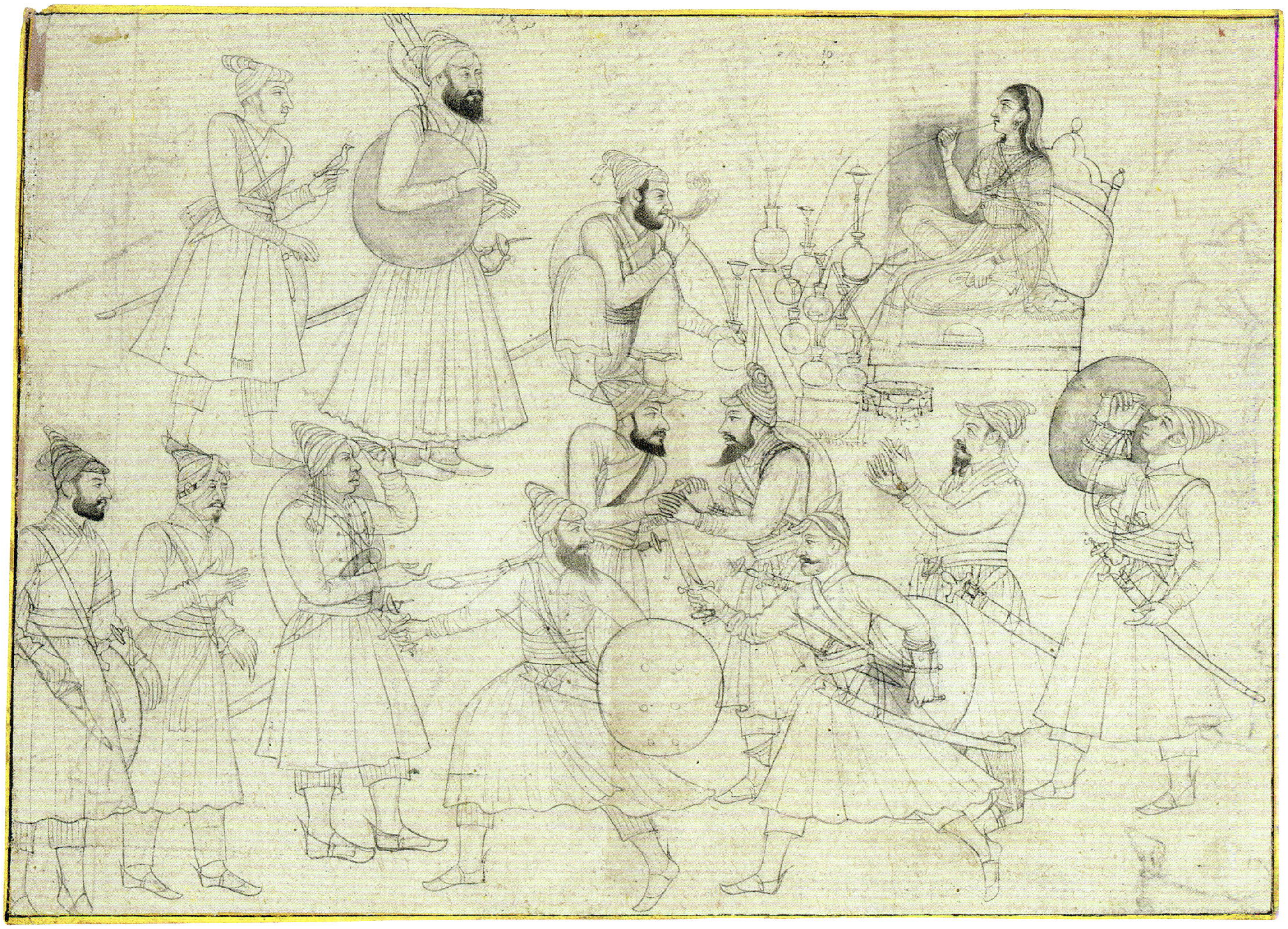

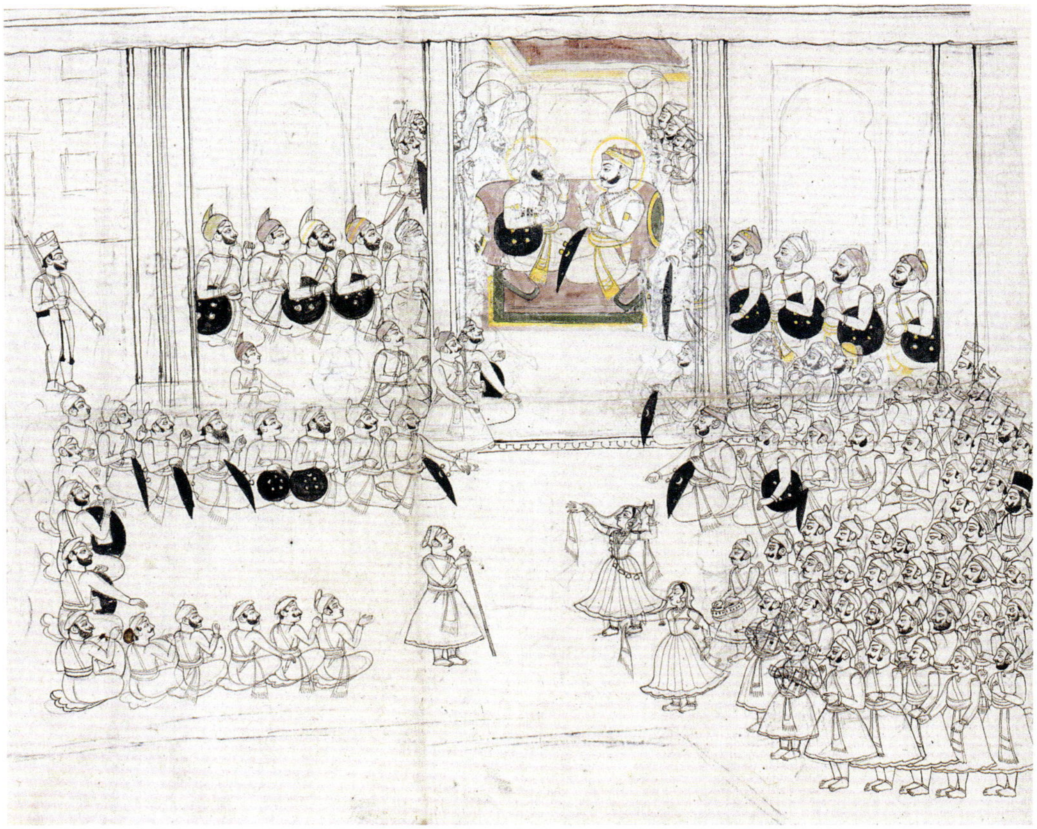

102

Maharao Ram Singh II receives a Raja in durbar

KOTAH, RAJASTHAN, CA. 1850

Brush drawing with watercolor on paper
49.5 × 56.5 cm (19 ½ × 22 ¼ in.)
Private collection

SEATED FACING LEFT ON THE CENTRAL ROYAL *GADDI* (throne seat), Maharao Ram Singh II of Kotah (r. 1827–65) receives another Rajput ruler in a formal durbar assembly. The portrait of the visiting prince is indistinct, but he may perhaps be the neighbouring ruler of Bundi, also called Ram Singh. Being of equal rank, the rulers (both with nimbuses) sit side by side against a huge bolster under a canopy, holding their shields. Near-symmetrically on either side, their attendants wave chowries (yak-tail fans) and their respective noblemen sit in facing rows, in order of hierarchy. In the main courtyard the visiting entourage sits on the left in a three-sided formation, while the more numerous local courtiers form a denser group on the right. In the foreground, a master of ceremonies stands holding a staff, while two nautch girls and their musicians provide entertainment.

While elsewhere in mid-nineteenth-century Rajasthan the art of painting was gradually losing its momentum, Ram Singh II of Kotah was a prolific and sometimes amusingly quirky patron, who encouraged his artists to paint court life with unusual verve and elan. This unfinished drawing with limited preliminary color is of a more conventional kind and was probably a study for a commemorative painting of this durbar.[1]

AT

1 For durbar scenes of Ram Singh II on paper, cloth and in wall-paintings, see Desai, 1985, no. 97 (for a preparatory drawing: J. Bautze, "Scenes of devotion and court life: Painting under Maharao Ram Singh of Kota," in A. Topsfield ed., *Court painting in Rajasthan*, Bombay, 2000, pp. 135–36, fig. 13); J. Bautze, "The Ajmer Darbar of 1832 and Kota painting," *South Asian Studies*, 6, 1990, figs. 2, 12, 14; J. Bautze, "Portraitmalerei unter Maharao Ram Singh von Kota," *Artibus Asiae*, XLIX, 3–4, 1988–89, pp. 316–50.

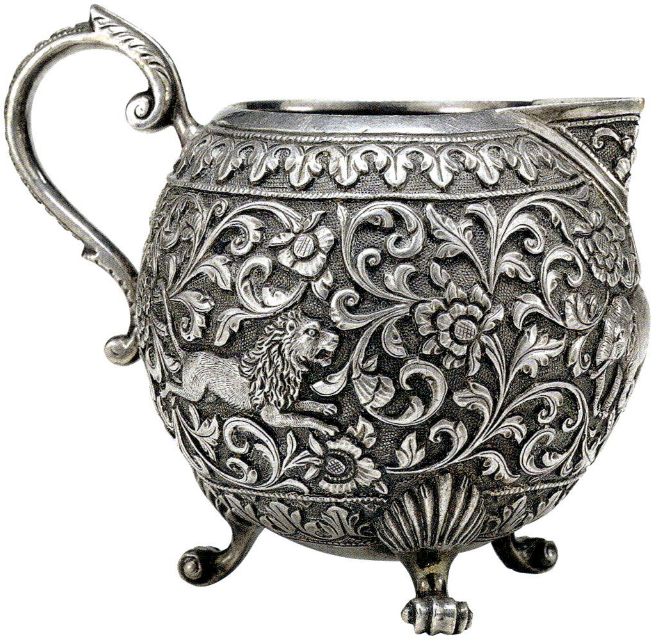

103

Silver cream jug

BHUJ, CUTCH, CA. 1880

Silver, marked "OM Bhuj"
H. 7.7 cm (3 ⅜ in.)

THIS CREAM JUG BELONGED TO a silver tea set of the European (British) type. Of globular form, it stands on three scrolling feet, with a handle and a small spout. The body has fine repoussé decoration of a running lion and an antelope amongst floral scrolls, against a punched ground. The jug was made by the silversmith Oomersi Mawji, who worked in Bhuj, the capital of Cutch. He was perhaps the best silversmith in late nineteenth-century India, and was appointed court silver-smith to the Maharao of Cutch.[1] His workshop was one of the few to mark their silver, using his maker's mark (OM Bhuj). Silver of a high purity was used,[2] and generally decorated with scrolling foliage, animals, and birds against a finely punched ground. Silverwork by Oomersi Mawji is in a number of collections, including the Musée Guimet, Paris.[3]

Cutch silverwork was exhibited in the International Exhibitions in Europe in the late nineteenth century, such as the Paris Universal Exposition of 1878. The catalogue for the Glasgow International Exhibition of 1888 records that no part of India was more celebrated for its work in precious metals than Cutch.[4] Such was the popularity of Cutch silver that it was imported into Britain by firms such as Proctor and Co. and Liberty's in London, and into the United States by Tiffany and Co.[5] The range of products included claret jugs, mugs, bowls, salt cellars, pepper pots, mustard pots, and tea sets.[6] Whereas firms such as Hamilton of Calcutta catered for the tastes of resident English patrons with silver entirely in the English style,[7] the Cutch silversmiths retained the vocabulary of traditional decoration but applied them skilfully to European forms, as with this jug.

MCS

1 Wilkinson, 1999, pp. 65–102, discusses Cutch silverwork; p. 69 for Oomersi Mawji.

2 *Ibid.*, p. 68.

3 Okada, Paris, 2000, p. 151.

4 Mukharji, 1974, p. 168.

5 Wilkinson, *op. cit.*, pp. 6, 8, 68; see pl. 12, p. 12, and pls. 107–08, p. 79, for examples of Cutch silver from Liberty catalogues of ca. 1890.

6 *Ibid.*, pls. 114–23, pp. 82–86; pl. 114 illustrates a jug of similar form to this example, part of a three piece tea set, with a variation for the handles.

7 Wilkinson, 1987.

104

A prince at play

MUGHAL, CA. 1605

Opaque watercolor and gold on paper
Image 13.8 × 9.5 cm (5 7/16 × 3 ¾ in.);
page 27.3 × 17.8 cm (10 ¾ × 7 in.)
Published: A. N. Heeramaneck, *Masterpieces of Indian painting from the former collection of Nasli M. Heeramaneck*, New York, 1984, pl. 182

IN THIS CHARMING IMAGE A YOUNG PRINCE seated on a cart is being dragged around a courtyard by two of his playmates. He is seated on a rich rug, and with one hand apparently directs the cart, while waving the stem of a hollyhock as a whip with the other. Two other boys rush around in the foreground. It is tempting to try to identify the prince with one of Jahangir's three sons. The confident handling of the open space of the court precludes a date before 1600, and we know the appearance of the three princes from the portraits of about this date of Akbar in old age with his grandsons and Murtaza Khan in the Cincinnati Museum and Chester Beatty Library.[1] Only the young Khurram, Akbar's favorite grandson and the future Shah Jahan, who is about ten years old in both of those paintings, would be the right age and appearance for this princeling in a cart of possibly a few years later.

JPL

1 See Beach, 1978, fig. 11, p. 133; and Leach, 1995, p. 340.

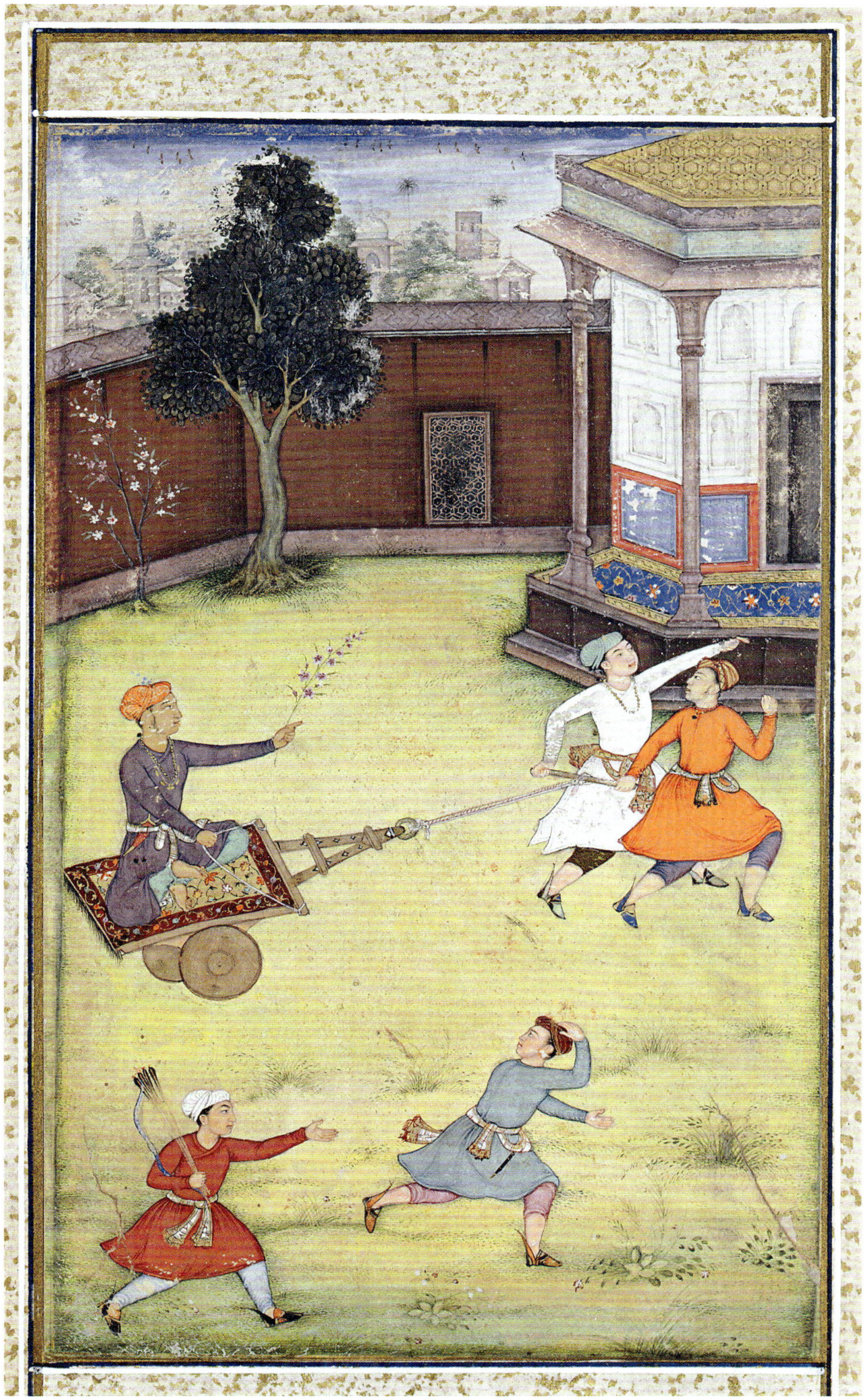

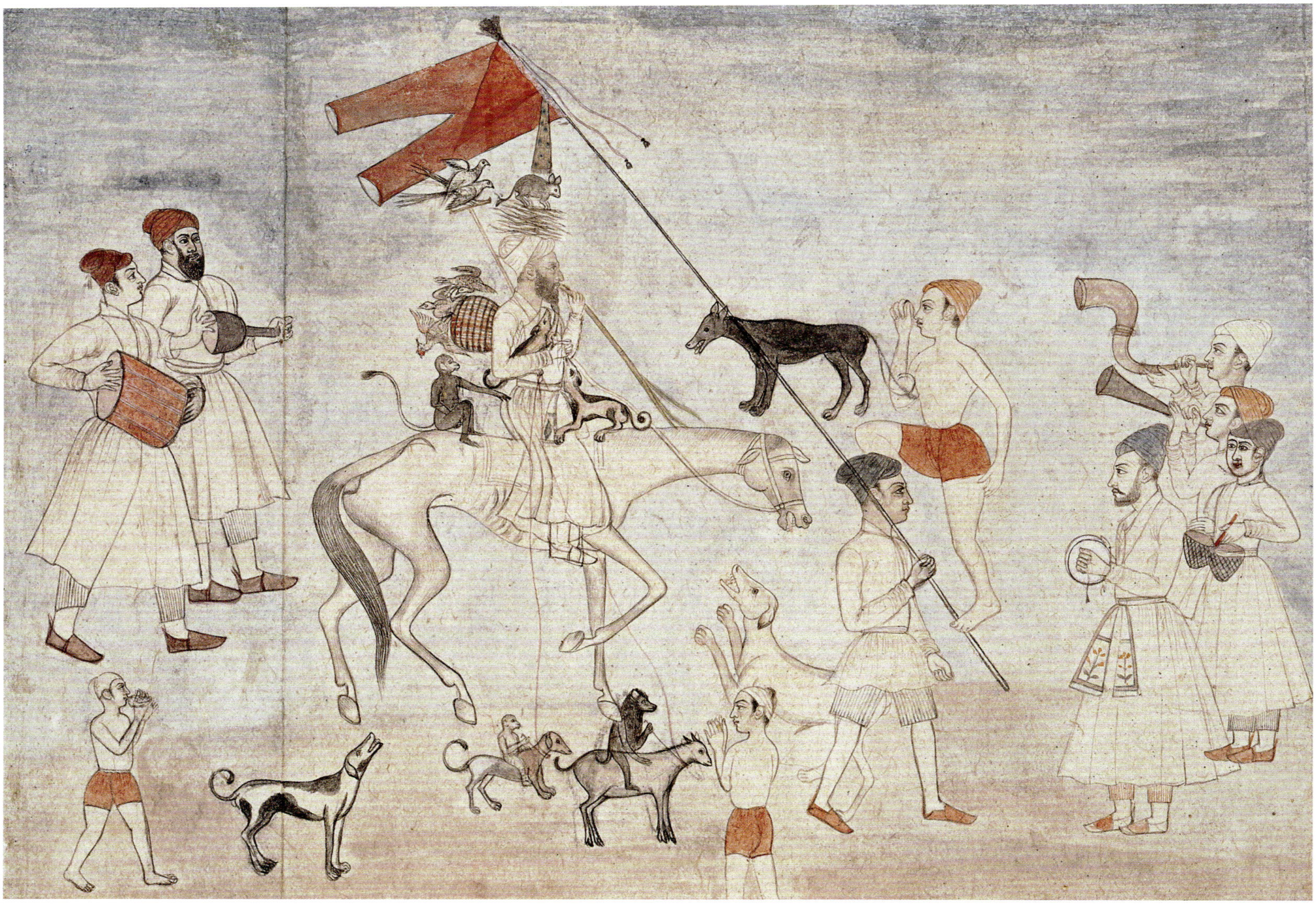

105

Traveling entertainers

RAJASTHAN, PROBABLY KISHANGARH, CA. 1740–50

Brush drawing with watercolor on paper
22.9 x 33 cm (9 x 13 in.)

TRAVELING ACROBATS, JUGGLERS, AND ENTERTAINERS with animals were and are a common feature of Indian street life. Here a very strange performing troupe travels in an almost stately procession. The principal figure is bearded, rides a horse, and smokes from a hookah tube in the manner of a nobleman; but no hookah is visible and his mount is a pathetic nag. His company of dogs, monkeys, and birds ride with him, and a rabbit(?) sits in a precarious nest on his turban. A monkey and a bear cub ride alongside on a dog and a goat, and a young assistant walks in front carrying a ballooning pyjama (*paijama*) on a pole for a banner. Musicians ceremoniously play horns, drums, and other instruments, while in the foreground a boy blows a conch and a dog howls, to complete the cheerful cacophony.

The image of the emaciated, broken-down horse is a familiar one from earlier Mughal models,[1] but otherwise this amusing slice of life seems to have been based on observation and is probably only a little exaggerated in its eccentricity. It may have been painted at Kishangarh, where such comic genre scenes were popular in the mid-eighteenth century (cat. no. 101).

AT

1 E.g. Welch, 1976, no. 8; Khandalavala and Chandra, 1965, no. 18.

106

Ivory plaque depicting a procession

CHANDRAKETUGARH, BENGAL, OR VIDISHA, MADHYA PRADESH, SECOND OR FIRST CENTURY BC

5 × 13.5 cm (2 × 5 ⅞ in.)

THIS IVORY PANEL IS CARVED IN RELIEF with a procession of musicians, dancers, and an elephant with two riders all moving to the right, with a beaded border above and below; the reverse side depicts six standing women. The elephant is shown with a saddle blanket and one of its riders holds up an elephant goad (*ankus*). In front of it, a procession of three musicians are playing drums and a horn, while above them are two figures carrying bundles of wood and another carrying a pot. All the figures have distinctive hair arrangement, with a high top-knot and a large coiffure to either side. The six standing women on the reverse also have this three-part hair arrangement. The function of this small decorative panel is not clear: it may have been part of an item of furniture or else a handle piece for a comb. It is believed to have been found at Chandraketugarh.

The narrative scene bears a very close relationship to a group of fragmentary terracotta panels from Chandraketugarh, which also have an elephant with a rider holding up an ankus facing right, two figures carrying bundles of firewood and musicians.[1] The link to the terracottas indicates that a specific narrative is represented, probably a scene from one of the Jataka stories. The coiffure is close to that seen on several of the terracotta figures reportedly found in Bengal,[2] and it is also found on the reliefs on the gateways (*toranas*) at Sanchi in Madhya Pradesh. Although Bautze suggests a close link between the terracotta and the Bharhut narrative scenes, this crowded scene is closer to the Sanchi reliefs, in particular to the two panels depicting the Wars of the Relics,[3] and it may therefore represent a precursor of the later Sanchi carvings. An inscription on the South Gate at Sanchi records that ivory carvers from Vidisha created the relief series on the toranas at that stupa.[4] An ivory comb attributed to the Vidisha workshops in the second century AD is in the Victoria and Albert Museum, London.[5]

MCS

1 Bautze, 1995, pl. XLVI; Haque, 2001, p. 337, nos. C868, C873, and p. 380, B870.

2 Bautze, *op. cit.*, pl. XIII.

3 Marshall, 1918, pls. V, VIII.

4 This widely quoted inscription is mentioned, *inter alia*, in P. Pal, *Elephants and ivories in South Asia*, Los Angeles, 1981, p. 73.

5 Acc. no. IM 21–1937; M. Chandra, "Ancient Indian ivories," *Bulletin of the Prince of Wales Museum*, 6, 1957–59, pl. 46.

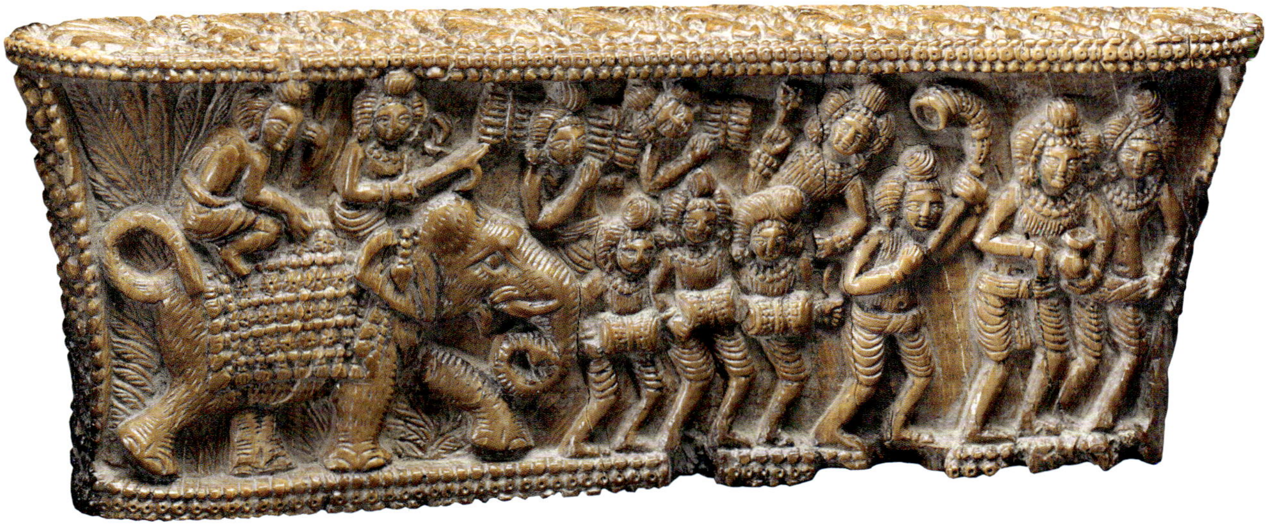

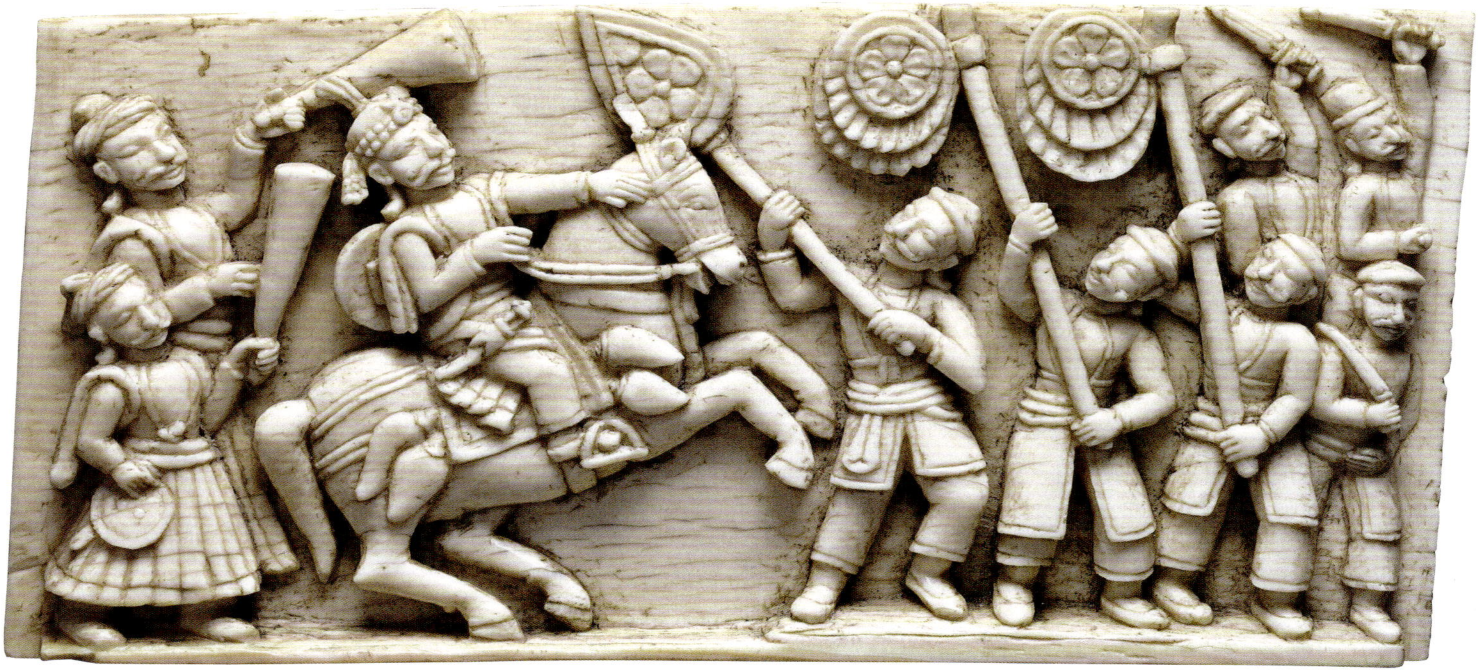

107

Ivory plaque with a Raja on horseback

SOUTH INDIA, EARLY NINETEENTH CENTURY

8.6 × 19.1 cm (3 ⅜ × 7 ½ in.)

THIS IVORY RELIEF PANEL DEPICTS A RAJA ON HORSEBACK riding in a procession with retainers, including two men walking behind his horse holding flywhisks, three carrying large fans in front of him, and a further three bearing swords. The figures can be compared to a group of small brass soldiers, probably made at Vizagapatam, examples of which are in the Ashmolean Museum, Oxford.[1] In particular, one of the three sword-bearers has similar headgear to that of a camel rider,[2] although the figures on the ivory panel do not have the bombast and swagger of the brass models. The small brass figures include riders and foot-soldiers, and were possibly made as a set of toys. Other small carved ivory soldiers were made as chess pieces, of which there are examples at Powis Castle.[3] This panel probably comes from a box, which we may speculate was perhaps associated with such model soldiers or chess pieces.

A painting of a procession at Tanjore with Raja Sarabhoji (r. 1798–1832) riding a horse, in the India Office Library collection, depicts soldiers with a similar range of uniforms and headgear.[4] The influence of European styles is evident in the realistic depiction of the figures both in the painting and on the ivory panel, replacing the Indian idioms of an earlier generation in paintings, such as a Tanjore procession of Raja Tulsaji (r. 1765–86).[5] The escort carries the emblems of royalty, including the fans and fly-whisks, indicating the status of the rider; such indications of rank were a jealously guarded privilege.

MCS

1 Digby and Harle, 1982.
2 *Ibid.*, pl. 9.
3 Archer et al., 1987, no. 114, p. 89; these examples are from Murshidabad.
4 Add. Or. 2954; Archer, 1972, no. 12, pl. 5, and p. 30.
5 Archer, 1992, no. 16, p. 49.

108

Nawab ʻAbd al-Rahman Khan of Jhajjar rides a tiger in his palace garden

DELHI, DATED 1849–50 (AH 1266).
BY GHULAM ʻALI KHAN

Opaque watercolor and gold on paper
Image 40.6 × 53.3 cm (16 × 21 in.);
page 48 × 60 cm (19 × 23 in.)
Persian inscriptions (among others): "dated 1266;" "work of Ghulam ʻAli Khan, resident of Shajahanabad;" "… he who subdued the lion (*shir*)"

GHULAM ʻALI KHAN, ACTIVE BETWEEN 1817 AND 1852, was the most versatile artist who worked in late Mughal Delhi. He was able to alter his style to suit the demands of the subject and of his various patrons, whether of the Mughal emperors, Company patrons such as Col. James Skinner, or local noblemen such as Raja Vinay Singh of Alwar and Nawab Muhammad ʻAbd al-Rahman Khan of Jhajjar.[1]

Jhajjar was a small principality thirty-five miles west of Delhi, which was assigned in 1803, after the British take-over of the area from the Marathas, to Nawab Nijabat ʻAli Khan, one of those local Muslim chieftains who had been helpful in the war. His great-grandson Nawab ʻAbd al-Rahman Khan (1827–57), on acceding to the throne in 1845 became a major patron of Ghulam ʻAli Khan. Two durbar scenes showing the Nawab in his court dated 1849 and 1852 are in the British Library, while a hunting scene in the Victoria and Albert Museum shows the Nawab spearing a tiger.[2] This extraordinary scene of the Nawab riding a tiger, surrounded by some of his courtiers in one of the palace gardens at Jhajjar, is perhaps a continuation of the last. As with the other Jhajjar paintings, helpful inscriptions above the characters inform us who they all are. Ghulam ʻAli Khan's tall elongated figures are instantly recognizable but also very imitable by his contemporaries; he adopted a naturalistic style and a freedom of composition from European models, but only so much of linear perspective as was needed to enable him to place his figures and buildings within the picture space.

Whether this is a metaphorical or an actual scene is for us to decide: tigers could be kept as pets from birth, but not ridden, unless the rider was divine like Satya Pir, the tiger god of the Santal people. Tiger skins are a common trait among Shaivite Hindu ascetics.[3] ʻAbd al-Rahman tried to "ride the tiger" in the Mutiny year of 1857: he made the mistake of hedging his bets, and paid for it with his life, being put on trial in Delhi and hanged on 23 December 1857, while his estates were confiscated. The graves of the Nawabs of Jhajjar are in the shrine of Qutb Saheb (d. 1235), the great saint of Mehrauli near the Qutb Minar.

JPL

1 For some of his other signed work, see Losty, 1982, no. 138; Bautze, 1998, no. 67; Bayley, 1990, no. 180; Leach, 1998, no. 45.

2 Published respectively in Hazlitt, Gooden & Fox, *Indian paintings for British patrons* 1770–1860, London, 1991 (also J. P. Losty, "The place of Company painting in Indian art," in Bautze, *op. cit.*, pp. 21–27); and Archer, 1992, no. 136 (incorrectly dated to ca. 1820 instead of ca. 1850).

3 Leach, 1995, pp. 442–45, discusses a portrait of a Muslim ascetic who wears a tiger skin over one shoulder and a hat made of the same material.

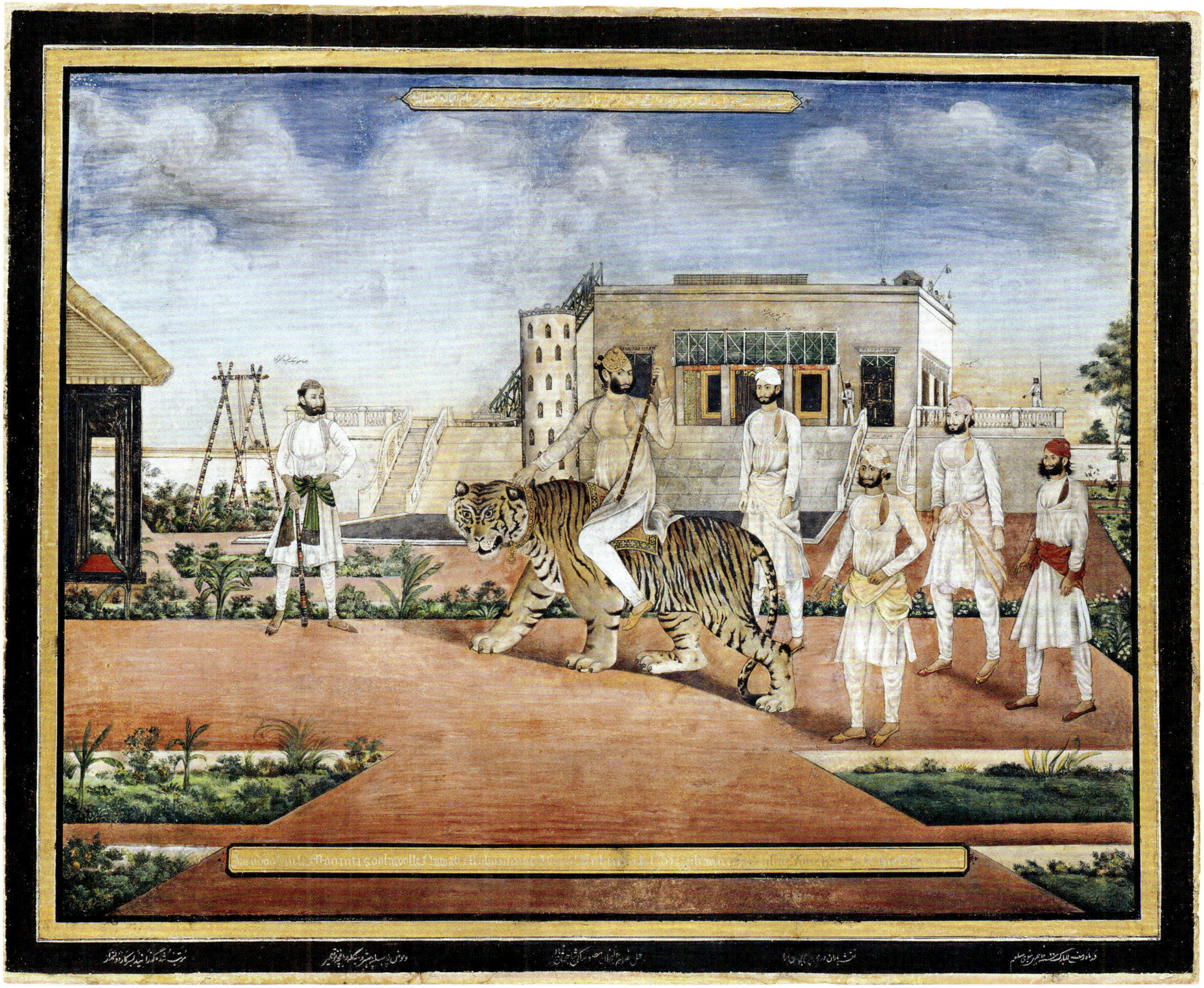

109

Maharana Sarup Singh of Mewar inspecting a horse on a festival day

UDAIPUR, RAJASTHAN, 1845, BY TARA

Opaque watercolor and gold on paper
Image 42.5 × 57.8 cm (16 ¾ × 22 ¾ in.);
page 48.6 × 63.5 cm (19 ⅛ × 25 in.)
On the reverse, a partly damaged thirteen-line devanagari inscription identifying the ruler, horse and other figures (ending: ... *kalami cataro taro / chha* 1902 *pos vid* 5...)
Metropolitan Museum of Art, New York, Cynthia Hazen Polsky and Leon B. Polsky Fund (2001.344)

IN THIS TOUR DE FORCE of his always meticulous style (see also cat. no. 110) the Udaipur painter Tara depicts his patron Maharana Sarup Singh (r. 1842–61) making an inspection of a royal horse on a festival occasion, attended by nobles, ministers and attendants under a richly patterned shamiana awning erected between red qanat cloth-screens in a grove. Although the festival (*mela*) is apparently mentioned in the first line of the inscription, its name is not clearly legible. It was, however, the custom on certain festival days for the ruler to make a formal inspection of royal horses or elephants.[1] Resplendent in pink and gold dress, Sarup Singh sits at his ease on an ornate couch of the same colors, smoking a gilt hookah in the form of a woman, with his shotgun and a jade-handled dagger lying before him. Almost everyone else present, down to the dancing girls, musicians, and even the saluki hound in the foreground, wears the same colors, giving a joyous effect of overwhelming pinkness, which offsets the otherwise stiff formality of the durbar ceremony. Adopting a particular uniform color of turban and jama for a specific festival day was a common custom at the Rajput courts.[2]

The royal stallion, named as Margchono, stands blinkered and tethered for inspection in a coat of red and white chevron pattern. This horse evidently became a royal favorite, as it is also known from later paintings.[3] The long and partly legible inscription lists those present, beginning with the two royal uncles (*kaka*) Anup Singh and Dal Singh, then Devi Singh, Baba Rasaluji, Baba Chand(?), Sirdar Singh, the Pancholi ministers Udai Chand and Shiv Karan, as well as the hookah and morchal (fan)-bearers, and many others.

AT

1 E.g. Topsfield, 1990, no. 69.

2 For example, the late nineteenth-century court historian Kaviraja Shyamaldas records that the whole Udaipur court wore clothes dyed red with the safflower (*kusum*) on the Maharana's birthday: Shyamaldas, *Vir Vinod*, Udaipur, 1886 (repr. Delhi, 1986), I, p. 133.

3 Topsfield, 1980, nos. 268–69; also Topsfield, 2002, fig. 233 (showing Sarup Singh playing Holi on this horse).

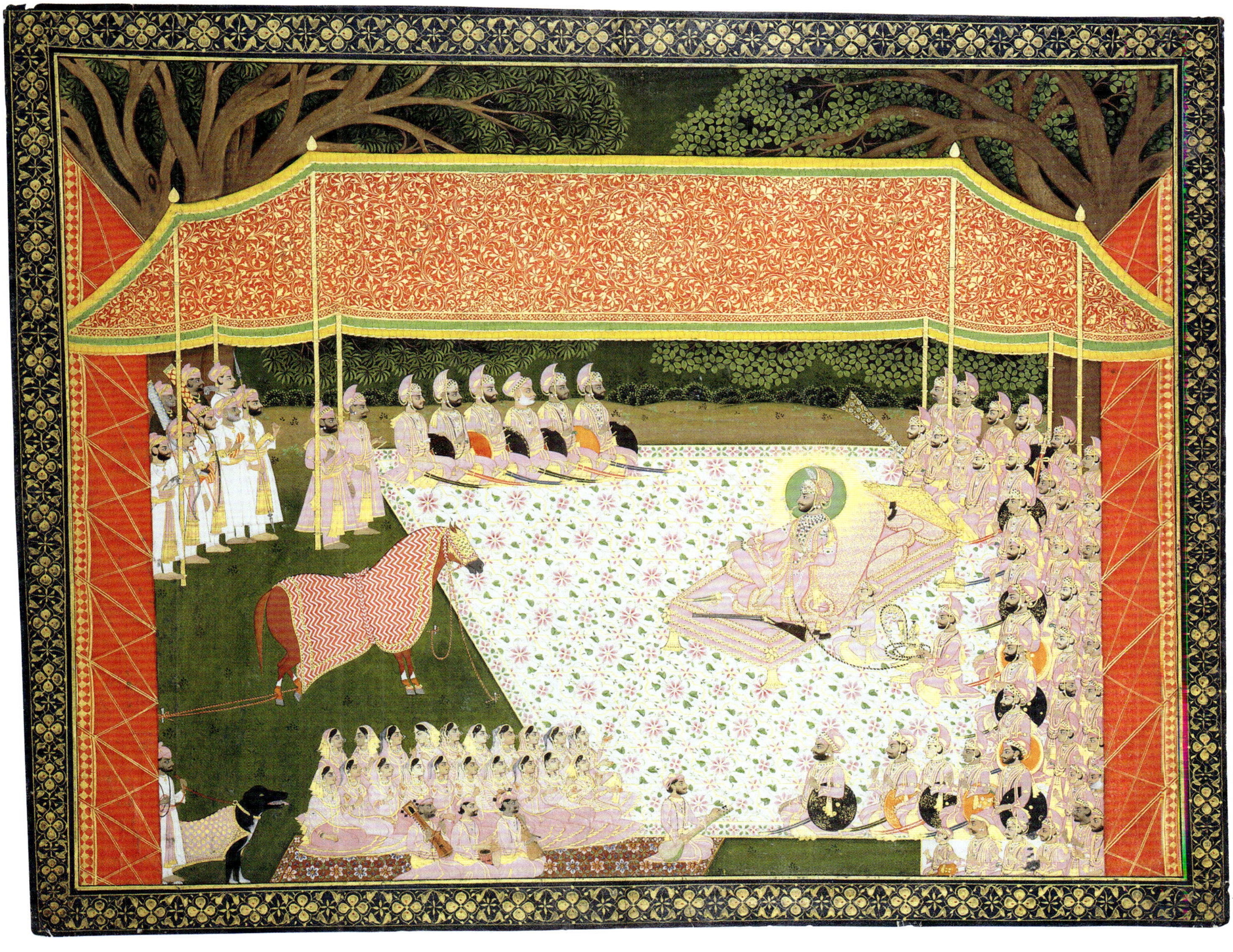

110

Maharana Sarup Singh of Mewar bathing at Jagniwas palace

UDAIPUR, RAJASTHAN, 1842,
ATTRIBUTED TO TARA

Opaque watercolor with gold and silver on paper
67.3 x 50.2 cm (26 ½ x 19 ¾ in.)
On verso, Mewar inventory no. 8/15 and long devanagari inscription identifying the ruler and other figures (with date: ... *sambat 1899 ra jath bi 7*); also numbered: 39
Published: A. Topsfield, *Court painting at Udaipur*, Zurich, 2002, fig. 227

ATTRIBUTABLE TO THE ARTIST TARA (cat. no. 109), this picture of Maharana Sarup Singh (r. 1842–61) bathing with courtiers was painted at the very start of his reign, in the summer of 1842. The Maharana, with gold and green nimbus, perches on a small *chatri* platform in the center of the ornamental pool at the lake palace of Jagniwas, with its water-surrounded, leaf- and flower-shaped parterres, planted with plantains and fruit-trees and flowering shrubs. Jagniwas had been built as his personal pleasure palace by Maharana Jagat Singh II in the 1740s,[1] and Tara's composition broadly follows a contemporary painting by Jai Ram in which that ruler bathes with his ladies in the same pool.[2]

The eighteen courtiers and attendants shown in the water here are grouped around Sarup Singh in respectful attitudes, one of them holding his hookah. Two figures are playfully riding statues of an elephant and horse, but the distrustful Sarup Singh, who became increasingly alienated from his nobles, was by all accounts not one to encourage too much levity in his presence. The courtiers are named as: Devi Singh, Ranavat Abhai Singh, Bagtavar Singh, Indar Singh, (the royal uncles) Chandji and Rasaluji, (his brother) Jagannath Singh, (a second) Bagtavar Singh, Moti Singh, the five Pancholi ministers Kishannath, Bishannath, Harnath, Prannath, and Akhainath, the Purohit (priest) Shyamnath, Ganga Ram, Achalo, and Jawara Chand. While the figures are stiffly executed, the architectural setting and gardens are rendered by Tara with his usual meticulous care.

AT

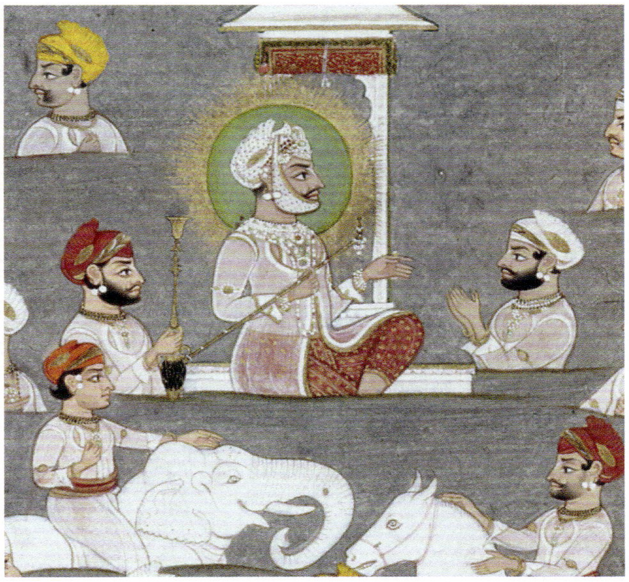

1 A pool of this type survives in the 1960s reincarnation of Jagniwas as the popular Lake Palace Hotel: e.g. J. Hegewald, "Water architecture in Rajasthan," in G. Tillotson ed., *Stones in the sand*, Bombay: Marg, 2001, fig. 12.

2 A. Topsfield, "City Palace and lake palaces," in Tillotson ed., *Stones in the sand*, fig. 15, and Topsfield, *Court paintings from Udaipur*, fig. 160; *ibid.*, fig. 201, for an early nineteenth-century painting of the more frolicsome Maharana Bhim Singh with nobles in the same pool (also Hurel and Okada, 2003, no. 16, there dated 1803).

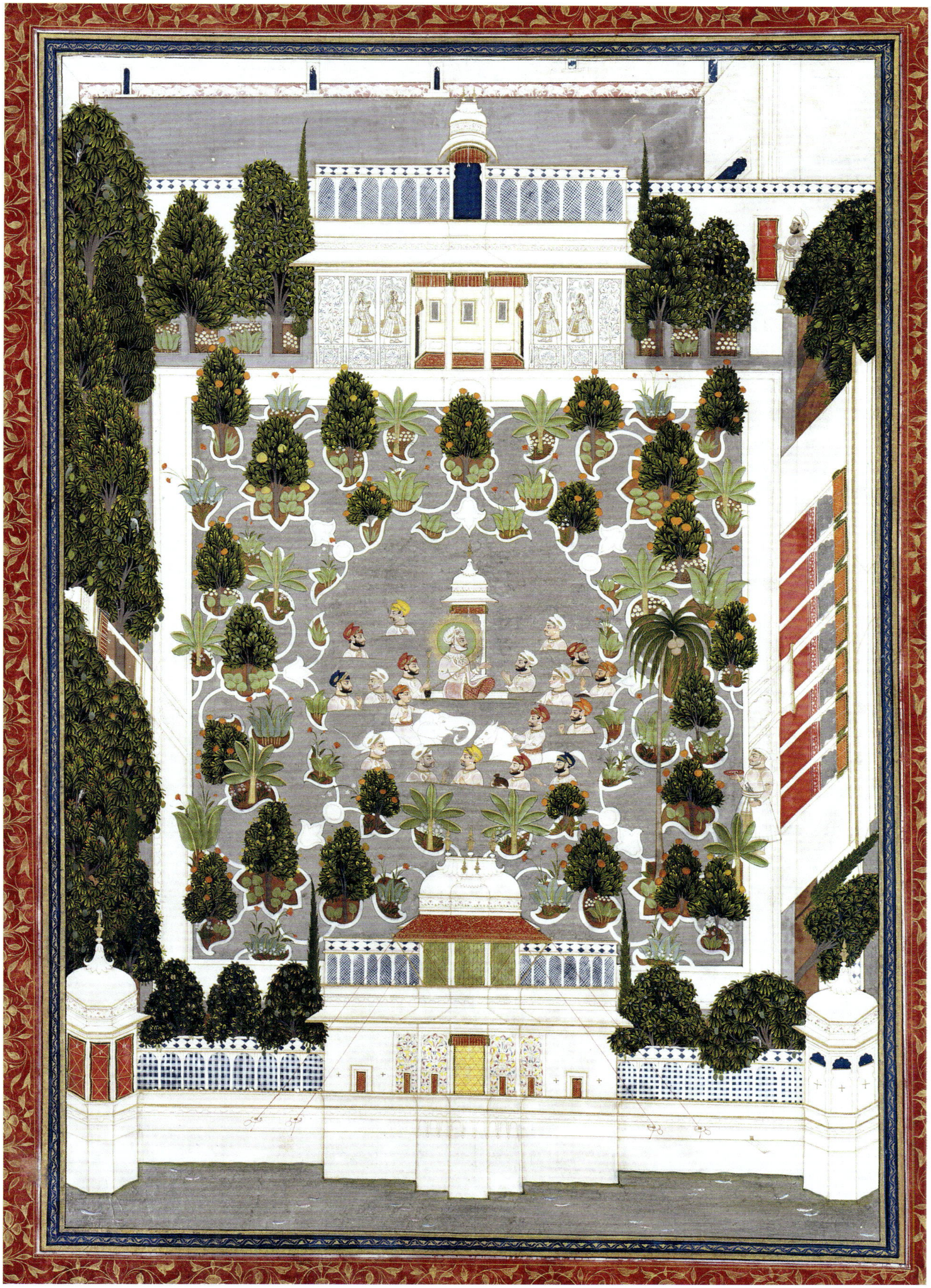

111

Maharana Bhupal Singh of Mewar with courtiers at a tank

UDAIPUR, RAJASTHAN, CA. 1930–35

Opaque watercolor and gold on paper
44.8 x 70.8 cm (17 ⅝ x 27 ⅞ in.)

IN THIS SPLENDIDLY DETAILED PAINTING, a mustached Maharana, with gold and green nimbus, takes his ease with his numerous entourage in a pavilion above a stepped reservoir or tank. Royal attendants (two bearing parasols) are dispersed around the ghats, which are modeled here with unusual care for spatial recession. In the center a pair of peacocks pose ornamentally, while below them bathers, fish, and turtles disport themselves in the water. As in the case of another, closely related painting, the picture is uninscribed, but the ruler is probably Maharana Bhupal Singh (r. 1930–55). He had suffered a paralysing illness in his youth, but this did not prevent him from going out on hunts and other excursions. Unlike his immediate predecessors as ruler, Bhupal Singh never adopted a beard.[1]

Deep-stepped basins (*kunds*) are common in the often arid regions of Western India including Rajasthan, where they provided a reliable source of water though the hot season, as well as a place for washing and bathing and also an occasional pleasure resort for the nobility.[2] This spacious and well-appointed reservoir, with its twin Persian wheels raising water in pots from a considerable depth to irrigate the surrounding wooded gardens, has an ornate *barahdari* (twelve-door) pavilion or summerhouse, with a large, open pillared hall for royal gatherings or picnics. It has been identified as the kund at the Indar Bagh (Garden of Indra), some distance from Udaipur in the direction of the Nahar Magra (Tiger Hill) hunting-ground.[3] It is likely that this picture dates from soon after Bhupal Singh's accession in 1930. It would probably have been painted by the leading artist Pannalal and his son Chaganlal, though the execution shows a sophistication and high level of finish which are sometimes lacking in their work, suggesting that the setting may have been partly based on a photographic model.[4]

AT

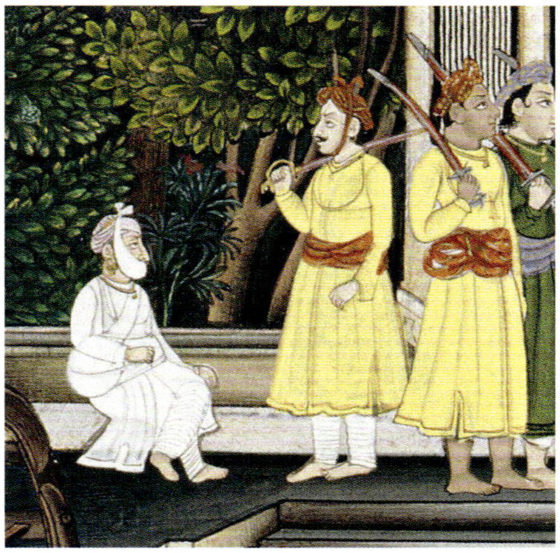

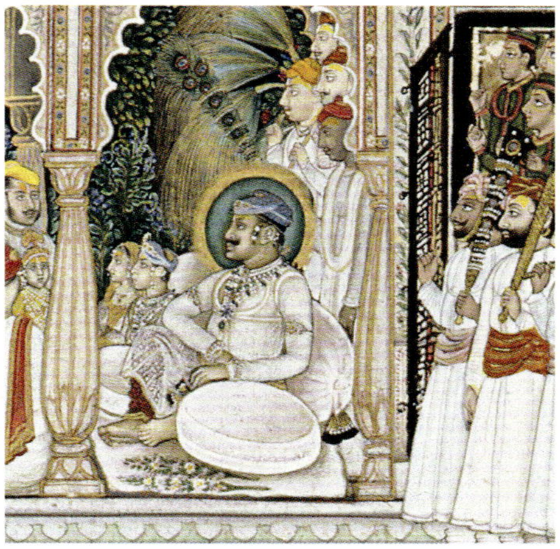

1 *Indian and Islamic works of art*, London: Simon Ray, March 2003, no. 57: evidently a contemporary or near-contemporary version of the same subject; its setting is just the same, but the Maharana there sits on the left side of the pavilion, facing right, and some other details also differ.

2 Topsfield, 1990, nos. 65–73; Topsfield, 2002, fig. 269.

3 J. Hegewald, "Water architecture in Rajasthan," in G. Tillotson ed., *Stones in the sand*, Bombay, 2001, pp. 78–89.

4 I am grateful to Thakur Sahib Bhupendra Singh Auwa for this identification, and to Sabina Bailey; an earlier identification for its near-identical counterpart picture (*Indian and Islamic works of art*, *loc. cit.*; and by a previous Sotheby's cataloguer), as showing a tank at the Shri Nathji Haveli (temple) at Nathdwara, is erroneous.

5 E.g. Topsfield, *City Palace Museum*, nos. 36, 62 *et seq.*

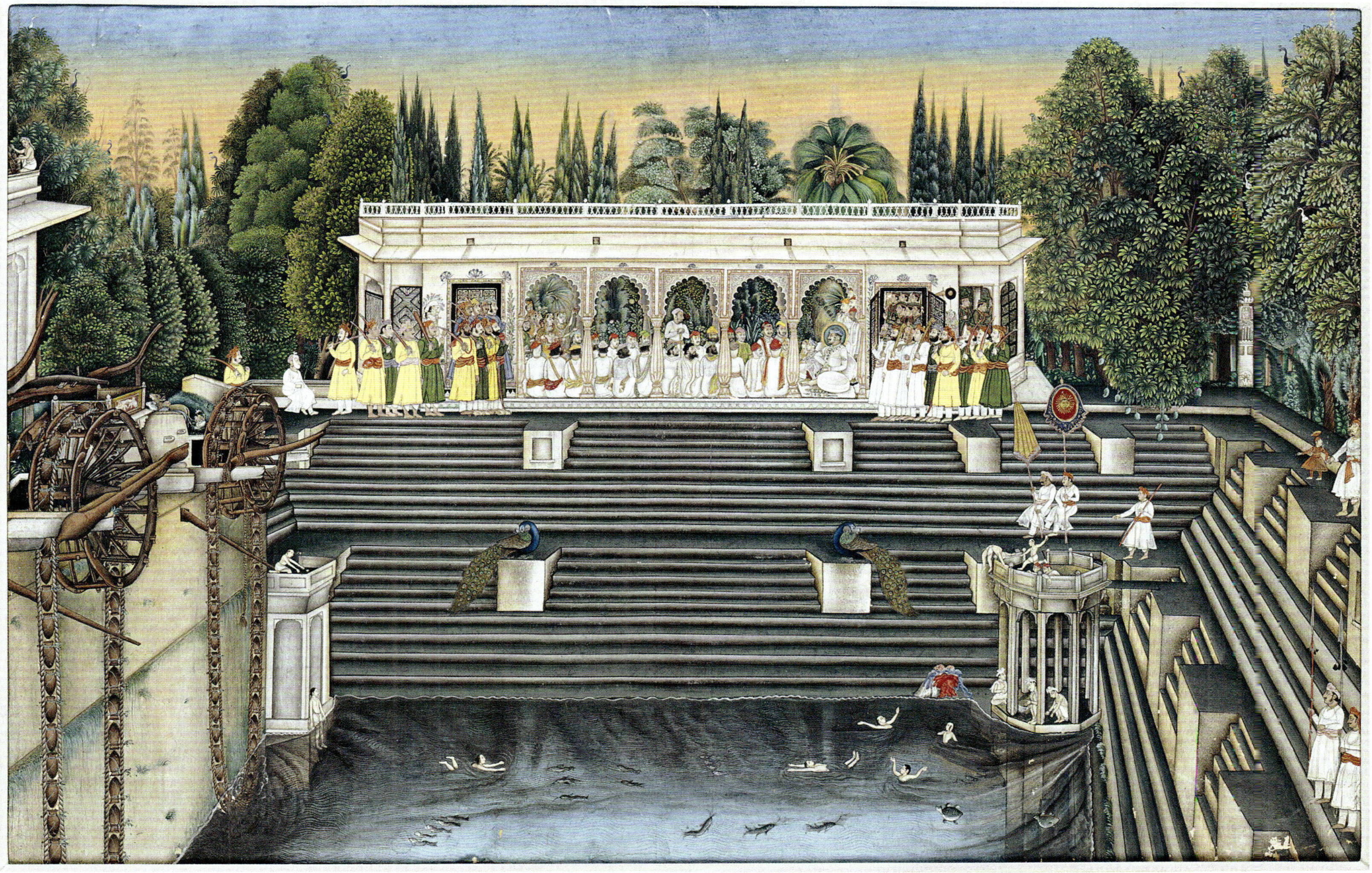

112

Coronation(?) of Prime Minister Juddha Shumsher Jang Bahadur Rana of Nepal

UNKNOWN PHOTOGRAPHER

Kathmandu, Nepal, 1942
Gelatin silver print
25.1 × 30.3 cm (9 7/8 × 11 15/16 in.)
Metropolitan Museum of Art, New York, Purchase, Cynthia Hazen Polsky Gift (1990.1025)

UNLIKE ITS NEIGHBOR INDIA, where the great public displays of a ruler's wealth and a subject's homage became a thing of the past after Independence, the determinedly isolated Kingdom of Nepal retains its royal rulers. But for over a century, the Nepal royal family ruled in name only, real power being held firmly in the control of the Rana family. The precise event celebrated in this view of a procession in Kathmandu has not been identified with certainty, but it appears to show the coronation procession of Maharaja Juddha Shumsher Rana (1875–1952), on his elevation to the post of Prime Minister in 1932. The Rana dynasty was established in Nepal in 1846, when Jang Bahadur Rana was appointed Prime Minister. On attaining office, he swiftly and ruthlessly suppressed the power of the royal family, establishing his own family as hereditary prime ministers and effective rulers. By the time of Juddha Shumsher's accession, however, Rana supremacy was declining in the face of increasing pressure for constitutional government, both from within the country and from abroad. The last of the Ranas to wield absolute power, Juddha Shumsher permitted some piecemeal reform, but remained adamant throughout his rule that constitutional government was neither possible nor desirable in Nepal. His attempts to suppress the rising tide of popular agitation for political reform—particularly his imprisonment and brutal execution of members of the Nepal People's Congress in 1941—only served further to inflame popular opposition.

Despite the colorful nature of his private life—a British official reported that he had fathered over a hundred sons and daughters across "the length and breadth of Nepal"—his later years were characterized by an increasing preoccupation with spiritual matters. In 1945, expressing a desire to retire from the world to a life of spiritual contemplation, he left office and spent his final years in India. There he survived just long enough to see the final toppling of the Rana dynasty and the restoration of the monarchy in 1951.

JF

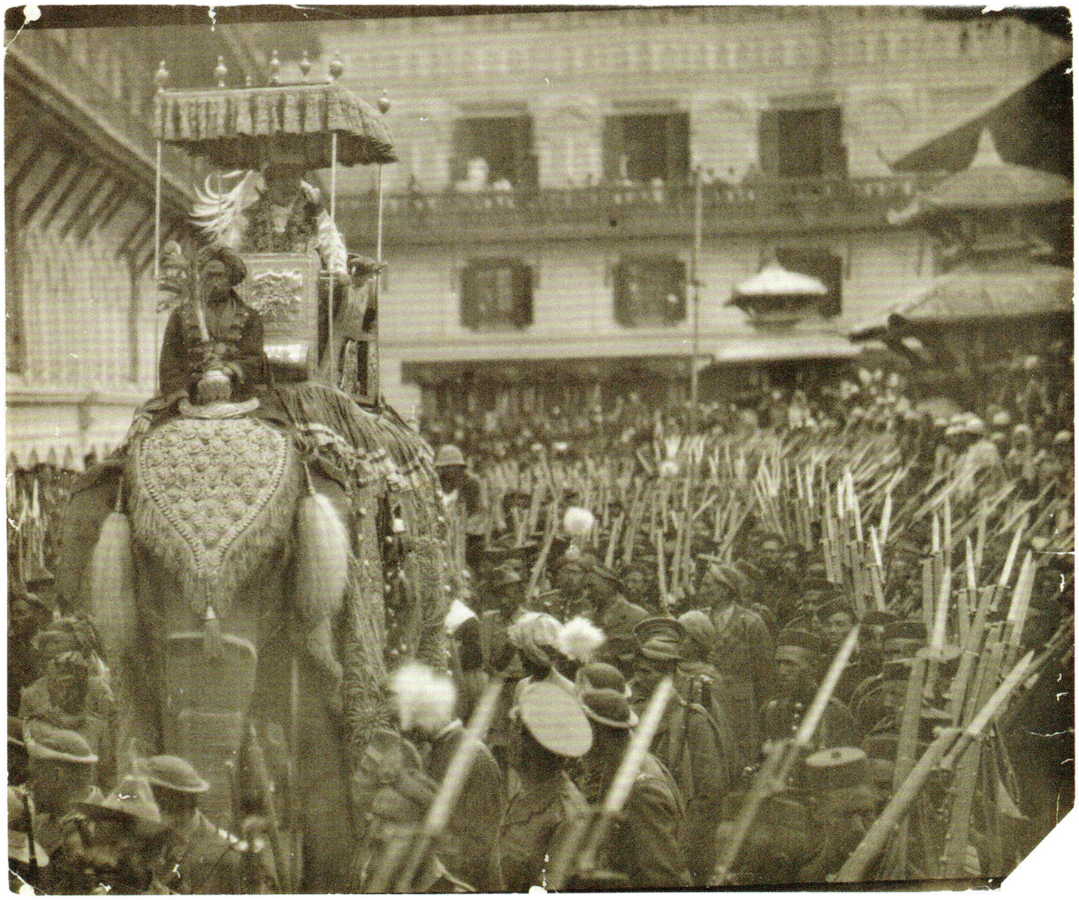

113

Ivory plaque with a female attendant figure

SRI LANKA, SEVENTEENTH OR EIGHTEENTH CENTURY

H. 21.6 cm (8 ½ in.)

THIS IVORY PLAQUE IS CARVED IN RELIEF with a standing female celestial attendant (*devata*), holding a flywhisk. She has an aureole behind her head and is heavily bejeweled, wearing a crown with a tiered finial, earrings, pearl necklaces, arm bands, a pearl belt, and jewelry hanging from her skirt. Around her are floral scrolls. Three sides of the rectangular plaque have a triple-banded molding. A similar plaque is illustrated by Coomaraswamy,[1] who states that such plaques are found on either side of the threshold of *vihara* (shrine) doors. It could also have been a panel attached to a box. The deep carving and the elaborate jewelry, including the tiered crown, recall the magnificent boxes made at Kotte in Sri Lanka in the sixteenth century and sent by the king to Portugal.[2] The background scrolls, however, are found on other Sri Lankan objects, including the hilts of the small daggers, *piha kaetta,*[3] and indicate a later date.

Ivory was highly valued in India and Sri Lanka in the later medieval period. The Mughal emperor Jahangir describes in his memoirs how Amanat Khan presented him with two tusks weighing over 165 lbs,[4] and Bernier describes Aurangzeb being sent two enormous tusks by the King of Ethiopia.[5] Ivory was principally imported from Africa. Ivory from Sri Lanka and Sumatra was valued as it did not become yellow, which was the tendency of Indian ivory according to Tavernier and Ovington.[6]

MCS

1 Coomaraswamy, 1913, p. 177, fig. 134.

2 A. Jaffer and M. A. Schwabe, "A group of 16th century ivory caskets from Ceylon," *Apollo*, CXLIX, March 1999, no. 445, pp. 3–14.

3 Archer et al., 1987, p. 45, no. 25.

4 *Tuzuk-i Jahangiri*, tr. A. Rogers, ed. H. Beveridge, repr. Delhi, 1989, p. 423. Today a tusk weighing over 70 lbs would be considered large: Webster, 1983, p. 587.

5 Aziz, 1942, p. 444.

6 *Ibid.*, p. 433.

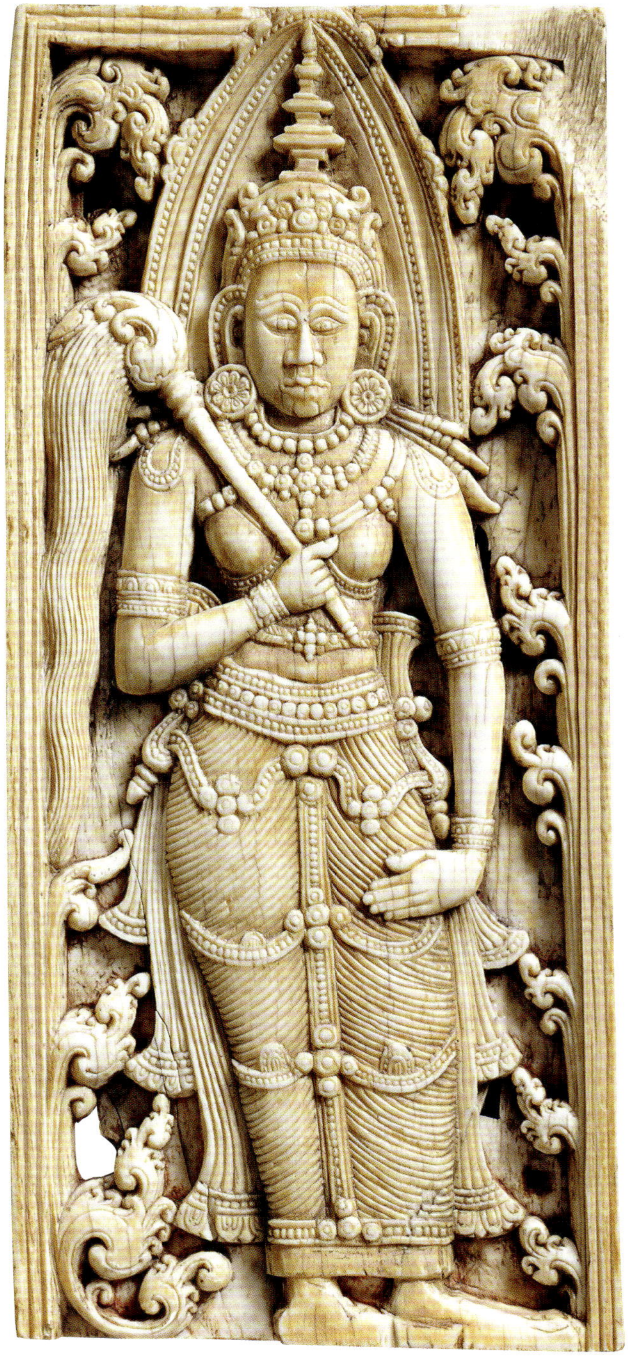

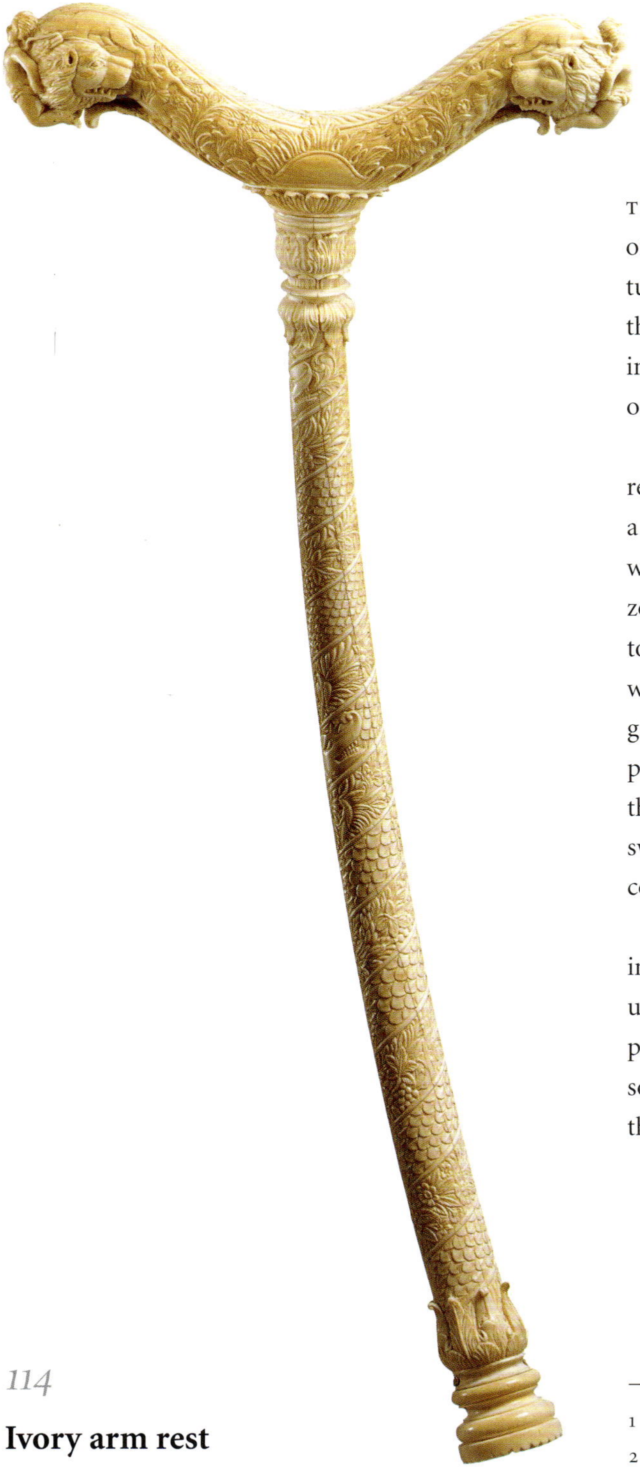

THIS LUXURIOUS ARM REST OR DERVISH CRUTCH is carved from sections of solid ivory. The curve of the support follows the curve of the original tusk. Although Sufi dervishes and Hindu sadhus professed a life of poverty, they could be supported by wealthy benefactors and so possess objects made in precious materials. Alternatively, artefacts such as this could be symbolic of devotion and be used as such by a royal patron.

The arm rest is made in two sections: a long, curved support, carved in relief, and the arm rest, also carved in relief and joined to the support with a threaded socket. The support has a double spiral design, one zone of which consists of two long aquatic creatures (*makaras*) with scales, the other zone having a leafy scroll. The foot is turned, with a hatched base and the top in the form of a capital with lotus flowers. The arm rest itself is carved with two lion head finials, to which cling putti carved in high relief. Its ground is carved in a low relief with flowers, lion heads, and further small putti. Although the form and several of the motifs in this design are Indian, the decorative scheme is heavily influenced by European work. An ivory sword hilt made for a European patron in South India shows a similar combination of European and Indian forms.[1]

Similar crutches are seen held by Sufis in the atlas prepared at Faizabad in 1770 for Col. Gentil, military advisor to the Nawab of Oudh.[2] They were used by both Hindu and Muslim mendicants, as seen in miniature paintings.[3] They occur in a variety of materials, including wood and steel, sometimes unscrewing to reveal a sharp stiletto blade.[4] Jade is also used for the arm rest, often carved with leafy buds and flowers.[5]

MCS

114

Ivory arm rest

SOUTH INDIA, EIGHTEENTH CENTURY

H. 51.5 cm (20 ¼ in.)
Metropolitan Museum of Art, New York,
Gift of Cynthia Hazen Polsky (1987.424.29)

1 Tchakaloff et al., 1998, no. 27, p. 103.

2 S. Gole, *Maps of India*, London, 1988, illustrating plates from Col. Gentil's atlas in the British Library (Or.4039): the Sufis are seen on the folio for Bidar.

3 E.g. Kossak, 1997, no. 33.

4 Alexander, 1992, nos. 132–33, pp. 198–99; a wooden example is in the Jagdish and Kamla Mittal Museum, Hyderabad, described in Victoria and Albert Museum, *The Indian Heritage: Court life and arts under Mughal rule*, London, 1982, no. 553.

5 Nigam, 1979, fig. 25.

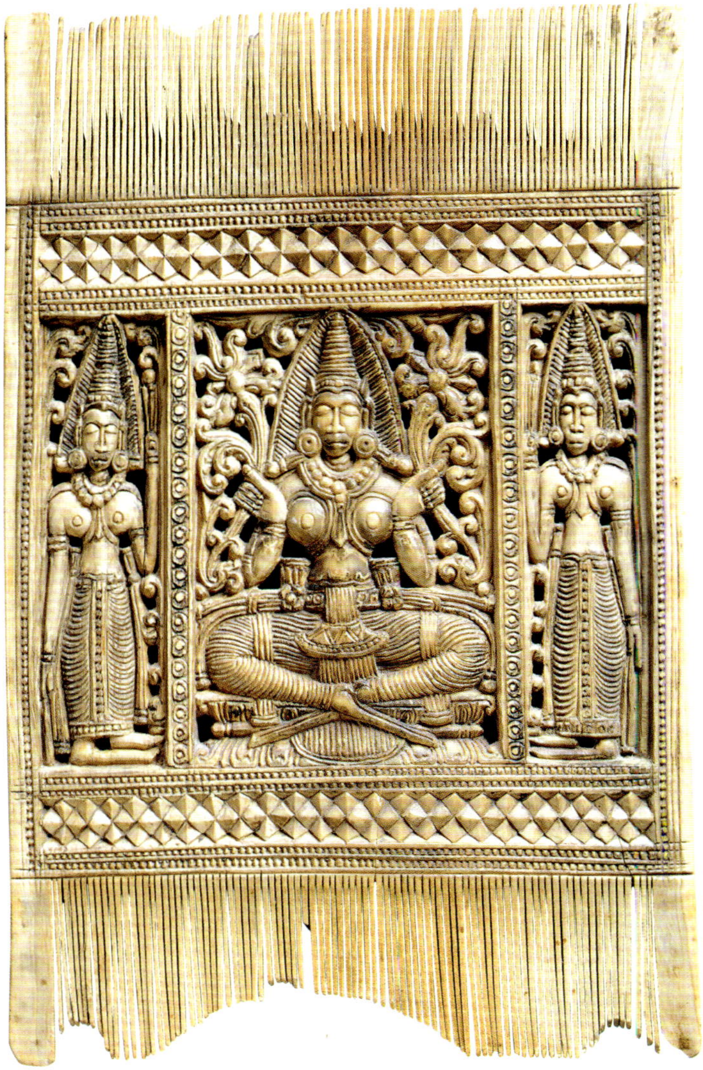

115

Ivory comb with Lakshmi and attendants

SRI LANKA, EIGHTEENTH CENTURY

H. 17.1 × W. 11.4 cm (6 ¾ × 4 ½ in.)
Metropolitan Museum of Art, New York,
Gift of Cynthia Hazen Polsky (2011.576.4)

THIS IVORY COMB (*PANAVA*) has a central panel with three female figures. The central figure is seated on a low throne, holding a leafy frond in each hand. She wears elaborate jewelry and a tall crown, and has long trousers falling to her ankles; her feet are heavily stylized. To either side, in separate panels, stands an attendant, each holding a flywhisk and wearing a long skirt, jewelry, and a tall headdress. Each section has a beaded inner border, and above and below are panels with a faceted diamond-patterned design (known as *kundi rakkan* in Tamil), and a further band of beading from which the teeth of the comb are then cut. This is a very elaborate comb, with a high degree of embellishment. The central figure probably represents Lakshmi, goddess of wealth and fertility. A comb with a similar arrangement of a central figure and two flanking figures is in the Los Angeles County Museum, and two further examples are in the collection of Powis Castle.[1]

Ivory combs from Sri Lanka have been highly valued in Europe since the first contacts made by the Portuguese. Garcia da Orto, an observer writing in the sixteenth century, stated that ivory was used in Ceylon for "caskets, combs and many other things."[2] Very few sixteenth-century combs survive, with the three earliest known dating from the 1540s, in the Munich Schatzkammer.[3] Queen Catherine (1507–78), wife of Dom João III of Portugal (r. 1521–57), acquired two ivory combs decorated "with gold and small rubies," brought on the ship Reis Magos from Goa in 1570.[4]

MCS

1 Pal, 1981, fig. 63, p. 74; Archer et al., 1987, p. 91, nos. 122–23.

2 Calouste Gulbenkian Museum, *Exotica: The Portuguese discoveries and the Renaissance Kunstkammer*, Lisbon, 2001, p. 84.

3 *Ibid.*, fig. 5, p. 89.

4 *Ibid.*, p. 141.

116

Ivory panel with Lakshmi and attendants

SRI LANKA OR SOUTH INDIA,
EIGHTEENTH CENTURY

9.5 × 10.2 cm (3 ¾ × 4 in.)

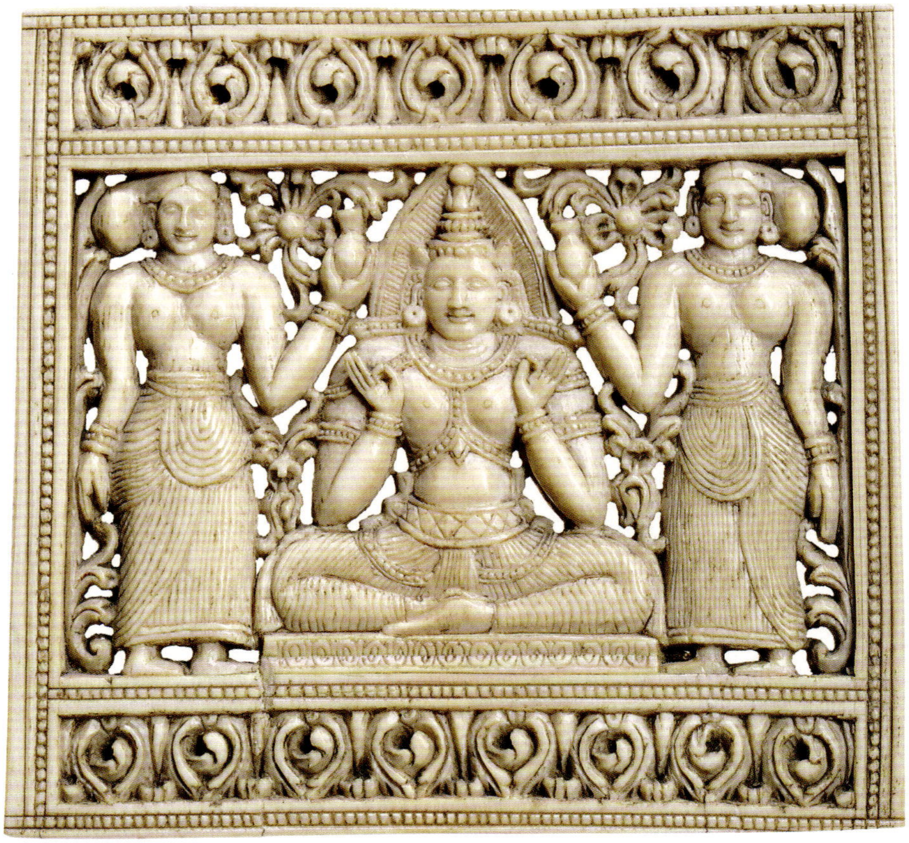

THIS RELIEF CARVING IS EITHER the center panel from a comb or a side panel on a box.[1] The central female figure (as in cat. no. 115), is Lakshmi, goddess of wealth and fertility and principal wife of Vishnu. Seated on a low, double-lotus throne, she has an aureole behind her head, elaborate jewelry, a tall-tiered crown and a long garment. Both hands are held up in the gesture of teaching. She is flanked by female attendants, each holding an auspicious water flask above the goddess; as Gajalakshmi, she is often depicted over the doors of houses and temples, flanked by two elephants holding water flasks above her head,[2] for water represents knowledge. Between the figures are floral scrolls, and above and below a panel with a stylized lotus-bud design, and a narrow beaded border.

The flanking figures have their hair gathered into a cloth, which is a style seen on Sri Lankan and South Indian ivories.[3] It was fashionable in Sri Lanka in the sixteenth century and in South India during the Nayak period in the seventeenth century and continuing into the eighteenth.[4]

MCS

1 A. Jaffer and M. A. Schwabe, "A group of 16th century ivory caskets from Ceylon," *Apollo*, CXLIX, March 1999, no. 445, pp. 3–14, fig. 1.

2 G. Michell ed., *Living Wood: Sculptural traditions of Southern India*, Bombay: Marg, 1992, p. 70.

3 Michell, 1995, fig. 155, p. 213.

4 The female figures on a sixteenth-century box from Kotte wear their hair in this manner: Calouste Gulbenkian Museum, *Exotica: The Portuguese discoveries and the Renaissance Kunstkammer*, Lisbon, 2001, fig. 3, p. 85; for South India. see A. Okada, *L'Inde des princes: La donation Jean et Krishna Riboud*, Paris, 2000, pp. 70–73, where the kneeling attendant female wears her hair in this style.

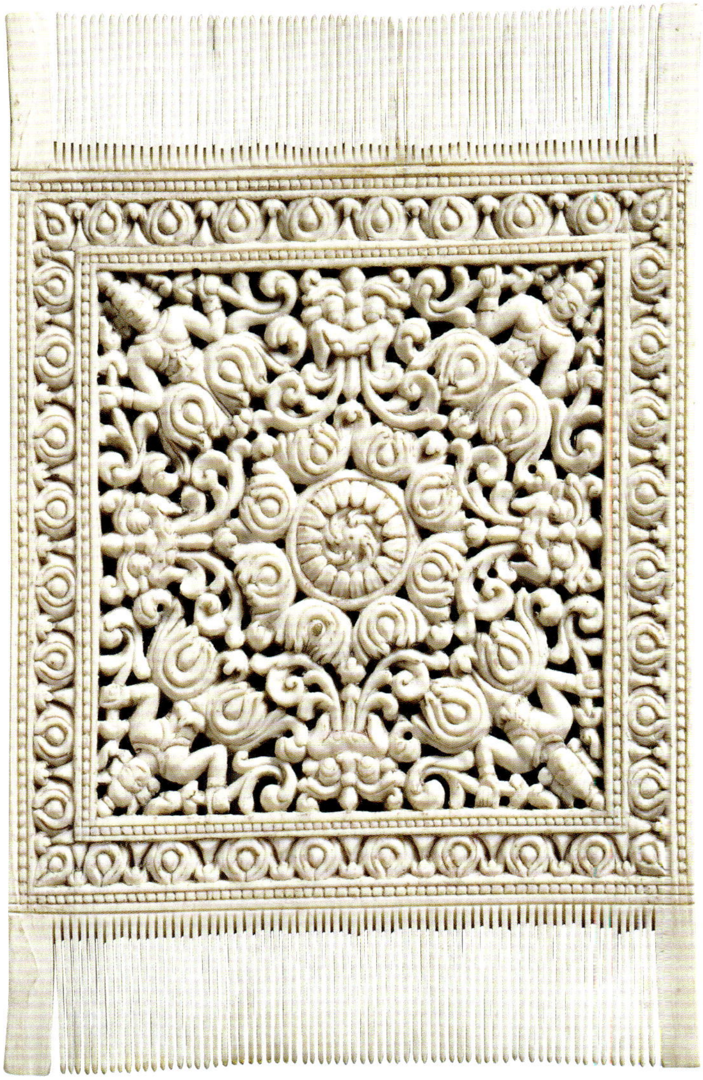

117

Ivory comb with flowers and figures

SRI LANKA, EIGHTEENTH CENTURY

15.2 × 10.2 cm (6 × 4 in.)

THE DECORATIVE PANEL OF THIS IVORY COMB (*PANAVA*) has a central floret, from which radiate floral scrolls, with a stylized figure holding plant stems in both hands emerging from the scrolls in each of the four corners, and lion masks between them on each side. Around the central panel there is a band of stylized scrolls, with an outer border of beading. The teeth of the comb are cut at both ends. The work on this comb is finely executed, and is closely related to the abstract and floral designs found on boxes, such as a round box, decorated with figures and scrolling vines, in the Victoria and Albert Museum, London.[1] The figures holding the plant stems probably represent Lakshmi, goddess of wealth and prosperity.

Combs from India and Sri Lanka carved from precious materials were greatly valued in the European royal courts. In addition to the ivory combs sent to Europe by the Portuguese in the sixteenth century (see cat. no. 115), were combs of tortoise shell. These came from Goa, the principle Portuguese trading post in India, where they were embellished with silver filigree.[2]

MCS

1 Jaffer, 2002, no. 19, p. 53, where other examples are also cited.

2 Six are listed in the inventory of Emperor Rudolf II's Kunstkammer carried out in Prague between 1607 and 1611: Calouste Gulbenkian Museum, *Exotica: The Portuguese discoveries and the Renaissance Kunstkammer*, Lisbon, 2001, p. 141, nos. 40–41.

THE HUNT

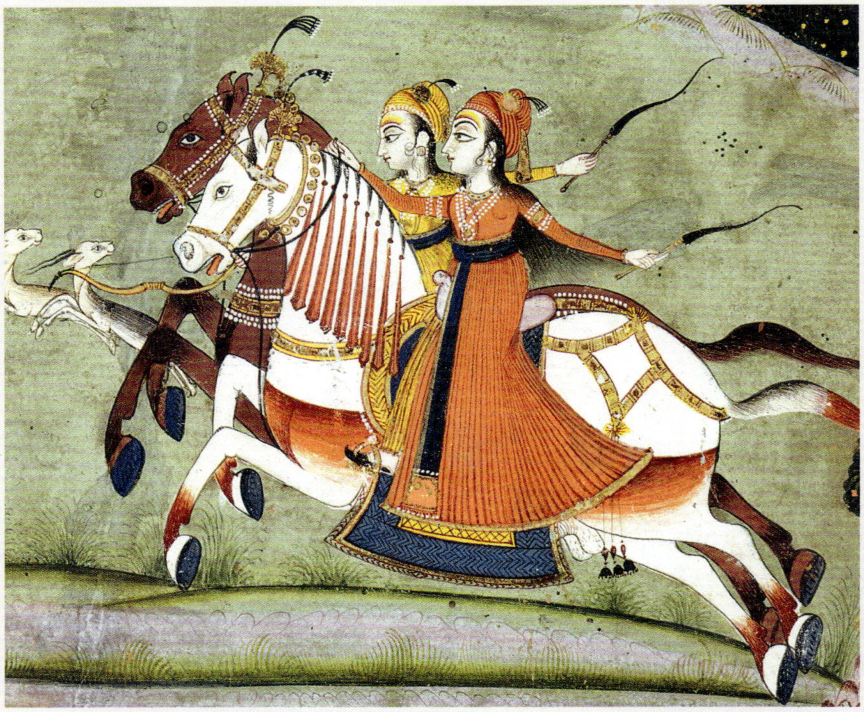

Superficial, worldly observers see in killing an animal a sort of pleasure, and in their ignorance stride about, as if senseless, on the field of their passions. But deep inquirers see in hunting a means of acquisition of knowledge, and the temple of their worship derives from it a peculiar lustre. This is the case with His Majesty [Akbar]. *He always makes hunting a means of increasing his knowledge, and besides, uses hunting parties as occasions to inquire, without first having given notice of his coming, into the conditions of the people and the army...*

ABU'L FAZL, *'Ain-i Akbari*[1]

In India, as elsewhere, hunting in its more developed forms has always been the sport of kings, as well as a substitute or a training for warfare. In the time of Akbar (1556–1605), the great qamargah hunt in particular was conducted on a grandiose military scale. An army of many thousands of beaters would be marched to a suitable area for game and then formed into an immense circle. As the beaters converged, they drove countless wild animals of all kinds into a confined space, around which screens were erected to form a pen. The killing then began and could last for days. As can be seen from contemporary paintings, the bold and energetic Emperor (to whom his chronicler Abu'l Fazl always imputes the wisest motives) participated in this carnage with gusto; until on one occasion, following a mystical experience just before the hunt began, he finally tired of the slaughter. In his treatise on Akbar's court administration, Abu'l Fazl gives a detailed account of the various hunting methods of the period, including hawking, different ways of capturing wild elephants, or the pursuit of tiger, leopard, deer, and buffalo. A favorite method of hunting deer was with trained cheetahs, which would first stalk and then swiftly outrun their prey. The enthusiasm for hunting continued under later Mughal rulers, and sometimes their queens also. The Empress Nur Jahan, when accompanying Jahangir in the elephant howdah on a lion hunt, distinguished herself highly, according to her husband's account, by rapidly dispatching a group of four lions with six well-placed shots.[2]

For the martial Rajput nobility, hunting (*shikar*) had an even stronger, ritualistic social importance. The coming of spring was celebrated with a royal hunt for wild boar, which if successful would be a good omen for the coming year. Tod (ca. 1820) describes the reckless courage shown by all on this occasion: "...Each cavalier impels his steed, and with lance or sword, regardless of rock, ravine, or tree, presses on the bristly foe, whose knowledge of the country is of no avail when thus circumvented, and the ground soon reeks with gore, in which not unfrequently is mixed that of horse and rider."[3] Game of every kind—boar, bear, deer, panther, crane and other fowl, rhinoceros, crocodile—was pursued by the Rajputs, but the tiger hunt held a special place. Killing a tiger was a royal prerogative, seldom granted to others. Tigers could be hunted on elephant-back, or else tree-hides (*machans*) were constructed, in which the Maharaja and his companions waited until the chosen animal, previously located by specialist shikari scouts, was driven within range of their guns by the ring of beaters. Depictions of such tiger hunts in dense forests by eighteenth century Kotah artists are among the most powerful of Indian hunting pictures. The most detailed and comprehensive shikar scenes of all were those of the Udaipur painters, who maintained an almost continuous pictorial record of royal hunts of all kinds, from the early 1700s until as late as the 1940s.

AT

1 Abu'l Fazl Allami, *The Ain-i Akbari*, tr. H. Blochmann, repr. Delhi, 1965, p. 292.

2 W. M. Thackston tr., *The Jahangirnama*, New York, 1999, p. 219.

3 J. Tod, *Annals and antiquities of Rajasthan*, ed. W. Crooke, repr. Delhi, 1971, II, p. 660.

118

A tiger hunt

KOTAH, RAJASTHAN, DATED 1777,
BY HANSRAJ JOSHI

Opaque watercolor and gold on paper
Image 38 × 54.5 cm (15 × 21 ½ in.)
page 41.2 × 57.7 cm (16 ¼ × 22 ½ in.)
Devanagari inscriptions on reverse (partly smudged and obscured), describing the hunt, with date (VS 1834) and artist's name
Published: M. C. Beach, *Rajput painting at Bundi and Kota*, Ascona, 1974, fig. 129

KOTAH WAS AT VARIOUS PERIODS the most energetic school of Rajasthani painting, excelling above all in its vigorous elephant studies and its dramatic hunting scenes, set among the dense forests and rocky ridges of the royal hunting grounds. Maharao Umed Singh I (r. 1770–1819), who had been largely relieved of the burdens of state by his dominant minister Zalim Singh, was devoted to hunting, and his reign is distinguished by a number of vividly conceived, large-scale tiger-hunt paintings.[1] They treat the local landscape, as here, with strong linear rhythms, sinuous tree and plant forms, a vivid palette and an intensity of vision which has sometimes been compared to that of the French painter Henri (Douanier) Rousseau.

A line of beaters, at far right, has driven the game into a fenced corral, within range of Maharao Umed Singh and his two companions waiting in a tree-hide (*machan*); the Maharao is taking aim at a tiger. Two more noblemen, seated in a machan below, fire at the boar which have also been trapped by the beaters. Among the legible names for these figures in the inscription are: Pandit Babaji, Bhagvat Singh, Thakur Sohan Singh, Sisodia Maharaja Nathji, and Dandavat(?) Bhavani Singh. The artist, Hansraj Joshi, is said to have been one of several who came to Kotah from Mewar,[2] presumably after patronage at Udaipur under Maharana Ari Singh had virtually dried up for another three decades, around 1767.[3] Other, still larger scale tiger hunts by this painter are in the Kotah Fort Museum[4] and the Benkaim Collection.[5]

AT

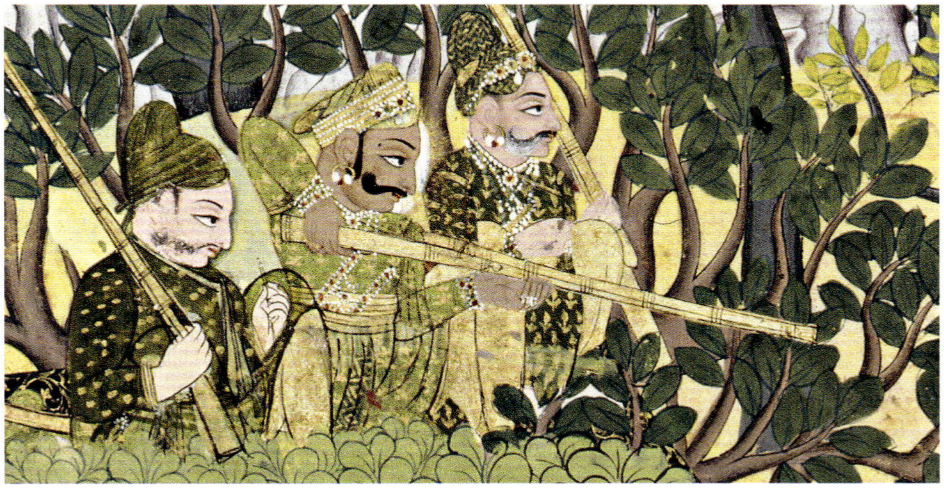

1 For examples in the Victoria and Albert Museum, see Archer, 1959, figs. 37–40.

2 Brijraj Singh, 1985, p. 23.

3 It has not so far been possible to identify them with artists known to have worked for Maharana Ari Singh (for a study of his reign, see Topsfield, 2002, Ch. 7).

4 Welch et al., 1997, no. 46.

5 Desai, 1985, no. 49.

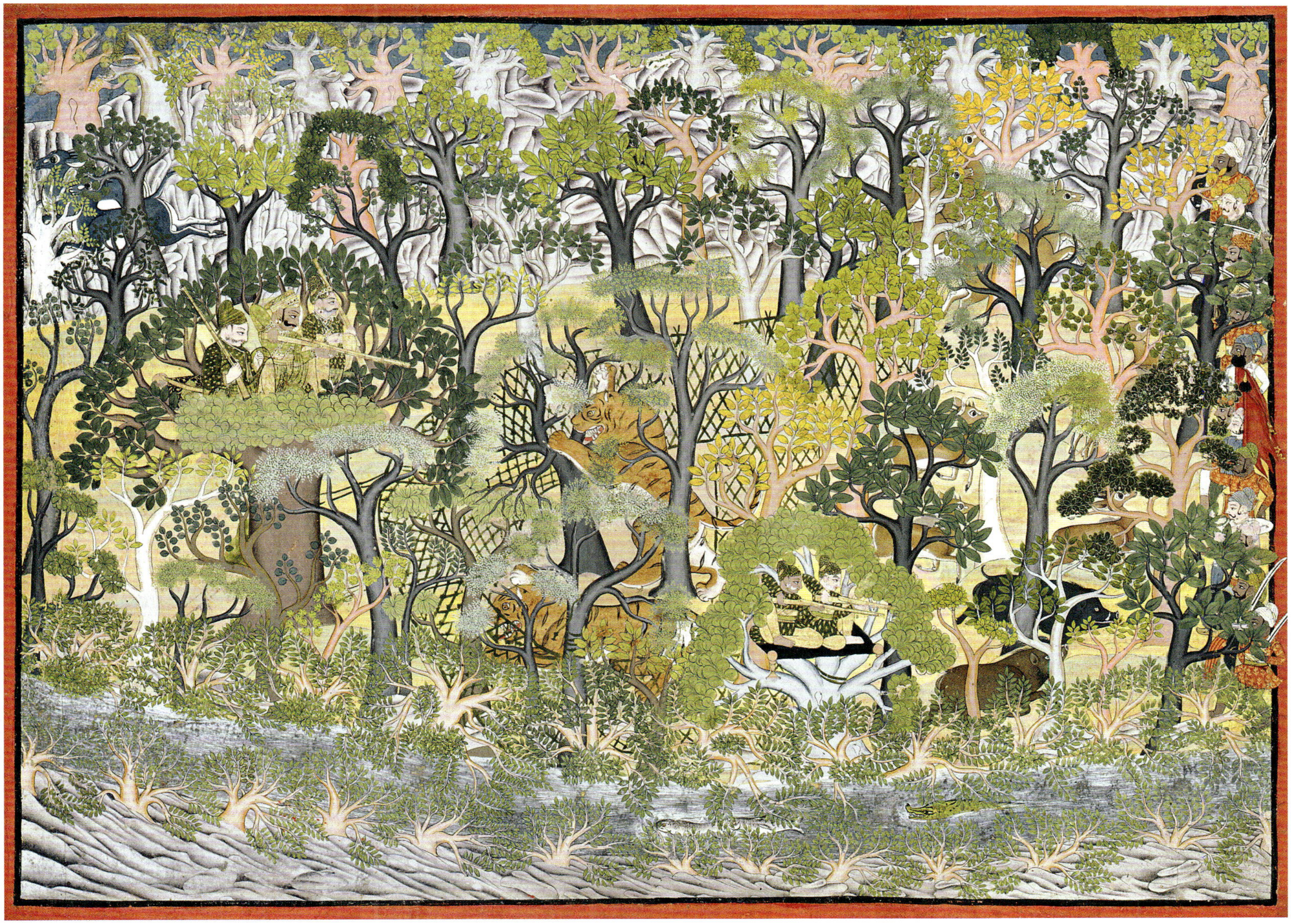

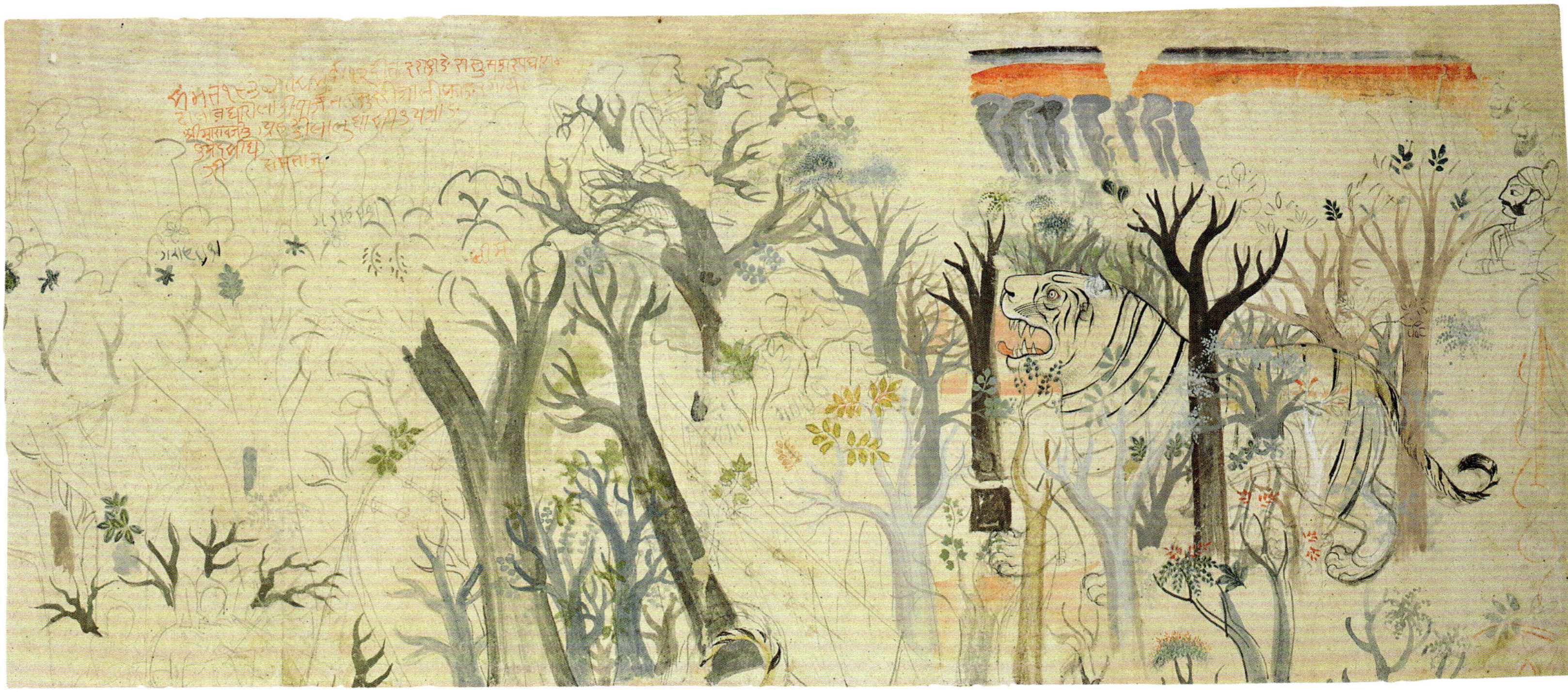

119

A tiger hunt

KOTAH, RAJASTHAN, 1780,
BY SHEIKH TAJU

Ink and watercolor on paper
29.5 × 69.5 cm (11 5/8 × 27 3/8 in.)
Devanagari inscription on picture surface describing the scene, with date VS 1837 and artist's name; also various color notations
Published: H. Hodgkin and T. McInerney, *Indian drawing*, London, 1983, no. 35;
S. Kossak, *Indian court painting, 16th–19th century*, London, 1997, no. 76
Metropolitan Museum of Art, New York, Promised Gift of Cynthia Hazen Polsky

UNFINISHED AS IT IS, THIS STUDY FOR A TIGER HUNT PAINTING by the artist Sheikh Taju has the power and immediacy of a master's confidently adumbrated first thoughts[1]. In a typical Kotah forest with a rocky cliff behind (see also cat. no. 118), the indistinct central figure of a Raja, possibly Maharao Umed Singh, takes aim from his machan. A mighty tiger, driven toward him by a line of beaters on the right, stands at bay with a wild eye and bared fangs. The head of this magnificent animal, seen among the rapidly brushed tree forms, is the most finished element and thus the focus of the picture, as it stands here. This rapidly conceived and fluently worked scene was in fact the upper part of a larger composition. Its matching lower section, showing further trees, a second tiger (the tip of whose striped tail appears here, in the center of the lower edge), and various fleeing animals, is in the Jagdish and Kamla Mittal Museum, Hyderabad.[2] Together, these pages are thought to have formed a study for a painting now in the collection of the Maharaja of Jodhpur.[3]

AT

1 S. C. Welch suggests that Sheikh Taju may have been as old as eighty when he painted it: Welch et al., *Gods, kings and tigers*, Munich, 1997, p. 38n.; no. 45, for another tiger hunt ascribed to Shaikh Taju, and pp. 30–34 *et passim*, for a consideration of this artist and further attributed works; also Welch, 1985, no. 258 .

2 Mittal, 1989, no. 36.

3 Kossak, *loc. cit.*

120

Ladies chasing blackbuck

BIKANER, RAJASTHAN, CA. 1775

Opaque watercolor on paper
15.9 × 27.6 (6 ¼ × 10 ⅞ in.)
Published: T. McInerney, *Indian paintings from the Polsky Collections*, Princeton, 1982, no. 11

TWO NOBLEWOMEN ON GALLOPING STEEDS pursue a herd of blackbuck, which they have surprised grazing in a pasture bounded by stylized rocks and small, regimented trees. The further lady has caught a fleeing buck by its neck with her bow, a proverbial feat of hunting dexterity. Both at the Mughal and other courts of India, queens or favourite concubines who were so inclined would sometimes accompany the rulers on their hunting expeditions. A few (such as Nur Jahan, the powerful wife of the Emperor Jahangir, who was a famous shot) even became renowned for their prowess. However, the restrictions of royal purdah were such that it would have been unusual for two princesses to be out careering on their own and in so carefree a manner. There may well therefore be a poetic symbolism here: not only the deer in flight, but also a lover's heart may have been ensnared by the peerless and valiant lady with the bow.

AT

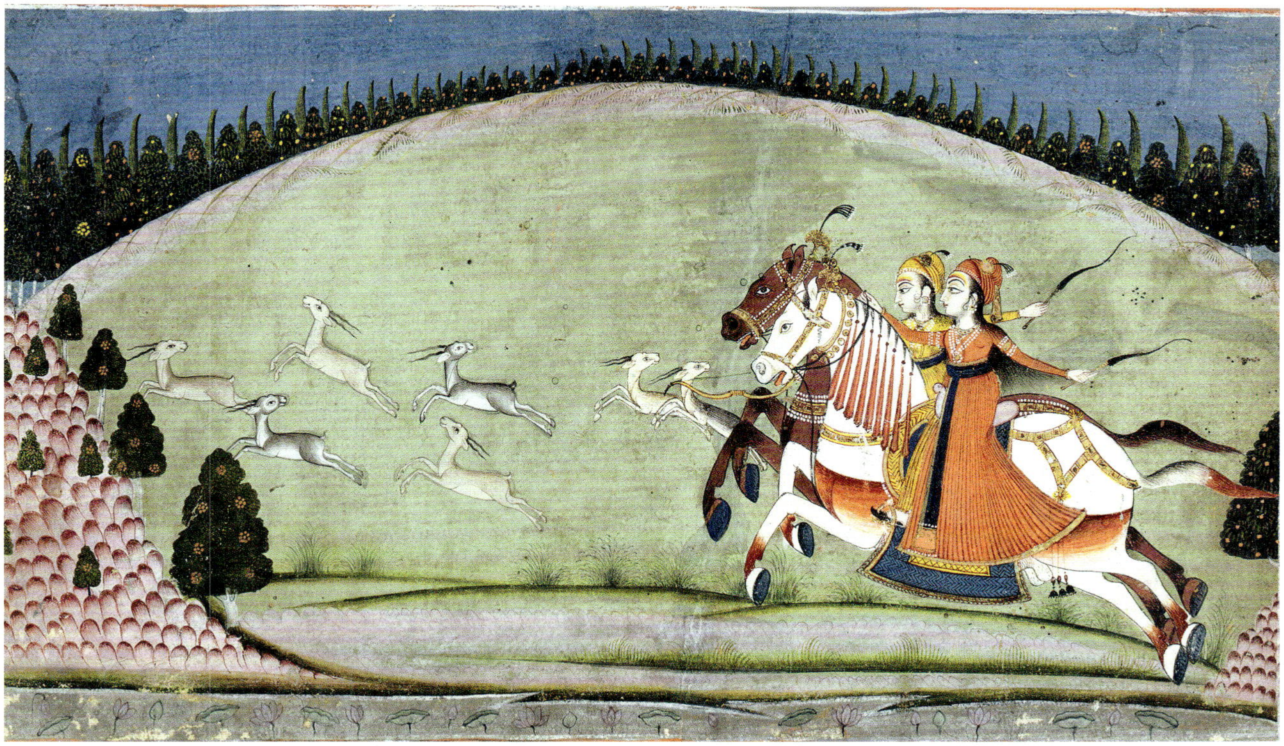

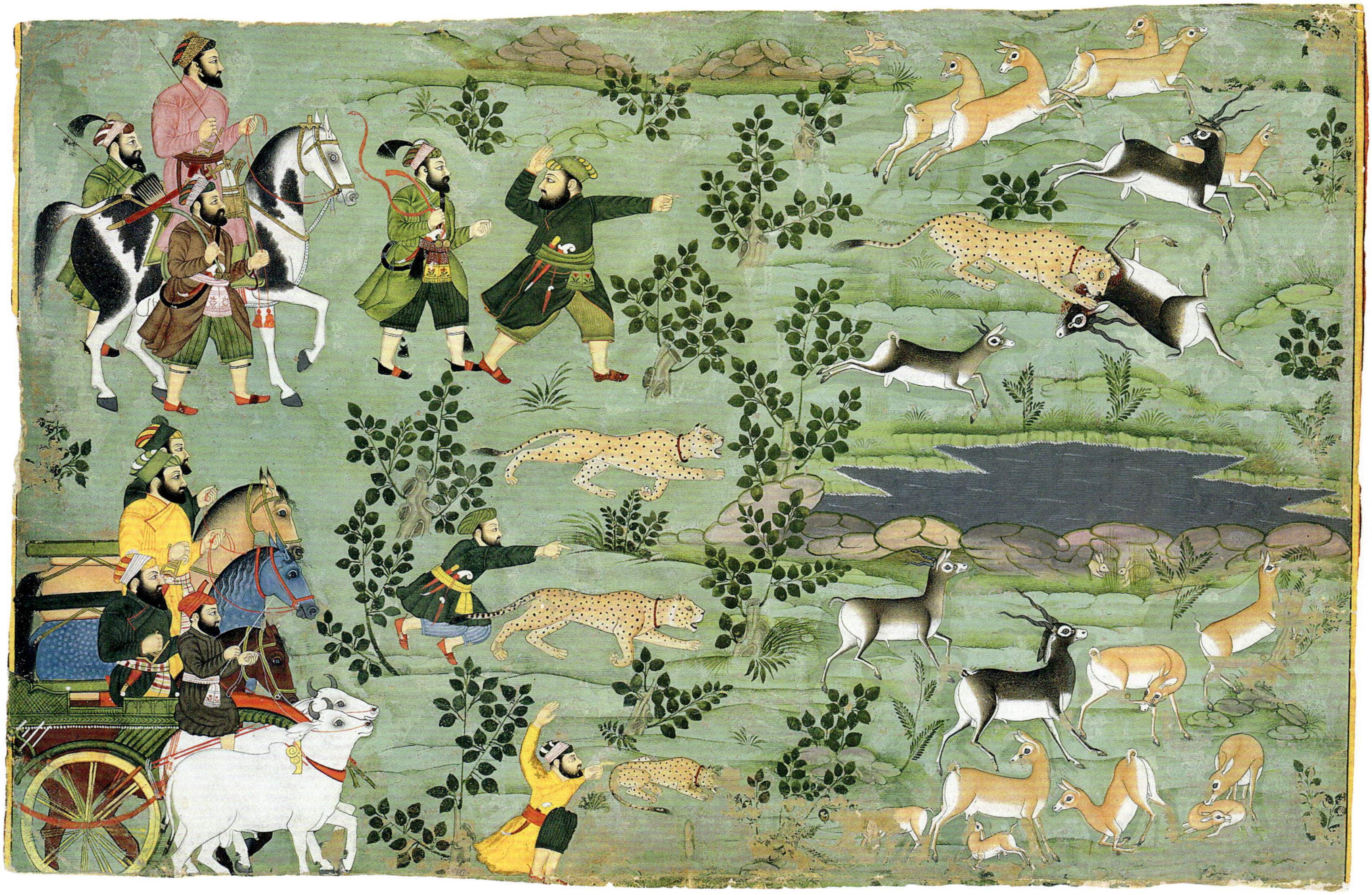

121

Shah Jahan hunting blackbuck with cheetahs

UDAIPUR, RAJASTHAN, CA. 1710–15

Opaque watercolor and gold on paper
27.9 × 42.2 cm (11 × 16 ⅛ in.); trimmed at upper and lower borders
Inscribed on reverse with Mewar royal inventory numbers 20/160, a valuation (Rs. 40) and other clerical marks
Published: S. Kossak, *Indian court painting*, London, 1997, no. 50
Metropolitan Museum of Art, New York, Promised Gift of Cynthia Hazen Polsky

THIS HUNTING SCENE SOMEWHAT UNUSUALLY depicts a seventeenth-century Mughal nobleman, possibly the Emperor Shah Jahan, in the Mewar idiom of the early eighteenth century. By that period, many imperial Mughal pictures are known to have entered the Udaipur Royal Collection,[1] and it was also no longer virtually unheard of to show the Maharanas' traditional enemies, the Mughals, in paintings. In the early years of the reign of Maharana Sangram Singh (r. 1710–34) several paintings reinterpreting Mughal durbar scenes and other subjects were undertaken, perhaps partly as technical exercises as well as for the interest of their subject matter.[2] This painting belongs to the same phase, though it is conceived in a more mainstream Mewar style.

The principal group of the Emperor on horseback with his huntsmen (*shikaris*) on foot and dressed mainly in hunting green, with one of them pointing forward to the kill, recalls Udaipur models of the previous decade.[3] Here the figure types have the short, thickset look of Sangram Singh's reign. The landscape, evenly dotted with rocks, short pollarded trees and a pool, is in the flattened Mewar manner. The use of the device of continuous narration makes it unclear whether two or more trained cheetahs are being used in the hunt. Taken from their bullock cart and then released, the cheetahs stalk a peacefully grazing herd of blackbuck and their young in the foreground. Above, the chase is over and a fine buck has been successfully brought down. As is sometimes the case, the Udaipur artist's human figures appear a little stiff and remote, but he brings a keener sympathy to his animals.

AT

1 A. Topsfield, "The royal paintings inventory at Udaipur," in J. Guy ed., *Indian art and connoisseurship: Essays in honour of Douglas Barrett*, Middletown NJ, 1995, pp. 189–99.

2 E.g. *Indian miniature painting*, London: Spink and Son, 1987, nos. 34–35; *Indian and Islamic works of art*, London: Simon Ray, 2003, no. 44; also Topsfield, 1980, no. 90, for a further ca. 1715 Udaipur painting of a Mughal officer hunting.

3 Topsfield, *op. cit.*, no. 57; Topsfield and Beach, 1991, nos. 19, 21.

122

Prince Ishvari Singh hunting crocodile

UNIARA OR SOUTHERN JAIPUR REGION,[1] RAJASTHAN, MID-EIGHTEENTH CENTURY

Opaque watercolor on paper
43 × 60 cm (17 × 23 ½ in.)
Mutilated devanagari inscription above:
...mharaj kunvar sri isari singhji hathi sut ?jasodev ch..........sighji magara ki sikar...lacha;
reverse uninscribed
Max Polsky collection

PRINCE ISHVARI SINGH[2] has arrived with his entourage at the embankment (*bund*) of a lake, in a cavalcade of elephants, horses, and a palanquin. He has come for a crocodile hunt. With his companions he shows his true Rajput mettle by wading in and meeting the dangerous beasts face to face with his twin-handled thrusting dagger; swords and spears are also being used. Meanwhile three marksmen take a few potshots at the ducks.

The crocodiles are clearly having the worst of it. With their exaggerated scaly fins and upturned snouts (like the classical makara), they have been drawn more from the artist's familiar repertoire of decorative motifs than from close observation. This serves to enhance the almost ritualistic aspect of the hunt in the context of Rajput life.

Crocodile hunting on this scale was an uncommon pastime in Rajasthan. At Udaipur, for example, the crocodiles which formerly flourished in the Pichola lake were occasionally shot for sport by the Maharanas, but generally were tolerated as a benign and even sacred presence, until their final extinction in the early 1960s. Feeding the lake crocodiles was a regular royal ritual,[3] and two beasts mentioned by Tod (ca. 1820) were well known for their prompt appearance when called to receive titbits.[4]

AT

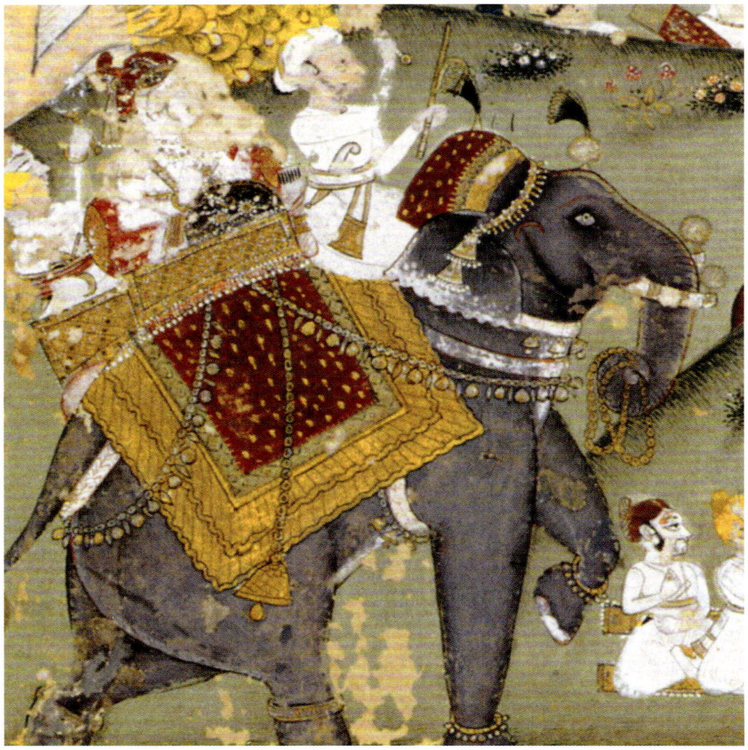

1 One authority has compared the style of this picture with eighteenth-century temple wall-paintings at Baroli, in the vicinity of Uniara.

2 This prince is not yet identified; he appears not to resemble Ishvari Singh of Jaipur, son of Maharaja Sawai Jai Singh, who ruled disastrously from 1743–50.

3 E.g. Topsfield, 1981, no. 72; Desai, 1985, no. 53.

4 Tod, 1920, vol. 2, pp. 753–54.

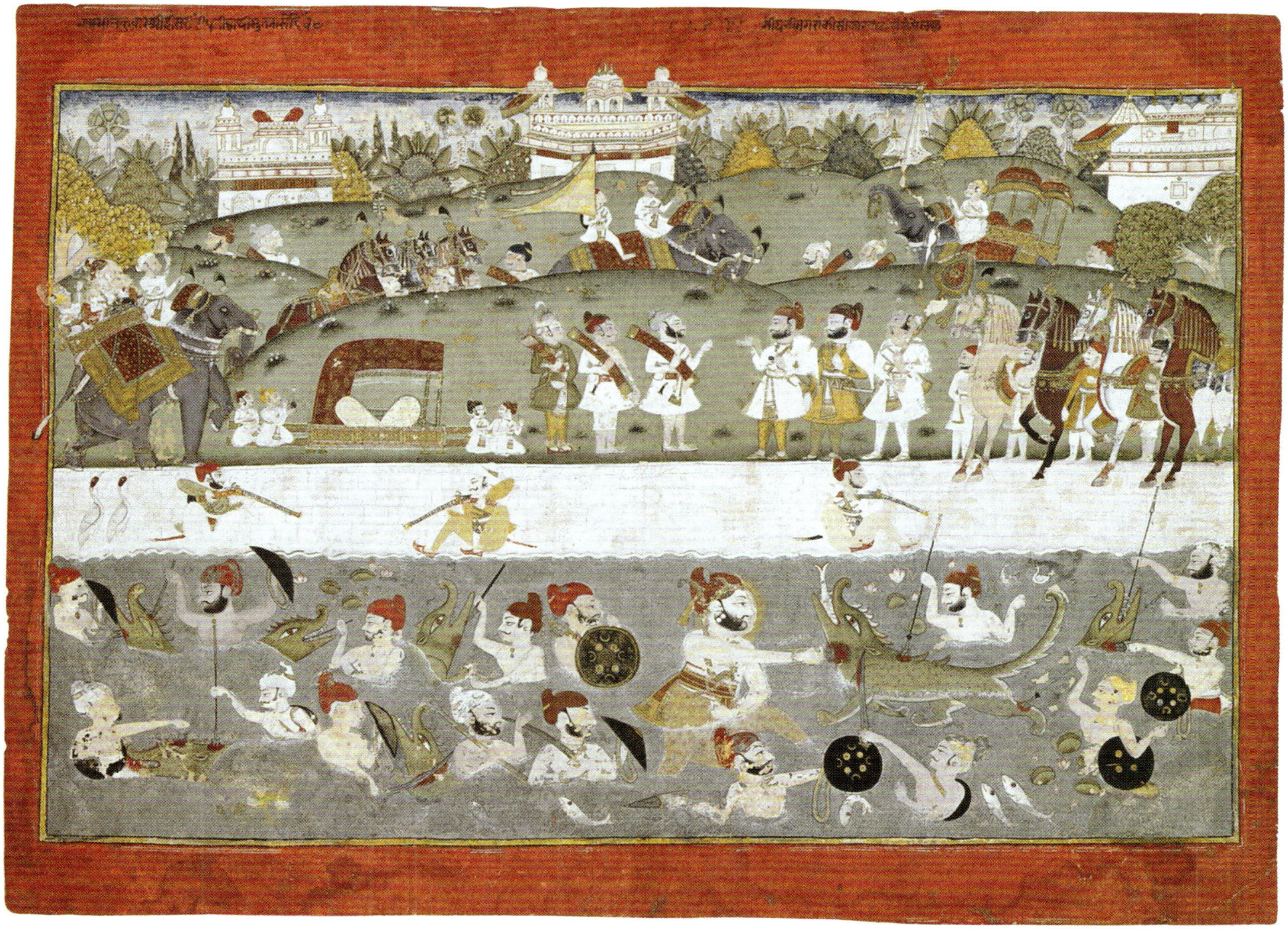

123

Skirmish with an elephant

GULER, PUNJAB HILLS, CA. 1800

Brush drawing with watercolor on paper
25.1 × 17.1 cm (9 7/8 × 6 3/4 in.)
Metropolitan Museum of Art, New York,
Gift of Cynthia Hazen Polsky (2011.576.8)

IN THIS FLUENT, UNFINISHED SKETCH by a Guler-trained artist, the prowess of a royal war elephant is shown. Guided by his mahout's calls and prods with the ankus, this mighty and imperturbable beast has engaged in a skirmish with a small posse of cavalry. He is more than a match for them. One unfortunate rider and his mount have been brought down and are being mauled and trampled; the others turn and flee to the ranks of their infantry.

For the rulers of India, the elephant combined, among other things, the functions of both the Rolls Royce and the tank. As well as being traditional symbols of kingship and the preferred royal mounts in state processions or on tiger shoots, elephants had from an early period formed a key element of the Maharajas' forces in battle, being able to terrify, trample, and scatter the opposition, as here, or else to break through the gates of fortresses. The Emperor Akbar's court historian Abu'l Fazl observed: "Experienced men of Hindustan put the value of a good elephant equal to five hundred horses; and they believe that when guided by a few bold men armed with matchlocks, such an elephant alone is worth double that number."[1]

AT

1 See also Pal, 1981.

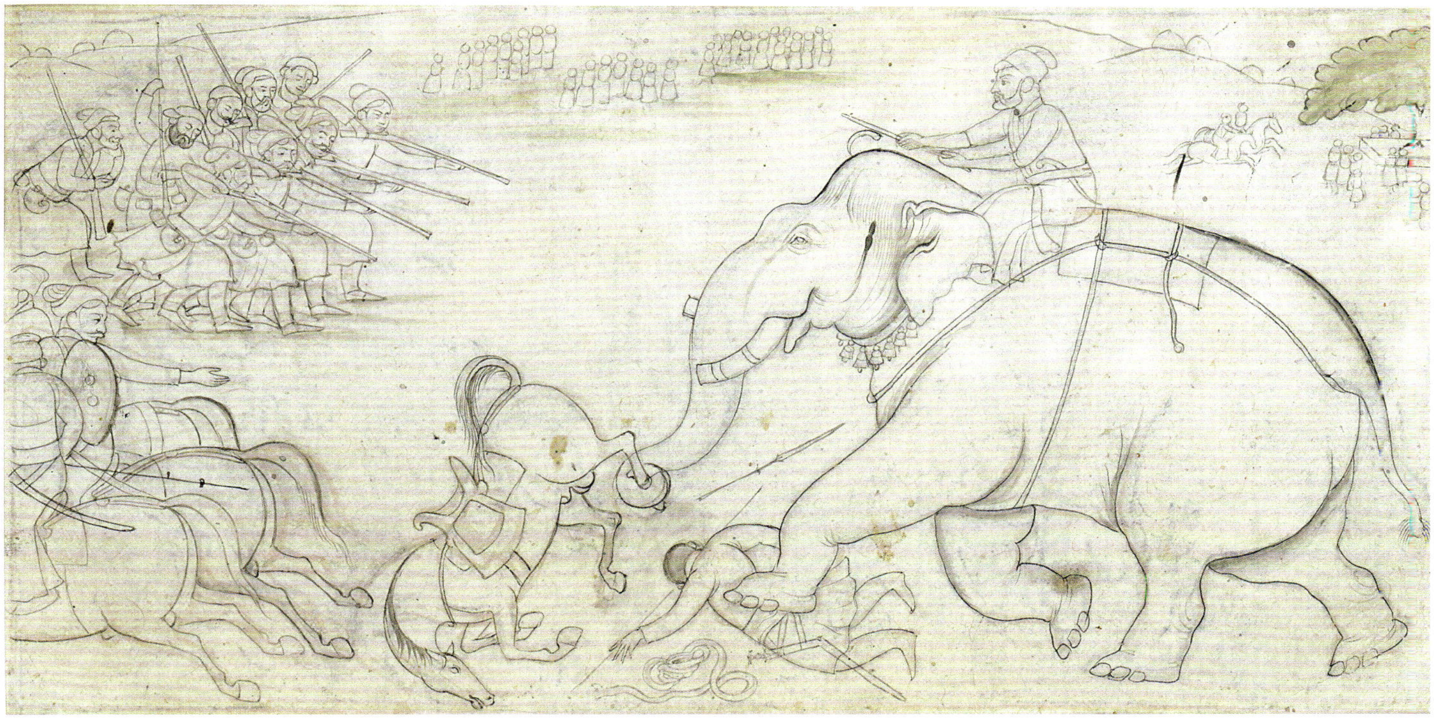

124

Maharana Fateh Singh shooting a bear

UDAIPUR, RAJASTHAN, CA. 1910–15, ATTRIBUTED TO PANNALAL

Opaque watercolor and gold on paper
55.6 × 45.6 cm (21 7/8 × 17 15/16 in.)
A Mewar clerical inscription on reverse, dated 1916 (VS 1973 *asoj sud* 10), with inventory no. 11/51
Metropolitan Museum of Art, New York, Purchase, Cynthia Hazen Polsky Gift (1992.7.1)

MAHARANA FATEH SINGH OF MEWAR (r. 1884–1930) was—to the despair of reformist British administrators—a deeply traditionalist ruler of the old school. Unlike many of his contemporaries among the Rajput rulers, he also led a simple and regular life, without indulgence or excess. His one great passion was for the hunts (*hikar*), and the first half of his reign saw a late flowering of the hunt painting genre at Udaipur,[1] first in the work of the painter Shivalal,[2] and later in that of his followers Pannalal and the latter's son Chaganlal.[3]

Here the Maharana and his hunting companion have waited patiently for game in a machan, in a semi-barren hilly landscape, rendered in Pannalal's hard-edged manner of this period. A passing bear (which is seen five times in all) approaches and investigates their tree, with fatal inquisitiveness. Fateh Singh fires a downward shot at close range, and the mortally wounded bear topples backward into a gully. This use of the ancient device of continuous narrative is effective in its simplicity, and this treatment of the subject clearly met with the approval of Fateh Singh himself. Two other versions of it are in the City Palace Museum, Udaipur.[4]

AT

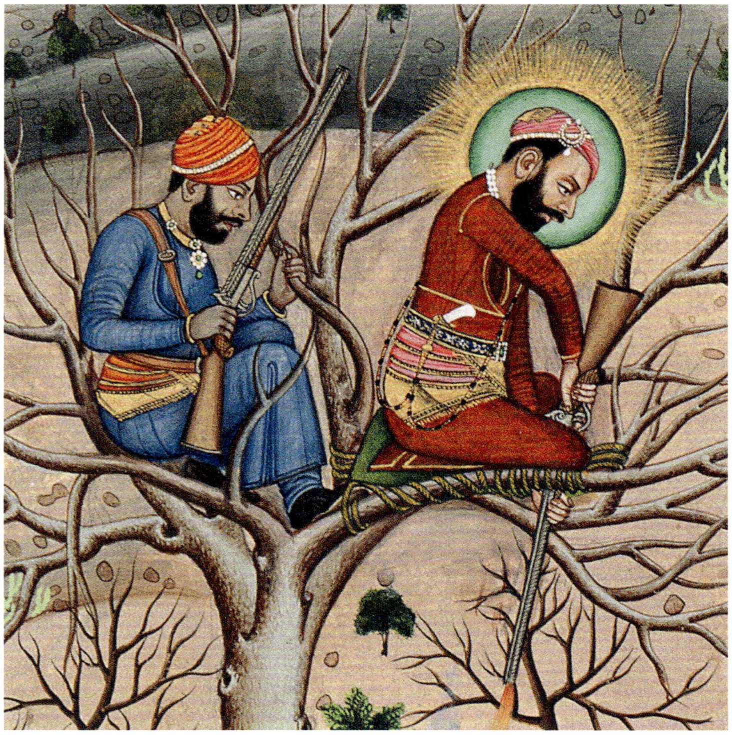

1 Topsfield, 2002, pp. 284–98, for a study of this period.

2 Topsfield, 1990, nos. 37–44.

3 *Ibid.*, nos. 53–56, 58–59, 61, 64–66.

4 *Ibid.*, no. 56; Vashistha, 1984, fig. 82.

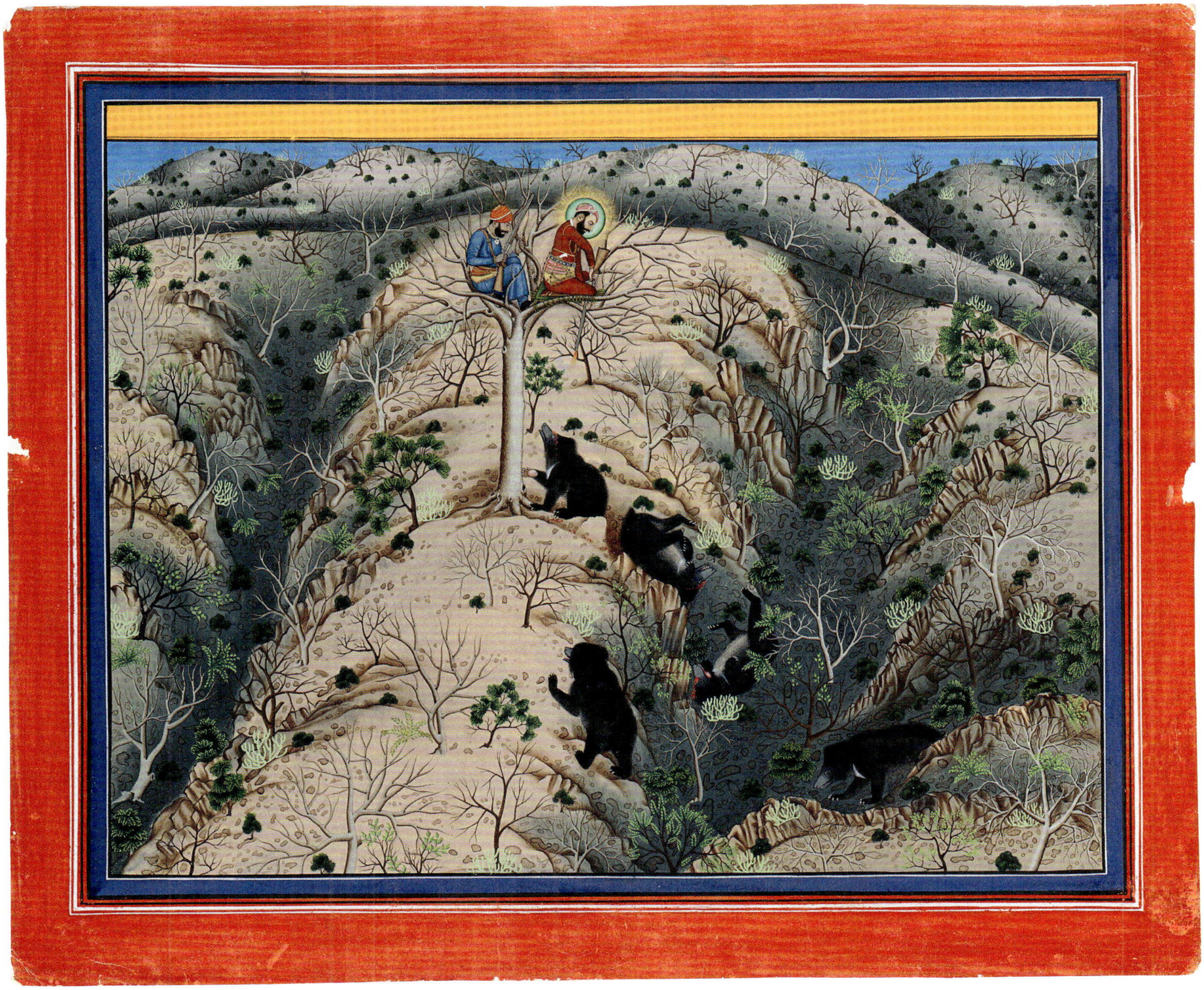

125

Box with hunting scenes

WESTERN INDIA, POSSIBLY AHMEDABAD, GUJARAT, LATE SIXTEENTH OR EARLY SEVENTEENTH CENTURY

Teak, ebony and lac, inlaid with stained ivory
H. 8.3 cm, W. 14.5 cm, L. 34 cm
(3 ¼ x 5 ¾ x 13 ½ in.)
Published: M. Castilho, *Na Rota do Oriente*, Lisbon, 1999, no. 4; N. Haidar, in *Recent acquisitions, a selection:* 2000–2001, *Metropolitan Museum of Art Bulletin*, Fall 2001, p. 15
Metropolitan Museum of Art, New York, Cynthia Hazen Polsky and Leon B. Polsky Fund (2001.301)

FINE PIECES OF IVORY INLAID FURNITURE SUCH AS THIS BOX represented an active market in luxury goods, made in part for a growing European presence in the subcontinent as well as for export to Europe, from the late sixteenth century onward. Such works were largely decorated with European or Indian figures, often engaged in hunting scenes, as in this example, where the forest setting is enlivened by the lyrically curving branches of the trees.

While many Europeanizing elements are evident in the decoration of this box, the idiom is essentially a Mughal one. Such hunting scenes find their ultimate inspiration in Persian compositions, which in turn became popular in Mughal painting. The types of furniture created ranged from large standing cabinets and tables to more portable fall-front cabinets and small boxes. Although several centers have been proposed for the production of this type of furniture, including Sind and the Deccan, Ahmedabad in Gujarat appears to have been a leader amongst them, as it had also been a notable area for the earlier production of inlay-in-lac furniture made for the Islamic Turkish and other export markets.[1]

This box can be related to a distinguished group of ivory inlaid furniture, possibly from the same workshop, which includes a cabinet in the Museu de Arte Antiga, Lisbon,[2] a "communion" table top in the Victoria and Albert Museum, London,[3] as well as two cabinets depicting hunting scenes in the Kuwait National Museum[4] and the Cincinatti Art Museum.[5] The distinctive S-shaped zoomorphized motifs along the edges are also seen on the V&A table and may derive from earlier Islamic precedents in metalwork, resembling Safavid dragon-headed hooks[6] and also Seljuq belt buckles. Its shape, long and narrow with a sliding drawer at one end (whose original interior has been replaced with European-style dovetail joints and screws, but exterior panel preserved), is unusual but can be related to an earlier calligraphic drawer-box in the inlay-in-lac technique at the Los Angeles County Museum.[7] While the Los Angeles box has been identified as a penbox by the Persian verses on its panels, the function of this box is less clear, though it may very well have originally had a drawer with compartments for smaller objects.

NHH

1 S. Digby, "The mother-of-pearl overlaid furniture of Gujarat: An Indian handicraft of the 16th and 17th centuries," in R. Skelton et al. eds., *Facets of Indian art*, London, 1986, pp. 213–23.

2 Bassini et al., 1991, p. 145.

3 Jaffer, 2002, pp. 33–34, no. 9.

4 Jenkins, 1983, p. 123.

5 Smart Walker, 1985, no. 58.

6 Taylor and Jail eds., 2001, p. 111, no. 76.

7 Victoria and Albert Museum, *The Indian Heritage*, London, 1982, no. 549.

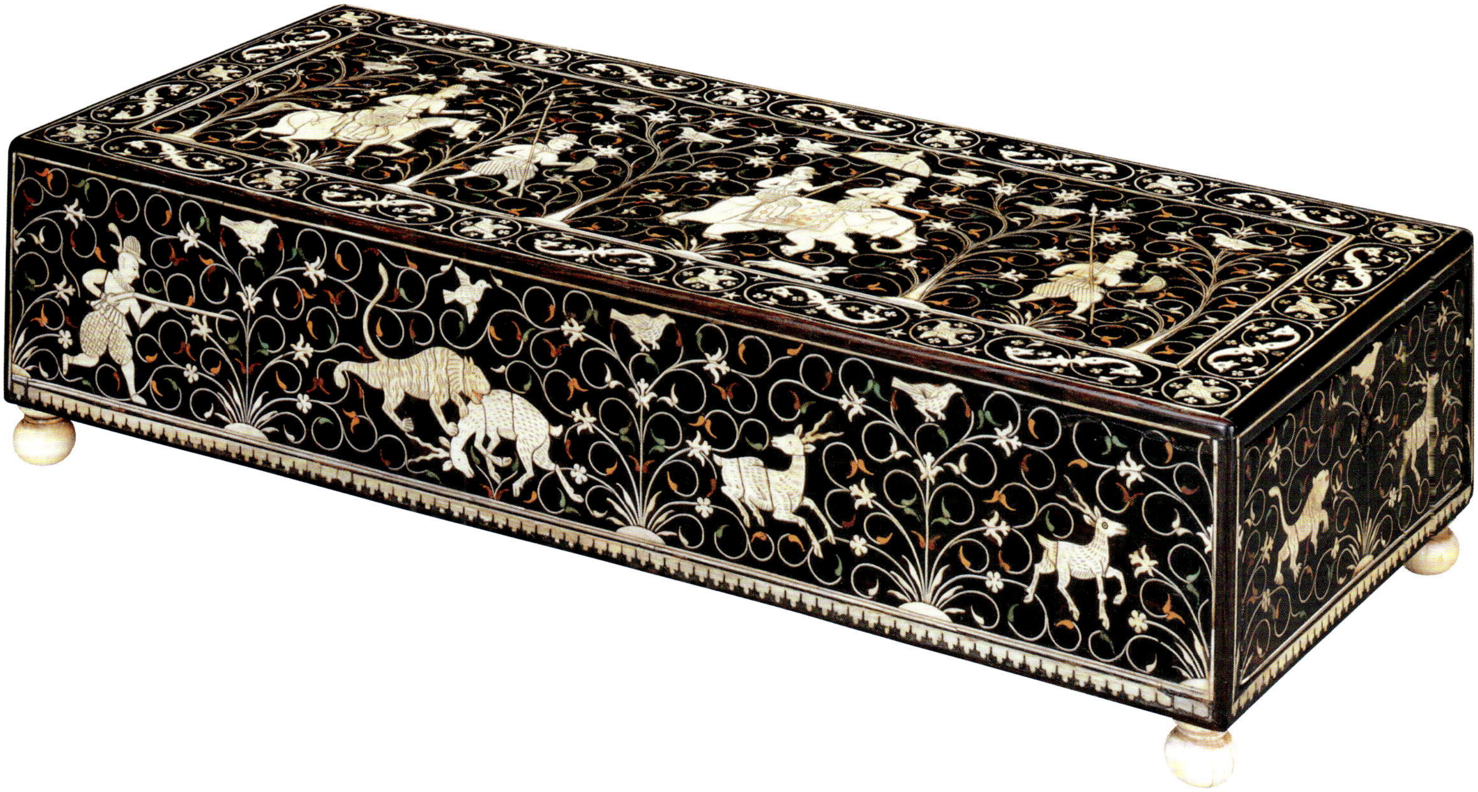

ROYAL PORTRAITS

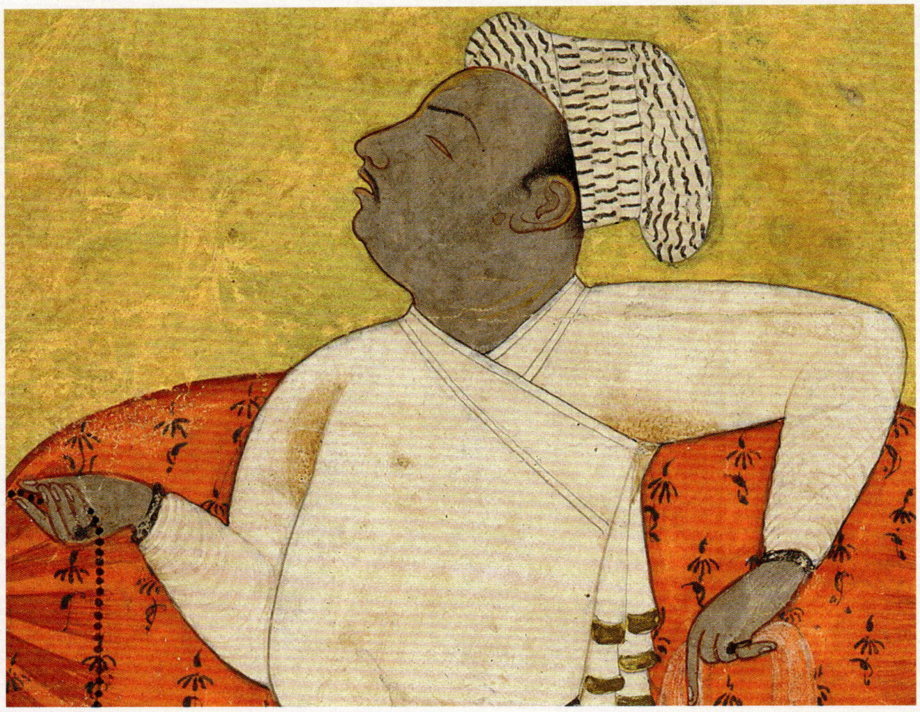

True portraiture in India was a Mughal invention. Traditional Indian representations of rulers and others had always tended to show them as idealized types, with little emphasis on the quirks of individual character. But from the Emperor Babur onward, the early Mughals showed a new and restless inquisitiveness about man and nature, focussing their attention on the individual, the particular, and the idiosyncratic. Akbar, above all, was able to nurture the novel naturalistic techniques which his artists were adapting from the European prints and paintings now reaching the court. In their highly organized collaborations on the great historical manuscripts produced in Akbar's reign, certain gifted artists were deputed to specialize in portraying the principal figures' faces, so bringing a new verisimilitude and actuality to these vigorous and teeming scenes of life at court.

Soon afterwards, the finely finished individual portrait became valued in its own right, a development which was strongly encouraged by the avowed connoisseur Jahangir. The ambassador Sir Thomas Roe reports Jahangir's fascination with the examples of English portrait miniatures that he carried in his belongings, and the Emperor's insistence that his painters should make copies of them. During Jahangir's reign portraiture reached an excellence of technique, and often of psychological insight, which was to a large degree maintained under his successor Shah Jahan. Accomplished individual or small group portraits of the ruler, princes, nobility, and courtiers, as well as plant and animal studies or paintings of women, holy men, or other subjects of interest, would be mounted in lavishly decorated borders and assembled in bound albums, for the Emperor and his family to study and enjoy at will. While they provided faithful portrayals of their subjects, such works remained highly conventional, often showing a solitary figure standing against a pale green ground, with a cursory treatment of grassy foreground and a band of sky. The depiction of the ruler himself, especially in Jahangir and Shah Jahan's time, also became increasingly replete with imperial symbolism. This tendency is seen not only in Mughal examples, but also in the derivative portrait idioms which soon developed at other regional courts during the seventeenth century, particularly those of the Deccani sultans and the Rajput rulers of Rajasthan and the Punjab Hills. In these too, the ruler is often shown with a radiant gold nimbus, carrying weapons to demonstrate his valor, and perhaps a flower to show his refinement. Also common are equestrian portraits, in which the ruler on a fine stallion is accompanied by a bevy of attendants carrying the parasol denoting kingship and other regalia. When a maharaja is shown taking his ease on a palace terrace, attendants will generally continue to fan him or to stand nearby with his hookah, betel (*pan*) or liquor at the ready. In Rajput painting, moreover, there remained an innate tendency to modify the new veracity with some reversion to the ancient idealizing tendency, presenting the ruler more as an archetype of the heroic or munificent monarch, than as a possibly fallible individual, with his own peculiarities. There are, of course, many exceptions, including the touching portrait of Raja Sital Dev of Mankot seen here (cat. no. 137).

In the nineteenth century, fine portraiture continued to be produced at many centers, often under increas-ing Western influence. Sometimes the subjects were the newly ascendant British governors or nabobs, many of whom, at least to begin with, adopted Indian customs, tastes, and manners. But by the middle of the century, the art of portraiture was in general decline and it was replaced soon after, except at the most conservative courts, by the sensational new art of photography.

AT

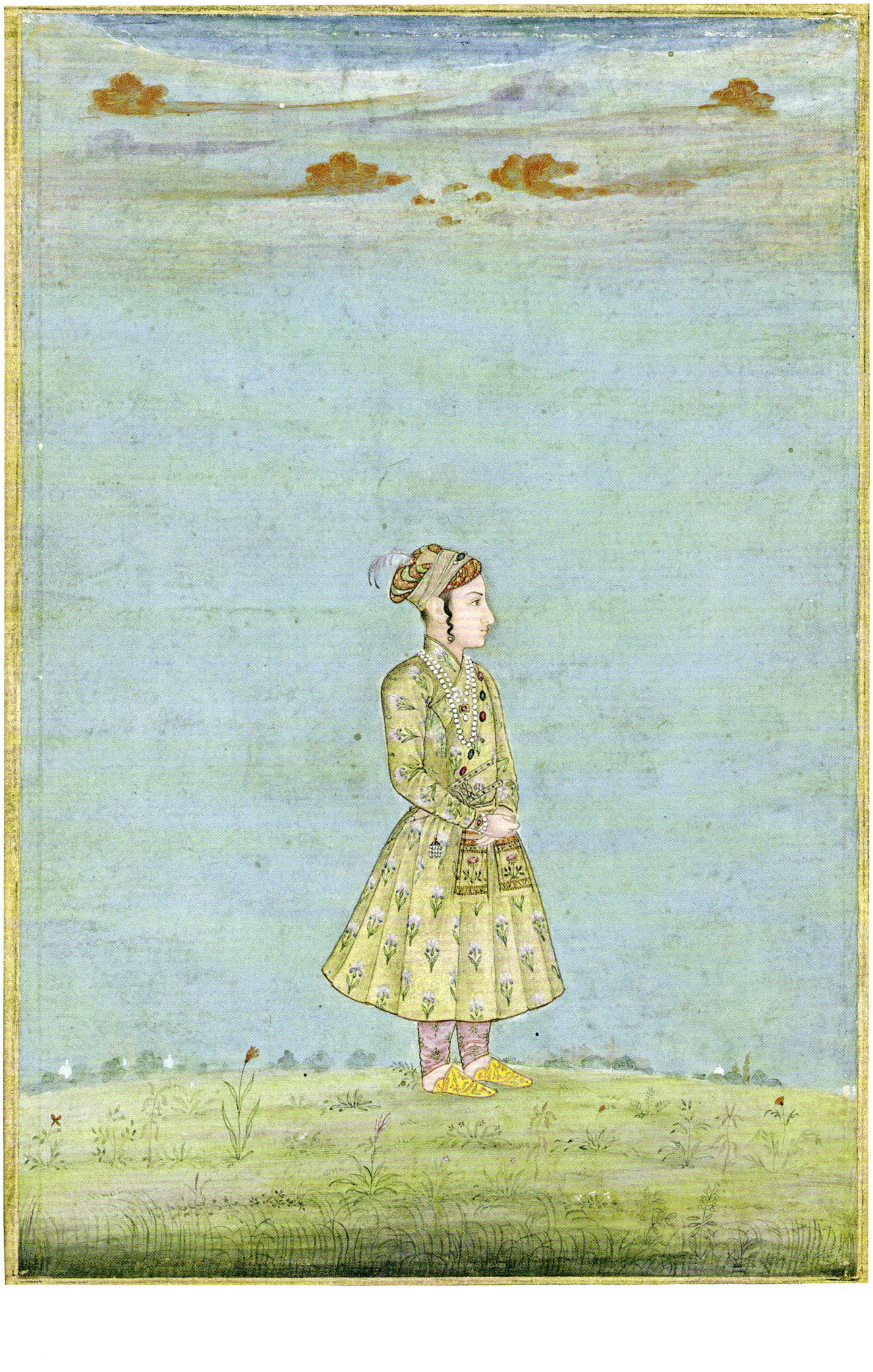

126

Portrait of a young prince

MUGHAL, 1681–82

Opaque watercolor and gold on paper
20.3 × 14 cm (8 × 5½ in.)
Inscribed on the reverse in devanagari (partly cut off): *s[h]ahzada azam…bedar sam 1738* ("Bedar [Bakht] [son of] Prince 'Azam [Shah] 1681–82")
Published: T. McInerney, *Indian paintings from the Polsky Collections*, Princeton, 1982, no. 3
Nicholas Polsky collection

A YOUNG MUGHAL PRINCE STANDS FACING RIGHT, his hands before him in the position used for courtiers in the Mughal court. This is then both a finished portrait and a study which could be used when this prince needed to be placed in a formal durbar scene. The richness of his costume indicates that he must be a grandson of the Emperor Aurangzeb (r. 1658–1707). Apart from his jama of gold brocade, and his standard pearl necklace, he has a single string of rubies and emeralds across his chest.[1] The difficult inscription confirms that this is indeed an imperial grandson and apparently Bedar Bakht, the eldest son of Aurangzeb's third son 'Azam Shah. 'Azam Shah and his son were both killed in 1701 in the war of succession following the Emperor's death. The devanagari inscription indicates that the portrait entered a Rajput collection shortly after it was painted; it is known that it was formerly in the Mewar Royal Collection.

Portraiture as a record of an individual's likeness, either as a decorative or commemorative object in its own right, or else as an aid for an artist when requiring likenesses of given subjects at the right age when portraying a larger composition, had long been a feature of the Mughal studio's output. Originally portrayed against an uncolored or a turquoise ground, by the 1630s thought was given seriously how to make the subjects appear more lifelike rather than like natural history specimens pinned to a board, and different types of background were devised. The album of Prince Dara Shikoh shows Mughal artists experimenting in Shah Jahan's reign with backgrounds.[2] One solution was to portray the subject standing on a flower-studded, deep-colored ground, which was then lightened as it retreated backward toward the top of the page, where streaks of color were introduced to indicate the sky. It would seem this came to be seen increasingly as unnaturalistic, and by the end of the decade, a clear distinction was drawn between the flower-studded ground, now green, and the background, often of turquoise with brightly colored swags above, as here. This became the standard background for portraits in the next reign.

JPL

1 For another probably contemporary portrait of a boy prince, see Poster, 1994, no. 44.

2 Falk and Archer, 1981, pp. 72–81, reproduced pp. 379–400.

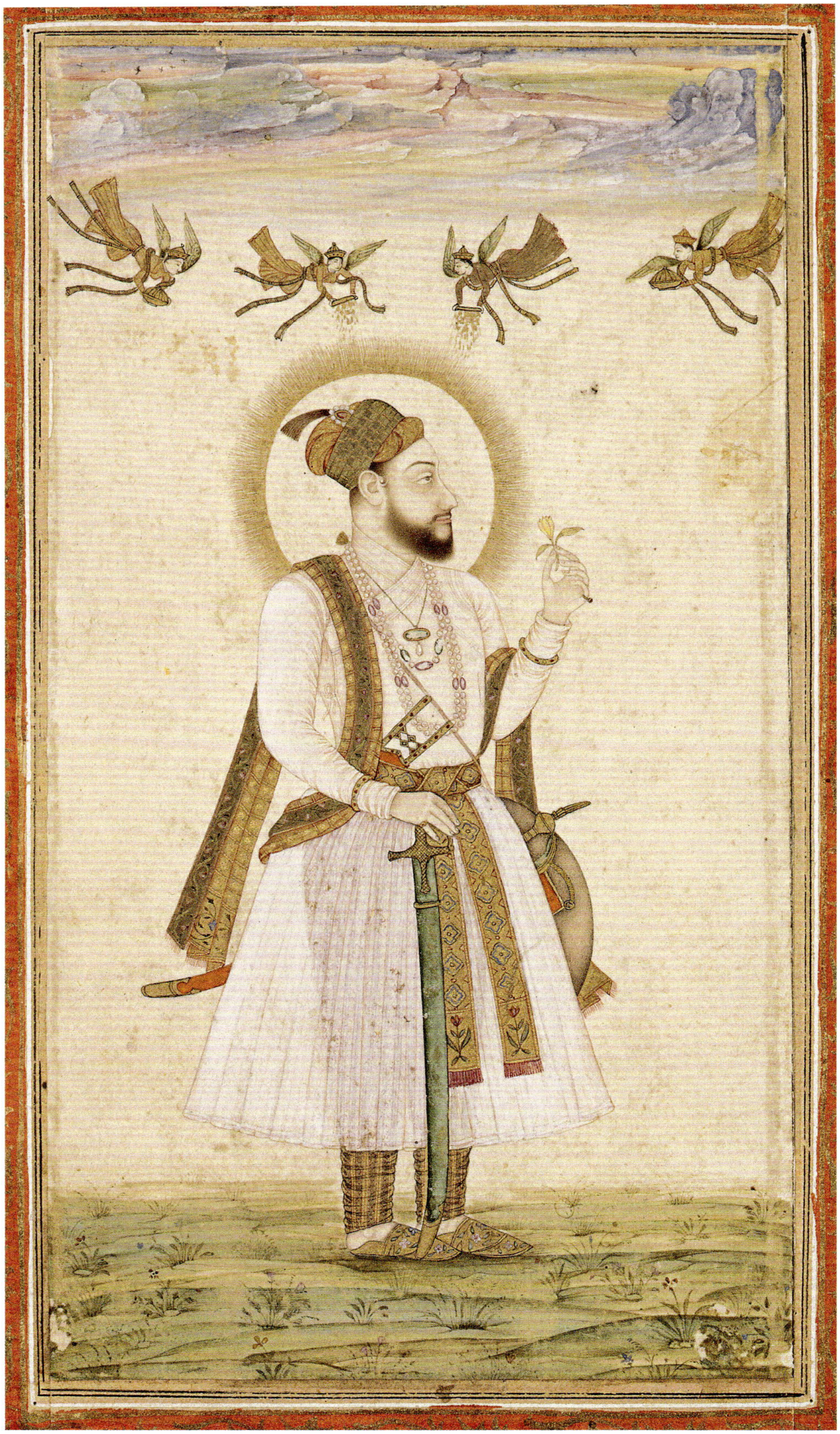

127

Muhammad 'Adil Shah II of Bijapur

BIJAPUR, DECCAN, CA. 1650

Opaque watercolor and gold on paper
Image 19.1 × 10.8 cm (7 ½ × 4 ¼ in.);
page 34.2 × 19.5 cm (13 ½ × 7 ⅝ in.)

MUHAMMAD 'ADIL SHAH II (r. 1627–56) came to the throne of Bijapur at the age of fourteen, and like his similarly young contemporary in Golconda (cat. no. 94) was unable to resist the increasing Mughal pressure on his kingdom after the fall of Ahmadnagar in 1636. All of his portraits are influenced by Mughal ideas of portraiture: in profile but naturalistic, whether in durbar or alone, and in poses familiar from northern examples. Here the Sultan stands in the conventional Mughal manner and in Mughal costume, and holds a flower. Royal fashions in shawls were less rigid in Bijapur than in Golconda (cat. no. 94), and the earlier Bijapur sultans were depicted wearing them in various ways, although the simple drape over the shoulders was the commonest.[1] Here, however, the shawl is wound round the Sultan's body in a northern manner, a fashion which he retained in his later portraits.[2] Beneath his feet is green grass studded with clumps of flowers, lightening toward the horizon, and behind is a neutral ground rising to a colorfully streaked sky. Four angels swoop from the clouds and scatter flower petals over the sovereign, who is nimbate in the manner of the Mughal emperors.

The two principal portrait painters of Muhammad's reign were Chand Muhammad and Muhammad Khan, who present their subjects in a hard-edged, wide-shouldered Mughal manner.[3] Our artist lacks the hardness of outline associated with these artists. The nimbus is found in two other portraits of Sultan Muhammad. In one, signed by Haidar 'Ali and Ibrahim Khan, he rides an elephant, although again our artist lacks their sumptuous style, and also in a double portrait with his prime minister Ikhlas Khan.[4] Angels had been bringing swords and crowns and such-like to the Mughal emperors since Jahangir's allegorical compositions of the 1610s.[5] Counter-reformation artists in Europe had depicted crowns of martyrdom being bestowed upon martyrs by angels, and this imagery was seized upon by Mughal artists concerned to transfer, not the imagery obviously, but the iconography, to bolster the status of their royal portrait subjects. Here again there has been a shift, as our Bijapuri artist has changed the European angels of Mughal imagery into ones wearing Indian "angelic" costume, and in the process reawakened imagery of Hindu apsarases, heavenly beings who shower flowers from above on triumphal occasions whether imperial or religious.[6]

JPL

1 Most illustrated in Zebrowski, 1983, pp. 65–123.

2 See Falk and Archer, 1981, p. 389, for young men from the Dara Shikoh Album wearing shawls in this fashion.

3 *Ibid.*, nos. 404–07; Zebrowski, *op. cit.*, pp. 126–31.

4 Zebrowski, *op. cit.*, pp. 131–32, and Pal, 1993, no. 99.

5 Leach, 1995, pp. 399–404, for example.

6 See also the "angels" in a Dakhni Urdu manuscript of about 1700 (Zebrowski, *op. cit.*, fig. 195).

128

Maharana Sangram Singh II of Mewar

UDAIPUR, RAJASTHAN, CA. 1715–20

Opaque watercolor and gold on paper
14 × 9.2 (5 ½ × 3 ⅝ in.)
Private collection

MAHARANA SANGRAM SINGH (r. 1710–34) stands formally with sword and shield, bejeweled and wearing a sash (*patka*) and jama with flaring muslin overskirt, against a streaked green ground with a row of plants in the foreground. The pose and setting follow standard conventions of seventeenth-century Mughal album portraiture. This Maharana's compact physique is here uncharacteristically elongated. The facial treatment and shadowy modeling of head and costume are also unusual for Sangram Singh's reign,[1] and seem to be the work of a painter who had come under the influence of the contemporary Bikaner artist Murad (cat. no. 174). At least one Bikaner portrait, depicting the young prince Zorawar Singh in Murad's style, probably entered the Mewar Royal Collection around this time or a little later.[2] Zorawar Singh's father Maharaja Sujan Singh (r. 1700–35) is known to have spent a month at Udaipur as Sangram Singh's guest in 1719 on his way back to Bikaner after ten years' service in the Deccan.[3] Presents would have been exchanged on that occasion, and the Bikaner Maharaja may also have been accompanied by one or more of his court painters.

The portrait of Maharana Sangram Singh most likely belongs in any case to the first decade of his reign, when (following the stylistic innovations of the previous decade 1700–10, under his father Amar Singh: cat. no. 129), some limited experimentation with Mughal and other exotic pictorial models continued for a time at Udaipur (cat. no. 121).[4]

AT

1 For a stylistically more normal solitary standing portrait of Sangram Singh, see e.g. Topsfield, 1980, no. 69.

2 *Ibid.*, no. 20.

3 Shyamaldas, *Vir Vinod*, Udaipur, 1886 (repr. Delhi, 1986), vol. 2, p. 500; Capt. P. W. Powlett, *Gazetteer of the Bikanir State*, Calcutta, 1874, p. 42.

4 Topsfield, 2002, pp. 153–54.

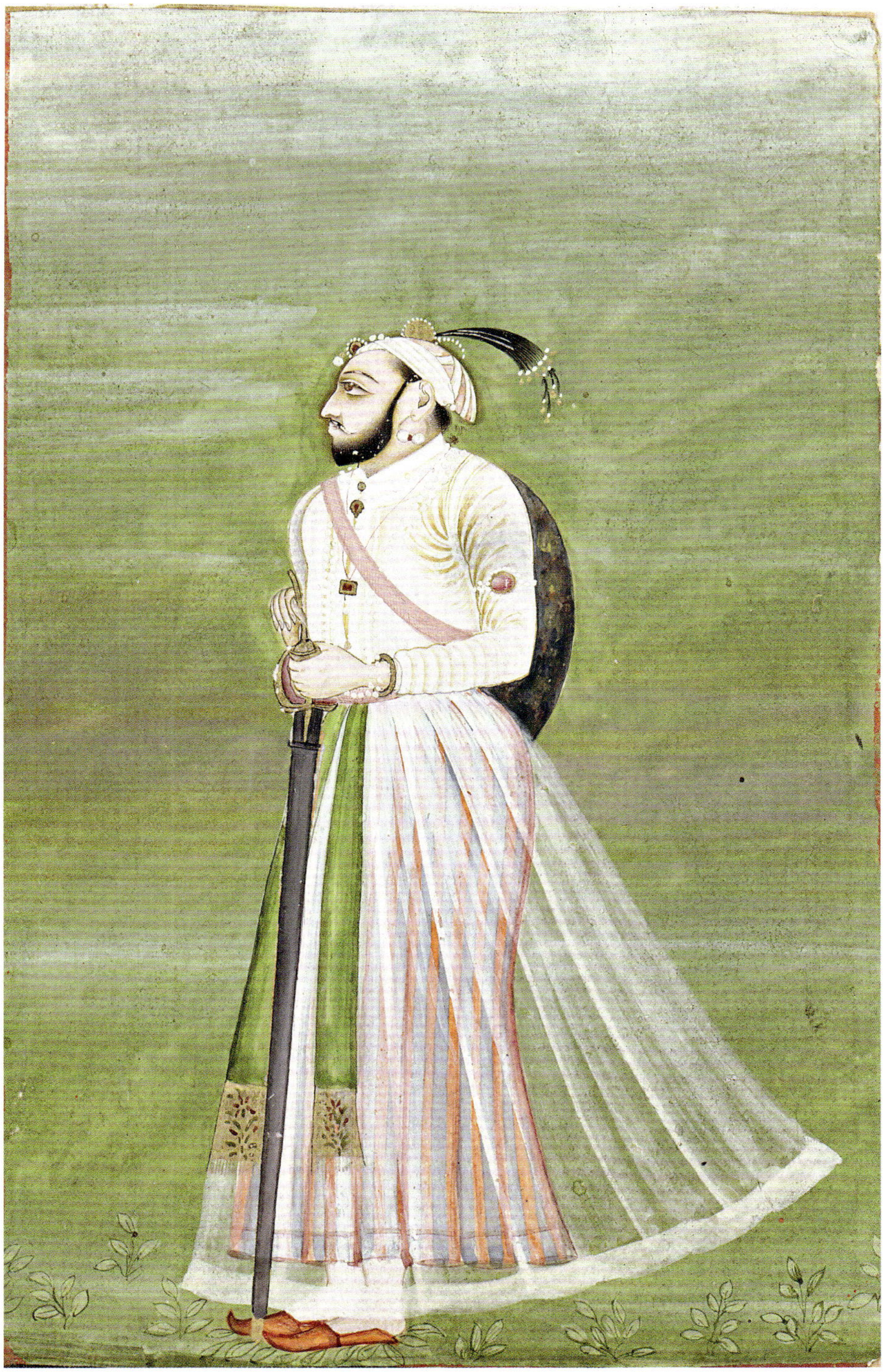

129

Maharana Amar Singh II of Mewar riding with retainers

UDAIPUR, RAJASTHAN, CA. 1705
ATTRIBUTED TO THE STIPPLE MASTER
(ACTIVE CA. 1690–1715)

Opaque watercolor and gold on paper
Image 34.6 × 28.3 cm (13 5/8 × 11 1/8 in.);
page 37.5 × 31.1 cm (14 3/4 × 12 1/4 in.)
Inscribed in devanagari on reverse:
jodpar ka che ("It is from Jodhpur")
Published: A. Topsfield, *Court painting at Udaipur*, Zurich, 2002, fig. 98
Metropolitan Museum of Art, New York, Cynthia Hazen Polsky and Leon B. Polsky Fund (2002.177)

UNDER MAHARANA AMAR SINGH II (r. 1698–1710) Udaipur painting took a crucial change of direction, away from the earlier traditional style of manuscript illustration, toward the more naturalistic, Mughal-inspired genres of court portraiture and reportage. Amar Singh's gifted leading painter (who is unnamed in any inscription) experimented boldly, not only with received conventions of portraiture but with a heavily stippled, grisaille modeling technique adapted from earlier Mughal and Deccani models, and also with restrained, semi-colored compositions. This portrait of the Maharana riding a rearing horse of an almost electric blue, with four attendants jogging rhythmically alongside him carrying a bow, chowries and the royal parasol, is a fine example of the type.[1] The intense color and shaded modeling of the centrally placed horse make it and its rider the focus of the picture, silhouetted against an uncolored, buff ground. Fine stallions were very highly prized by the Rajput nobility, and the inscription on the reverse, "It is from Jodhpur," could perhaps refer to the horse's origin as a state gift from the neighboring Maharaja of Jodhpur, to the west. Beyond the conventional, rounded hill outline above, a delicately observed Mewari landscape stretches away, with a serpentine river, a walled royal pleasure garden and pool and, on the right, a village with a Shiva temple.

AT

1 See Topsfield, 2002, figs. 96–97, 99, for comparable Amar Singh equestrian subjects; also R. Skelton, *Indian miniatures*, Venice, 1961, pl. 11; Ehnbom, 1985, no. 50.

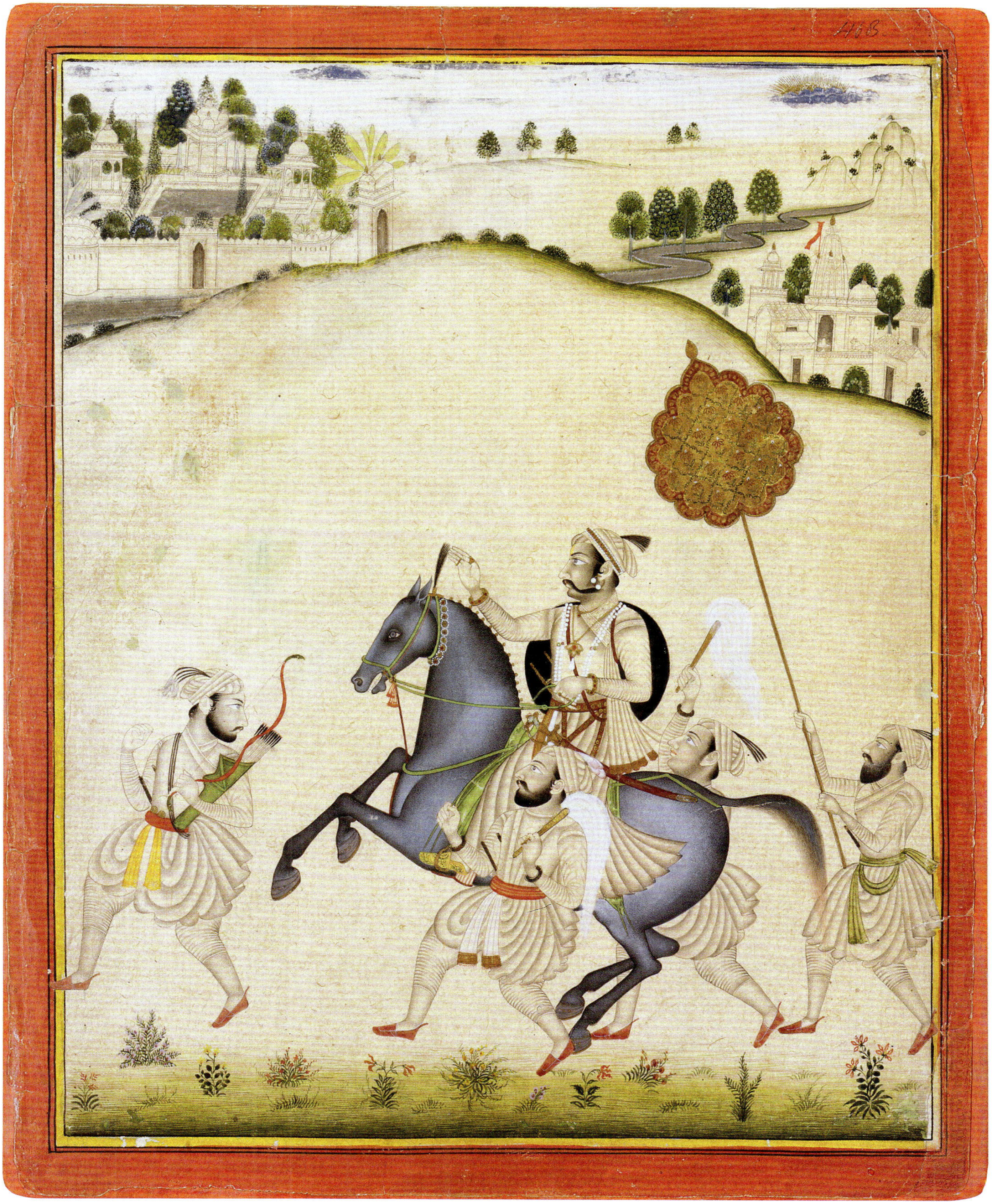

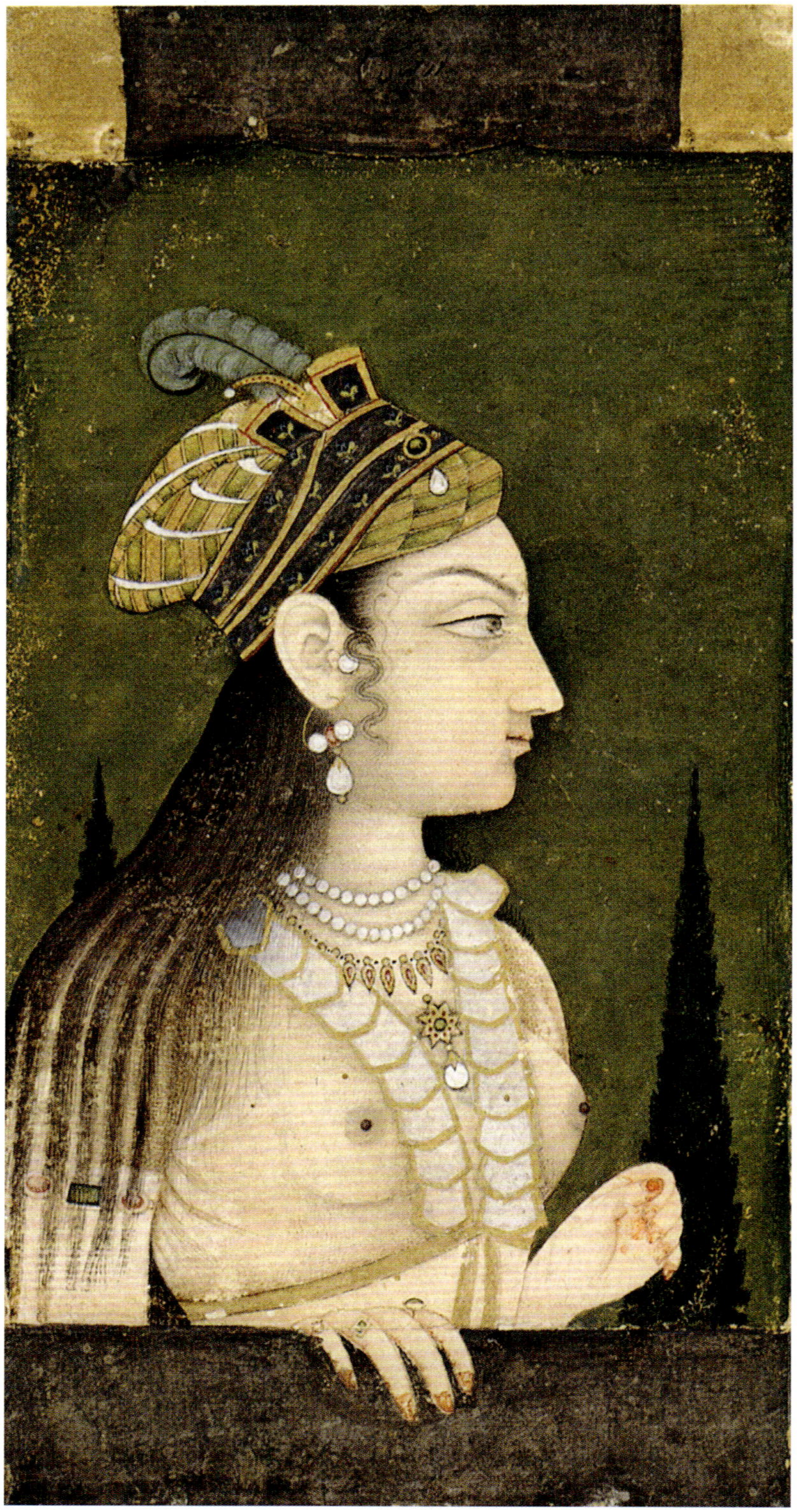

130

A lady at a window

MUGHAL, CA. 1750

Opaque watercolor and gold on paper
16.5 × 8.9 cm (6½ × 3½ in.)
Inscribed in Persian above: *nur mahal*
Published: T. McInerney, *Indian paintings from the Polsky Collections*, Princeton, 1982, no. 13

WITH RARE EXCEPTIONS, THERE ARE NO Mughal portraits of royal or even respectable women. There are some female portraits with inscriptions naming them as women of the royal household (see also cat. no. 142), but these are idealized renderings, unless of course the artist was a woman, so we need not take too seriously the identification of the subject here as Nur Mahal, the all-powerful queen of Jahangir. If any woman had her portrait taken by a male artist, she was by definition not respectable, and to reinforce the point, many such female portraits show the subject carrying a wine bottle and a cup. Although lacking these latter attributes, our beauty here wears such a transparent shift as to bare all beneath it, but such garments are common in zenana scenes.[1] Her long tresses fall from her elegant turban over her shoulders, and her slightly plump features are exquisitely modeled, although the lower part of the painting is much rubbed.

Window portraits had been a feature of Mughal art since the seventeenth century, painted in imitation of Renaissance portraits transmitted to India via the medium of prints. Like their models, a parapet beneath converts the open frame into an architectural space and a rolled up curtain above completes the illusion that we are looking through a window. Here, the subject places a delicate hand on the parapet, suggesting the intermediate space above the parapet that is between her and the viewer, another Renaissance conceit transferred to India. Window portraits of such ladies became very fashionable in the mid-eighteenth century.[2]

JPL

1 Leach, 1995, col. pl. 73 and p. 496, for example.

2 For comparable portraits, see Falk and Archer, 1981, nos. 179, 182, 199, and 203.

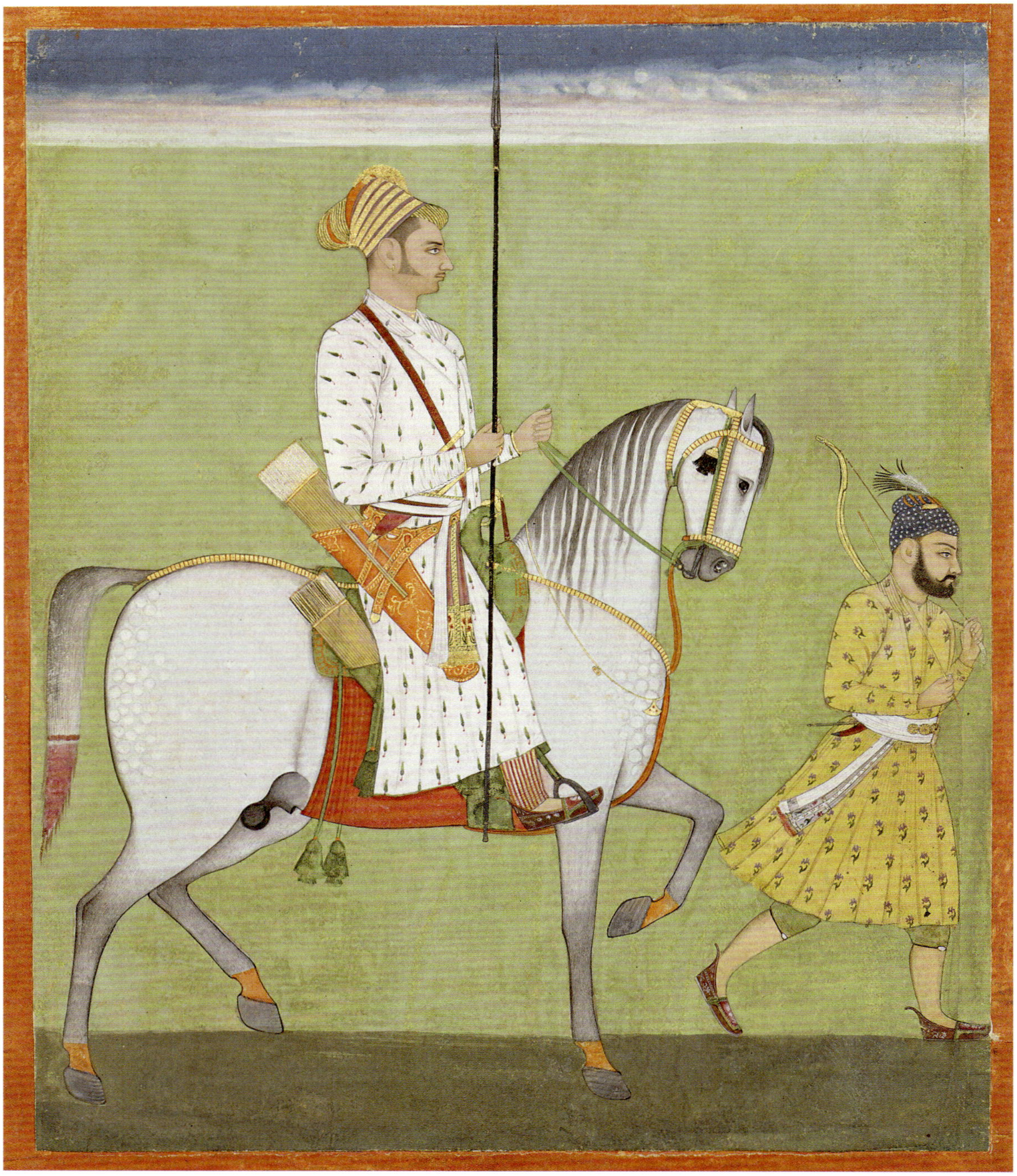

131

Maharaja Jhujhar Singh riding

MARWAR OR BIKANER, RAJASTHAN, CA. 1720

Opaque watercolor and gold on paper
20.3 × 20.3 cm (8 × 8 in.)
Inscribed in devanagari on reverse: *rathor jhujhar sigh sujan sighot gam phulyai*;
Mewar royal inventory no. 16/233
Metropolitan Museum of Art, New York, Cynthia Hazen Polsky and Leon B. Polsky Fund (2002.349)

WITH ITS PLAIN GREEN GROUND and band of sky above, this dignified equestrian portrait of a Rajput nobleman of the Rathor clan follows a classic Mughal model. The youthful Jhujhar Singh, son of Sujan Singh, sits erect as he rides a fine dappled gray stallion. He bears a lance, dagger and two quivers of arrows. His attendant precedes him on foot, carrying his bow. Both men wear court jamas with sprigged patterns.

The identifying inscription on the reverse is in a contemporary Udaipur clerk's hand, suggesting that the painting had very soon entered the royal Mewar collection, perhaps as a gift from another ruler. It names the youthful Rathor, his father, and the as yet unidentified village of Phulya(?), which he held as chief. (His father's name, Sujan Singh, is also that of the contemporary Bikaner Maharaja, but if Jhujhar Singh had been of royal descent this would have been made explicit in the inscription).[1]

AT

1 A Jhujhar Singh was appointed by Maharaja Zorawar Singh (son of Sujan Singh) of Bikaner early in his reign (1736–45) to the *jagir* (fief) of Churu: Singh, 1974, p. 102.

132

Raja Udai Singh smoking on a terrace

MARWAR REGION, RAJASTHAN, CA. 1710

Opaque watercolor on paper
22.2 × 30 cm (8 ¾ × 12 in.)
Inscription (slightly obscured) in devanagari on reverse: *raj sri ude saghji ?lal*[..]*irot campavat* ("Raja Shri Udai Singh son of Lalbir?[1] Champavat")

A RATHOR NOBLEMAN, OF PORTLY PHYSIQUE and flamboyant mustache and side-whiskers, smokes his hookah on a garden terrace. Seated against a flowered bolster on a quilted and embroidered coverlet, he wears a white turban and jama and a dagger tucked in his waist-sash (*patka*). An attendant holds up his sword, emblematic of his valor, while waving a chowry over his master. A younger attendant offers a flask of wine or strong liquor on a tray. As court etiquette demands, the manner and expressions of all are serious and dignified. A pool and flower-bed appear in a schematic band in the foreground. The cool white tones combined with an otherwise typically muted Marwar palette make this a pleasing study of a proud Rathor taking his ease.

Identifying early eighteenth-century Rathor nobles can be problematic, as they are seldom well documented and they often look quite similar. This Raja is identified as Udai Singh (son of Lalbir?) of the Champavat clan. It has been suggested that he is an Udai Singh said to have been a late seventeenth century-Thakur (chief) of Pali, an important commercial town in eastern Marwar, but this remains uncertain. He does resemble, even down to the long drooping mustache, the Rathor noble riding in a palanquin in a painting, possibly even by the same artist, in the Victoria and Albert Museum.[2] However, that picture's subject is identified by inscription as a Jaswant Singh (*sri jasot sighji*), and the drooping mustache may simply have been a common Rathor vogue at the time.

AT

1 Reading *lalvirot*? [son of Lalbir]; Crill, 1999, p. 115, n. 36 reads: *lalkishot* [son of Lalkishan?].

2 W. G. Archer, *Indian miniatures*, London 1960, pl. 53; Crill, *op. cit.*, fig. 44, pp. 74–75.

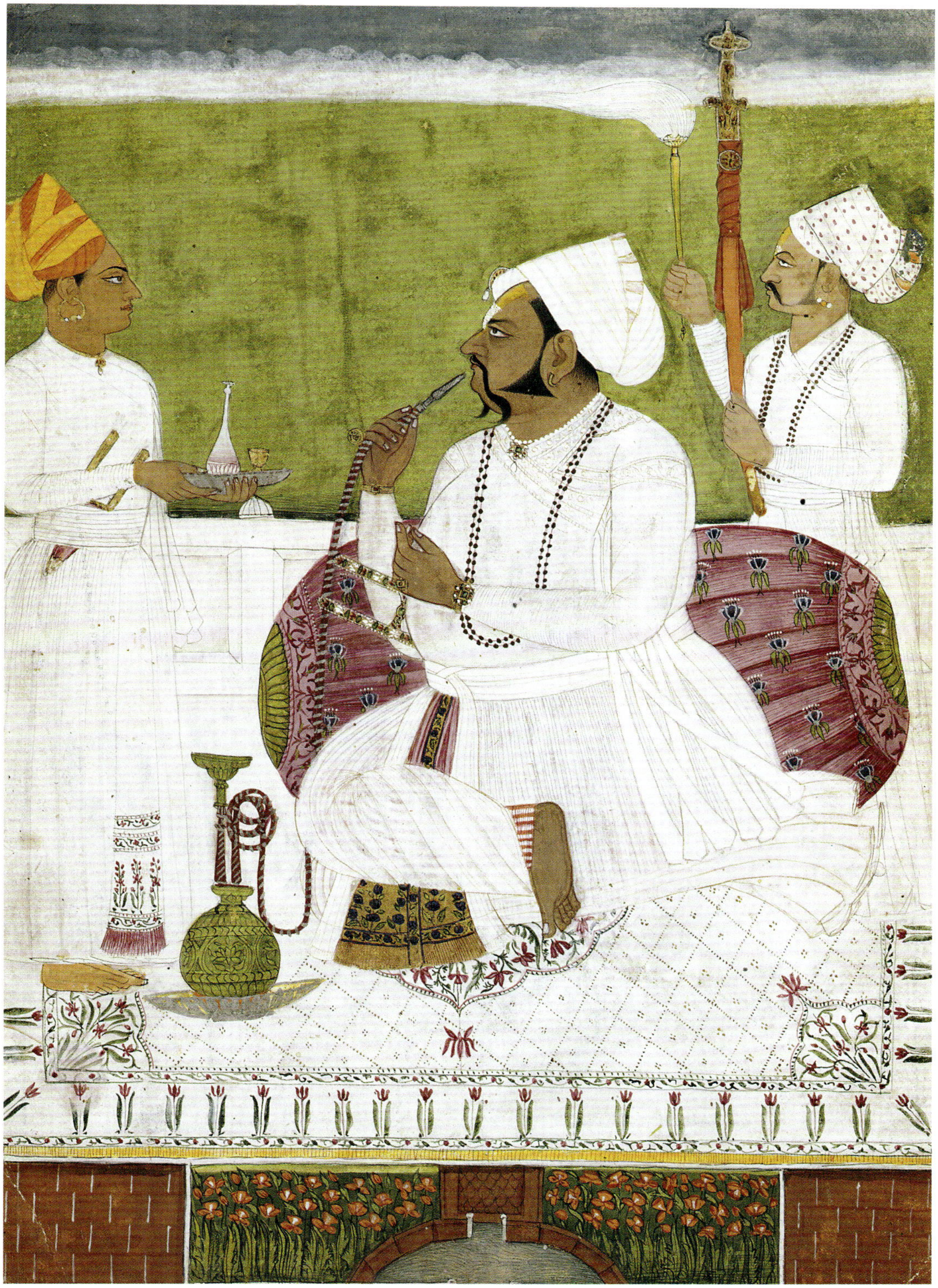

133

Prince Padam Singh of Bikaner and the bard Gordhan

KISHANGARH, RAJASTHAN, CA. 1725, ATTRIBUTED TO BHAVANI DAS OR A CLOSE FOLLOWER

Opaque watercolor, gold and silver on paper
29.5 × 35.6 cm (11 ⅜ × 14 in.)
On the reverse two parallel inscriptions (each in two columns, in devanagari and Persian) naming the Charan Gordhan son of (?) Lakshmi Das of Bikaner, "a singer of good songs" who recited verses (*kundaliya*) to Padam Singh; followed by Hindi and Persian verses in praise of Padam Singh
Published: S. Kramrisch, *Painted delight*, Philadelphia, 1986, no. 72; S. Kossak, *Indian court painting*, London, 1997, no. 55
Metropolitan Museum of Art, New York, Promised Gift of Cynthia Hazen Polsky

THE CHARANS OR TRADITIONAL BARDS enjoyed an influential role and privileged status at the Rajput courts, as official recorders of the rulers' ancestors and narrators of their heroic deeds. At public ceremonies or else more informally, they would be called on to recite for the princes' entertainment and edification. Being immune from censure, they could also on occasion produce biting lampoons about their patrons, if warranted.[1] The bard Gordhan is said to have composed many poems in praise of Prince Padam Singh (1645–83), a legendary Bikaner warrior famed for his strength and courage,[2] whose huge sword, according to the British *Gazetteer* of 1874, is "reverently preserved, and at certain seasons 'puja' [worship] is performed before it."[3] The Hindi verses inscribed here extol him as: "the eternally risen sun of intelligence, Dharma and fame; his like is unknown in the world for generosity and compassion...The greatly wise Raja Padam Singh [who] in the eyes of his heart contemplates Hari [Vishnu]; a thorn to the Kali Yuga; protector of his kinsmen; uprooter of the enemy's house."[4] The Persian verses also praise him with similar effusiveness.[5]

This Kishangarh painting of half a century later recreates one of the private audiences of the Prince and the Charan. Padam Singh sits on a low throne on a lakeside terrace smoking a hand-held pipe, while Gordhan sings or declaims with one hand raised in an expressive gesture. Like the prince, he wears full court dress including dagger, sword, and shield, as well as a surcoat and shawl. Two manuscripts lie beside him and, between the men, two bees hover over a bowl of flowers or sweets. The intent expressions of reciter and listener are delicately caught by the artist, probably either Bhavani Das, one of the foremost Kishangarh masters, or a close follower. His debt to the imperial Mughal idiom is shown in the wooded horizon with a distant fort and figures of elephants bathing. This painting recalls other psychologically charged confrontations of figures on terraces attributable to Bhavani Das, such as "Anand Singh and Joshi Shyam," formerly in the Ehrenfeld Collection.[6]

AT

1 Sharma, 1968, pp. 94–96; Kathuria, 1987, pp. 212–14.

2 Singh, 1974, pp. 94–95; for anecdotes of Padam Singh's feats in battle and his generosity to Charans ("minstrels"), see Capt. P. W. Powlett, *Gazetteer of the Bikanir State*, Calcutta, 1874, pp. 38–40; among names of seventeenth-century Bikaner Charans listed by Powlett (*ibid.*, p. iv) is Gordhan Gadan, cited as having composed verses on Padam Singh's heroic death in battle.

3 *Ibid.*, p. 38.

4 Adapted from a translation kindly provided by Imre Bangha.

5 Beginning: "Source of greatness of disposition and embodiment of virtues of the horizons; light of the seat of worship and source of bountiful knowledge; pinnacle of munificence and chancellor of the bearers of the sword; commander of courageous fighters; essence of the brave and chief of royal servants..." (adapted from a translation kindly provided by Maryam Ekhtiar).

6 Ehnbom, 1985, no. 71; also discussed by T. Falk, "The Kishangarh artist Bhavani Das," *Artibus Asiae*, LII, 1/2, 1992, Notice 1; and, with other comparable works, by N. Haidar, *The Kishangarh school of painting ca. 1680-1850*, Oxford University D.Phil thesis, 1995, fig. 77.

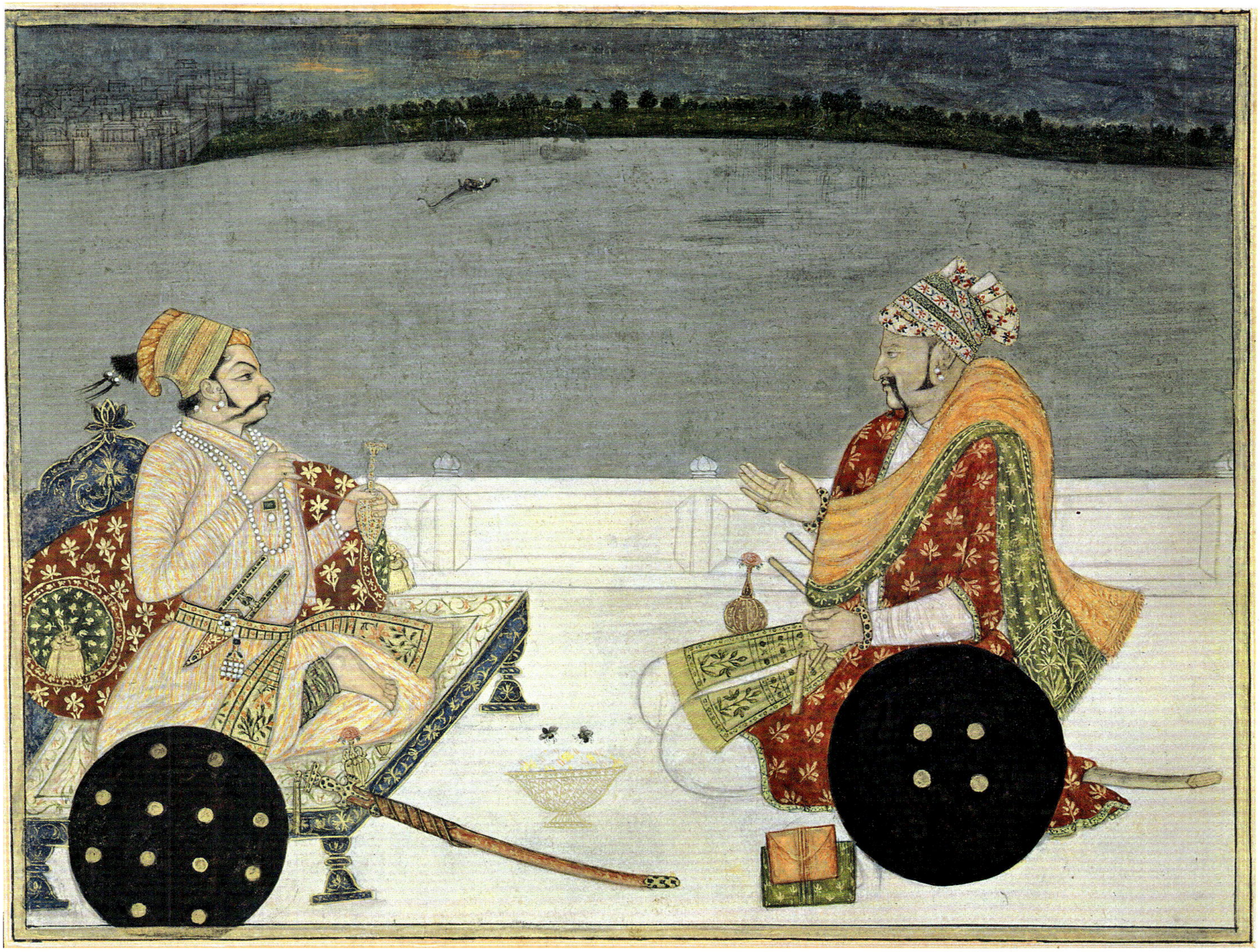

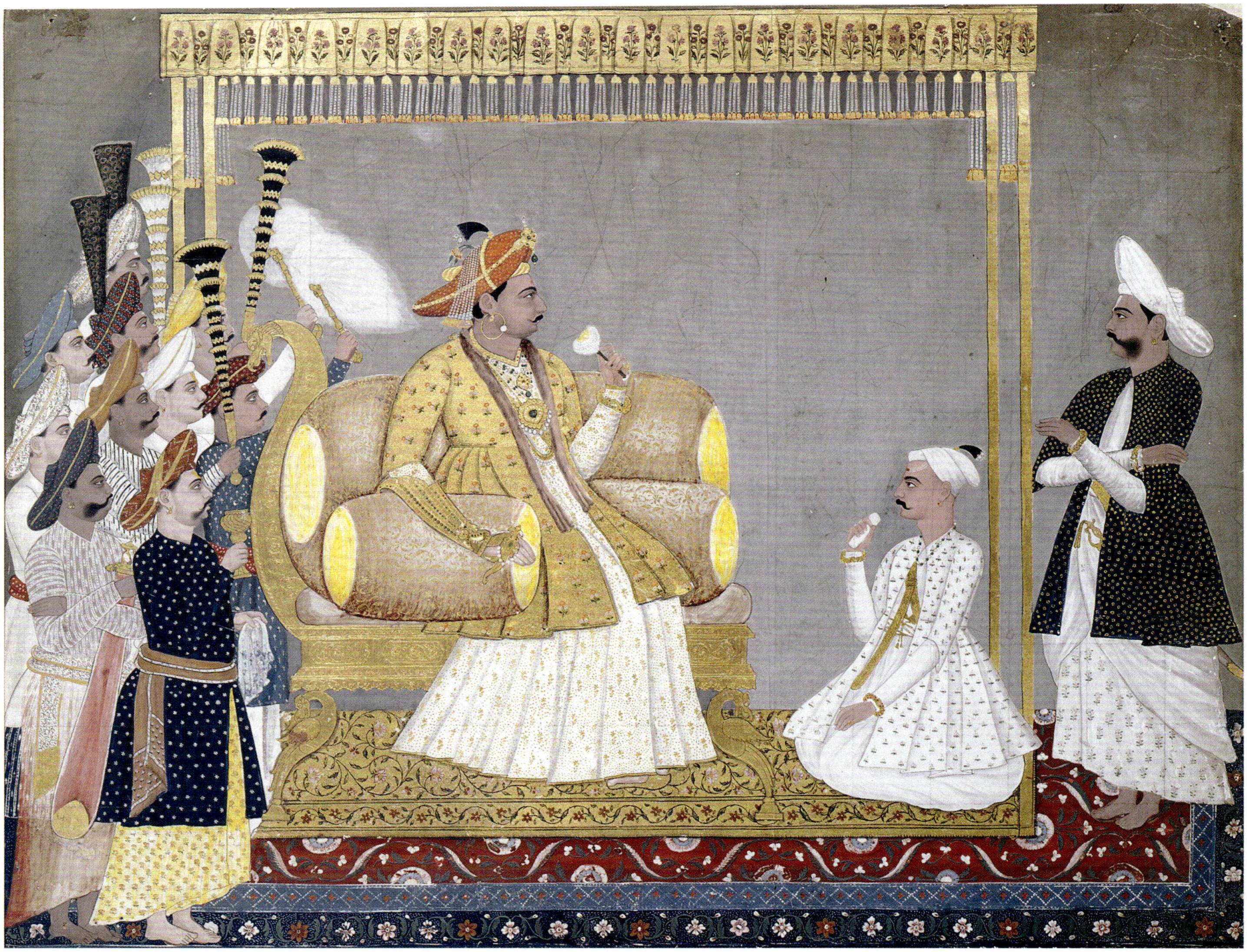

134

Durbar of Raja Amar Singh of Tanjore

TANJORE, SOUTH INDIA, 1787–98

Opaque watercolor heightened with gold on paper
43.2 × 57.2 cm (17 × 22 ½ in.)

SEATED ON A THRONE PLATFORM between monstrous cushions and under a gilded canopy supported by four poles from which hang swags of pearls, Raja Amar Singh of Tanjore (r. 1787–98) sniffs delicately at a pomander, while his chief minister or *Divan* is seated before him, with his *Peshwa* or deputy standing behind. Behind the Raja stand court officials with their fans (*morchals*), while the nearer two hold a great sword and a gilded cup.

The Maratha dynasty of Tanjore was established in 1674 by Venkaji, the brother of the Maratha leader Shivaji, who drove out the last of the Nayak dynasty from that place. The Raja and his noblemen therefore are always depicted wearing the wide Maratha turban from the northern Deccan. The British East India Company based in Madras interfered constantly in Tanjore's affairs. In 1787 they refused to recognise the adoption by Raja Tulsaji (1765–86) of the young Sarabhoji, and accordingly placed the late Raja's brother Amar Singh on the throne. In 1798 the British reversed their policy, pensioned off Amar Singh, and recognized Sarabhoji as Raja.

The court painting style of Tanjore in the far south is indebted to the northern Deccan and to the style of Bijapur as filtered through its Maratha sub-style. No court paintings are dated and many seem to have been copied at a later date, but a procession scene in the Victoria and Albert Museum, London, with Amar Singh's brother Tulsaji seems to have been executed just before our painting.[1] The delicate modeling of the faces in the painting and the purity of the colors mark it as one least influenced by European styles. Another processional scene in the same museum shows Amar Singh with this same chief minister as in this painting and with Sarabhoji his successor, but seems on grounds of style to have been done in the latter's reign.[2]

JPL

1 Archer, 1992, no. 16.
2 *Ibid.*, no. 18.

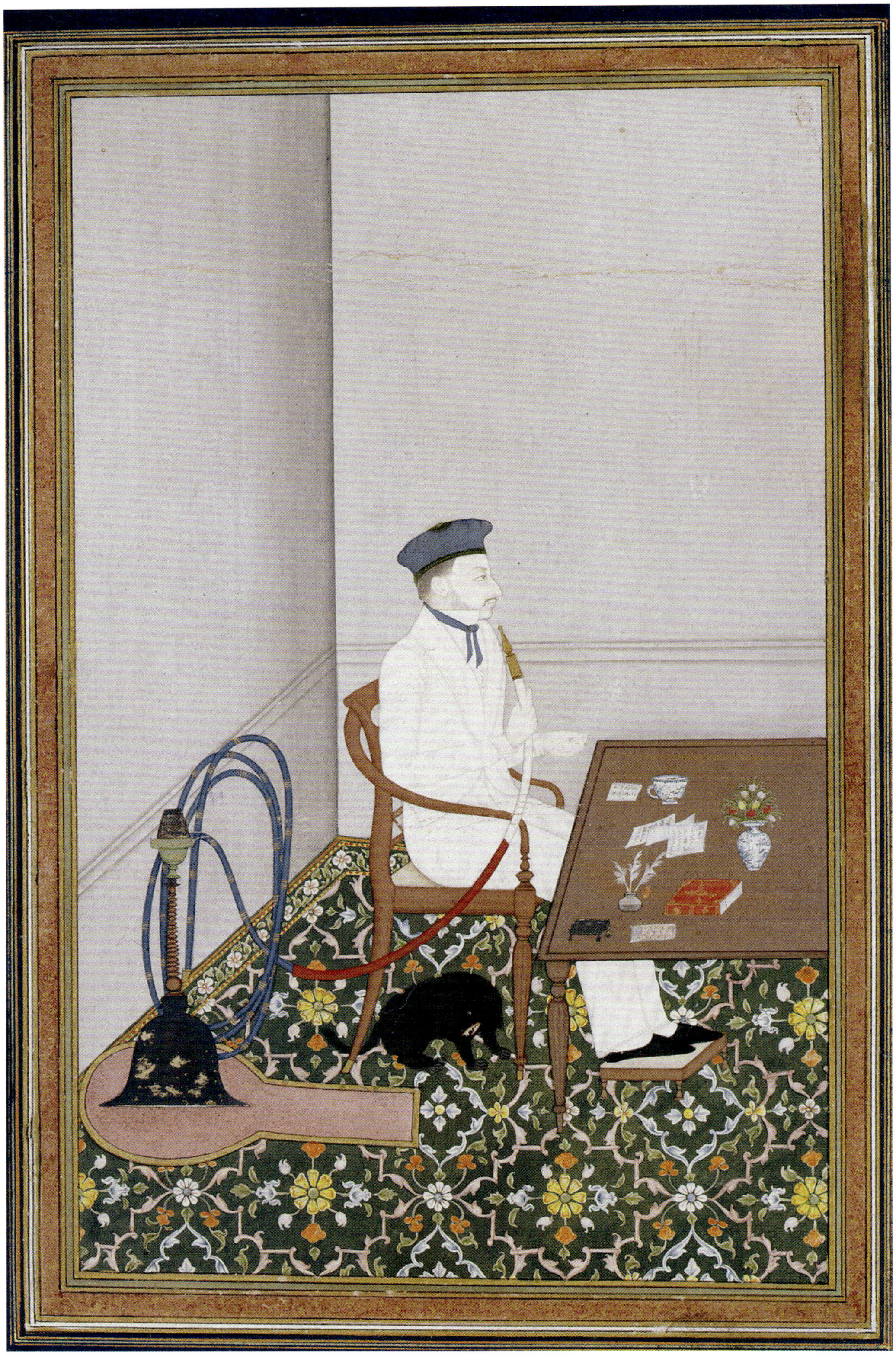

135

An Briton seated at a table

DELHI, 1830–40

Opaque watercolor and gold on paper
Image 19.7 × 11.7 cm (7 ¼ × 4 ⅝ in.);
page 22.5 × 16.5 cm (8 ⅞ × 6 ½ in.)
Published: T. McInerney, *Indian paintings from the Polsky Collections*, Princeton, 1982, no. 26

AN IMAGE OF CONTROLLED SELF-DISCIPLINE far above the swirling cartouches of his carpet and the arabesques of his hookah snake, our servant of the East India Company sits calmly smoking at his desk, on which sit his cup of tea, his morning letters, and his pens, while his dog lies beneath his Regency style chair. The traditional high viewpoint of the Mughal artist has been beautifully exploited to enable the viewer to see everything on the table and to create a three-dimensional room setting around the subject. Only the carpet is drawn traditionally in plan rather than perspective, but artfully so as to appear on the slant. Dressed in white, and with a Scottish bonnet on his head, he seems the epitome of coolness within the recesses of his house with its high white walls. Although the painting could have been created any time between 1820 and 1850, the subject's whiskers suggest a date about 1830–40, before fuller sets became more fashionable.

The Company's armies had taken over Delhi in 1803, and the Mughal Emperor exchanged his Maratha master for a British one. The Company administered the city of Delhi and the territory around it, while the Emperor remained master only in his own palace. The Company's Resident headed the administration and conducted negotiations with the Emperor. We know the appearance of many of these men through their portraits by Delhi artists—Ochterlony, Seton, Metcalfe, Fraser—but our portrait subject here is unknown. Mughal artists in nineteenth-century Delhi adapted easily to their new patrons' requirements for greater naturalism, which they sometimes combined with traditional portraiture conventions as here, an intriguing cultural amalgam.

JPL

136

End (anchla) of a Baluchari sari

BALUCHAR, MURSHIDABAD, BENGAL, EARLY NINETEENTH CENTURY

Woven silk with purple ground
65.1 × 94.6 cm (25 5/8 × 37 1/4 in.)
Metropolitan Museum of Art, New York, Gift of Cynthia Hazen Polsky (2011.576.9)

COLORFUL AND SUMPTUOUS INDIAN SILK FABRICS were woven at Baluchar, near Murshidabad, the eighteenth-century capital of the important Mughal province of Bengal. Artist-weavers lavished their perfect sense of ornamental design and technical skills on the decoration of the skirt of the cloth (*anchla*).

As in this work, decoration of the anchla usually comprised an enclosed rectangle with stylized leaves (*kalkas*) at the center and compartments with figures in niches arranged in rows around the outside border. In this sari, the figure is a seated European, dressed in an exotic, make-believe fashion, who is smoking a hookah beneath the emblem of an inverted bird.

TM

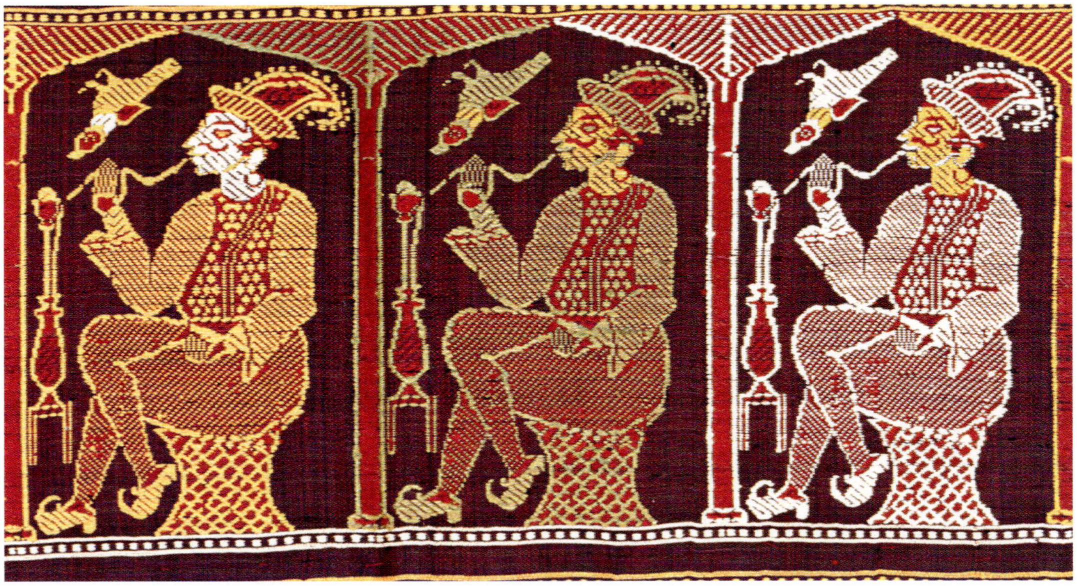

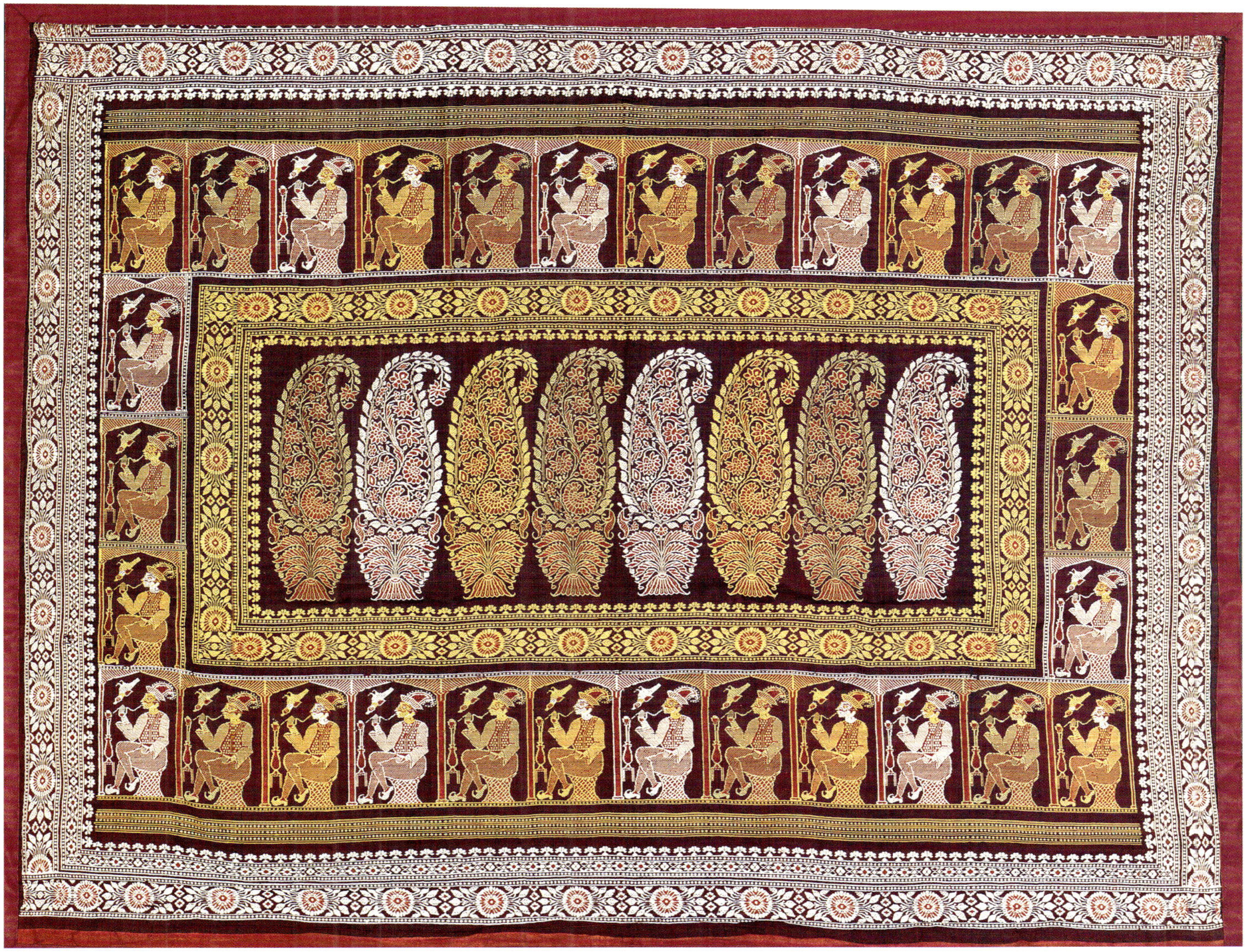

137

Maharaja Sital Dev of Mankot at prayer

BASOHLI, PUNJAB HILLS, CA. 1690

Opaque watercolor with silver on paper
18.4 × 15.9 cm (7 ¼ × 6 ¼ in.)
Inscribed above in takri script: *sri raj sital mankotia*; similar Persian inscription on reverse in a late hand (with various takri numerals and inscriptions)
Published: Sir Leigh Ashton ed., *The art of India and Pakistan*, London, 1950, no. 515, pl. 106; W. G. Archer, *Indian paintings from the Punjab Hills*, London, 1973, s.v. Mankot, no. 1
Metropolitan Museum of Art, New York, Purchase, Cynthia Hazen Polsky Gift (2000.24)

PAINTED SOME THIRTY YEARS AFTER HIS DEATH, this refined and moving portrait of the blind Raja Sital Dev of Mankot (r. ca. 1630–60) shows him at his private prayers. Seated cross-legged against a cushion in a schematic palace interior, he inclines his head backward, outlined against a plain yellow ground, as he perhaps intones a mantra while counting his *mala* (rosary) beads with his right hand. His other arm rests on the large bolster, his hand holding a muslin kerchief. Intimate portraits of Rajas at their private devotions are not uncommon in Rajput painting, but this image is an unusual and poignant one, in view of Sital Dev's reported blindness during most of his mature life. Though he is insensible to the rich ambient world of color, form, and pattern represented here, he seems nevertheless to move in an inward realm of spiritual vision. This backward inclination of his head was evidently habitual, as it also appears in a standing portrait in which he is led by two courtiers holding his arms.[1]

AT

1 Archer, 1973, s.v. Mankot, no. 3.

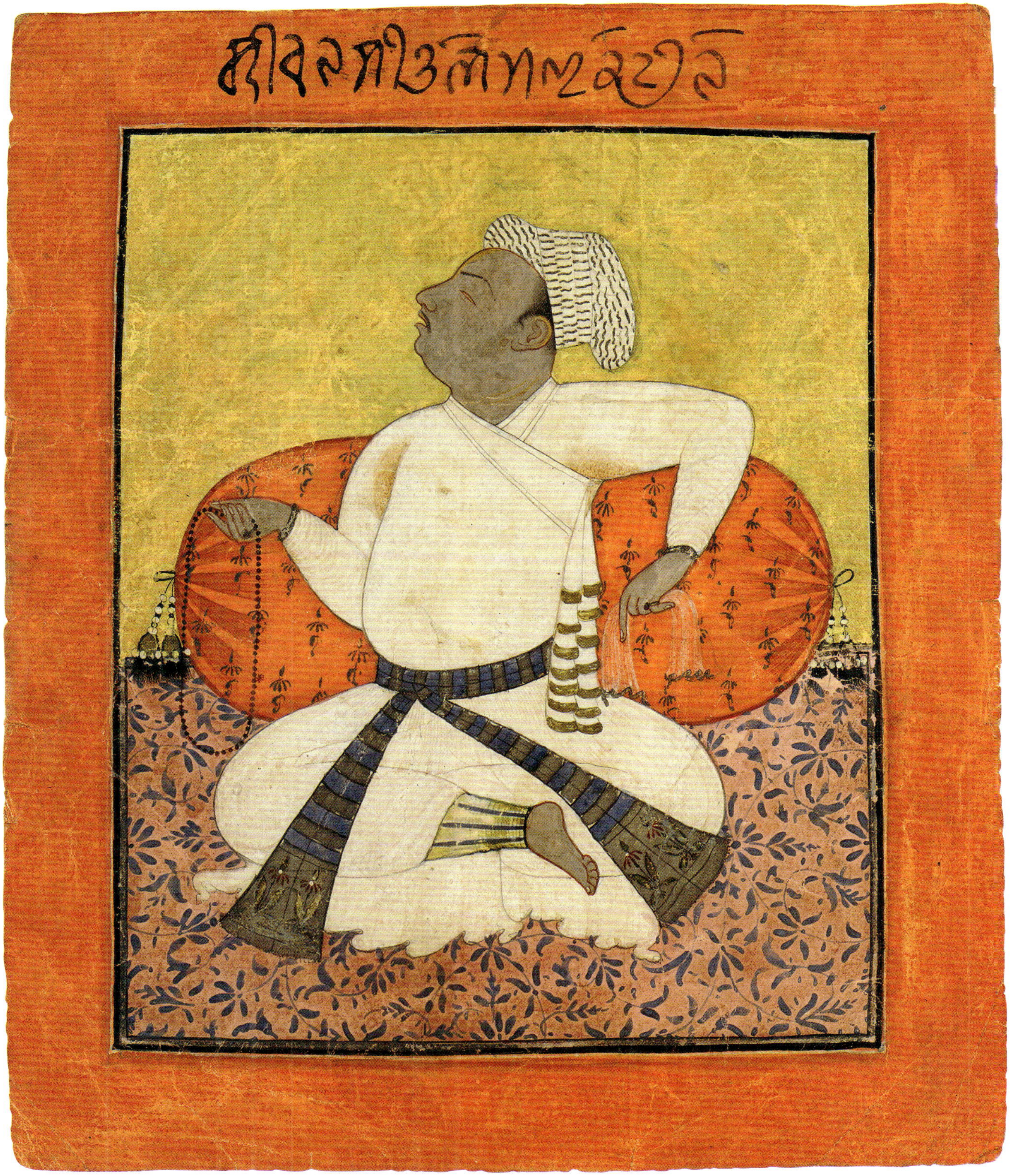

COUPLES & WOMEN

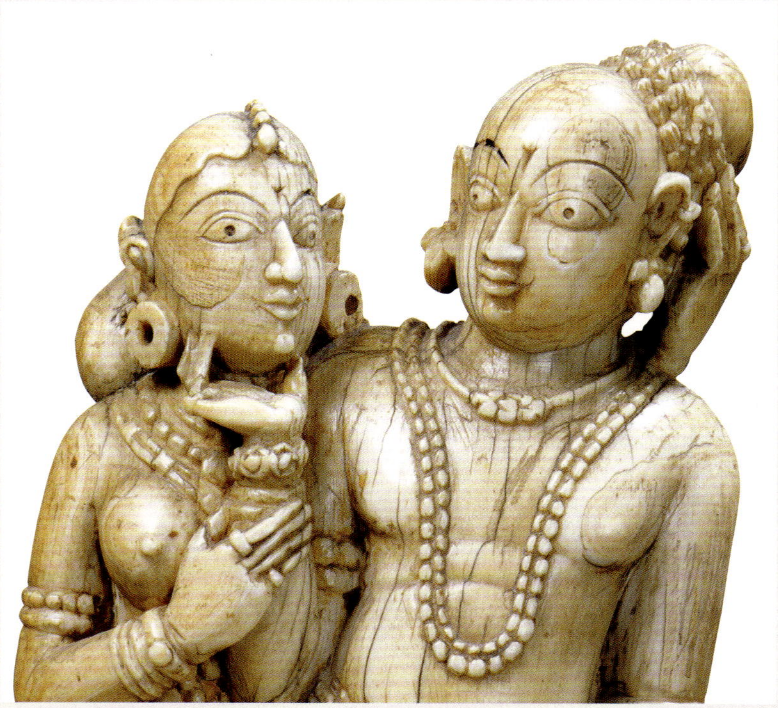

Auspicious images of beautiful, alluring women—*yakshis* or nature spirits, and *shalabhanjika* nymphs, whose very touch coaxes trees into blossom—are often found in early Indian sculpture as bearers of fertility and good fortune. Similarly, in later periods, stone temple reliefs or carvings on furniture and decorative objects frequently include graceful celestial nymphs (*apsarases*), dancers, and musicians, or idealized figures of ladies engaged in their toilet or other pastimes. Loving (*mithuna*) couples also are a common subject in sculpture, whether standing together in joyful serenity, or engaged in love-making, sometimes in a variety of postures, embodying in their sensuous bliss the creative energy of nature and the transcendence of self through union with another. In the ideal world of art at least, the sexes generally stand in a relationship of equality and tender respect.

In life, the position of women was of course far more complex. While enjoying certain property and other rights in ancient times, they were considered inferior to men in religious terms and were thus debarred from access to the scriptures and Brahminical learning. A woman traditionally lived her life in dependence on the will of men: first of her father, then her husband and, thereafter, her sons. However deplorable the husband, a good wife must always defer to him as her lord. She must keep house and wait on him, massage his feet when he is weary, and only eat and sleep after him. The ever-loyal Sita, who calmly underwent the hardships of exile with Rama and her subsequent captivity, remains a major cultural model of Indian female virtue. Taken to an extreme, the self-effacement enjoined on wives made tolerable or even encouraged the tradition of *sati* or self-immolation of a widow on her husband's funeral pyre, a practice eventually proscribed under British rule. Needless to say, however, Indian history has also had its share of redoubtable, powerful women, such as Nur Jahan, the empress of Jahangir who dominated court life from behind the scenes; the warrior Rani of Jhansi, a famous adversary of the British; or, in recent memory, the late Indira Gandhi.

The seclusion of noblewomen in harems began at a relatively early period in India, though the evidence of art and literature suggests that their freedom of movement was at first not as restricted as it became in the period of Islamic rule, when the institution of purdah was observed by both Hindus and Muslims, particularly in the north. The palace complexes of the Rajput nobility, as of the Mughals, were divided into the *mardana*, the male or public areas, and the *zenana* (female quarters), which lay behind high, windowless walls, with guarded doorways. The enforced separation of the sexes which resulted served to encourage—and to make all the more piquant—the romantic and erotic themes of contemporary court literature and painting, dwelling on the meetings and separations of youthful lovers, for which, as we have seen, the amorous adventures of Krishna and Radha in the eternal world of Vrindaban provided a versatile literary paradigm.

AT

138

Stone roundel with a female riding a horse

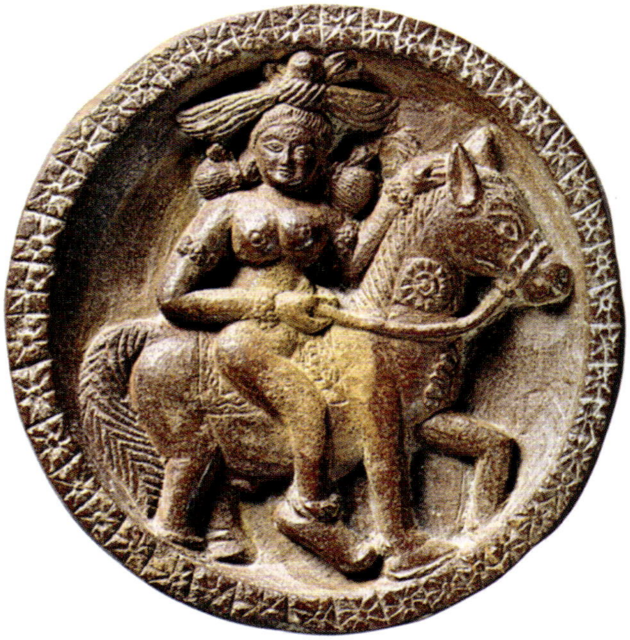

CHANDRAKETUGARH AREA, BENGAL, SECOND OR FIRST CENTURY BC

Diam. 6.2 cm (2 ½ in.)
Private collection

THIS STONE ROUNDEL depicts a naked female figure on horseback, with one hand holding the reins and the other reaching forward to touch the top of the horse's head. Her hair is gathered in large plaits to either side and in a large bow as a top-knot, while the horse has a rosette on the side of its neck and a saddle-cloth. The border has a design of stylized florets. The iconography of a naked female rider is unusual and may have been transmitted (with substantial changes) from the classical world, where naked figures of nereids riding hippocamps, or fantastic sea creatures, are depicted as decorative figures.[1] The nereid image appears elsewhere in the Hellenistic and post-Hellenistic periods: for instance, on Gandharan schist palettes in various forms.[2] Variations on this theme include a naked figure of a yakshi riding a lion which is found on a Kushan period capital in the Alsdorf collection.[3] Naked female dancing figures on Sasanian silver objects may be interpreted as representations of the fertility goddess Anahita,[4] while depictions of naked females probably representing goddesses on early Indian terracottas are also linked to fertility and fecundity.[5] It is possible that such a link is intended with this roundel. Horses are generally associated with male riders and hunting scenes, such as those on the later Sasanian silver dishes.[6]

The function of the roundel could have been decorative: a Gandhara period ivory roundel in the Kronos collection which shows Greek or Roman inspiration in its portrayal of a young male was possibly part of a piece of jewelry.[7] It could also have been an object for a small shrine.

MCS

1 Allchin et al. eds., 1992, no. 156, p. 156.
2 *Ibid.*; also Lerner and Kossak, 1991, nos. 20–21, p. 63; Czuma, 1985, no. 70, p. 152.
3 Pal, 1997, no. 339, p. 348.
4 Gunter and Jett, 1992, p. 200.
5 Bautze, 1995, pp. 12–13; Poster, 1986, no. 79, p. 161.
6 Harper and Meyers, 1981.
7 Lerner, 1984, no. 6, p. 28.

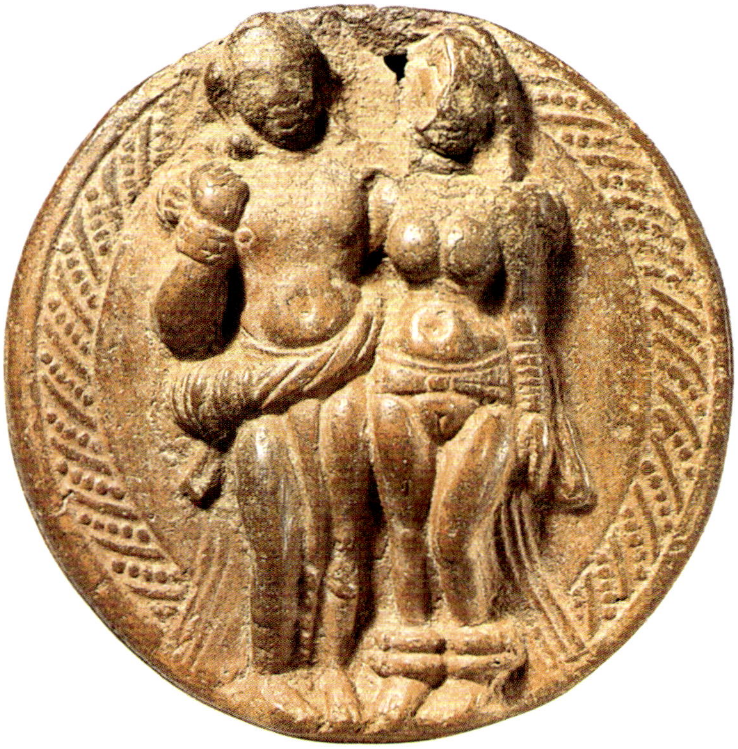

139

Terracotta rattle with a mithuna couple

MATHURA, KUSHAN PERIOD, SECOND CENTURY AD

Diam. 10 cm (3 15/16 in.)
Published: S. Czuma, *Kushan sculpture: Images from early India*, Cleveland, 1985, p. 128, no. 55
Metropolitan Museum of Art, New York, Gift of Cynthia Hazen Polsky (1986.506.11)

THE AMOROUS *MITHUNA* COUPLE is a motif found in numerous forms in Indian sculpture. An early appearance is on a pillar from Bharhut,[1] and on terracotta panels found at Chandraketugargh.[2] This molded terracotta rattle of hollow cylindrical form, containing a small pebble, depicts two standing figures of nature deities, a *yaksha* and *yakshi*. The male has his arm around the waist of the female, and she in turn has her arm across his shoulders. She stands naked except for her jewelry, with armbands, earrings, heavy anklets, a jeweled belt, and a sash that falls to her feet. The male figure stands with his right arm raised and the palm turned toward his body, wearing a sash with a large knot tied to one side, and a thin garment that clings to his legs; this large sash-knot is found in stone sculpture of the Kushan period.[3] Around the circular border is a band with alternate dots and lines. The reverse is decorated with a central open lotus flower and an incised floral pattern around the edge.

Rattles occur widely in Northern India from the second century BC to the second century AD. They occur with various motifs, including single figures of yakshas and yakshis,[4] Kubera,[5] and animals such as monkeys.[6] The rattles are molded, as are other terracottas such as plaques, toys, and figurines from the first century BC onward. They were made in two halves, and many have a small pebble inside. An example of a terracotta rattle from Kaushambi is in The Metropolitan Museum, New York,[7] and another probably from Chandraketugarh is in the Los Angeles County Museum.[8] Terracotta was a popular medium in India, lending itself to easy modeling and carving prior to firing.

MCS

1 Pal, 2003, no. 12, p. 45.

2 Bautze, 1995, pl. XXIX, p. 20.

3 Czuma, 1985, no. 17, p. 74, and no. 25, p. 84.

4 P. Pal, Introduction, in Pal ed., *Indian terracotta sculpture: The early period*, *Marg* vol. 54, 1, 2002, p. 11, fig. 4; also Bautze, *op. cit.*, p.8, pls. XXVIIIc-d.

5 A. K. Bhattacharya, "Terracotta of Bengal," in Pal ed., *Indian terracotta sculpture*, pp. 62-63, fig. 5; another example in Los Angeles is shown in Pal, 1986, no. S25, p. 145.

6 Bhattacharya, *op. cit.*, p. 64, fig. 6.

7 Poster, 1986, p. 118, no. 52; also discussed in Lerner and Kossak, 1991, no. 15, p. 58.

8 Pal, 1986, *Indian sculpture*, no. S23, p. 143.

140

Box lid depicting a loving couple

GANDHARA REGION, PAKISTAN, CA. FIFTH CENTURY AD

Gray-green steatite
W. 11.4 cm (4 ½ in.)

THIS OVAL STEATITE BOX LID is carved in low relief with a banqueting couple. The bearded, semi-naked male figure, wearing a narrow diadem and a cloth around his thighs, is seated on a couch holding a drinking vessel to his lips, while a seated female figure, wearing jewelry and a long dress, with her clothing falling from her shoulders, holds his wrist with her hand. Above her head, a bird bends its neck toward the bowl. An indentation at the top indicates the remains of a hinge.

Another box lid showing a couple drinking is in the British Museum,[1] while a group of schist box lids in The Metropolitan Museum, New York, formerly in the Eilenberg Collection, depict various animals, both real and fantastic, amidst scrolling foliage.[2] These objects are secular in nature, with a North-west Indian provenance, and are possibly versions of silver box lids in a less expensive material. The imagery of two banqueting figures seated on a couch is based on Sasanian prototypes, with few known Gandharan examples, although a steatite tray depicting a drinking scene with a seated couple was excavated at Taxila.[3] A Sasanian silver bowl in the Sackler Gallery, Washington, depicts a man and a woman seated together at a banquet holding a large wreath or diadem, symbolic of marriage, a motif which is found on other vessels and on Sasanian gems.[4] Another dish with a banqueting royal couple is in the Walters Art Gallery, Baltimore,[5] and the scene appears on a Kushano-Sasanian silver gilt dish in the British Museum.[6] The motif on this box lid is a variation on the royal banquet theme, with the nakedness of the couple and the shared wine cup having Bacchic overtones. Royal drinking scenes have been linked to the Sasanian New Year celebrations, the *Nauruz* festival, and the iconography was transmitted as far as China.[7] The female figure may represent the fertility goddess Anahita, and the bird could be a symbol of her domination over water, or she could be a Bacchant figure of seasonal significance.[8]

MCS

1 Acc. no. 1920.5–17.1.

2 Lerner and Kossak, 1991, nos. 57–61.

3 Marshall, 1951, vol. 3, pl. 144, no. 65; vol. 2, p. 495; see also note 1 above.

4 Gunter and Jett, 1992, no. 18, pp. 131–35, and no. 25, pp. 161–65.

5 Grabar, 1967, no. 13, pp. 100–01, illustrates the Walters dish.

6: Harper and Meyers, 1981, p. 109, fig. 35; the dish formed part of the Oxus Treasure (acc. no. 124093). Another silver gilt bowl with a drinking scene depicting a semi-naked seated male with a female seated in front of him was found at Buddhigharra, near Tank in Pakistan, dating from the third to fourth century (British Museum, OA 1937.3-19.1).

7 M. Carter, "Royal festal themes in Sasanian silverwork and their Central Asian parallels," *Acta Iranica*, 1, pp. 171–202, Leiden, 1974, pp. 188–90. The scene is found on a mid-sixth century Northern Qi tomb carving: *ibid.*, pl. X.

8 *Ibid.*, pp. 198–200.

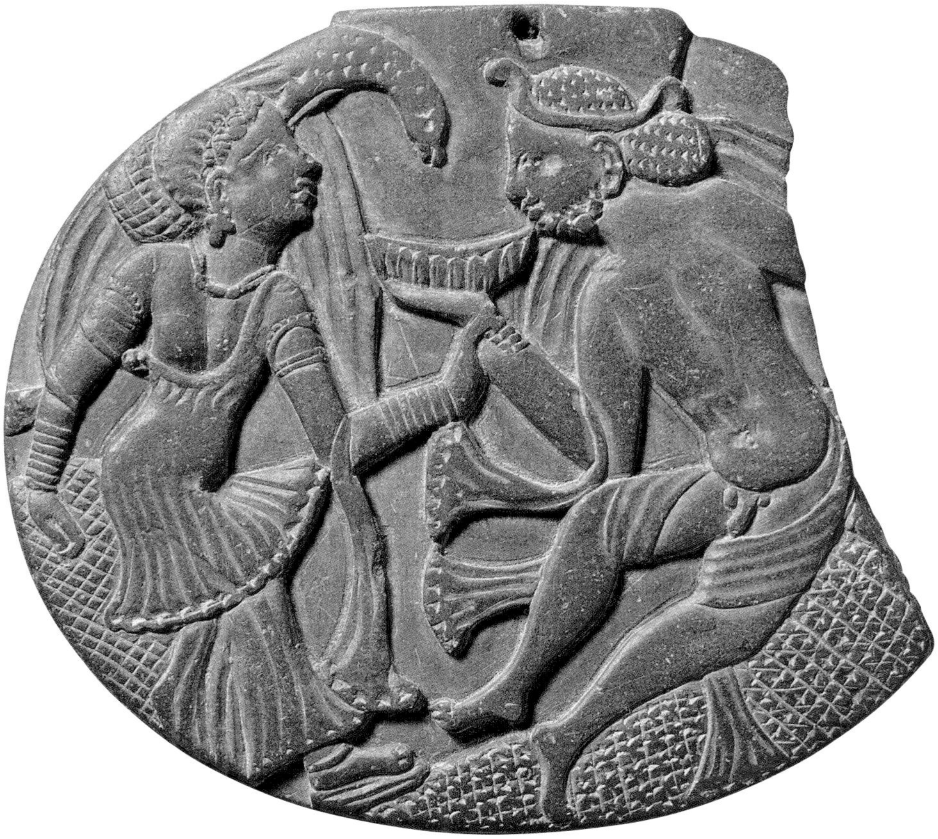

141

Three ladies in a palace interior

FROM A DISPERSED MANUSCRIPT OF THE LAUR CHANDA

Sultanate India, ca. 1520–30
Opaque watercolor and gold on paper
22.1 x 19.1 cm (8 11/16 x 7½ in.)
Metropolitan Museum of Art, New York, Purchase, Cynthia Hazen Polsky Gift (1990.82)

THE BULK OF THE SURVIVING PORTION of this manuscript in Avadhi Hindi of the *Laur Chanda* of Maulana Da'ud is in the Prince of Wales Museum, Bombay, with other dispersed pages in various collections.[1] It is the finest surviving example of the sixteenth-century Sultanate style of pre-Mughal Islamic India, in which Indian artists have incorporated elements of Iranian painting into a new synthesized style. From Iran come the cool colors, the arabesques and decorative features, and the architectural style. Not happy with the way an Iranian artist would have shown his figures existing in space within a palace complex from an overhead viewpoint, the Indian artist has instead, preferring his frontal viewpoint, conceptualized the space and moved one of the essential parts of the room, its doorway, as well as such contents as the watercoolers, into a different register.

Within a palace interior in the heat of summer, Chanda is being fanned by one of her attendants as she prepares for bed. Incense burners and water coolers testify to the heat, and to the heat of the heroine's passion as she awaits her lover. The story is a Hindu pastoral story converted by Da'ud in the late fourteenth century into a mystical poem symbolic of the soul's search for the divine: Laur, who is already married to Maina, is drawn irresistibly to the beautiful Chanda. It was the first important Indian Muslim text written in an Indian language (eastern Hindi), and five versions from the fifteenth and sixteenth centuries illustrated in greatly differing styles, apparently from many different parts of India, albeit all in the Arabic script, testify to its immense popularity in this period. All adopt the Indian narrative technique of having pictures on every folio which carry the story independently of the text. The text on the verso, which is in a distinctive version of naskhi script, is arranged in five panels, three single verses in red alternate with two double verses in black. Scholarly opinion remains divided over the provenance of this version.[2]

JPL

1 Other pages from this manuscript are published in Khandalavala and Chandra, 1969, pp. 94–99, figs. 156–75; Leach, 1986, no. 7; Poster, 1994, no. 17.

2 Jaunpur, as preferred by Khandalavala and M. Chandra, is really ruled out of court by the collapse of its culture and independence at this time. Mandu is suggested in Losty, 1982, pp. 52–53, and 69, while Chandra, 1976, pp. 48–49, and Leach, *op. cit.*, pp. 19–20, prefer not to be specific.

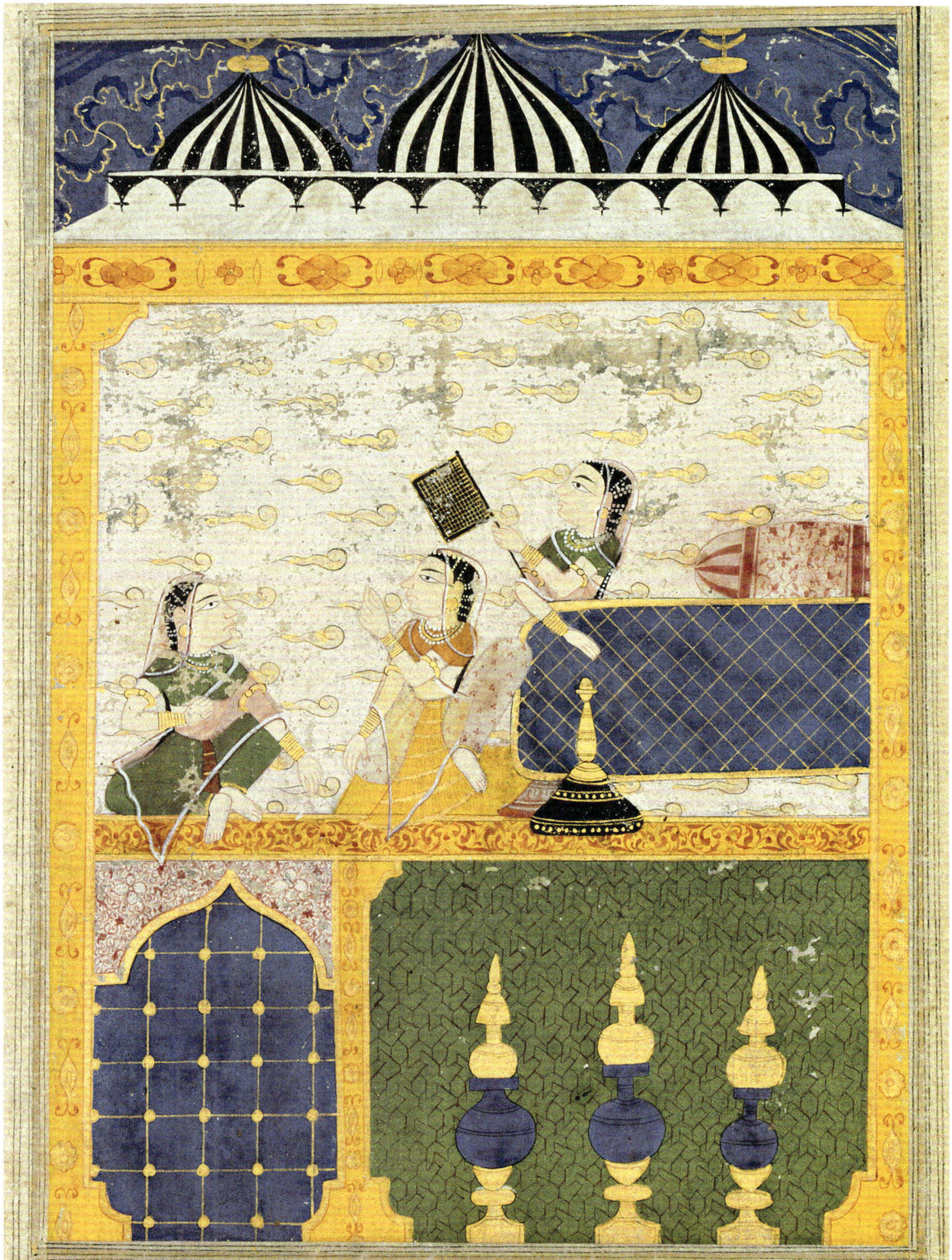

142

A lady with a parakeet

GOLCONDA, DECCAN, 1670–1700

Opaque watercolor and gold on paper
Image 23.8 × 15.9 cm (9 3⁄8 × 6¼ in.);
page 30.8 × 22.2 cm (12 1⁄5 × 8¾ in.)
Inscribed above in Persian: "Portrait of Zib al-Nisa, daughter of 'Alamgir"
Metropolitan Museum of Art, New York, Gift of Cynthia Hazen Polsky (2011.585)

RATHER THAN SEEING THIS LADY FRAMED BY A WINDOW, as occurs in cat. no. 130, we view her through an architectural niche looking out on to the terrace on which she sits. Traditional Deccani flatness has, however, vitiated this spatial innovation. She is perhaps dreaming of her lover, her parakeet as a substitute on her hand. This image of a courtesan has been idealized as the Princess Zebunnisa, daughter of Aurangzeb, and given jewels to match this status. Ladies with parakeets were con-ventionalized in late seventeenth-century Golconda painting.[1]

JPL

1 Comparable examples are illustrated in Zebrowski, 1983, no. 179, and Falk and Archer, 1981, no. 478.

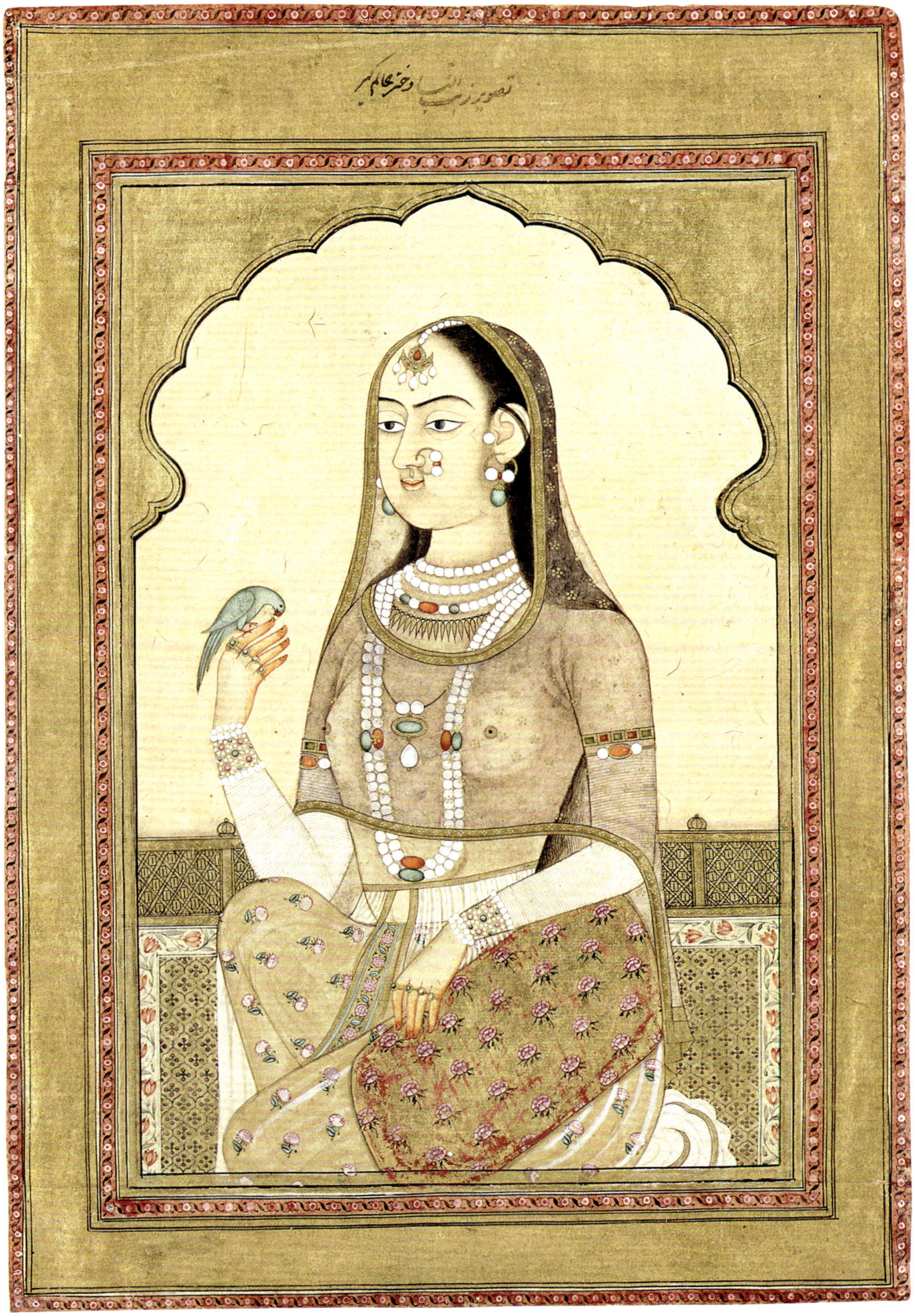

143

A lady adorning herself before a mirror

ILLUSTRATION TO THE MUSICAL MODE VILAVAL RAGINI

Sirohi, southern Rajasthan, ca. 1670–80
Opaque watercolor on paper
22.2 × 19.1 cm (8 ¾ × 7 ½ in.)
Inscribed above in devanagari: *ka*[?];
and *velaval ragani* 14
Published: T. McInerney, *Indian paintings from the Polsky Collections*, Princeton, 1982, no. 7
Metropolitan Museum of Art, New York, Gift of Cynthia Hazen Polsky (1985.398.11)

THE MODE VILAVAL IS A MORNING RAGA, performed between the hours of 9 and 12. Its essential nature is conceived in poetry and painting as a lady who adorns herself before a mirror as she awaits her lover. Here she is carefully fixing her earrings and other pearled and jeweled ornaments, while a maid holds up a small square mirror for her and another maid stands by with a morchal . From behind the three-storeyed palace, with its multiple arched niches, sharply projecting eaves and spiky roof finials, the face of the sun-god Surya shines out (as is also found in Udaipur paintings of the period).

With its hot orange borders and the complementary red and green palace interiors, combined with a confident delineation of architectural details, this is a characteristic page (numbered 14) from the finest[1] of a group of *ragamalas* from a center in southern Rajasthan in the late seventeenth century. These are generally attributed, albeit as yet without conclusive evidence, to the small court of Sirohi,[2] near Mount Abu. Wall-paintings of *ragamala* and *Rasikapriya* subjects in the mid-seventeenth century Udaipur style of Sahibdin and his followers still survive in the palace at Sirohi. Here a later, local artist has evidently adapted his architectural setting from Udaipur models, while imbuing his subject with a simplified, vibrant palette and an emotional intensity which are all his own.

AT

1 Nearly half of its (originally thirty-six) pages are extant: many are listed (as set 36) in Ebeling, 1973, p. 182, col. pl. 31; compare also e.g. Czuma, 1975, no. 79; Pal, 1978, no. 18; *Indian painting*, London: Colnaghi & Co, 1978, no. 64; Kramrisch, 1986, no. 59; Leach, 1986, no. 95; Beach, 1992, col. pl. I, p. 158; Pal et al., 1993, no. 35; Mason et al., 2001, no. 56; Pal and Seid, 2002, fig. 15.
2 J. Bautze, "Sirohi-Malerei in der Mitte des 17. Jahrhunderts," *Indo-Asiatische Zeitschrift: Mitteilungen der Gesellschaft fur Indo-Asiatische Kunst, Berlin*, 4–5, 2000–01, pp. 56–71.

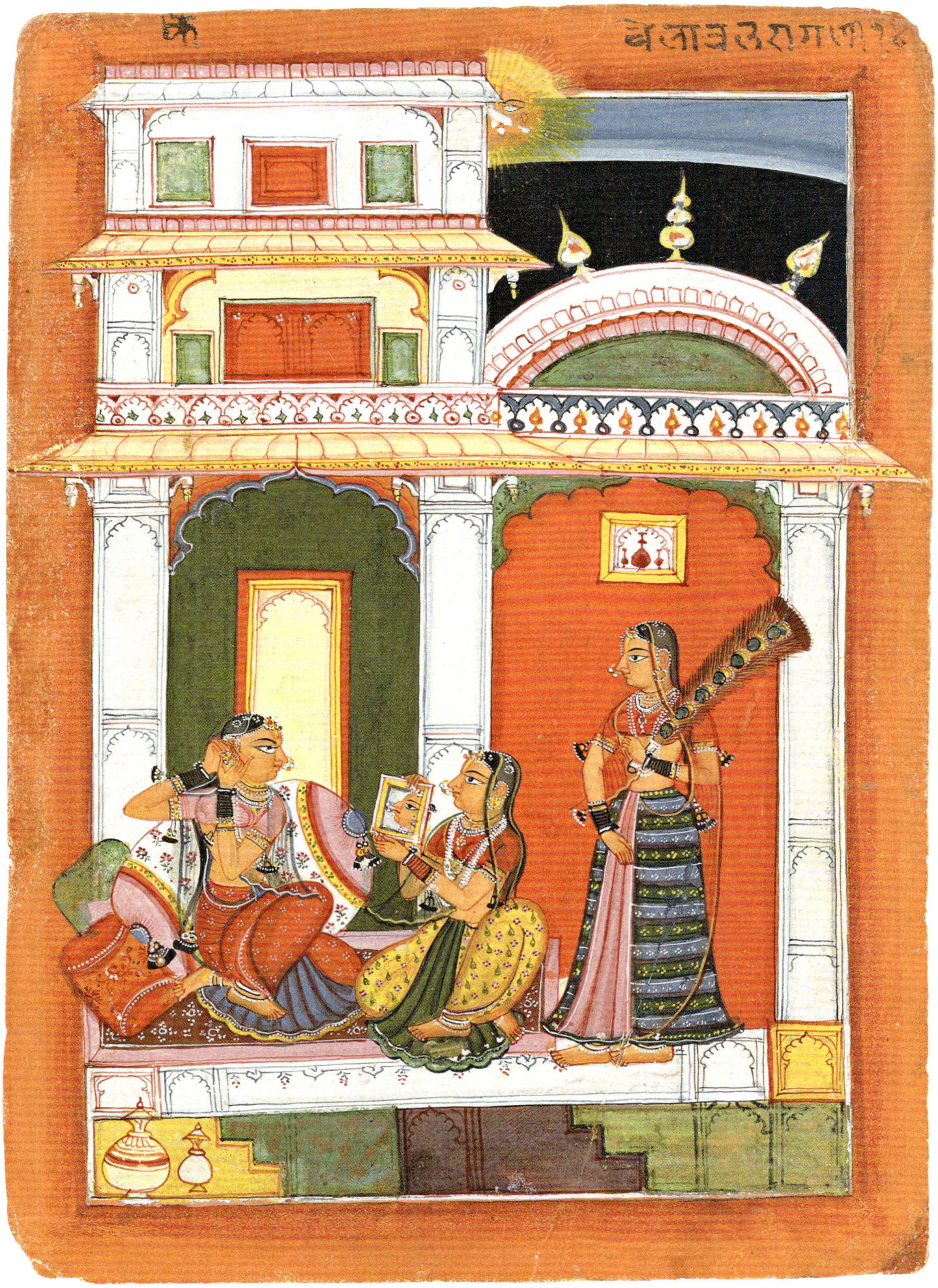

144

Two ladies on a terrace

MUGHAL, CA. 1700–05, BY RAI DALCHAND

Opaque watercolor and gold on paper
Image 22.2 × 14.9 cm (8 ¾ × 5 ⅞ in.);
page 36.2 × 23.6 cm (4 ¼ × 9 ⅜ in.)
Inscribed in Persian on the reverse: "The portrait of … and Gul Safa, the two-eyed;" "work of Rai Dalchand;" seals of an official of the time of Aurangzeb, and of Sayyid Nijabat Khan Bahadur 'Ali of the time of Muhammad Shah dated 1152 / 1739–40

TWO LADIES, APPARENTLY OF EQUAL RANK, sit opposite each other on a marble terrace. The one on the left holds a small jade wine cup in her hand while her companion on the right is holding the long straight stem of her hookah. Each is attended by three ladies who hold fly-whisks, food, wine, and so on, formally balancing the composition. An enigmatic note is struck by the lady in white, who appears to be an ascetic. Behind the terrace a river winds its way into the distance, where may be seen a city on a hill and white mountains beyond. This suggests a place of production for the painting near the northern mountains such as Lahore, an interpretation reinforced by a Punjabi inscription on the reverse. The recession of the landscape is beautifully handled. This exquisite painting is superbly mounted in an album page with margins of alternating tulips and poppies. The album page format is that of the "Small Clive Album" in the Victoria and Albert Museum, Londond, indicating that this drawing was once in the collection of Nawab Shuja' al-Daula of Avadh, who assembled the album as a gift to Robert Clive during his final period in India 1765–67.[1]

An inscription on the reverse identifies the lady on the left as Gul Safa, while the other identification has been erased. Gul Safa is known from a portrait in the British Library[2] as the sweetheart of Prince Dara Shikoh, eldest son of Shah Jahan, who was executed by his victorious younger brother Aurangzeb in 1659 for apostasy. Many of the inscriptions relating to Dara Shikoh were erased after the triumph of Aurangzeb. On the other hand, the painting is not contemporary with Dara Shikoh but rather seems to date late in the reign of Aurangzeb in the new century. Rai Dalchand is known as an artist working in Delhi in the first half of the eighteenth century.[3]

JPL

1 See Pal, 1993, no. 80, for another page with the same border.

2 Falk and Archer, 1981, no. 73.

3 A portrait of him is in the British Library (Falk and Archer, *op. cit.*, no. 287).

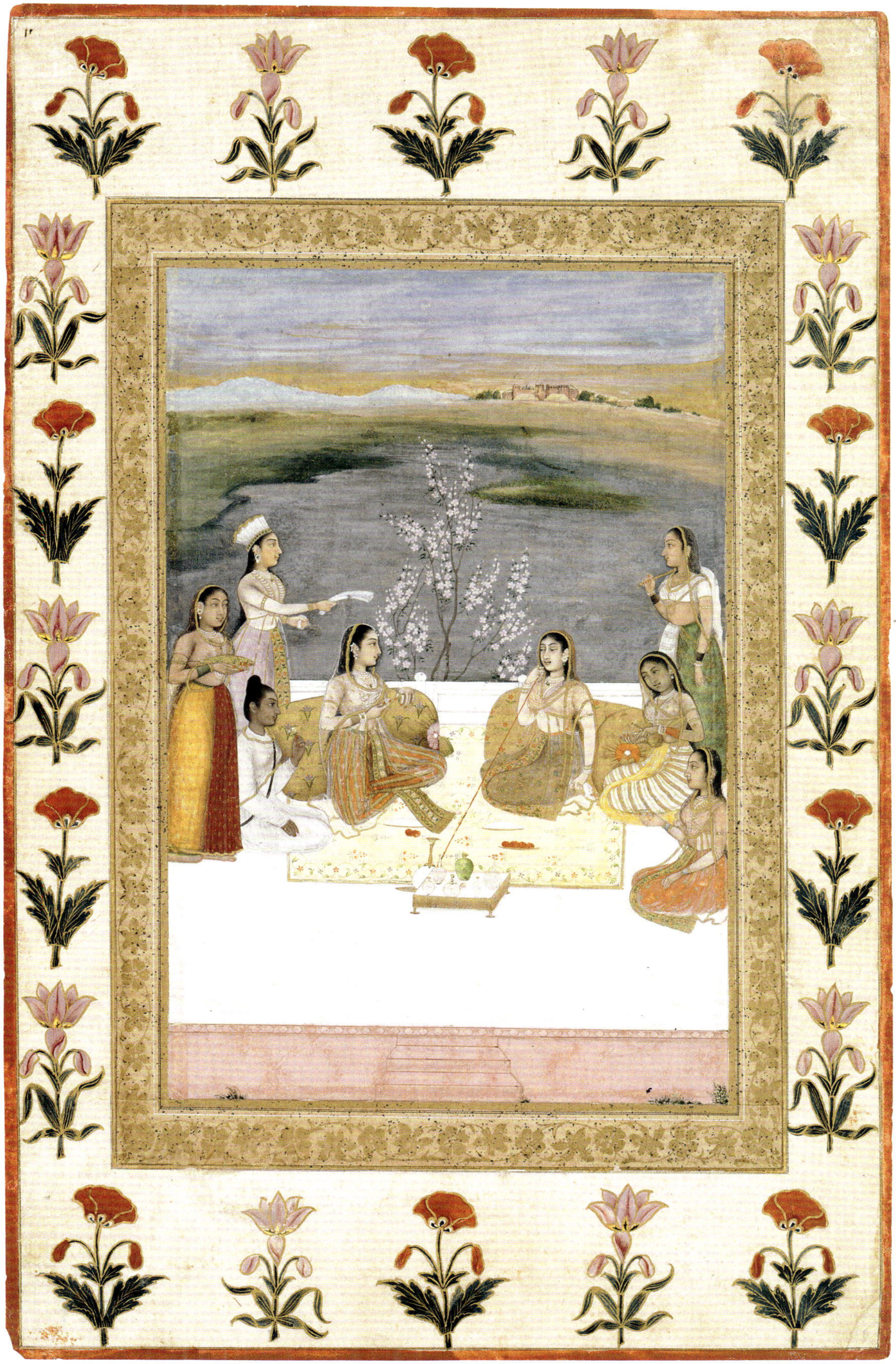

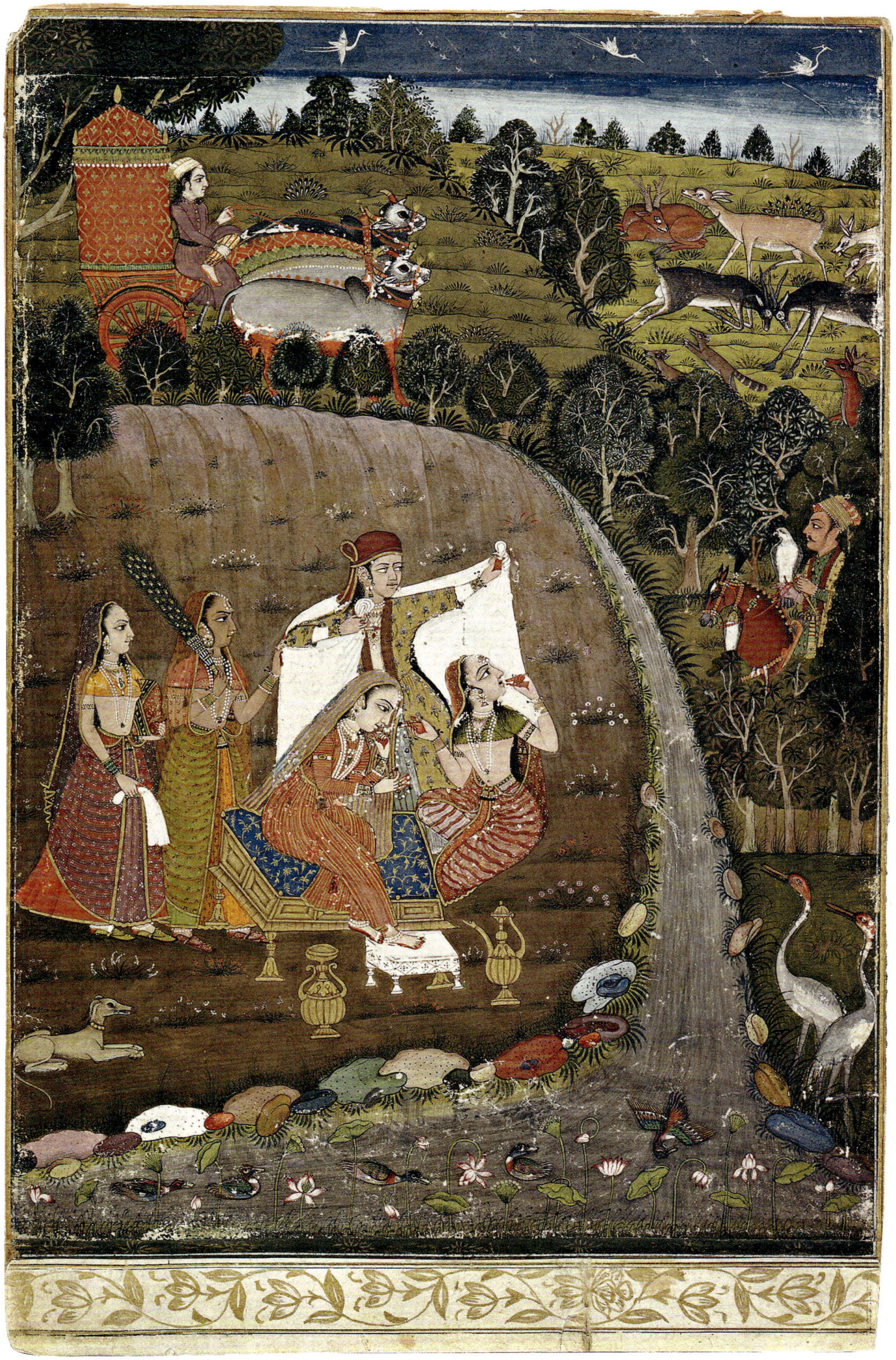

145

Khusrau spies Shirin bathing

HYDERABAD, DECCAN, CA. 1750–75

Opaque watercolor and gold on paper
Image 26.7 × 19.1 cm (10½ × 7½ in.);
page 29.2 × 19.1 cm (11½ × 7½ in.)

A PRINCESS SURROUNDED BY HER WOMEN is preparing herself for a bath in a stream, which runs between an idyllic flower-strewn meadow and a wood. Beyond the wood waits her *rath* or covered purdah-wagon drawn by oxen. Into the wood comes a prince out hawking who spies the princess, despite one of her women indignantly trying to cover her by extending a cloak out. Beyond, deer roam, two blackbuck fight, two jackals run near them, while crane fly overhead, and duck and crane occupy the foreground space.

The legendary first setting eyes on each other of Prince Khusrau Parviz and Princess Shirin of Armenia is part of one of the great romances of Persian literature, first told in the Iranian epic the *Shahnama*. Its most memorable exponent was the late twelfth century poet Nizami, in the form of one of the mathnavis in his *Khamsa* or Quintet of poems. The tale has been illustrated in innumerable manuscripts, both Iranian and Indian. Here it has been given a decorous Indian twist, for Shirin was actually bathing in a pool, not sitting clothed beside it, and the reason for the attendant's taking offence here would seem to be that her mistress is in purdah and so not to be seen by any man.

The flatness of the landscape recalls much earlier work from Golconda, as in a *Prince out hawking* in London,[1] in that the vertical rendering of the stream, similarly encased by colored rocks, is meant to indicate recession. Themes from poems which used to be illustrated by complete manuscripts were taken up by late eighteenth-century artists and made into genre scenes as here. The same subject, combined with another famous poetical theme of Laila visiting the starving Majnun, were combined in one magnificent page by a Farrukhabad artist 1770–80 with an expansive landscape encompassing palaces, estuaries, and mountains.[2]

JPL

1 Falk and Archer, 1981, no. 414.

2 Heeramaneck, 1984, pl. 245, now in Los Angeles.

146

A loving couple

MADURAI, SOUTH INDIA, NAYAK PERIOD, SEVENTEENTH CENTURY

Ivory
H. 24.1 cm (9 ½ in.)

THIS IVORY SCULPTURE DEPICTS A COUPLE standing gracefully and tenderly together. The male figure, to the front, wears earrings, a jeweled belt, and necklaces and holds a sword in his left hand. He gently holds the chin of the lady with his right hand, as she stands slightly behind him, wearing large earrings, necklaces, armbands, and a long dress which falls with a gathered pleat to the ground. This sculpture closely relates to a group of ivories of loving couples carved in South India in the Madurai area under the Nayak rulers.[1] Details of the faces, hair, and jewelry display small variations within this group, but they are clearly from the same workshop. They must have been commissioned by courtly patrons, possibly Tirumala Nayak himself (r. 1623–59). The ivories can also be compared to Nayak bronze donor figures of the seventeenth century,[2] and to bronze portraits of Tirumala Nayak and his queen portraits made to stand at the entrance to a temple on a door jamb.[3] The ivory figures are dressed as royalty, and although they may be secular sculptures, possibly even portraits, they could also represent epic figures such as Rama and Sita (though the male figure here has a sword, not Rama's bow).

Tirumala Nayak was one of the most powerful rulers in Southern India during the seventeenth century, establishing the strength of Madurai at the expense of other rulers in the region, such as the Wodeyars of Mysore. Considerable building programs were undertaken during his reign and that of his successor Chokkanatha (r. 1659–82), including the temples at Srirangam, near the second Madurai Nayak capital of Tiruchirapalli.[4]

MCS

1 Several examples are in the Srirangam Museum: Michell, 1995, fig. 154, p. 212; Bussagli and Sivaramamurti, 1971, figs. 332–33, p. 266; a later example is in the Berlin Museum: *Museum für Indische Kunst, Berlin: Katalog* 1976, Berlin, 1976, no. 169 (cover photo).

2 Michell, *op. cit.*, fig. 151, p. 208.

3 Bussagli and Sivaramamurti, *op. cit.*, fig. 331, p. 265; C. Branfoot, "Royal portrait sculpture in the South Indian temple," *South Asian Studies*, 16, 2000, pp. 11–36.

4 Michell, *op. cit.*, p. 108.

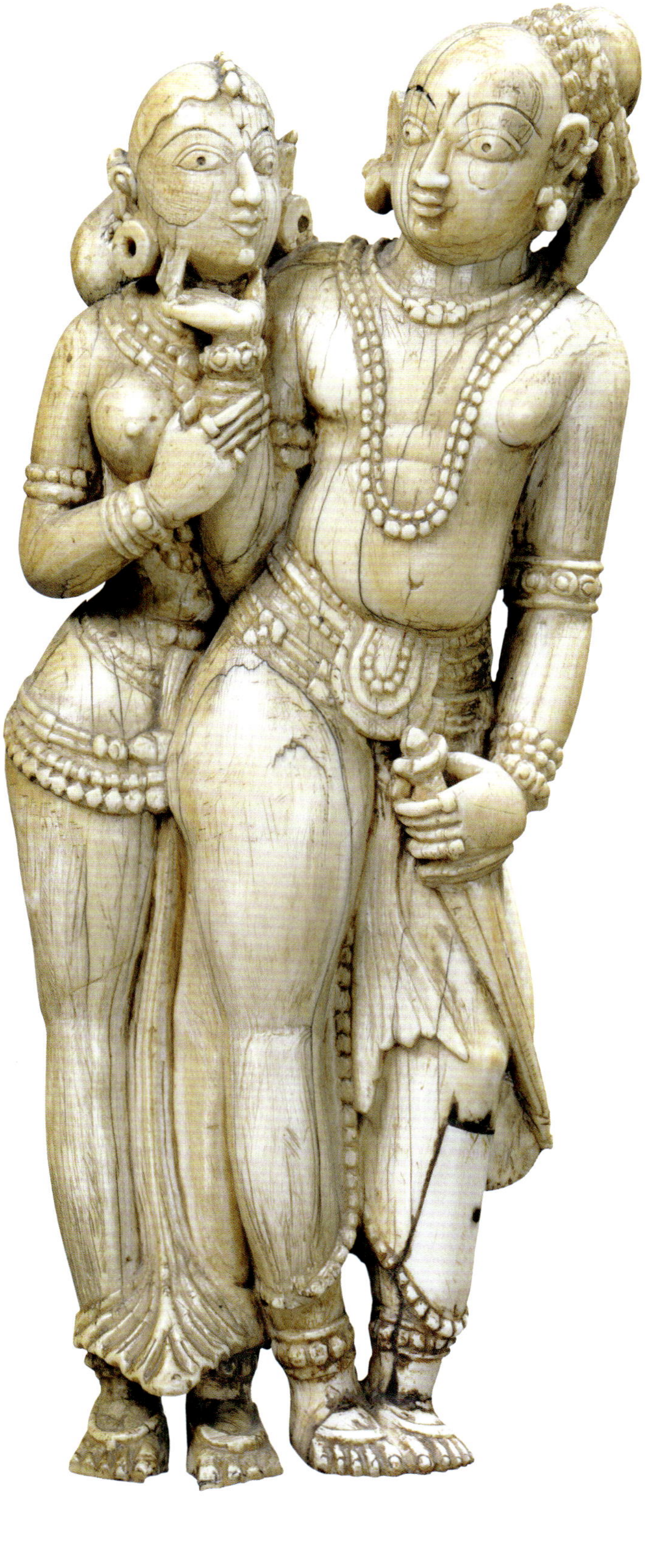

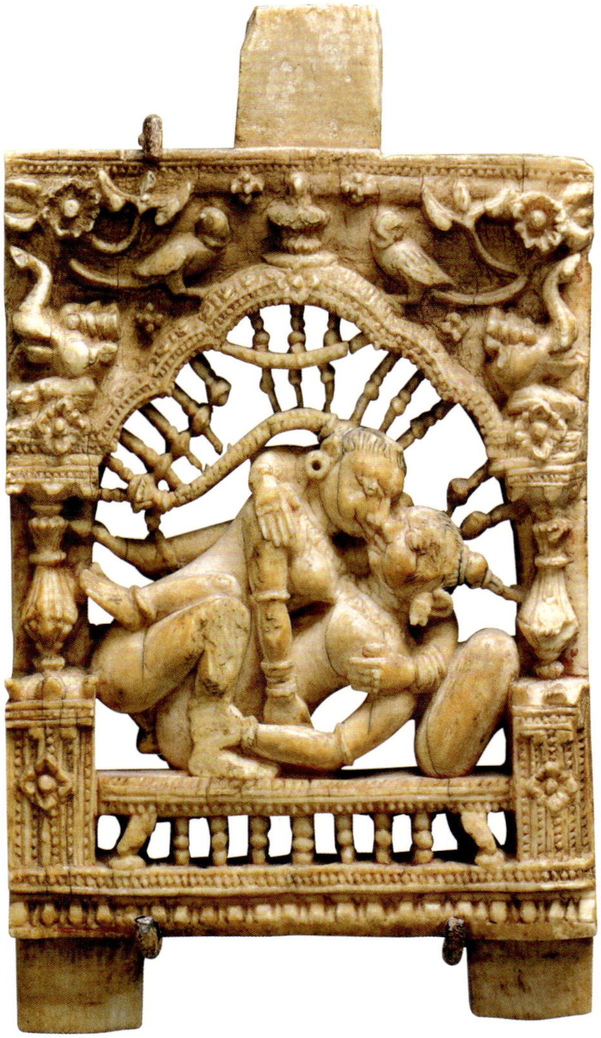

147

Ivory panel with a loving couple

ORISSA, SIXTEENTH CENTURY

H. 7.6 × W. 5.7 cm (3 × 2 ¼ in.)

THIS IVORY PANEL IS CARVED WITH A LOVING COUPLE (*MITHUNA*), entwined on a low bed with a bolster behind the woman's shoulders. The two figures are contained within an architectural frame under a cusped arch, with elephant heads, birds, and flowers in the spandrels. The panel is carved from a piece of solid tusk, with a single lug on the top edge and a double lug on the bottom for assembly into a larger panel, probably part of a bed or chair. The remains of pigment indicate that the panel was originally painted.

Erotic panels such as this example were produced both as expressions of human pleasure and as symbols of eternal unity. There is a long tradition of erotic sculpture in India, and particularly in Orissa. Orissan palm-leaf manuscripts of the *Kama Sutra* and other erotic treatises illustrate a variety of sexual postures,[1] and the magnificent temple carvings at Konarak and Bhuvaneswara in Orissa illustrate the metaphysical meaning of love-making as well as the earthly pleasures.[2] The depiction in temples of maithuna couples (so called when physically engaged in the act of love) was specified by the sacred texts, with emphasis that such scenes should be placed on the doorframes,[3] and from the twelfth to thirteenth centuries they came to dominate the decorative schemes in certain temples.[4]

A number of similar ivory panels are known, the earliest possibly dating from the fourteenth century.[5] A closely related example is in the British Museum.[6] Stone sculptures with maithuna couples from Orissa are in various museums, including the Metropolitan Museum and the Norton Simon Museum.[7]

MCS

1 E.g. Guy, 1982, no. 10, discussing a manuscript in the National Gallery of Victoria.
2 Donaldson,1987, vol. 3, p. 1167.
3 *Ibid.*, p. 1164.
4 *Ibid.*, p. 1165.
5 British Museum (OA 1972.12-13.2): M. Willis, "Early Indian ivory," *Arts of Asia*, vol. 28, 2, March–April 1998, figs. 134–35; Pal, 1981, figs. 75–76.
6 Willis, *op. cit.*, fig. 134.
7 Pal, 2003, p. 206, no. 161; Lerner and Kossak, 1994, fig. 46.

148

Maharaja Raj Singh cosseted by his ladies

SAWAR, RAJASTHAN, CA. 1715–20

Opaque watecolor on paper
34 × 43.8 cm (13 3/8 × 17 1/4 in.)
Inscribed in devanagari on reverse: *maharaj sri raj sinhaji ki chabi hai* ("It is a picture of Maharaja Raj Singh")
Metropolitan Museum of Art, New York, Cynthia Hazen Polsky and Leon B. Polsky Fund (2002.65ab)

UNDER MAHARAJA RAJ SINGH (r. 1705–30) the small court of Sawar in central Rajasthan saw a flowering of scenes of court life, painted in a distinctive manner which combines naive charm with a subtle refinement.[1] Its spare, semi-colored compositions show affinities with similar developments at Udaipur under Maharana Amar Singh[2] of Mewar (1698–1710; cat. no. 129), who was head of the Sisodia Rajput clan to which the Sawar chiefs belonged.

Raj Singh is known to have enjoyed gardens and birds, music and the company of women, interests which are united in two paintings showing him listening to female musicians in bird-filled gardens where all is formal, spacious, and serene.[2] In this picture there is a more unusual, even urgent feeling. Within a schematically outlined pavilion, Raj Singh is almost hemmed in by the attentive, adoring ladies who cluster round him. Large and impassive, he stands holding a long staff, while a lady in front of him makes an imploring gesture. Other women adjust or dust his turban and jama, and maids behind carry a morchal, *pandan* (box for *pan*). and trays of delicacies in readiness. After this thorough cosseting, Raj Singh will be ready to stride forth immaculate as he promenades in his gardens or graces some public ceremony.

AT

1 E.g. Topsfield and Beach, 1991, nos. 23–24.

2 Weber, 1982, Abb. 110; Patnaik, 1985, pl. 27 (also Welch, 1997, col. pl., p. 21).

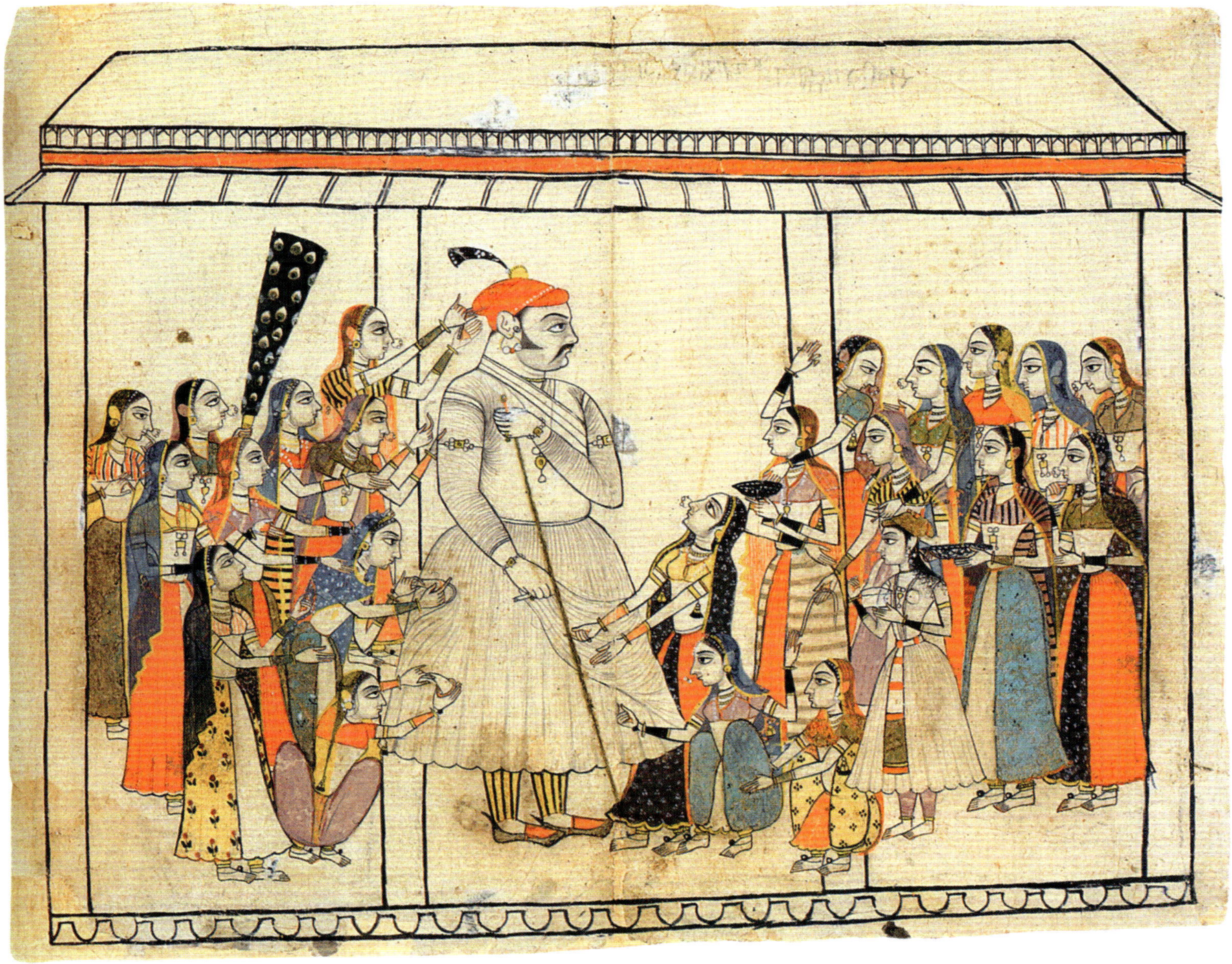

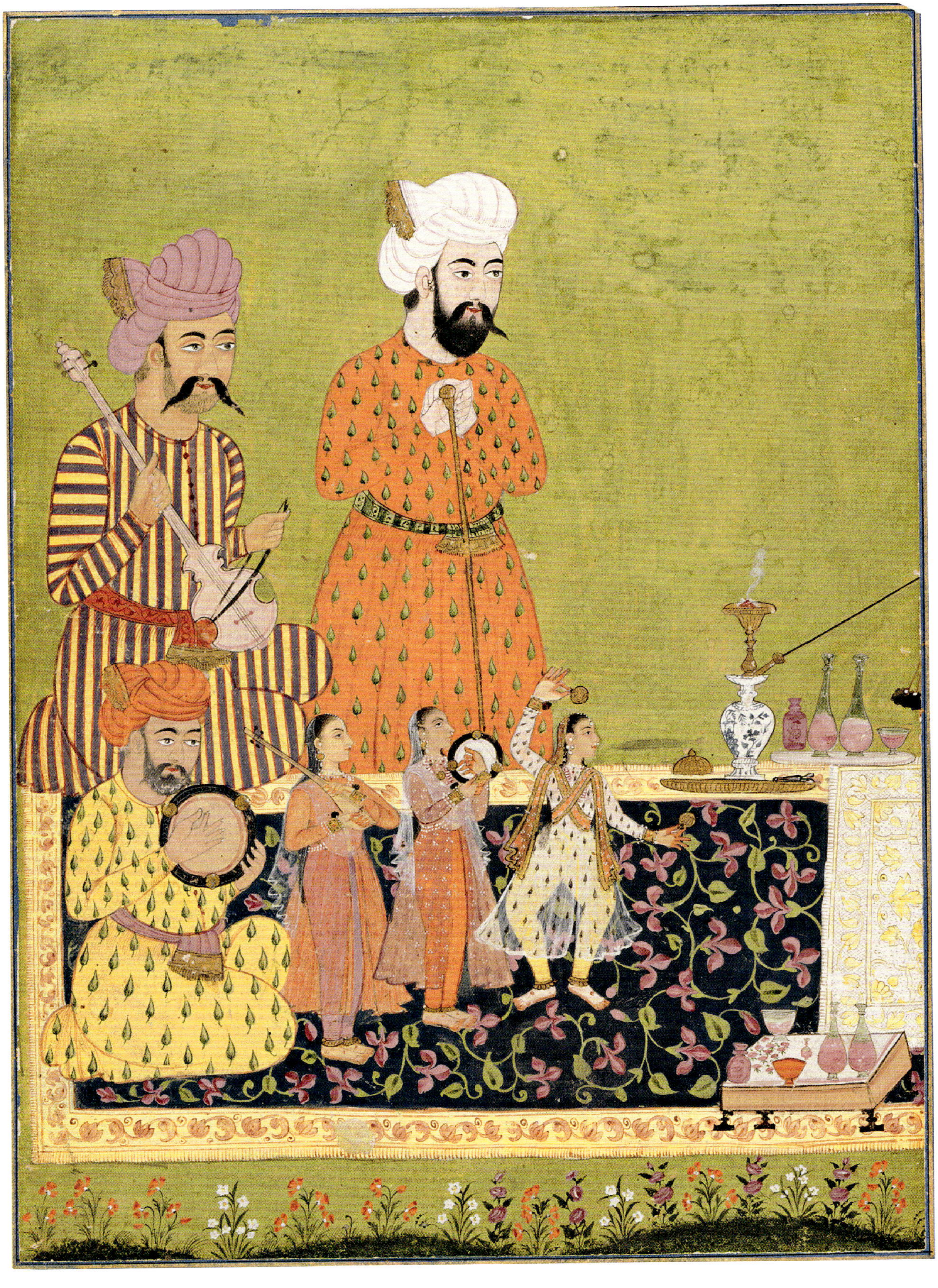

160

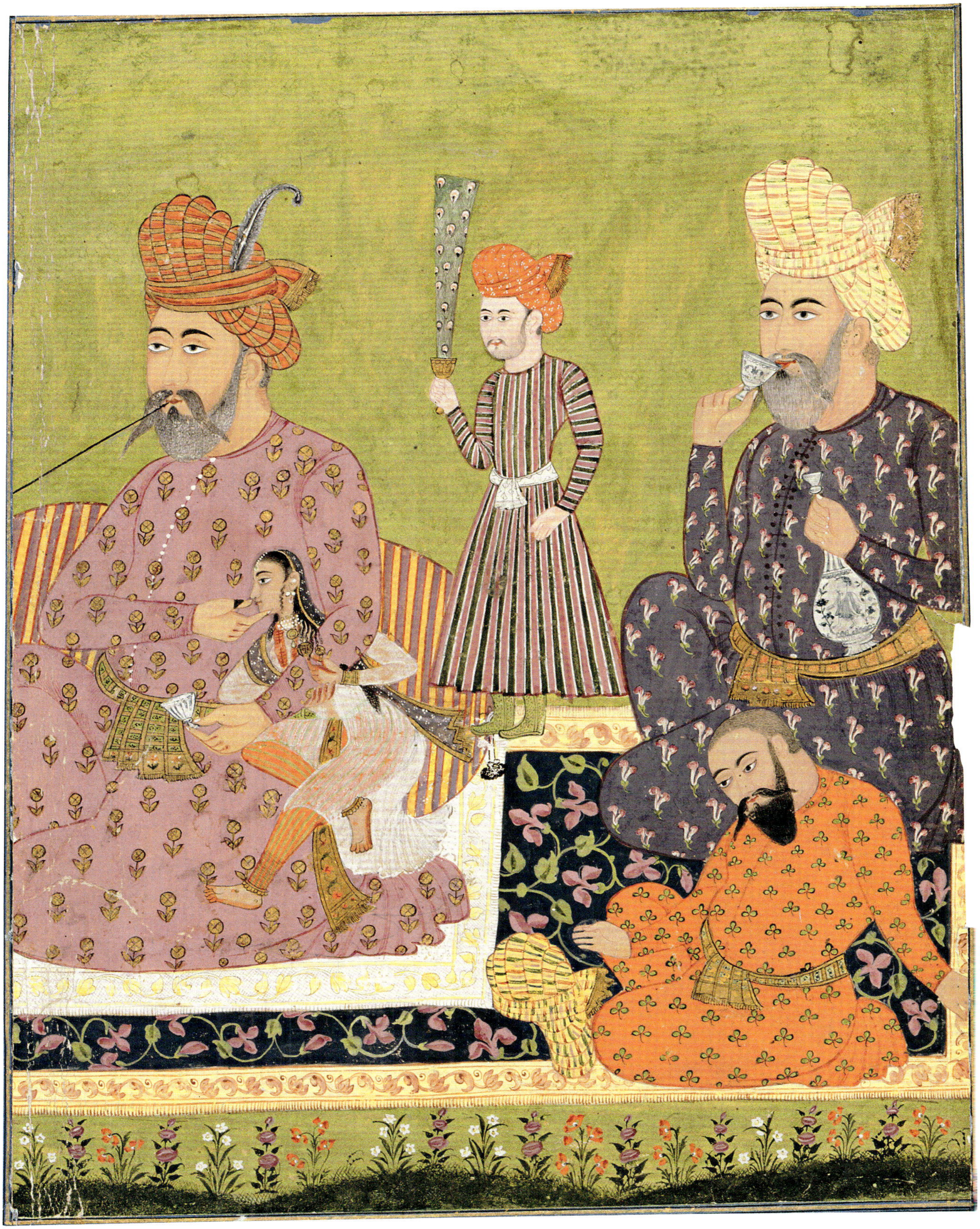

149

A nobleman and courtiers entertained by musicians

SIND, WESTERN INDIA, 1750–75

Opaque watercolor and gold on paper
Left painting 35.6 × 25.4 cm (14 × 10 in.); right painting 34.3 × 27.9 cm (13½ × 11 in.)

A SEATED NOBLEMAN IS SIMULTANEOUSLY ENJOYING HIS HOOKAH, his wine, and his girlfriend, whom, seated on his knee, he tickles under the chin with his right hand. Meanwhile, his left holds on to his wine cup, but fortunately the straight pipe of his hookah can manage without support. A page behind him waves a *morchal* (fan), while on the right one courtier has been helping himself from the flask of wine, and another, his turban fallen off, is lapsing into unconsciousness. On the left stands the doorkeeper with his long staff, while two musicians accompany the three female dancers, who all wear the costume of northern court dancers. The females are diminutive in size compared with the men, who all differ in size on account of their relative importance and their positions within the composition. The scene is apparently set on a carpeted terrace by a garden, with delicately painted flowers running along the foot. The two parts of this large painting were clearly once joined as one, and were perhaps separated to form facing pages in an album.

The lack of sophistication both of the participants and of the artist suggest a very provincial court indeed. The over-large turbans with cockades, the simple textiles of stripes and sprigs, the front-opening gowns with very short cummerbunds, the bright colors, as well as of course the naive compositions, and the discrepancy in size between the figures, all point to a provincial court in the north-west in the area of what is now Pakistan. Here in the eighteenth century the naive local styles were overlaid by influences both from Iran and from late Mughal India. The Kalhora dynasty had established themselves as de facto rulers in the southern Indus valley in the reign of Aurangzeb, but in 1739 with Nadir Shah's conquest of Delhi, all the Mughal provinces west of the Indus were afterwards tributary to him and his successors. The Kalhoras were dispossessed of the area in 1783 by the Talpur Mirs. Little is known about painting in this area until 1775, which is the date of a Persian manuscript in the British Library from Sind.[1] Its naive miniatures exhibit all of the stylistic traits of our painting, its differential sizes, its costumes, textiles, and turbans (although here the ladies wear local costumes), as well as some scenes of delicately painted gardens like the lower border here. The present painting then could be attributable to the court of the Kalhora rulers of Sind a few decades earlier than the manuscript, when the culture of the late Mughal court still had some influence on this area.

JPL

1 British Library Or. 8758: see M. I. Siddiqi, "An illustrated manuscript from Sind," in R. Pinder-Wilson ed., *Paintings from Islamic lands*, Oxford, 1969.

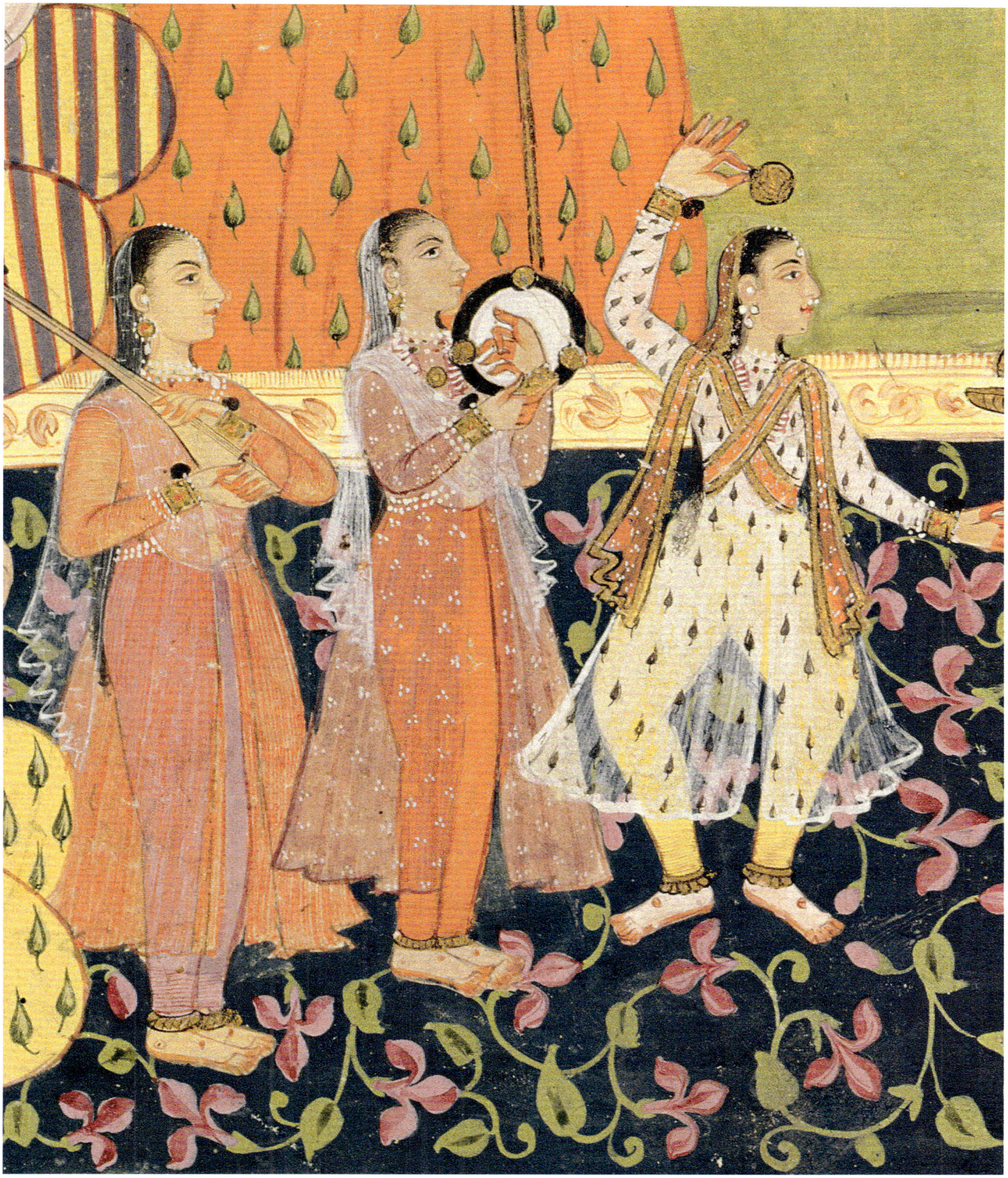

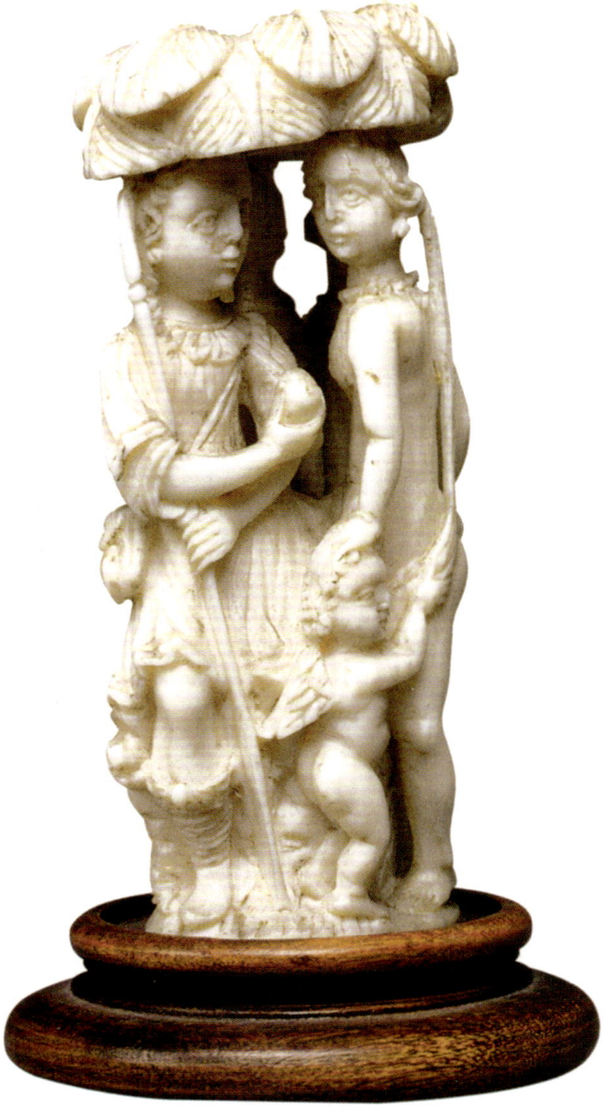

150

The Judgment of Paris

GOA, NINETEENTH CENTURY

Ivory
7 × 3.8 cm (2 ¾ × 1 ½ in.)

THE SUBJECT OF THIS IVORY SCULPTURE is the Judgment of Paris, from the myths of ancient Greece. Paris was herding cattle on Mount Ida when he was approached by Hermes and asked to decide which of the goddesses, Hera, Athene, or Aphrodite, was the fairest and should thus win the golden apple. The goddesses tempted Paris respectively with wealth, victory in battle, or the most beautiful woman in the world. He chose beauty and was promised the love of Helen of Sparta, thus setting in motion the cause of the Trojan War. Paris set off for Sparta with Eros, the god of love and son of Aphrodite.[1]

The sculpture depicts the three goddesses and the winged Eros standing together under the stylized branches of a tree. Athene is depicted holding an apple and a spear, Hera with a bejeweled garment, and Aphrodite partly clothed, with the figure of the winged Eros holding on to her. European subject matter of this type was popular in the Portuguese colony of Goa, where ivories depicting Christian themes in particular, such as the Crucifixion or the Good Shepherd, were relatively common. These figures were initially inspired in the sixteenth century by the devotional objects of the Jesuits, and were carved on occasion in precious materials including crystal[2] and ivory.[3] Their Indian origin is evident in the fullness of the figures and the heavily stylized drapery, contrasting with the more matter-of-fact precision of contemporary European carving.

MCS

1 R. Graves, *The Greek myths*, London: Penguin, 1975, p. 270, no. 159i.

2 Calouste Gulbenkian Museum, *Exotica: The Portuguese discoveries and the Renaissance Kunstkammer*, Lisbon, 2001, p. 187, no. 75.

3 Pal, 1981, no. 105, p. 102.

151

Princesses gather at a fountain

WATERCOLOR AND GOLD ON PAPER

Provincial Mughal, probably at Farrukhabad, 1750–75
22.9 × 34.6 cm (9 × 13 5/8 in.)
On reverse, four lines of Persian calligraphy
Metropolitan Museum of Art, New York, Cynthia Hazen Polsky and Leon B. Polsky Fund (2001.421)

THIS IDYLLIC SCENE OF LADIES gathered around a fountain may once have been part of a series relating to an unknown text, or formed a section of a larger album of such works. The attenuated forms of the long-legged figures and slightly stiff treatment of the marble pavilion and fountain are typical of images from the provincial Mughal center of Farrukhabad, which had a lively painting tradition in the later part of the eighteenth century. The rendering of the background, however, shows a strong Deccani flavor, particularly in the great receding views with hills and lakes dotted with animals and birds.[1] A comparable painting in the India Office Library, London, is close in mode to this work, thus possibly from the same series, and also combines these stylistic features.[2] Interestingly the animals and birds seen in the background of this scene nearly all occur in pairs, a metaphor of love in poetry and painting: the tree on the right contains three sets of colored birds and the background shows a couple of swan-like storks, whose long necks are curled into rings. Further pairs of birds can be seen around the lake, which also has deer, goats, and rabbits in its vicinity. An illustrated Deccani manuscript of the Urdu text of *Nal Daman*, dated 1698, shows a folio entirely filled with numerous birds in pairs, resembling those seen here.[3] The city of Farrukhabad was founded in the early eighteenth century but it was during the second half of the century that it enjoyed the wealth and security that allowed its painting traditions to flourish.

NHH

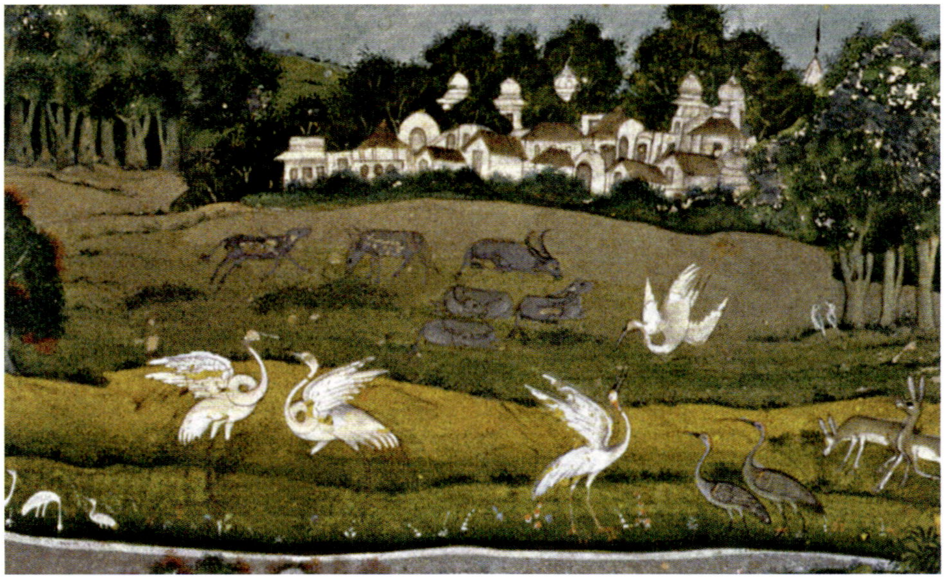

1 Zebrowski, 1983, figs. 183 and 185, for comparable backgrounds in Deccani paintings.

2 Falk and Archer, 1981, no. 362, col. pl. 11.

3 Zebrowski, *op. cit.*, p. 218, fig. 188.

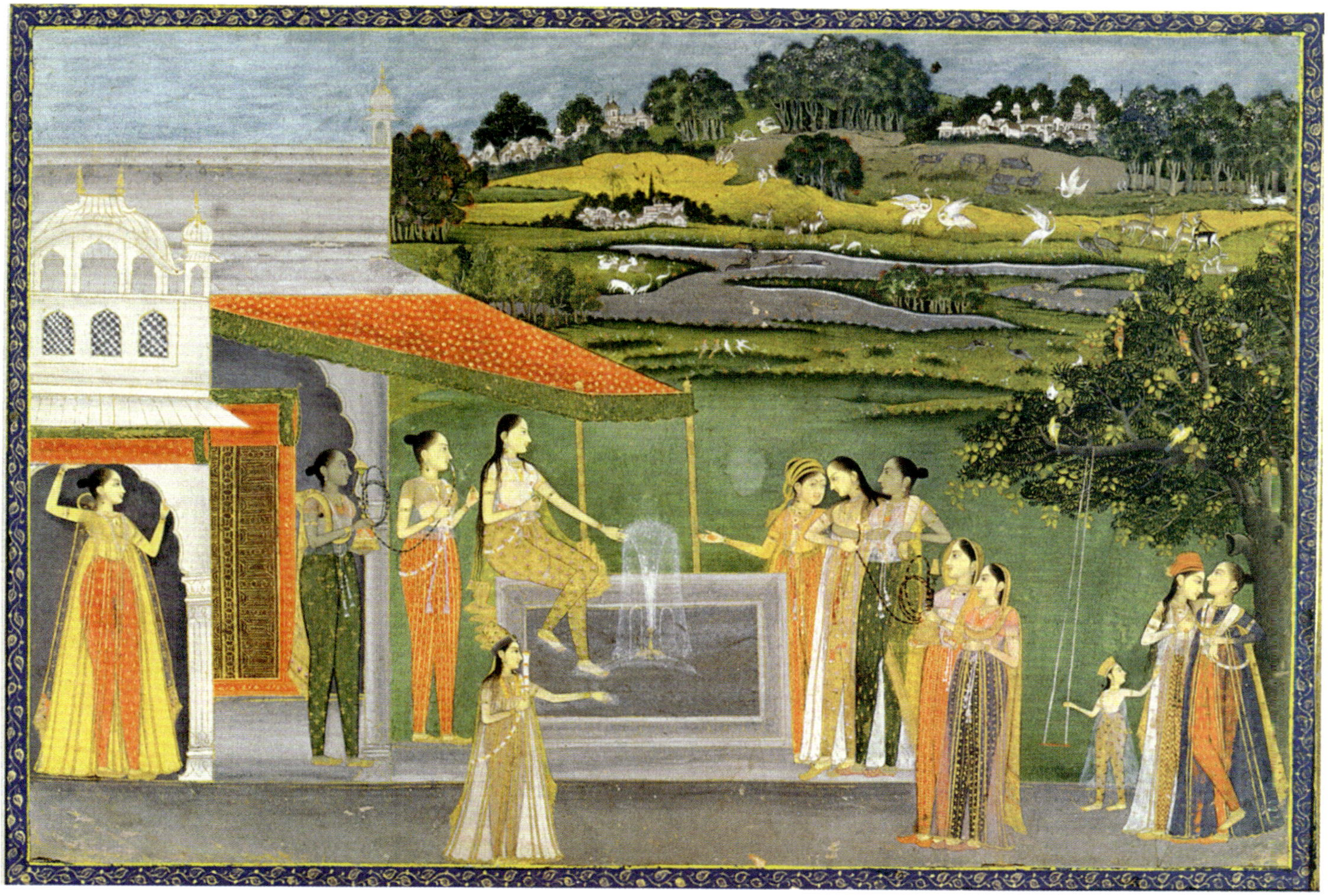

152

A lady riding with female attendants

BUNDI OR UNIARA, RAJASTHAN, CA. 1770

Opaque watercolor on paper
29.8 x 21.3 cm (11 ¾ x 8 ⅛ in.)
Published: T. McInerney, *Indian paintings from the Polsky Collections*, Princeton, 1982, no. 16
Maya Polsky collection

PAINTINGS OF LADIES AT THEIR TOILET or taking their leisure in various ways in the secluded, inviolate zone of the zenana of the palace were a popular genre with the late eighteenth-century Hara Rajput rulers of the Bundi region. These subjects generally have a strong romantic or erotic undercurrent, occasionally made more explicit by the furtive appearance, at one side, of a kingly figure (or sometimes Krishna) as an onlooker or voyeur.

In this carefree scene, a group of princesses and a small dog playfully enact a royal procession in a walled garden courtyard. One, riding the caparisoned, dappled stallion, turns her head as a maid offers her a cup of wine. Another lady follows behind carrying a ceremonial parasol, of the kind held behind the ruler when riding in a cavalcade. This subject is also known in other versions.[1] Here, a blossoming tree and the broad fleshy leaves and pendulous pink flower of the plantains in the adjoining gardens seem to spill over the courtyard wall and strain inward through its doorways, as though irresistibly drawn by the lovely lady and her maids.

AT

1 E.g. Archer, 1959, fig. 18; Welch and Beach, 1965, no. 66.

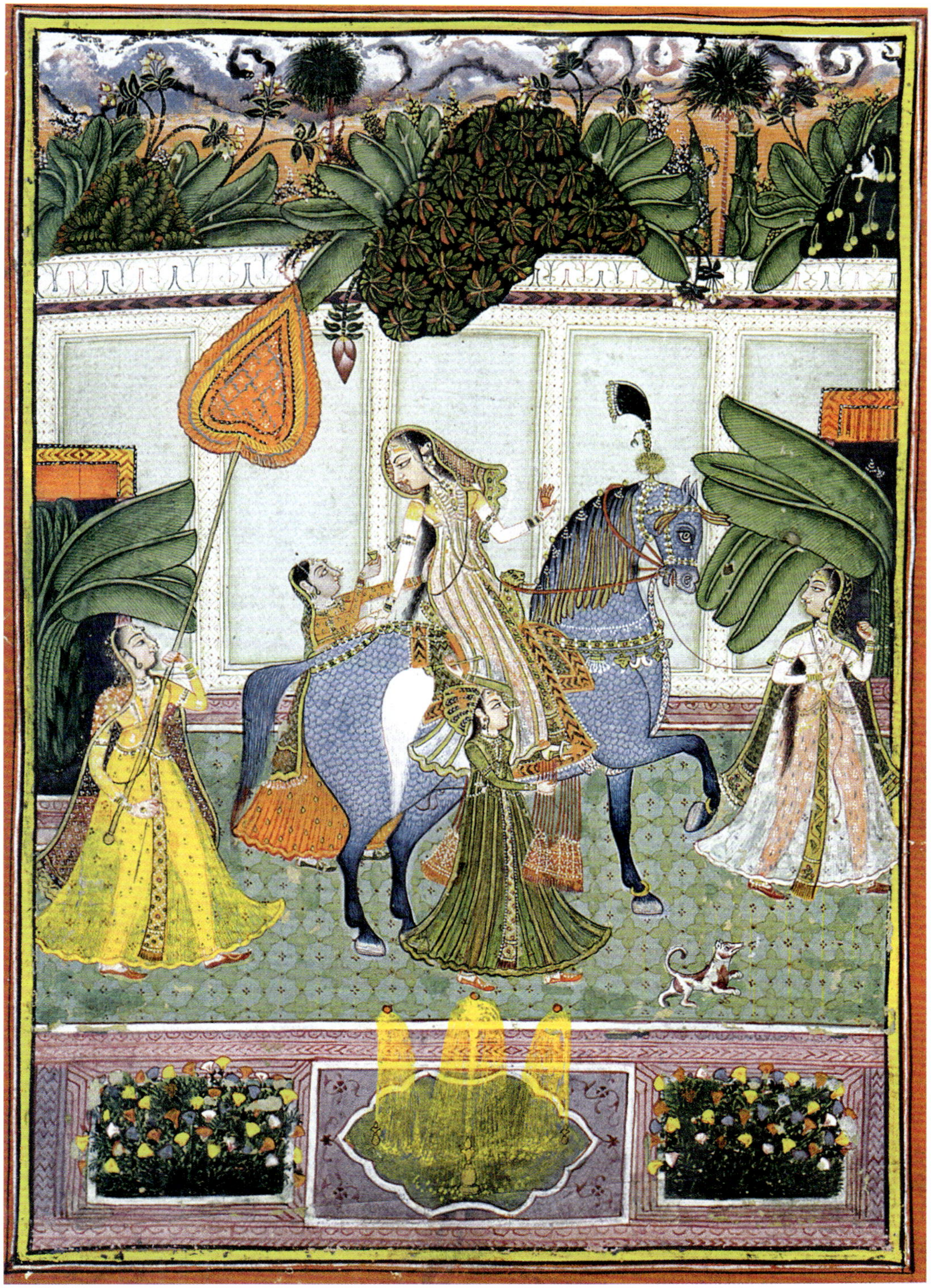

153

Ivory panels with dancing girls and musicians

SRI LANKA, SEVENTEENTH CENTURY

Each panel 3.2 x 7.9 cm (1¼ x 3 ⅛ in.)

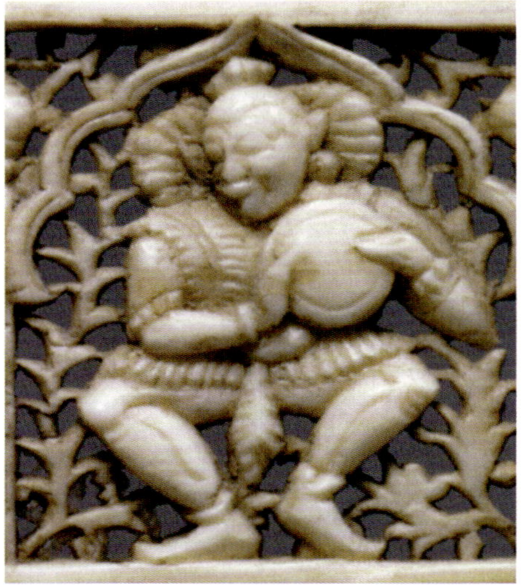

THESE FIVE IVORY PANELS WITH OPENWORK carved decoration were formerly attached to a piece of furniture, probably a box.[1] The group possibly comprises almost the entire principal decorative scheme of a single box of rectangular form, forming the long and short sides of the body. The lid may have been pitched, as is found on Portuguese boxes, or the box could have been flat-topped.[2] Each panel has a series of four figures, all dancing, within an arcade of columns and arches; each figure is surrounded by floral scrolls. From top to bottom: panel (a) has three women and a man; panel (b) has two women and two men, one playing a tambourine; panel (c) comprises a single panel now in two parts, with two dancing women on each part; panel (d) has two women and two men, one playing a tambourine; panel (e) has two women and two men each playing the tambourine. Each panel has three columns with rounded capitals, and cusped arches, which create a series of four niches for the figures. Each of the figures is bejeweled. The women are dressed in long diaphanous garments, several with a small bag over one arm, and the men in short dhotis, with the tambourine players also wearing a jacket with a high collar.

The ivory boxes of Ceylon came to European attention through the Portuguese, who sent embassies to the Kingdom of Kotte in Ceylon in the sixteenth century. Magnificent boxes were sent to the Portuguese court by the embassy, and some were sent as gifts by Queen Catherine (1507–78) to other royal families in Europe, including the Habsburg princes Philip II, Rudolph II, and Albrecht V of Bavaria. These boxes can be dated through surviving inventories taken in the sixteenth and seventeenth centuries.[3]

MCS

1 A box in the British Museum has ivory panels of dancing figures: M.Willis, "Early Indian ivory," *Arts of Asia*, vol. 28, 2, March–April 1998, fig. 126. Another panel with women dancing and playing instruments is in the Berlin Museum: *Museum für Indische Kunst Berlin: Katalog* 1976, Berlin, 1976, no. 173.

2 A rectangular box with openwork ivory panels is in Lisbon (inv. 66 cx): Tchakaloff et al., 1998, no. 26, p. 102, while the box in the British Museum (see note 1) has a pitched lid.

3 Calouste Gulbenkian Museum, *Exotica: The Portuguese discoveries and the Renaissance Kunstkammer*, Lisbon, 2001, p. 41; and A. Jaffer and M. A. Schwabe, "A group of 16th century ivory caskets from Ceylon," *Apollo*, CXLIX, 445, March 1999, p. 8.

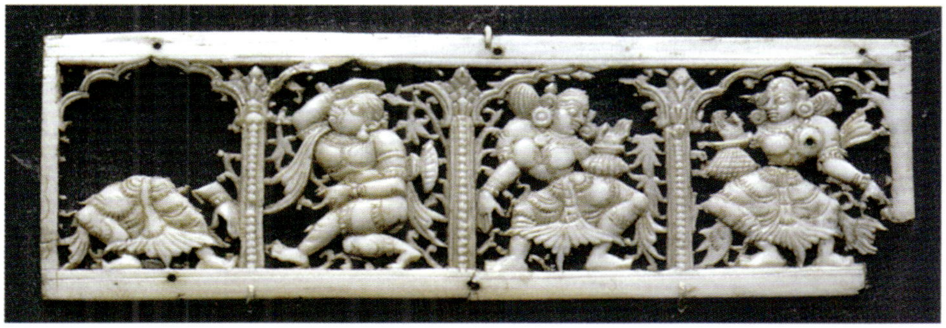

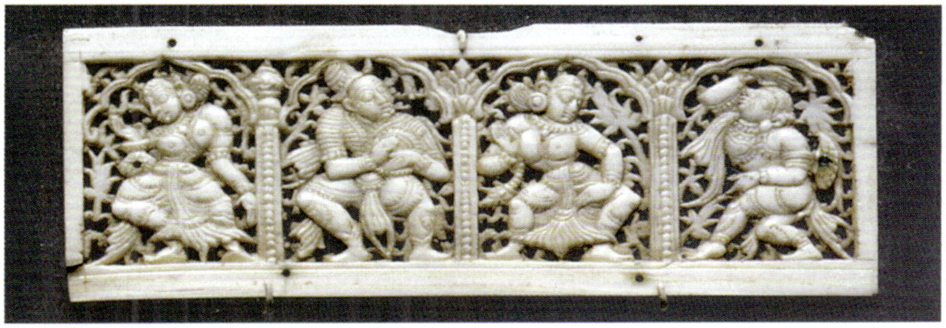

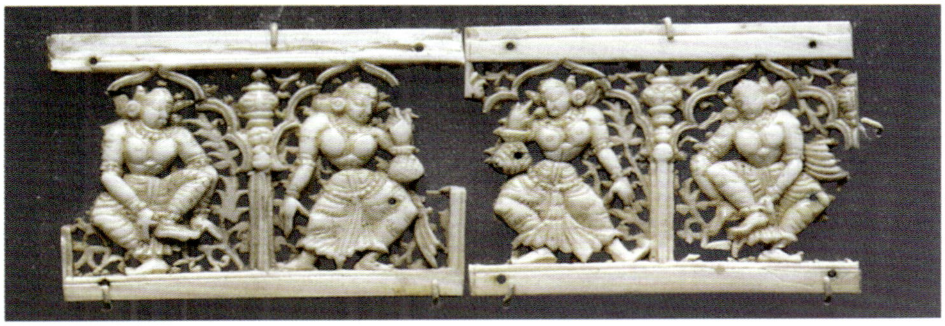

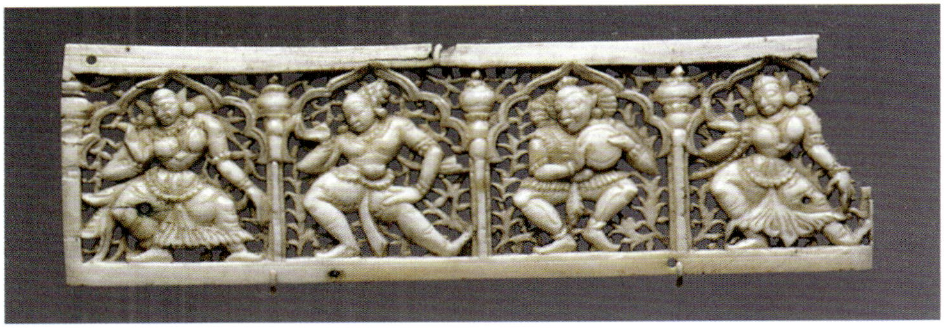

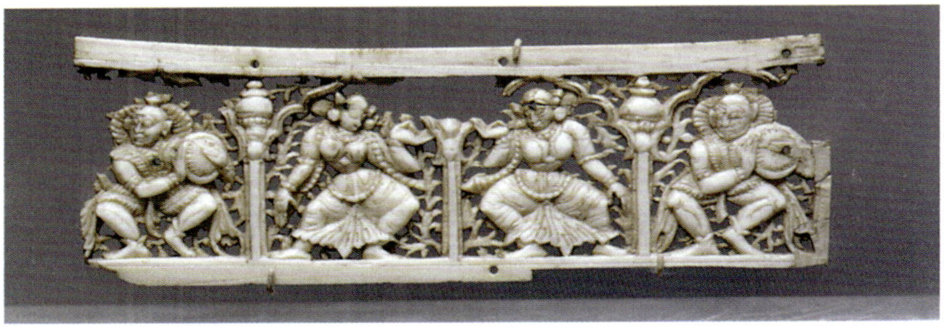

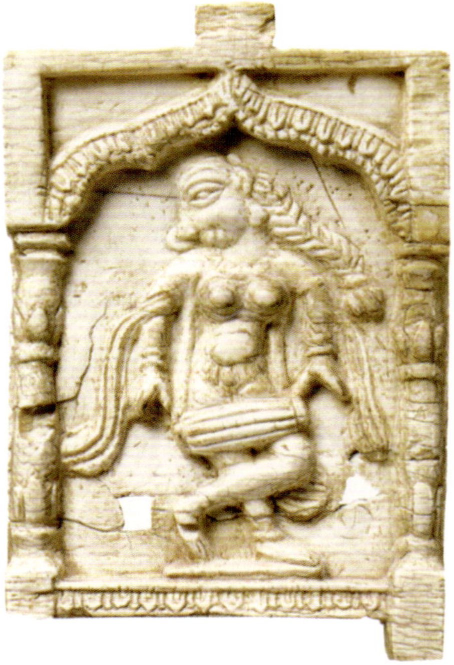

154

Ivory panel depicting a female drummer

ORISSA, EIGHTEENTH CENTURY

6.4 × 7.9 cm (2 ½ × 3 ⅛ in.)
Metropolitan Museum of Art, New York,
Gift of Cynthia Hazen Polsky

THIS IVORY PANEL DEPICTS A WOMAN DANCING as she plays a drum. She is scantily dressed, and has her hair in a long plait, as she stands in an architectural frame with columns to either side and a cusped arch above her. The panel is carved from a single piece of ivory, and has lugs on the bottom and one on the top for assembly into a larger panel, probably a bed-head or other piece of furniture.

Musical instruments are extensively represented in Indian paintings and sculpture, indicating that in the past, as today, music was an important part of ceremony and social functions; the paintings of the seventeenth-century Mughal *Padshahnama* manuscript notably depict musicians with stringed instruments, trumpets and drums playing at the royal receptions and weddings of Shah Jahan and his sons.[1] The female musician here is playing the cylindrical drum known as *pakhavaj*, which is suspended around the neck and has a drum-skin at both ends.[2] Other drums traditionally played in India include the *tabla* (since the eighteenth century), which sits on the floor, and the older *dhol* or *dholak*, which was also suspended around the neck.[3] The pakhavaj is described in the *Ghunyat al-Munya*, a fourteenth-century Gujarati manuscript, and a closely similar instrument is described in the *'Ain-i Akbari* of Abu'l Fazl.[4] Larger *naqqara* or kettle drums were also used at court, sometimes mounted on elephants.

Nautch girls, or dancers, who are often depicted semi-naked, commonly provided entertainment for the Mughal and Rajput nobility and, later on, for European visitors. A painting from the Fraser Album is inscribed by Edward Fraser, father of James: "Kander Buksh a celebrated dancing woman of Dehlee, once considered very beautiful. In the usual undress."[5]

MCS

1 Beach and Koch, 1997, no. 22, p. 62–63, and no. 26, p. 68.
2 Bor and Bruguière eds., 2003, p. 157.
3: *Ibid.*, p. 161.
4 *Ibid.*, pp. 155, 157.
5 Archer and Falk, 1989, no. 127, p. 129.

155

Ivory plaque with Krishna and gopis

ORISSA, SEVENTEENTH CENTURY

6.4 × 4.5 cm (2 ½ × 1 ¾ in.)
Metropolitan Museum of Art, New York,
Gift of Cynthia Hazen Polsky (2011.576.5)

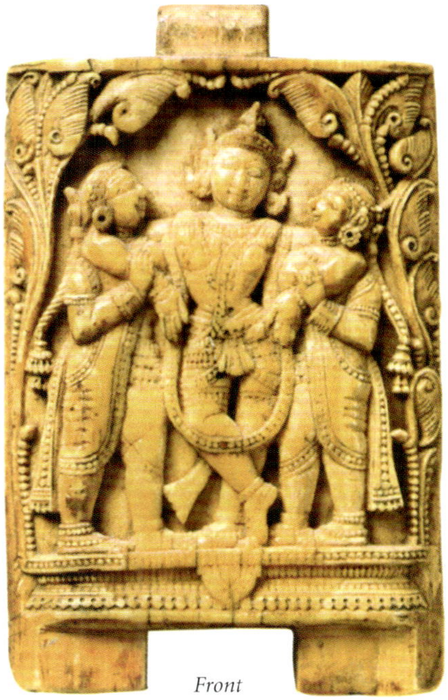

Front

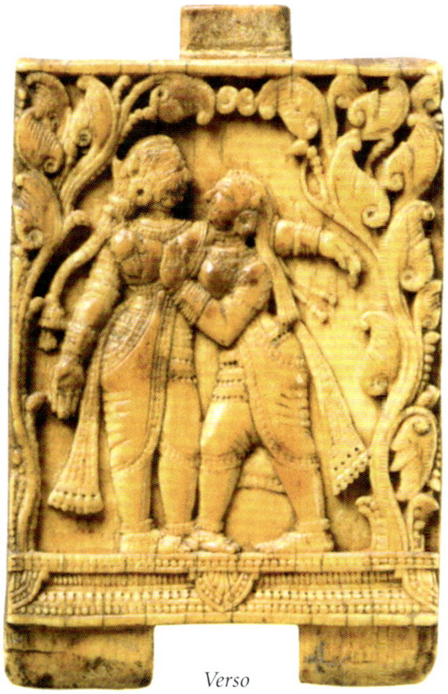

Verso

ON ONE SIDE OF THIS DOUBLE-SIDED IVORY PLAQUE carved in relief, two lovelorn gopis stand together framed by foliage, one with her left arm outstretched, the other holding up her left hand. On the other side, Krishna stands, dressed in a short garment, elaborate jewelry, and a garland, with his arms around the shoulders of two gopis, who have their hair in long plaits with bells. Rich plant fronds and foliage appear to either side. This ivory alludes to the episode from the *Bhagavata Purana* in which Krishna dances with the ladies of Vrindaban, and then disappears.[1] They search the forest for him, calling out to the trees and animals to enquire after their beloved Krishna. He then suddenly reappears before the distraught women, and after praising their devotion to him, begins to dance with them. Using his divine power, he stands simultaneously between each pair of women, his arms around their necks, while they press his hands to their breasts. The ivory depicts the women searching for Krishna on one side, and dancing with the god on the other. This episode is depicted in an Orissan manuscript in the British Library,[2] in which the same specific iconography of the dancing scene appears;[3] other similarities include the women's hairstyles, garments, and jewelry, and the distinctive foliage.[4] The local artists and ivory carvers worked from a common repertory of stories and scenes, ensuring that anyone would instantly recognize the narrative.

The panel is carved from a single piece of ivory, with a lug on the top and two on the bottom for assembly into a larger panel, possibly a bed-head or other item of furniture, which would have narrated further episodes from the *Bhagavata Purana*. Together with the erotic scenes carved on similar small panels (cat. no. 147), these assembled furniture panels would have formed splendid overall narrative sequences.

MCS

1 *Bhagavata Purana*, Book X, chapters 29–33.

2 Or. 11689: Losty, 1980, there dated to the early eighteenth century.

3 *Ibid.*, f.23a, p. 30, depicts Krishna dancing with the pairs of women, and ff.13b and 14a, pp. 22–23, show the women searching the forest.

4 *Ibid.*, f.9a and f.25a for the foliage; f.22b for the long plaits with bells; f.22a for the garments.

156

Wedding party, Jodhpur-Jaisalmer road

RAGHUBIR SINGH (1942–99)

Rajasthan, 1980–81
Chromogenic color print
25.3 × 37.6 cm (9 15⁄16 × 14 13⁄16 in.)
Metropolitan Museum of Art, New York, Purchase, Cynthia Hazen Polsky Gift (1991.1281)

THIS SEEMINGLY UNSTRUCTURED MOMENT of intense and startling color, caught against a washed out desert landscape, comes close to the essence of Raghubir Singh's work. Such bright flashes of color in this stark setting are wholly characteristic of both the photographer's home state of Rajasthan and his own ambition to illuminate through photography "the lyric poetry inherent in the life of India."[1] Singh has been both praised and criticized for his use of intense and vivid color, and in the revealing essay that prefaces the last collection of his work to appear before his death in 1999, he articulates a credo that places its use at the centre of his artistic vision. Discussing the European introduction of photography to India in the mid-nineteenth century, he revealingly refers to the medium's "illusion of documentary realism,"[2] and in a modern context to the prevalence in the West of the idea that only black-and-white photography can attain a seriousness that transcends the "vulgarity" of color. But for Singh, photography was an attempt to move beyond mere documentation in order to reach a deeper vision of his homeland. For this the use of color was not just one of many available tools, but the essential expression of a specifically Indian reality: "the eyes of India see only in color."[3] Repudiating "the angst, the alienation and guilt of recent nihilistic photography in the West,"[4] a world-view that has in the past expressed itself predominantly in monochrome, Singh saw in color his true means of capturing "the lyric poetry inherent in the life of India: the high range of the coloratura of everyday India."[5]

JF

1 Singh, 1998, introduction, p. 15.
2 *Ibid*, p. 11.
3 *Ibid*, p. 10.
4 *Ibid*, p. 13.
5 *Ibid*, p. 15.

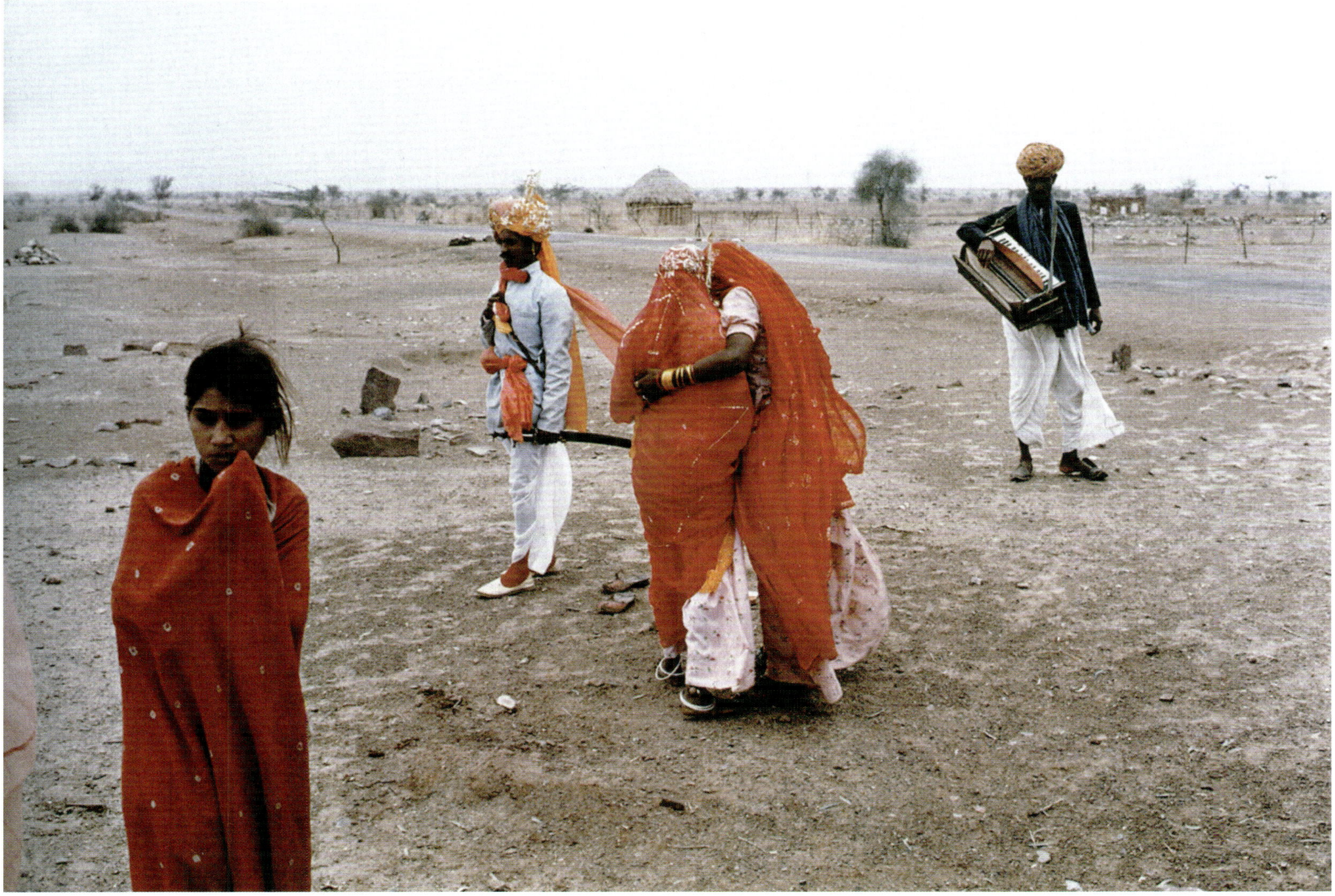

COURTLY MANUSCRIPTS

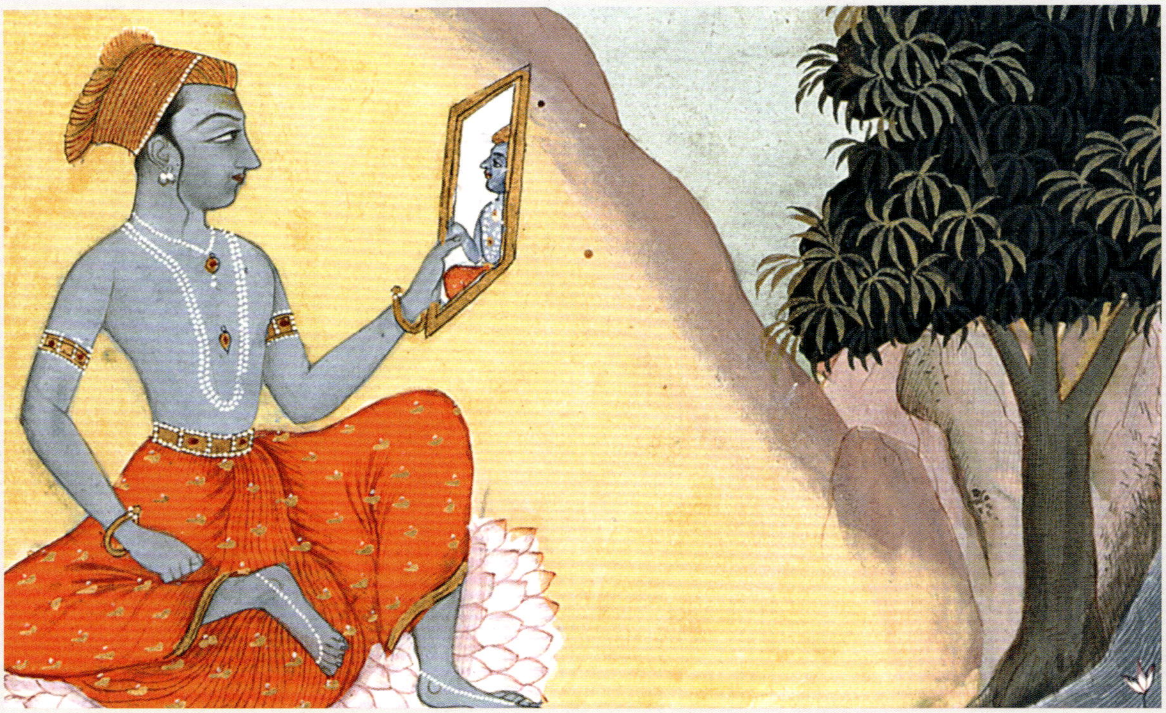

Because of the ravages of the Indian climate and the accidents of history, very little Indian manuscript material survives from before ca. AD 1000. The written text in any case seems to have played a subordinate role in India in early times, when the preferred mode of preservation and transmission of sacred scriptures was through their memorization and recitation by Brahmin priests or Buddhist and Jain monks. Before its gradual replacement by paper around the fourteenth century, the most commonly used material for manuscripts was the leaf of the talipot palm, which provided a long, narrow rectangular surface for writing and any additional embellishment. Even after the introduction of paper from Central Asia, which allowed an expansion of the page size, the conservative Western Indian illustrators of the Jain scriptural texts still adhered to the old, narrower format (cat. nos. 30–32).

Elsewhere, at the Hindu courts of the Rajput rulers, a vigorous and expressive new style developed in the fifteenth to sixteenth centuries, devoted to the illustration of devotional texts such as the tenth book of the *Bhagavata Purana*, relating the life story of Krishna (cat. nos. 54–55), as well as secular, courtly subjects such as *ragamala* ("Garland of Ragas"), or the systematic illustration of the North Indian musical modes (*ragas* and *raginis*) according to received poetic tradition. This robust Early Rajput style in turn contributed to the formation of the dynamic and influential early Mughal school. The new imperial studio established by Akbar under the direction of his imported Persian masters included many native Indian painters, recruited from Gwalior and other earlier centers of production. Within a few years, as the new commissions for Akbar's library multiplied, the refined Iranian tradition of illustrated manuscript production in a vertical codex format had become integrated with the vigorous Indian tradition and with the new currents of naturalism deriving from the study of European prints. The texts illustrated for Akbar included the chronicles of his own life (cat. no. 165) and the memoirs of his grandfather Babur, founder of the dynasty, with their unusually vivid and original observations on human and natural life. Not only were the familiar classics of Persian poetry superbly illustrated, but also the newly commissioned Persian translations of Indian narrative or religious texts, including the *Ramayana* epic, whose mythological subjects were treated with an unprecedented dramatic realism in imperial examples (cat. nos. 163–64), and with a simpler vigor and decorative charm in versions of sub-imperial quality (cat. nos. 157–62).

With the steady dispersal of Mughal-trained painters to work at provincial courts, the Akbari revolution in manuscript illustration gave a new impetus to the local schools of Rajput painting in Rajasthan and the Punjab Hills, whose individual histories begin to be traceable from the early seventeenth century onward. Prominent among the more popular mythological subjects for illustration, as before, were the tenth book of the *Bhagavata Purana* and also the *Gita Govinda* of Jayadeva, with its impassioned celebration of the love of Krishna and Radha. Its theme of the apotheosis of romantic love was carried over also into Hindi literary texts, such as the *Rasikapriya*, the poetic treatise on idealized types of lovers composed by Keshav Das in 1591 at the court of Orccha, and the *Sat Sai* of Bihari Lal, court poet of Amber in Rajasthan in the mid-seventeenth century. At many courts, however, *ragamala* remained the most commonly depicted genre of all, especially during the seventeenth century. Its unique distillation and fusion of the separate arts of music, poetry, and painting, in a well-ordered classification of sometimes intriguing or mysterious imagery, appealed greatly to the taste of cultured royal connoisseurs.

AT

Six folios from a dispersed series of the Ramayana

Northern India, sub-imperial Mughal, ca. 1595–1605
Opaque watercolor and gold on paper
Each folio with Sanskrit text on reverse, and some lines of Bundeli Hindi
Two folios in the Cynthia Hazen Polsky collection; four folios in The Metropolitan Museum of Art, New York

THESE SIX PAINTED FOLIOS are all from a well-known dispersed series illustrating the epic of the *Ramayana*, made in all likelihood for Bir Singh Deo of Datia in the sub-imperial Mughal style, denoting works commissioned by patrons of lesser status than the Emperor, usually high-ranking court officials.[1] There are four known lavishly illustrated late sixteenth century Mughal manuscripts of the *Ramayana*, two being made for members of the imperial family: for Akbar (in 1588–92), now in the City Palace Museum, Jaipur, and for his mother Hamida Banu Begum (in 1594), now dispersed. The other two manuscripts were made for members of the imperial court: ʿAbd al-Rahim (in 1597–1605), now in the Freer Gallery of Art, Washington D.C., and the dispersed series to which these pages belong. Since this series has a Sanskrit text, unlike the others which are written in Persian, and also comes from the Datia palace collection, it has been plausibly suggested that it was made for the wealthy Hindu patron Bir Singh Deo Bundela, an important courtier in the late Akbar (r. 1556–1605) and Jahangir (r. 1605–27) periods.

Painting of this kind, created outside the circles of royal patronage, while often the work of lesser known artists, was also somewhat freed from the formality of imperial painting, thus often appearing more lively, if somewhat simpler.[2] The *Ramayana* to which these folios belong exemplifies this in its distinctive fusion of Mughal and Rajput artistic sensibilities, joined with unexpectedly bold decorative elements from Chinese and Persian painting. The resulting effect is that almost every folio has a fresh and original combination of stylistic features, many with rich passages of illogical but striking patterning. Seyller's efforts to trace the workshop where these pages were made have brought to light the names of several artists who may have worked on this series, based on similar compositions in the National Museum *Baburnama* of 1597–99 and a *Razmnama* of 1598–1600; these include Jagjivana, Makara, Lohanka, Khemana, and Bhora.[3] This *Ramayana* series suffered damage while it was still intact, and all of its pages have been affected to some degree. Dispersed pages from it are found in a number of museum holdings, including the Prince of Wales Museum, Bombay; National Museum, New Delhi; Bharat Kala Bhavan, Varanasi; Los Angeles County Museum of Art; Virginia Museum, Richmond; as well as in various private collections.

NHH

1 Mason et al., 2001, pp. 62–63, no. 16, illustrates another leaf from the series and provides an overview by J. Seyller, who acknowledges T. McInerney's suggestion for the patron.

2 Beach, 1981, p. 134.

3 Seyller, in Mason et al., *op. cit.*, p. 62.

See pages 356-67

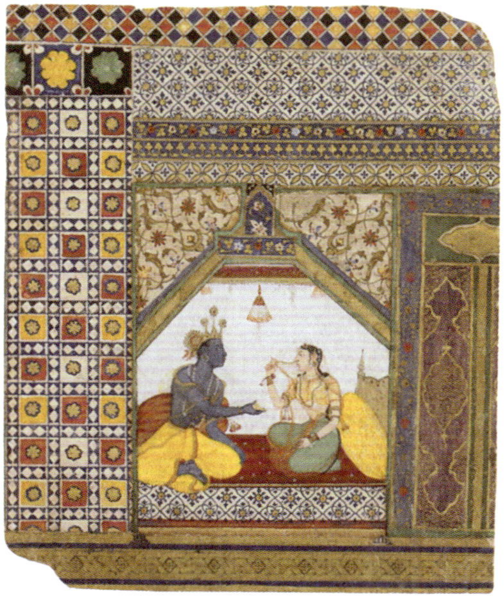

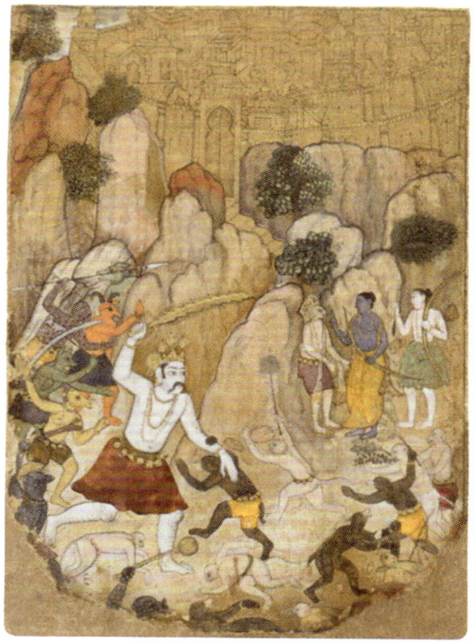

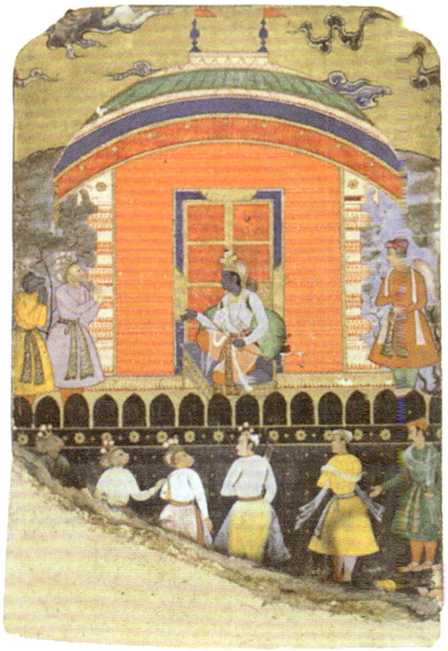

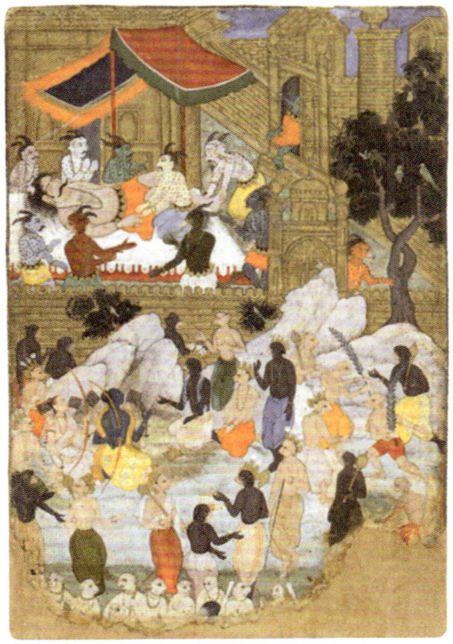

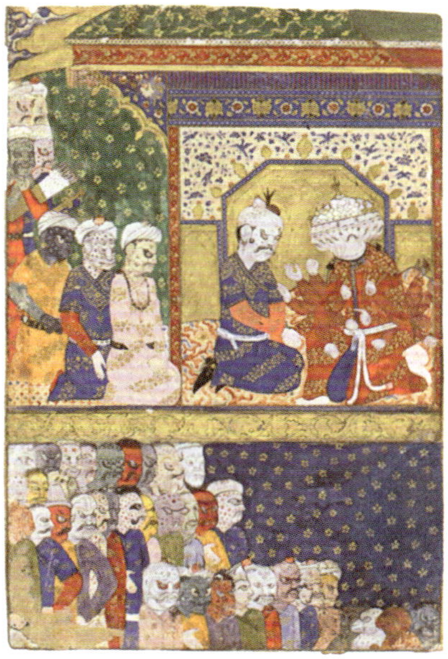

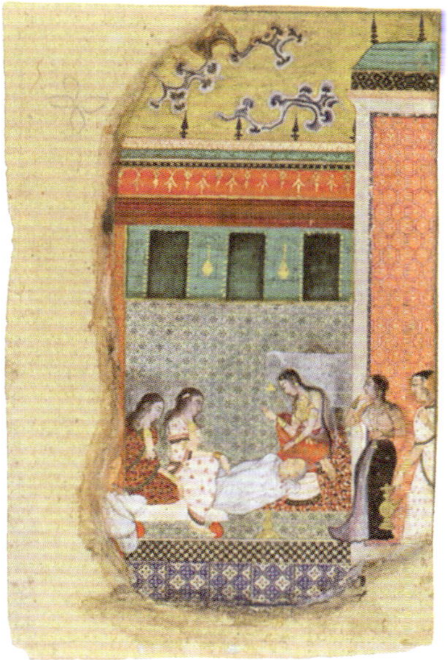

157

Rama justifies to Sita his earlier repudiation of her

FROM A DISPERSED RAMAYANA SERIES

Sub-imperial Mughal, ca. 1595–1605
Watercolor and gold on paper
On verso, five lines of Sanskrit text and one line of Bundeli Hindi
15.6 × 13.3 cm; (6 ⅛ × 5 ¼ in.)

RAMA'S REPUDIATION OF SITA after her rescue from Lanka was based on his fear that dishonor would befall him and his family due to defamatory rumors of her association with her captor, the demon Ravana. The blameless Sita, whose virtuous conduct while in Ravana's captivity was a testament to her devotion to Rama, was ultimately reconciled with her husband, much to the delight of all the gods and mortals. Here, surrounded by heavy swathes of patterning, Ram and Sita are seated against cushions, face to face while Rama holds out his arm as he explains his actions. For her part, Sita pulls her veil over her face, displaying the modesty and composure for which she has come to be regarded as the perfect woman and wife. Her profile form and costume recall earlier models in the widespread sixteenth-century Early Rajput (or *Chaurapanchasika*) style, whereas the depiction of Krishna is more in the Mughal taste.[1] Among the assorted patterns and designs all around, the right side of the folio contains a rectangular cartouche which resembles Mughal leather book bindings, both in form and color scheme. The spandrels above the figures contain Persianized scrolling arabesques, while the outer borders are filled with brightly colored, repeating geometric forms. This variety of decorative panels reflects the fact that sections of the damaged painting were pieced together in close proximity, but the overall effect of areas of contrasting pattern is in keeping with the character of other folios from the same series.

NHH

1 P. Chandra, "A series of *Ramayana* paintings of the Popular Mughal school," *Bulletin of the Prince of Wales Museum*, Bombay, no. 6, 1957, pp. 64–70, figs. 18–27.

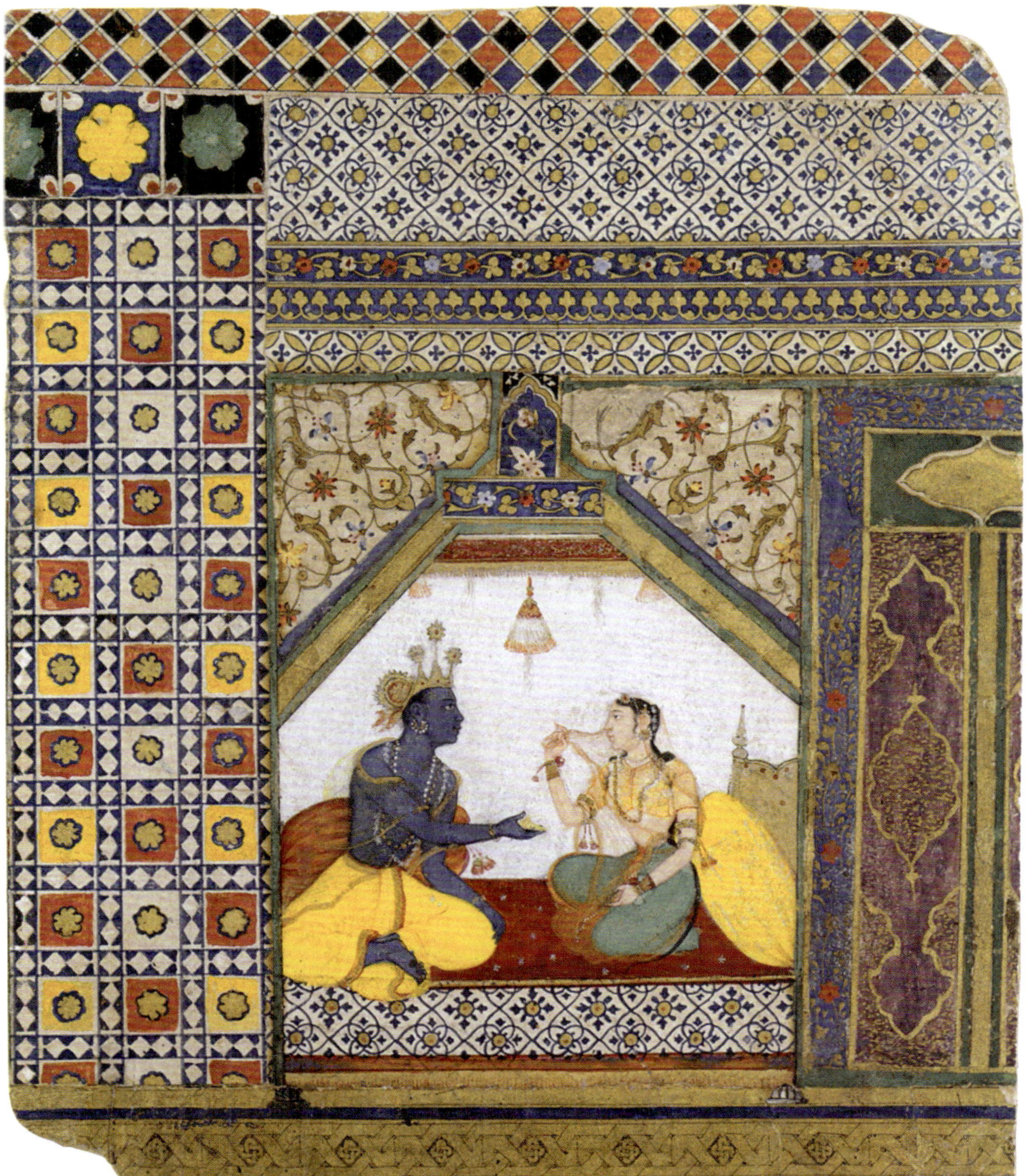

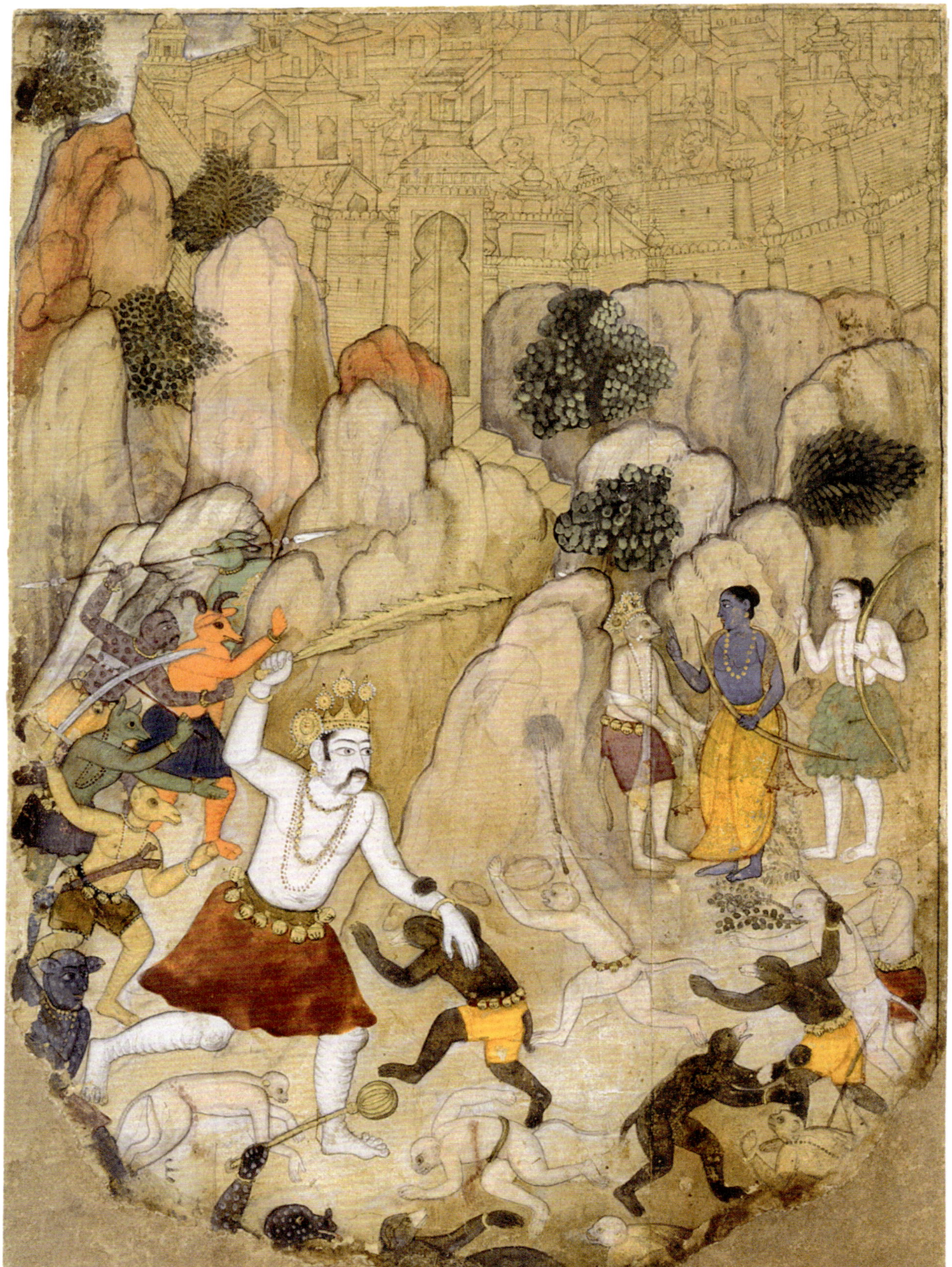

158

A giant demon, possibly Atikaya, confronts Rama's army

FROM A DISPERSED RAMAYANA SERIES

Sub-imperial Mughal, ca. 1595–1605
Watercolor and gold on paper
On verso, thirteen lines of Sanskrit text
27.3 × 18.1 cm (10 ¾ × 7 ⅛ in.)

DURING THE COURSE OF THEIR LONG BATTLE, the demon king Ravana sent out several of his chief Titans or giant demons in succession to fight Rama's army, Atikaya being among the most powerful of them. Having decimated many of the bear and monkey fighters, he was finally defeated by Rama's brother Lakshmana. The name of Atikaya appears in the text on the reverse, hence the present identification of the scene, which does also recall another great battle, between the Titan Akampana and Hanuman. Here Rama and Lakshmana can be seen conferring with Hanuman, while Ravana's warrior combats the army. The golden city of Lanka can be seen in the background. The text mentions Atikaya as having two immensely powerful, broad and long swords:[1] the unusual, serrated-edge weapon wielded by the giant here may illustrate of one of these.

NHH

1 Shastri tr., 1959, vol. 3, pp. 201–3.

159

Rama receives Sugriva and Jambavat, the monkey and bear kings

FROM A DISPERSED RAMAYANA SERIES

Sub-imperial Mughal, ca. 1595–1605
Watercolor and gold on paper
On verso, four lines of Sanskrit text and one line of Bundeli Hindi, with three pale pencil sketches of men and a faintly written number 10
28.2 x 19.1 cm (11 ⅛ x 7 ½ in.)
Published: N. Haidar, in *Recent acquisitions, a selection:* 2003, *Metropolitan Museum of Art Bulletin*, Fall 2003, p. 9
Metropolitan Museum of Art, New York, Cynthia Hazen Polsky and Leon B. Polsky Fund (2002.503)

THE BATTLE BETWEEN THE PRINCE RAMA and the demon king Ravana was fought and won with the aid of the monkey and bear armies. Here the blue-skinned Rama is seated under a brilliantly colored curved bangla-style pavilion with the monkey and bear kings, Sugriva and Jambavat, who stand before him with folded hands. A row of courtly figures below comprises three monkey and three human figures. Bold, Chinese-inspired ribbon-style cloud forms float in a golden sky above; these are a feature seen in several pages from this series. The strong coloring of this folio is probably inspired by earlier Hindu and Jain painting traditions, while the delicately painted figures are more in the Mughal taste.

The martial help provided by the armies of Sugriva and Jambavat was crucial to Rama in his efforts to rescue Sita. With their help a great bridge was built across the water to Lanka and Ravana's island citadel was stormed. The monkey and bear figures were a popular subject in *Ramayana* illustrations in many Indian painting traditions, with the image of the monkey chief Hanuman, around whom a strong cult of worship exists until the present day, being a favorite subject.[1]

NHH

1 E.g. Welch, 1985, pp. 399–401, no. 272, for a similar scene in a Pahari manuscript; Seyller, 1999, p. 202, no. 236a, shows Hanuman carrying the mountain.

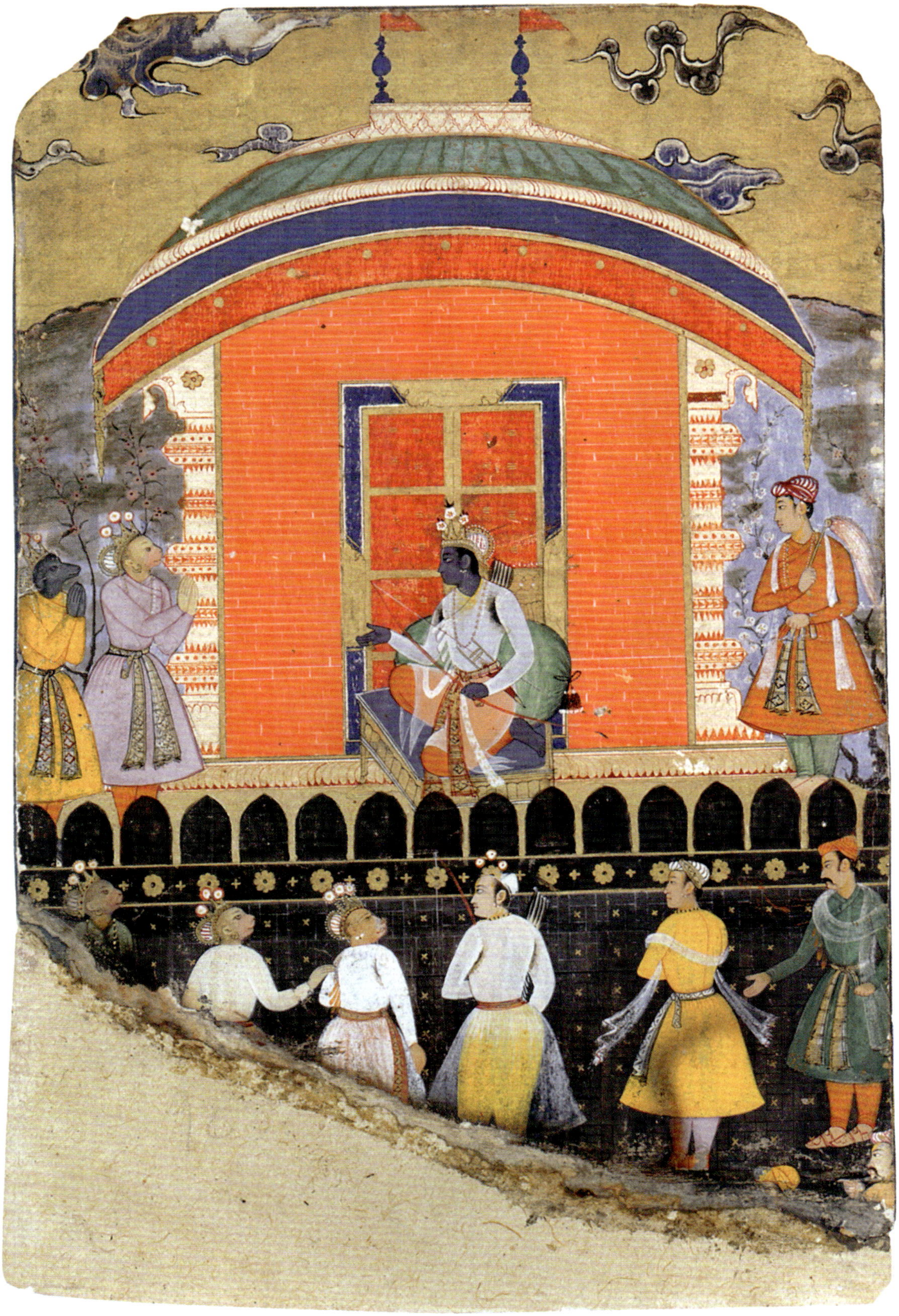

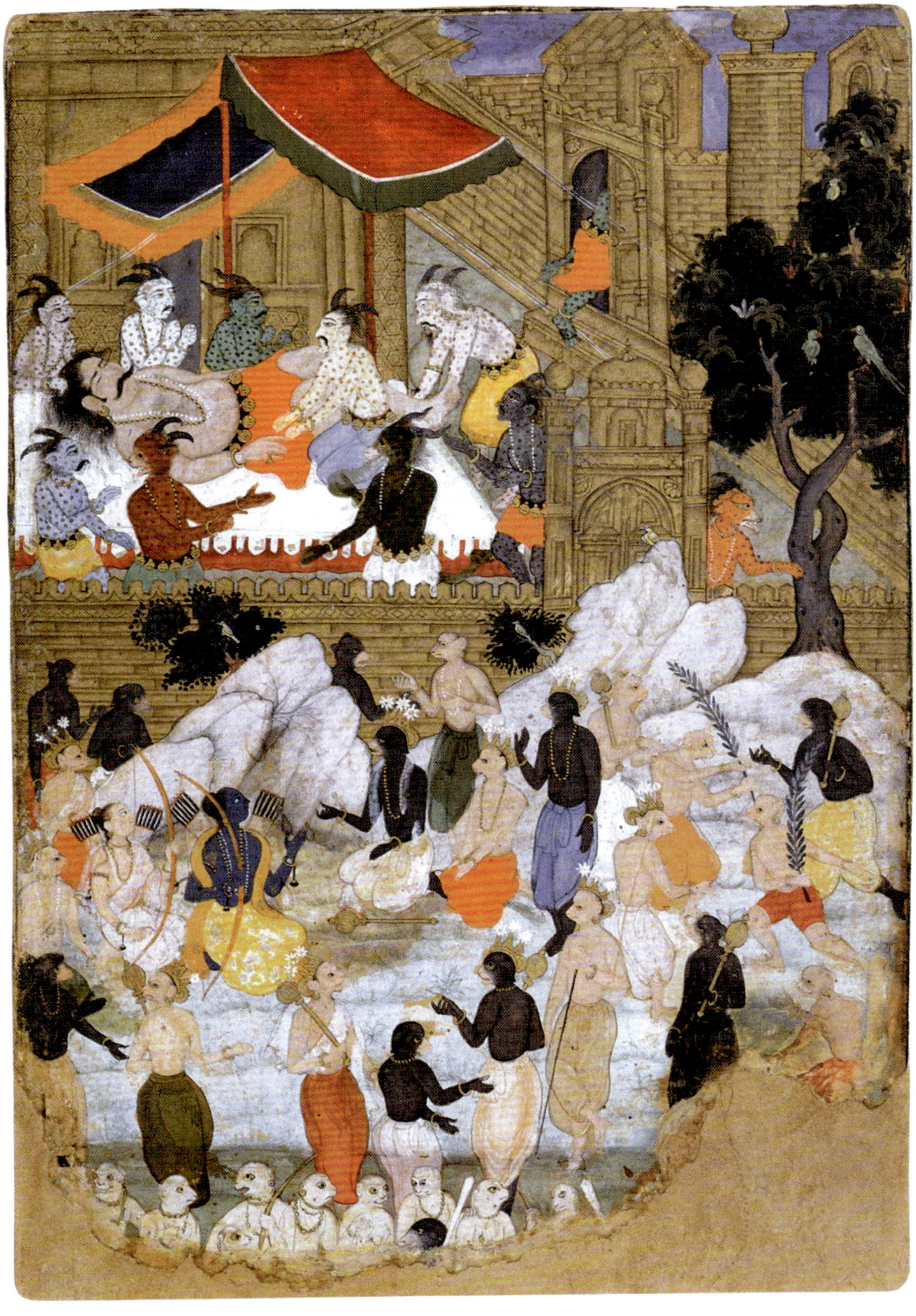

160

The awakening of Kumbhakarna

FROM A DISPERSED RAMAYANA SERIES

Sub-imperial Mughal, ca. 1595–1605
Watercolor and gold on paper
On verso, twelve lines of Sanskrit text and one further damaged line at the bottom of the page; an ink stamp reads *tasvirkhana datia state* (Datia State picture house), with the number 48(?)
27.4 × 19.3 cm (10 7/8 × 7 3/8 in.)
Metropolitan Museum of Art, New York, Cynthia Hazen Polsky and Leon B. Polsky Fund (2002.504)

Kumbhakarna was the giant brother of the demon Ravana, who had been tricked by the gods into asking Brahma for the boon of interminable sleep.[1] At his request, Ravana built him a lavishly adorned palace in which Kumbhakarna slumbered, it is said, for a hundred years. He is awakened by his demon attendants in the episode shown here. Rama and his brother Lakshmana, along with the monkey and bear armies, have laid siege to the city of Lanka. Within its golden walls, his attendants, whose figures with horns, pointed ears, and spotted bodies are modeled on those of *divs* in classical Persian painting, try to rouse him from his deep sleep. They beat drums and cymbals, blare trumpets, strike gongs and even rain blows upon him. When Kumbhakarna finally wakes (out of hunger rather than awareness of this commotion), he fights a fierce battle with Rama's army, crushing many soldiers under his gigantic feet, until the hero, after severing some of the demon's limbs, ultimately beheads him with a powerful arrow.[2]

With its refined brushwork, pale coloring, and complex composition of interior and exterior spaces, this page is among the more classically Mughal in character from the series. The Freer *Ramayana* contains a folio depicting Kumbhakarna asleep which is much simpler in detail and composition than this painting.[3]

NHH

1 Shastri tr., 1959, vol. 3, pp. 156–78.

2 Seyller, 1999, pp. 190–95, for several episodes of the story of Kumbhakarna, including his death, in the Freer manuscript.

3 *Ibid.*, p. 227, refers to a similar composition in the Jaipur *Ramayana*.

161

Ravana with his son Indrajit and demon courtiers

FROM A DISPERSED RAMAYANA SERIES

Sub-imperial Mughal, ca. 1595–1605
Watercolor and gold on paper
On verso, ten lines of Sanskrit text and two lines of Bundeli Hindi; seal or stamp (probably of the Datia Palace) overlaid with paper
27.6 x 19.0 cm (10 ⅞ x 7 ⅜ in.)
Metropolitan Museum of Art, New York, Cynthia Hazen Polsky and Leon B. Polsky Fund (2002.505)

THIS PARTICULAR FOLIO IS DISTINGUISHED from all others in the manuscript by its remarkable style, which seems to be looking to fifteenth-century Indian and Persian painting for inspiration. The composition is divided into two registers, with the ten-headed demon Ravana and another figure, probably his son Indrajit, seated in a pavilion area above. While Ravana's many faces resemble human visages, his son and their demon courtiers form an array of Persianate *div* figures, many in Safavid dress. The scene is rendered in a slightly naive manner, with areas of patterning and a golden sky with Chinese-style cloud forms. The spandrels of the pavilion are decorated with blue and white patterns, resembling Persian tile decoration seen in manuscript painting, particularly of the Shiraz school.[1] In contrast to other pages, this folio represents a distinct style which is archaizing and more provincial, yet also markedly fresh.

According to the description provided in the text, Ravana's appearance was dazzling but terrible: he wore costly linen daubed with sandalwood, with a pearl necklace and arms laden with bracelets. His eyes were reddened and had a fierce gaze, and behind his protruding lips were brilliantly sharp teeth. His seat was a gem-studded crystal throne, surrounded by his four advisors and beautiful women.[2] While the painting does not represent all these details, it attempts to the show the splendor of the demon court in its varied depiction of individual figures.

NHH

1 Soudavar, 1992, p. 247, fig. 98b, shows a Shiraz painting with similar architectural elements.

2 Shastri tr., 1959, vol. 2, p. 454.

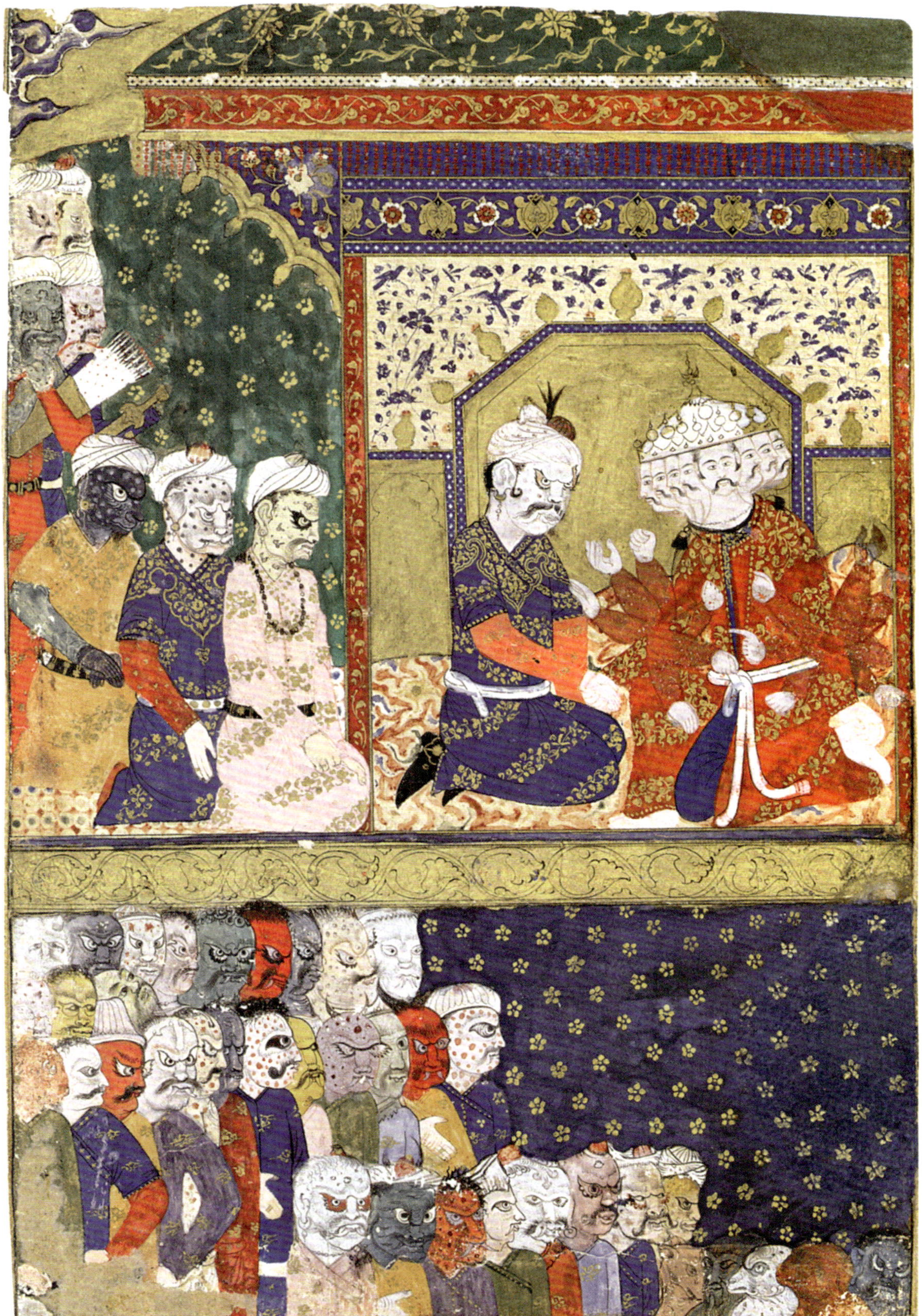

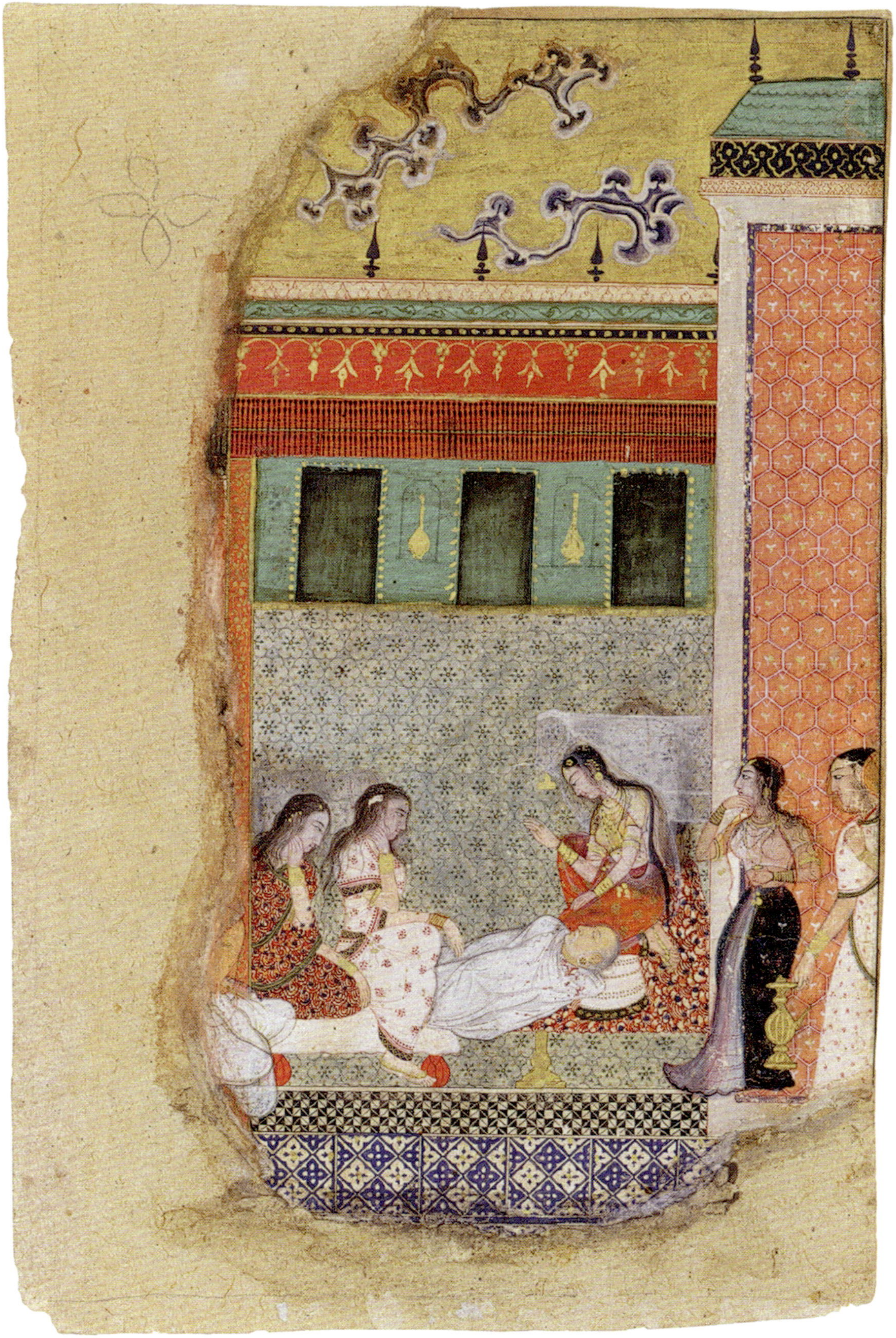

162

The death of King Dasharatha, father of Rama

FROM A DISPERSED RAMAYANA SERIES

Sub-imperial Mughal, ca. 1595–1605
Watercolor and gold on paper
On verso, eight lines of Sanskrit text; seal or stamp (probably of the Datia Palace) overlaid with paper
19 × 29 cm; (7 ½ × 11 ½ in.)
Metropolitan Museum of Art, New York, Cynthia Hazen Polsky and Leon B. Polsky Fund (2002.506)

KING DASHARATHA EMERGES IN THE *RAMAYANA* as essentially a noble character, though flawed by the weakness which allowed him to be swayed by his second wife Kaikeyi, whose ambitions for her own son caused the king to banish the crown prince Rama for fourteen years. Having succumbed to this pressure, Dasharatha took to his sickbed, plagued by regrets, where eventually he died of grief.[1] This folio shows the passing away of the king, draped with a simple white shroud and surrounded by his queens Kaushalya, Sumitra, and Kaikeyi, and female attendants. The women's grief is conveyed by their loose, disheveled hair and by the raising of their hands to the cheek in gestures of sorrow and disbelief. The damaged left side of the composition shows part of the folded legs and upper body of a male figure, possibly a priest. The intimacy of the scene and the focus of the figures around the delicately painted face of the king imbue the painting with a marked intensity of feeling.

The areas of dense patterning for which this *Ramayana* series is notable are seen here in the multiple panels all around the figures, and even the decorated textiles worn by the women. This patterning recalls folios from a much larger, imperial level manuscript of about thirty years earlier, the *Hamzanama*, which although different in scale and medium, also has striking passages of repeating designs as in this example.[2] The bold clouds in the gold sky above appear in other pages from the series.

NHH

1 H. P. Shastri tr., 1959, vol. 1, p. 318.

2 J. Seyller, 2002, pp. 206–7, no. 67, for similar designs on architecture.

163

Rama and his allies arrive at the shores of the ocean

FOLIO FROM A MANUSCRIPT OF THE RAMAYANA IN PERSIAN TRANSLATION

Mughal, ca. 1594
Opaque watercolor and gold on paper
38 x 26.5 cm (15 x 10 ½ in.)

THE SANSKRIT TEXT OF THE *RAMAYANA* was first translated into Persian under Akbar's command and finished in 1588: this is the lavishly illustrated imperial version now in Jaipur. Akbar also ordered other copies made for distribution around his court. This recently discovered *Ramayana*,[1] however, seems to have been translated anew in 1594 according to the colophon, and concentrates on key portions of the story rather than the more discursive original translation.[2] It was translated by Akbar's order, and seems to have been specifically meant for Akbar's mother, Hamida Banu Begum known as Mariyam Makani (see cat. no. 165). Two librarians' notes record that it was taken out for her in 1603, shortly before her death that same year, while another records it as part of her estate. It was then returned to the imperial library, since Jahangir records its coming into his possession on his accession in 1605, with the same inscription that he wrote on many other manuscripts in his father's great library. Stylistically all the known paintings from this manuscript are from the hands of lesser masters, and have a rather old-fashioned air to them, although text panels are kept to a minimum in accordance with the latest fashion of book illustrations of the 1590s. Leach suggests that the hands of only a small number of artists are present, and only one folio has an artistic attribution on it.[3]

This open and attractive folio from the end of the fifth book of the epic illustrates the arrival of Rama and Lakshmana with their allies, the monkeys and bears of Kishkindha, at the shores of the ocean opposite Lanka, where Sita has been taken by the demon Ravana. Rama and his brother Lakshmana have been borne all the way on the backs of the monkey leaders Hanuman and Angada. Rama and the monkey king Sugriva and the other leaders are discussing the size of the rocks which will be needed to build a causeway across the ocean to Lanka. Some monkeys rush around excitedly on seeing the ocean and even taste its waters, while others swing from trees in the background.

JPL

1 Other pages from this manuscript are published in Leach, 1998, pp. 40–49.

2 *Ibid.*, p. 43.

3 To an otherwise unknown Nur Muhammad; sold at Christie's, London, *Islamic art* sale, October 2000.

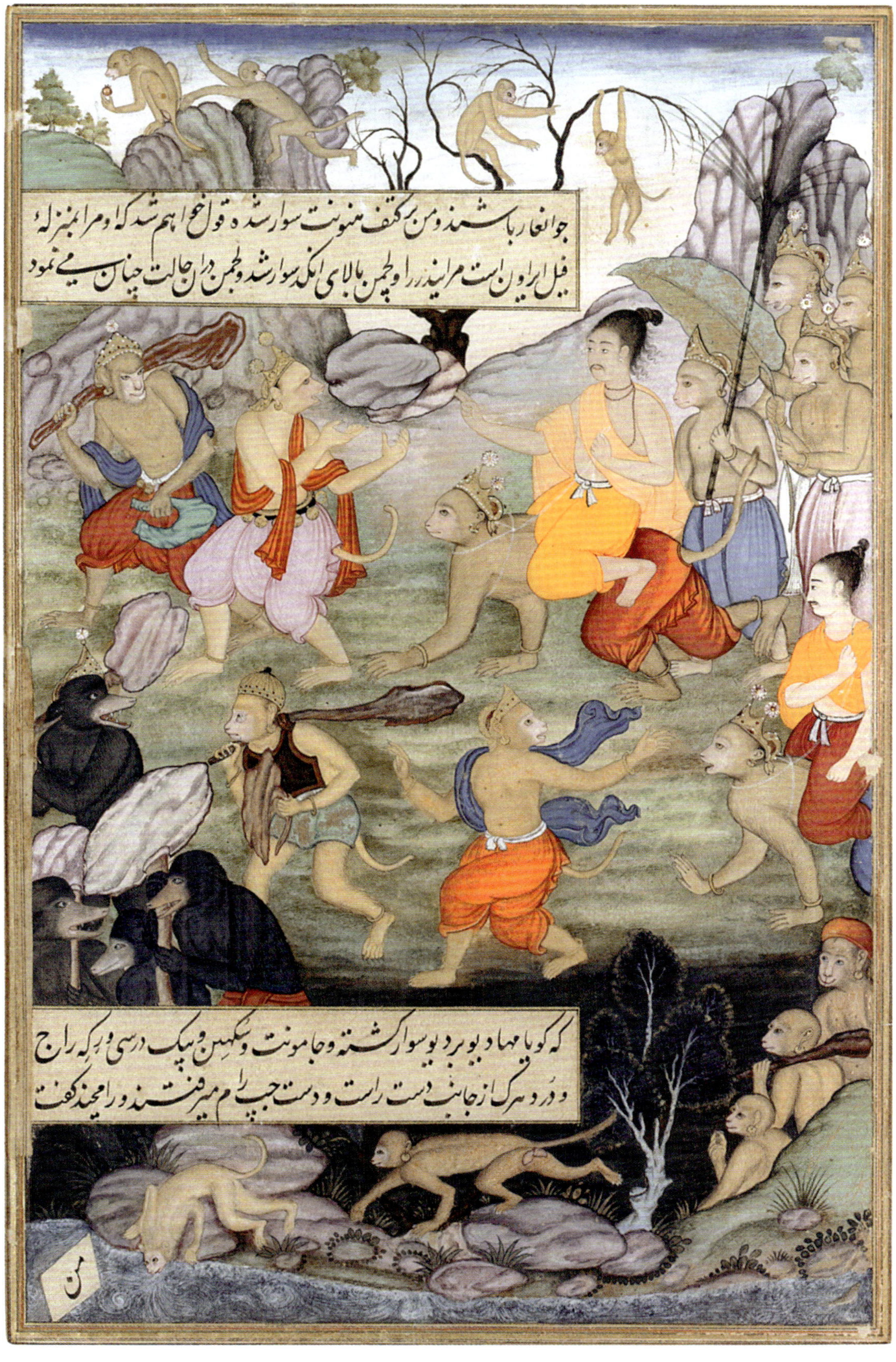

164

The siege of Ravana's palace at Lanka

FOLIO FROM A MANUSCRIPT OF THE RAMAYANA IN PERSIAN TRANSLATION

Mughal, ca. 1594
Opaque watercolor and gold on paper
38 × 26.5 cm (15 × 10 ¼ in.)

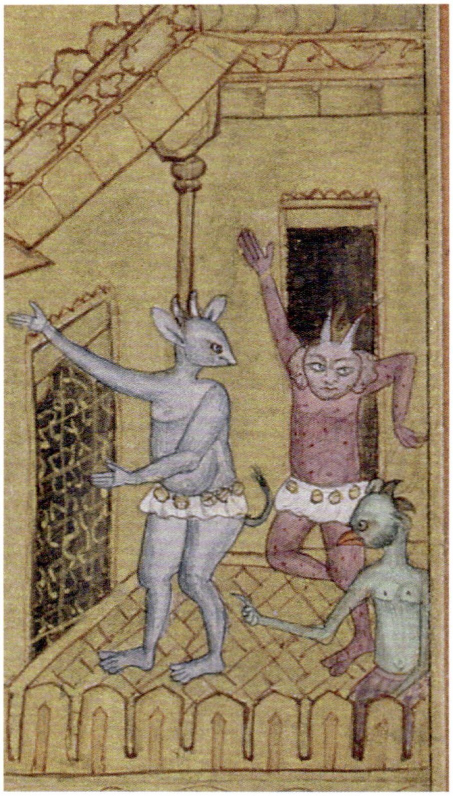

IN THIS FURTHER PAGE FROM A MUGHAL *RAMAYANA* probably made for Akbar's mother (see cat. no. 163), Rama and his allies have crossed the ocean and begin to besiege the great golden city of Lanka, at the beginning of the sixth book of the epic. They hold a conference outside the city, having been joined there by Ravana's brother Vibhishana, who is always depicted in human form. While the conference is going on the monkeys range around the outside of the city, but the serious fighting has yet to begin. The gates are still open, and through them and over the walls we can see the animal-headed demons within. Deer and jackals go about their business unconcernedly in the foreground. The buildings and pavilions within the city are all based on Akbari architecture of such palaces as Fatehpur Sikri. Only the spires would have been unfamiliar as buildings, since they are borrowed from the backgrounds of the European prints and paintings which had been flooding into the Mughal court since 1580.

Stylistically this, like the other illustrations in the manuscript, is very old-fashioned for the 1590s. While the more progressive artists in the studio were concentrating in this decade on the production of the great illustrated poetical manuscripts, other artists who had worked on the historical and epic manuscripts of the 1580s were presumably kept on to work on second versions of texts such as this, the *Akbarnama* (cat. no. 165), the *Baburnama* and so on, for distribution around the imperial household.

JPL

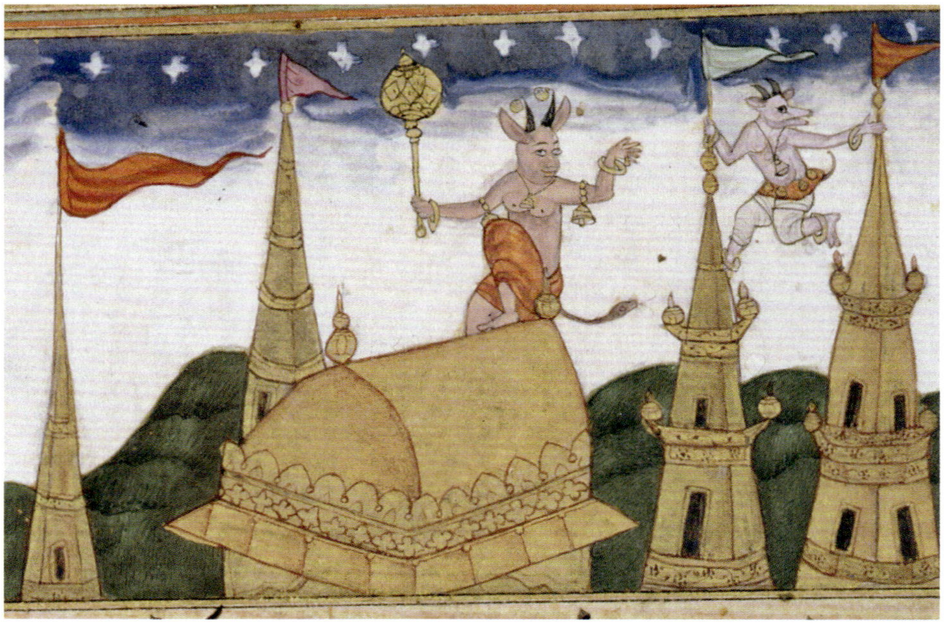

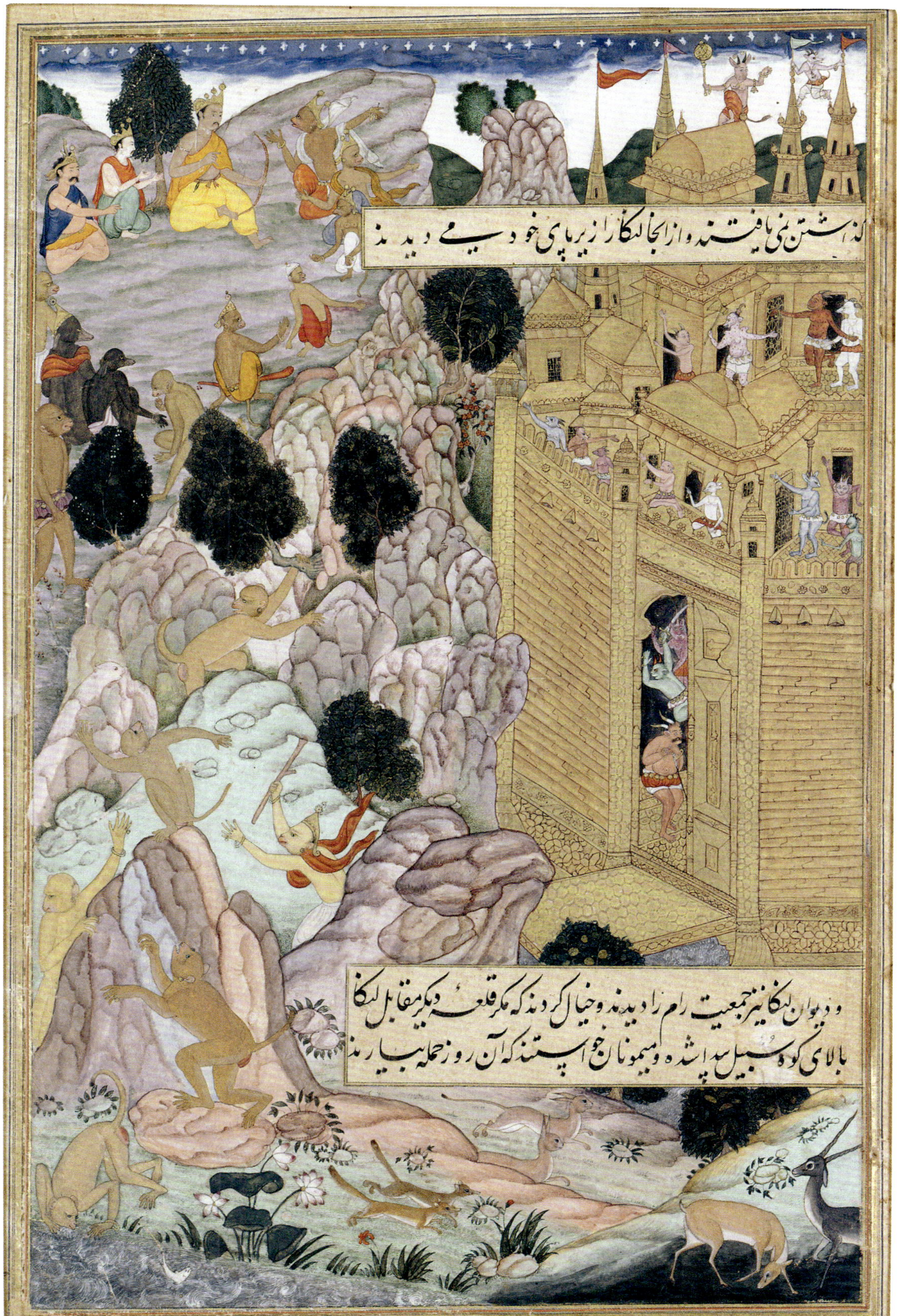
گذشتن نمی یافتند و از انجا لنکا را زیر پای خود می دیدند
و دیوان لنکا نیز جمعیت رام را دیدند و خیال کردند که مگر قلعهٔ دیگر مقابل لنکا
بالای کوه سُبیل پیدا شده و هیمونان خواستند که آن روز حمله بیارند

165

Festivities at the wedding of the Emperor Humayun and Hamida Banu Begum

FOLIO FROM AN AKBARNAMA MANUSCRIPT, NOW WITHIN A RED ALBUM BORDER

Mughal, ca. 1595. By the artist As, with portraits by Daulat
Opaque watercolor and gold on paper
Image 32.5 × 19 cm (12 ¾ × 7 ½ in.);
page 36 × 24 cm (14 × 9 ½ in.)
Inscribed in Persian below: "The [damaged] of His Majesty—the one whose abode is in Paradise—in the garden and the performing of the rites and the ladies who were in His Majesty's attendance;" "Work of As;" on the incense burner: "The portraits of both the distinguished faces are the work of Daulat;" inscribed above: "no. 76" (not related to its original position in the manuscript)

THIS FOLIO[1] COMES FROM NEITHER OF the well-known manuscripts of the *Akbarnama* (Abu'l Fazl's history of the reigns of Humayun and Akbar), named after their respective institutions the Victoria and Albert Museum and the British Library/Chester Beatty *Akbarnamas*, although many folios had previously escaped from both manuscripts. The former is the first illustrated version ca. 1590–95, presented to the Emperor as his friend Abu'l Fazl was still working on the text, the second is datable to around 1604, the date on one of the miniatures, and was probably begun after the murder of the author in 1602.[2] The present manuscript is known from a small number of folios, some of them such as this dispersed into album formats. Stylistically it is closer to the Victoria and Labert Museum manuscript than to the later one, and may be one of those ordered for members of the imperial family such as the Emperor's mother.

The inscription naming As as artist and describing the scene has of course been rewritten, since the page has been removed from the manuscript and mounted up in an album format with a new border. The rewritten description is slightly damaged, but there seems no doubt that this charming scene represents festivities shortly after the marriage of Humayun with the fourteen-year-old Hamida. The Emperor was fleeing westwards in 1540 into what is now Pakistan after his defeat by the Afghan Sher Shah Sur, and had reached Bhakkar on the Indus in the southern Punjab when his marriage took place around the middle of August 1541: "They pitched their tents at Rohri which is on the river bank and opposite Bukkur. His Majesty took up his quarters in a garden on the environs which was unequalled for pleasantness and delight. Charming houses had been erected there and were made illustrious by his presence."[3] Akbar was born in 1542 in the deserts of Sind as Humayun tried to reach safety in Iran.

In a pavilion within a garden walled off from the outside world, Humayun and Hamida sit opposite ladies of the imperial family while food is brought to them and music plays. Other ladies of the zenana amuse themselves within the cubicles around the walls by reading and other means—one has a child clinging to her. Details of costume and instruments reflect the Iranian and Chagatai Turkish culture of the early Mughal court, although the buildings are contemporary Mughal, while the curtain swags are borrowed from Renaissance art. The artist As has adopted, like other artists in the historical manuscripts forced to depict events within zenanas, the very high viewpoint that allows us to see over the walls and what is happening within. In this form of his name, As is known only from two paintings in the sub-imperial *Razmnama* of 1598.[4] It is debatable whether he is the same artist as 'Asi, who is known as the son of the early Akbari artist Mahesh and brother of the more celebrated Miskin; he worked mostly on the lesser historical manuscripts.[5] The only reliable inscription here, however, is that on the incense burner, where Daulat, just coming into prominence as a portraitist, writes that he did the principal faces.[6] The expression of happiness on the face of Humayun and of Hamida is indeed remarkable.

JPL

1 Other pages from this manuscript are published in Ashton ed., 1950, pl. 127, no. 664; Leach, 1998, no. 10; while a third has recently been acquired by the Cleveland Museum of Art (2003.38); see also L. Y. Leach, "Pages from an *Akbarnama*," in Crill et al. eds., (forthcoming, 2004).

2 Stronge, 2002, pp. 58–85; Losty, 1982, nos. 70–71; Leach, 1995, pp. 232–300.

3 The precise date of the wedding is unspecified in the *Akbarnama* (H. Beveridge tr., Calcutta, 1903–39, vol. 1, pp. 362–64).

4 British Library Or. 12076, ff. 35v and 62v; see S. P. Verma, *Mughal painters and their work*, Delhi, 1994, p. 69.

5 *Ibid.*, pp. 69–70; and Beach, 1981, p. 124 and *passim*.

6 For Daulat, see M. C. Beach, *The Grand Mogul*, Williamstown, 1978, pp. 113–16.

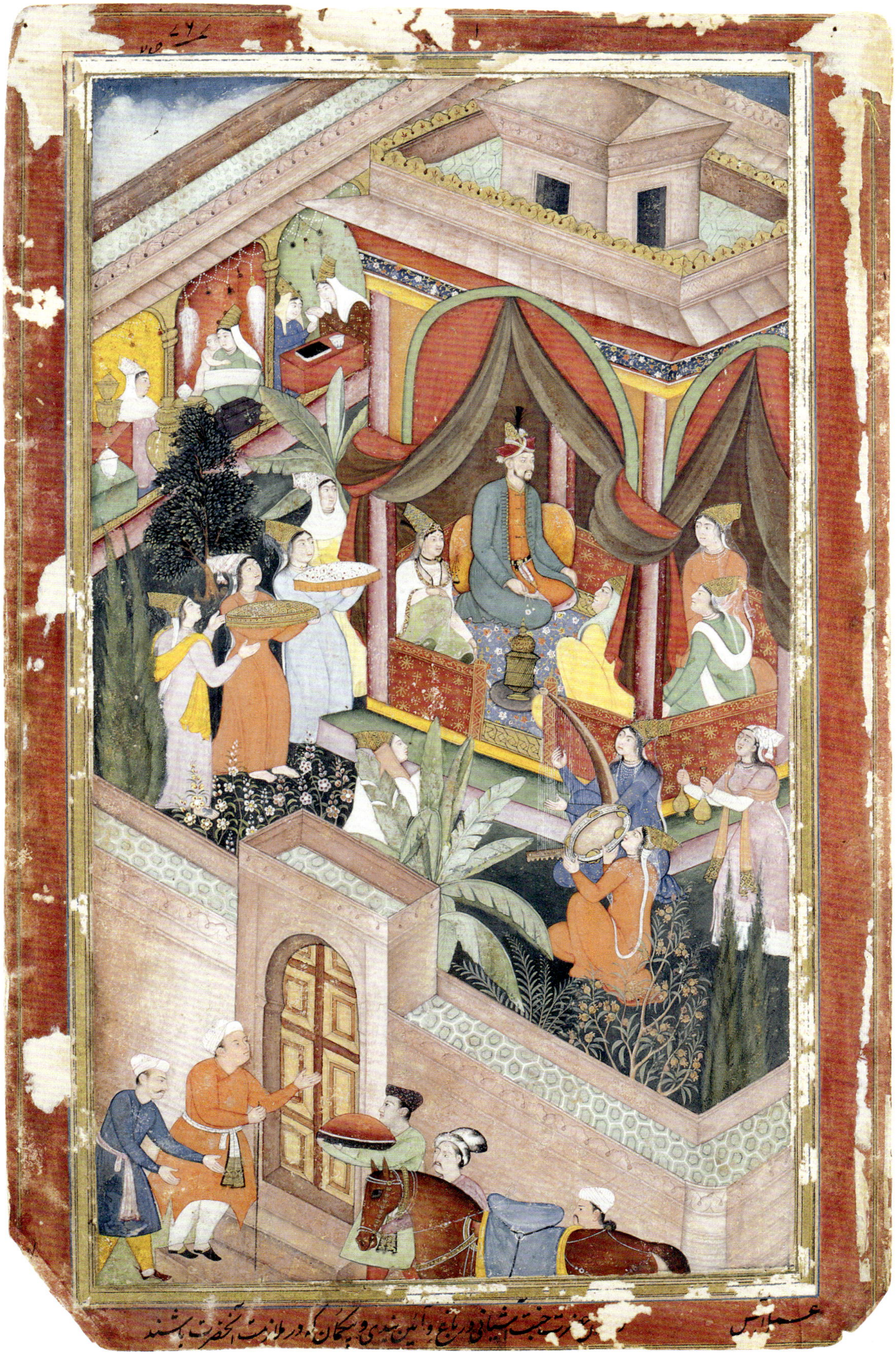
جنت آشیانی در باغ و آیین بندی و بیگمان که در ملازمت آنحضرت باشند

166

Krishna invites Radha to make love

ILLUSTRATION TO THE GITA GOVINDA OF JAYADEVA, PART XII

Udaipur, Rajasthan, ca. 1655–60. Style of Manohar
Opaque watercolor on paper
26 x 21 cm (10 ¼ x 8 ¼ in.)
Inscribed above with Hindi paraphrase text of the 23rd Canto; numbered 23
Published: T. McInerney, *Indian paintings from the Polsky Collections*, Princeton, 1982, no. 6
Metropolitan Museum of Art, New York, Gift of Cynthia Hazen Polsky (1985.398.12)

IN THE CLIMACTIC FINAL SECTION of Jayadeva's great poem, Radha has come to join Krishna in a forest grove. There, in the 23rd Canto, he woos her in impassioned terms:

> *Throbbing breasts aching for loving embrace are hard to touch.*
> *Rest these vessels on my chest! Quench love's burning fire!...*[1]

Krishna makes a (slightly archaic) *mudra* or hand-gesture of speech or exposition, while Radha sits demurely listening to his amorous discourse and her companions behind the trees exchange a meaning glance. The mood of erotic expectation is conveyed less by the figures' attitudes than by the intensity of color—in the hot orange ground and the red interior of the love-bower with its water-vessels and hanging garlands—and by the rhythmic patterns of the plantains, palms, cypresses and other trees. This boldly simplified but expressive style, which reverts to some extent to the Early Rajput conventions of the sixteenth century (cat. nos. 54–55), is typical of the work-shop of Manohar, an artist active at Udaipur in the 1640s and '50s.[2] The series to which it belongs is a reworking of the compositions of the 1629 *Gita Govinda* series by Sahibdin,[3] the leading Udaipur master of the period. In Sahibdin's treatment of this subject,[4] the landscape is considerably lusher and, instead of sitting apart, Krishna is already reaching out to embrace Radha. The reinterpretation of the subject by the Manohar workshop is drier and more static but still has a clarity and emotional force of its own.

AT

---

1 *Gita Govinda*, XII, v.5; Miller tr., 1977, p. 122.

2 Topsfield, 2002, pp. 75–76, 88–91.

3 A. Topsfield, "Sahibdin's illustrations to the *Gita-Govinda*," in A. Krishna ed., *Chhavi-2: Rai Krishnadasa Felicitation Volume*, Varanasi, 1981, pp. 236–37, figs. 511, 513–14.

4 *Ibid.*, fig. 507 (in the Palace Library, Jodhpur).

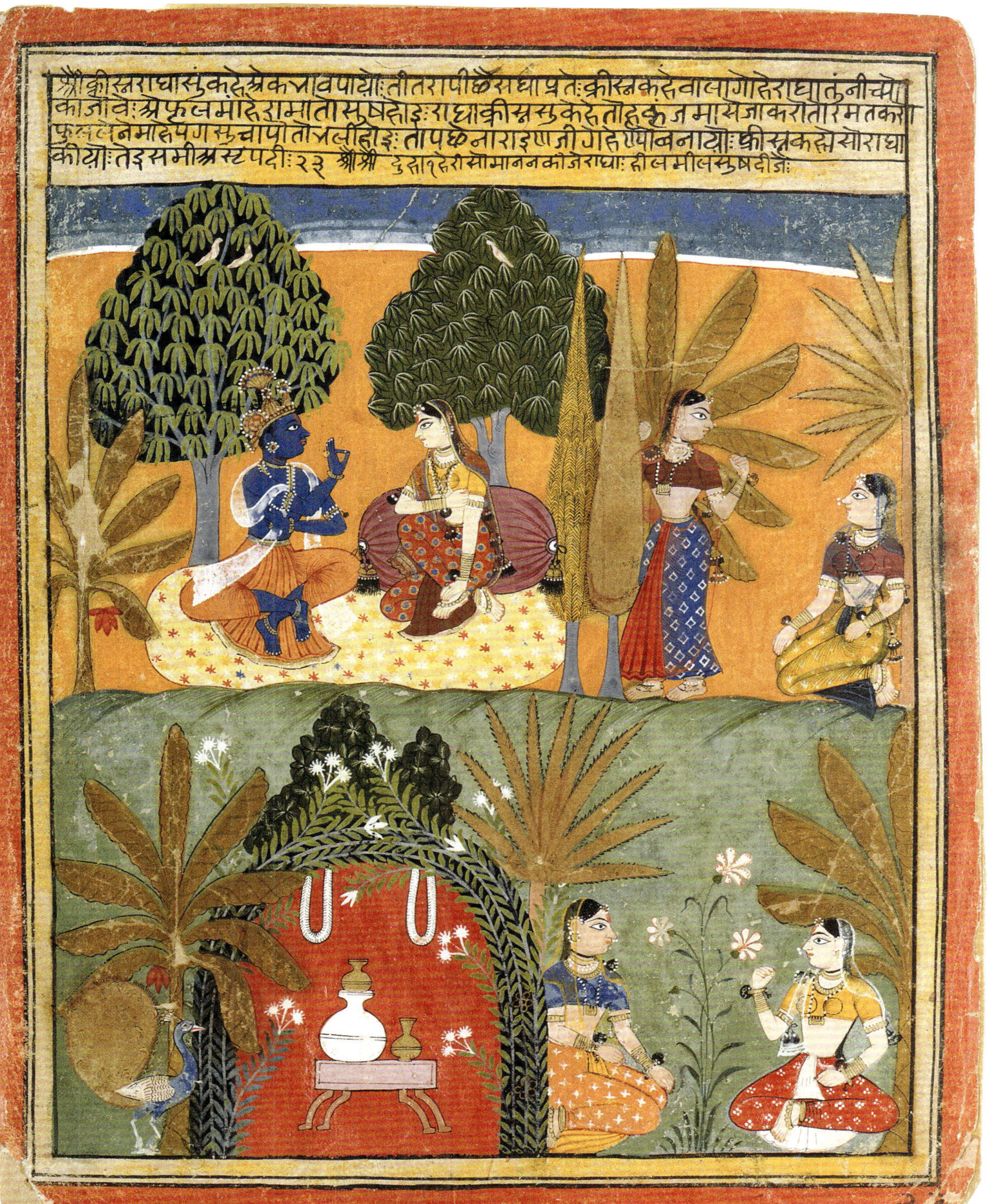

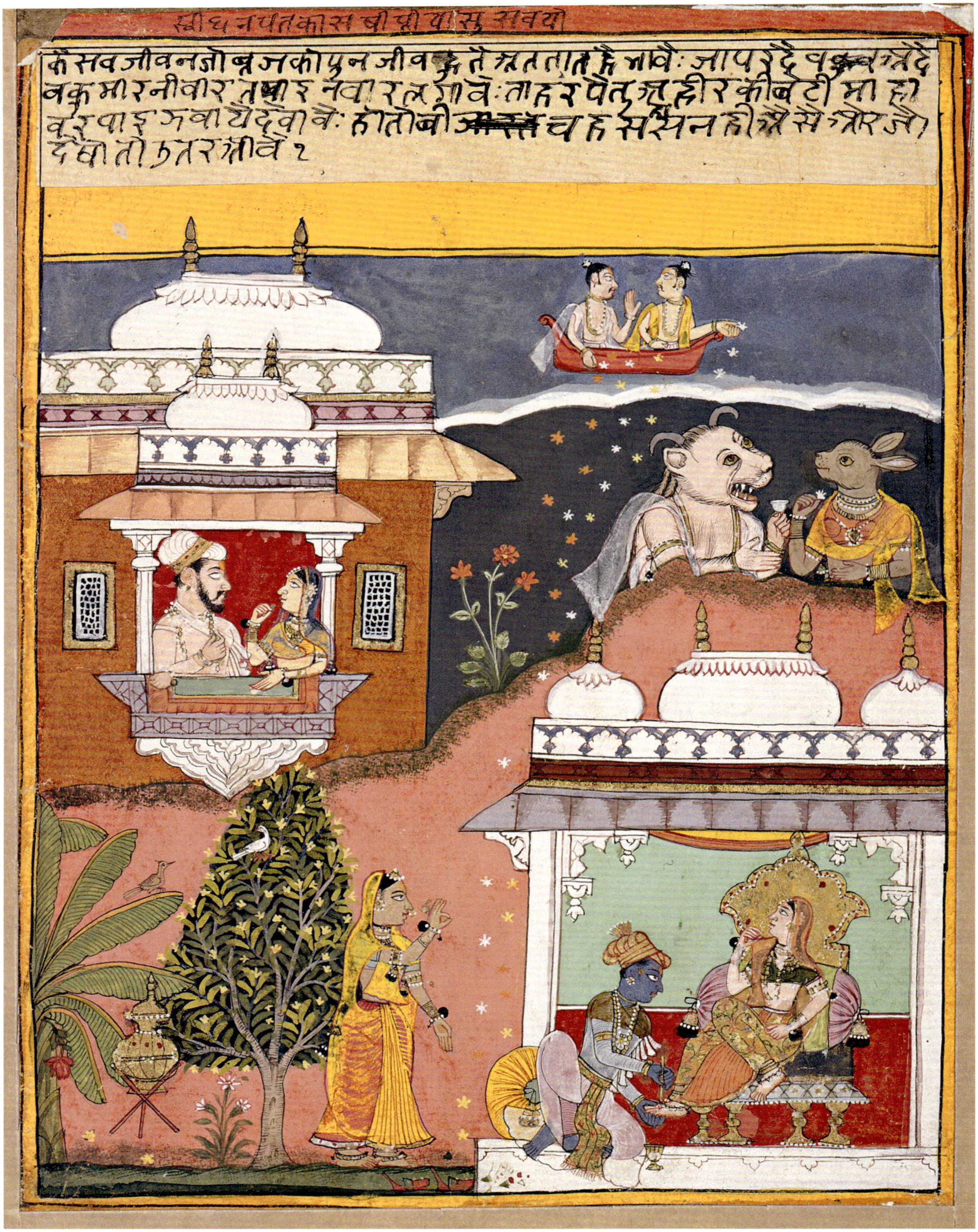

167

Krishna cleans and adorns Radha's feet

ILLUSTRATION TO THE RASIKAPRIYA OF KESHAV DAS

Udaipur, Rajasthan, ca. 1660
Opaque watercolor on paper
27.3 × 21 cm (10 ¼ × 8 ¼ in.)
Inscribed above with Hindi verses (*RP* VII.5) on added paper; Bikaner inventory date on reverse (VS 1751 / 1694 AD)
Private collection

IN THE *RASIKAPRIYA*, A POETICAL TREATISE on types of lovers and their emotions, Keshav offers two classifications of *nayikas* or ideal heroines. One is based on their physical characteristics, the other on their typical conduct and behavior. First in the latter category is the svadhinapatika, the nayika who is loyally loved by her husband and whose virtues bind him to her will. In an example of this type, Radha (as the nayika) sits enthroned while Krishna devotedly performs the humble task of cleaning her soles with a pumice stone and painting her toes. Her female companion (*sakhi*), standing to the left, remarks wonderingly to Radha that she, a mere cowherd's daughter, is having her feet cleaned by the Lord of the Universe:

> *. . . by that beloved*
> *Krishna, O daughter of an Ahir!*
> *By pumice stone you get your soles scrubbed,*
> *And with red dye get stained your feet!*[1]

To elaborate the point, two further harmonious couples appear in the painting, exemplifying further conjugal harmony in the human and demonic realms: a Raja and lady converse at a palace window, while a horned demon and a winsome demoness engage in a pleasant chat behind a hill. Above, celestial deities shower petals which fall to earth near Krishna.

This page belongs to one of several mid-seventeenth century *Rasikapriya* series from Udaipur[2] which are based on compositions devised by the leading local master Sahibdin in the 1630s[3]. As in cat. no. 166, the later artist here has a flatter and coarser style than that of Sahibdin, but his interpretation retains a robust charm.

AT

1 *RP* VII, v.5; Bahadur tr., 1972, p. 112; e.g. compare also for this subject, Randhawa, 1962, fig. 31, pp. 63–64.

2 Fify-four pages from this series were formerly in the Bikaner Royal Collection, and were inventoried there in 1694; see Topsfield, 2002, pp. 90–91, fig. 53b, for discussion and references.

3 *Ibid.*, pp. 65–67, 91, figs. 35–37, 53a; also A. Topsfield, "Sahibdin's illustrations to the *Rasikapriya*," *Orientations*, 17, 3, March 1986, pp. 18–31; V. Desai, "From illustrations to icons: The changing context of the *Rasikapriya* paintings in Mewar," in B. N. Goswamy ed., *Indian painting: Essays in honour of Karl J. Khandalavala*, New Delhi, 1995, pp. 97–127.

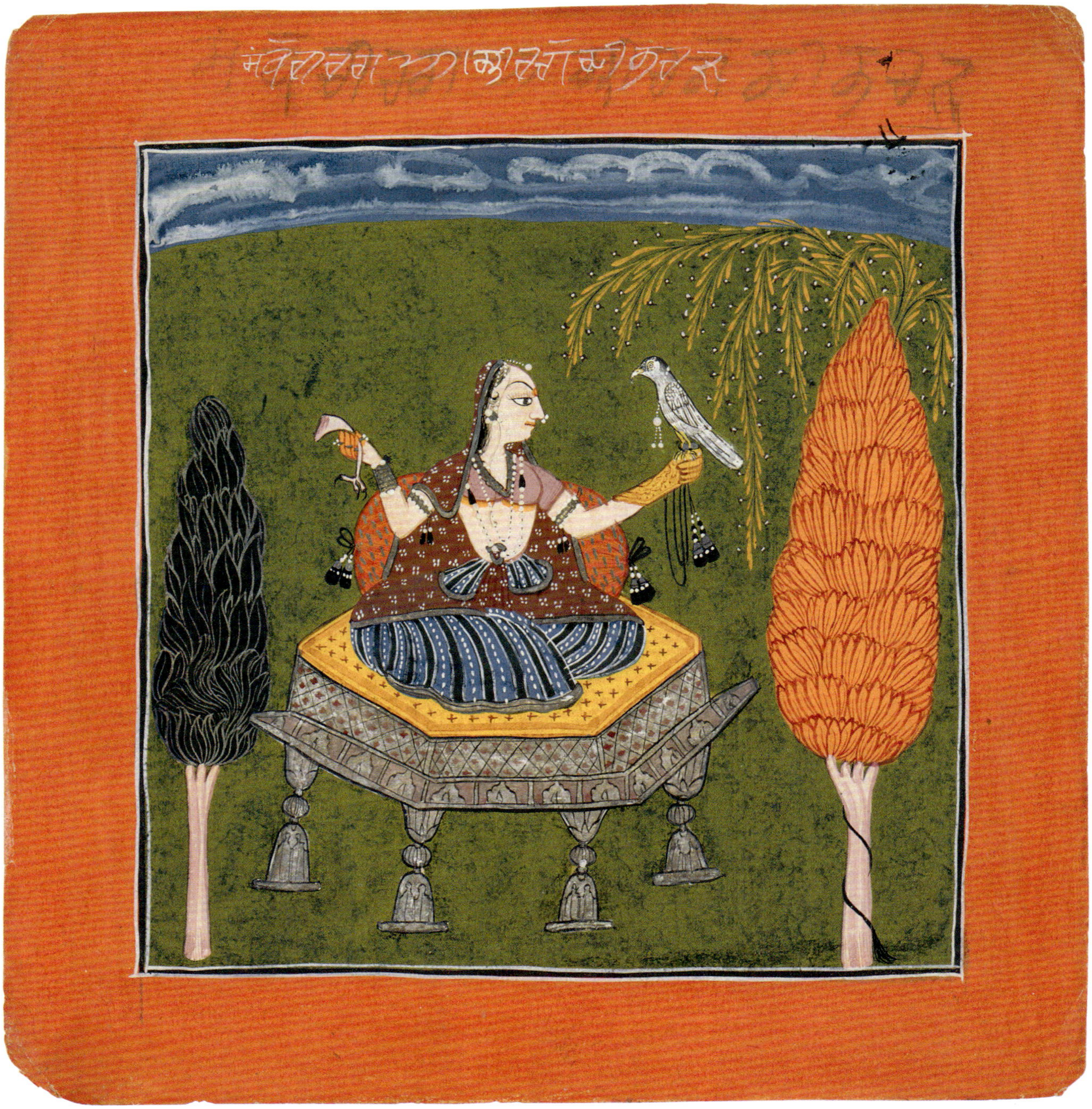

168

A lady with a hawk

ILLUSTRATION TO THE MUSICAL MODE SAMVERI RAGINI

Bahu or Kulu, Punjab Hills, ca. 1700–1710
Opaque watercolor with silver on paper
Image 15.9 × 15.6 cm (6 ¼ × 6 ⅛ in.);
page 20.6 × 20.6 cm (8 ⅛ × 8 ⅛ in.)
Inscribed above twice in takri script: *samveri ragani sri rage di bharaja* ("Samveri *ragini*, wife of Shri")
Published: D. J. Ehnbom, *Indian miniatures: The Ehrenfeld Collection*, New York, 1985, no. 94
Metropolitan Museum of Art, New York, Cynthia Hazen Polsky and Leon B. Polsky Fund (2002.178)

THE MUSICAL MODE SAMVERI is depicted as a lady sitting on a hexagonal seat, holding a hawk on her gloved wrist. In her other hand she holds the leg of a large bird such as a crane: she will presumably feed this titbit to her hawk.[1] On each side are tightly bunched, tapering trees of contrasting color, with a trailing willow spray. A narrow band of sky appears above the deep green ground color. This painting belongs to a dispersed *ragamala* ("Garland of Ragas") series, originally of eight-four pages.[2] In the Pahari *ragamala* system followed here, each of the six male ragas is given five 'wives' (*ragini*) and eight subordinate ragas or "sons" (*ragaputra*). Samveri ragini is a wife of Shri Raga, and in this series she shares with other members of that family the same matching background and border colors. Such solitary ragini figures are sometimes also interpreted as representing *virahini nayikas* or heroines who experience the pain of separation from their lover (for whom the hawk, in this case, may perhaps stand as a surrogate). The style of this artist, which shows strong affinities with the earlier phase (Archer's "Style I") of the contemporary Shangri *Ramayana* series project (cat. nos.47–49), has a powerful, nervous intensity, using rich and unusual color combinations and an energetic, wiry line.

AT

1 The unusual detail of the bird-leg does not appear in the drawing of Samveri in K. Ebeling, 1973, fig. 333, p. 282; and other Pahari versions of Samveri sometimes show a lady with a dog, not a bird.

2 Thirty-two pages are in the Victoria and Albert Museum, London, and six in the Boston Museum of Fine Arts; see Archer, 1973, s.v. Kulu, nos. 13 (i–xxxii); also e.g. Coomaraswany, 1926, nos. 67–72, pls. 232–33; Archer and Binney, 1968, no. 59; Archer, 1976, pl. 53; Goswamy and Fischer, 1992, nos. 34–35.

169

A prince and lady in a chamber

ILLUSTRATION TO THE MUSICAL MODE HARSHA RAGAPUTRA

Basohli, Punjab Hills, ca. 1700–10
Opaque watercolor with silver, gold, and beetle-wing case on paper
Image 15.6 × 17.5 (6 ⅛ × 6 ⅞ in.);
page 20.3 × 20 cm (8 × 7 ⅞ in.)
Inscribed above in takri and devanagari with the name of Harsha *ragaputra*, son of Bhairava
Published: R. K. Tandan, *Pahari ragamalas*, Bangalore, 1983, fig. 10; P. Pal et al., *Pleasure gardens of the mind: Indian paintings from the Jane Greenough Green Collection*, Los Angeles, 1993, no. 37.

THE MUSICAL MODE HARSHA, whose name means joy or rapture, is classified in the Pahari *ragamala* system (see also cat. no. 168) as a son (*ragaputra*) of Bhairava raga; its essential sound is compared by the theorist Kshemakarna to that of running water.[1] Harsha appears in Pahari painting as a standing or seated nobleman dallying with a lady, sometimes in or near a chamber. Here, within a pavilion in a Mughal-derived decorative style, next to a pencil-thin cypress standing against a hot orange ground, a young prince with large, expressive eye makes overtures with a delicate hand gesture to his willing lady. The sense of amorous tension is enhanced by the rich concatenations of color and pattern, almost like expressive musical phrases and rhythmic runs to which the yellow border acts as a constant tonic drone note. The prince's flaring sash-ends make a dramatic foreground accent, against the fluid, converging stripes of his jama and the lady's half-revealed paijama.

Discovered relatively recently, this *ragamala* series with sixty-five extant pages once belonged to the family of a former Basohli court astrologer. As with cat. no. 168, the border and background colors are coordinated throughout the series according to the raga family (here yellow and orange, respectively, for a Bhairava family member).[2]

AT

1 Tandan, *Pahari ragamalas*, pp. 72–73.
2 *Ibid.*, pp. 49–50.

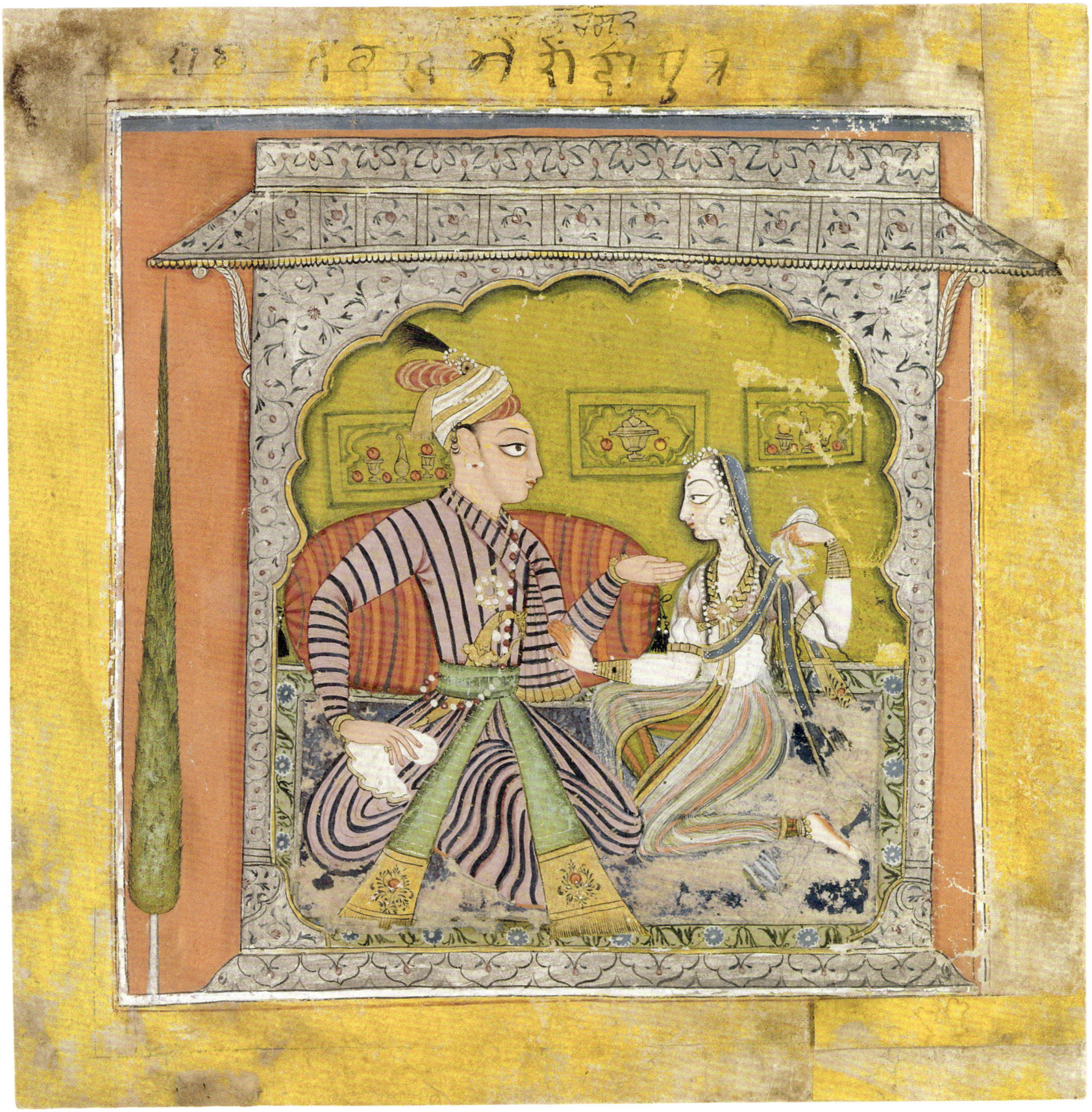

170

A prince chewing betel while being fanned

ILLUSTRATION TO THE MUSICAL MODE MALKOS RAGA

Popular Mughal style, perhaps in Rajasthan, ca. 1610–20
Opaque watercolor and gold on paper
25.4 × 20 cm. (9 ¾ × 7 ¾ in.)
Inscribed above in Sanskrit:
[ni]tambinicamaracalanena labdhanicolam krtahemapithah / gandharvarat kancanakanti[radhyah] sriman ayam malayapancamakhyah //7// malavakausikaraga ("His coat moved by the fanning from the fan of the lovely-hipped lady, a throne of gold made for him, the handsome and wealthy Lord of the Gandharvas is that lord known as the fifth Malaya. [This is] Malavakaushika Raga")
Published: P. Pal, *Indo-Asian art: The John Gilmore Ford collection*, Baltimore, 1971, no. 31; T. McInerney, *Indian paintings from the Polsky collections*, Princeton, 1982, no. 2
Metropolitan Museum of Art, New York, Gift of Cynthia Hazen Polsky (1987.424.14)

THIS PAGE COMES FROM A DISPERSED *RAGAMALA* ("Garland of the Ragas") series illustrating the thirty-six modes of Indian music, with Sanskrit poetical inscriptions.[1] *Ragamala* paintings illustrate not the mood of the musical mode, but rather the verses, anonymous as well as authored, which had become attached to that mode over the centuries. There were various systems of classification of the modes of *ragamalas*, but those most in common use identified six major ragas, each with five dependent 'wives' or raginis. Malkos is the second raga of the Painters' system (hence numbered 7 in this set), and the verse describes, and the painter illustrates, a prince, as handsome as a king of the Gandharvas (musicians of the gods), seated on a golden throne, his back to the lovely lady waving a chowry over him as he chews his betel. Undescribed in the text is the ardent look which the lady gives him, and the adjacent empty bed which awaits them. Both betel-chewing and fanning are conceits used in Indian poetry to cool the ardour of love. The iconography, with the prince's back to the lady who fans him, follows the earliest known visualizations of this raga, whereas later ones make the erotic flavour more obvious as the prince dallies with one lady while others surround them waving fans or playing instruments. The iconography of this painting is very close to that in the slightly earlier Popular Mughal "Manley" *ragamala*, which has almost the same verse.[2] Our scribe has attempted to make better sense of the verse's conclusion by substituting Malaya or 'perfumed breeze from the south' for the Malava or "prince from Malwa" of the Manley verse.[3]

Various sets of *ragamalas* and similar short Sanskrit texts were produced from the 1590s into the early seventeenth century in which the Mughal style has been adapted to fit Hindu sensibilities. Instead, however, of the flat backdrop colors and conceptualized architecture of Early Rajput painting, which continue into some Rajput schools such as that of Mewar, some elements of landscape and three-dimensional architecture have been introduced, although the paintings remain very simple in their compositions and coloring. Some seem to have been done for the Rajput courtiers based in Agra, others very likely in Rajput courts such as Amber and Bikaner. The iconography of this raga, and of another from the same set in Los Angeles, are closely replicated in a *ragamala* from Bikaner of about 1650 in the British Library.[4] It contrasts with the iconography of Malkos Raga from other contemporary sets such as that from Chawand in Mewar of 1605.[5]

JPL

1 Other pages from this set are published in Pal, *Indo-Asian art: The John Gilmore Ford collection*, no. 31; and Pal, 1993, no. 90.

2 Now in the British Museum, reproduced A. Dahmen-Dallapiccola, *Ragamala-Miniaturen von 1475 bis 1700*, Wiesbaden, 1975, p. 127. An imperial quality Malkos Raga of ca. 1600 following this subtle iconography, but apparently without text (see also cat. no. 172), is reproduced in Maggs Bros., *Bulletin* no. 14, London, 1968, no. 63.

3 See Ebeling, 1973, pp. 118–28, for a discussion of this *ragamala* text and its importance for the Rajasthani and other traditions of *ragamala* painting; Ebeling does not note this textual variant.

4 Pal, *Indian painting*, no. 90, for the Los Angeles painting; and Falk and Archer, 1981, nos. 505, xii and xv, for the Bikaner set.

5 Reproduced in Dahmen-Dallapiccola, *op. cit.*, p. 125; this has two fanning ladies and male musicians.

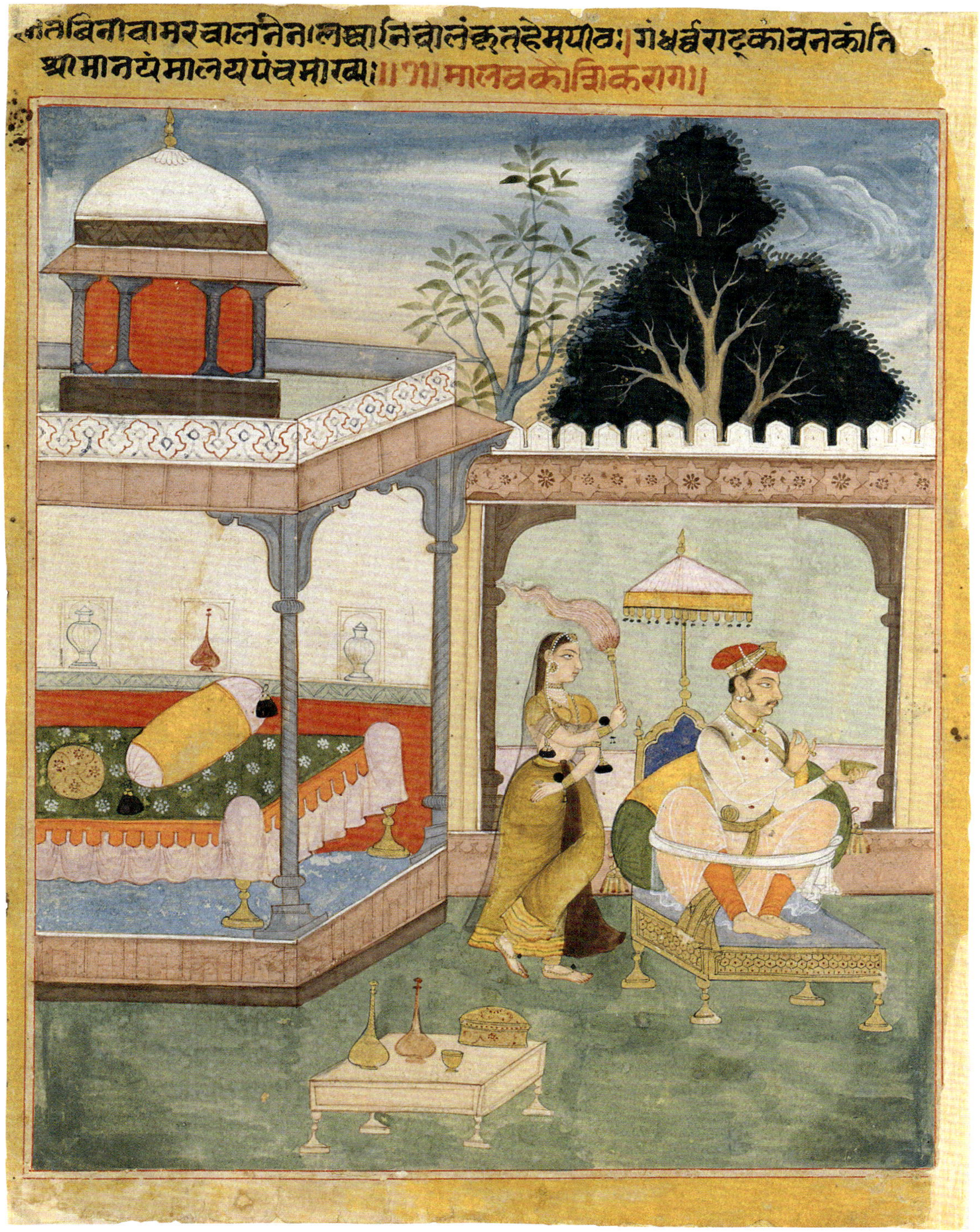
मालवकोशिकराग

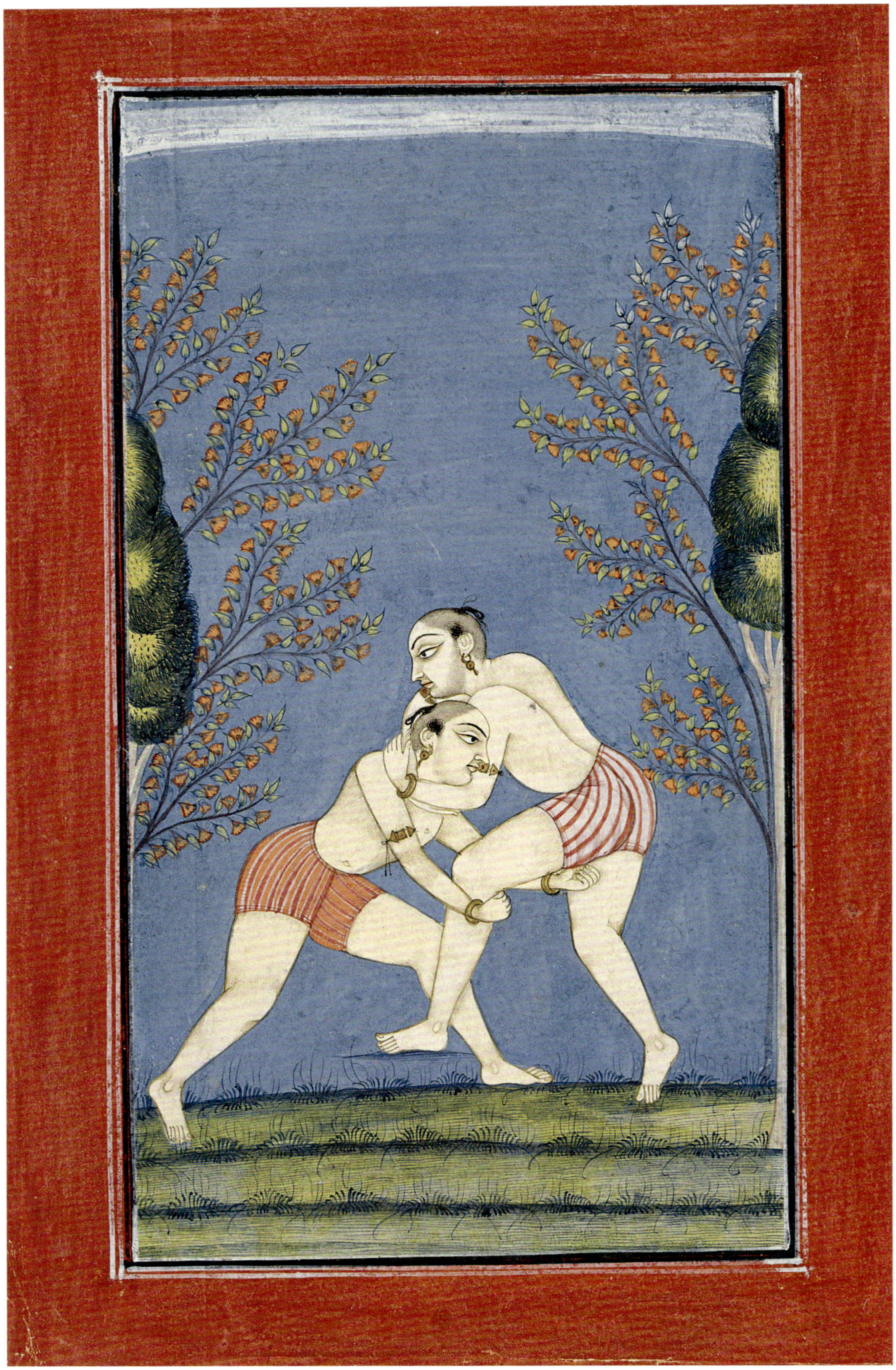

171

Two wrestlers

ILLUSTRATION TO THE MUSICAL MODE MALAVA RAGAPUTRA

Bilaspur, Punjab Hills, ca. 1730–40
Opaque watercolor on paper
26 × 17.1 cm (10 ¼ × 6 ¾ in.)
On reverse, identifying inscriptions in takri and devanagari (*sri rage da putra rag malava duva* 2 / *patra* 8)
Published: T. McInerney, *Indian paintings from the Polsky Collections,* Princeton, 1982, no. 19

THE MUSICAL MODE MALAVA is classified as a son (*ragaputra*) of Shri Raga; according to the theorist Kshemakarna, its essential sound is like that made by the stewing of food.[1] Malava is depicted in Pahari painting as a pair of wrestlers in combat; in one variant, in a slightly later Bilaspur *ragamala* in Berlin, they comprise a male and a female wrestler,[2] adding a further level of suggestion to the image. The present painting has been identified as belonging to the earliest of the several related *ragamala* sets painted at Bilaspur in the mid-eighteenth century.[3] Wearing striped drawers, the two wrestlers grapple decorously in a pleasant grove with blossoming fronds spilling out across the blue ground.

Wrestling has always been a popular sport in India (cat. no. 86), and professional wrestlers (*Jethi*) were a common feature of Rajput court life in former times. Each Raja would retain his own corps of wrestlers to provide regular entertainment for the court, or to take part in occasional challenge matches against neighboring courts.[4]

AT

1 Waldschmidt, 1967, p. 45.

2 *Ibid.*, fig. 8.

3 McInerney, 1982, pp. 29–30; Archer, 1973, s.v. Kahlur (Bilaspur), nos. 31 (i-ii).

4 E.g. Topsfield, 1990, no. 1.

172

A prince dancing in a grove with musicians

ILLUSTRATION TO THE MUSICAL MODE VASANTA RAGINI

Mughal, ca. 1610
Opaque watercolor and gold on paper
21.5 × 15 cm (8 ½ × 6 in.)

IN THIS PAGE FROM A *RAGAMALA* SERIES, a prince holding a vina and a vase of flowers is dancing to the rhythm of the drum and the cymbals played by his female companions. Vasanta is the epitome of spring, when new life is springing in the bud and all of nature dances. One of the most joyous of the *ragamala* subjects, it became associated in the Rajasthani tradition with Krishna dancing with the milkmaids of Vrindavan, but at the early date of this painting Vasanta is still conceived of as a prince. The iconography here is close to that of other early *ragamala* sets in the Popular Mughal tradition such as the "Manley" *Ragamala* and the early Johnson *Ragamala*, which both include a landscape retreating to finely formed hills on the horizon.[1]

There is no text accompanying this raga subject. It is an exceptionally refined painting which belongs more to the imperial Mughal tradition than to the Popular or sub-imperial Mughal styles associated with Agra and the northern Rajput courts (cat. no. 170).[2] The vigor of the dancing which can be seen in examples from the latter styles of this period is here also, but conveyed not through linear means but through the physical displacements of these modeled forms. The depth within the landscape behind the dancers is most beautifully conveyed through subtle shading and shadows. Vasanta and the player of the double-ended drum (*pakhavaj*) are gazing at each other ardently: she is slightly behind him, so there is a reason, not just convention, for his being portrayed in full profile.

JPL

1 See A. Dahmen-Dallapiccola, *Ragamala-Miniaturen von 1475 bis 1700*, Wiesbaden, 1975, pp. 267–68.

2 There is some evidence for imperial-quality *ragamala* subjects, e.g. a Malkos Raga from Jahangir's Allahabad period (1599–1604), as noted in cat. no. 170, n.2.

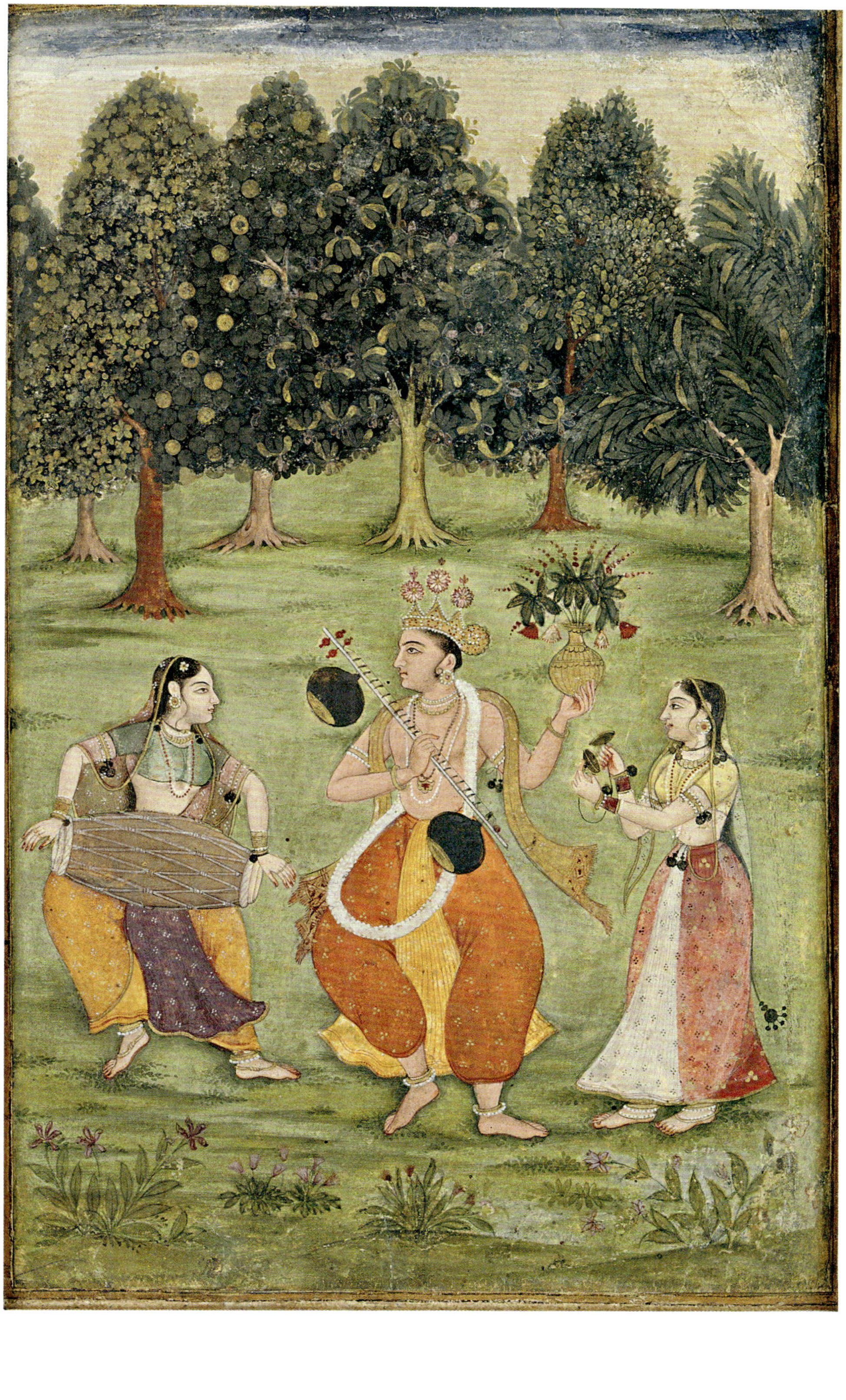

173

The swing

DECCAN, 1700–25

Opaque watercolor and gold on paper
Image 20 × 15.1 cm, (7 7/8 × 6 in.);
page 24.4 × 18.7 cm, (9 5/8 × 7 3/8 in.)

AN ARTIST HAS TAKEN ADVANTAGE of our understanding of painters' conventions to startle us. Instead of merging his blue-green ground into his yellowish background and so suggesting the landscape behind the subject, he starkly differentiates them, thereby turning his yellow background into the sky and the subject into a starkly beautiful silhouette. We are ravished by the cool palette—the pink and dull blue of the swing pusher, the grey and green of the tree—and so the mauve and red garments of the girls on the swing stands out the more. Pairs of hoopoes and crows on the tree and a pair of deer below gaze at the girls in wonderment that they have no menfolk. The subject is as it were trying to be Hindola Raga, in which a lord sits in a swing with his lady: this is a spring raga, so nature is waiting for the cold weather to be over and for spring to arrive. The composition is developed out of more generic paintings of girls on swings, such as an early eighteenth-century Mughal painting in the Bibliothèque Nationale, Paris.[1]

Although the spirit of this enchanting painting, with its flying shawls and ravishing colors, seems to come from the late seventeenth-century Deccan, its general flatness indicates a later date. The girls are wearing the skirt and bodice of the eighteenth century, but instead of the enveloping transparent sari, they still retain their earlier shawls (see cat. nos. 94, 127). Trees in this starkly bare manner seem a feature of Hyderabad painting in the eighteenth century.[2] It seems then best to place it for the moment in the early eighteenth century.

JPL

1 Bibliothèque Nationale, *A la cour du Grand Moghol*, Paris, 1986, no. 81.

2 Examples in Falk and Archer, 1981, include nos. 426–xxiv (ca. 1760), 427–iv (ca. 1770) and 429 (ca. 1780).

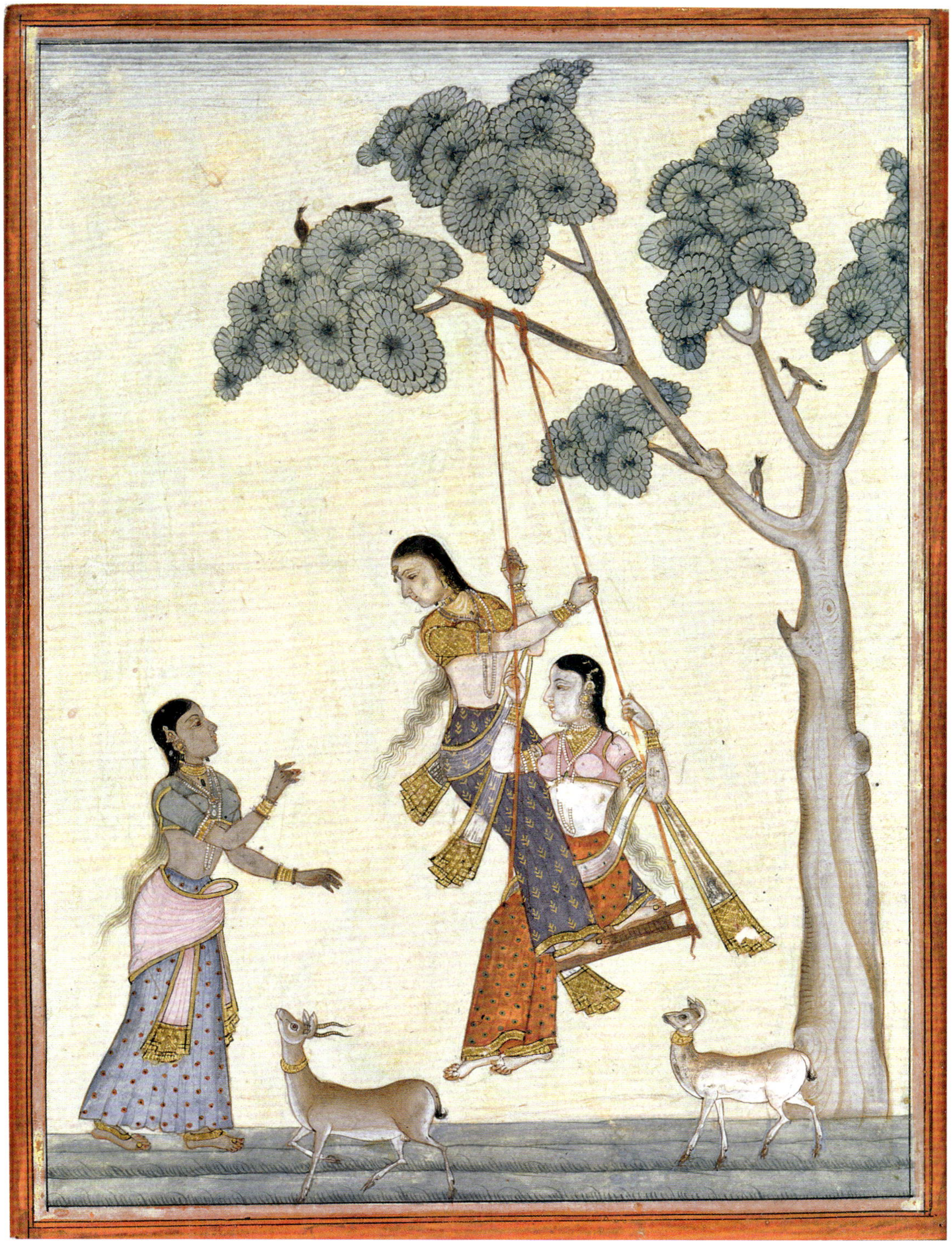

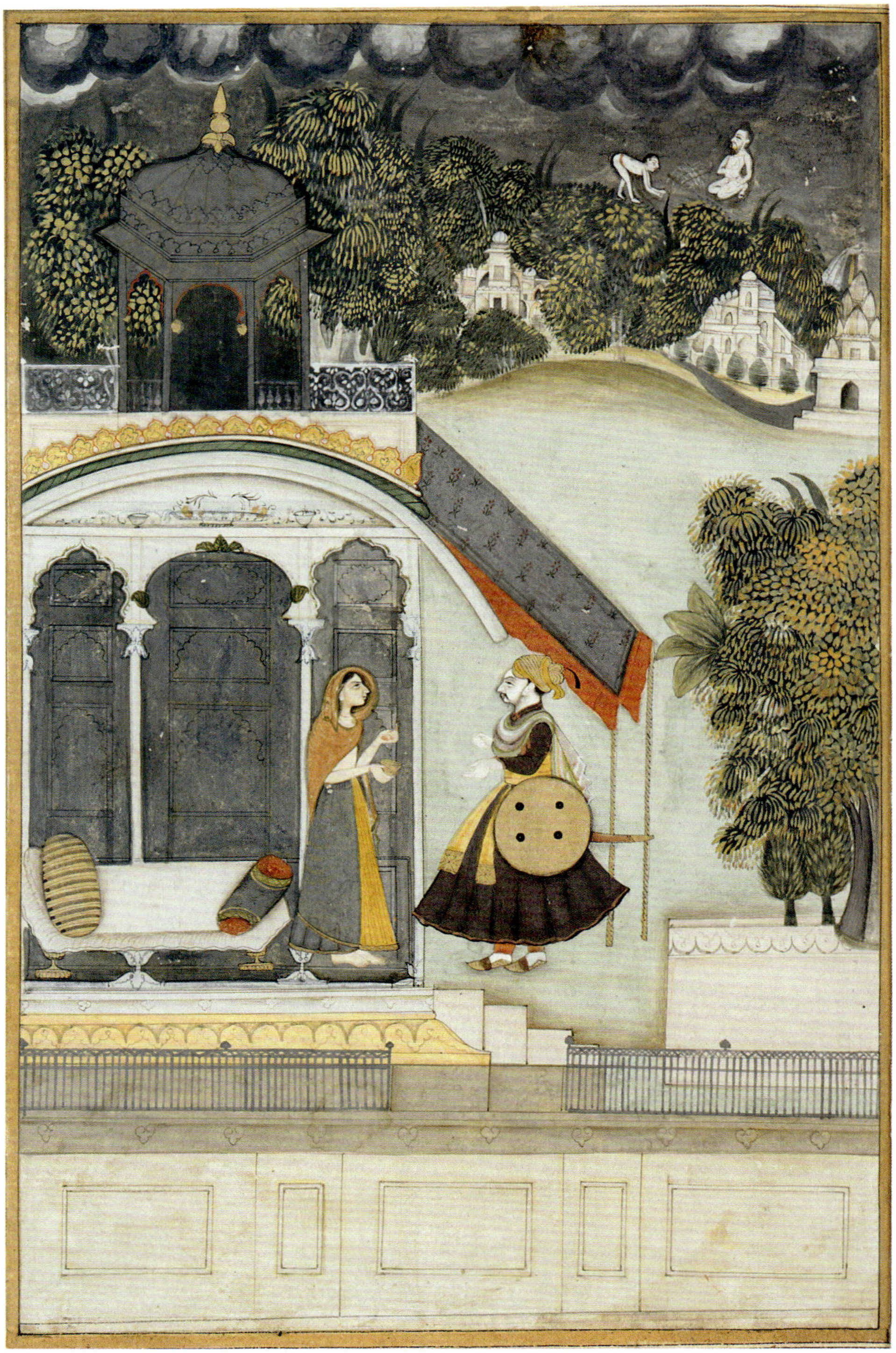

174

Lovers meeting in the rainy season

ILLUSTRATION TO A SERIES OF BARAMASA

Bikaner, Rajasthan, ca. 1725.
Attributed to Murad
Opaque watercolor with silver and gold on paper
On verso, several lines from an unrelated Persian narrative describing a Raja's encounter with a fantastical horse
26.7 × 17.1 cm (10 ½ × 6 ¾ in.)
Published: T. McInerney, *Indian paintings from the Polsky collections*, Princeton, 1982, no. 10

THE BARAMASA ("*TWELVE MONTHS*") GENRE IN POETRY AND PAINTING describes the behavior and feelings of lovers in the successive months and changing seasons of the year. The monsoon rains, a time of fertile regeneration and refreshment after the long drought of the hot season, are a season when travel became more difficult and when lovers above all are exhorted to remain united and enjoy each other's company. In his popular treatment of the *Baramasa* theme in the *Kavipriya* of 1601, Keshav Das writes of the rainy month of Bhadon (August–September):

> *The purple clouds are gathering, the thunder rolls and rain pours in torrents...*
> *The day is dark like the night, and one's own home is the best.*
> *Pray leave me not in the month of Bhadon, for separation pains like poison.*[1]

This painting evidently illustrates either Bhadon or the preceding month of Shravan (July–August). Under a sky of dense monsoon cloud, a nobleman and a lady meet in front of a pavilion on a palace terrace. Its shamiana awning is steeply tilted, like the curving bangla roof-eaves, to drain off the rainwater. The lady offers her lord a wine-cup, and a bed stands invitingly ready within. The trees have become luxuriant again and begin to envelop the mansion (*haveli*) buildings and temple in the background. The only incidental figures in the landscape are two hardy ascetics. Otherwise, whites and grays predominate, and the muted, pallid light contrasts effectively, for example, with the sultry, yellow glow suffusing the same artist's rendering of the hot, dry summer month of Jyestha.[2] This series of twelve illustrations[3] (of which half are said to survive) can be attributed to the Bikaner painter Murad, who employed a distinctive facial type with a rounded brow, drooping eye, and small mouth.[4]

AT

1 Randhawa, 1962, p. 142.

2 Welch and Beach, 1965, no. 30; S. C. Welch, *Rajasthani miniatures*, New York, 1997, col. pl. p. 29.

3 See also Guy and Swallow eds., 1990, pl. 120.

4 Goetz, 1950, fig. 88.

175

A murder in the bedchamber

PAGE FROM AN UNKNOWN MANUSCRIPT

Mughal, ca. 1600. Attributed here to Rahman Quli
Image 10.8 × 12.7 cm (4 ¼ × 5 in.);
page 14.6 × 22.9 cm (5 ¾ × 9 in.)

THIS SMALL MINIATURE IS, UNUSUALLY FOR THIS PERIOD, in horizontal format, and lacks any text whereby to help identify it. A man lies murdered on his bed, a woman tears her hair in grief, and the murderer runs away. This stark tale seems to come from one of the collections of Indian stories which were extremely popular at the Mughal court. Two versions of Ziya' al-Din Nakhshabi's *Tutinama* or Tales of a Parrot were illustrated in the early Akbari period, an otherwise almost entirely lost manuscript of the Persian translation from the *Kathasaritsagara* of Somadeva ("The Ocean of Story") is known from a few miniatures of about 1590, while several illustrated versions of the mostly animal fables of the *Anvar-i Suhaili* were made throughout Akbar's reign. Our painting dates from towards the end of Akbar's reign, when cooler tonalities and larger figures relative to the picture size were becoming standard features, developments sometimes associated with the type of work commissioned by Akbar's eldest son Salim when in rebellion and based at Allahabad in 1599–1604. The work of the rarely found artist Rahman Quli seems relevant here, whose equally dramatic painting from Jahangir's *Anvar-i Suhaili* of the favorite monkey trying to stab the sleeping king and being restrained by the thief displays a similar interest in interior perspective and male profile portraiture.[1]

A miniature in the *Tutinama* in Cleveland is perhaps relevant to the subject of our painting, from the thirty-second of the fifty-two nights in which the parrot tells tales to prevent his mistress Khojasta straying from the straight and narrow path while her husband is away. This shows Latif, who has murdered his young brother, falsely accusing his adopted sister Khurshid of the murder, since he wanted to cover his tracks in previously making advances to her. In that miniature the brother lies dead in bed, while Latif raises his hands in horror, and Khurshid sits dejectedly outside the chamber.[2] Here perhaps is an earlier stage of this story. In both, the little brother of Nakhshabi's text has been changed to an adult, so the other slight discrepancies from the text here are perhaps not too important.[3] No further miniatures, however, from a *Tutinama* manuscript of this date would appear to be known. The artist has a nice sense of drama and balances his composition beautifully. The eye-level viewpoint is also noteworthy, something very rare in Mughal narrative illustration. The perspective is naturalistic, apart from the cupola on the building on the left.

JPL

1 British Library Add. 18579, f. 244v, reproduced in Wilkinson, 1929, pl. XXII.

2 Chandra, 1976, p. 132, and f.211 of the manuscript facsimile.

3 Simsar tr., 1978, p. 203.

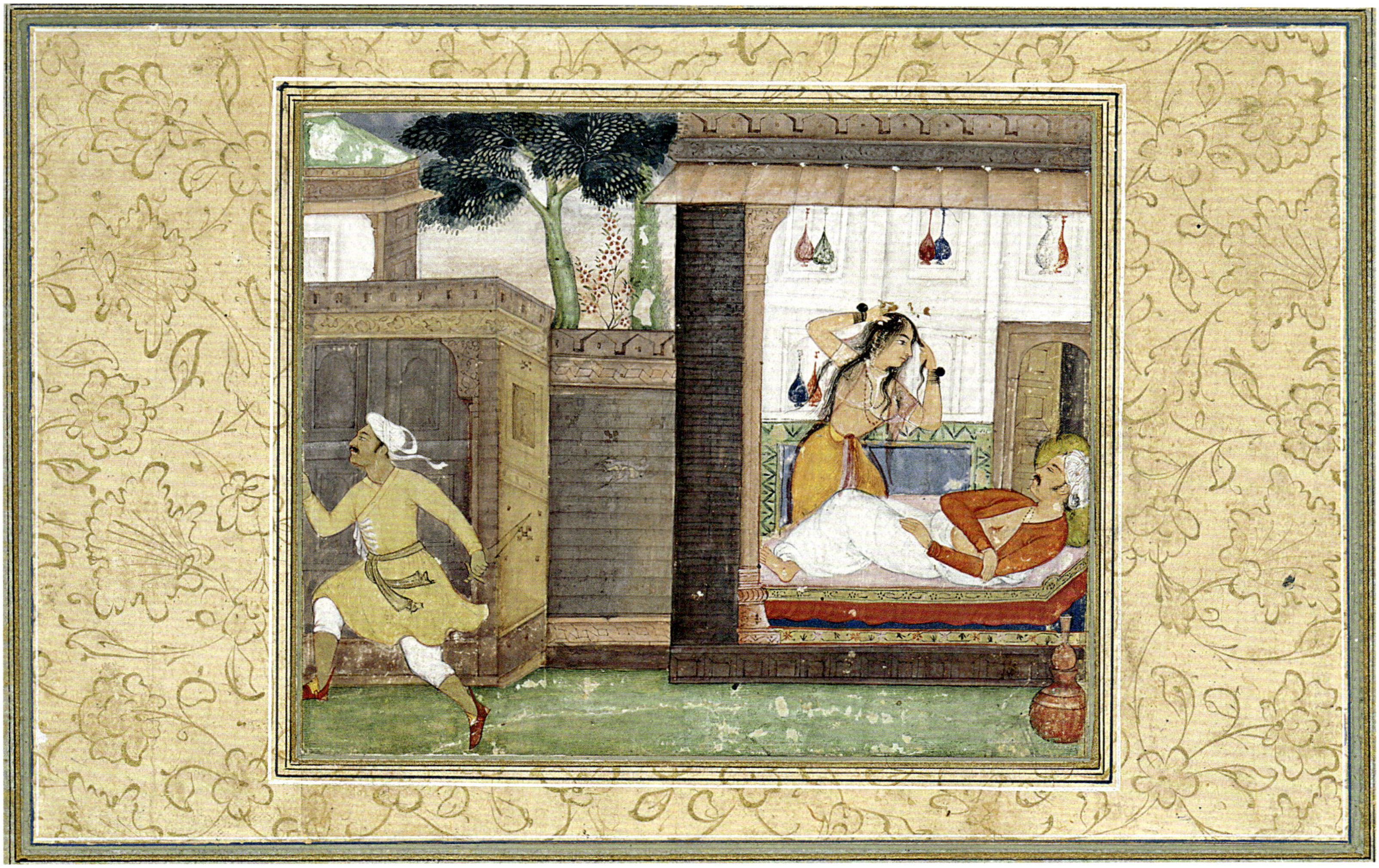

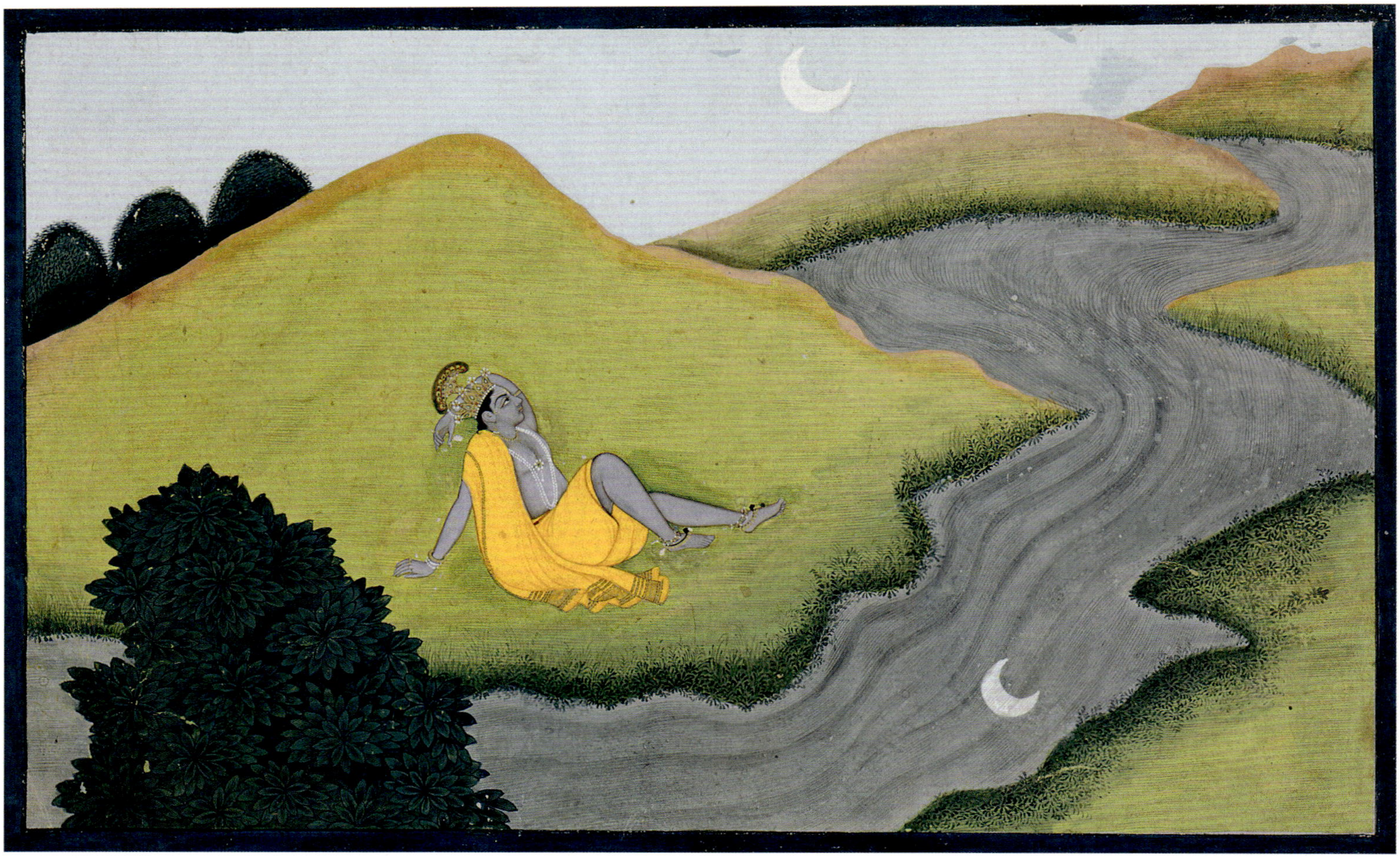

176

Krishna in solitude

ILLUSTRATION TO THE GITA GOVINDA OF JAYADEVA

Kangra, Punjab Hills, ca. 1780
15.2 × 25.4 cm (6 × 10 in.)
Sanskrit text, with a vernacular paraphrase, on verso (*GG*, V.3)

IN THE FIFTH PART OF JAYADEVA'S GITA GOVINDA, the lovelorn Radha is exhorted by her friend to go to Krishna. All alone by the river Jumna, he too is suffering intensely the pain of separation from her:

Cool moon rays scorch him,
Threatening death.
Love's arrow falls
And he laments his weakness.
Wild-flower-garlanded Krishna
Suffers in your desertion, friend.[1]

In an appropriately empty and largely featureless landscape of gently rolling hills, the desolate Krishna reclines in a languishing posture on the riverbank, wearing his peacock crown, jewelry and yellow robe. The swirling river which undulates past him through the landscape reflects the pale moon whose cool light afflicts him so badly in his inner torment of *viraha* (separation from the beloved). This expressive page comes from the well-known dispersed *Gita Govinda* series[2] which was probably painted for Maharaja Sansar Chand of Kangra not long after his accession in 1775 (see also cat. no. 69).

AT

1 Miller tr., 1977, p. 90.

2 E.g. Randhawa, 1963; Archer, 1973, s.v. Kangra, no. 33.

177

Krishna and Radha exchange glances

ILLUSTRATION TO THE SAT SAI OF BIHARI LAL

Kangra, Punjab Hills, ca. 1785
19.7 × 14 cm; 7 ¾ × 5 ½ in
Hindi text on verso[1]
Published: M. S. Randhawa, *Kangra paintings of the Bihari Sat Sai*, New Delhi, 1966, pl. 3

COMPOSED IN 1662 FOR MAHARAJA SAI SINGH OF AMBER, the *Sat Sai* ("Seven Hundred" verses) of Bihari Lal is a famous poetic cycle in the Braj Bhasha dialect of Hindi. Like the earlier *Rasikapriya* of Keshav Das, but in more concentrated, gnomic verses, it explores with subtle rhetorical conceits the emotions and behavior of idealized, courtly lovers (*nayakas* and *nayikas*), often personified as Krishna and Radha. During the eighteenth century it became a favorite text for illustration by painters at many courts. One of its most refined treatments is in this Kangra series of the mid-1780s,[2] probably painted for Maharaja Sansar Chand (r. 1775–1823) a few years after his great illustrated series of the *Bhagavata Purana* and *Gita Govinda* (cat. nos. 68, 176). It is likely that Fattu, son of the Guler painter Manaku, was one of the artists working on the series. In its pages the gist of each verse is elegantly distilled, with romantic charm and psychological wit, in a compact vignette enclosed by an oval cartouche with decorative spandrels.

This verse evokes the restlessness caused by love. Two female companions, seen in the far gateway of a palace courtyard, have noticed their friend Radha's agitation, and one of them remarks:

She swiftly climbed her balcony
to glance at him
but fearing prying eyes
ran down the next minute
not tiring a bit,
as though she was a yoyo
in her sweetheart's hand
whirled up and down
on the string of love![3]

As Krishna (or the nayaka) looks up tenderly at the palace where she dwells, Radha is also shown regarding him from different vantage points on three levels, as she hastens up and down in her excitement. Below, she stands coyly in the doorway, grasping its lintel; above, she bends to peep covertly through a small latticed jali window; at the top, she leans over a window-ledge to gaze down at Krishna.

AT

1 Ratnakar ed., 1969, no. 194.

2 Formerly in the Tehri-Garhwal Royal Collection: Randhawa, *Kangra paintings of the Bihari Sat Sai*; also Archer, 1973, s.v. Kangra, no. 39 (i-iv); Bautze, 1991, nos. 74–76; Goswamy and Fischer, 1992, no. 150.

3 Bahadur tr., 1992, no. 44, p. 59.

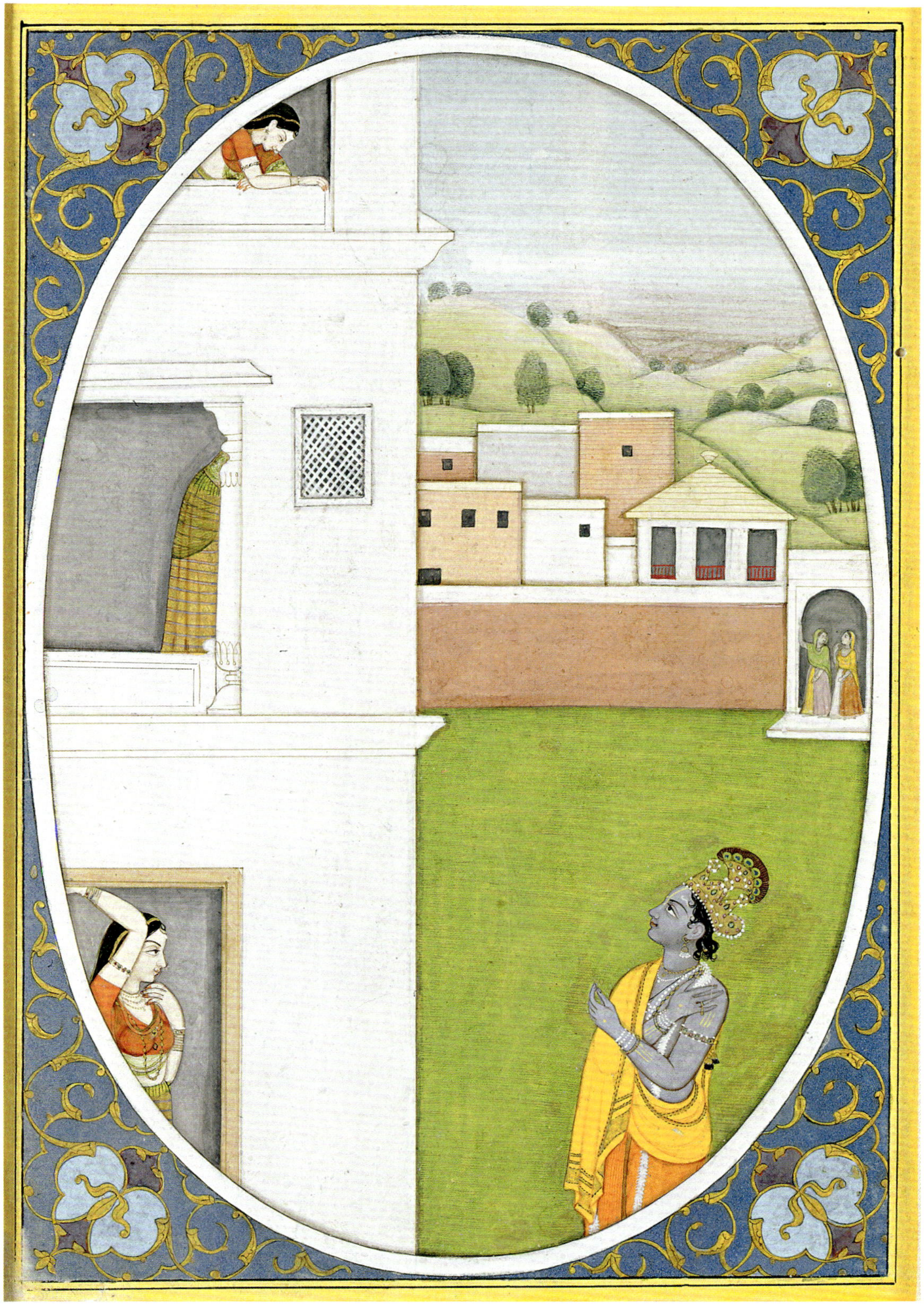

178

Radha's companion exhorts Krishna

ILLUSTRATION TO THE RASIKAPRIYA OF KESHAV DAS

Udaipur, Rajasthan, ca. 1720–30
Opaque watercolor on paper
30.8 x 19.1 cm (12 ⅛ x 7 ½ in.)
Numbered 120 on upper border; text on verso (partly obscured by gauze) giving a Rajasthani Hindi paraphrase of the subject; Mewar royal inventory no. 35/393

ON THE LEFT, RADHA LINGERS IN THE FOREST, holding a lover's garland and accompanied only by a crane. Meanwhile, her companion (*sakhi*) addresses Krishna, seated like a Raja in a pavilion enjoying wine and *pan*. Presumably she is telling him of Radha's pain in her separation (*viraha*) from him. The love-god Kama appears in a tree above, with his bow and flower arrow. A celestial deity in a sky-boat and a humble potter working his wheel round out the composition. From its numbering (120), this page probably illustrates an as yet unidentified verse from the fifth chapter of the *Rasikapriya*, describing the ways in which lovers meet. Radha may perhaps be playing the role of the inexperienced, unmarried woman who is too shy to try to meet her lover, so that her companion must act as a go-between for her:

> *Her friend to him somehow conveys*
> *The passion that burns through her frame.*[1]

As with most other Udaipur *Rasikapriya* series (cat. no. 167), the compositional elements recall the models established for the illustration of this text in the 1630s by Sahibdin (fl. 1628–55), court painter to Maharana Jagat Singh I of Mewar (r. 1628–52). By the early eighteenth century, the local style of manuscript illustration had coarsened considerably, following two generations of increasing mass production.[2] Over twenty pages from the present series are known to survive (some of them in a mutilated condition); seven are in the National Gallery of Victoria, Melbourne.[3]

AT

1 *Rasikapriya* V, v.21; Bahadur tr., 1972, pp. 78–79.

2 Topsfield, 2002, ch. 4, for a survey.

3 Topsfield, 1980, nos. 100–06 (nos. 104–5 are folios 118–19, which precede this one). Other examples of Udaipur *Rasikapriya* illustrations of the late seventeenth or early eighteenth century are in the Government Museum, Udaipur.

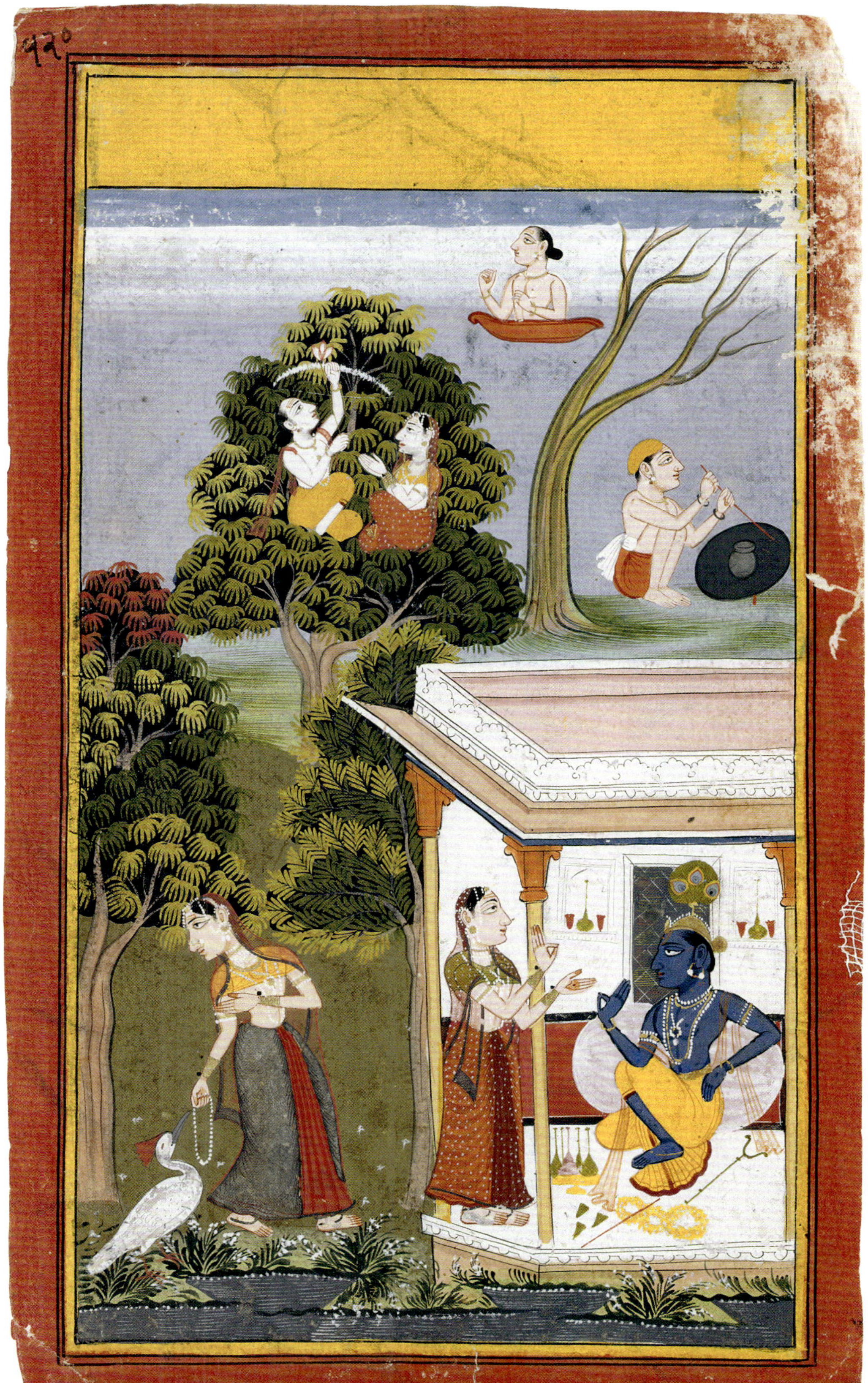

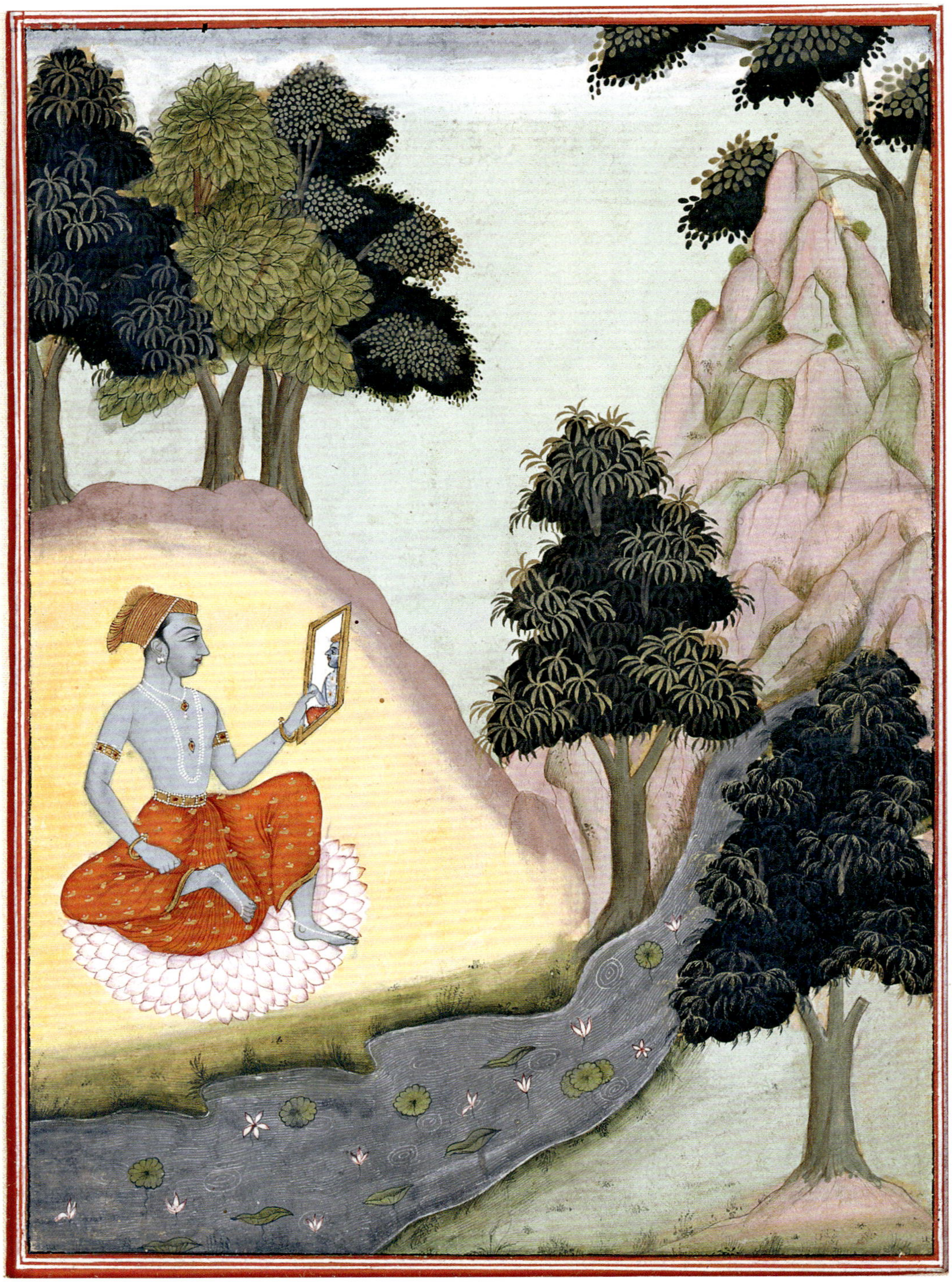

179

Seeing the beloved in absence

ILLUSTRATION TO THE RASIKAPRIYA OF KESHAV DAS

Bikaner, Rajasthan, ca. 1690
Opaque watercolor and gold on paper
19.7 × 14.6 cm; (7 ¾ × 5 in.)
Inscribed on verso with the beginning of the verse *Rasikapriya* IV.11; Bikaner inspection date 1694 (VS 1751) and Bikaner royal stamp

THE FOURTH BOOK OF KESHAV DAS'S POETIC TREATISE on ideal lovers deals with various types of "meeting" the beloved, in absence as well as in her or his presence. One method of such 'distant' meeting is by seeing the loved one's portrait, although this can be less than satisfying:

How can her lifeless picture show
Her varying moods...?
...How long shall my eyes I feed
On her insipid picture framed?
Deprived of water how can fish
Their restfulness retain? Even so
When on her picture I look, 'tis
As if my mind does burn fourfold.[1]

In this late seventeenth-century Bikaner illustration, the nayaka sits alone by a river, silhouetted against an area of pale yellow set within a hillside. Blue-skinned and seated on a couch of lotus petals like Krishna, he however wears here a flame-red (instead of yellow) lower garment and a turban (not a peacock crown).[2] It would seem moreover that (unless some repainting may have occurred) the artist has misunderstood the sense of the verse, or has chosen to subvert it. Instead of contemplating the picture of his lover (Radha), the nayaka holds a small mirror which shows us, and presumably him, his own reflection. Such an act of introspection or vanity is not usual for the male hero, though it is normal to the heroine, to whom it gives a chance not only to beautify herself but perchance to catch her lurking lover's reflection in the mirror's image, constituting another variety of "distant" meeting.[3]

AT

1 Bahadur tr., 1972, p. 64.

2 In Bikaner *Rasikapriya* illustrations of the 1680s by the leading master Ruknuddin and his followers, Krishna tends to wear a crown: e.g. Goetz, 1950, fig. 78; K. Khandalavala et al., 1960, fig. 72; A. Topsfield, "Painting for the Rajput courts," in B. Gray ed., *The arts of India*, Oxford, 1981, fig. 174.

3 Bahadur tr., *Rasikapriya*, pp. 61–62 (*RP* IV.5–7): Khandalavala et al., 1960, no. 91 (not illus.), for the Bikaner artist Ibrahim's version of that theme, dated 1685 (also *ibid.*, fig. 34, for an earlier Mewar version).

180

Krishna's revels with the gopis

ILLUSTRATION TO THE GITA GOVINDA OF JAYADEVA

Malwa, Central India, early seventeenth century
Opaque watercolor and silver on paper
Inscribed in text panel above with *Gita Govinda*, I, v.41
20.3 × 11.4 cm (8 × 4 ½ in.)
Metropolitan Museum of Art, New York, Cynthia Hazen Polsky and Leon B. Polsky Fund (2003.165)

IN THE FOURTH SONG FROM THE FIRST SECTION OF JAYADEVA'S POEM, Krishna is drawn one day into amorous frolics by several gopis. The present verse relates:

A girl with curving hips, bending to whisper in his ear,
Cherishes her kiss on her lover's tingling cheek.
Hari revels here as the crowd of charming girls
Revels in seducing him to play.[1]

Krishna's embrace with this forward young maiden is depicted, against a red ground, in a pleasing, stylized riverside grove comprising four "lollipop" trees in green and pink, with flowering creepers, monkeys, birds and a peacock. Krishna wears a transparent muslin jama over a yellow paijama, like a Mughal period courtier. But other, archaic features recall the pre-Mughal Early Rajput style of the sixteenth century, such as the band of pink lotus petal chevrons on which the figures are standing, the water with its curlicue eddies, and the wavy white skyline above, all of which suggest a date relatively early in the seventeenth century.

AT

1 Miller tr., 1977, p. 76.

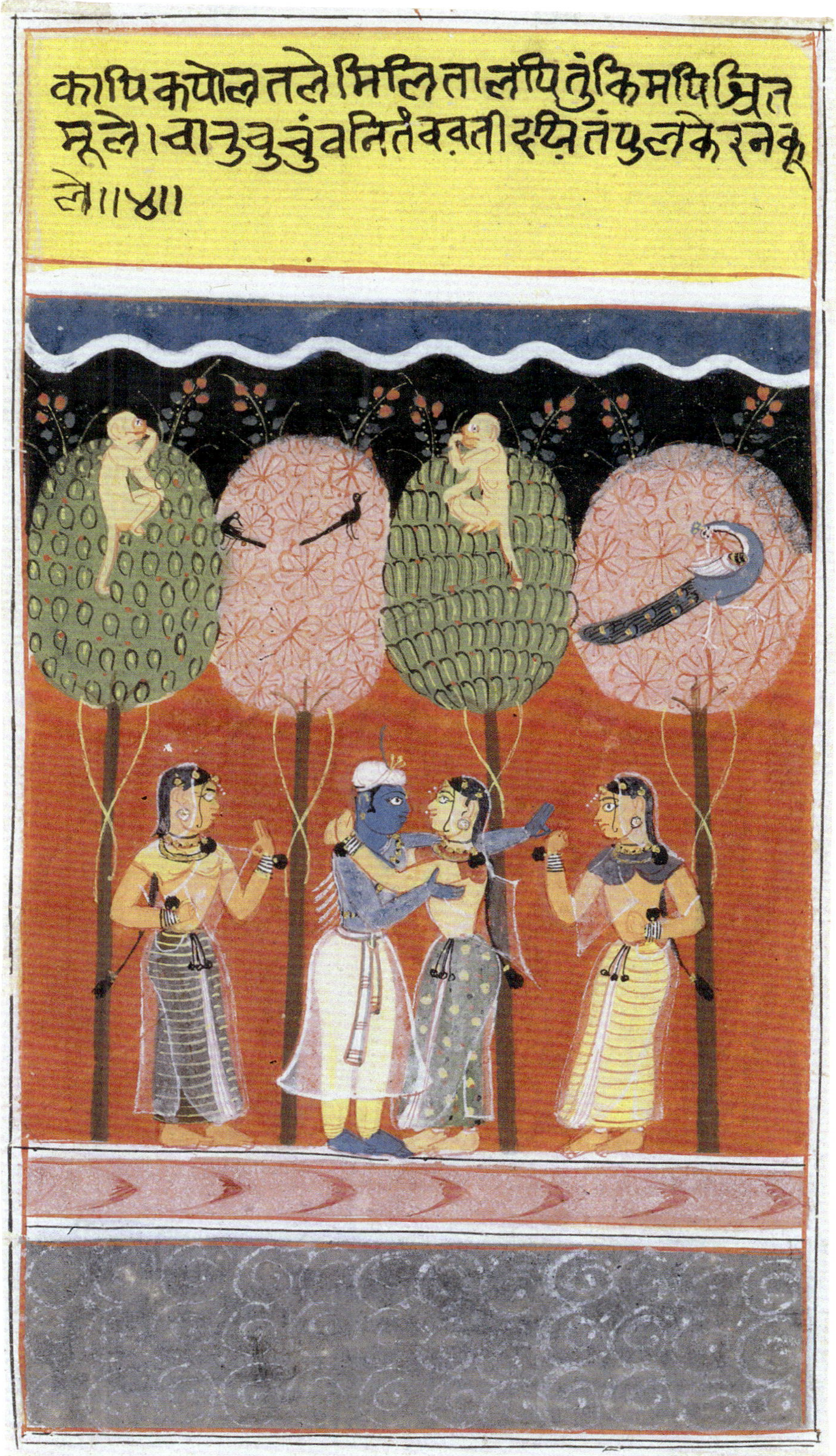
कापि कपोलतले मिलिता लपितुं किमपि श्रुत
मूले। चारु चुचुंब नितंबवती दयितं पुलकैरनुकू
ले॥४॥

181

Monsoon rain, Monghyr, Bihar

RAGHUBIR SINGH (1942–99)

Monghyr, Bihar, 1967
Chromogenic color print
38.2 × 25.3 cm (15 × 10 in.)
Published: Raghubir Singh, *The Ganges*, London, 1992, pl. 77

THIS ELEGANT COMPOSITION, of a group of women huddled together and braced against the force of the monsoon rains at Monghyr, as the rising waters of the Ganges threaten their fields, was one of Raghubir Singh's earliest published works. The image reflects his abiding fascination both with the river Ganges itself and the elemental force of the rains which bring both life and destruction to the subcontinent. As a native of Rajasthan, a land of little rain, Singh wrote often of his abiding love of the monsoon, "the most dramatic, sad and beautiful seasons on the Ganga," a devotion which persists among Indians despite the often overwhelmingly cruel power of the season. The river itself was a source of inspiration from his early days as a photographer: 'by 1966,' he wrote, 'photographing the Ganga had become my passion,'[1] and in the acknowledgements to the work in which this photograph appears, Singh paid tribute 'to the true protagonists of India's life: the mountain, the river and the plain.' As his book unfolds, in the form of a narrative tracing the river's journey to the sea from its source in the glaciers of the Himalayas, it becomes clear that the Ganges in its many moods—as spiritual focus and inspiration, destroyer, supplier of nourishment, or as a briefly glimpsed backdrop to the daily life along its course—is the central and unifying character in the drama of India's life.

JF

1 Raghubir Singh, *The Ganges*, pp. 7–8.

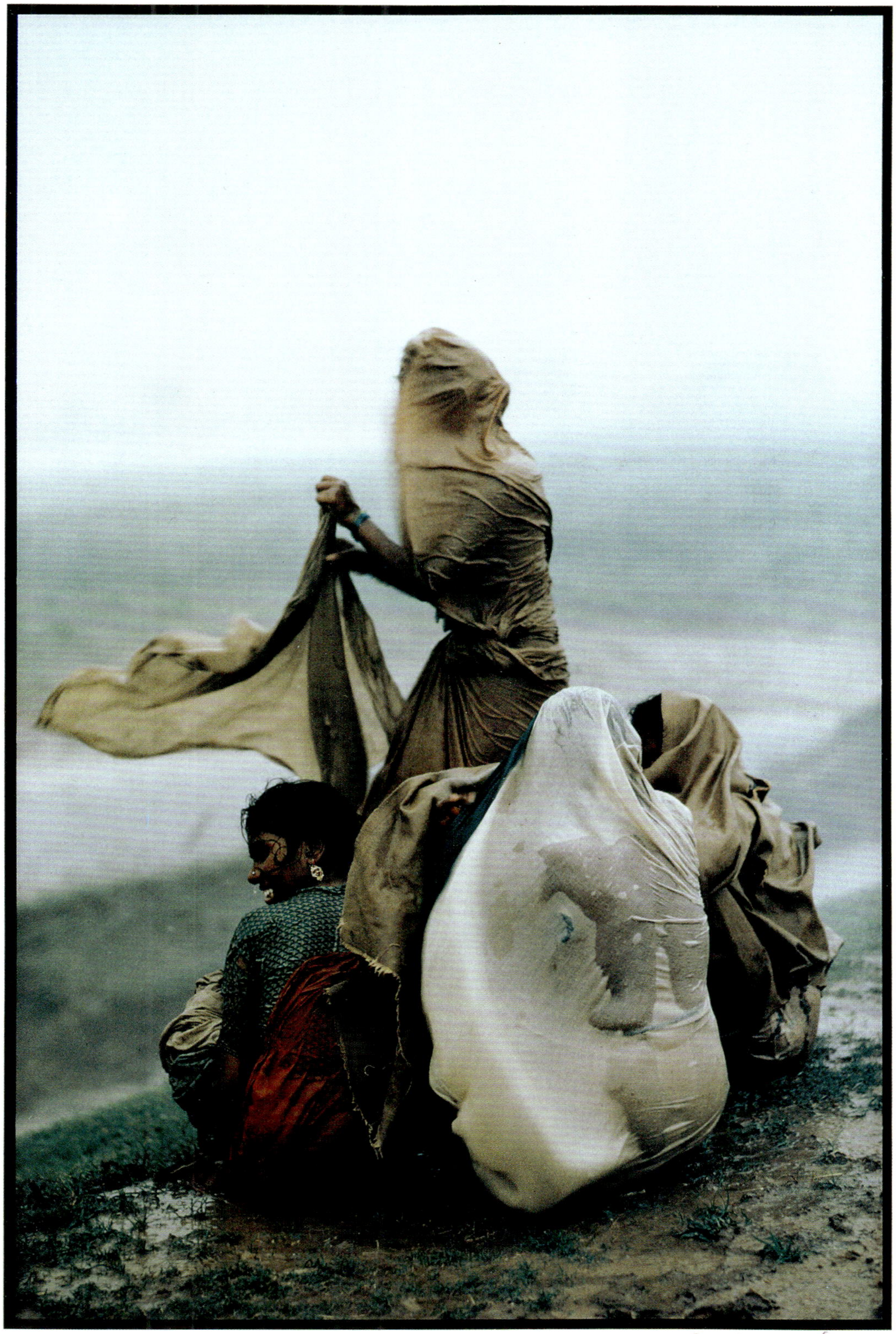

Raghubir Singh

LIST OF CONTRIBUTORS

AT	Andrew Topsfield
JE/JC	John Eskenazi/Jane Casey
JF	John Falconer
JPL	Jeremiah P. Losty
MCS	Michael Spink
ML	Martin Lerner
NHH	Navina Haidar Haykel
TM	Terence McInerney

SELECTED BIBLIOGRAPHY

Adamova, A. T., *Persian painting and drawing of the 15th–19th centuries from the Hermitage Museum*, St Petersburg, 1996.

Aijazuddin, F. S., *Pahari paintings and Sikh portraits in the Lahore Museum*, London, 1977.

Alexander, D., *Arts of war: Arms and armour of the 7th to 19th centuries: The Nasser D. Khalili collection of Islamic art*, London, 1992.

Allchin, F. R. et al., *The Crossroads of Asia: Transformation in image and symbol*, Cambridge, 1992.

Archer, M., *Company drawings in the India Office Library*, London, 1972.

Archer, M., *Company paintings: Indian paintings of the British period*, London, 1992.

Archer, M., *Indian miniatures and folk paintings*, London, 1967.

Archer, M., et al., *Treasures from India: The Clive collection at Powis Castle*, London 1987.

Archer, M and Falk, T., *India revealed: The art and adventures of James and William Fraser 1801–35*, London, 1989.

Archer, W. G., *Indian painting in Bundi and Kotah*, London, 1959.

Archer, W. G., *Indian paintings fom the Punjab Hills*, London, 1973.

Archer, W. G., *Pahari miniatures: A concise history*, Bombay, 1975

Archer, W. G., *Visions of courtly India*, Washington, D. C., 1976.

Archer, W. G. and Binney, E., *Rajput miniatures from the collection of Edwin Binney, 3rd*, Portland, Or., 1968.

Asher, C., *Architecture of Mughal India, (New Cambridge History of India 1:4)*, Cambridge, 1992.

Ashton, Sir Leigh ed., *The art of India and Pakistan*, London, 1950.

Aziz, A., *The imperial treasury of the Indian Mughals*, Lahore, 1942.

Bahadur, K. P. tr., *Bihari: The Satasai*, London: Penguin, 1992.

Bahadur, K. P. tr., *The Rasikapriya of Keshavadasa*, Delhi, 1972.

Barnes, R. et al., *Trade, temple and court*, Bombay, 2002.

Barrett, D. and Gray, B., *Painting of India*, Lausanne, 1963

Bassini, E. et al., *Via Orientalis*, Brussels, 1991

Bautze, J., *Drei "Bundi"-Ragamalas: Ein Beitrag zur Geschichte der Rajputischen Wandmalerei*, Stuttgart, 1987.

Bautze, J., *Early Indian terracottas*, Leiden, 1995.

Bautze, J., *Interaction of cultures: Indian and western painting 1780–1910*, Alexandria, Va., 1998.

Bautze, J., *Lotosmond und Löwenritt*, Stuttgart, 1991.

Bayley, C. A., *The Raj: India and the British 1600–1947*, London, 1990.

Beach, M. C., *Mughal and Rajput painting*, (New Cambridge History of India 1:3), Cambridge, 1992.

Beach, M. C., *Rajput painting at Bundi and Kota*, Ascona, 1974.

Beach, M. C., *The Grand Mogul*, Williamstown, 1978.

Beach, M. C., *The imperial image: Paintings for the Mughal court*, Washington, D. C., 1981.

Beach, M. C. and Koch, E., *King of the World: The Padshahnama*, Washington, D. C. and London, 1997.

Béguin, G., *L'Inde et le monde indianisé au Musée National des Arts Asiatiques—Guimet*, Paris, 1992.

Binney, E., *Indian miniature painting from the collection of Edwin Binney 3rd*, Portland, 1973.

Binney, E., *Panorama de la miniatura da India*, Monterey, 1979.

Boner, G., Fischer, E., and Goswamy, B. N., *Sammlung Alice Boner*, Zurich, 1994.

Bor, J. and Bruguière, P. eds., *Gloire des princes, louange des dieux*, Paris, 2003.

Brijraj Singh, M. K., *The kingdom that was Kotah*, New Delhi, 1985.

Brown, W. N., *The story of Kalaka*, Washington, D. C., 1933.

Bryant E. F., tr., *Krishna: The beautiful legend of God (Srimad Bhagavata Purana Book X)*, London, 2003.

Bussagli, M. and Sivaramamurti, C., *5000 years of the art of India*, New York, 1971.

Carboni, S., *Glass from Islamic lands*, New York, 2001.

Carboni, S., *Glass of the Sultans*, New York, 2002.

Chandra, P., *The Tuti-nama manuscript of the Cleveland Museum of Art*, Graz, 1976.

Chandra, P. and Ehnbom, D., *The Cleveland Tutinama manuscript and the origins of Mughal painting*, Chicago, 1976.

Colnaghi & Co, *Indian painting*, London, 1978.

Coomaraswamy, A., *Arts and crafts of India and Ceylon*, London, 1913.

Coomaraswany, A., *Catalogue of the Indian collection of the Museum of Fine Arts, Boston, Part V: Rajput painting*,

Cambridge, Mass., 1926.
Crill, R., *Marwar painting*, Bombay, 1999.
Crill, R. et al. eds., *Arts of Mughal India: Studies in honour of Robert Skelton*, London (forthcoming, 2004).
Czuma, S., *Indian art from the George P. Bickford collection*, Cleveland, 1975.
Czuma, S. *Kushan sculpture: Images from early India*, Cleveland, 1985.
Desai, V., *Life at Court: Art for India's rulers, 16th–19th centuries,* Boston, 1985.
Desai, V. and Mason, D. eds., *Gods, guardians and lovers: Temple sculptures in North India*, New York, 1993.
Digby, S. and Harle, J. C., *Toy soldiers and ceremonial in post-Mughal India*, Oxford, 1982.
Dikshit, M. G., *History of Indian glass*, Bombay, 1969.
Donaldson, T., *Hindu temple art of Orissa*, Leiden, 1987.
Dwivedi, V. P., *Indian ivories*, Delhi, 1976.
Dye, J. M. *The arts of India: Virginia Museum of Fine Arts*, Richmond, 2001.
Ebeling, K., *Ragamala painting*, Basel, 1973.
Ehnbom, D. J., *Indian miniatures: The Ehrenfeld collection*, New York, 1985.
Eskenazi, J., *Inaugural exhibition: Images of faith*, London, 1995.
Falk, T. et al., *Indian Painting*, London, Colnaghi & Co., 1978.
Falk, T. et al., *Paintings from Mughal India*, London: Colnaghi & Co, 1979.
Falk, T. and Archer, M. *Indian miniatures in the India Office Library*, London, 1981.
Fantoni, G., *Indian paintings and manuscripts*, London: Sam Fogg, 1999.
Filliozat, J., and Pattabiramin, P. Z., *Parures divines du Sud de l'Inde*, Pondicherry, 1966.
Gittinger, M., *Master dyers to the world*, Washington, D. C., 1982.
Goetz, H., *The art and architecture of Bikaner State*, Oxford, 1950.
Gole, S., *Maps of India*, London, 1988.
Goswamy, B. N., *Nainsukh of Guler*, Zurich, 1997.
Goswamy, B. N., *Painted visions: The Goenka Collection of Indian painting*, New Delhi, 1999.
Goswamy, B. N., *Rasa: Les neuf visages de l'art indien*, Paris, 1986; (English ed.) *Essence of Indian art*, San Francisco, 1986.
Goswamy, B. N. and Bhatia, U., *Painted visions*, New Delhi, 1999.
Goswamy, B. N.and Fischer, E., *Pahari masters: Court painters of northern India*, Zurich, 1992.
Grabar, O., *Sasanian silver*, Ann Arbor, 1967.
Gunter, A. and Jett, P., *Ancient Iranian metalwork in the Arthur M. Sackler Gallery and the Freer Gallery of Art*, Washington D. C., 1992.
Guy, J., *Palm-leaf and paper: Illustrated manuscripts of India and South East Asia*, Melbourne, 1982.
Guy, J. and Swallow, D. eds., *Arts of India 1550–1900, London: Victoria and Albert Museum*, 1990.
Haque, E., *Chandraketugarh: A treasure house of Bengal terracottas*, Dhaka, 2001.
Harle, J. C., *Gupta sculpture*, Oxford, 1974.
Harper, P. and Meyers, P., *Silver vessels of the Sasanian period*, New York, 1981.
Heeramaneck, A., *Masterpieces of Indian painting from the former collection of Nasli M. Heeramaneck*, New York, 1984.
Huntington, S. L. and J. C., *Leaves from the Bodhi tree*, Dayton, 1990.
Hurel, R. and Okada, A., *Pouvoir et désir: Miniatures indiennes du San Diego Museum of Art*, Paris, 2002.
Isacco, E. and Dallapiccola, A., *Krishna, the Divine Lover*, London, 1982.
Jacob, S. S., *Jeypore portfolio of architectural details*, Jaipur, 1890.
Jaffer, A., *Furniture from British India and Ceylon*, London, 2001.
Jaffer, A., *Luxury goods from India, The art of the Indian cabinet maker*, London, 2002.
Jenkins, M., *Islamic art in the Kuwait National Museum*, London, 1983.
Kak, R. C., *Ancient monuments of Kashmir*, London, 1933.
Kathuria, R. P., *Life in the courts of Rajasthan*, New Delhi, 1987.
Khandalavala, K. and Chandra, M., *Miniatures and sculptures from the collection of the late Sir Cowasji Jehangir, Bart.*, Bombay, 1965.
Khandalavala, K. and Chandra, M., *New documents of Indian painting: A reappraisal*, Bombay, 1969.
Khandalavala, K. et al., *Miniature paintings from the Sri Motichand Khajanchi collection*, New Delhi, 1960.
Knox, R., *Amaravati: Buddhist sculpture from the Great Stupa*, London, 1992.
Kossak, S., *Indian court painting 16th–19th century*, London, 1997.
Kramrisch, S., *Manifestations of Shiva*, Philadelphia, 1981.
Kramrisch, S., *Painted delight*, Philadelphia, 1986.
Krishna, A. ed., *Chhavi: Golden Jubilee Volume*, Varanasi, 1971.
Krishna, A. ed., *Chhavi-2: Rai Krishnadasa Felicitation Volume*, Varanasi, 1981.
Kurita, I., *Gandharan art*, Tokyo, 1990.

Lawton, T. and Lentz, T. W., *Beyond the legacy: Anniversary acquisitions for the Freer Gallery of Art and the Arthur M. Sackler Gallery*, Washington, D. C., 1998.
Leach, L. Y., *Indian miniature paintings and drawings: The Cleveland Museum of Art*, Cleveland, 1986.
Leach, L. Y., *Mughal and other Indian paintings from the Chester Beatty Library*, London, 1995.
Leach, L. Y. *Paintings from India: The Nasser D. Khalili collection of Islamic art*, London, 1998.
Lerner, M., *The flame and the lotus*, New York, 1984.
Lerner, M. and Kossak, S., *The arts of South and Southeast Asia*, New York, 1994.
Lerner, M. and Kossak, S., *The Lotus transcendent*, New York, 1991.
Lippe, A., *The Freer Indian sculptures*, Washington, D. C., 1970.
Losty, J. P., *Indian book painting*, London, 1986.
Losty, J. P., *Krishna: A Hindu vision of God*, London, 1980.
Losty, J. P., *The art of the book in India*, London, 1982.
Luce, G. H., *Old Burma—Early Pagan*, New York, 1969–70.
Marshall, Sir John, *A guide to Sanchi*, Calcutta, 1918.
Marshall, Sir John, *Taxila: An illustrated account of the archaeological excavation carried out at Taxila*, Cambridge, 1951.
Mason, D. et al., *Intimate worlds: Indian paintings from the Alvin O. Bellak collection*, Philadelphia, 2001.
McInerney, T., *Indian painting* 1525–1825, London, 1982.
McInerney, T., *Indian paintings from the Polsky collections*, Princeton, 1982.
Mele, P., *Tibet*, Calcutta, 1975.
Michell, G., *Architecture and art of Southern India: Vijayanagara and the successor states (New Cambridge History of India*, I:6), Cambridge, 1995.
Miller B. S., tr., *Love song of the Dark Lord: Jayadeva's Gitagovinda*, New York, 1977.
Mittal, J., *Andhra paintings of the Ramayana*, Hyderabad, 1969.
Mittal, J., *Indian drawings 16th–19th century*, New Delhi, 1989.
Mittal, J., *Indian folk paintings 15th to 19th century*, New Delhi, 1990.
Mukharji, T. N., *Art-manufactures of India*, Calcutta, 1888.
Neven, A., *Peintures des Indes: Mythologie et légendes*, Brussels, 1976.
Nigam, M. L., *Jade collection in the Salar Jang Museum*, Hyderabad, 1979.
Okada, A. and Joshi, M. C., *Taj Mahal*, New York, 1993.
Okada, A., *A la cour du Grand Moghol*, Paris, 1986.
Okada, A., *L'Inde des princes: La donation Jean et Krishna Riboud*, Paris, 2000.
Okada, A., *Un joyau de l'Inde Moghole: Le mausolée d'Itimad ud-Daulah*, Milan, 2003.
Pal, P., *A Collecting Odyssey: Indian, Himalayan and South East Asian Art from the James and Marilynn Alsdorf Collection*, Chicago, 1997.
Pal, P., *Art from the Indian subcontinent: Asian art at the Norton Simon Museum*, vol. 1, Yale, 2003.
Pal, P., *Desire and devotion*, London, 2001.
Pal, P., *Elephants and ivories in South Asia*, Los Angeles, 1981.
Pal, P., *Indian painting: Catalogue of the Los Angeles County Museum of Art collection*, Los Angeles, 1993.
Pal, P., *Indian sculpture*, vol. 1, Los Angeles, 1986.
Pal, P., *Indian sculpture*, vol. 2, Los Angeles, 1988.
Pal, P., *The classical tradition in Rajput painting*, New York, 1978.
Pal, P., *The flute and the brush*, Newport Beach, 1976.
Pal, P., *The sensuous immortals*, Los Angeles, 1977.
Pal, P. and Glynn, C., *The sensuous line: Indian drawings from the Paul F. Walter collection*, Los Angeles, 1976.
Pal, P. and Seid, B., *The holy cow and other animals*, Chicago, 2002
Pal, P. et al., *Pleasure gardens of the mind*, Los Angeles, 1993.
Patnaik, N., *A second paradise*, New York, 1985.
Poster, A., *From Indian earth: 4,000 years of terracotta art*, Brooklyn, 1986.
Poster, A. et al., *Realms of heroism: Indian paintings at the Brooklyn Museum*, New York, 1994.
Randhawa, M. S., *Kangra paintings of the Gita Govinda*, New Delhi, 1963.
Ratnakar, J. ed., *Bihari-Ratnakar*, Varanasi, 1969.
Rowland, B., *Ancient art from Afghanistan*, New York, 1966.
Schmitz, B., *Islamic manuscripts in the New York Public Library*, New York, 1992.
Seyller, J., *The Adventures of Hamza*, Washington, D. C., 2002.
Seyller, J., *Workshop and patron in Mughal India*, Zurich, 1999.
Sharma, G. N., *Social life in medieval Rajasthan*, Agra, 1968.
Shastri tr., H. P., *The Ramayana of Valmiki*, London, 1952.
Simsar, M. A. tr., *Tales of a parrot by Ziya' ud-din Nakhshabi*, Cleveland and Graz, 1978.
Singh, K., *The relations of the house of Bikaner with the central powers*, New Delhi, 1974.
Singh, R., *River of Colour: The India of Raghubir Singh*, London, 1998.
Sivaramamurti, C., *Tthe art of India*. New York, 1966.

Sivaramamurti, C., *Nataraja in art, thought and literature*, New Delhi, 1974.

Skelton, R., *Indian miniatures from the XVth to XIXth centuries*, Venice, 1961.

Skelton R., et al., *The Indian Heritage: Court life and arts under Mughal rule*, London, 1982.

Smart, E. and Walker, D., *Pride of the princes*, Cincinatti, 1985.

Soudavar, A., *Art of the Persian courts*, New York, 1992.

Spink, W., *Krishnamandala*, Ann Arbor, 1971.

Stchoukine, I., *La peinture indienne a l'époque des Grands Moghols*, Paris, 1929.

Stronge, S., *Bidri ware: Inlaid metalwork from India*, London, 1985, p. 94.

Stronge, S., *Painting for the Mughal Emperor: The art of the book 1560–1660*, London, 2002.

Stronge, S., Smith, N., and Harle, J. C., *A golden treasury: Jewellery from the Indian subcontinent*, London, 1988.

Tandan, R. K., *Indian miniature painting*, Bangalore, 1982.

Taylor, M. B. and Jail, C. eds., *L'etrange et le merveilleux en terres d'Islam*, Paris, 2001.

Tchakaloff, T-N. et al., *La Route des Indes*, Bordeaux, 1998.

Tod, J., *Annals and antiquities of Rajasthan*, ed. W. Crooke, London, 1920.

Topsfield, A., *Court painting at Udaipur: Art under the patronage of the Maharanas of Mewar*, Zurich, 2002.

Topsfield, A., *Paintings from Rajasthan in the National Gallery of Victoria*, Melbourne, 1980.

Topsfield, A., *Paintings from the Rajput courts*, London: Indar Pasricha Gallery, 1986.

Topsfield, A., *The City Palace Museum, Udaipur: Paintings of Mewar court life*, Ahmedabad, 1990.

Topsfield, A. and Beach, M. C., *Indian paintings and drawings from the collection of Howard Hodgkin*, New York, 1991.

Untracht, O., *Traditional Jewelry of India*, London, 1997.

Vashistha, R. K., *Mewar ki citrankan parampara*, Jaipur, 1984.

von Schroeder, U., *Buddhist sculptures in Tibet, vol. 1: India and Nepal*, Hong Kong, 2001.

von Schroeder, U., *Indo-Tibetan bronzes*, Hong Kong, 1981.

Waldschmidt, E. and R., *Miniatures of musical inspiration*, I, Bombay, 1967.

Waldschmidt, E. and R., *Miniatures of musical inspiration*, 2, Berlin, 1975.

Watt, Sir George, *Indian art at Delhi*, Calcutta, 1903.

Weber, H., *La Compagnie Française des Indes*, Paris, 1904.

Weber, R., *Porträts und historische Darstellungen*, Berlin, 1982.

Webster, A. R., *Gems: Their sources, descriptions and identification*, 4th ed., London, 1983.

Welch, S. C., *A flower from every meadow*, New York, 1973.

Welch, S. C., *India: Art and culture 1300–1900*, New York, 1985.

Welch, S. C., *Indian drawings and painted sketches*, New York, 1976.

Welch, S. C., *Rajasthani miniatures: The Welch Collection*, New York, 1997.

Welch, S. C. and Beach, M. C., *Gods, thrones and peacocks*, New York, 1965.

Welch, S. C. et al., *Gods, kings and tigers: The art of Kotah*, Munich and New York, 1997.

Welch, S. C. et al., *The Emperor's Album: Images of Mughal India*, New York, 1987.

Welch, S. C., *The art of Mughal India*, New York, 1963.

Wilkinson, J. V. S., *The lights of Canopus*, London, 1929.

Wilkinson, W., *Indian silver 1858–1947*, London, 1999.

Wilkinson, W., *The makers of Indian colonial silver 1760–1860*, London, 1987.

Zaehner, R. C. tr., *The Bhagavad-Gita*, Oxford, 1969.

Zebrowski, M., *Deccani painting*, London, 1983.

Zebrowski, M., *Gold, silver and bronze from Mughal India*, London, 1997.

Zimmer, H., *Myths and symbols in Indian art and civilization*, New York, repr. 1963.

Zwalf, W., *Catalogue of the Gandhara sculpture in the British Museum*, London, 1996.

INDEX

E

F

G

H

I

J